STUDIES IN IMPERIALISM

general editor John M. MacKenzie and Andrew S. Thompson

When the 'Studies in Imperialism' series was founded more than twenty-five years ago, emphasis was laid upon the conviction that 'imperialism as a cultural phenomenon had as significant an effect on the dominant as on the subordinate societies'. With more than ninety books published, this remains the prime concern of the series. Cross-disciplinary work has indeed appeared covering the full spectrum of cultural phenomena, as well as examining aspects of gender and sex, frontiers and law, science and the environment, language and literature, migration and patriotic societies, and much else. Moreover, the series has always wished to present comparative work on European and American imperialism, and particularly welcomes the submission of books in these areas. The fascination with imperialism, in all its aspects, shows no sign of abating, and this series will continue to lead the way in encouraging the widest possible range of studies in the field. 'Studies in Imperialism' is fully organic in its development, always seeking to be at the cutting edge, responding to the latest interests of scholars and the needs of this ever-expanding area of scholarship.

Developing Africa

MANCHESTER
1824

Manchester University Press

FWF Der Wissenschaftsfonds.

Developing Africa

CONCEPTS AND PRACTICES
IN TWENTIETH-CENTURY
COLONIALISM

Edited by Joseph M. Hodge, Gerald Hödl, and Martina Kopf

MANCHESTER
UNIVERSITY PRESS

Published by MANCHESTER UNIVERSITY PRESS
ALTRINCHAM STREET, MANCHESTER, M1 7JA, UK
www.manchesteruniversitypress.co.uk

British Library Cataloguing-in-Publication Data
A catalogue record for this book is available from the British Library

Library of Congress Cataloging-in-Publication Data applied for

ISBN   978 1 5261 0676 6   paperback

First published by Manchester University Press in 2014
This edition first published 2017

Typeset in 10/12pt Trump Mediaeval
by Graphicraft Limited, Hong Kong

To Marta, Benjamin, and Olivia – JMH

To Irmgard Kirchner, Werner Hörtner, Brigitte Pilz,
and all friends at *Südwind Magazin* – MK

Figure 1 Field assistants training for survey work at the Land-planning
Training Centre, Morogoro, Tanganyika, 1960s
Source: British National Archives, CO1069/164 (34).

CONTENTS

[vii]

CONTENTS

FIGURES AND TABLES

Figure

Table

GENERAL EDITOR'S INTRODUCTION

Development is a complex concept. The interests served, the actors involved, the communities targeted, as well as the actual effects (intended or otherwise), vary tremendously according to the 'where', 'when' and 'how' of development policy and practice. As the editors of this very valuable addition to the 'Studies in Imperialism' series rightly argue, development is emphatically not, therefore, a concept which we can afford to take for granted. Rather, development demands to be historicised. And, for it to be historicised, we need to be mindful of the full extent of development's involvement and investment in the colonial and post-colonial state. For just as the legitimacy of colonial regimes and their post-colonial successors might be bolstered by development projects and programmes undertaken in their name, so the reach of bureaucratic and military state power could be extended by these very same projects and programmes. It is not simply that under colonialism coercion and conciliation went hand in hand; in terms of colonial development they were, in fact, entwined. By ranging widely across European empires, the African continent, and the twentieth century, this book opens up important new perspectives on development as it was conceived by its proponents and experienced by its (supposed) beneficiaries. It alerts us to the persistent dangers of hubris in development planning, to contrasting and conflicting development paradigms within European and African societies, to the gendered dynamics and dimensions of development, and to how development was defined in relation to other discourses, modernity in particular. At the start of the twentieth century development was embryonic; by the final quarter of that century it had become a central orthodoxy of national planning and United Nations thinking. In the intervening decades the word 'development' gradually gathered layers of significance – as a form of welfare and philanthropy, as a strategy for promoting industrial growth, as a tool for tackling rural poverty, as an offshoot of economic thinking, and as an academic discipline. Within these different manifestations of development many perspectives, priorities and paradoxes were contained. In this wide-ranging enquiry the expansive nature of the development concept, in its African and colonial settings, is not only crisply captured for the reader, but carefully and critically appraised.

CONTRIBUTORS

Caio Simões de Araújo holds a BA in International Relations, and minor in Sociology, from the University of Coimbra, Portugal. He obtained an MA in Sociology and Social Anthropology from the Central European University, Hungary. He is currently pursuing a PhD at the International History Department of the Graduate Institute for International and Development Studies, Switzerland. He has conducted research in different areas of interest in both Brazil and Portugal and has presented his work at academic conferences in Brazil, Europe, India, and South Africa. His research interests involve histories of colonialism and decolonisation, historical anthropologies, anthropology of the body, anthropology of development, history of racism and racial ideologies, and post-colonial studies.

Walter Bruchhausen, Priv.-Doz. Dr med., Dipl. theol., MPhil, is Vice-Director of the Institute for the History of Medicine, University of Bonn, and Research Fellow at the Institute for the History, Theory and Ethics of Medicine, University of Aachen. He has done studies in medicine, theology, philosophy of medicine/health care ethics and anthropology at Bonn, Würzburg, and Glasgow; medical work in Germany and East Africa (1990–97); and habilitation for 'History, Anthropology and Ethics of Medicine' (2004) with field and archival research in Tanzania on 'Past and Present Medical Pluralism in Southeastern Tanzania' (2000–4). He is currently researching the 'History of German Development Cooperation in Health'. He has also published on 'traditional', colonial, and mission medicine in East Africa, development and emergency assistance, religion and medicine, cultural and anthropological historiography of medicine, and global health ethics.

Barbara Bush is an Emeritus Professor of History at Sheffield Hallam University, UK. She is the author of *Imperialism and Postcolonialism* (Harlow: Pearson 2006), 'Gender and Empire: The Twentieth Century', in Philippa Levine (ed.), *Gender and Empire* (Oxford: Oxford University Press 2004), and *Imperialism, Race and Resistance: Africa and Britain, 1919–1945* (London: Routledge 1999). She also has a number of key publications on gender, culture, and resistance in slave and post-slave societies in the African diaspora. Her current research focuses on the academic social sciences, colonial research, and development in the late colonial era.

Cláudia Castelo is a Research Fellow at Centro Interuniversitário de História das Ciências e da Tecnologia, Faculdade de Ciências, Universidade de Lisboa, Lisbon, Portugal. She graduated in History in 1992 and concluded her MA in History of the Twentieth Century in 1997 (both degrees at the Universidade Nova de Lisboa, Lisbon, Portugal). She holds a PhD in Social Sciences from the Instituto de Ciências Sociais, Universidade de Lisboa, Lisbon, Portugal (2005). Currently, she coordinates the project 'Field Scientists in the "Luso-tropical Setting": Knowledge, Ideology and Governance in Late Portuguese Empire'. Her research interests include the history of the Portuguese Colonial Empire in the twentieth century, white settlement in Angola and Mozambique, and 'colonial science'. She is the author of *'O modo português de estar no mundo': o luso-tropicalismo e a ideologia colonial portuguesa, 1933–1961* (Porto: Afrontamente 1998); *Passagens para África: o povoamento de Angola e Moçambique com naturais da metrópole, 1920–1974* (Porto: Afrontamento 2007); and 'Scientific Research and Portuguese Colonial Policy: Developments and Articulations, 1936–1974', *História, Ciências, Saúde – Manguinhos* (2012).

Françoise Dufour is a researcher in linguistics at Montpellier 3, University Paul Valéry, France. She specialises in discourse analysis. Her research involves the analysis of discursive modalities of French colonial dominance over West Africa and its reformulations into development discourses. More generally she analyses the links between discourse, language, notions, and ideology. She is the author of *De l'idéologie coloniale à celle du développement: une analyse du discours* (Paris: L'Harmattan 2010) and 'Développement durable, humain: la cohérence des contradictions', *Mots* (2011).

Billy Frank is a Senior Lecturer in the School of Education and Social Science at the University of Central Lancashire (UCLan), UK. His doctoral thesis examined Britain's colonial development policy in Central and Southern Africa in the trans-World War Two period with special reference to Barclays Bank (Dominion, Colonies and Overseas). He is currently researching the lives and careers of empire bankers, developers, and 'experts' in post-1945 Southern Africa. He has co-edited *The British Labour Movement and Imperialism* (Newcastle: Cambridge Scholars 2010).

Joseph M. Hodge is an Associate Professor of Modern British and British Imperial History in the Department of History at West Virginia University in Morgantown, West Virginia, USA. He is author of *Triumph of the Expert: Agrarian Doctrines of Development and the Legacies of British Colonialism* (Athens, OH: Ohio University Press

2007). He is also co-editor along with Brett Bennett of *Science and Empire: Knowledge and Networks of Science across the British Empire, 1800–1970* (Basingstoke: Palgrave Macmillan 2011). He has published several articles in leading historical journals including the *Journal of Imperial and Commonwealth History*, the *Journal of Southern African Studies*, *Agricultural History*, and the *Journal of Modern European History*. He is currently researching the post-colonial careers of British colonial officers who worked subsequently for various international organisations after retiring from the colonial service, including the United Nations and the World Bank, or else for British donor agencies and consultancy firms.

Gerald Hödl is a historian who has published several books and articles on development theory, Austrian foreign policy and development assistance, and on global sports. From 2001 to 2009, he taught extensively on these subjects at the University of Vienna's development studies programme. From 2009 to 2012 he was a member of the research project 'Colonial Concepts of Development, 1920–1960' at the Department of African Studies, University of Vienna, funded by the Austrian Science Fund. His publications include *Österreich und die Dritte Welt: Außen- und Entwicklungspolitik der Zweiten Republik bis zum EU-Beitritt 1995* (Vienna: Promedia 2004). He has also translated books by Immanuel Wallerstein and Andre Gunder Frank into German.

Emma Hunter has been a Lecturer in History and Fellow of Gonville and Caius College, Cambridge, since 2008. Her current book project is called 'Languages of Freedom: Making Tanzanian Political Society in an International Age'. Major publications include '"Our Common Humanity": Print, Power and the Colonial Press in Interwar Tanganyika and French Cameroun', *Journal of Global History* (2012) and 'Dutiful Subjects, Patriotic Citizens and the Concept of "Good Citizenship" in Twentieth-Century Tanzania', *Historical Journal* (2013). She is also working on a new project, funded by the British Academy, called 'Concepts of Democracy in Mid-Twentieth-Century Africa'.

Martina Kopf, PhD, is a researcher and Lecturer in African Literature Studies at the University of Vienna. Her current research is on development discourse in Francophone and Anglophone twentieth-century colonial literature on and from Africa. From 2009 to 2012 she was a member of the research project 'Colonial Concepts of Development, 1920–1960' at the Department of African Studies, University of Vienna. She is the author of *Trauma und Literatur: Das Nicht-Erzählbare erzählen – Assia Djebar und Yvonne Vera* (Frankfurt-on-Main: Brandes

& Apsel 2005) and 'The Ethics of Fiction: African Writers on the Genocide in Rwanda', *Journal of Literary Theory* (2012).

Juhani Koponen was Professor of Development Studies at the University of Helsinki until his retirement in 2012. As emeritus, he continues teaching and researching. A historian by training, his main research interest is the history of development and developmentalism, with the long-term development history of Tanzania and the formation of Finnish development policy as the main empirical cases. He has published on Tanzanian history – for example *Development for Exploitation. German Colonial Policies in Mainland Tanzania, 1884–1914* (Helsinki, Hamburg: Lit 1994), and on development issues elsewhere, such as in Nepal, and has led several major research projects on different aspects of development. He has also undertaken commissioned research on topical development policy issues and participates actively in development policy discussions.

E. Kushinga Makombe is Lecturer in the Department of Economic History at the University of Zimbabwe, where he teaches courses on the economic history of Zimbabwe, Southern Africa, and East Africa as well as the development of economic thought. He has been a member of the department since 2003 beginning as a Graduate Teaching Assistant. Makombe earned his BA and MA degrees from the University of Zimbabwe, and he recently received his doctorate degree from the University of Witwatersrand in South Africa in 2013. His doctoral research focused on the history of rural-urban interaction in colonial Zimbabwe, conceptualising rural immigrants to the city as agents operating in a social field that extends beyond the rural-urban divide. Makombe has strong interests in the role of human agency in the economy and his research focus includes: agrarian, gender, labour histories, post-colonialism and development discourses.

Céline Pessis is currently preparing her PhD dissertation in the history of science and technology on rural development knowledge, experts and politics in West Africa from 1945 to the 1970s, at the Ecole des Hautes Etudes en Sciences Sociales/Centre A. Koyré, Paris. She is also interested in environmental discourses and movements in mainland France and the African colonies. She has co-edited, with Christophe Bonneuil and Sezin Topçu, *Une autre histoire des 'Trente Glorieuses': modernisation, alertes environnementales et contestations du 'progrès' dans la France d'après-guerre, 1945–1968* (Paris: La Découverte 2013).

Walter Schicho is the retired Chair of African History at the Department of African Studies, University of Vienna. His fields of research and teaching include African contemporary history, global history, development studies, North-South relations and inter-cultural communication. He was director of the research projects 'Colonial Concepts of Development' and 'Plurilingual Speakers in Unilingual Environments' (the latter jointly with Brigitta Busch). His publications include *Handbuch Afrika* (3 vols, Frankfurt: Brandes & Apsel; Vienna: Südwind 1999–2004) and *Geschichte Afrikas* (Stuttgart: Theiss 2010).

Sven M. Speek has studied history and philosophy at the Ludwig-Maximilians-University of Munich. His current research as a doctoral candidate in environmental history at Ruhr University Bochum focuses on the intertwined histories of science and empire in colonial sub-Saharan Africa. He is particularly concerned with the histories of ecology and soil science.

Uyilawa Usuanlele, PhD, had his academic education in Nigeria, Sweden, and Canada, concentrating on African history. He worked as a researcher and administrator with the National Council for Arts and Culture, Nigeria. He was a founding member and Coordinator of the Institute for Benin Studies, Benin City, Nigeria. He is a recipient of the Swedish International Development Fellowship award and has presented papers at conferences in Africa, Europe, and the Americas. He has contributed articles and chapters to journals and books. He presently teaches African History at State University of New York (SUNY) Oswego, New York State, USA.

Iolanda Vasile holds a BA in Portuguese and Japanese Studies from the Faculty of Foreign Languages of the University of Bucharest, Romania. She is currently a PhD candidate at the Centre for Social Studies (CES) of the Faculty of Economics of the University of Coimbra, Portugal, in the programme 'Postcolonialisms and Global Citizenship'. In 2012, she was an exchange student at the Centre for African Studies at the University of São Paulo, Brazil, and currently is a tutor for an e-learning course on post-colonialisms for the Latin American Council of Social Sciences (CLACSO). She is also working as a research assistant in a project carried out by CES on the Portuguese Colonial War.

ACKNOWLEDGEMENTS

The idea for this book grew out of the international workshop 'Developing Africa – Development Discourse(s) in Late Colonialism', organised by Gerald Hödl and Martina Kopf, and held at the University of Vienna in January of 2011. Many of the following essays were presented first at the workshop, which brought together scholars from varied disciplinary backgrounds working and studying at universities across three continents: Africa, Europe, and North America. This made for three days of stimulating discussion and debate, not only concerning different approaches to the study of development, but also about the very meaning of development itself. We wish to thank the workshop participants whose work, for various reasons, does not appear in the volume: Aram Ziai, Regina Finsterhölzl, Cyrus Veeser, Susan Zimmerman, Julian Reid, Mamadou Fall, Karlheinz Spitzl, Hubertus Büschel, Suzanne Hanson, and Ewald Blocher. We also wish to give thanks to the convenors, discussants, and roundtable participants for their hard work: Heike Schmidt, Hanna Hacker, Berthold Unfried, Birgit Englert, Henning Melber, Marie Rodet, Margarete Grandner, Walter Schicho, Andreas Eckert, Odile Goerg, and David Simon.

A number of other people deserve credit for inspiring and supporting the publication of this volume. A special word of acknowledgement goes to Robert W. Shenton, one of the pioneers of development history, who gave one of the keynote addresses at the workshop. In light of the central role his ideas have played, not only for the book but in our thinking about the history of development generally, we wish to express our much-deserved appreciation: thank you, Bob. This publication would also not have come to fruition without the support of Walter Schicho, one of the founders of the Development Studies Programme at the University of Vienna and director of the research project 'Colonial Concepts of Development in Africa, 1920–1960'. Not only did Walter contribute one of the chapters to this collection, but he was instrumental in the editing and revisions of several other essays as well as offering valuable feedback and advice on the volume as a whole. We also would like to thank Matthew Vester and Marta Hodge for their assistance in translating Céline Pessis's chapter and Cláudia Castelo's chapter respectively, and to Billy Frank, whose friendship, humour, and constructive criticism helped us stay on track throughout the process.

Credit must also be reserved for the Austrian Science Fund, who financed three years of research into colonial concepts of development in Africa and made the workshop and this publication possible. Joe Hodge would like to acknowledge the support of West Virginia University for providing faculty development and travel funding during the time he spent working on the book project. Finally, our gratitude goes to the history editor, Emma Brennan, for working with us on the book and for guiding us patiently through every stage in the process. This book is also part of the larger series, 'Studies in Imperialism'. We would like to thank the series editors, John M. MacKenzie and Andrew S. Thompson for their support for the project. It is an honour to be associated with this long-standing and prestigious body of work.

ABBREVIATIONS

AEF   Afrique-Équatoriale Française (French Equatorial Africa)
AOF   Afrique Occidentale Française (French West Africa)
BIS   Bureau International des Sols
CDC   Colonial Development Corporation
CDWA   Colonial Development and Welfare Act
CEAC   Colonial Economic Advisory Committee
CFA   Communauté Financière d'Afrique
CGOT   Compagnie Générale des Oléagineux Tropicaux
CGP   Commissariat Général au Plan
CIRAD   Centre de Coopération Internationale en Recherche Agrono-
           mique pour de Développement
CO   Colonial Office
CRAM   Collectivités Rurales Autochtones Modernisées (Madagascar)
CSSRC   Colonial Social Science Research Council
DCO   (Barclays Bank) Dominion, Colonial and Overseas
EMB   Empire Marketing Board
FAO   Food and Agriculture Organization of the United Nations
FERDES   Fonds d'Équipement Rural et de Développement Économique
           et Social
FIDES   Fonds d'Investissement pour le Développement Économique
           et Social
IFAN   Institut Français d'Afrique Noire
JIU   Junta de Investigações do Ultramar
LTA   Land Tenure Act
MNHN   Muséum National d'Histoire Naturelle
NAD   Native Affairs Department, Southern Rhodesia
NLHA   Native Land Husbandry Act
NPTC   Native Production and Trade Commission
NRB   Natural Resources Board
ORSC   Office de la Recherche Scientifique Coloniale
ORSOM/ORSTOM   Office de la Recherche Scientifique et Technique
           Outre-Mer
RLI   Rhodes-Livingstone Institute for Social Research
SEMA   Secteurs Expérimentaux de Modernisation Agricole
STAT   Section Technique d'Agriculture Tropicale
TANU   Tanganyika African National Union
TOM   Territoires d'Outre-Mer
UNSCCUR   United Nations Scientific Conference on the Conservation
           and Utilization of Resources

Introduction

Joseph M. Hodge and Gerald Hödl

There is a new sense of optimism today about the future of sub-Saharan Africa. After being written off as hopeless by international donors for much of the 1980s and 1990s, sub-Saharan Africa has seen a remarkable reversal of economic fortunes in recent years. Between 2004 and 2008 African economies grew an average of 6.5 per cent annually, and while growth slowed during the global financial crisis, rates have rebounded to more than 5 per cent a year since 2010.[1] What is more, Africa's poverty rate has been falling steadily since the 1990s, with the percentage of people living in extreme poverty declining from 58 per cent in 1999 to 48 per cent by 2008.[2] There also have been important improvements in rates of educational completion and life expectancy. In the last decade in fact, eight of the top ten performers on the non-income dimensions of the United Nation's Human Development Index were countries in sub-Saharan Africa.[3] These and other indicators, such as the increase in private sector investment and market-oriented economic reforms, has led the World Bank to declare 'that Africa could be on the brink of an economic take-off, much like China was 30 years ago, and India 20 years ago'.[4]

After the setbacks and hardships of the age of structural adjustment, one hopes this is finally Africa's moment. But as the reference to Rostowian modernisation theory reminds us, this is not the first time foreign interests and powers have waxed about the unprecedented opportunities for transformation in Africa. Nor would it be the first if such possibilities, which by the Bank's own admission face considerable challenges,[5] should end in disappointment. It is worth recalling the heady optimism of the years immediately following the Second World War, when as Nicholas White has shown, the leading European colonial powers embarked on extensive development plans in Africa and Southeast Asia.[6] Such plans were designed both to raise purchasing power and standards of living in the overseas territories and to alleviate US dollar shortages by stimulating colonial exports that would help pay for metropolitan reconstruction. As the British Colonial Secretary, Oliver Stanley, put it in 1944, 'here we have an opportunity which may never recur, at a cost which is not extravagant, of setting the Colonial Empire on lines of development which will keep it in close and loyal contact with us'.[7] Yet within a few short years much of the enthusiasm had waned, prompting business leaders like Frank Samuel, the Managing Director of the United Africa Company, to complain: 'there has been a great deal of wishful thinking on the part of many writers and speakers who have, since the war, created an impression that Tropical Africa is an El Dorado of wealth sorely neglected in the past and capable of being developed rapidly on a grand scale. I take a far more sober view of the position'.[8] For Samuel, it was the barriers and challenges to progress, rather than the possibilities, that were most striking.[9]

In many ways, the post-war colonial development drives of Britain, France, and the other European colonial empires, represent the culmination of a much deeper history of concepts, practices, and debates about the prospects and setbacks of developing Africa. It is a history whose beginning stretches back to the *mission civilisatrice* and constructive imperialism doctrines of the late nineteenth century, and whose legacy, as the inter-governmental reports cited above remind us, continues to be felt to this day. Gradually over the course of the twentieth century, the concept of development superseded earlier notions of Europe's civilising mission until by the late 1930s and 1940s, as Frederick Cooper and Randall Packard observe, it had become 'a framing device bringing together a range of interventionist policies and metropolitan finance with the explicit goal of raising colonial standards of living'.[10] That development rose to such prominence during the closing stages of colonial rule is a testament to its semantic ambiguity, which enabled it to engage the desires and aspirations of diverse groups of African and European actors, and lent itself to being appropriated by a great variety of interests.[11]

This book is about the history of development during the colonial period in sub-Saharan Africa from the 1890s through to the end of empire. It is centred on British colonial Africa, the most extensively documented of the colonial empires in Africa in the twentieth century, but several chapters also study French and Portuguese colonial development or draw comparisons between the British and French experiences. It examines how the concept of development became an increasingly important element of colonial policies and mentalities and how its meaning was transformed over the course of the twentieth century. Much of the focus of the histories of development assembled in this volume is on the final decades of colonial rule in Africa, especially the period from the 1920s onwards, when development gradually if unevenly became the central, organising concept underpinning the relationship between metropolitan Europe and colonial Africa.[12]

What is development?

Given the amorphous quality of development, and its many and varied usages, it is imperative that we begin by making some clear distinctions. Development is a murky and often contentious term. Its ambiguity reflects, in large measure, the fact that it encompasses more aims than just achieving modernity and it refers not only to an intransitive, self-evolving process of change, but also, increasingly, to intentional practices and actions initiated most often by state agencies. Much of the confusion surrounding 'development' is attributable to the fact that most books and articles written on the subject fail to explain coherently what is meant by the term, or they define the concept so broadly that it becomes devoid of substantive meaning. The first crucial distinction that needs to be made, following Michael Cowen and Robert Shenton, is between 'development' as an action or process, and 'development' as a goal or product.[13] Development as a process refers to the actions that are taken or the measures implemented in order to become 'developed'. This is development as a verb, whereas development as a product or goal refers to the results of development; what is achieved once one has experienced 'development' as a process.

Having goals is important. The problem arises when studies of development routinely conflate the means with the goal, by suggesting for example, that development 'is empowering in the sense that the people concerned have a substantial degree of control ... over the process through access to the means of accumulating social power'.[14] In other words, one must be empowered in order to become more empowered, but if one is already empowered is one really in need of development? A more useful definition, for our purposes, might be to describe development simply as an intentional, organised intervention in collective affairs according to a general (if not universal) standard of improvement.[15]

We might also note that from the colonial period to the present day, development has been oscillating between two distinct poles: raising production and productivity on the one hand, and raising the living standards of people regarded as backward or underdeveloped on the other. The normative contents or 'goals' of development have shifted over time between these two poles, between the aim of making fuller or more efficient use of given economic resources – usually by employing capitalist or market forces – and the objective of improving the living conditions or welfare of a given population. Toward which of these ends of development policies the pendulum is swinging depends in large measure on the power relations among and between the various actors involved. Closely related to this is another dimension of development: its potential to serve purposes of control.

And this leads us to Cowen and Shenton's second distinction between 'development' as an immanent and objective process, and 'development' as a subjective course of action or intentional practice. The emergence and expansion of market capitalism is perhaps the most relevant example of a natural or spontaneous process of development. Enlightenment thinkers such as Adam Smith popularised the idea of unlimited and universal progress whereby human economic activity progressed through a succession of different stages from hunting and gathering to commerce and manufacturing.[16] The problem is that this apparently universal movement of progress does not always unfold as effortlessly and as spontaneously as Enlightenment thinkers predicted. There is, as Marshall Berman reminds us, a darker side to development; one that turns out 'to exact great human costs . . . human powers can be developed only through what Marx called "the powers of the underworld", dark and fearful energies that may erupt with a horrible force beyond all human control'.[17]

It is the disorder and chaos of immanent development, Cowen and Shenton suggest, that leads to the modern idea of development as a planned and intentional course of actions. They insist that the idea of development as a means by which the state could impose order on the uncertainty thrown up by material transformation emerged first as a response to the growing fears of rapid urbanisation, poverty, and unemployment during the early industrialisation of Europe in the nineteenth century. It thus emerged not as the equivalent of progress but 'as the counterpoint to progress . . . based upon the idea that "development" may be used to ameliorate the disordered faults of progress'.[18] As long as there is the historical process of immanent, materialist development, to paraphrase Cowen and Shenton, there will be conscious and intentional attempts to bring order to the disorder and chaos which inevitably follows in its wake.[19]

But just as important, one might add, has been the desire to use development to create and to intensify productive forces. In regions being integrated into a capitalist world system and where capitalist relations of production increasingly predominate, this has entailed the expansion of market-oriented production and the commodification of both human labour and its products. Here, we come to understand that development is both constructive and destructive, both positive and negative at the same time; like two sides of the same coin. Therefore the practices that were subsumed under the concept of development from its inception in the nineteenth century both unleashed social and economic forces and tried to manage and rein them in. The two polarities – higher production/better living conditions, stimulating material production/trying to control its destructive effects – are closely interrelated and inseparable.

Development and twentieth-century colonialism in Africa: a short history

Central to the idea of development as an intentional practice is the principle of 'trusteeship': only if those who possess the necessary knowledge and who understand the goals that should guide intervention are empowered to operate as 'trustees' for humanity, can the reconciliation of progress with order follow.[20] For the Saint-Simonians this meant placing society's resources in the hands of bankers, through the creation of a central government bank. For Auguste Comte, a student of Saint-Simon and founder of the doctrine of positivism, bankers would be aided by experts in the science of history or 'sociology' who understood the laws of social evolution. This doctrine of trusteeship would in time become the central ideological foundation of European colonial empire. For societies in which the conditions of development were not present and thus had to be made to happen, the process would be guided by trustees from societies where development had already taken place.

In the nineteenth century various imperial doctrines were formulated in which the principle of trusteeship was implicit. European colonialism, as Frederick Cooper observes, was constructed around ideologies of difference that justified foreign rule.[21] Non-European native peoples were perceived as 'backward', static, and trapped in their traditional or customary ways. Colonial conquest led to demands to incorporate and transform colonial societies through the introduction of Western cultural norms and practices, especially the spread of Christianity and Western education and medicine. Nevertheless, throughout the colonial period, authorities continued to emphasise the distinctiveness of non-European native peoples as a way of legitimising European claims of cultural and political superiority.

Most prominent among these ideologies was the French doctrine of a *mission civilisatrice* associated with the Third Republic.[22] Before the First World War, the most important tenet on which the French civilising mission rested was the *mise en valeur* or rational development of the colonies' natural and human resources. The term *mise en valeur* was first popularised in the 1880s by Jules Ferry, a French government minister and Prime Minister under the Third Republic, who stressed that French colonial expansion was necessary because in a world of increasing international competition the growth of production and accumulation of capital required access to new outlets and control of new sources of raw materials. However, Ferry also believed the 'higher races' had rights and duties towards the 'lower races' and were obligated to share the benefits of science and progress, to help spread civilisation and republican values, and to help improve native living conditions. In other words, colonisation was not simply a question of French interests, though these were important, but it was also a matter of duty.[23]

The new concept of 'constructive exploitation' rather than mere expansion and plunder gained prominence in the 1890s, becoming official policy in 1895.[24] It reflected the republican belief in science and technology as key to the mastery and rational control of nature, as well as a new interest in the role of the state in managing overseas resources. The aim, first and foremost, was to build a modern trans-portation network through railways, ports, and other lines of com-munication, in order to 'open up' the interiors of Indochina and West Africa. It also sought to improve health conditions in the colonies through the introduction of medical research and sanitary services, although most resources benefited Europeans and urban areas. In its widest sense, the *mission civilisatrice* envisioned the uplifting of France's colonial subjects through the eradication of native institutions such as slavery and chieftaincies considered antithetical to republican values, and the creation of a federal school system in West Africa to provide free, secular education to all Africans.[25] In keeping with the demands of *mise en valeur* the emphasis was placed on primary educa-tion and practical training, such as learning manual trades and studying agriculture. Nevertheless, assimilationist principles endured through the retaining of French as the language of instruction and the implicit belief that French civilisation and culture were superior.[26]

The French were not alone in constructing imperial ideologies. In the 1890s, the British Secretary of State for Colonies, Joseph Chamberlain, promoted what he called the doctrine of 'constructive imperialism'. Like Ferry, Chamberlain pushed for state intervention and assistance to develop what he referred to as the 'imperial estates':

> Great Britain, the little centre of a vaster Empire than the world has ever seen, owns great possessions in every part of the globe, and many of those possessions are still unexplored, entirely undeveloped. What would a great landlord do in a similar case with a great estate? We know perfectly well, if he had the money, he would expend some of it, at any rate, in improving the property, in making communications, in making outlets for the prod-ucts of his land, and that, it seems to me, is what a wealthy country ought to do with regard to these territories which it is called upon to control and govern. That is why I am an advocate of the extension of Empire.[27]

Chamberlain called for the British imperial government to provide the necessary financial and technical assistance for the extension of imperial communications, especially railways, and other infrastructural projects in order to tap into the largely unexplored wealth of Britain's colonial dependencies in tropical Africa and the West Indies.[28] As Colonial Secretary from 1895 to 1903, he pushed the Colonial Office to make greater use of scientific knowledge and technical expertise, especially in the fields of tropical medical and tropical agricultural research and training. He was instrumental, for example, in the establishment of the London and Liverpool Schools of Tropical Medicine and in the setting up of the West India Royal Commission, which recommended grants and subsidies to aid the declining sugar industry and to encourage economic diversification of the islands.[29]

The goal for Chamberlain was to strengthen British industry and trade by harnessing the untapped resources and raw materials of the empire and by opening up lucrative new markets for British manufactured goods. But there was a dark side to Chamberlain's development doctrine, which as many contemporaries observed, involved the increasing exploitation of the colonies, and the sacrifice of the rights of indigenous peoples. And while he maintained that his policies would benefit both the 'cause of civilization' and the prosperity of the indigenous population, he nevertheless acknowledged that' you cannot make omelettes without breaking eggs. You cannot exercise control over barbarous countries, which previous to your arrival have been in a state of constant anarchy and disorder, without occasionally coming into conflict with their savage rulers and having to shed some blood'.[30] In time, criticism and opposition to Chamberlain's brand of development would mount and demands for greater attention and protection of native people's rights and welfare would escalate. Liberal critics, in particular, argued that intervention was necessary, not to create the conditions for private capitalist development, but rather to halt the destruction of native ways of life and the erosion of communal land ownership on which traditional African society was said to be based.[31]

The 1920s represents a transitional phase from the predatory, if increasingly more systematic, economic exploitation of the colonies, to a significantly reformed and modified system of colonial governance.[32] The latter's main feature, a substantially enhanced role for government action, had its roots in earlier imperial ideologies, as noted above, but would gather speed in the aftermath of the First World War when the hegemony of the colonial state 'was consolidated and its rule thoroughly institutionalized'.[33] It is no coincidence that the two most important programmatic texts sketching out the outlines for a revamped colonialism were published in the early 1920s.[34] French colonial doctrine reached its height with the publishing of Albert Sarraut's *La mise en valeur des colonies françaises* in 1923. Sarraut was a French statesman, Governor-General of the Indochina federation and minister in several governments including Prime Minister twice between 1906 and 1940. During his tenure as Minister of Colonies from January 1920 to March 1924, and then as a member of various coalition governments in the late 1920s, Sarraut was the leading spokesman of the French colonial lobby, campaigning for state investment for the economic and social development of the French overseas possessions, especially Francophone Africa. His views are perhaps best captured in *La mise en valeur*, in which he called on government and parliamentary leaders to give greater attention to colonial policy, asserting that: 'It should not be forgotten that we are centuries ahead of them, long centuries during which – slowly and painfully, through lengthy effort of research, invention and intellectual progress aided by the very influence of our temperate climate – a magnificent heritage of science, experience and moral superiority has taken shape, which makes us eminently entitled to protect and lead the races lagging behind us'.[35]

One year earlier, in 1922, Sir Frederick Lugard wrote *The Dual Mandate in British Tropical Africa*. Lugard had played a vital role within British colonialism in the late nineteenth and early twentieth centuries, both as an ideologue and as an administrator holding key posts in Africa and Asia. In *The Dual Mandate*, which is widely credited with formulating the doctrine of British Indirect Rule in Africa, Lugard argued that Britain had a dual responsibility in Africa, both to the indigenous peoples whose interests and welfare had to be taken into account, and towards the whole of humankind since the immense resources of the continent had to be exploited for the benefit of all.[36] Lugard was critical of past efforts to impose Western models of government and education which he considered ill-suited to African beliefs and customs. Instead, he favoured an 'appropriate native policy' that emphasised administration 'along native lines' through the use of local indigenous chiefs and authorities and the creation of local courts.[37]

The writings of Sarraut and Lugard on colonial rule reflect the growing importance attached to the principle of trusteeship in the 1920s, especially by the League of Nations, whose covenant proclaimed 'that the well-being and development of . . . peoples [not yet able to stand by themselves under the strenuous conditions of the modern world] form a sacred trust of civilisation'.[38] Under the influence of the League, French and British attitudes towards their overseas dependencies began to change.[39] It is worth noting, for example, that Lugard

[8]

was appointed the British representative on the League's Permanent Mandates Commission (PMC) from 1919 to 1936. The PMC was set up to guarantee protection for the rights and interests of the 'natives' of the Mandated Territories, as they were termed, while also serving to regulate the relations of imperialist nations in these territories. However, the tutelage of the Mandated Territories continued to be entrusted to the advanced nations by virtue of their proximity, resources, and experience. What trusteeship actually meant in practice remained vague and unclear. Nevertheless, there was increasing pressure on colonial authorities in the 1920s to show that trusteeship, however defined, was being taken seriously.

Several new plans and programmes were introduced by both the French and the British in the 1920s. As was the case before the First World War, much importance was attached to investing in public works and communications, as well as scientific research, to increase the production and productivity of African agriculture. Sarraut, for example, proposed a fifteen-year investment programme to the National Assembly in 1921 to provide more than one billion francs in government loans to build additional railways, ports, telegraph networks, roads, irrigation as well as schools, public health care, and research facilities.[40] The programme included funds for the expansion of cash crop production, including one of the largest rice and cotton irrigation schemes ever envisioned in colonial Africa, the Office du Niger project in the French Soudan. Office planners anticipated the reclamation of some 1,850,000 hectares of under-utilised land on the borders of the Sahara desert by resettling farmers on irrigated plots and introducing intensive plough agriculture and crop rotations.[41] The goal was not only to produce more crops for the export market, but to generate a total social transformation of African society.

In the 1920s, French colonial authorities such as Jules Carde, the Governor-General of French West Africa, also began to stress the *mise en valeur* of Africa's human resources as the key to tapping the continent's material potential. Carde advocated greater social investment in public health, education, and labour productivity in order to increase the efficiency of Africa's 'native producers' and expand its human power. Modest steps were taken to prevent disease and mortality among the African population by, for example, setting up a new medical training centre for African doctors and midwives, the opening of medical dispensaries and maternity homes, and by organising mobile assistance units staffed with African auxiliaries to carry medical care into remote rural areas.[42] French officials also allocated more resources to vocational education and training, which they saw as more appropriate for local circumstances in which traditional methods could be reinforced with nursery school practices to teach, for example, new agricultural techniques.[43]

As the emphasis on adapting to local conditions and reinforcing tradition suggests, one of the distinctive features of French colonial policy after 1919 was the fusing of *mise en valeur* economic development with associationism – the French version of Indirect Rule, which held a more positive view of African cultures and was more receptive to working through indigenous chiefs and political institutions.[44] The renewed interest of the French in 'development along native lines' (and this applies to British Indirect Rule as well), had less to do with a genuine desire to understand African cultures, than it did with imperial security and limiting the growth of anti-colonial discontent. As Martin Thomas argues: 'Harmonious interracial contact required a common appreciation that colonialism amounted to more than untrammelled economic exploitation. Improved colonial living standards, vaccination programs, declining infant mortality, and higher life expectancy all promoted national efficiency, which, in turn, generated greater political loyalty to France among dependent populations'.[45] Or at least this is what proponents such as Sarraut believed.

There was also growing recognition in Britain in the 1920s of the need for closer imperial economic integration and greater metropolitan responsibility for a more coordinated colonial development policy. In 1925, a parliamentary commission on East Africa, headed by William Ormsby-Gore, urged the imperial government to develop the vast productive areas of the region by investing in transport facilities, and to this end, London agreed to guarantee a £10 million East Africa Transport Loan over ten years for railway extension, harbour developments, the construction of main roads, and mechanical transport.[46] In the Sudan, the British government financed a £3 million loan for the Gezira Cotton Scheme, granted in 1913 but delayed by the war until 1920.[47] The scheme was a joint agreement between the state, which undertook the construction of the Sennar dam and irrigation canals, and the Sudan Plantation Syndicate, a commercial consortium who managed the project and ran the ginneries. Initially, the dam and canals provided irrigation to 80,000 feddans (or 83,040 acres) of land.[48]

As was the case in Francophone Africa, British colonial administrators also began to turn their attention to what may be termed the 'human side' of colonial development, introducing programmes for 'native' education and public health in the 1920s that included the creation of rural medical dispensaries, centres for child and mother welfare, and the deployment of mobile laboratory and vaccination units for preventing the spread of epidemic diseases.[49] In the Gold Coast, the Prince of Wales' College at Achimota, the first secondary school and teachers training college in British West Africa, was founded in 1924–25 at a cost of more than £500,000. According to Gordon Guggisberg, the Governor of the Gold Coast, Achimota was intended to serve as an educational model for the region, and in time to develop into the first university.[50] The British also set up several regional agricultural research and experimental stations, the most prominent of which was the East African Agricultural Research Station at Amani, Tanganyika, originally founded by the Germans before the First World War but re-established after years of neglect as a centre for basic, long-range research in 1927.[51] Among other things, scientists at Amani conducted surveys of the region's basic soil types, and carried out trials on new crop varieties and cultivation methods to help boost African agricultural production.

In truth, both *mise en valeur* and the dual mandate were more rhetoric than reality, largely because the necessary political will and financial resources were lacking. Such efforts were tightly constrained by the doctrine of colonial financial self-sufficiency. The severe spending limits imposed on the colonies under this doctrine meant that in the 1920s and 1930s neither the British and French, nor the Belgian and Portuguese imperial governments for that matter, were able to initiate and sustain major development projects. As a result, any development had to be paid for out of each colony's own revenues generated from taxes on Africans and from custom duties imposed on imports and exports. Sarraut's proposed investment programme, for example, failed to gain parliamentary backing, as France's financial troubles and eventual devaluation of the franc in 1926 undercut official enthusiasm for *mise en valeur*. The Office du Niger project refered to earlier, had to rely initially on local funds only, which limited what could be done to opening two small farming centres in 1925 and 1929 and constructing a barrage at Sotuba, near Bamako.[52] Overall, as Cooper notes, before 1940 the major European colonial powers in Africa rejected any development plans that would have entailed the significant use of metropolitan funding.[53] The parsimonious attitude of metropolitan governments meant that most colonies had very little in the way of investment funding and what they did have tended to be spent on railways and physical infrastructure that benefited the economic exploitation of natural resources, rather than on social services and welfare for Africans.

It is important to stress, moreover, that the meagre attempts to improve African living conditions and welfare existed in tandem with other less savoury characteristics of the colonial system that were no less integral to colonial development, such as the use of forced labour, the raising of hut and poll taxes, the displacement and movement of populations, and in some areas, the forced cultivation of cash crops like cotton.[54] In all colonial systems between the wars, public infrastructure projects such as railways or irrigation works were built by what amounted to a labour tax, forced African labour (what the French refered to as the prestation policy and the British as 'communal' labour), often with extremely high mortality and attrition rates.[55]

Given the externally oriented and trade-dependent nature of colonial African states, it is not surprising that the world economic depression that began in 1929 exposed the contradictions and tensions inherent in European colonial rule. Changes began to gather pace and gradually assumed a new complexion in the wake of the crisis. The British government's initial response was the Colonial Development Act of 1929, which largely followed the tradition of earlier policies, still representing a narrow economic conception of development mainly geared towards supporting the metropolitan economy. At the same time, the Act, which provided up to £1 million per year in Treasury grants and loans to aid a range of colonial government schemes, showed the increasing readiness of the imperial centre to make additional funds available in the name of development.[56] This reaction to the Great Depression, which had strong neo-mercantilist undertones, can also be witnessed in the case of France where the crisis magnified the importance of the empire as a *réservoir colonial*, providing a secure market, as well as an exclusive source of raw materials, for French industries.[57] The beginnings of a new departure in French colonial policy, aimed at accelerating the economic integration of the empire, can be detected in the 1930s as government expenditure for the *plans d'équipement* multiplied and the need for a programme of public funding to finance major construction projects was recognised.[58] In 1931, for example, the metropolitan government finally agreed to include funds for the Office du Niger irrigation scheme as part of its colonial loans programme, albeit at a much reduced level. A special administration was established a year later to manage the project, and in 1934 construction began on a new and larger barrage at Markala near Segu.[59]

The Office du Niger was the most high-profile agricultural project in all of French West Africa, foreshadowing many of the developmentalist ambitions of the post-Second World War period. Indeed, as Christophe Bonneuil remarks: 'One can locate the birth of the developmentalist state in tropical Africa in the 1930s, when colonial governments confronted the disorders and the threats of the Great Depression, adopted a more *dirigiste* agenda, intervened more directly in the economy, and took steps towards planning and state regulation. Major welfare and development policies also emerged in the 1930s and were key milestones in state building in Africa'.[60] Indeed, if John Darwin is correct in suggesting that 'the proactive or developmental state' is one of the most striking features of late colonialism, then we can fairly situate the origins of the late colonial state in the fallout of the world economic crisis of the early 1930s.[61]

Several other contributing factors may be identified in the turn from the 'preservationist colonialism of the 1930s' to the 'developmentalist colonialism of the 1940s and 1950s'.[62] Throughout the 1930s and 1940s, the volume of criticism of the old colonial system and calls for its reform magnified, not only from inside (for example, from members of the British Labour Party and the Section Française de l'Internationale Ouvrière) but also from the international community outside Britain, France, and the other colonial powers. Disapproval was heard both from moderate groups, such as the Aborigines Protection Society and other philanthropic non-governmental organisations, as well as multilateral organisations such as the International Labour Office, and from more radical forums like the International African Service Bureau and the Pan-African Congresses. Compounding such criticism were the pressures of the Second World War, which created new demands on colonial states to mobilise Africans for military service and to intensify colonial food and economic production for the war effort. Forced labour and recruitment was used extensively by both the British and French to meet the heightened strains of war, while consumption was reduced drastically by restricting imports and raising taxes. All of this entailed severe hardships and food shortages in many parts of colonial Africa.[63]

But perhaps most crucial of all, as Cooper notes, in the 1930s and 1940s 'colonial rule [in Africa] choked on the narrowness of the pathways it had created'.[64] Simply put, Africans were increasingly unwilling to stay in the limited roles that colonial rulers had assigned to them. The result, as has been well documented, was widespread labour unrest and strikes between 1935 and 1950 across British and French Africa that crippled the key nodal points of empire: ports, mines, railways, and commercial centres.[65] In 1935 there was a strike in the copper mines and towns of Northern Rhodesia, and between 1935 and 1938, a series of strikes, demonstrations, and riots swept across the British West Indies, including an island wide rebellion in Jamaica. Strikes occurred on the docks of Mombasa and Dar es Salaam, and on the railways and mines of the Gold Coast in the late 1930s, and again on the Rhodesian Copperbelt in 1940. The strikes and riots continued after the war in the gold mines of South Africa in 1946, in Mombasa and Dar es Salaam in 1947, and in Accra and Southern Rhodesia in 1948. In Francophone Africa, strikes occurred in Senegal in 1945, and the entire railway system of French West Africa was shut down in 1947–48.

Unrest and conflict erupted in rural areas as well over government soil conservation measures in East and Southern Africa, and after the war, there was a large protest of cocoa farmers in the Gold Coast over the government's swollen-shoot eradication campaign which forcibly destroyed diseased cocoa trees.[66] This groundswell of resistance coming from Africans would eventually feed into the political movements and independence struggles of the 1950s, but initially these diverse grievances were more about demanding equal rights and entitlements such as equal work for equal pay or family allowances. As Cooper writes: 'The demands were not, at first, focused on taking over the state. But they were focused on what states actually did: on education, on taxation, on investment in social services and productive resources, on judicial systems, and on the question of who was to participate in the making of vital decisions'.[67]

The European colonial powers responded to these pressures from above and below in various ways designed to regain the initiative. Most notably, they sought to expand the scope of colonial development both by committing greater financial resources to the endeavour and by broadening the definition of development to include novel forms of social welfare services. In 1940, Britain enacted the Colonial Development and Welfare Act, which provided £5 million per year for ten years for development and welfare projects, plus £500,000 per year for ten years for research. The Fund was enhanced substantially by the 1945 Act which provided £120 million (amended to £140 million in 1950) to be made available over the next ten years with up to £17.5 million available in any one year. Up to £1 million per year was also provided for research with no time limit imposed on schemes of investigation.[68]

The French passed a similar Act, known as the Fonds d'Investissement pour le Développement Économique et Social (Economic and Social Development Investment Fund: FIDES) in April 1946, with a budget of 200 million CFA francs in 1947 increasing to 9,300 million CFA francs by 1950. In addition, the government established the Fonds d'Équipement Rural et de Développement Économique et Social (Rural Economic and Social Development Fund: FERDES) in 1949, which invested a further 2,500 million CFA francs in French West Africa between 1949 and 1954.[69] Overall for the period 1940–58, Jacques Marseille estimates public sector funding outpaced private investment in the French empire by a ratio of 5 to 1.[70] Despite the new public credits, a great deal of French colonial development funding continued to come from internal revenues, raised through public borrowing and local taxation, as FIDES expected colonial states to match metropolitan funding at a rate of 45 per cent.[71] Nevertheless, for the first time, both the British and French metropolitan governments were prepared to provide substantial subventions of metropolitan funds and resources to undertake programmes of social and economic development in Africa, not only to build infrastructure and make economic production more efficient, but specifically to raise the standard of living of colonial peoples by investing in housing, water, schools, health services, and so on.[72]

With these policies, British and French colonial officials and rulers aimed not only to hold on to the colonial state, but to reinvigorate it by transforming it into a more effective instrument for development as a way of re-legitimising the colonial mission. Correspondingly, state planning and administrative services were expanded dramatically in the 1940s.[73] All overseas British territories were instructed to prepare comprehensive ten-year development plans. At the same time, the Colonial Office was revamped by the formation of nearly two dozen specialist advisers and consultants and an equal number of specialised advisory bodies in areas such as social welfare, labour, economics, and cooperation. In the field, colonial technical and research services were enlarged and coordinated, and colonial service recruitment, especially technical personnel, was increased substantially. Between 1945 and 1952 over 10,000 new colonial service recruits were hired, 60 per cent of whom were technical experts in areas such as agriculture, engineering, surveying, medicine, education, forestry, and town planning.[74] Under the framework of the post-war French Union, the Ministry for Overseas France was now joined by the technical ministries such as the Finance Ministry, the Ministry of Agriculture, and the Education Ministry, who provided expertise and consultation in their respective areas of government intervention, sometimes through joint committees. At the same time, a specialised entity, the *Commission de Modernisation et d'Équipement aux Territoires d'Outre-Mer* was formed to administer the FIDES, and housed in the *Commissariat Général du Plan* so as to operate outside of the control of the Ministry for Overseas France and the Government-General in Dakar.[75] And in Dakar, the government set up a planning directorate to examine development proposals prior to sending them on to the federal level.[76]

Planning was thus part and parcel of the grandiose attempts at economic and social engineering in the post-war years. As Britain and France faced the loss of their possessions in Asia, their colonies in Africa promised to fill the gap and supply resources for post-war reconstruction. Fearing another global depression, European metropolitan governments sought to intensify colonial primary production in the hopes of meeting essential food and raw material shortages and securing protected markets for home industries and European investors. But more than this, as Nicholas White explains, 'the real attraction of the colonial empires in the era of reconstruction lay in the contribution they could make to relieving acute balance of payment deficits, and especially plugging the US dollar gap'.[77] Colonial exports would act as 'dollar earners' providing much needed foreign exchange to purchase food and goods for metropolitan reconstruction, while simultaneously serving as 'dollar savers' by supplying raw materials and commodities directly to the home market. Both Britain and France controlled financial and monetary policy through currency zones, coordinated by the Bank of England and the Banque de France, in order to centrally pool foreign exchange generated from colonial exports.

The British government also established two new public corporations: the Colonial Development Corporation (CDC), which was given the authority to borrow up to £100 million, and the Overseas Food Corporation (OFC), with up to £50 million. The new public corporations were designed specifically to increase the supply of colonial products for export as quickly as possible. The onset of the Cold War compounded this trend, leading the United States to include the colonies in the European Recovery Programme (ERP) in 1949 on the grounds that stimulating colonial export production would not only aid the economic recovery of their European allies, but also increase the supply of strategically valuable commodities.[78] Some 10 billion francs of Marshall Aid spending, for example, was funnelled into French West Africa between 1948 and 1952, mostly for the construction of railways, ports, and roads.[79]

Much of the public funding provided by the European metropolitan governments in the 1940s and 1950s went towards high prestige, capital intensive projects for infrastructure and agricultural development. Development projects of enormous proportions were drawn up and realised. In British colonial Africa, the two most notorious schemes were the East African Groundnut Scheme in Tanganyika, and the gigantic poultry farm designed to mass produce eggs in the Gambia. Both schemes proved to be dismal failures. In the case of the Groundnut Scheme, over 3 million acres were to be cleared and transformed into a hundred 30,000 acre farming units, at a cost of £40 million. Every aspect of the vast project was to be mechanised, which at full capacity was projected to produce between 600,000 and 800,000 tons of groundnuts annually. The scheme, however, turned out to be a white elephant from the very beginning due, in large measure, to the insufficient examination of soil and climatic conditions, and an under-estimation of the difficulties involved in supplying and operating heavy tractors and planting machinery under tropical conditions.[80]

For Francophone Africa, it is estimated that over 65 per cent of the FIDES credits under the first four-year plan, and 45 per cent under the second, went to infrastructure, much of it to high-profile projects, such as the Vridi Canal in the Côte d'Ivoire, which by providing access to the sea transformed Abidjan into the major shipping and financial centre for French West Africa.[81] Another major example was the Office du Niger irrigation scheme, which as we have seen had been in existence since before the Second World War, but was expanded substantially after the war with FIDES and FERDES support. An extensive project evaluation, commissioned in 1945, initated a shake-up of the scheme leading to the appointment of a new director, more in depth research on soil types and crop varieties, and the introduction of mechanised deep ploughing and experimental trials with chemical fertilisers.[82] By 1959 roughly 35,000 African tenants had been settled on 36,000 hectares of irrigated land.[83] In the end, however, mechanisation proved to be too expensive and had to be abandoned in favour of a return to oxen-drawn ploughs. The costs of artificial fertilisers also proved prohibitively high, and in consequence Office managers increasingly relied on organic manuring by allowing nomadic pastoralists to graze their cattle on Office lands during the dry season. These various schemes in both British and French colonial Africa increased the number of technicians, administrators, and other European employees, as well as the largess of financial resources and bureaucratic machinery. The scale of the colonial development policies after 1945, and the level of state intervention that such policies entailed, have led historians to refer to a 'second colonial occupation' in Africa.[84]

Although the 'second colonial occupation' is associated primarily with Britain and France, it is important to see the emergence of the 'developmentalist state' as a common trend occurring across sub-Saharan Africa in the late colonial period. This is not to say that important differences in periodisation and experience do not exist between the British and French empires on the one hand, and some of the other colonial regimes such as the Belgians and Portuguese on the other. Nonetheless, in this as in several other respects the Belgian and Portuguese governments lagged behind but would eventually follow suit; Belgium introduced its ten-year plan for the Congo in 1949, while Portugal turned to planning in the early 1950s.

Although the Belgian government never warmed to the idea of a metropolitan development fund, the Belgian Congo was nevertheless able to provide substantial welfare provisions funded through its own revenues, which expanded dramatically during the post-war commodity boom.[85] The Belgian Congo invested considerably in an African school system, which in 1945 was almost non-existent, achieving

70 per cent enrolment of primary school-age children by 1959. By the late 1950s, the Belgian colonial administration also boasted of having instituted the best health services in the tropics.[86] Higher education, however, was woefully neglected, such that at independence in 1960 only 16 Congolese students had graduated from the colony's two, infant universities at Lovanium and Elizabethville.[87]

In the field of rural development, the Belgian colonial state began re-making African agriculture as early as 1936 with the introduction of large-scale land utilisation schemes, known as *paysannats*, which by the mid-1950s had become home to some 140,000 resettled African farmers.[88] Like the Office du Niger, however, the Congolese *paysannats* turned out to be less than successful in practice as officials seldom took adequate account either of the challenging and variable environmental conditions at each site, or of farmers' own livelihood strategies and responses to the schemes. On the Paysannat Turumbu near Yangambi, for example, Belgian agronomists developed a land-use and cropping system known as the 'corridor system' in which rectangular bands of cleared land alternated with bands of forest, and crop rotations included a twelve-year fallow period. Despite years of testing, however, the experiment failed to maintain soil fertility, and in the end, farmers were advised to return to the traditional Turumbu farming practice of twenty-year-long fallow periods.[89]

Portugal's commitment to maintaining its African colonies in the twentieth century has often been portrayed as an abberation, as something running against the tide of change that rolled across the other colonial powers in the late 1950s as they came to grips with the reality of African nationalism.[90] Portugal's late colonial experience together with the timing of its demise is certainly distinctive. At the same time, as the chapters by Castelo and Araújo and Vasile demonstrate, it is equally clear that the colonial policies and practices of the Estado Novo (1933–74)[91] must be viewed as part of the wider history of the era of the developmentalist state in Africa, which as Bonneuil observes, began in the 1930s but endured despite various alterations until the end of the 1970s.[92] Portugal's African colonies took on a new importance during the Estado Novo under the dictatorship of António de Oliveira Salazar, and later Marcello Caetano, who insisted that Angola and Mozambique be regarded as an integral part of a single, unified Portuguese nation and thus designated administratively as 'overseas provinces'. Similar to Britain and France, the Salazar regime maintained, as Martin Thomas writes, 'that its colonial administration was a "scientific occupation", informed by the rational study of dependent peoples, the maximization of their economic potential, and benevolent, but authoritarian, governance. Where the Portuguese empire differed was in its stubborn adherence to this ideology of domination after 1945, at a time when other imperial states were adopting strategies of colonial development and greater political inclusion of subject populations, in an effort to assuage international criticism and breathe new life into their empires'.[93]

That Portugal was able to sustain its predatory form of colonial rule unreformed for so long is attributable partly to the skilful use of ideology. In the early 1950s, the Minister of Overseas Provinces, Manuel Maria Sarmento Rodrigues, began promoting the concept of lusotropicalism, an idea first articulated by the Brazilian sociologist Gilberto Freyre, who was invited by Rodrigues to visit the Portuguese overseas provinces in 1951–52.[94] According to Freyre, the Portuguese had a unique ability for 'civilising' peoples of the tropical world by blending and assimilating indigenous cultures and values with their own, rather than denigrating and discounting them.[95] The Salazar regime appropriated the concept of lusotropicalism as a 'useful ideological veneer', to borrow Penvenne's term, in order to gloss over the continuing exploitation and colonisation of its African colonies.[96] In a sense they attempted to deflect criticism by arguing that their empire was a post-racial, post-imperial community of Lusophone peoples.

Determined to reinvigorate their colonial mission, the Portuguese finally began emulating the other colonial powers in the 1950s by introducing a series of ambitious six-year development plans. The first *Plano de Fomento para o Ultramar* (Overseas Development Plan) for 1953–58 provided roughly $55 million in funding to Mozambique and $100 million to Angola for investment on roads, ports, railways, and other infrastructure and communication projects. Funding more than doubled under the second plan for 1959–64, and investment diversified into health services, secondary and university education, and agricultural development.[97] And similar to the other colonial powers, much of the investment in agriculture committed by Portugal in the 1950s and 1960s went to high-profile, large-scale settlement schemes, such as the agricultural and irrigation settlements at Cela and Cunene in Angola, and similar projects on the Limpopo and Umbeluzi Rivers in Mozambique, which received the lion's share of agricultural investment funds under the second Overseas Development Plan – 71 per cent of Angola's budget and 84 per cent of Mozambique's.[98]

Portugal's state-sponsored settlement schemes were distinctive, however, in that they were designed primarily for white settlers rather than Africans tenants. Indeed, the schemes were closely tied to the promotion of Portuguese overseas migration to Angola and Mozambique from the 1950s to the early 1970s. As a result of both economic incentives and government colonisation programmes, the white population living in Angola and Mozambique grew quickly after 1945, increasing from 71,521 in 1940 to 514,000 by 1973, with migratory flows reaching their peak in the mid-1960s.[99] Even though most of the new settlers came from peasant backgrounds, the government's ambitious agricultural settlement schemes were not very successful with only a small fraction of the *colonos* remaining on farms and ranches in the countryside. Ironically, despite the rural bias propagated by official propaganda, the vast majority of the white population of Portuguese Africa was concentrated in urban centres.[100] As Cláudia Castelo observes, 'the migration to Africa corresponded . . . to the wish of leaving the countryside. Few metropolitan peasants wanted to remain peasants in Africa; often they had previously migrated to the cities, within Portugal. Only a tiny minority went to the State sponsored rural settlements (*"colonatos"*) in Angola and Mozambique and a significant percentage eventually gave up, settling down in the major cities'.[101]

Of all the interventions of the colonial state in Africa, those designed for agricultural intensification and rural modernisation, such as the groundnut scheme, the Office du Niger, the Congolese *paysannats* or the Portuguese *colonatos*, were perhaps the greatest debacles of the age. They consumed massive amounts of investment funds and resources, including technical and administrative staff, while offering up very little in return. The Office du Niger, for example, was absorbing more than half of French West Africa's total agricultural budget by 1961, and yet only managed to produce 0.3 per cent of the cotton it was projected to, while only 50,000 acres of the 3.2 million originally planned had been planted under the groundnut scheme by 1949 before it was shut down.[102] These schemes came to epitomise the failings of the post-war colonial development drive, often exacerbating the social unrest and discontent they had been designed to mitigate. The compulsory measures and regulations, harsh conditions, and often forcible recruitment of settlers, provoked deep hostility among African farmers and rural communities, and in turn, helped fuel anti-colonial political mobilisation in the 1940s and 1950s that accelerated decolonisation.[103]

It is important to emphasise, however, that not all the initiatives of the developmentalist colonial state in Africa ended in collapse or disappointment. Important advances were made in education, with for example the establishment of the first universities after the Second World War, and in the expansion of medical facilities, hospitals, and infrastructure. There was greater political liberalisation by allowing Africans to unionise and form political organisations. The French created a unified Labour Code in 1952 that guaranteed all wage workers in the private sector a forty-hour work week, paid vacations, the right to organise, and other benefits. The British introduced local government reforms and later internal self-government in many of its dependencies. Colonial development, as Frederick Cooper stresses, opened up new possibilities and spaces for African farmers and urban workers, while anticipations of the future inspired African political leaders to imagine alternatives 'that were neither continuation of colonialism nor the break-up of empire into territorial nation states'.[104]

At the same time, there were also clear limits to this reforming, modernising imperialism. During the 1950s the metropolitan states (and their publics, including prominent business leaders) grew more and more disillusioned with colonial development as it failed both to live up to the economic promises and to stem the growing tide of political discontent in the colonies themselves. Fissures and competing visions emerged within the metropolitan and colonial state and among governing elites which produced policy confusion and contributed to the sense of bureaucratic impasse.[105] Yet, in many ways, it was not the British or French or Belgian rulers who decided the limits, but the emerging African nationalist leaders, as well as the diverse groups of Africans whose desires and energies they tried to channel. Colonial subjects turned the promise of development back on the colonisers, viewing development as an entitlement and right, the logic of which began to rapidly outstrip the boundaries of colonial rule itself.[106]

In the final years of colonialism in Africa, the British, French, and Belgians found themselves scrambling to guide the economic and social changes taking place as best they could and to strengthen informal ties to the metropolitan centre in such a way that they would survive political decolonisation. The Portuguese empire, because of its economic weakness and authoritarian political system, as well as the settler colonies in Southern Africa, tried to repress the anti-colonial uprisings but eventually they too were compelled to relinquish political power to African liberation movements. Only by the mid-1990s, after the decolonisation of Namibia and the end of apartheid in South Africa, had the African continent in its entirety entered the post-colonial era.

The continuities between colonial and post-colonial concepts and practices of development are striking, which makes the current volume a significant contribution to understanding the origins of modern development policies and their underlying mental and material structures. Nevertheless, it is important not to forget the crucial difference between colonial and post-colonial concepts of development. Colonialism as a 'complex of philosophical exclusions'[107] created a system in which coloniser and colonised 'belonged to two different and opposed universes'.[108] Under post-colonial conditions, however, 'conceptually, *the "development"/"underdevelopment" contrast introduced the idea of a continuity of substance*, so that now the two terms of the binomial differed only relatively'.[109] To what extent the colonial hierarchies really have disappeared is open to debate. Undoubtedly, however, European colonialism in Africa sought to establish a rigid and formal hierarchical order with clearly demarcated barriers between coloniser and colonised. This formal distancing influenced and shaped colonial development and the overall goals it set out to achieve in profound and contradictory ways. The ultimate end for colonial modernisers was not to fashion an industrial society modelled on the metropole, but rather, an agrarian society with an efficient export production sector and pockets of mining, and with Africans firmly tied to the land as peasant farmers or stabilised in towns as urban labourers.

The aims of the book: writing the history of development concepts and practices in colonial Africa

Development as a concept has been increasingly challenged in recent decades, particularly in the West. In the wake of the neo-liberal turn and the debt crisis of the 1980s, market fundamentalists launched a sustained attack on developmentalism. Their critique, together with the demise of the developmentalist state in most parts of the world, seemed to have an intellectually liberating effect to the extent that from the late 1980s onwards scholars began to look at development from a new angle: not from a partisan position within the various churches of development theory, but from a detached viewpoint which tried to de-naturalise and contextualise development. This historicist approach, as Nick Cullather observed more than a decade ago, 'puts the framework inside the frame. It treats development *as* history, as an artifact' and makes history the methodology for studying development, rather than the other way around.[110] In other words, instead of being taken for granted, development came to be seen as a historically specific set of ideas and practices that linked the metropolitan centres and peripheries of the twentieth century world together.[111]

The exponents of the 'post-development' approach played a major role in these endeavours. Authors such as Alberto Arce, Arturo Escobar and Gilbert Rist focused on the discursive side of development and analysed it as an essential pillar of global economic, social, and cultural hierarchies.[112] The rather selective use of sources by these and similar authors, and their treatment of development as a unitary, hegemonic discourse drew substantial criticism from historians such as Frederick Cooper, who demanded 'a more rigorous historical practice'.[113] The neglect of development as practice may also have led these authors to pay less attention to the colonial history of development, a short-coming that characterised many early historiographies of development which took the rise of the United States to global hegemony and the onset of the Cold War in the later 1940s and 1950s as their start-ing point.[114] The earliest explorations into the intellectual history of development go back in time several centuries at least, and include post-colonial uses of the term, yet remarkably, omit the colonial period altogether.[115] Perhaps the most ambitious genealogy of development, Michael Cowen and Robert Shenton's *Doctrines of Development*, touches on colonial history at various moments – India in the early nineteenth century, Joseph Chamberlain's constructive imperialism and the negation of Chamberlainite development in Africa in the form of the failed Fabian colonial offensive of 1947–50 – but their focus remains squarely on the genesis and invention of development as a quintessentially and unapologetically Eurocentric conception.[116]

Often forgotten in this debate is the work of historians such as J. M. Lee, David Morgan, Stephen Constantine, Javier Alcalde, Michael Havinden, and David Meredith, who from an older, more empirically based or economic history approach, pioneered the study of colonial development well before the post-colonial moment.[117] Over the past decade or so a new generation of authors have added valuable insights and broken new ground.[118] But apart from a few exceptions, historians of colonial development have tended to be more interested in the 'colonial' than in 'development' per se. Rather than enquire into the various and changing meanings of development, they have largely taken the idea as given and treated it as just another, if only more recent, administrative task performed by the colonial administrations. More often than not they have contented themselves with a vague notion of development oscillating somewhere between economic stimulus/ exploitation and social welfare. Even more recent studies touching on the history of colonial development policies have not given sufficient thought to clarifying or problematicising the idea of development itself. Careful investigations have been made into the nexus between colonialism, development, and the production of scientific knowledge,[119] between colonial and post-colonial development and conservation projects,[120] and into the relationship between the developmental state and the politics of decolonisation.[121] Although such studies often acknowledge the shifting cultural and perceptual meanings and con-texts in which development is embedded, rarely do they go beyond this to decipher the complexities of these meanings and contexts.

In other words, there remain important gaps or blind spots in the historical literature: those scholars searching for the genesis and intellectual roots of *development* rarely venture into its colonial history; while those researching *colonial* development rarely enquire into its shifting meanings and content. To this we might add a third blind spot in most historical analyses, at least in English-speaking publications: the overwhelming majority of studies focus on British colonialism, and most of these studies focus exclusively on the metropolitan centre. Other European colonial empires and/or perspectives emanating from within specific colonies or from colonised peoples are largely missing from the growing body of writing on the history of development.

This book aims to address these shortcomings at least in part. It begins from an understanding of development as a conscious process of ideas, interventions, and practices – one filled with contradictions and fuelled by crises, but also amorphous enough to encompass a wide spectrum of expressions and experiences. The geographical focus of the book is on sub-Saharan Africa, which despite its vastness and great diversity shares a common history of the colonial, and indeed post-colonial, 'development regime' during the twentieth century. Nevertheless, one may legitimately question whether development concepts employed in the Caribbean or South Asian context were so substantially different as to constitute a separate subject. David Ludden's description of colonial (and post-colonial) development in India as 'an ideology of science that controls principles and techniques to effect and measure progress' sounds remarkably similar to the imperial ideologies employed in Africa.[122] This resonance reflects the fact that colonial development was to a large extent formulated and directed by imperial governments, and thus it is not surprising to find a multitude of related phenomena across the European empires. On the other hand, different regions of the world provided different backdrops to the conception and perception of development. In Asia and the Middle East development discourse was inscribed into a powerful orientalist tradition which regarded the societies in question as culturally refined but as technically and economically backward.[123]

Sub-Saharan Africa, by contrast, was associated with an imagery that differed significantly from that of the Middle Eastern and Asian parts of the colonised world. European racism placed Africans at the bottom of humanity's hierarchy; the distance between the European 'self' and the African 'other' seemed unbridgeable in several respects. Africa was seen as a much more powerful antithesis to what European development intended to achieve than Asia had ever been. Darkness, as the essence of the continent, not only embodied the threat, but also the unique epistemic challenge that Africa posed to its European conquerors – there was a lack and in many cases a complete absence of the knowledge which was deemed necessary to put development into effect.[124] As one senior official at the British Colonial Office remarked as late as 1945: 'it must be recognised that in the prevailing absence of the bulk of the fundamental data required for sound planning, much of the purely developmental expenditure cannot fail to be misdirected and so wasted, together with the man-power diverted thereto. We must reconcile ourselves to a period of building upon sand, and to some extent of pouring money into the sand'.[125] This mixture of hubris and humility, the sense of unfettered power and of the permanent risk of failure, though characteristic of every colonial encounter, was probably nowhere else as marked and as widespread as in the African context. This very attitude towards Africa and Africans may have informed concepts of development within the African colonies in specific ways. In turn, the response by Africans to development may have differed from responses in other parts of the colonial world. It is hoped that our focus on the African continent, which today figures most prominently as the object of development's efforts, may help to shed greater light on this core concept of the twentieth century.

Although the focus is on sub-Saharan Africa as the locality of various planned interventions and the object of various colonial ideologies, it is important to acknowledge that the book should not be read strictly or primarily as a contribution to African history. It is, rather, a history of development and how it linked the African continent to other parts of the world and to Europe in particular. As many of the contributions to this volume stress, the presence of Western Europe as the place where colonial ministries were headquartered and where the vast underlying networks of businessmen and diplomats, missionaries and academics, philanthropists and administrators had their centres and their origins, needs to be acknowledged. Western Europe, following Cowen and Shenton, is also where the idea of development as an intentional and willed course of action was first imagined and elaborated.[126] But as the twentieth century unfolded, development began to play an increasingly central and critical role in shaping relations between Africa and Europe. Development policies and practices became the nexus around which the history of sub-Saharan Africa and the history of European colonialism was bound, and as Bonneuil argues, became the keystone in the construction of the colonial (and postcolonial) state itself.[127]

Structure of the book

Developing Africa examines a range of historical contexts in which development emerged as a powerful, ideological, and mental framework shaping both policies and practices in colonial Africa. A wide array of sources have been made use of – from fictional texts and newspapers to political statements and administrative documents. An equally wide span of actors are investigated, from scientists, bankers, members of metropolitan and colonial governments, administrators, and farmers to intellectuals, novelists, missionaries, teachers, and doctors – African and European, men and women – all of whom sought to shape and appropriate development in their efforts to confront and transform colonial realities. Although the majority of case studies assembled here examine the more familiar experience of British colonialism, several chapters are devoted to French and Portuguese concepts of colonial development. Others seek a comparative analysis of specific dimensions of British and French colonial development, such as education and literature.

Most of the contributions to this collection seek to understand how discursive and non-discursive practices intersected, by analysing development not simply as a concept in abstract terms, but also as a social practice whose meaning was closely tied to the specific historical context in which it was embedded.[128] And while the timing was not entirely synchronised, in all three colonial empires – Britain, France, and Portugal – the 'colonising', expansive nature of 'development' led to the gradual inclusion of new elements within its conceptual and ideological frame, especially in the areas of ecology, social welfare, and the 'human factor'. As the chief promoter of development, the colonial state across Africa increased the scope of its authority and extended its reach, and in the name of development new instruments such as planning and external subventions of aid were introduced. Government policies and administrative machinery were based increasingly on the use of science, technology, and expert knowledge.

The structure of the book reflects the main spheres in which development played out and the main agencies who promoted it. It is not organised along imperial boundaries but instead takes account of different sectors and actors. Part I engages the conceptual history of development in different colonial settings and contexts. Each author (Koponen, Castelo, Hunter) explores, from a long-term perspective, the historical roots and changing meanings of development. Much emphasis is placed on the evolving meaning of certain key words, such as *fomento* or *maendeleo*, or the different uses to which the word 'development' was put in colonial and post-colonial relations. This initial, conceptual section is followed by three thematic sections, each examining a different dimension of colonial development in Africa: economic and rural, social and welfare, discursive and literary.

Part II consists of a set of essays interested broadly in economic and rural development. Private bankers, for example, had a vital interest in African economic and agricultural development and believed that banks with their network of local branches were ideal development partners situated between the state and the people (Frank). The introduction of new farming systems or the improvement of existing ones was seen by many colonial governments as key to expanding agricultural production, which in many ways stood at the very heart of the development project in Africa. Several chapters in this section explore different aspects of the project, from the new concerns with ecology (Speek), to the depoliticisation of the land question in colonial Zimbabwe through the sharp demarcation of 'modern' settler and 'traditional' African farming sectors (Makombe), to the introduction of tractors as part of a new plan for the technicisation of agricultural production in French West Africa (Pessis).

Part III offers another set of chapters which concentrate on the social or 'human' side of colonial development and on women as actors and objects of development. The focus is on the two main pillars of colonial social development, health (Bruchhausen) and education (Schicho, Usuanlele), which as noted above became increasingly integrated into state development doctrines in the late 1930s and 1940s when colonial 'welfare' emerged as a focal tenet of colonial administrations. Despite the official concern, however, two of the chapters (Bruchhausen, Usuanlele) argue that at no point were social services viewed as goals of development in and of themselves, and that there was more continuity than change after 1940 at the level of practice. This section also highlights the gendered nature of colonial, and indeed post-colonial, development discourse and practice. Here too, despite the construction of a new bio-medical discourse in the 1930s which enabled more women to serve as advisers or to be trained as nurses and welfare providers, biases against African women as passive, non-agents of development persisted (Bush).

Although the majority of contributions to this collection approach the subject from a historical perspective, the inclusion of literary studies and linguistics offers a unique angle on colonial development that serves as an important counterweight to more empirically based enquiries. The final section, Part IV, therefore opens the field to research from language and literature studies, post-colonial studies, and cultural anthropology. From different points of view the contributors (Aráujo and Vasile, Dufour, Kopf) engage in methodological questions by approaching the history of development via the texts and narratives that produced and continue to produce what we might call 'development knowledge'. The book concludes with an epilogue, in which we offer our reflections on the contribution of the essays to the history of colonial development as well as our thoughts on new directions for future research.

Notes

1 United Nations Development Programme, *Africa Human Development Report 2012: Towards a Food Secure Future* (New York: United Nations 2012), pp. 17–18.
2 Ibid., p. 19.
3 Ibid., p. 17.
4 World Bank, *Africa's Future and the World Bank's Support to It* (n.p.: s.n. 2011), p. 4. Available at: http://siteresources.worldbank.org/INTAFRICA/Resources/AFR_Regional_Strategy_3-2-11.pdf (accessed 24 March 2013).
5 Ibid., pp. 4–5.
6 Nicholas J. White, 'Reconstructing Europe through Rejuvenating Empire: The British, French, and Dutch Experiences Compared', *Past and Present* 210, suppl. 6 (2011), pp. 211–36.
7 'Future provision for colonial development and welfare: War Cabinet memorandum by Mr. Stanley, 15 Nov. 1944', in S. R. Ashton and S. E. Stockwell (eds), *Imperial Policy and Colonial Practice 1925–1945: British Documents on the End of Empire*, vol. 1/A (London: HMSO 1996), p. 205.
8 Frank Samuel, 'Economic Potential of Colonial Africa', *Tropical Agriculture* 28, 7–12 (1951), p. 150.
9 A similar response was aired by spokesmen for French and Dutch imperial business interests such as Paul Bernard, managing director of Sociétié Financière Française et Coloniale and Paul Rijkens, chairman of Unilever NV. See White, 'Reconstructing Europe through Rejuvenating Empire', pp. 235–6.
10 Frederick Cooper and Randall Packard, 'Introduction', in Frederick Cooper and Randall Packard (eds), *International Development and the Social Sciences: Essays on the History and Politics of Knowledge* (Berkeley, Los Angeles, London: University of California Press 1997), p. 7.
11 This is a point that Fred Cooper has made with great force. See Frederick Cooper, *Africa since 1940: The Past of the Present* (Cambridge: Cambridge University Press 2002), pp. 38–65.
12 To provide some necessary historical context, a few of the case studies, particularly the two chapters on Portuguese colonialism, reach back to the origins of colonial development in the late nineteenth century.
13 Michael Cowen and Robert Shenton, 'The Invention of Development', in Jonathan Crush (ed.), *Power of Development* (London, New York: Routledge 1995), p. 28.
14 David Simon, 'Development Reconsidered: New Directions in Development Thinking', *Geografiska Annaler. Series B, Human Geography* 79, 4 (1997), pp. 183–4.
15 Jan Nederveen Pieterse, *Development Theory: Deconstructions/Reconstructions* (New Delhi: Vistaar 2001), p. 3.
16 Adam Smith, *An Inquiry into the Nature and Causes of the Wealth of Nations* (2 vols, London: W. Strahan and T. Cadell 1776).
17 Marshall Berman, *All that is Solid Melts into Air: The Experience of Modernity* (Harmondsworth: Penguin 1988), p. 40.
18 Michael Cowen and Robert Shenton, *Doctrines of Development* (London, New York: Routledge 1996), p. 7.
19 Ibid., p. 173.
20 Ibid., pp. 34–5.
21 Cooper, *Africa since 1940*, p. 16.
22 Alice L. Conklin, *A Mission to Civilize: The Republican Idea of Empire in France and West Africa, 1895–1930* (Stanford, CA: Stanford University Press 1997), p. 1.

23 Gilbert Rist, *The History of Development: From Western Origins to Global Faith* (London: Zed Books; New York: St. Martin's Press 1997), pp. 51–5.

24 Conklin, *A Mission to Civilize*, pp. 11, 41.

25 Ibid., pp. 77–9.

26 Martin D. Lewis, 'One Hundred Million Frenchmen: The "Assimilation" Theory in French Colonial Policy', *Comparative Studies in Society and History* 4, 2 (1962), pp. 129–49.

27 Joseph Chamberlain, 'Speech at Walsall, 15 July 1895', in George Bennett (ed.), *The Concept of Empire: Burke to Attlee, 1774–1947* (London: Adam & Charles Black 1953), p. 314.

28 Robert V. Kubicek, *The Administration of Imperialism: Joseph Chamberlain at the Colonial Office* (Durham, NC: Duke University Press 1969), p. 69.

29 Michael Worboys, 'Science and British Colonial Imperialism' (PhD dissertation, University of Sussex, 1979), pp. 29–142; Michael Worboys, 'The Emergence of Tropical Medicine: A Study in the Establishment of a Scientific Specialty', in Gerard Lemaine et al. (eds), *Perspectives on the Emergence of Scientific Disciplines* (The Hague: Mouton; Paris: Maison des Sciences de l'Homme 1976), pp. 75–98; Michael Worboys, 'Manson, Ross and Colonial Medical Policy: Tropical Medicine in London and Liverpool, 1899–1914', in Roy MacLeod and Milton Lewis (eds), *Disease, Medicine and Empire: Perspectives on Western Medicine and the Experience of European Expansion* (London, New York: Routledge 1988), pp. 21–37.

30 Joseph Chamberlain, 'British Trade and the Expansion of Empire: Speech given before the Birmingham Chamber of Commerce, 13 November 1896', in Joseph Chamberlain, *Foreign and Colonial Speeches* (London: Routledge 1897), p. 146.

31 Bernard Porter, *Critics of Empire: British Radical Attitudes to Colonialism in Africa, 1895–1914* (London: Macmillan; New York: St. Martin's Press 1968).

32 See Catherine Coquery-Vidrovitch, 'La mise en dépendance de l'Afrique noire: essai de périodisation, 1800–1970', *Cahiers d'Études Africaines* 16, 61 (1976), p. 28.

33 Crawford Young, *The African Colonial State in Comparative Perspective* (New Haven, CT, London: Yale University Press 1994), p. 141.

34 Frederick D. Lugard, *The Dual Mandate in British Tropical Africa* (Edinburgh, London: Blackwood 1922); Albert Sarraut, *La mise en valeur des colonies françaises* (Paris: Payot 1923).

35 Sarraut, *Le mise en valeur*, pp. 118–19, as quoted in Rist, *The History of Development*, p. 58.

36 Lugard, *The Dual Mandate in British Tropical Africa*, p. 617.

37 Frederick D. Lugard, 'Education in Tropical Africa', *Edinburgh Review* 242, 493 (1925), pp. 3–4.

38 League of Nations, 'The Covenant of the League of Nations', 28 April 1919. Available at: http://avalon.law.yale.edu/20th_century/leagcov.asp (accessed 14 April 2013).

39 Penelope Hetherington, *British Paternalism and Africa, 1920–1940* (London: Frank Cass 1978), p. 45; Rist, *The History of Development*, pp. 58–65; Susan Pedersen, 'Settler Colonialism at the Bar of the League of Nations', in Caroline Elkins and Susan Pedersen (eds), *Settler Colonialism in the Twentieth Century: Projects, Practices, Legacies* (New York, London: Routledge 2005), pp. 113–34.

40 Conklin, *A Mission to Civilize*, p. 217; Martin Thomas, 'Albert Sarraut, French Colonial Development, and the Communist Threat, 1919–1930', *Journal of Modern History* 77, 4 (2005), p. 926.

41 Monica M. van Beusekom, 'Colonisation *Indigène*: French Rural Development Ideology at the Office du Niger, 1920–1940', *International Journal of African Historical Studies* 30, 2 (1997), pp. 299–323; Monica M. van Beusekom, 'Disjunctures in Theory and Practice: Making Sense of Change in Agricultural Development at the Office du Niger, 1920–1960', *Journal of African History* 41, 1 (2000), pp. 79–99; Monica M. van Beusekom, *Negotiating Development: African Farmers and Colonial Experts at the Office du Niger, 1920–1960* (Portsmouth, NH: Heinemann; Oxford: James Currey; Cape Town: D. Philip 2002).

[29]

42 Conklin, *A Mission to Civilize*, pp. 218–22.
43 Rist, *The History of Development*, p. 57.
44 Conklin, *A Mission to Civilize*, pp. 174–202.
45 Thomas, 'Sarraut, French Colonial Development, and the Communist Threat', p. 928.
46 Great Britain, 'Parliamentary Papers, Report of the East Africa Commission', April 1925; 'East African development loan: Cabinet memorandum by Mr. Amery, 15 Oct 1925', in Ashton and Stockwell (eds), *Imperial Policy and Colonial Practice 1925–1945*, pp. 1–7.
47 Stephen Constantine, *The Making of British Colonial Development Policy, 1914–1940* (London: Frank Cass 1984), pp. 23–4.
48 The area covered by the scheme would continue to expand, especially after 1945, increasing to over 1.9 million feddans when the 1957 Managil extension was constructed. By the mid-1960s when the Al Roseires dam was completed, the scheme had become the centre of the Sudanese economy. See Arthur Gaitskill, *Gezira: A Story of Development in the Sudan* (London: Faber and Faber 1959); Tony Barnett, *The Gezira Scheme: An Illusion of Development* (London: Frank Cass 1977).
49 Joseph Morgan Hodge, *Triumph of the Expert: Agrarian Doctrines of Development and the Legacies of British Colonialism* (Athens, OH: Ohio University Press 2007), pp. 117–43.
50 Apollos O. Nwauwa, 'University Education for Africans, 1900–1935: An "Anathema" to British Colonial Administrative Policy', *Asian and African Studies* 27, 3 (1993), p. 282.
51 Hodge, *Triumph of the Expert*, pp. 109–11.
52 van Beusekom, 'Disjunctures in Theory and Practice', p. 82.
53 Cooper, *Africa since 1940*, p. 17.
54 Conklin, *A Mission to Civilize*, pp. 212–45.
55 Young, *The African Colonial State in Comparative Perspective*, pp. 174–6.
56 The best source on the Colonial Development Act of 1929 is Stephen Constantine, who notes that most of the funds were given to defray the interest on loans raised by colonial governments. He calculates the total cost of schemes assisted by the Colonial Development Fund to be £17,286,773 by March 1939. See Constantine, *The Making of British Colonial Development Policy*, pp. 164–226.
57 By 1939, the empire absorbed over 40 per cent of French exports, and supplied 37 per cent of France's imports. See Martin Thomas, 'The Roots of French Decolonization: Ideas, Economics, and Reform, 1900–1916', in Martin Thomas, Bob Moore, and L. J. Butler (eds), *Crises of Empire: Decolonization and Europe's Imperial States, 1918–1975* (London: Hodder Education 2008), p. 133. See also Jacques Marseille, 'The Phases of French Colonial Imperialism: Towards a New Periodization', *Journal of Imperial and Commonwealth History* 13, 3 (1985), p. 132. Similarly for Britain, the proportion of domestic exports bound for empire destinations increased from 43.5 percent in 1930 to 49.85 per cent in 1938. See S. R. Ashton and S. E. Stockwell, 'Introduction', in Ashton and Stockwell (eds), *Imperial Policy and Colonial Practice 1925–1945*, p. lxiii.
58 Coquery-Vidrovitch, 'La mise en dépendance de l'Afrique noire, pp. 39–40; Jean Suret-Canale, 'From Colonization to Independence in French Tropical Africa: The Economic Background', in Prosser Gifford and William Roger Louis (eds), *The Transfer of Power in Africa: Decolonization 1940–1960* (New Haven, CT: Yale University Press 1982), p. 450.
59 van Beusekom, 'Disjunctures in Theory and Practice', p. 82.
60 Christophe Bonneuil, 'Development as Experiment: Science and State Building in Late Colonial and Postcolonial Africa, 1930–1970', *Osiris*, 2nd series, 15 (2000), p. 259. A number of other historians have also identified the Great Depression and the 1930s as the criticial watershed in the emergence of the developmentalist state in Africa. See Coquery-Vidrovitch, 'La Mise en dépendance de l'Afrique noire', pp. 28, 38–42; D. K. Fieldhouse, 'Decolonization, Development, and Dependence:

A Survey of Changing Attitudes', in Gifford and Louis (eds), *The Transfer of Power in Africa*, pp. 483–515; Hodge, *Triumph of the Expert*, pp. 144–206.

61 John Darwin, 'What was the Late Colonial State?', *Itinerario* 23, 3–4 (1999), pp. 76–7.

62 Cooper, *Africa since 1940*, p. 197.

63 Martin Shipway, *Decolonization and Its Impact: A Comparative Approach to the End of the Colonial Empires* (Malden, MA: Blackwell 2008), pp. 65–8.

64 Cooper, *Africa since 1940*, p. 20.

65 Frederick Cooper, *Decolonization and African Society: The Labor Question in French and British Africa* (Cambridge: Cambridge University Press 1996), pp. 57–65, 124–41, 225–60; Cooper, *Africa since 1940*, pp. 30–2.

66 William Beinart, 'Soil Erosion, Conservationism and Ideas about Development: A Southern African Exploration, 1900–1960', *Journal of Southern African Studies* 11, 1 (1984), pp. 52–83; David Throup, *Economic and Social Origins of Mau Mau, 1945–53* (London: James Currey 1987), pp. 149–50; Francis K. Danquah, 'Rural Discontent and Decolonization in Ghana, 1945–51', *Agricultural History* 68, 1 (1994), pp. 1–19.

67 Cooper, *Africa since 1940*, p. 37.

68 Great Britain, 'Parliamentary Papers, Statement of Policy on Colonial Development and Welfare, 1940'; 'Future provision for colonial development and welfare: War Cabinet memorandum by Mr. Stanley, 15 Nov. 1944', in Ashton and Stockwell (eds), *Imperial Policy and Colonial Practice 1925–1945*, pp. 203–5. The Colonial Office was able to persuade the Treasury to grant a further £115 million extension to cover the fund an additional five years from 1955–60. See L. J. Butler, 'British Decolonization, Insurgency and Strategic Reverse: The Middle East, Africa and Malaya, 1951–1957', in Thomas, Moore, and Butler (eds), *Crises of Empire*, p. 77.

69 Tony Chafer, 'Friend or Foe? Competing Visions of Empire in French West Africa in the Run-up to Independence', in Martin Thomas (ed.), *French Colonial Mind*, vol. 1, *Mental Maps of Empire and Colonial Encounters* (Lincoln, NE, London: University of Nebraska Press 2012), pp. 285–6.

70 Jacques Marseille, *Empire colonial et capitalisme français: histoire d'un divorce* (Paris: Albin Michel 1984), p. 105.

71 Shipway, *Decolonization and Its Impact*, p. 118. Jean Suret-Canale estimates that of the 820.9 billion CFA francs in public investment in Francophone Africa for the period 1946–60, 569.8 billion came from the metropole, while 251.1 billion was derived from local budgets. See Suret-Canale, 'From Colonization to Independence in French Tropical Africa', p. 455.

72 Cooper, *Africa since 1940*, p. 31.

73 D. K. Fieldhouse, *The West and the Third World: Trade, Colonialism, Dependence, and Development* (Oxford, Malden, MA: Blackwell 1999), p. 85.

74 Hodge, *Triumph of the Expert*, pp. 196–206.

75 Chafer, 'Friend or Foe?', pp. 281–8.

76 Thomas, 'The Roots of French Decolonization', p. 160.

77 White, 'Reconstructing Europe through Rejuvenating Empire', p. 214.

78 Ibid., p. 219.

79 Martin Thomas, 'Decolonizing the French African Federations after 1945', in Thomas, Moore, and Butler (eds), *Crises of Empire*, p. 161.

80 Hodge, *Triumph of the Expert*, pp. 209–13.

81 Suret-Canale, 'From Colonization to Independence in French Tropical Africa', p. 452; Shipway, *Decolonization and Its Impact*, p. 119; Bill Freund, *The Making of Contemporary Africa: The Development of African Society since 1800* (Boulder, CO: Lynne Rienner 1998), p. 170.

82 van Beusekom, 'Disjunctures in Theory and Practice', pp. 93–6; van Beusekom, *Negotiating Development*, pp. 126–9.

83 Bonneuil, 'Development as Experiment', p. 262.

84 D. A. Low and John Lonsdale, 'Introduction: Towards the New Order, 1945–63', in D. A. Low and A. Smith (eds), *History of East Africa*, vol. 3 (Oxford: Clarendon Press 1976), pp. 1–63.

85 Shipway, *Decolonization and Its Impact*, p. 118.
86 Young, *The African Colonial State in Comparative Perspective*, p. 212.
87 Martin Thomas, 'Contrasting Patterns of Decolonization: Belgian and Portuguese Africa', in Thomas, Moore, and Butler (eds), *Crises of Empire*, p. 387.
88 Bonneuil, 'Development as Experiment', p. 264.
89 Ibid., p. 272.
90 See, for example, Jeanne Marie Penvenne, 'Settling Against the Tide: The Layered Contradictions of Twentieth-Century Portuguese Settlement in Mozambique', in Elkins and Pedersen (eds), *Settler Colonialism in the Twentieth Century*, pp. 79–94.
91 The Estado Novo (New State) was a conservative, Catholic, and colonialist dictatorship which ruled in Portugal, from 1933 (date of approval of new Constitution of the Portuguese Republic) to 1974. It emerged following the military coup of 28 May 1926, which toppled the First Republic (1910–26). Until 1968, its figurehead was António de Oliveira Salazar, president of the Council, who was succeeded by Marcello Caetano. The military coup of 25 April 25 1974 overthrew the Estado Novo and paved the way for democracy in Portugal and independence for its African colonies. 1975 marks the end of the Portuguese colonial empire in Africa, with the liberation of Angola, Cape Verde, Guinea-Bissau, Mozambique and São Tomé, and Príncipe.
92 Bonneuil, 'Development as Experiment', p. 259.
93 Thomas, 'Contrasting Patterns of Decolonization', p. 394.
94 Email correspondence with Cláudia Castelo, 7 June 2013.
95 Kenneth Maxwell, 'Portugal and Africa: The Last Empire', in Gifford and Louis (eds), *The Transfer of Power in Africa*, pp. 337–8; Cláudia Castelo, '*O modo português de estar no mundo': o luso-tropicalismo e a ideologia colonial portuguesa, 1933–1961* (Porto: Afrontamento 1998).
96 Penvenne, 'Settling against the Tide', p. 81.
97 Ibid., p. 84.
98 Ibid.
99 Cláudia Castelo, *Passagens para África: o povoamento de Angola e Moçambique com naturais da metrópole, 1920–1974* (Porto: Afrontamento 2007), pp. 59, 97, 143.
100 Maxwell, 'Portugal and Africa', p. 339; Thomas, 'Contrasting Patterns of Decolonization', p. 397.
101 Cláudia Castelo, 'Colonial Migration into Angola and Mozambique: Constraints and Illusions', in Eric Morier-Genoud and Michael Cahen (eds), *Imperial Migrations: Colonial Communities and Diasporas in the Portuguese World* (Basingstoke: Palgrave Macmillan 2012), p. 12.
102 White, 'Reconstructing Europe through Rejuvenating Empire', p. 221; Hodge, *Triumph of the Expert*, p. 211.
103 Hodge, *Triumph of the Expert*, pp. 214–26. See also Monica M. van Beusekom and Dorothy L. Hodgson, 'Lessons Learned? Development Experiences in the Late Colonial Period', *Journal of African History* 41, 1 (2000), pp. 29–30.
104 Frederick Cooper, 'Reconstructing Empire in British and French Africa', *Past and Present* 210, suppl. 6 (2011), p. 208.
105 The importance of competing policy agendas and bureaucratic confusion in the late colonial mission has been noted in both the French and the British case. See Chafer, 'Friend or Foe?', pp. 276, 280–8; Hodge, *Triumph of the Expert*, pp. 226–30.
106 Cooper, *Africa since 1940*, pp. 20–37.
107 Olúfémi Táíwò, *How Colonialism Preempted Modernity in Africa* (Bloomington, IN: Indiana University Press 2010), p. 39.
108 Rist, *The History of Development*, p. 73.
109 Ibid., p. 74. Emphasis in the original.
110 Nick Cullather, 'Development? It's History', *Diplomatic History* 24, 4 (2000), p. 642.
111 It is worth noting that this also applied to internal peripheries within Europe and North America.

112 Alberto Arce and Norman Long, *Anthropology, Development, and Modernities: Exploring Discourses, Counter-Tendencies, and Violence* (London, New York: Routledge 1999); Arturo Escobar, *Encountering Development: The Making and Unmaking of the Third World* (Princeton, NJ: Princeton University Press 1995); Rist, *The History of Development.*

113 Frederick Cooper, *Colonialism in Question: Theory, Knowledge, History* (Berkeley, London: University of California Press 2005), p. 13.

114 Michael Adas, *Dominance by Design: Technological Imperatives and America's Civilizing Mission* (London, Cambridge, MA: Belknap 2006); Crush (ed.), *Power of Development*; Cullather, 'Development? It's History'; David C. Engerman et al. (eds), *Staging Growth: Modernization, Development, and the Global Cold War* (Amherst, MA: University of Massachusetts Press; London: Eurospan 2003); Nils Gilman, *Mandarins of the Future: Modernization Theory in Cold War America* (Baltimore, London: Johns Hopkins University Press 2003); Colin Leys, *The Rise and Fall of Development Theory* (Nairobi: EAEP; Bloomington and Indianapolis: Indiana University Press; London: James Currey 1996); Philip McMichael, *Development and Social Change: A Global Perspective*, 2nd edn (London, Thousand Oaks, CA: Pine Forge 2000); David B. Moore, 'Development Discourse as Hegemony: Towards an Ideological History, 1945–1995', in David B. Moore and Gerald J. Schmitz (eds), *Debating Development Discourse: Institutional and Popular Perspectives* (Basingstoke, London: Macmillan Press; New York: St. Martin's Press 1995), pp. 1–53; Amy L. S. Staples, *The Birth of Development: How the World Bank, Food and Agriculture Organization, and World Health Organization Have Changed the World, 1945–1965* (Kent, OH: Kent State University Press 2006).

115 Robert A. Nisbet, *Social Change and History: Aspects of the Western Theory of Development* (New York, London: Oxford University Press 1969).

116 Cowen and Shenton, *Doctrines of Development*. See also Cowen and Shenton, 'The Invention of Development', pp. 27–43.

117 Javier Gonzalo Alcalde, *The Idea of Third World Development: Emerging Perspectives in the United States and Britain, 1900–1950* (Lanham, New York, London: University Press of America 1987); Constantine, *The Making of British Colonial Development Policy*; Michael Ashley Havinden and David Meredith, *Colonialism and Development: Britain and Its Tropical Colonies, 1850–1960* (London, New York: Routledge 1993); J. M. Lee, *Colonial Development and Good Government: A Study of the Ideas Expressed by the British Official Classes in Planning Decolonization, 1939–1964* (Oxford: Clarendon Press 1967); David John Morgan, *The Official History of Colonial Development*, vol. 1, *The Origins of British Aid Policy, 1924–1945* (London: Macmillan 1980).

118 David Anderson, *Eroding the Commons: The Politics of Ecology in Baringo, Kenya, 1890s–1963* (Athens, OH: Ohio University Press 2003); Hodge, *Triumph of the Expert*; Rohland Schuknecht, *British Colonial Development Policy after the Second World War: The Case of Sukumaland, Tanganyika* (Berlin: Lit 2011); van Beusekom, *Negotiating Development.*

119 Helen Tilley, *Africa as a Living Laboratory: Empire, Development, and the Problem of Scientific Knowledge, 1870–1950* (Chicago: University of Chicago Press 2011), p. 73; Christian Jennings, 'Unexploited Assets: Imperial Imagination, Practical Limitations, and Marine Fisheries Research in East Africa, 1917–53', in Brett Bennett and Joseph Hodge (eds), *Science and Empire: Knowledge and Networks of Science across the British Empire, 1800–1979* (Basingstoke: Palgrave Macmillan 2011), pp. 253–74.

120 Elizabeth Lunstrum, 'State Rationality, Development, and the Making of State Territory: From Colonial Extraction to Postcolonial Conservation in Southern Mozambique', in Christina Folke Ax et al. (eds), *Cultivating the Colonies: Colonial States and their Environmental Legacies* (Athens, OH: Ohio University Press 2011), pp. 209–74.

121 Shipway, *Decolonization and Its Impact*, pp. 114–39.

122 David Ludden, 'India's Development Regime', in Nicholas B. Dirks (ed.), *Colonialism and Culture* (Ann Arbor, MI: University of Michigan Press 1992), p. 251. See also Benjamin Zachariah, *Developing India: An Intellectual and Social History, c. 1930–50* (New Delhi, Oxford: Oxford University Press 2005).

123 Bernard S. Cohn, *Colonialism and Its Forms of Knowledge: The British in India* (Princeton, NJ, Chichester: Princeton University Press 1996); Edward W. Said, *Orientalism* (New York: Pantheon Books 1978).

124 Patrick Brantlinger, *Rule of Darkness: British Literature and Imperialism, 1830–1914* (Ithaca, NY, London: Cornell University Press 1988).

125 British National Archives, London, CO 927/1/3 Research Policy, Relation of Research to Development Plans, C.Y. Carstairs, 'The Place of Surveys in Colonial Development Plans', 1945.

126 Cowen and Shenton, *Doctrines of Development*, p. 5.

127 Bonneuil, 'Development as Experiment', p. 259.

128 On the importance of development practice and context see v Van Beusekom and Hodgson, 'Lessons Learned?', pp. 29–33.

PART I

Meanings of development in twentieth-century colonialism

From dead end to new lease of life: development in South-Eastern Tanganyika from the late 1930s to the 1950s

Juhani Koponen

In this chapter I examine the changing ideas and practices of development in Tanganyika, especially its remote South-Eastern corners, from
the late 1930s to the 1950s.[1] The chapter shows the variety of meanings of development in colonial discourse and practice and spells out
their implications for the history of the idea of development more
broadly. The focus is on three development endeavours, very different
in themselves: (1) the Groundnut Scheme, (2) the promotion and expansion of cashew nut as a cash crop, and (3) the post-war colonial development plans across the country and in the South-East. By exploring
and comparing these three different approaches to development under
colonialism, I argue that colonial development reached its limits and
met a dead end in the hands of rising African nationalism, although
the very same nationalism subsequently gave a new lease of life to
development more generally.

Meanings of development and their colonial history

To set the scene for the discussion, two points must be made at the
outset. The first concerns the meaning of development. A notion
notorious for the multiplicity of its meanings, 'development' is used
differently in differing languages and in the same languages in different
periods. In our case in particular, the etymology and connotations of
Swahili *maendeleo* and English 'development', and the latter's European
equivalents such as *Entwicklung* and *développement*, are rather different. *Maendeleo* means basically progress while 'development' has
a much more activist ring: it also means *doing* things for something,
often for progress but sometimes against it.[2] Similarly there are important differences in the way 'development' was perceived and how it
actually worked in the colonial period compared to the post-colonial era.

This argument eschews the quest for a 'correct' meaning of development in terms of its contents; something that I think is a chimera anyway. Instead, it takes its cue from Wittgenstein and traces the multifarious ways in which the word development is actually used in practice.[3] By doing so, a benchmark can be established: in the combination of its different uses, development can be seen to have a core meaning, which turns out to have remained remarkably stable from the early colonial times till today. What can be called the modern notion of development has both empirical and normative reference points. It is used in three basic senses, referring to (1) normative goals, (2) an actual social process, and (3) intentional activity. That is, development denotes an intentional intervention, the process (or processes) triggered or affected by that intervention, and the goal of the intervention which also serves as its ideological justification. As I see it, the power of the notion of development derives from the fact that it embraces these very different uses under the same term and binds them together: it promises that the intentional development intervention will lead to a process which can be taken as development in the normative sense. It is the same notion of development which guides contemporary development efforts that also laid the basis for colonial exploitation. As exploitation obviously also could produce development in the normative sense, development was soon elevated to the goal of the very exploitation and brought in to justify it. Yet in spite of these crucial functions, under colonialism development remained one notion among many; only after independence did it acquire its present status of a foundational concept, shaping an entire discourse and the practices drawing on it.

The second point, following from the first, is that at the start of our inspection, the 1930s, development, understood in the sense sketched above, was by no means a new feature in British colonial ideology and practice. The claims that development entered colonialism only in its late stage notwithstanding,[4] it is obvious that it had been around much longer, basically from the onset of colonialism.[5] In Africa at least, development must be regarded as an unacknowledged condition of colonialism. In retrospect, colonialism has been judged as a system of exploitation, geared primarily to benefit the colonisers, and to me rightly so. But the point is that only development made colonial exploitation possible: rather than opposites they form a dialectical unity. In places like Tanganyika there was not much to be exploited before the exploitable resources were developed. European colonialism saw that its mission was to make the whole world exploitable, and development provided it with both the means and the justification to do so. This was perfectly clear to the historical agents concerned, but has been obscured in our post-war development discourse with its conflation of development with welfare and all other good things. As long as colonialism continued, there was no way to give up 'development for exploitation', but it alone was not enough to tackle the political challenges it faced when it matured.

In British colonial ideology, an ingenious attempt to make sense of and accommodate the competing policy demands to which development was offered as an answer was made in the guise of the dual mandate. Colonies could be seen as 'undeveloped estates' as Joseph Chamberlain did in his famous speech back in 1895. But the British Treasury was always afraid that starting to develop the faraway possessions would require expenditure which would doom the colonies to become a drain on the imperial finances. In addition, there were always influential colonial officials on the ground, who were afraid that development would upset the forces which kept the African societies stable and wanted to preserve and consolidate rather than undermine them. Under the conflicting pressures, the dual mandate provided what came nearest to an official doctrine. As articulated by Lord Lugard in 1922, the colonial power was placed in a trusteeship position in two respects: towards the Africans; and towards the 'rest of mankind', meaning Europeans. Colonialism thus had to work for the African advancement while at the same time developing the material resources of Africa so that everyone could enjoy them.[6] This idea, expressed in slightly different formulations, also guided British colonialism in Tanganyika from the start to the end.

The shift in the meanings of development took place within the dual mandate. In earlier colonialism, it was the development of resources that figured most prominently. The basic claim underlying this, originating from the time of colonisation, was that the local people were incapable of developing the resources of their countries. Thus the colonialists took, on behalf of humankind, not only the right but the duty to take over and initiate 'development'. This was a pervasive lamentation in late pre-colonial and early colonial literature, not only in Britain but elsewhere, and provided a major pillar for the justification of the colonial conquest.[7] The other half of the dual mandate, the idea of colonialism working for the advancement of Africans, was gaining strength as colonialism progressed, but it too had been expressed right from the beginning. At first it was a demand of humanitarians but soon the idea had been taken over by more farsighted colonialists. Ove time, it became an increasingly political demand – first from outside and then from inside the colony. 'The advancement of the African' became a major prop in legitimising colonialism. The British made the point by adding the term 'welfare' to development in the Colonial Development and Welfare Acts of 1940 and 1945.

With these acts, His Majesty's government gave up what was then called 'good government' according to which the colonies had to aim at balanced budgets to be financially self-sufficient and endorsed the necessity to transfer resources on a grant basis to the colonies. Again, the recognition of the need for imperial assistance was not new. The early colonial railways had mostly been built by loans guaranteed by the imperial government. Some grant assistance had even been given under the first Colonial Development Act of 1929, although in trifling sums and with the view of getting orders from the colonies to stimulate the flagging British economy and relieve the rising unemployment back in Britain.[8] What was new was that development was now elevated to official policy by attempting to systematise the scattered efforts and backing them up by more substantial resources. Although funding in practice was considered and granted on a project basis, the projects had to be collated into more comprehensive plans before they could be applied for. Although it never totally materialised, the sums committed under the Colonial Development and Welfare Acts seemed to come very close to the modern international aid target of 0.7 per cent of the donor GDP.[9]

'Welfare' was added to development in the title of the 1940 and 1945 Acts to make development politically more attractive and get rid of the view that it was about the exploitation of resources only. As put by Sir Henry Moore, assistant colonial secretary, 'if it is just going to be mainly "development" on the old lines, it will look merely as if we are going to exploit the Colonies in order to get money to pay for the war!' Including welfare in the title, another official remarked, was 'to add to [Britain's] moral prestige' and 'make a big thing out of it' politically.[10]

In the sections that follow, I provide more detailed empirical knowledge and a fuller understanding of the historical processes involved through an examination of the three cases refered to at the beginning of this chapter, although here I can only sketch the broad outlines. These endeavours are not only quite varied, but they are also unevenly known in the historical literature. The Groundnut Scheme, of course, is popularly presented as a paradigm case of an uninformed and short-sighted colonial productive push but its place in the colonial development framework has been frequently misunderstood and its broader ramifications to the actual development of the area have not received much attention. The spread and promotion of cashew is virtually a virgin topic in Tanzanian historiography and has to be constructed from archival and other primary source materials. The existence of the post-war colonial development plans has been known in historical literature and some local plans have been discussed in more detail in specific works.[11] It is not well known that a similar plan was attempted in the South as well. Nor is it well known how it was related to the planning exercise more generally and to some of the better-known local plans. In particular, I try to trace to what extent these interventions were conceptualised in terms of development, and what other notions, such as advancement or improvement, were used by the colonialists and what we know about the conceptualisations among the local people (which is not much).

The Groundnut Scheme: development operation located in a colony

The Groundnut Scheme ranks as perhaps the leading candidate for the prize of the best publicised development failure in Africa. As 'everybody' knows, it was a gigantic effort to launch mechanised cultivation of groundnuts in three widely separated areas in Tanganyika, one of them Nachingwea in the South. The eponymous township grew up from a few scattered huts to a settlement of 600 European inhabitants in 1951 to cater for it. A railway was built from there to Mtwara at the coast where a new deepwater port was established for the expected massive outflow of groundnuts. The modern town was carved out of the bush – 'one of the few towns in Africa planned before any building was commenced'.[12] Within a few years, the expectations of mass production of groundnuts proved entirely unrealistic. The project was scrapped and the colonial government was left to wonder what to do with the under-utilised infrastructure. Everybody agreed and continues to agree that the scheme was an utter failure – but a failure of what? Of 'socialism', as claimed by the British conservatives in the subsequent election campaign? Or that of large-scale agriculture in Africa, or even of a more general 'capitalist high modernism of the utopian kind' as suggested by later researchers?[13] Or perhaps simply that of planned development?

The Groundnut Scheme has had a pride of place in most accounts of British post-war colonial development and is often taken to be emblematic of its fallacies and fantasies.[14] It plainly was a development scheme, and is understood and habitually referred to as such, but its colonial credentials are feebler. It did not grow up from any inherent needs and interests of the colonial state and administration let alone those of local people and societies. Rather, it was conceived and planted from outside and always remained an outgrowth foisted on the colonial body. It was not even run by the Colonial Office and the government of Tanganyika but by the Ministry of Food and the Overseas Food Corporation (OFC), a public entity established for this purpose. I would suggest that rather than seeing it as part of generic 'colonial development', the Groundnut Scheme should be considered a single and very exceptional development operation physically located in a colony (which, legally speaking, was not even a colony but a United Nations Trust Territory).

A mixture of business planning, Labour development thinking, and political expediency, the scheme was undertaken in the atmosphere of general post-war euphoria. Initiated by Frank Samuel, the head of the United Africa Company, a subsidiary of Unilever, it was sold to the Labour administration in London and the lukewarm colonial administration in Dar es Salaam and Lindi. The company aimed at opening up fresh sources of raw materials for their vegetable oils and fats, the demand of which seemed limitless in the post-war global shortage. The imperial government wanted to do away with rationing of food at home and gain dollar revenues in order to ease its balance of payments predicament.[15] After the victories on the battlefields of the Second World War, it did not seem much of a task to clear a few hundred thousands hectares of bush in remote Tanganyika and grow groundnuts there. Britain had capital, Tanganyika had land, and machines would do the work. 'The African interest' was definitely subdued but the project was at pains to assure potential critics that they had not been forgotten. It was meant to give the Africans an 'ocular demonstration' of the superiority of mechanised agriculture. In the words of John Wakefield, the former Director of Agriculture of Tanganyika and the key planner of the scheme, it would contribute to the 'provision of an economic foundation for social advance' by clearing tsetse bush and controlling sleeping sickness, establishing water sources, and improving communications. Later, after an undefined but obviously very long period, the project could be handed over to the local, colonial government, and, ultimately, to the African communities themselves.[16]

It was a magnificent scheme indeed. The plan was to clear for groundnut cultivation 107 units of 12,000 hectares each (some 1,300,000 hectares in all), located in three different places (to avert the possibility of simultaneous drought): in Kongwa and Urambo along the central railway, and in Nachingwea. Each of the units was meant to be an independent community of its own with modern houses, welfare centres, schools, and hospitals. The cultivation areas would be self-contained with roads, ditching systems, and anti-erosion earthworks. Work was to be undertaken by machines, especially by bulldozers whose war-time exploits were fresh in mind. But thousands of labourers were still needed, first for clearing and construction, and later for cultivation itself.

There was no lack of innovative ideas. When the old second-hand tractors that had been ordered first proved to be scrap, it was decided to beat the swords into ploughshares. 580 Sherman surplus tanks were ordered from the British Army and the Vickers Armstrong Company turned them into Shervick tractors. The areas to be cleared were nearly uninhabited but this was only considered an advantage. Relatively few people needed to be chased from their land – 400 households was the estimate for Lindi, local food production would not be interfered with, and the scheme could get off to a flying start. It was widely seen as a brave but not unrealistic endeavour, especially if it was undertaken with 'the same determination . . . as was needed, and found, for the major operations of war'.[17] For *The Economist*, not exactly a fan of planned development, the scheme represented 'the sort of economic planning that is needed to change the face of the colonial empire'. The magazine lauded not only its wide vision but its 'hard-headed practical thinking and costing'.[18]

The rise and fall of the scheme took barely four years. Implementation started in early 1947. Problems began almost immediately. While the 'Groundnutters' came and filled the few existing hotels, trains, and planes, machines were delayed and soon turned out to be unusable. Many of the original tractors, gathered from surplus dumps all over the world, broke down before they reached the fields. At the end of the year, three-quarters were out of order. Work had to be undertaken manually and only a fraction of the designed area was actually cleared. Workers were hard to obtain. The second year of the scheme was a repetition of the first, the story of one crisis succeeding another. The 'Shervicks' did not do any better than the original tractors; rather the contrary: the Sherman had been designed for fast breakthroughs on European roads, not for the dust and mud of Africa. Another sup-posedly epoch-making mechanical device, the Blaw Knox root cutter, turned out as inefficient – a prototype that had not been properly tested. Groundnut yields remained low. In 1949, it was clear that the scheme was foundering. With costs of £1 million per month, the Treasury declined to put more funds in and elections approached at home. The *coup de grâce* came in 1949 which was a drought year both in Kongwa and Urambo and the yields were largely destroyed. In Nachingwea, weather was not a problem but only a small area had been planted. In the next year, it was decided to wind up the scheme. It was abandoned as hastily as it was stitched together.

In terms of what is nowadays called development effectiveness – the attainment of the expected results – the scheme was nothing short of a disaster. It spent almost £36 million of the British taxpayers' money instead of the budgeted 24 million – roughly equivalent to all the expenditure of the Tanganyika government from 1946 to 1950. Only 20,000 hectares were cleared instead of the projected 1,300,000. It produced much less groundnuts for export than the African peasants had produced before the war – indeed, less than had been imported to Tanganyika as seed.[19] In addition to the cleared land, it left behind heaps of rusting machines, an underused railway (later demolished), an idle harbour, and a deep suspicion towards grand plans. Most ironically, even if it had been a success it may have been futile. At the time when land clearing was starting in Tanganyika, one hundred tons of groundnuts were found rotting in Northern Nigeria waiting in vain to be transported out.[20]

This is not to say that the Groundnut Scheme had no wider, largely unintended impacts or nobody benefited from it. Wherever ample amounts of extra money are pumped in, somebody is bound to benefit. Many British contractors obviously made good business but also a number of local people got their share. This happened mainly through labour market participation. At its height, the scheme employed more than 23,000 African labourers in 1949 in the Southern Province alone. Because the colonial administration was reluctant to use extra-economic measures of compulsion in the recruitment of local labour for the scheme, and a considerable amount of labourers migrated out from the South anyway, the Groundnut Scheme had to attract labourers by paying better than its competitors. The great majority of the workers must have been unskilled but scattered evidence suggests that the number of skilled, and better remunerated, employees was also significant. Although it is not clear how the workers used their incomes, the influx of money obviously stimulated the local economy at least for a while. This can be seen in the rising trend not only of wages but of prices as well. Some more influential and better positioned men even could accumulate some starting capital and diversify into trade, transport, and farming. To the most enthusiastic African employees these appeared to be 'days of great prosperity'.[21]

In retrospect it is not difficult to locate the faults of the Groundnut Scheme. Haste, poor planning, and over-reliance on the power of agricultural mechanisation have been commonly singled out. Rather than planned development it resembled a military operation. But it has been less appreciated how the modernist development philosophy behind the scheme dovetailed with the persistence of some major colonial myths on the means of and obstacles to development. The drive towards mechanised production was accompanied by two deep-seated beliefs: that the railway is the key to opening up virgin lands and that the presence of tsetse fly keeps the people away from fertile land in Africa. The production areas were explicitly chosen along or nearby the existing railways (Urambo and Kongwa) or where it was feasible to build a new one (Nachingwea), not only to get the expected products out but to get the needed machines in. And what was deliberately sought after was uninhabited land which would be turned cultivable by clearing the bush and chasing tsetse away. Lonely dissenting voices arguing that where large tracts had remained uninhabited and uncultivated the root cause was rather a lack of surface water than the presence of tsetse went unheeded.[22]

Many development lessons have been drawn from the fate of the scheme. Perhaps the safest is that it is not only the shortage of capital and the lack of human will which prevent human societies from turning the deserts into agricultural paradises.[23] Technology works in a physical and social context and an endeavour like the Groundnut Scheme would have required an entirely different, more controllable environment. Even the small-scale experimental farms that were set up in the cleared areas after the closing down of the scheme to explore the conditions for mechanised agriculture failed to produce noteworthy results.[24] An obvious conclusion was that the sun and the soil and the mud of Africa forced the harassed Europeans with their technologies to follow the same rhythm that the local people had been forced to follow. And in the end it chased them away. The most poetic commentators thought that at the demise of the scheme they almost heard a voice in the background, a 'low mocking voice as old as the centuries, the voice of Africa'.[25]

The cashew expansion: market-led development?

An intriguing contrast to the capital-intensive development drive of the Groundnut Scheme is provided by the spread of cashew nuts and their emergence as a major cash crop in the Tanzanian South. The commercial expansion of Tanzania's cashew production and export started in a small way in the 1930s and boomed in the 1950s and 1960s. The bulk of the production came from African peasants, and eventually cashew came to be by far the most important source of cash for the majority of the people. The causes and mechanisms of this spectacular expansion still call for further research and I can present only a first overview compiled from scattered archival and secondary sources.[26] For our analysis of development discourse, the respective roles of market forces on one hand and the extra-economic measures of 'encouragement' and 'push' by the colonial state on the other merit attention. Although the officials were ready to intervene in African cashew cultivation since the 1930s and did so, the intervention was rather unsystematic and always overshadowed by the fear that the production might surpass the demand. It never did: the basic momentum for the cashew expansion was generated by the play of market forces, fuelled by the demand of raw nuts from India. Cashew expansion in East Africa provides an early example of South-South trade.

Cashew is a tree crop the cultivation of which is easy to enter into as it demands few, if any, specialised production inputs. When, where, and how the first cashew tree appeared on Tanganyikan soil will never be known but it must have been centuries ago. It is usually assumed that it had been brought to Mozambique by the Portuguese seafarers and colonialists, became naturalised there, and spread to Tanganyika. In Northern Mozambique, some responsibility for its introduction is credited to Arab slavers.[27] At first the trees appear to have been used to keep soil erosion in check along the coast and perhaps also as a food reserve. Local people gradually found other uses. In addition to processing and eating the 'nut' kernels they also made more or less potent alcoholic drinks from the apples by fermentation (*ulaka*) or distillation (*zarambo*). When the cashew first appears in our colonial sources in the 1930s one of the concerns of the officials was that its possible encouragement among the African cultivators might lead to an increase of drunkenness. In Mozambique the colonial government was reported to have for this reason once tried to ban cashew cultivation, an attempt which naturally was unenforceable. Such concerns soon faded when cashew gained increasing commercial value because of the growing demand from India.[28]

India was and has since been the pivot of international cashew trade. It was the first country to build up a processing industry for export.[29] The introduction of simple technologies raised the productivity in the 1920s and 1930s. When the Indian domestic production of raw nuts fell short of meeting the requirements of the country's cashew industry, East Africa was an obvious place to turn for imports. Not only was it conveniently located along the old maritime routes across the Arabian Sea but the harvest times there were complementary to India's own. Although the East African nuts were considered of lower quality, the processors were often willing to bid a decent price to keep their factories going. In the early 1930s, some 9,000–10,000 tons of raw cashew were annually exported to India from East Africa, the bulk of this coming from the Portuguese colony where the first recorded exports are from 1921.

The interest of the Tanganyika administration in the potentialities of cashew was first raised in the early 1930s in the wake of the territory-wide grow-more-crops campaign. In 1934, it was estimated that there were some 30,000 cashew trees in the country with an annual production of around 600 tons. These trees grew predominantly on the coast: some 20,000 on the island of Mafia, 8,000 in the Southern Province, and 1,000 in Dar es Salaam. The harvest was consumed on the domestic market; nothing was known to go abroad. For officials in the Southern Province it appeared a good idea 'to develop the production of this commodity both as a cash crop and as a potential auxillary [sic] food reserve'.[30] They had in mind the coastal people, who were dependent for their cash income on copra from coconut, the price of which was steadily declining. Cashew's prospects were much brighter. Taking his data from Mozambique, an official estimated that to earn the cash needed to pay his tax, a man had to work 100 days on a sisal estate while it was possible to get the same amount of money with two to three weeks' work of a man and his wife in cashew cultivation. However, he was hesitant to rely entirely on market forces. It was 'necessary to upset the present static production by definite Government intervention and stimulus before normal trade demand can be relied upon to further stimulate production'. In practice, what could be done was to issue seedlings to cultivators free of charge, to plan a moderate number of trees at all Court Houses and other centres, and to conduct 'direct propaganda'.[31] Force was not specifically mentioned but everybody knew that in different guises it belonged to the policy arsenal of the colonial state.

What actually happened is patchily known but definitely the production of cashew nuts started to grow and soon led to exports. The first exports were recorded in 1939 when 928 tons of raw nuts were shipped to India. The war years brought a backlash but planting was intensified because of high prices, and when the new trees started to bear fruit after the war the growth of production accelerated during the 1950s. In 1950 the Provincial Commissioner rejoiced that in cashew the Southern Province had its first perennial crop of any value and told his District Commissioners to 'press forward' with its planting 'as vigorously as possible'.[32] The exports reached 11,700 tons in 1952 and 40,700 tons in 1961. By then cashew had risen to the fourth most important export crop of Tanganyika and the country was producing one-fourth of the world's raw cashew nuts. The bulk of it came from the South-East.[33]

The detailed mechanisms of this spectacular expansion remain speculative. Government intervention did play a part but the role of the state was hardly as decisive as most officials wanted to believe. The intensity and nature of 'encouragement' varied from district to district and slackened in the early 1950s. The main growth did not take place on the coast as originally envisaged by the colonial administration but inland. It appears to have started on the Western Makonde plateau and then spread northwards into present Lindi and Coast regions and westwards into Masasi and Tunduru. In 1961, roughly half of the Southern production came from the Makonde plateau and a quarter from Masasi.[34] To this day, the highest concentration of cashew trees remains on the Makonde plateau. Elders interviewed by researchers commonly maintain that the first trees were grown from seed materials brought from Mozambique, either by migrants from there or by Tanzanian villagers themselves.[35] Most had a few dozen trees and managed their fields with their own household labour. Yet there also emerged some large-scale cultivators with several hundred trees who regularly used hired labour. As with so many other early large-scale cash crop growers in Tanzania, these were men who had accumulated some starting capital in the colonial service or elsewhere – perhaps in the Groundnut Scheme – and disproportionately many were Christians, a small minority among the Makonde. They hired labourers not only from among the local population but also migrants from Mozambique.[36]

Although India belonged to the same colonial empire as Tanganyika, the colonial officials of Tanganyika were unhappy that 'their' cashew nuts were taken raw to India and that the trade was dominated by Indian companies. That the nuts should have been processed domestically was a common concern already at that time. The issue, however, was not the price paid to the producer but the prospect that if the processed kernels could have been exported directly to the United States it would have diverted eagerly sought dollars from India to Tanganyika. Here, again, Portuguese East Africa showed the way: in small quantities manually processed kernels were exported to the US in the early 1930s. At the same time, a small plant was established near Mombasa by a British-Indian company, although it exported to the UK. The owners of that plant approached the Tanganyika government to establish a factory in the Southern Province but the attempt was foiled by the refusal of the government to grant it a 'preferential licence', meaning virtually a monopoly to buy nuts. After the war, Governor Twining attempted to induce the Colonial Development Corporation, the newly created public company which was to promote the supply of colonial foodstuffs, raw materials, and other commodities, to establish a processing facility in Mtwara. The representatives of the company politely listened to the proposal but no action followed. Instead, a small processing plant was established in Dar es Salaam in 1948 by a British citizen without any governmental support.

It processed some 200 to 300 tons of raw nuts per year. Later, another small private plant was set up in Mtwara. As far as can be seen from the scattered references in documents, the plants worked erratically, the main problems being the very small profit margins by which they were forced to operate as the Indian buyers set the general price level, and the low skill levels of the labour force, which made it difficult to compete with the well-established Indian processors.[37]

The Africans clearly appreciated the spread of cashew and the cash income it brought and in the politically charged atmosphere of rising nationalism in the 1950s cashew became politicised. It was always a crop dominated by African peasants and the colonial administration wanted to keep it as such. But there were half a dozen large-scale European and Asian farmers in Lindi and Mikindani, and cashew was also an important crop in the 'production farms' left over by the Groundnut Scheme in Nachingwea. When the non-African cultivators started to organise themselves in the early 1950s and set out to form an association, the Africans grew concerned about the fate of their land. A rare glimpse of African understanding can be gained from a letter that an articulate African OFC welfare officer in Nachingwea sent to his colonial superiors. Southern people had long been poor, he wrote. They had no cattle, no coffee trees, no wheat – things that other Provinces had. Finally, God has given them cashew, 'this sprout for uplifting ourselves (kujiinuka)'. The coming generations would have a better life on the strength of it. Now the planned association threatened to overtake their land and reduce them back to boys and servants of the Asians and Europeans. The writer invoked the civilising mission of the colonial power. English rule had the reputation 'to uplift people, to civilize them, to liberate them, but if this Association will be allowed we cannot stand up (inuka)'.

It is noteworthy that the discourse employed was more that of civilisation and modernity than of development: maendeleo was not yet part of the local vocabulary. Still the writer advocated a forceful intervention. Instead of allowing the association, he said, the colonial administration should promote the cashew cultivation by Africans even by force – by adding cashew to cassava among those crops the cultivation of which was made obligatory by local regulations: 'this is the way to elevate us to become people of the world', i.e. modern people. But force was now regarded as futile by the colonial government, which by this time had grown more concerned with the possible overproduction of cashew and concluded that nobody – neither Africans nor Europeans – needed any 'encouragement' any longer.[38]

Development plans: development as colonial policy

Both the Groundnut Scheme and the expansion of cashew cultivation represent major manifestations of development although in quite different ways: the former can be seen as a climax of its interventionist thrust while the latter resulted more spontaneously from a fortuitous coincidence of international and internal market forces of demand and supply, brought together by the people's own agency and some support by the colonial state. As should be clear from the above, contemporaries associated both occurrences with development but also used other designations to discuss them: advancement, progress, even civilisation. The dual mandate had been there from the outset of British rule, but starting from the late 1930s, development gained a more specific meaning in British colonialism in general and in Tanganyika in particular. This was 'colonial development' understood as colonial policy: something intentionally undertaken by the state and distinguished by three features. It consisted of schemes or projects explicitly undertaken to improve the economic and social conditions of the country and its inhabitants, i.e. their welfare; these went beyond the normal 'maintenance' tasks of the administration (although it was admitted that the line between the two was always blurred); and they were something for which it was possible to seek and gain some extra resources from outside, meaning the metropolitan country. This concept was very similar to the modern project approach, and soon even conjured up a modern caricature: in the public imagination 'development' was seen as 'grandiose projects embarked upon with the highest hopes and financed from the bottomless purse, with eventual disillusionment and a heavy loss to the taxpayer'.[39]

Colonial Development and Welfare Acts: old and new

The development project approach made, as has been noted above, its breakthrough in the Colonial Development and Welfare Acts of 1940 and 1945. Although development had served politically justificatory purposes before, the British decision-makers now felt an increasing need to assure their developmental credentials both outside and inside the colonies. Parts of the empire were plagued by strikes and other 'disturbances' and Tanganyika's international status as a mandated territory was uncertain, with the Germans paying close attention to their former colonies and accusing the present masters of their neglect. The Colonial Office had for quite some time demanded more funds for colonial development but the Treasury remained unconvinced. Only after the outbreak of the war was the tug-of-war finally resolved in favour of the Colonial Office. Development backed by imperial grant assistance was made an official, imperial policy.[40]

Once launched, the new policy gained a momentum of its own. As the war progressed, colonial resources – men, money, and raw materials – were needed ever more urgently. Britain grew more indebted to the United States and after the war colonial products could be sold for dollars. The war also acted as a catalyst for intensifying nationalist aspirations among the Africans who were taken to the frontlines in countries such as Burma and Malaysia which were more advanced in their efforts at self-government. The German criticisms of lackadaisical colonial development were replaced by American ones echoing the aspirations of the colonised peoples. The new United Nations organisation was much keener to lend its ear to the demands of the colonised than the League of Nations ever had been.

In Britain, the voters returned the Labour Party back to power in 1945. An active state and extensive planning had been the order of the day during the war and Labour was ready to go along and make colonial development a policy of its own. Although the Conservatives in their 1951 election campaign made a big noise over the groundnut folly and some leftish Labour politicians and writers showed considerable sympathy for the nationalist aspirations much earlier than any Conservatives, in colonial development the basic policy lines of the parties converged. After their electoral victory the Conservatives carried on with colonial development and even intensified it. Both parties saw it as a means to continue developing exploitable resources but also increasingly, with its newly introduced political embellishments, as a surrogate for having to seriously start to talk about self-government. In the very long run, it was seen as something more: as a means to make sure that 'when the African Territories attain self-government they do so as a part of the Western world'.[41]

Development plans in Tanganyika

The lofty principles of development as welfare reached colonial practice through many mediating mechanisms and the colonial exigencies sometimes shaped them beyond recognition. 'Planning' is a case in point. Its introduction ostensibly was a big change in colonial administrative practice and a number of documents called plans proliferated at both national and provincial levels. Yet it was readily acknowledged that what such documents amounted to was really not a plan but 'an outline sketch of the developments proposed . . . in effect [consisting] of a series of objectives with an approximation of their costs'.[42] In Tanganyika, it took almost a decade to start implementing them and they kept being revised.

The first steps were taken before the war. At the end of 1938, a Central Development Committee was set up to investigate 'how the development of the Territory can be encouraged by the enterprise of the Non-natives and the natives'. Its report, which concluded that 'Tanganyika is capable of great development', was revised to *Outlines of Post-war Development* in 1944 and both were replaced by a *Ten-Year Development and Welfare Plan* in 1946, and an *Education Plan* closely connected to it. This drew on the Colonial Development and Welfare Act of 1945 and was to be implemented from 1947 to 1955. It, too, was soon rendered outdated by the unprecedented economic activity and rising prices. A new plan was drafted in 1955 and revised in 1957.[43] In addition, a number of local agricultural development plans, with emphasis on soil conservation, were launched.

The flaws of the first development plans of Tanganyika were not lost on contemporaries. It was quickly pointed out by a perceptive critic that they were based on shaky or non-existent data and '"the Pilgrim Fathers Complex", an attitude of boundless optimism founded on faith, courage and lack of knowledge'.[44] Julius Nyerere, a new African member of the Legislative Council in 1957, dismissed them as plans as they had set no production targets.[45] Governor Twining admitted that in practice the plans 'contained a number of schemes, which for long had been apparent as being necessary, but which could only be put forward in a modest way because of the limited sums available'.[46] The contrast between the centralising ambitions – the Central Development Committee in 1938 famously set out 'to make Tanganyika a country'[47] – and the inevitably scattered and isolated efforts actually taken on the ground was striking indeed. Their impact was sniffed at. The most important economic expansion in East Africa had taken place regardless of the plans and in no way in consequence of them, the East Africa Royal Commission declared in 1953.[48]

But the Colonial Development and Welfare funds, accessed through the plans, were never meant to do more than to 'prime the pump'.[49] Further financing was to be sought from imperially guaranteed loans raised by colonial governments on the London capital market, by local agricultural surplus funds and revenue, and by private investment, in the case of Tanganyika mainly from the first two. As pump primer, they can in fact claim some success. In post-war Tanganyika, considerably larger sums were used for development purposes than the totals of development plans indicate. While the expenditure of the last plans was about three times more than that of the first, the total expenditure of the colonial administration increased fivefold from 1947 to 1959.[50]

What interests us most here is the interpretation of development the plans portrayed. It had the element of bringing in extra resources but this was always subordinate to the dominant policy line of the day. The Central Development Committee advocated mainly measures that would have facilitated white settlement but after the war an unabashedly pro-settler line was no longer politically possible. All the plans, starting from the 1938 one, talked about the need of defining development broadly and promoting in addition to 'economic' also 'social' development. A key aim was to get Africans – long understood as male – to work beyond the minimum of fulfilling their tax obligations. 'An understanding by the African of the need for more wealth that he can at present see use for, which is undoubtedly essential for his welfare, is necessary to give him an incentive to produce more'. The people 'must . . . increase the efficiency and output of their labour'.[51]

The low standard of productivity of the African peasant was 'at the root of the economic problem' in Africa, argued Colonial Secretary Arthur Creech Jones, a Labour colonial expert. The question was what to do about it, and whether compulsion should and could be resorted to. Creech Jones did not rule out compulsory measures, as it was mandatory to ensure that proper methods of cultivation were adopted and the soil was conserved although he wondered whether they might be effective. Anyway the local native administrations should be 'induced' to secure efficient agricultural practices. Among Tanganyika officials some noted that compulsion was already there in the form of Native Authorities' orders and rules. The District Commissioner of Mikindani interpreted that 'the Trustee power is in loco parentis, it should be able to enforce a policy of development against the wishes of wazee [elders] if satisfied as to the urgency of its need'.[52]

Looking at the actual projects undertaken and expenditure spent on them, it is evident that at the territorial level a dominant understanding of development in these plans was that of building up physical assets of which the colonial state felt a need. Creech Jones urged the primacy of economic development, as 'advance in other directions is largely consequential'.[53] Economic schemes were contrasted to social ones which did not 'immediately show a productive return'.[54] Yet in practice in Tanganyika, most of development expenditure was allocated to infrastructural projects equally slow in their return. The major part went to communications, especially to the construction of roads, which every plan had given as a priority. The Orwellian doublespeak common to modern development interventions had its first antecedents here. What was ostensibly earmarked for social services was in fact used for related capital works. 'Township development' meant basically the water supply in Dar es Salaam while the funds for 'public building and works' were spent to provide housing for government officers.[55] Although later a greater part of the funds was used for health and education, especially in the late 1950s, these were regarded as separate issues: investment in human capital as a basic prerequisite for economic growth was not part of this development thinking.

Local development schemes interfered with people's basic ways of life and production more directly, in the spirit of Creech Jones's vision. Their predominant concern was with soil erosion. Tanganyika was an agricultural country but over most of the country the soil was poor and rainfall badly distributed. The attitude that 'the ravages of the tsetse fly are the greatest menace to the development of Tropical Africa' reigned unchallenged: two-thirds of Tanganyika was seen as 'closed to cultivation' owing to the presence of the fly. The result was over-cultivation of the remaining areas with consequent soil deterioration and diminishing returns, aggravated by occasional drives for intensified production during the depression and war. Thus 'the main objective of any development plan must be a rebuilding of the soil and of conditions which make stable agriculture possible'.[56]

The local schemes were funded mainly from sources inside Tanganyika, either from the central government agricultural surpluses or the native authorities concerned, and to some extent from Colonial Development and Welfare funds. The first, and by far the most important, of the local schemes was started in 1947 in Sukumaland. It was followed by smaller schemes in Mbulu in 1948 and later in Uluguru, Usambara, and Pare as well as in Bukoba, Maasailand, and North Mara. In the mid-1950s they covered one-sixth of the land area with some two million people, which is more than a quarter of the population of Tanganyika (see Table 1). The intention was to extend a scheme to every district of the country.[57]

Table 1 Local development schemes in Tanganyika, 1955

District	Area covered (square mile)	Population affected
1 Sukumaland	20,000	1,115,000
2 Uluguru	500	50,000
3 Usambara	8,500	220,000
4 Bukoba	6,000	300,000
5 Maasailand	23,000	57,000
6 Mbulu	6,000	150,000
7 North-Mara	1,500	110,000
8 Pare	3,000	85,000
Total	68,500	2,087,000

Source: J. F. R. Hill and J. P. Moffett (eds), *Tanganyika: A Review of its Resources and their Development* (Dar es Salaam: Government of Tanganyika 1955), p. 514

The schemes were implemented and administered in different ways but they were predicated on the same basic logic. As the root causes for land degradation were identified as too high densities of human and cattle population and deficient methods of cultivation, mostly by Africans, the plans aimed at (a) reducing the population pressure by opening up new areas for settlement and urging people to move into them, (b) reducing the numbers of cattle by demanding the cattle-owning people to sell off more cattle than before, and (c) improving cultivation methods and introducing new ones. Many of the efforts may have been sound in a narrow technical sense, but all entailed social and cultural changes which the large majority of the peasants felt were threatening their ways of life and were unwilling to go along with voluntarily. This meant that to enforce the plans the colonial state had to employ its repressive machinery. Local authorities were ordered to introduce by-laws on agriculture. Those who did not obey them were punished. In the words of a colonial official turned post-colonial researcher, 'for many years before the war and for some years after 1945, the agricultural staff tended to be policemen rather than advisers, largely responsible for the enforcement of the multitude of agricultural rules and for bringing offenders to court'.[58] The resistance towards the schemes grew and at the same time contributed to and gained extra force from the spreading nationalist agitation. Finally they had to be given up.

Colonial development planning in the South-East

The new breed of colonial development entered South-Eastern Tanganyika rather late, only after the collapse of the Groundnut Scheme and when the expansion of cashew was already in full swing. Historically, the region had suffered from erratic development efforts even more than many other parts of Tanganyika. The grafting of enforced German developmental measures on an ailing commercial economy had contributed to the eruption of the great Maji Maji rebellion in 1905–7 whose suppression destroyed what little was left from the earlier prosperity.[59] Under British rule, the developmental impact of the alien administration made itself gradually felt in the area as an increasing number of technical staff were added to the administrative officials. Yet the direction of development efforts was seen to depend largely on the personal idiosyncrasies of the rapidly changing local officials. Often well intentioned, they were paternalistic and constrained by ignorance. Liebenow, with a pardonable degree of exaggeration, speaks of administrative behaviour referred to by Africans as *wazimu wa mzungu* or 'white man's madness':

This was the 'disease' which seemed to compel each new district commissioner to make his own special imprint upon a district during his brief tenure in the area. The special 'madness' of one man might be road construction, while that of his successor might be soil conservation. These in turn would be followed by a district commissioner with a penchant for getting the people to breed hybrid chickens, perhaps, or dig latrines, or dig wells. [After] the arrival of a new European . . . all energies could be directed to pleasing his idiosyncrasy and ignoring the pet projects of his predecessors. The elaborate network of paths and roads established . . . could be surrendered to the jungle; the latrines could become chicken houses; and the hybrid chicken could revert to their primitive type.[60]

The Southern Province Development Plan, which was launched in 1951, was meant to bring some method to this madness. The local Africans had already been pressed to produce surplus food by forcing them to plant a number of acres, normally two, of cassava or other food crops. The plan was to intensify the production drive. Soil erosion was not seen as much of a concern as the peripheral province had earlier been spared unduly intensified production pushes. Underlying the plan was the need to make use of the resources left by the Groundnut Scheme. The colonial government had inherited the infrastructure investment, i.e. the port of Mtwara and the railway from there to Nachingwea and had to cover their operational losses. The railway obviously would become profitable only if the annual amount of the freight could be drastically raised to 100,000 tons, a far cry from some 26,500 tons produced in 1949. The government committed itself to 'develop' the Southern Province so as to attain this target. The Southern Province Development Plan assumed that although some further land could be alienated for non-native cultivation, especially of sisal, most of the increase had to come from African production. Basically any existing crop, from cassava to cashew, would do; the latter was sometimes singled out but was not given any consistent priority. The need for water supplies and even the possibility of agricultural mechanisation were fleetingly mentioned, but two fundamental problems were seen in communications and staff. Road improvement needed a heavy injection of capital. New administrative and agricultural staff were required; the present ones were only able to do 'care and maintenance' and it was impossible to carry out a development plan with them: 'for the African, abstract principles, however lofty, are no substitute of direct personal contact, and . . . success of a production drive eventually depends on adequate and competent field staff'.[61]

Again, the existing sources are scarce and it is difficult to know what actually took place on the ground but it is evident that the production drive did not live up to expectations and eventually petered out. The natural and cultural environment obviously was too intractable even for this kind of approach. The agricultural staff were increased although at a slower pace and to a lesser extent than planned and a major part of the expenditure went to their personal emoluments. Their costs were transferred to the normal departmental budget and the provincial agricultural officer could note that in this respect the plan had achieved what it had been devised to: 'to raise an inadequate establishment of the Agricultural Department in the Province to a normal one'.[62] Investment in roads was confounded by the need to protect the freight prospects of the railway from road competition. Road-building efforts were concentrated on building feeder roads for the railway, whereas the upgrading of the main Songea-Lindi road was neglected. In the late 1950s it was clear that the overall production targets would never be attained. The plan withered away. The railway tracks were scrapped in 1964. Among the wildly over-optimistic production targets only one had been badly underestimated: cashew tonnage, which had been foreseen at 10,000, was more than double that in 1961.

Conclusion: dead end and rebirth of development

Thus, development was put to many uses and had different meanings in late colonial South-Eastern Tanganyika whereas some things that we might recognise as development did not qualify as such. The country as a whole had been caught in a drive of colonial development in which the old dominant colonial notion of development for exploitation of resources was accommodating another, that of development for the welfare of the people. This shift was shoring up the politically legitimising function of development at the cost of its economically instrumentalist task. Yet its practical manifestations were much more mundane, ranging from building infrastructure for colonialists to interfering with the basics of local people's lives. They remained unfinished and often worked against the overall political purposes.

The South-East had its idiosyncrasies. The Groundnut Scheme was not part of generic colonial development but a development endeavour located in a colony, a metropolitan initiative for metropolitan purposes. The spectacular expansion of cashew production was referred to as development only for the part of the involvement of the colonial state, as it was otherwise fuelled by market forces, mainly demand from India, and executed by the people's agency. The Southern Province development plan deviated from the local plans in other parts of the country in that its interference with local life was more superficial, for example it did not entail any relocation of population (or cattle, practically non-existent in the South). In our terms they all represent development, understood as a combination of intervention, process, and goal. But their different conceptualisations and the fact that development remained one notion among many and could be used interchangeably with them shows that a colonial discourse development had not acquired the hegemonic status it was to gain in the post-colonial discourse.

This leads to the following concluding suggestion: as the meanings of development ramified, the notion of development was reaching the limits of its usability in the colonial context. Development did not and could not upkeep a colonial discourse. This was for a simple reason: it could not undo the basic colonial premise of an unbridgeable difference between the coloniser and the colonised. It rather reinforced it. Governor Twining invoked the dual mandate again: 'Tanganyika possesses many rich potentials, and these must be developed, first for the benefit of the local population, but also to make their contribution to the ever growing needs of the world'.[63] For African nationalists, this would no longer do. For them, the main problem with colonialism was the 'difference' on which it was based: its denial of human equality and of the capacity of the Africans to govern themselves. There was no way for colonial development to undo this, particularly if its purpose was to make African resources contribute to the 'growing needs of the world'.

Yet the dead end of colonial development did not toll the death knell for development as a whole – on the contrary. The African nationalists seized development as a potent notion for another purpose: it gave them grounds to attack the colonial government. In taking it over they rescued development from its colonial dead end and gave it a new lease of life in associating it with *maendeleo*, or progress.[64] They turned the tables by charging that development did not and could not happen under colonialism. The fate of the Groundnut Scheme was well known. Nyerere complained in the Legislative Council in 1957 that in spite of the elaborate colonial development set-up there was 'no policy for economic development, there were no production targets for crops or minerals'. What achievements in production there were, such as the increase of the cotton crop in Sukumaland or the promise of cashew in the South, had been achieved haphazardly, and largely due to the work of the people and not because of any government plan. During independence, development was to provide them the main prop of their rule. On the eve of it, Nyerere promised to 'transform' the country: in ten years Tanganyika would achieve most of the things the colonialists had failed to achieve during their rule.[65]

Now we of course know that it was not so simple. Despite all colonial and post-colonial development efforts, not only the South-East but almost the whole of Tanzania is impoverished, a few pockets of affluence notwithstanding. After colonialism, development became the loadstar of all policy but the post-colonial development interventions have not been able to overcome the forces that produce effects contrary to the proclaimed aims. Although the goals and motivations of post-colonial development differ from those of colonial development the means remain much the same. The ideology of colonial development is now duly condemned and transcended but many of its forms continue to be relied upon in differing guises. And although nobody any longer mentions the dual mandate, its basic thrust is intact and maintains the allure of development. Today's Tanzania, of course, is being developed primarily to the benefit and welfare of its inhabitants, but outsiders who support it by means of development cooperation are also meant to benefit.

Notes

1 I wish to thank the editors of this book for their constructive comments in revising the chapter for publication.

2 Or rather against the consequences of 'progress'. This important point is made, with considerable overgeneralisation, by Michael Cowen and Robert Shenton, *Doctrines of Development* (London, New York: Routledge 1996), pp. 6ff.

3 See Ludwig Wittgenstein, *Philosophical Investigations* (Oxford: Blackwell 1995 [1953]), p. 43: 'The meaning of a word is its use in the language'.

4 Recently notably Frederick Cooper, who takes development as a product of the need to counteract the economic contraction during the Great Depression. See Frederick Cooper, *Africa since 1940: The Past of the Present* (Cambridge: Cambridge University Press 2002), especially pp. 91–131.

5 This has been my argument for quite a time and the rest of this paragraph is based on my previous work. For the Tanganyika case, see Juhani Koponen, *Development for Exploitation: German Colonial Policies in Mainland Tanzania, 1884–1914* (Helsinki, Hamburg: Lit 1994).

6 Frederick D. Lugard, *The Dual Mandate in British Tropical Africa* (Edinburgh, London: Blackwood 1922), pp. 606–19. In the original formulation, it stated that the task of the colonial power was to act as 'trustee, on the one hand, for the advancement of the subject races, and on the other, for the development of its material resources for the benefit of mankind' (p. 606).

7 For British attitudes, see Alan C. Cairns, *Prelude to Imperialism: British Reactions to Central African Society, 1840–1890* (London: Routledge and Kegan Paul 1965), pp. 78, 234–5. For German arguments, see Koponen, *Development for Exploitation*, pp. 176–7.

8 George C. Abbott, 'Re-examination of the 1929 Colonial Development Act', *Economic History Review*, New Series, 24, 1 (1971), pp. 68–81.

9 See David John Morgan, *The Official History of Colonial Development*, vol. 1, *The Origins of British Aid Policy, 1924–1945* (London: Macmillan 1980), pp. 199–200.

10 British National Archives, London (hereafter BNA), CO 859/19/7475, Correspondence between Colonial Office and Treasury from November 1939 to February 1940, as quoted in Michael Ashley Havinden and David Meredith, *Colonialism and Development: Britain and Its Tropical Colonies, 1850–1960* (London, New York: Routledge 1993), p. 203.

11 The most successful of the schemes was probably that of Sukumaland. See, for example, D. W. Malcom, *Sukumaland: An African People and Their Country. A Study of Land Use in Tanganyika* (London: Oxford University Press 1953); G. Andrew Maguire, *Towards 'Uhuru' in Tanzania: The Politics of Participation* (London: Cambridge University Press 1969); John Charles de Wilde, assisted by Peter F. M. McLoughlin et al., *Experiences with Agricultural Development in Tropical Africa*, vol. 2, *The Case Studies* (Baltimore: Johns Hopkins Press 1967), pp. 415–50. Contemporary information on the Uluguru Scheme can be found in Roland Young and Henry Fosbrooke, *Land and Politics among the Luguru of Tanganyika* (London: Routledge and Kegan Paul 1960), while the Usambara scheme is discussed with more historical distance by Steven Feierman, *Peasant Intellectuals: Anthropology and History in Tanzania* (Madison, WI: University of Wisconsin Press 1990), chapters 6 and 7.

12 Ralph Jätzold, 'Die Nachwirkungen des fehlgeschlagenen Erdnuss-Projekts in Ostafrika', *Erdkunde* 19, 3 (1965), pp. 229–30; J. F. R. Hill and J. P. Moffett (eds), *Tanganyika: A Review of its Resources and their Development* (Dar es Salaam: Government of Tanganyika 1955), p. 820.

13 The first suggestion is by Jan S. Hogendorn and K. M. Scott, 'Very Large-Scale Agricultural Projects: The Lessons of the East African Groundnut Scheme', in Robert I. Rotberg (ed.), *Imperialism, Colonialism and Hunger: East and Central Africa* (Lexington, MA: Lexington Books 1983), pp. 167–98; the latter is by James C. Scott, *Seeing Like a State: How Certain Schemes to Improve the Human Condition Have Failed* (New Haven, CT, London: Yale University Press 1998), p. 229.

14 See, for example, Matteo Rizzo, 'What Was Left of the Groundnut Scheme? Development Disaster and Labour Market in Southern Tanganyika, 1946–1952', *Journal of Agrarian Change* 6, 2 (2006), p. 207.

15 The best contemporary eye-witness account of the early phases of the scheme comes from Alan Wood, who was head of information of the scheme at that time. See Alan Wood, *The Groundnut Affair* (London: The Bodley Head 1950). Other useful overviews, based on archival sources, include D. J. Morgan, *The Offical History of Colonial Development*, vol. 2, *Developing British Colonial Resources 1945–1951* (London: Macmillan 1980), pp. 285–319; Havinden and Meredith, *Colonialism and Development*, pp. 276–83. If not otherwise indicated, much of the subsequent discussion draws on these sources.

16 The first quotation is from 'A Plan for the Mechanized Production of Groundnuts in East and Central Africa', as quoted in Havinden and Meredith, *Colonialism and Development*, p. 277; and the latter is from 'The Summary of the Wakefield Report', reprinted in Wood, *Groundnut Affair*, p. 255.

17 In addition to Wood, see correspondence in the Tanzania National Archives, Dar es Salaam (hereafter TNA), 16/15/104. The quotation is from 'A Plan for the Mechanized Production of Groundnuts in East and Central Africa', in John Iliffe, *A Modern History of Tanganyika* (Cambrige: Cambridge University Press 1979), pp. 440–1.

18 *The Economist*, 5 March 1947, as quoted in Cyril Ehrlich, 'The Poor Country: The Tanganyika Economy from 1945 to Independence', in D. A. Low and Alison Smith (eds), *History of East Africa*, vol. 3 (Oxford: Clarendon Press 1976), p. 310.

19 For statistics, see Hill and Moffett (eds), *Tanganyika*, p. 389.

20 See Anwarul Haque Haqqi, *The Colonial Policy of the Labour Government, 1945–51* (Aligarh: Muslim University 1960), p. 187.

21 Quoted in Rizzo, 'What Was Left of the Groundnut Scheme?', p. 212.

22 For one such warning, see TNA 16/15/104/252, letter from an unidentifiable provincial official to the Chief Secretary, 15 February 1947.

23 See Herbert S. Frankel, 'The Kongwa Experiment: Lessons of the East African Groundnut Scheme', in Herbert S. Frankel (ed.), *The Economic Impact on Underdeveloped Societies: Essays on International Investment and Social Change* (Cambridge, MA: Harvard University Press 1953), pp. 141–53.

24 For these, see for example, Jätzold, 'Nachwirkungen', and Morgan, *The Official History of Colonial Development*, vol. 4, *Changes in British Aid Policy, 1951–1970*, pp. 54–91.
25 Wood, *Groundnut Affair*, p. 182.
26 The most important archival sources are from TNA, Cashew Nut Industry, complemented by the BNA at Kew.
27 TNA, Cashew Nut Industry. Information on the history of cashew nuts in Northern Mozambique below is taken from the report of the British official who was sent from Tanganyika to study it – District Agricultural Officer, Lindi, 'Report of the Cashew Nut Industry in Portuguese East Africa', 8 January 1935.
28 Most of this and what follows is taken from discussions between the Provincial Commissioners in Lindi (Williams and Kitching) and the Senior Agricultural Officer in Lindi (Latham) between November 1933 and October 1934; see TNA, Cashew Nut Industry.
29 The sketch of the history of cashew in India is collated from bits and pieces in R. C. Mandal, *Cashew Production and Processing Technology* (Jodhpur: Agrobios 2007), and documentation in TNA, Cashew Nut Industry, and BNA CO852/1176/2.
30 TNA, Cashew Nut Industry, Acting Provincial Commissioner, Lindi (Williams) to Chief Secretary, 23 November 1933.
31 The latter proposals were made by Latham and endorsed by Kitching from February to October 1934, see note 28 above.
32 TNA, 16/44/3, Provincial Commissioner, Lindi, to all District Commissioners, 29 November 1950.
33 Statistics in Herbert C. Kriesel et al., *Agricultural Marketing in Tanzania: Background Research and Policy Proposals* (East Lansing, MI: Michigan State University 1970), p. 133.
34 TNA, Production figures in 'Regional Commissioner's Annual Report: Southern Region', probably 1961.
35 Clive P. Topper, 'The Historical and Institutional Background of the Tanzanian Cashew Industry', in Clive P. Topper et al. (eds), *Proceedings of the International Cashew and Coconut Conference: Trees for Life – the Key to Development. Held at Kilimanjaro Hotel, Dar es Salaam, 17–21 February 1997* (Reading: BioHybrids International 1998), p. 79; E. S. S. Adamu, 'Small-holder Cashew Farmers in Mtwara Region: A Case Study', *Journal of the Geographical Association of Tanzania* 5 (1969), p. 76.
36 J. Gus Liebenow, *Colonial Rule and Political Development in Tanzania: The Case of the Makonde* (Nairobi: East African Publishing House 1971), p. 329, note 15.
37 See discussions in TNA, Cashew Nut Industry, and BNA CO 852/1176/2.
38 TNA, Cashew Nut Industry, 'Huko ndio kuinuka tuwe watu kama watu Duniani', G. C. Kasembe to Provincial Commissioner, Lindi, 5 February 1953; Hill and Moffett (eds), *Tanganyika*, p. 452. My translation.
39 BNA EAF 53/2, Part B, Discussions between colonial officials and members of the Royal Commission of East Africa in Dar es Salaam in June 1953, as quoted in Morgan, *The Official History of Colonial Development*, vol. 4, p. 66. As the outcome of the discussions, the successor of the Overseas Food Corporation was named the Tanganyika Agricultural Corporation, dropping 'development' from the title.
40 For the history of the Acts, see Morgan, *The Official History of Colonial Development*, vol. 1, esp. p. xvii and chapters 2–8.
41 BNA CAB 21/1690, Arthur Creech Jones, 'Memorandum', 9 June 1948, as quoted in Havinden and Meredith, *Colonialism and Development*, pp. 231–2.
42 Tanganyika Territory, *A Ten-Year Development and Welfare Plan for Tanganyika Territory: Report by the Development Commission* (Dar es Salaam: Government Printer 1946), p. 2.
43 For an overview, see Hill and Moffett (eds), *Tanganyika*, pp. 841–5.
44 BNA CO 691/190, extract from C. Gillman, 'Planned Development', *Tanganyika Standard*, 30 April 1944.
45 BNA CO 822/1575, extract from *Tanganyika Standard*, probably 1957.

46 Sir Edward Twining, 'The Situation in Tanganyika', *African Affairs* 50, 201 (1951), p. 304.
47 Tanganyika Territory, *Report of the Central Development Committee* (Dar es Salaam: Government Printer 1940), p. 7.
48 *Report of the East Africa Royal Commission 1953–1955* (London: HMSO 1955), p. 94.
49 See, for example, Andrew Cohen, *British Policy in Changing Africa* (London: Routledge and Kegan Paul 1959), pp. 31–2.
50 Ehrlich, 'The Poor Country', p. 323.
51 Tanganyika Territory, *Report of the Central Development Committee*, p. 14; Tanganyika Territory, *Ten-Year Development and Welfare Plan*, p. 12.
52 Discussion in TNA 16/44/1, esp. Creech Jones to Governor Battershill, 2 February 1947, and comments by the District Commissioners of Masasi, 14 May 1947, and of Mikindani, 13 May 1947.
53 As quoted in Haqqi, *Colonial Policy of the Labour Government*, p. 164.
54 *Tanganyika Annual Report for 1950*, as quoted in Ehrlich, 'The Poor Country', p. 322.
55 Hill and Moffett (eds), *Tanganyika*, pp. 841–7.
56 Tanganyika Territory, *Ten-Year Development and Welfare Plan*, p. 14. The quotation concerning the tsetse menace is from *Report of the East Africa Commission* (London: HMSO 1925), p. 70.
57 Hill and Moffett (eds), *Tanganyika*, pp. 513–14.
58 N. R. Fuggles-Couchman, *Agricultural Change in Tanganyika, 1945–1960* (Stanford, CA: Stanford University, Food Research Institute 1964), p. 75.
59 Juhani Koponen, 'Maji Maji and the Making of the South', *Tanzania Zamani* 7, 1 (2010), pp. 1–58.
60 Liebenow, *Colonial Rule*, p. 143.
61 BNA CO 691/208, 'Southern Province Development Plan 1950–1960'.
62 TNA 16/44/3, Provincial Agricultural Officer (Brett) to Director of Agriculture, Dar es Salaam, 20 November 1955.
63 Twining, 'The Situation in Tanganyika', p. 307.
64 This is where I part company with Cowen and Shenton, see note 2 above. Whatever the merits of regarding development as a counterpoint to progress in Europe, such a function cannot be found in post-colonial, and, I believe, colonial development.
65 BNA CO 822/1575, extract from *Tanganyika Standard* [ca. 1957]; Julius Nyerere, *Freedom and Unity – Uhuru na umoja: A Selection from Writings and Speeches, 1952–65* (London: Oxford University Press 1967), p. 183.

CHAPTER TWO

Developing 'Portuguese Africa' in late colonialism: confronting discourses[1]

Cláudia Castelo

This chapter examines the shifting contours and ambiguities of African development discourses during the Estado Novo,[2] in order to include the Portuguese case in the international debate on the colonial roots of development narratives.[3] Special attention is given to development ideas raised around Angola and Mozambique. In addition to being the two most significant territories of the Portuguese empire, both politically and economically, they also became areas of white settlement. This last characteristic held strong sway in the development model that the regime devised for those colonies. Although this text will give priority to the perspectives and strategies of the Portuguese state, it will also reflect on the views of experts. The study is based on political documents, such as governmental statements (namely of Ministers of Colonies/Ministers of Overseas Provinces and colonial officials), parliamentary debates, colonial legislation, Development Plans (*Planos de Fomento*); and on scientific surveys and reports, especially of the Overseas Provinces Research Board (*Junta de Investigações do Ultramar*, JIU).

Before proceeding, it is important to explain that in Portuguese there are two different words that can be used to refer to development: *desenvolvimento* (that may also be translated as growth) and *fomento* (that may also be translated as promotion or support). They both may signify an act and an effect. The word *fomento* is a word of Latin origin – *fomentum* ('material to feed the fire') – and is derived from the Latin word *fovere* (keep warm; favour, cherish).[4] It means, in particular, an 'act or effect of promoting the development or progress of something'.[5] Other dictionaries describe it as 'government action aimed at facilitating the development of a country, region or economic sector: agricultural development',[6] or simply as 'development (of material progress, by the governments' beneficial action)'.[7]

During the Estado Novo, *fomento* was the word more often used in the political discourse to signify development produced by the state, both as an action and as a goal of action.[8] From 1936 onwards a number of specialised bodies and high posts of *fomento colonial* were created by the Ministry of Colonies, including the Director General of Development (*Direcção Geral do Fomento*), the Chief Inspector of Development (*Inspecção Superior do Fomento*), and the Assistant-Secretary of State of Development (*Subsecretário de Estado do Fomento*). The word *desenvolvimento* was viewed with suspicion by the Estado Novo[9] and was used only belatedly (after 1945) and less frequently than *fomento*. In turn, the democratic opposition would advocate for the development of the country. The political programme of the Armed Forces Movement (*Movimento das Forças Armadas*, MFA), which overthrew the dictatorship on 25 April 1974 is often cited as the '3Ds' programme due to its three main goals: democratisation, decolonisation, developing (*Democratizar, Descolonizar, Desenvolver*). After the democratisation process the word *fomento* was gradually replaced by the word *desenvolvimento* in the Portuguese political discourse.

The spiritual nature of the imperial project: colonial fomento in standby (1930s)

Although this chapter focuses on the period of the Estado Novo, the roots of the discourse on the development of Portuguese Africa within Portuguese political thought can be traced back to the last decades of the nineteenth century and the early twentieth century. An analysis of parliamentary activity during the Constitutional Monarchy (1821–1910) reveals that the problem of colonial development entered into the political debate in the last quarter of the nineteenth century.[10] Throughout the First Republic (1910–26) the issue remained on the agenda and was discussed in several parliamentary sessions.

The subject of colonial development was discussed in the parliament especially when the deputies were asked to approve the government's legislative initiatives on the matter. It was discussed, for instance, in the debates on the loan for overseas public works in 1878; the 'public works expeditions' in 1880; agricultural and military colonisation in 1896; industrial development in the colonies in 1899; and the colonial *fomento* of the Angola province in 1921. Closely tied to the theme of colonial development, which was mainly envisaged as material development of the colonies, invariably were the themes of public works, the exploitation of natural resources, and white settlement.

With the advent of the Estado Novo, colonial *fomento* continued to refer in the political discourse to the material development of the colonies and, specifically, to public works. Nevertheless, in the 1930s, aiming to confront the crisis provoked by the Great Depression and to stabilise the country's budget, Salazar[11] made the decision to terminate the colonial *fomento* policies of the First Republic.[12] The official discourse stressed that 'development work' ('uma obra de fomento') would only be 'reproductive and beneficial' ('reprodutiva e benéfica') if it was subordinated 'to strict principles of financial order' ('a rígidos princípios de ordem financeira').[13]

The Estado Novo colonial ideology during the 1930s sacralised the empire, by emphasising the spiritual nature of Portuguese colonisation, and turning its back on materialist concerns.[14] But this did not happen without a large degree of ambiguity. Its 'civilising and evangelising mission' was claimed to be based on 'the high principles of the Christian civilisation' ('nos mais altos princípios da civilização cristã').[15] Nevertheless, beyond self-proclaimed universalist and humanitarian ideals, the official colonial discourse was often explicitly racist. Africans were considered backward people, lazy, prone to multiple vices, and inferior to the European. They were only capable of a slow and limited evolution through the benign influence of (compulsory) work, Catholicism, and the example of the Portuguese settler. Those who advocated for the health care and well-being of the native populations did so from an instrumentalist vantage point, arguing that better health would lead to greater productivity: 'It is essential to treat them as if they were precious reservoirs of energy'.[16] Moreover, the 'civilising mission' would consist of practices that in augmenting the needs of the natives, did so for the sake of the metropolitan, capitalist economy. As Armindo Monteiro argued: 'We must increase the needs of black people. Herein lies civilisation. Each new need that the black [sic] acquires (in clothing, food and health, objects of everyday use), will also benefit commerce and industry'.[17]

The Colonial Act of 1930 reaffirmed that 'Portugal [had] an historical and essential mission of possessing, civilising and colonising overseas dominions'.[18] But it also stated that: 'The metropole and the colonies, by their moral and political ties, have based their economy on a natural community and solidarity ... The economic systems of the colonies are established in accordance with the needs of their development ... and the rights and legitimate conveniences of the metropole and the Portuguese colonial empire'.[19] The prevailing nationalist, Catholic, traditionalist, and ruralist ideology was very reluctant to entertain to any degree industrialisation, urbanisation or any other aspect of modernity, not only in the empire, but within the metropole as well. Having few financial resources available to pursue its 'civilising mission', the Estado Novo dismissed its responsibilities in promoting colonial development. Salazar would emphasise instead that Portuguese Africa was a wide open field to private entrepreneurs and he would discourage claims for public expenditure in the colonies. As he proclaimed in 1937:

> One understands that the civilised man, knowing from experience the full range of modern needs and the formidable scientific and technical apparatus existing to address them in the old countries, placed before large extensions of virgin land, its resources within his arm's reach, and the potential and unexplored wealth of the natural forces, longs for civilisation to be fully transplanted, envisions the magical transformation of the backward countries in the face of others who took millennia to make themselves, and appeals to the state as the great divinity of our days.[20]

The empire, in the Estado Novo narrative, was placed 'above finances, economy and politics' ('acima das finanças, da economia e da política'), in communion with the national past, moral and feeling, as a 'consubstantiation of the proper Portuguese ideal' ('consubstanciaçao do próprio ideal português').[21] While the *fomento* promoted by the central state, and the investment of metropolitan funds that it implied, was put on standby until the early 1950s, the 'civilising mission' was largely left to the private enterprise and the 'virtues' of settlers and missionaries. While the first possessed a 'singular talent to cope with *inferior races*' ('talento singular para lidar com as raças inferiores') and could serve as an example to the Africans, the second ensured the 'education of the indigenous peoples' in the 'values of the civilisation' ('valores da civilização'), including work, the Portuguese language, patriotism, and religion.[22] The true 'civilising mission' of the Portuguese in Africa was to educate the natives' bodies and souls for work.[23]

Even in the early 1940s, senior colonial officials were still insisting that 'the main engine of the colonies' progress will always be private activity, exerted by labour and capital, and driven by self-interest'.[24] The central state should only create a favourable environment for the private sector, by drawing up development plans, passing legislation that promoted production, and stimulating useful scientific work.

Colonial fomento: *beyond public works*

In a speech delivered in 1942, the Director General of *Fomento Colonial* and Secretary General of the Ministry of Colonies explained that the expression *fomento* was normally used 'in the sense of equipping the territory through the construction of public works'. However, he added, that way of seeing things had become too restricted. Instead, a *fomento* policy had to be seen from a higher level. He could find no better definition of *fomento* than the one attributed to the Direcção Geral de Fomento Colonial and included in the organic law of the Ministry of Colonies: 'guidance and supervision of all the services and activities related to the development of the colonies' public wealth, the defence of the national economic unity and the equipping of all that was needed for enhancing the value of the natural resources and possibilities of the overseas territories'.[25] The *fomento* policy thus represented something more than the politics of public works to high officials like the Director General.

Three years later in 1945, the Minister of Colonies, Marcello Caetano, recognised that although the word *fomento* was being used as the expression for one of the main pillars of colonial policy, it often did not have a precise meaning.[26] He noted that *fomento* being such a 'broad concept', encompasses 'all that, directly or indirectly, facilitates, encourages and promotes the creation of wealth, but when implemented it becomes impractical and suffers inevitable restrictions'. Moreover, Caetano continued: 'In the tradition of Portuguese administrative policy, *fomento* primarily aimed at public works, and among these, especially communications. The rest faded away, even against the will of the rulers, before the overt utility and brilliance of the roads, ports, [and] railway construction'.[27]

A discursive shift was then introduced by the Minister of Colonies: colonial *fomento*, Caetano suggested, should mean the economic policy of empire, concerned with production, commerce, industry, credit, transports, and communications.[28] Moreover, *fomento* should mean modernisation and should require technical expertise. The mission of a colonial country like Portugal was to 'create new values – to optimise the value of wild lands, and the populations still not awakened for modern civilisation'.[29] Caetano would claim: 'Africa needs technicians!' and regretted that 'the vacancies for colonial technical staff remained unfilled'.[30]

This is probably the first sign of the Estado Novo turning towards a modernising and technocratic discourse on Portuguese African development that would deepen in the 1950s and 1960s. The origins of this turn should be sought in the crisis of the colonial system after the Second World War, as well as in domestic policy. Regarding the international context, Portugal faced a strong campaign against its colonialism, above all in the United Nations. In the revised Constitution of 1951 the Estado Novo replaced the term 'colonies' with 'overseas provinces' and the term 'colonial empire' with 'Portuguese overseas'. Thenceforth, the official discourse would affirm that Portugal did not have colonies but metropolitan and overseas provinces, which formed a single nation, regardless of its geographic discontinuity. The inhabitants of the European provinces and the inhabitants of the overseas provinces (in Africa and Asia) were all Portuguese, despite their degree of civilisation.

With regard to the domestic policy, one must bear in mind that after 1945 the Estado Novo opened (albeit slowly) the country to economic modernisation and industrialisation despite the permanence of an anti-modernist discourse.[31] During the presentation of the first National Development Plan, conceived for the benefit of both the metropole and the overseas territories, Salazar stressed that the plan was 'son of the same principles and [was] integrated in the noble thought of achieving . . . with concrete and attainable realities, for each arm a hoe, for each family its home, for each mouth its bread'.[32] Nevertheless, it is important to observe that during the 1950s the *fomento* of the overseas provinces – namely all the big engineering works – would be largely accomplished through the system of forced recruitment and forced labour of African people.

The Planos de Fomento: *from economic to social meaning*

In the 1950s the Estado Novo assumed central responsibility for promoting economic growth in Portuguese Africa.[33] Re-invoking a modernising discourse that had its roots in the parliamentary debates of the Constitutional Monarchy, the new concept of economic development gained influence as a justification for state interventionist policies in the overseas provinces and as a device of reinforcement and legitimisation of Portuguese colonial rule. This condition was not specifically Portuguese. As emphasised elsewhere in this volume, Portugal followed a trend that could be observed in all the European colonial powers, although admittedly with some delay, fewer technical resources, a different set of priorities, and from a lower level of investment.

The Development Plans (*Planos de Fomento*) launched by the Estado Novo began in 1953 and lasted until the end of the dictatorship. Conceived with a six-year period in mind – with the exception of the Midterm Plan (*Plano Intercalar*) covering three years – they derived from the Lisbon government's will to rationalise public investment, and to formulate and coordinate general and sectoral economic and social policies both for the metropole and for its overseas provinces. The intention was to develop in the overseas territories an economy complementary to that of the mother country and ultimately to support the economic integration of all the territories of the Portuguese community 'from Minho to Timor' as a single economic unit.[34] In spite of censorship and the conservative nature of the regime, the preparatory work of the *Planos de Fomento* contributed to a better understanding of colonial reality, in its economic and social aspects.[35]

A brief analysis of the *Planos de Fomento* regarding the overseas provinces allows us to understand the evolution of the Estado Novo's ideas regarding the development of the Portuguese territories in Africa, particularly Angola and Mozambique.[36] The first National Development Plan (1953–58) assigned four and an half million *escudos* for investment in the overseas provinces, which was directed towards three main sectors: communications and transportation, the exploitation of resources, and white settlement.[37] In Angola, these sections of the budget received 66 per cent of the expenditure; and in Mozambique, 57.7 per cent. The intention, in the case of Angola, was to make possible the exportation of raw materials, produced in the colony and valued in the international exchange market: coffee, oil, diamonds, and iron. In the case of Mozambique, the development of the territory's infrastructure anticipated not only the exportation of materials produced in the province but also greater economic regional integration with South Africa and Rhodesia. Investments in white settlement schemes, related to agricultural irrigation schemes, were also planned for both colonies.

According to Sarmento Rodrigues, Minister of Overseas Provinces, although the plan did not include any special reference to the indigenous populations, they would be the first to benefit from the improvements and 'teachings' ('ensinamentos') of the plan. He justified the omission by claiming that

> the new native farmers in Angola and Mozambique, those who have launched themselves in an informed use of ploughs and tractors, those who exchanged the winding footpath for the broad road and infallible bicycle; at the very least, those who instead of queuing in large caravans searching for work weeks away, are now served by fast and convenient transport, and those who no longer hide in the virgin jungle, but work in the factories and come to the capital of the nation flying in modern airplanes. We must not forget [them in] the plan ... but it also does not seem justifiable to give them a special place within our egalitarian system.[38]

It is obvious that the minister's statements can only be understood within the realm of intentions, if not in the field of pure propaganda.

According to Marcello Caetano, at the time Minister of the Presidency (*Ministro da Presidência*), the main goals of the Second Development Plan (1959–64) were augmenting the gross domestic product and increasing the standard of living of the Portuguese population.[39] By 'standard of living' the Minister meant 'the basic consumption needs of an individual or family such as nutrition, housing, lighting, heating, water supply, clothing, health care and hygiene, and cultural and recreational opportunities'.[40] By highlighting the need for raising standards of living, the Minister was pointing to the fact 'that one should not rely solely on the automatic increase in national product to ensure a balanced distribution'.[41]

The global expenditure of the Second Development Plan (1959–64) for the overseas provinces was over nine million *contos* (1 *conto* was 1,000 *escudos*). The highest expenditure in the plan was earmarked for communications and transportation (at 44.7 per cent), followed by the expenditure for the 'exploitation of resources' ('aproveitamento dos recursos') (at 26.7 per cent) and for settlement (at 11.9 per cent). Scientific surveys of the territories were expected to absorb 4.4 per cent of the expenditure and included general cartography, geological studies, pedology studies, population studies, and economic studies associated with the Development Plan (these last two only covered Angola and Mozambique). The plan also included, for the first time, appropriations for education and health (7.2 per cent) and for 'local improvements' ('melhoramentos locais') (4.5 per cent).[42]

The beginning of the colonial wars, first in Angola in 1961, and soon after in Guinea in 1963 and Mozambique in 1964, led to increasing international pressure on Portugal regarding decolonisation. In response, the political discourse on the development of Portuguese Africa took a more technocratic turn, without giving up its Christian and Lusotropical imprints. The new internal and external context and the influence of social expertise would force a social turn in the discursive and non-discursive practices of the Estado Novo after 1961.

When Adriano Moreira, an academic with experience in colonial education and research, assumed control of the Ministry of Overseas Provinces in 1961–62, he produced several laws that abolished the main discriminatory aspects of the Portuguese colonial system: the unequal status of indigenous people from the provinces of Angola, Guinea, and Mozambique, forced labour, and forced cultivation of cash crops (cotton and rice). The preamble to the law that abolished the *indigenato* stated that throughout their history of expansion, the Portuguese showed no colour prejudices but respect for the cultural manifestations of the people they met (with the exception of practices that were deemed contrary to the morals and laws of mankind). The Portuguese claimed to have developed 'the only humanism that until now has been able to implant human democracy in the areas of the world where the West has expanded and colonised'.[43] To justify the measure, it was argued that 'the development and progress' ('a evolução e progresso') of overseas populations in continental Africa allowed 'waiving many of the rules and mechanisms for protecting defined populations wholly entrusted to the State and would benefit from the use of broader means for the management and safeguarding of their own interests and also for participating in the management of local interests'.[44]

The Under-Secretary of State of *Fomento Ultramarino*, Rafael Amaro da Costa, in a 1962 speech entitled – not coincidentally – 'Economic humanism in the overseas provinces', argued that in the Third Development Plan for the overseas provinces, still in preparation at the time, there needed to be 'greater emphasis given to everything related to the improvement of Man [sic] and the promotion of industries, mines and fisheries, and [to] all agriculture, forestry and animal husbandry along with the necessary infrastructure, particularly the plans for roads and ports and the production, transmission and distribution of electricity'.[45] Two years later, his successor, Mário Oliveira, would claim that 'the technical surveys would be empty of pragmatic content' if they did not include 'a conceptual attitude' in which 'Man as social being and God's creature was very present with all its complexity of needs and aspirations'.[46] In stating this, Oliveira also had in mind the social environment. Notwithstanding the continuing need for the development of infrastructure, which was necessary to ensure the colonial security strategy, 'a better position relative to "human and social investment"' was also recognised.[47]

In the Midterm Plan (1965–67) and the Third Development Plan (1968–73) for the overseas territories, one notes an increasing attention given to the industrial sector.[48] At the same time, a larger investment was made in 'social promotion' ('promoção social'), meaning education, health, and welfare ('educação, saúde e assistência') of the native populations.[49] It was assumed that social investments were particularly necessary in the 'underdeveloped territories' and that the 'human factors' that shaped and constrained development ought to be taken into account. The government believed that increasing the living standards of the native populations was closely tied to their social advancement in terms of making them participate in the circuits of the monetary economy.[50] The new development engine would be a more rational economy based on widespread wage labour (once forced labour had been finally abolished).

Having as the overall objective 'the economic and social progress of the Portuguese people' ('o progresso económico e social do povo português'), state economic planning in the late 1960s was aimed specifically at 'accelerating the rate of increase in national product'; and 'a more equal distribution of national income'.[51] It was recognised that the overseas provinces – by then also referred to as underdeveloped territories – were in different stages of development. In order to reduce the disparities between the parts that comprised the Portuguese Economic Area (Espaço Económico Português), it was the government's intention to promote 'polarised development' ('desenvolvimento polarizado') through concentrating its investment effort in 'growth poles' ('pólos de crescimento').[52]

In the Third Development Plan, a larger portion of the expenditure continued to be channelled to the transport and communications sector.[53] Nevertheless, in Angola and the remaining overseas territories, the agriculture, forestry, and cattle-ranching sectors (which since the Midterm Plan included irrigation and settlement schemes) were surpassed by the education and research sectors, which occupied the second tier in terms of money allocated.[54]

The third and last executed Development Plan of the Estado Novo (the Fourth Development Plan intended for the 1974–79 period was never put in practice due to the end of the dictatorship) had as its main goals: 'the progressive elevation and dignifying of the human being within the Portuguese community', a 'fairer redistribution of wealth', and a 'progressive correction of regional inequalities of development', which were means to achieve that spiritual purpose.[55] The concept of 'regional development' ('desenvolvimento regional') was perhaps the main discursive novelty of the Midterm and Third Development Plans.

During the thirteen years of colonial war, the need to coordinate the development of the overseas provinces with the counter-insurgency effort was continually stressed in the political discourse. In everyday communication it was repeated that war had been the true engine of Angola's and Mozambique's economic development. As FRELIMO, the liberation movement in Mozambique, began to make serious gains however, Estado Novo officials had to admit that the war would not be won by military means but only with a concerted development effort.[56] In the early 1970s, Angola high officials and economic associations came to recognise that only through peace could 'promoção social' be achieved.[57]

White settlement: means and goal of the development of 'Portuguese Africa'

As we have seen earlier in this chapter, the relation between white colonisation of Portuguese Africa, the indigenous civilisation, and the development of the overseas economy had deep historical roots in Portuguese colonial discourse. Moreover, this linkage perpetuated itself, even against the tide of other European colonial empires, during the era of decolonisation.[58]

During the 1950s, not only was the 'assimilationist principle' ('princípio assimilacionista') enshrined in the Constitution of the Portuguese Republic, but a 'luso-tropical vulgate', as one scholar puts it,[59] began to be implemented as the official discourse of the Portuguese state. Gilberto Freyre[60] coined the term lusotropicalism[61] during an official visit to Portugal and the Portuguese colonies in 1951–52 at the invitation of the Minister of Overseas Provinces, Sarmento Rodrigues. Freyre claimed that the Portuguese possessed a unique relationship with the tropics through ties of love rather than material interest, and a capacity for constituting there multi-racial societies of mixed race and cultural interpenetration.[62] This predisposition resulted from Portugal's ethnic and cultural past, which was situated between Europe and Africa and subject to long contact with Arabic populations. Brazil was, in Freyre's opinion, the greatest example of Portuguese colonial genius. However, in Angola and Mozambique, the Brazilian social scientist believed he had found new 'Brazils' in the making.[63]

It was also during the 1950s that the Estado Novo committed itself fully to the promotion of white settlement in Portuguese Africa. Sarmento Rodrigues argued that white migration to the colonies would not only help solve the problem of metropolitan demographic surplus, but also simultaneously empower the Portuguese overseas provinces. The minister did not show preference for any settlement system in particular. As he declared: 'I accept every system, all approaches, seeing only the settlement at the end of every act. I go so far as subordinating everything to it, like a master idea. Pure deception. It is just a road – a long road – to achieve the greatness of the Nation . . . It is possible that not everyone is aware of this historic moment we are crossing'.[64] He therefore endorsed a diverse range of modalities: agricultural, military, or penal colonisation directed or oriented by the state; agricultural colonisation directed by private companies; free colonisation destined to agriculture, industry, trade, and liberal professions; and even permanent settlement deriving from public, civilian, and military services.

The nationalisation and defence of overseas territories demanded, from the minister's point of view, a greater presence of Portuguese settlers. The fundamental idea of increasing the Portuguese population in the overseas territories was closely associated with the goal of progress and development of the Portuguese overseas provinces.[65] In a conference held to discuss the first Plano de Fomento for the overseas provinces, Sarmento Rodrigues suggested that Portuguese settlement was one of the most crucial elements of the plan. As Rodrigues explained:

Without an increase in the Portuguese population, specifically the metro-politan – which radiates a power of assimilation that shall gather around itself the remaining elements, growingly identifiable with the original Lusitanian standard – one cannot count on any real progress, including the efficient and permanent defence of the territories and their perfect nationalisation. On the other hand, settlement leads to a re-evaluation and consequent resolving of all regional problems. It is life in its highest representation and [with] theoretical demands that are the impelling stimulus of civilisation.[66]

In the Organic Law of the Portuguese Overseas Provinces (1953), it was established that the social and economic life of the overseas provinces would be regulated and coordinated in particular conformity with the following goals: the 'rational use of resources and natural possibilities of the territory' and 'settlement in the territory, namely through the incitement of colonisation by national families'.[67]

While other colonial regimes in post-war Africa planned and intro-duced schemes of resettlement and agricultural development aimed at Africans,[68] the Portuguese Estado Novo invested massive sums in the creation of rural settlements associated with irrigation schemes that were exclusively directed (for example at Cela, Angola) or mostly directed (for example at Cunene, Angola, and Limpopo, Mozambique) towards rural working class families from the metropole, and which were relocated at public expense. These settlements were established on small agricultural properties and were modelled on the metro-politan rural parish. Impoverished peasants were settled on the land, which would be worked upon by the family unit without the aid of native salaried labourers and, initially, using routine techniques such as bull-wagons and ploughs. The schemes involved the removal of all native populations who used these lands from the areas that underwent this sort of intervention, thus aggravating social tensions between settlers and the colonised. Presented in the official discourse as agents of Portuguese civilisation in Africa and as models for the indigenous populations, in actuality the settlers constituted the poorer and most illiterate group among the so-called 'civilised'. In the region of Limpopo, they served as very poor examples, not only to the *assimilados*, but even to those who did not intend to apply for Portuguese citizenship.[69]

As mentioned earlier, the beginning of the colonial war in Angola determined, on an internal level, the initiation of reformist legislation by Adriano Moreira, the Minister of Overseas Provinces, and the rein-forcement of investment in Angola and Mozambique. At this time, the Provincial Settlement Boards (*Juntas Provinciais de Povoamento, JPP*) of Angola and Mozambique were created, to act as high organs of public administration responsible, in each overseas province, for the orientation and conduct of all matters related to settlement in the territory and the coordination of private and public initiatives. Aiming to promote the so-called multi-racial integration, investments in the creation of mixed settlements were begun, in which natives of Angola, Mozambique, and Cape-Verde were admitted. In the preamble of the decree on the creation of the JPP of Angola and Mozambique, Adriano Moreira revealed the government's thinking on overseas settlement, resorting to an argument clearly Lusotropicalist in nature. As seen in the quote below, it reveals in a particularly eloquent way the rigid articulation that the official doctrine made between settlement and the development of the overseas provinces:

> In the state of development achieved by the African provinces and which requires acceleration . . . the issues of settlement assume particular relevance and careful growth. They [the issues of resettlement] are the base, not just for social-economic improvement of territory and peoples, but for their [peoples'] genuine elevation and integration with alien ethnic elements of the common Motherland, in the harmonious multi-racial community that we traditionally have proposed to ourselves and built with effort, and without which there shall be no more peace or progress in this unstable African land.

Moreira went on to assert that:

> In societies that are evolving – as are or should be those of Black Africa – the evolution process cannot do without a permanent inflow of these specialised workers of all levels and all sectors, whether as an indispensable tool for projects of economic development, or for diversified work of civilised life; whether for the professional training of increasingly wide layers of aboriginal populations, called to progress and, themselves, participating in all those activities; whether, still for social support and moral assistance of these populations.[70]

The Portuguese government would, shortly afterwards, come to terms with the fact that the introduct on of legislation and large sums of funding invested in maintaining Portuguese settlement in Angola and Mozambique were not having the results that were expected. Government-assisted emigration to Africa was no match to emigration elsewhere (only one out of every four emigrants would go to the overseas provinces). Even the efforts of the JPP in promoting an agrarian model of settlement could not achieve the goal of extensive and consolidated colonisation. As a result, Silva Cunha, then Minister of Overseas Provinces, requested during 31 March 1965 session that the Overseas Council analyse matters related to the reform of the JPP. In its report, the Council stressed that European settlement should result primarily from the development of economic activities, increased productivity, and the intensity of investments planned and programmed by the government through entities of planning and coordination. Thus, white settlement was, simultaneously, both a means to development and a goal of development.

In the commentaries prepared by the Office of Political Affairs of the Ministry of Overseas Provinces (*Gabinete de Negócios Políticos do Ministério do Ultramar*), which were broadcasted by the state-owned radio station (*Emissora Nacional*), it was asserted that Portugal was creating 'whole communities' ('comunidades integrais') in the overseas provinces which were said to be a 'factor of mult-ethnic stability' ('factor de estabilidade poliétnica') on the African continent. People were told that white settlement was not a stratagem to ensure white supremacy; rather, its fundamental purpose was 'the social advancement of native populations' ('a promoção social das populações autóctones').[71] It was presented as a valid way for attaining the material, social, and cultural evolution of the indigenous populations, with the intention of integrating all in a new composite society.[72] The settlement of metropolitan Portuguese in the overseas territories would homogenise otherwise heterogeneous human groups, elevating those less gifted.[73] Measures of incentive for white settlement, it was argued, would not just promote the migration of Portuguese from Europe to Africa, it would give rise to a process of ethnic and cultural dialogue between the different communities, thus resembling the symbiosis of people of diverse origins that formed the foundation of the Portuguese nation.[74]

Alternative views on the development of 'Portuguese Africa'

As other scholars have noted, British state interventionism in the colonies required technical and scientific knowledge and there was an increasing need of experts for advice and guidance in a wide range of areas.[75] Additionally there was an 'ascendancy of economists and engineering experts as advisers to development plans'.[76] In the Portuguese case, although the politicians recognised the importance of technical expertise and practice, the state faced a lack of technicians in the overseas provinces which was considered to be a national problem.[77] In 1962, it was estimated that: 'A thousand technicians in the agricultural, forestry and husbandry field would be needed in the overseas technical services in the next 10 or 12 years, in other words the number of all the agricultural and forestry engineers that work nowadays in the metropole'.[78] Yet, in the early 1960s the metropolitan universities were producing less than fifty agricultural and forest engineers and thirteen veterinaries annually, which gives us a sense of the severe shortage of technical staff that existed at the time.[79]

Given the scarcity of scientific and technical staff in the overseas provinces for conducting surveys and advising on state planning, about a hundred missions and technical brigades were created within the Overseas Provinces Research Board (*Junta de Investigações do Ultramar*, JIU).[80] These missions and brigades conducted fieldwork in the colonies and gathered a large amount of research in several scientific and technical domains.[81] The Estado Novo used science and technology to establish and legitimise its major development schemes in Africa.[82] The evolution traced above regarding the *Planos de Fomento* – from an economic view (in the first and second plans) to a social understanding of development (from the Midterm Plan onwards) – was determined in great measure by the scientific and technical expertise mobilised to support policy making.

Experts from several research fields contested the prioritisation of infrastructure and white rural settlement in the first two development plans. As the economist João Salgueiro pointed out in the colloquium on the Second Development Plan organised by the JIU's Centre of Political and Social Studies (*Centro de Estudos Políticos e Sociais*), the intention of increasing white settlement had no parallel in any other foreign development plan.[83] He also stressed that the centrality of infrastructure and the lack of social investment directly beneficial to the African population were other anachronisms of Portuguese planning.[84] In 1961, Orlando Ribeiro, a distinguished geographer and university professor, and head of the JIU's Mission of Overseas Physical and Human Geography (*Missão de Geografia Física e Humana do Ultramar Português*) and Hélder Lains e Silva, an agronomist and head of the JIU's Mission of Overseas Agricultural Studies (*Missão de Estudos Agronómicos do Ultramar*), would condemn the rural white settlement schemes of Limpopo and Cela due to their narrow, somewhat idyllic, and unscientific view of development.[85] The professor of economics, Alfredo de Sousa, drew attention to a major prejudice of the colonial administration regarding community development (a method of action that the United Nations encouraged), noting that it was seen as 'an English-style means of directing people to absolute self-management'.[86] Such suspicions help explain its mis-application by the colonial administration and the armed forces in Angola and Mozambique, whom de Sousa accused of imposing an economic and social development model on the African people with no concern for their active and conscious collaboration.[87]

Although this subject requires further extensive research, empirical evidence collected so far indicates that during the 1950s and 1960s experts from several technical and scientific fields linked to research units based in the metropole and in the overseas territories, produced alternative visions on the development of 'Portuguese Africa'. Previous fieldwork experience and participation in international bodies of technical and scientific cooperation were fundamental in this process.[88] Conducted studies, involving shorter or longer periods of fieldwork in the colonies, detailed surveys, direct observation, interviews, enquiries, and other methods of agricultural and social research revealed the shortcomings of a strictly economic model of development that would only benefit the colonial administration and the settlers. Social researchers, human geographers, and agricultural engineers endeavoured to convey a doctrine of development that took into account social justice and the improvement of the living conditions of African populations. The experts' views, translated in both confidential and public reports on colonial realities, uncovered abuses and illegal practicies (of officials and employers) and called into question political measures, such as the rural settlements (colonatos), the strategic hamlets (aldeamentos estratégicos), and paternalist approaches to agricultural technical assistance. They also pushed political actors to recognise the importance of social justice, of social investments, especially in the public educational system, of community development programmes (involving local populations in the decisions about their own lives), of the recognition and use of local knowledge and related practices, and of effective policies of racial equality within Portuguese Africa. At the centre of development (as a state practice), they argued, should be human concerns: this was an idea that the political discourse of the Estado Novo would borrow from the technical and scientific discourse of the 1960s. Some of those specialists would come to accept high political responsibilities or enter the Overseas Provinces Administration, and later, return to the academy and to scientific research.[89]

Conclusion

The Portuguese political discourse on colonial development evolved gradually over the years from a model that focused on the economy and infrastructure to one that eventually embraced other sides of development. In the 1950s the Estado Novo would affirm itself as a *pluricontinental* and multi-racial state, empoying an instrumental reading of Lusotropicalism as its ideological anchor. It would never abdicate the role of white settlement in Angola's and Mozambique's development, not even after the onset of anti-colonial uprisings which demanded a more rapid and multi-faceted approach to development that placed Africans at the centre of government concerns.

After the Second World War, scientific research conducted in the overseas provinces would be mobilised to serve their modernisation and economic development and, finally, the 'social advancement' ('promoção social') of the indigenous population. Since the overseas provinces were essentially agricultural economies and the emerging questions in the colonial setting were human problems, agronomic and social research gained importance. Experts involved in social and agricultural research on and in the overseas provinces produced critical analyses on the most discriminating aspects of the colonial system, and on political practices imposed on Africans with no regard for local specificities, knowledge, and practices. The adoption of community development programmes was advocated as well as the promotion of an endogenous development of the indigenous peoples. The shift towards the 'human side' of development, especially an increasing investment in African education, which is evident in the Midterm Plan and the Third Development Plan, was to a large extent a consequence of the criticisms, views, and advice of experts. Nonetheless, the further step towards an integrated development plan that accepted the right of African populations to self-determination was never taken, at least not explicitly. The limitations imposed by the nature of Estado Novo – the official view on the uncompromising defence of the integrity of the nation dispersed over several continents; censorship and self-censorship to which researchers and technicians submitted to; values and myths about the supposed uniqueness of Portuguese colonialism that many of them (probably the majority) shared – help to explain why.

Notes

1 I would like to thank Marta Hodge for her assistance in editing and translating the chapter. I also thank Catarina Trigo Pereira for her collaboration in the translation of a first draft, and the book editors for all their help.
2 See 'Introduction', note 91.
3 Development is a concept with a vast semantic content; therefore, it is difficult to define with precision. Concerning development and colonialism, see, for example, Frederick Cooper and Randall Packard (eds), *International Development and the Social Sciences: Essays in the History and Politics of Knowledge* (Berkeley, Los Angeles, London: University of California Press 1997); Frederick Cooper, 'Writing the History of Development', *Journal of Modern European History* 8, 1 (2010), pp. 5–23; Joseph Morgan Hodge, *Triumph of the Expert: Agrarian Doctrines of Development and the Legacies of British Colonialism* (Athens, OH: Ohio University Press 2007); Helen Tilley, *Africa as a Living Laboratory: Empire, Development, and the Problem of Scientific Knowledge, 1870–1950* (Chicago: University of Chicago Press 2011). For a historical account of the development doctrine, especially that which stems from the European setting, see Michael Cowen and Robert Shenton, *Doctrines of Development* (London, New York: Routledge 1996), chapter 1.
4 My Etymology. Available at: www.myetymology.com/latin/fomentum.html (accessed 16 May 2013).

5 In Portuguese it is: 'Ato ou efeito de promover o desenvolvimento ou o progresso de algo'. See *Dicionário de Língua Portuguesa*, Porto Editora. Available at: www. infopedia.pt/pesquisa.jsp?qsFiltro=0&qsExpr=fomento (accessed 3 May 2013). Hereafter, the original Portuguese quotations for all English translations that are one line or more are given in the notes.

6 'Ação do governo que visa a facilitar o desenvolvimento de um país, de uma região ou de um setor económico: fomento agrícola'. See *Dicionário online de Português*. Available at: www.dicio.com.br/fomento (accessed 15 May 2012).

7 'Desenvolvimento (de progressos materiais, pela acção benéfica dos governos)'. See, 'Dicionário Priberam da Língua Portuguesa'. Available at: www.priberam.pt/dlpo/default.aspx?pal=fomento (accessed 15 May 2012).

8 Cowen and Shenton have stressed that whatever definition of development is used, it appears both as means and as goal. See Cowen and Shenton, *Doctrines of Development*, p. 3.

9 Mário Murteira notes that during the Estado Novo, 'The word *fomento*, after all, was hiding the theme of development'. See José Manuel Rolo, 'Entrevista a Mário Murteira', *Análise Social* 46, 200 (2011), p. 567.

10 Regarding the colonial question, the parliament during the Constitutional Monarchy was not the centre of political decision-making but acted as a space for ideology production and was thereby able to define the parameters of policy options. See Valentim Alexandre, *A questão Colonial no Parlamento, 1821–1910* (Lisbon: Publicações Dom Quixote 2008), p. 194.

11 António de Oliveira Salazar (1889–1970) was Minister of Finance (1928–32) of the military dictatorship and president of the Council (1932–68) of the Estado Novo regime.

12 This was not a Portuguese peculiarity. Cooper reminds us that 'Interwar colonialism refused to follow a developmentalist vision of itself'. See Cooper, 'Writing the History of Development', p. 10.

13 Armindo Monteiro, 'Directrizes duma política ultramarina', *Boletim Geral das Colónias* 9, 97 (1933), p. 17.

14 In the interwar period, the mythification of the empire, through arguments of universal nature based on religion or the Enlightenment, was common to other countries such as Britain, France, and Belgium. However, in the Portuguese case, a close link was established between the colonial question, the political regime and national identity, which facilitated the process of sacralisation of the empire and withdrew space from anti-colonial currents which only gained prominence in the last years of Estado Novo. See Valentim Alexandre, *Velho Brasil, novas Áfricas: Portugal e o Império, 1808–1975* (Porto: Afrontamento 2000), p. 229.

15 Decreto [Decree] no. 18570 [Approval of the Colonial Act], *Diário do Governo*, 1st series, 156, 7 August 1930, p. 1308.

16 'É indispensável tratá-los como se fossem preciosos reservatórios de energia'. Armindo Monteiro, *Da Governação de Angola* (Lisbon: Agência Geral das Colónias 1935), p. 43.

17 'Cumpre-nos aumentar as necessidades do negro. Nisto consiste a civilização. Cada necessidade nova que o preto adquira (no vestuário, na alimentação, nos objectos de uso comum), terá repercussões felizes no comércio e na indústria'. Monteiro, *Da Governação de Angola*, p. 44.

18 'Portugal tem a função histórica e essencial de possuir, civilizar e colonizar domínios ultramarinos'. Decreto [Decree] no. 18570 [Approval of the Colonial Act], p. 1308.

19 'A metrópole e das colónias, pelos seus laços morais e políticos, têm na base da sua economia uma comunidade e solidariedade natural . . . Os sistemas económicos das colónias são estabelecidas de harmonia com as necessidades do seu desenvolvimento . . . e com os direitos e legítimas conveniências da metrópole e do império colonial Português'. Decreto [Decree] no. 18570 [Approval of the Colonial Act], p. 1311.

20 'Compreende-se que o homem civilizado, conhecendo por experiência toda a gama das necessidades modernas e a formidável aparelhagem científica e técnica existente

para lhes fazer face nos velhos países, colocado ante extensões intérminas de ter-renos virgens, tesoiros ao alcance dos braços, e a riqueza potencial, inexplorada das forças naturais, anseie pela transplantação integral de toda a civilização, visione a mágica transformação de países atrasados na feição de outros que levaram milénios a fazer-se e apele para o estado como a grande divindade dos nossos dias'. António de Oliveira Salazar, 'O império colonial na economia da Nação', in António de Oliveira Salazar, *Discursos e notas políticas*, vol. 2 (Coimbra: Coimbra Editora 1937), p. 163.

21 Armindo Monteiro, *Para uma política imperial: alguns discursos do Ministro das Colónias Doutor Armindo Monteiro* (Lisbon: Agência Geral das Colónias 1933), p. 5.

22 João Carlos Paulo, 'Vantagens da instrução e do trabalho: "Escola de massas" e imagens de uma "educação colonial portuguesa"', *Educação, Sociedade e Culturas* 5 (1996), p. 109. Emphasis in the original.

23 Miguel Bandeira Jerónimo, *Livros brancos, almas negras: a 'missão civilizadora' do colonialismo português, c. 1870–1930* (Lisbon: Imprensa de Ciências Sociais 2010), pp. 46–7.

24 'Será sempre a actividade particular, exercida pelo trabalho e pelo capital, e movida pelo próprio interesse, que representará a principal alavanca do progresso das coló-nias'. Rui de Sá Carneiro, 'Fomento colonial', *Boletim Geral das Colónias* 18, 204 (1942), p. 48.

25 'Quando se fala de fomento colonial toma-se geralmente a expressão no sentido do apetrechamento do território por meio da construção de obras públicas. Na verdade, porém, essa maneira de ver é demasiado restrita porque uma política de fomento tem que ser encarada um pouco de mais alto. Não encontro para ela melhor definição do que a que se pode extrair do diploma fundamental da organização do Ministério quando nele se atribui à Direcção Geral de Fomento o papel de orientar e fiscalizar superiormente todos os serviços e actividades ligadas ao desenvolvimento da riqueza pública nas colónias, à defesa da unidade económica nacional e ao apetrechamento necessário para a progressiva valorização dos recursos e possibilidades naturais dos territórios ultramarinos'. Ibid., p. 38.

26 Marcello Caetano, 'Discurso de S. Ex.ª o Ministro das Colónias no acto de posse do Director Geral, Interino, de Fomento Colonial e do Inspector Superior de Fomento Colonial', *Boletim Geral das Colónias* 21, 236 (1945), p. 3.

27 'É fomento tudo quanto, directa ou indirectamente, facilite, estimule, promova, a criação de riqueza. Conceito amplíssimo, este, que, ao traduzir-se para a prática, sofre inevitáveis restrições. Na tradição administrativa portuguesa a política de fomento visou sobretudo as obras públicas e, de entre estas, elegeu especialmente as comunicações. O resto apagava-se, mesmo contra a vontade dos governantes, perante a ostensiva utilidade e o brilho da construção das estradas, dos portos, dos caminhos de ferro'. Ibid., p. 4.

28 Ibid.

29 'A missão de um país colonial, como o nosso, é criar valores novos – valorizar as terras bravias, valorizar as populações ainda não acordadas para a civilização moderna'. Ibid., p. 8.

30 'A África precisa de técnicos! E não é sem profunda tristeza que vejo desertos os concursos para os quadros técnicos coloniais'. Ibid.

31 Fernando Rosas, *Portugal entre a paz e a guerra, 1939–1945* (Lisbon: Estampa 1990).

32 'podemos sentir orgulho em afirmar que [o Plano] é filho dos mesmos princípios e se integra no nobre pensamento de alcançar, não com frases literárias mas com realidades concretas e atingíveis, para cada braço uma enxada, para cada família o seu lar, para cada boca o seu pão'. António de Oliveira Salazar, 'Plano de Fomento Nacional', *Boletim Geral do Ultramar* 29, 336–7 (1953), p. 53.

33 The development plans of the late 1930s and 1940s in Mozambique and Angola were financed by the colonial budgets. The great novelty of the *Planos de Fomento* regarding the overseas provinces would be the investment of metropolitan funds in those territories.

34 As Cowen and Shenton have shown, development was a mid-century state practice rooted in the nineteenth century with fundamentally European intellectual origins. In the Portuguese case, after 1945, development was conceived by state initiative to address and solve problems in the metropole and in the overseas territories. See Cowen and Shenton, *Doctrines of Development*, chapter 1.

35 Mário Murteira, 'Formação e colapso de uma economia nacional', in Francisco Bethencourt and Kirti Chaudhuri (eds), *História da expansão portuguesa*, vol. 5, *Último império e recentramento, 1930–1998* (Lisbon: Círculo de Leitores, 1999), p. 110.

36 Although the development plans were intended to cover all territories under Portuguese sovereignty, Angola and Mozambique received the majority of investments made overseas: 86 per cent in the first and second plans, 87 per cent in the intermediate plan and 91 per cent in the third plan. See Victor Pereira, 'A economia do Império e os Planos de Fomento', in Miguel Bandeira Jerónimo (ed.), *O Império Colonial em questão, sécs. XIX–XX* (Lisbon: Edições 70 2012), pp. 251–86.

37 Secretariado Técnico de Presidência do Conselho de Ministros [Technical Secretariat of Presidency of the Council of Ministers], Inspecção Superior do Plano de Fomento, *Relatório final da execução do I Plano de Fomento, 1953–1958* (Lisbon: Imprensa Nacional 1959), pp. 694–5.

38 'Que o digam os novos agricultores indígenas de Angola e Moçambique, que se lançaram esclarecidamente no uso de charruas e tractores; os que trocaram a pista sinuosa do caminho de pé posto pela estrada larga e a infalível bicicleta, pelo menos; os que, em vez de enfileirarem nas grandes caravanas à busca de trabalho a semanas *de distância*, são servidos agora por transportes rápidos e cómodos; os que já não se escondem no mato virgem, mas trabalham nas fábricas e vêm à capital da Nação voando nos modernos aviões. O plano não os podia esquecer ... Mas dedicar-lhes uma secção especial não nos pareceu justificável, dentro do nosso sistema igualitário'. Manuel Maria Sarmento Rodrigues, 'Plano de fomento do ultramar', *Boletim Geral do Ultramar* 29, 336–7 (1953), p. 67.

39 Marcello Caetano, 'Plano de fomento para 1959–64: exposição do sr. prof. dr. Marcelo Caetano ao Conselho Económico', *Boletim Geral do Ultramar* 33, 379 (1957), p. 16.

40 'O nível de vida é uma expressão ligada sobretudo a realidades de consumo, sintetizando a situação do indivíduo ou da família quanto ao teor da sua alimentação, às comodidades de habitação, iluminação, aquecimento e abastecimento de água, às facilidades de vestuário, aos cuidados de saúde e higiene, às possibilidades de cultura e diversão'. Ibid.

41 'Ao destacar a elevação do nível de vida pretende-se significar que não se deve unicamente confiar no automatismo do aumento do produto nacional para assegurar uma equilibrada distribuição'. Ibid.

42 Secretariado Técnico de Presidência do Conselho de Ministros, *Relatório de execução do II Plano de Fomento: Ultramar, 1959–1964* (Lisbon: Imprensa Nacional 1970), p. 635.

43 'o único humanismo que até hoje se mostrou capaz de implantar a democracia humana no Mundo para onde se expandiu o Ocidente'. Decreto-Lei [Decree-Law] no.43893, *Diário do Governo*, 6 September 1961, p. 1102.

44 'dispensar muitas das normas que definiam um mecanismo de protecção das populações inteiramente confiado ao Estado e haveria vantagem em generalizar o uso de mais meios para a gestão e defesa dos seus próprios interesses e, também, para a participação na gestão dos interesses locais'. Ibid., p. 1103.

45 'No Terceiro Plano de Fomento para o Ultramar ... prosseguir-se-ão os objectivos do vigente, dando maior relevo a tudo o que respeita à valorização do Homem e ao fomento das indústrias, minas e pescas e de todas as actividades agro-silvo-pecuárias em necessário enquadramento com as infra-estruturas, designadamente as dos planos rodoviários e portuários e de produção, transporte e distribuição de electricidade'. Manuel Rafael Amaro da Costa, *Humanismo económico no Ultramar: conferência proferida pelo Subsecretário de Estado do Fomento Ultramarino, Eng.º Manuel Rafael Amaro da Costa, em 5 de Junho de 1962, no anfiteatro do Instituto de Medicina Tropical* (Lisbon: Agência Geral do Ultramar 1962), p. 15.

46 'os estudos técnicos ficariam vazios de conteúdo pragmático se neles se não inserisse uma atitude conceptual onde se sintetizasse uma ordem de princípios orientadores, em que o Homem, como ser social e criatura de Deus, estivesse bem presente com todo o seu complexo de necessidades e aspirações, na sistemática consideração da peculiaridade do meio em que vive e convive'. Mário de Oliveira, *Problemas do ultramar no Plano Intercalar de Fomento: comunicação feita por Sua Excelência o Subsecretário de Estado do Fomento Ultramarino na sessão plena do Conselho Ultramarino do dia 5 de Novembro de 1964, seguida do colóquio que teve lugar no final da mesma* (Lisbon: Agência Geral do Ultramar 1964), pp. 6–7.

47 'uma maior posição relativa do "investimento humano e social"'. Ibid., p. 16.

48 In 1972, the Overseas Council (Conselho Ultramarino) was made responsible for studying the role of the manufacturing industry as an engine of economic progress and social development of the overseas provinces. See Arquivo Histórico Ultramarino, Lisbon (hereafter AHU), Ministério do Ultramar, Direcção Geral de Economia, Grupo de Trabalho do Povoamento, Pareceres sobre diversos estudos, vol. 3 (1971–72), p. 264.

49 In the conclusions and recommendations of the Congress on Settlement and Social Promotion (Congresso de Povoamento e Promoção Social) that took place in Luanda in 1970, social promotion was defined as: 'the granting to all populations of the opportunity to perform themselves fully so that every individual passes to have a minimum consistent with human dignity. The social promotion is based mainly on education and a better settling of the legal and economic sense of property by the populations' ('a concessão a todas as populações da oportunidade de se realiza-rem integralmente por forma a que todo o indivíduo passe a dispor de um mínimo compatível com a dignidade humana. A promoção social assenta fundamentalmente na educação bem como numa melhor sedimentação do sentido jurídico-económico da propriedade por parte das populações'). *Congresso de Povoamento e Promoção Social, Luanda, 4 a 9 de Outubro de 1970* (Luanda: Associações Económicas de Angola 1970), p. 517. Curiously, Norton de Matos in a speech delivered in Angola, in 1913, had already put forward the argument that the civilisation of the indigenous populations depended on granting them the full ownership of the land they cultiv-ated. That speech was reproduced in Norton de Matos, *A nação una: organização política e administrativa dos territórios do ultramar português* (Lisbon: Paulino Ferreira Filhos 1953), p. 73.

50 Oliveira, *Problemas do ultramar no Plano Intercalar de Fomento*, pp. 6–7.

51 'a) a aceleração do ritmo de acréscimo do produto nacional; b) a repartição mais equilibrada do rendimento nacional'. Lei [Law] no. 2123, *Diário do Governo*, 1st series, 291, 14 December 1964, p. 1173.

52 Oliveira, *Problemas do ultramar no Plano Intercalar de Fomento*, pp. 20, 49–50.

53 One must recall that within the colonial war effort it was crucial to open roads that ensured rapid and safe communications for the Portuguese troops in Angola. See Douglas L. Wheeler and René Pélissier, *Angola* (London: Pall Mall Press 1971), p. 232.

54 Although the allocation for education was substantial, one must keep in mind the low starting point at the beginning of the 1960s. See Eduardo de Sousa Ferreira, 'A lógica da consolidação da economia de mercado em Angola, 1930–74', *Análise Social* 21, 1 (1985), p. 103.

55 'progressiva elevação e dignificação da pessoa humana dentro da comunidade por-tuguesa'; 'repartição mais equilibrada do rendimento'; 'correcção progressiva dos desequilíbrios regionais do desenvolvimento'. Presidência do Conselho, *III Plano de Fomento para 1968–1973*, vol. 1 (Lisbon: Presidência do Conselho 1968), p. 36. See also, *Base III* of Lei [Law] no. 2133, *Diário do Governo*, 1st series, 294, 20 December 1967.

56 Michael Mahoney, '*Estado Novo, Homem Novo* (New State, New Man): Colonial and Anticolonial Development Ideologies in Mozambique, 1930–1977', in David C. Engerman et al. (eds), *Staging Growth: Modernization, Development, and the Global Cold War* (Amherst, MA: University of Massachusetts Press 2003), p. 179.

57 *Congresso de Povoamento e Promoção Social*, pp. 522–3.
58 As Jeanne Marie Penvenne has pointed out, by promoting substantial state-sponsored white settlement projects, Portugal was running counter to the tide of other colonial powers (that began to reconsider their colonial empires and to restrain settler efforts to secure and extend their authority) and of African nationalism. See Jeanne Marie Penvenne, 'Settling Against the Tide: The Layered Contradictions of Twentieth-Century Portuguese Settlement in Mozambique', in Caroline Elkins and Susan Pedersen (eds), *Settler Colonialism in the Twentieth Century: Projects, Practices, Legacies* (New York, London: Routledge 2005), pp. 79–94.
59 Yves Léonard, 'Salazarisme et lusotropicalisme: histoire d'une appropriation', *Lusotopie* (1997), p. 223. Available at: www.lusotopie.sciencespobordeaux.fr/l%C3%A9onard97.pdf (accessed 20 May 2013).
60 Gilberto Freyre, one of the leading Brazilian intellectuals of the twentieth century, was a social scientist whose ideas had a major national and international impact. His most famous work is *Casa-grande e senzala: formação da família Brasileira sob o regime de economia patriarcal* (Rio de Janeiro: Maia & Schmidt 1933), translated into English by Samuel Putnam as *The Masters and the Slaves: A Study in the Development of Brazilian Civilization* (New York: Knopf 1946).
61 On lusotropicalism and development discourse in late Portuguese colonialism see Araújo and Vasile's chapter in this book.
62 Gilberto Freyre, *Um brasileiro em terras portuguesas* (Rio de Janeiro: José Olympio 1953).
63 Lusotropicalist ideas easily penetrated the discourse of the Portuguese elites and the general public because it reworked earlier ideas about the specificity of Portuguese colonisation, giving them a supposedly scientific credibility. See C. Castelo, 'O modo português de estar no mundo': o luso-tropicalismo e a ideologia colonial portuguesa, 1933–1961 (Porto: Afrontamento 1998).
64 'Aceito todos os sistemas, todas as achegas, só vejo o povoamento no fim de todos os actos. Chego a subordinar-lhe tudo, como a uma ideia mestra. Puro engano. É apenas um caminho – um largo caminho – para se alcançar a grandeza una da Nação... É possível que nem toda a gente se aperceba deste momento histórico, genésico, que estamos atravessando'. Manuel Maria Sarmento Rodrigues, *Unidade da nação portuguesa*, vol. 1 (2 vols, Lisbon: Agência Geral do Ultramar 1956), pp. x–xi.
65 Rodrigues, *Unidade da nação portuguesa*, vol. 2, p. 743.
66 'Sem o aumento da população portuguesa, sobretudo metropolitana – irradiante de poder assimilador, que há-de aglutinar à sua volta os restantes elementos, cada vez mais os identificando com o padrão original lusitano – não se pode contar com o verdadeiro progresso, incluindo nele a defesa eficiente e permanente dos territórios e sua perfeita nacionalização. Por outro lado, o povoamento conduz ao equacionamento e consequente resolução de todos os problemas regionais. É a vida na sua representação mais alta e na teoria de exigências que são o estímulo impulsionador da civilização'. Manuel Maria Sarmento Rodrigues, 'O plano de fomento no ultramar: aproveitamento de recursos e povoamento', in Secretariado Nacional da Informação (ed.), *O plano de fomento: conferências ministeriais inauguradas pelo Presidente do Conselho em 28 de Maio* (Lisbon: SNI 1953), p. 92.
67 'O metódico aproveitamento dos recursos e possibilidades naturais do território' and 'O povoamento do territórios, designadamente promovendo a fixação de famílias nacionais'. Lei [Law] no. 2066, *Diário do Governo*, 1st series, 135, 27 June 1953, p. 888.
68 See, for example, Christophe Bonneuil, 'Development as Experiment: Science and State Building in Late Colonial and Postcolonial Africa, 1930–1970', *Osiris*, 2nd series, 15 (2000), pp. 258–81; Hodge, *Triumph of the Expert*.
69 'In Limpopo Colonato ... many of the settlers were simple hoe diggers, and despite all the selection made, many were illiterate who asked the black man to write for them the letter to the family ... The black man, in his simplicity, solved the problem as follows: there is the white of Lisbon and there is the white of Lisbon's bush'.

This situation is denounced by Commander Gabriel Teixeira at the Overseas Council meeting on white settlement held in 1965. See, Conselho Ultramarino, *Sessão Plenária de Outubro de 1965: Parecer e Actas* (Lisbon: Conselho Ultramarino, 1965), p. 13.

70 'No estado de desenvolvimento atingido pelas províncias de África e que é mister acelerar ... assumem singular relevância e crescente acuidade os problemas de povo-amento, que estão na base não só da valorização económico-social de territórios e gentes, como da real elevação destas e sua integração com os elementos étnicos alienígenas na Pátria comum, naquela harmoniosa comunidade multirrial que tradi-cionalmente nos temos proposto e esforçado por criar e sem a qual não mais haverá paz nem efectivo progresso na conturbada terra africana'. 'Nas sociedades em evolução, como são ou se pretende que sejam as da África Negra, o processo evolu-tivo não pode dispensar um permanente afluxo destes trabalhadores especializados de todos os graus e em todos os sectores, quer como instrumento imprescindível dos projectos de desenvolvimento económico, quer para as mais variadas tarefas da vida civilizada, quer para o enquadramento e formação profissional de camadas cada vez mais extensas das populações aborígenes, chamadas a elevar-se e a participar elas próprias em todas aquelas actividades, quer ainda para apoio social e amparo moral destas mesmas populações'. Decreto [Decree] no. 43895, *Diário do Governo*, 1st series, 207, 6 September 1961, p. 1128.

71 AHU, Ministério do Ultramar, Gabinete de Negócios Políticos, Comentários (here-after MU/GNP)/161/pt. 6, *Comentário* no. 52, 2 February 1966, of Júlio Augusto Dá Mesquita Gonçalves, entitled 'Promoção social nas províncias de África' ['Social promotion in the African provinces'].

72 'o povoamento é uma forma válida para a evolução material, social e cultural das populações' ... 'no sentido da integração numa nova sociedade compósita'. AHU MU/GNP/161/pt. 6, *Comentário* no. 37, 12 February 1966, of Júlio Augusto Dá Mesquita Gonçalves, entitled 'Aspectos do povoamento ultramarino' ['Aspects of overseas settlement'].

73 'Uma das tarefas que se impõe às Nações constituídas por grupos humanos hetero-géneos é justamente a de procurar nivelá-los. Por isso mesmo, impõe-se-nos, par-ticularmente no Portugal africano, elevar social, cultural e materialmente os menos dotados'. AHU MU/GNP/161/pt. 7, *Comentário* no. 157, 6 July 1967, of Rui Manuel Soares de Campos Pessoa de Amorim, entitled 'Prioridade que se justifica' ['Priority that is justified'].

74 AHU MU/GNP/161/pt. 7, *Comentário* no. 178, 1 August 1967, of José Alberto Pereira Monteiro, entitled 'Um servidor da Portugalidade' ['A servant of Portugality'].

75 Hodge, *Triumph of the Expert*, pp. 24–6.

76 Tilley, *Africa as a Living Laboratory*, p. 325.

77 Costa, *Humanismo económico no Ultramar*, p. 19.

78 'A sua gravidade pode aferir-se pelo número de 350 técnicos necessários para satisfazer as necessidades imediatas dos serviços de obras públicas, incluindo o preenchimento das vagas actuais dos respectivos quadros e pelo milhar de técnicos que no campo agro-silvo-pecuário deveriam entrar para os serviços do Ultramar nos próximos dez ou doze anos, ou seja quase o número de agrónomos e silvicultores existentes actualmente na Metrópole'. Ibid.

79 Ibid.

80 The Junta de Investigações Coloniais/do Ultramar (JIU) (1936–74) was a central research institution within the Ministry for Colonies/Overseas Territories, which coordinated and promoted scientific research in and on the Portuguese colonies, within various areas of knowledge (except in medical sciences). JIU organised research expeditions on a vast number of subjects. It operated along similar lines to the French Office de la Recherche Scientifique et Technique dans les territories d'Outre-Mer (ORSTOM); see Christophe Bonneuil, *Des savants pour l'empire: la structuration des recherches scientifiques colonials au temps de 'La mise en valeur des colonies françaises', 1917–1945* (Paris : L'ORSTOM 1991). Britain expanded the system of the British Research Council to its colonial empire, but never created a

research service integrated into the Colonial Office; see Sabine Clarke, 'A Technocratic Imperial State? The Colonial Office and Scientific Research, 1940–1960', *Twentieth Century British History* 18, 4 (2007), pp. 453–80; Tilley, *Africa as a Living Laboratory*, p. 128.

81 See Costa, *Humanismo económico no Ultramar*, pp. 16–17.

82 For instance, the construction of the Cabora Bassa hydro-electric dam, 'the biggest one in Africa and the fifth in the world', was 'a starting point for the systematic evaluation of the land and of its people, in a wide area of the Zambezi basin', and 'an undeniable proof of confidence in the destinies of the Portuguese Africa'. It was, according to Cunha, presented as 'the conscious application of the modern techniques for regional planning in order to form a base for decisions and to clear the way for accomplishment'. The overseas minister, in a speech delivered at the signing ceremony of the Cabora Bassa agreement in September 1969, highlighted the fact that 'since 1957 technicians of all kinds [had] devoted themselves to the exhaustive analysis and study of the region'. Joaquim Moreira da Silva Cunha, *Cabora-Bassa: The Signing of the Cabora Bassa Agreement on the 19th September 1969* (Lisbon: Agência Geral do Ultramar 1970), pp. 9–10.

83 See João Salgueiro, 'Política de investimentos nos territórios do Ultramar', in Junta de Investigações do Ultramar (ed.), *Colóquios sobre o II Plano de Fomento: Ultramar* (Lisbon:Junta de Investigações do Ultramar – Centro de Estudos Políticos e Sociais 1959), pp. 55–6. During the 1950s the French and British governments were no longer committed to sending new colonists to Algeria and Kenya as a means to develop those white settlement colonies.

84 In 1951, more than 43 per cent of the funds from the development plans for the British colonial territories aimed at social development, e.g. social services, particularly education and health; in the Belgian Congo social projects absorbed 31 per cent of the budget; in the French empire, in the first four years of its plan, the spending on this type of expenditure was between 14 and 29 per cent; see [Lord] William Malcolm Hailey, *An African Survey: A Study of Problems Arising in Africa South of the Sahara*, rev. edn (London: Oxford University Press 1957 [1938]), pp. 1325–6.

85 Both of these missions were created in support of the agricultural development programmes of the second *Plano de Fomento*.

86 'meio de, ao estilo inglês, encaminhar as populações à autogestão absoluta'. Alfredo de Sousa, 'Desenvolvimento comunitário em Angola', in Instituto Superior de Ciências Sociais e Politica Ultramarina (ed.), *Angola: Curso de extensão universitária ano lectivo de 1963–1964* (Lisbon: Junta de Investigações do Ultramar 1964), p. 22.

87 Ibid.

88 Agronomists and technicians, with vast field knowledge and prolonged and close contact with African populations, tend to be open to endogenous knowledge and understanding of local agriculture and livestock systems. In such cases, as Beinart et al. have pointed out, they did not shut themselves off in an office or lab or claim European methods are scientifically superior. See William Beinart, Karen Brown, and Daniel Gilfoyle, 'Experts and Expertise in Colonial Africa Reconsidered: Science and the Interpenetration of Knowledge', *African Affairs* 108, 432 (2009), p. 428.

89 The two major examples are: Adriano Moreira, Professor and Director of the Higher Institute of Overseas Studies/Higher Institute of Social Sciences and Overseas Policy (Instituto Superior de Estudos Ultramarinos – ISEU/Instituto Superior de Ciências Sociais e Política Ultramarina – ISCSPU) and Director of the Centre for Political and Social Studies (Centro de Estudos Políticos e Sociais – CEPS) of the JIU, would be Undersecretary of State for Overseas Administration (1960–61) and Overseas Minister (1961–62); and Joaquim da Silva Cunha, ISEU/ISCSPU teacher, CEPS researcher, would become Undersecretary of State for Overseas Administration (1962–65) and Minister of Overseas Provinces (1965–73).

CHAPTER THREE

A history of *maendeleo*: the concept of 'development' in Tanganyika's late colonial public sphere

Emma Hunter

The starting point for this chapter is a dictionary, or more accurately, a series of dictionaries and wordlists, and the translations which they offer for the Swahili word *maendeleo*. The 1903 edition of Madan's Swahili-English dictionary translated *maendeleo* as meaning 'going on, progress, advance, success'.[1] Frederick Johnson's Swahili-English dictionary, published in 1939 and based on Madan though with some definitions rephrased, offered a similar definition. Of the noun 'endeleo' he wrote that it generally appeared in the plural form and had a meaning of 'going on, progress, advance, success'.[2] But by 1967, after the post-war period of what is increasingly known as 'late colonialism' and six years after independence, a list of newspaper terminology defined *maendeleo* as meaning 'community development' or 'progress', and a study of political vocabulary published four years later similarly translated *maendeleo* as development or progress.[3] Thus, over the course of the period with which we are concerned, a new meaning of 'development' had been added to translations of *maendeleo*.

This chapter tells the story of the changing use of the term *maendeleo* in colonial Tanganyika between Madan's 1903 dictionary and independence in 1961. I argue that it is only by appreciating the broad way in which *maendeleo* was understood in local contexts and the way that it served in part as a space in which to reflect on the meaning of modernity that we can make sense of its power then and now. In other words, the history of this keyword provides a crucial context for understanding development discourse in late colonial Tanganyika.

To make this argument, I will draw on a close reading of the editorial comment and letters pages of three Swahili-language newspapers – *Mambo Leo*, *Mwafrika*, and the Kilimanjaro newspaper *Komkya*, as well as a set of district newspapers published in 1952 by district offices around Tanganyika. With the exception of *Mwafrika*, which was a nationalist newspaper published commercially, all were published by the colonial government. *Mambo Leo* was published by the education department, and was for a long time the newspaper with the widest circulation in Tanganyika, with demand always outstripping available supply.[4] The district newspapers from 1952 and *Komkya* were published by local district offices, and while their circulation figures are more difficult to ascertain, the proportion of space given over to letters from readers suggests that they are an important source in which to uncover the public intellectual world of colonial officials and a growing number of Africans for whom the press provided both a source of information and a channel of communication with government.[5] After a brief overview of late colonial development policy and the emergence of a language of development in the Anglophone public sphere, I then move on to explore public discussions of *maendeleo* in the late colonial period and reflect on what this meant for colonial developers and nationalists. I end by considering the broader lessons which this case study might offer.[6]

Of groundnuts and prosperity

Colonial Tanganyika has long attracted the attention of scholars writing about late colonial development, thanks in large part to the supreme ambition and folly of the Groundnut Scheme which seemed to sum up all that was wrong with post-1945 development projects.[7] The scheme, which was intended to solve Britain's post-war shortage of fats but which famously resulted in a loss of £36 million to the British government and the production of only 9,120 tons of groundnuts by the time it began to be wound down in 1951, serves as a textbook example of the unintended consequences which could ensue when metropolitan planners imposed their grand designs on unsuspecting colonies.[8] At the other end of the country, the Sukumaland Development Scheme was equally ambitious in its attempt to remake social, economic and political life in the region. It too was abandoned, having fallen victim to changing intellectual and political fashions and to local resistance to agricultural measures which demanded farmers work harder and sacrifice their stock, in the name of combating soil erosion.[9] With some justification, Havinden and Meredith describe the Territory as having borne 'the brunt of the "new colonialism"'.[10]

Unsurprisingly, ambitious schemes provoked serious responses. Across the Territory, from Uluguru district in Central Tanganyika to the Usambara mountains in the North-East and Sukumaland in the North-West, new political organisations were formed, in part to resist the destocking policies, soil erosion measures, and reforms which were central to colonial development plans but which seemed to strike at the heart of established systems of land ownership, wealth, and division of labour.[11] Conflict was not only anti-colonial, but also reflected the exclusion of emerging elites from political power, and anger at those who supported and promoted the colonial system that was responsible for newly interventionist policies.[12] This was a revolt of the traders and clerks against the chiefs as much as a revolt of a colonised population against the colonial power.

A great deal of recent work has focused on the conflict which ensued between colonial officials seeking to implement controversial development schemes and Africans who mobilised against them. Work exploring the colonial minds and networks of knowledge responsible for these schemes and the local resistance they encountered has cast important new light on colonial rule in the period of its demise and the ways in which Africans took advantage of cracks in the colonial system to mobilise against it.[13] But recent work on both the Groundnut Scheme and the Sukumaland Scheme suggest that there is another story to be told, and that there may be more to this process than a dichotomy of colonial action and African resistance.

In a 2006 article which considers the effects of the Groundnut Scheme on the local labour market, Matteo Rizzo shows that for many Africans the period was understood as one of prosperity, wealth, and the change which had long been hoped for.[14] He cites an account by Mr Makwinja, an African Field Assistant working on the scheme, in the local newspaper *Habari za Nachingwea katika Kiswahili* which described the way in which rumours had spread about 'White men coming to cultivate large farms of groundnuts and that people would get the chance to go and offer themselves for work and be paid very good salaries'.[15] These rumours, Mr Makwinja continued, 'turned out to be true', and he described the period in which he was living as 'these days of great prosperity'.[16]

Similarly capturing echoes of contemporary perceptions of development beyond colonial officialdom, Rohland Schuknecht's study of colonial development in Sukumaland is intended both as a study of development policy and a study of the concept of development. He shows that the Sukuma Union, a political association concerned with uniting and representing the Sukuma people which was first founded in 1945 then refounded with renewed purpose in 1950, was as concerned with 'development' as colonial planners, but understood it as something much broader than simply destocking or cotton production.[17] As Schuknecht writes, 'The declared aim of the Sukuma Union – to promote the development of Sukumaland and the material and social progress of the Sukuma people – was the same as that of the colonial administration. The vital question was which kind of "development" one deemed to be desirable and necessary and in which way it should be implemented'.[18]

Both of these examples suggest that we might profitably look beyond the history of failed development plans and a politics of conflict and nationalist mobilisation in order to reach a better understanding of how languages of development were deployed. Both instances reveal hints of a shared intellectual world which crossed colonial and nationalist divides, manifested in the appeals made to colonial officials and in the tightly controlled local press. They encourage us to look more deeply, and enquire into the context in which a language of development, which came to be used by both the Sukuma Union and the Groundnut Scheme, was discussed in positive tones in the district newspaper of Nachingwea.

'Where there is no vision, the people perish'

As global thinking about the state and its functions began to shift around 1940, particularly in terms of the expectations laid upon the state to deliver economic development and social welfare, we can, as Frederick Cooper and others have shown, see the emerging importance of the idea of 'development' in Anglophone colonial discourse.[19] For while rethinking the role of the state was a process taking place in both European metropoles and overseas colonies, in colonial settings changing thinking about the role of the state was closely tied to questions of how to strengthen colonial rule for a new era. There were echoes in this process of an earlier moment when the European colonial system had come under threat. The 'Wilsonian moment' of 1919 which galvanised anti-colonial activity around the world coupled with the challenges which the war posed to European economies and colonial systems had inspired efforts to reframe the colonial mission as one of development and trusteeship.[20] But these efforts swiftly foundered against the priorities of national reconstruction at home in the case of France and re-establishing political control through effective alliances in the case of Britain.[21]

After the Depression, thinking turned again to the problem of how to enact far-reaching social and economic change, and it did so in a context in which states were becoming more ambitious in what they thought they could achieve. The concept of development reappeared as a means of describing this vision of change. For some parts of the British empire, the rapid post-1945 unravelling of authority meant that the plans drawn up in the late 1930s became the responsibility of the post-colonial state, but in East Africa, the Second World War provided an impetus for a new colonial effort.[22]

We can see this process very clearly in Tanganyika, where the expectation of new capital funding for development schemes at the end of the war meant that the files relating to schemes which had been proposed before the war but frozen when war broke out were dusted off and once again became the subject of active consideration. A Post-War Planning Committee was established by the Tanganyika Government in the spring of 1944 and invited to use the 1940 *Report of the Central Development Committee* as a basis from which to prepare for the post-war era.[23] In Kilimanjaro, where, in the late 1930s, ideas had been considered to make the area below the mountain suitable for farming, to relieve land pressure on the mountain and to enable the 'progressive' farmer to fulfil his potential, officials returned to the question with new urgency and with plans for an ambitious development scheme which went beyond simply making new land available.[24] But the end of the war also saw a new priority attached to 'welfare' or social development, as calls for more social services from below chimed with new visions of the state and the meaning of citizenship from above.[25] The availability of Colonial Development and Welfare funds, and the establishment of new development commissions ensured that a language of development entered public discussion.

Beyond the immediate imperial context, Tanganyika was also a League of Nations mandate, which after the Second World War became a United Nations Trust Territory. In contrast to the League of Nations which understood its role to be one of long-term but arm's-length paternalism, the Trusteeship Council of the United Nations understood its role to lie in keeping a watchful eye on administering powers as they worked to secure rapid economic, social, and political development. In his speech opening the Trusteeship Council, the Secretary General of the United Nations explicitly defined the mission of the Trusteeship Council as time-limited, noting that 'Full success . . . will automatically put this organ out of existence, since your ultimate goal is to give the Trust Territories full statehood'.[26] The Secretary General went further, and tied the Trusteeship Council to the success of the new body of the United Nations itself, for 'a really successful Trusteeship system' will 'provide further proof of the fact that this Organization is ready to transform its high principles and noble objectives into positive action'.[27] Unlike the Permanent Mandates Commission of the League of Nations, the United Nations Trusteeship Council included members from the newly decolonised world and from the USSR. It was far easier to transmit petitions to the Trusteeship

[91]

Council than it had been to the Permanent Mandates Commission, either by sending petitions to New York, or by transmitting them to the members of the Visiting Missions on their regular visits to the Territory. Their concern was with monitoring the progress being made by the administering authority in the spheres of economic, social, and political development, and we see a focus on these elements both in British submissions and appearances before the Council, and in the petitions received by the Council.

This rapid tour through the colonial archive and the records of the Trusteeship Council has suggested that a language of development was becoming increasingly important in the Anglophone public sphere, both within Tanganyika and in discussions about Tanganyika in London and New York. But if a language of development was becoming increasingly important in Anglophone discussions, what of the Swahili public sphere?

Progress and maendeleo

The idea of progress, or *maendeleo*, had been important in the Swahili public sphere since the interwar period, as part of a cluster of ideas about modernity, but it was generally framed in terms of progress towards *ustaarabu* or civilisation, rather than as an end in itself. As Katrin Bromber and others have shown, the term *ustaarabu* was itself redefined by the colonial government, reinscribed not as a set of cultural attributes which could be claimed only by coastal, urban, and Islamic elites but as open to all who embraced values of good citizenship, cleanliness, and hard work.[28] Within this broad cluster of ideas about progress, newspaper editors tended to use the term *maendeleo* in a fairly straightforward way to describe what had changed from one year to the next, as in an annual report concerning the education department, originally written in English but published in *Mambo Leo* in Swahili, headed 'Education Department: Habari za Maendeleo'. The report of the year's activities concentrated on comparing how things were in the past (*zamani*) to how they were today.[29] But in the letters pages we see a concern with 'good progress', or *maendeleo mema*, which often related to material signs of progress. For example, a letter entitled 'Maendeleo Mema' celebrated the fact that a growing number of people in the town of Kahama, in Western Tanganyika, now read a newspaper. In similar vein, a letter published in 1929 measured *maendeleo* in terms of the number of motor-cars now owned in up-country areas.[30] More generally, the term would appear as a way of discussing the progress made towards an end, the end being *ustaarabu*.

It is worth pausing here for a moment to reflect on the importance of ideas of progress in the interwar period, because we often think of this period in Tanganyika as defined not by movement forwards but by re-traditionalisation. This was, after all, the period when the dominant ideology which drove local government reforms was one of 'Indirect Rule' which involved a focus on finding the 'traditional' authorities in a local area, and when there was a relative lack of spending on social and economic projects.[31] But even the numerous 'ethno-histories' produced in the period and often taken as evidence of such re-traditionalisation were themselves focused on comparing the past with the present, and with telling a story of increasing political unity over time.[32]

Two points about conceptions of progress should be made here. The first is that there were clear Christian undertones even in spaces, such as *Mambo Leo*, which were intended to be secular and which had a policy of not discussing religion. On a broad scale this is not surprising, given the strong belief in the period, manifested in the language of the League of Nations, that the Western version of civilisation, with its Christian undertones, was applicable as a universal standard. But the link between Christianity, progress, and development projects can also be traced at the local level, as has been shown by studies of other regions, such as in interwar India.[33] The second, and related, point is that this was an idea of what progress and civilisation meant that was deliberately exclusionary. In a highly divided society like Tanganyika, adopting these ideas for oneself served as a means of differentiating oneself from others.

But if *maendeleo* was used in a general sense of progress towards *ustaarabu* or 'good progress', after 1945 it became something more than that as *maendeleo* was used increasingly to signify new forms of social services and new types of economic arrangements. Thus for example, the generic term for a female development officer was 'Bibi Maendeleo'. The word became a commonplace in local council reports and as elections began to be introduced; bringing development or *maendeleo*, particularly in the form of medical dispensaries and schools, came to be accepted as one of the core duties of any chief or elected representative.[34]

To see this expansion of meaning towards including the social and material senses of 'development' in practice, we might look in some detail at a text published in 1947. The text, published by the East African Literature Bureau as a contribution to the growing genre of ethno-histories, was both an account by the Kilimanjaro chief Petro Itosi Marealle of the customs and traditions of the Chagga people, and an account of recent political changes and his hopes for the future.

The district had recently undergone a reorganisation, which had seen Petro Itosi Marealle elevated to the new position of 'Divisional Chief', charged with governing a third of the mountain of Kilimanjaro.

In his book, entitled *Maisha ya Mchagga Hapa Duniani na Ahera*, Marealle used the term *maendeleo* in a series of different senses. In the first place, it was employed in the general sense as meaning social change associated with modernity. 'The proper development (*maendeleo*) of a tribe' depended, he argued, on making far-reaching changes. This meant adopting new customs from outside and either abandoning or improving existing bad customs. 'In this way by combining good foreign customs with our own good customs we will have true *ustaarabu* [civilization] in Africa'.[35] But *maendeleo* was also used in the specific senses which reflected the emphasis in colonial discourse on development projects. Marealle referred to the need to cooperate in 'kazi za maendeleo' or 'development work' to solve problems of landlessness, health, and education.[36] He also engaged with the idea of political development, much under discussion in the district in the 1940s, writing that 'In the development of governance, Britain has been a famous example for the people of the entire world', and he went on to discuss the potential for building 'democracy' at the local level.[37] Yet elsewhere in the text, *maendeleo* also had a sense of human flourishing, as an organic development rather than one planned from above. Thus Marealle expressed his concerns that the erosion of chiefly power would be a great loss for the '*maendeleo mema* of the people'.[38] In this text we see a web of meanings associated with the term *maendeleo*. Some of these uses reflect colonial discourse regarding political steps towards self-rule and the 'social development' of solving society's ills. But there are also traces of the broader sense of progress which we saw in Frederick Johnson's dictionary and in *Mambo Leo* in the interwar years.

Thus the new sense acquired by *maendeleo* by virtue of its employment as a translation of 'development' was quickly absorbed into a wider set of meanings carried by the word *maendeleo* and new meanings were in turn sparked by this development. In this way it followed a similar trajectory to a related term in Nigeria, the term *olaju*. In an article published in 1978 called 'Olaju: A Yoruba Concept of Development', J. D. Y. Peel identified a term which he understood to be the central 'indigenous concept of development' among Yoruba speakers, and tracked its shifting meanings since the late nineteenth century, as it became increasingly linked to Western education.[39] *Olaju*, he argued, did not only refer to social change but also suggested historical causes for that change. It carried a sense of 'enlightenment', which gave it a range of associations much broader than the term 'development' might suggest. Interviews with Yoruba speakers demonstrated that it was linked with Christianity and Islam and the renunciation of certain elements of 'traditional' culture, as well as with accessing amenities such as roads, housing, health care, and education.[40]

In summary, in the late colonial period the word used in the Swahili public sphere was employed both to talk about 'development' in the sense of managed schemes with economic, social, and political aims, and for a wider discussion of progress linked to conceptions of modernity. This is a crucial basis for understanding its enduring power. But in the next section we go on to consider the ways in which a shared shorthand of *maendeleo* could conceal very different agendas.

Maendeleo *and modernity*

By the early 1950s, *maendeleo* had the status of a word which was both descriptive and evaluative, so that claiming that a particular course of action was desirable for reasons of 'development' also implied a statement that it was an unproblematic good.[41] As we have seen, the colonial state claimed that it was charged with encouraging the development of Tanganyika, and the Trusteeship Council claimed that its role was to monitor that development. This shaped the language employed by those without power as they sought to appeal to the state. To see this in practice, we might consider the ways in which appeals to the central government and to the United Nations were framed by their writers.

In 1956, the officers of a branch of the nationalist party TANU which the government had refused to register wrote to the territory's Chief Secretary appealing against this refusal. They argued that: 'The people of this part of Nassa Mwanza District feel great sadness as a result of being without a Political Party (*Chama cha Utetezi*)', for 'even the Government itself understands' that such parties were the best way to achieve 'the *maendeleo* of every country'.[42] Achieving 'development' was understood to be a shared goal, one which new associations and political parties as well as the colonial state were engaged in striving towards.

If we look at the district newspapers created by district offices across the country in 1952, we see the same shared focus on *maendeleo*. In the Usambara mountains, the focus of one of the government's most controversial development schemes, the district newspaper was called *Maendeleo ya Shambalai*. The editorial line, pursued by the editor C. A. Sangai, was to explain and promote colonial development policies, as well as providing a space for questions and letters to the editor.[43] In June 1952, the agricultural officer responsible for the scheme, Mr

Silcock, was congratulated for his OBE and praised for his hard work preventing soil erosion which was, it was claimed, a problem faced across the world.[44] Editorials sought to defend the decision of elders to support the terracing policy pursued as part of the development scheme against their critics, and argued that the district risked falling back if young people did not support the scheme.[45] There was an assumption that all could agree that *maendeleo* was the desired end; the question was how to achieve it.

But beneath apparent agreement that *maendeleo* was a goal on which all could agree was a tension between the idea of progress as a universal and the idea that *maendeleo* was a goal associated with specific cultural attributes. Some saw *maendeleo* as integral to what it meant to be human. In a study of political discourse after independence, Jan Blommaert draws attention to *maendeleo* as a distinguishing feature between humans and animals, and this sense is present in the earlier period too.[46] An editorial in the Catholic newspaper *Kiongozi* in 1953 entitled 'Are we going backwards?' stressed the centrality of *maendeleo* to human existence. The editor wrote: 'We Africans have been given reason, like Europeans, in order that we should progress'. Honouring God meant pushing forwards, protecting those traditions which should be protected while 'following the good examples of other nations, as we cooperate in the progress of the world (*maendeleo ya dunia*)'.[47] The Assistant Welfare Officer Hamza Mwapachu, serving on Ukerewe Island in the Lake Province, agreed. In an article published in the Ukerewe district newspaper in 1952 he exhorted Ukerewe farmers to plant more so as to feed those living in the towns.[48] He argued that central to humanity was *maendeleo* and the enemy of humanity was being satisfied. He challenged his readers to ask themselves whether they were 'satisfied with [their] income last year?' If they were then they were in danger, for they had lost sight of the importance of *maendeleo*.[49]

But in mid-twentieth-century Tanganyika, as elsewhere in twentieth-century Swahiliphone Africa, this broad sense of progress as human flourishing ran counter to the more material or social senses of *maendeleo* with their more exclusionary overtones.[50] In March 1950, a correspondent wrote to *Mambo Leo* from the Northern Province with news of a new appearance in Moshi. A Welfare Centre had been established which, this correspondent wrote, offered a great deal to those 'who want to achieve progress (*maendeleo*)'. In particular, the Welfare Centre offered evening lessons in English to enthusiastic seekers of *maendeleo*, including, the correspondent noted, men and women, young and old.[51] In this sense, a desire for *maendeleo* was not a universal aspect of being human, but was specific to a particular form of human flourishing.

A similar use of the term appears in the mid-1950s. In the aftermath of the East African Royal Commission which sought to outline a path towards economic development in Africa resting on private property and the market, a press release from the Public Relations Department proclaimed the existence of cash loans for 'Africans who like *maendeleo*'.[52] Here, a desire for *maendeleo* appears not as a universal attribute, but as part of a construction of personhood which not all accepted, tied to an idea of social change as leading inexorably towards a Western version of modernity in which an individual would borrow money to enhance his own prosperity.

We therefore see an association of *maendeleo* with a particular set of cultural and economic practices which some had adopted and others had not. Very often a desire for *maendeleo* was associated with youth and was appealed to by the young in their battles with an older generation. In Kilimanjaro in the 1950s, a growing political divide emerged between an older generation and a younger generation. In the newspaper *Komkya*, the old were accused of fomenting jealousy and discrimination. Younger correspondents called on 'the youth of today' to 'work together with those leaders with authority in the country to take further the development we have today'.[53] Progress and development were associated with imagery of moving from darkness to light, as they wrote: 'The darkness is gone and the light has appeared; there is no one who prefers to remain in darkness any longer'.[54]

But a sense of *maendeleo* as involving the adoption of the attributes of economic man, with the assumptions about private property rights and land use which that entailed, led to arguments that this vision of the future was inappropriate in Tanganyika and that it was based on misunderstandings of the ways in which local society operated. A letter published in the Kondoa newspaper *Kondoa News* in 1957 and entitled 'Lack of Development' blamed government destocking policies, intended to bring about *maendeleo*, for in fact endangering hopes of development. 'No nation can achieve *maendeleo* if there is no money', and for the people of that region their capital was in cattle, which was, in the view of this correspondent, being destroyed by government policies to reduce cattle stocks. One specific government policy for development, cattle destocking, was destroying local hopes for social development through education. The author went on: 'Therefore you should not be surprised if there is little education here in Irangi. Many of us want higher development (*maendeleo ya juu*) but we receive no help'.[55]

Similarly, attempts to encourage private property and cash loans inspired the criticism that this was one version of development, but it was not the only one. Appearing before the East Africa Royal Commission

[97]

in 1953, the Tanganyika African Association argued strongly against the idea that freehold land tenure was an essential prerequisite for economic development. Julius Nyerere attacked the idea of making it possible for a person to sell land in the 'same way as he sells his chair', fearing the landlessness and loss of community spirit which he believed would result from such a model.[56]

But there was also a more fundamental question to be asked of *maendeleo*. Just as the question had been asked in the 1920s and 1930s of whether *ustaarabu* or civilisation was even desirable, or whether it meant the irreversible loss of much which was positive about society and social life, so colonial officials and African correspondents asked whether *maendeleo* posed similar dangers.[57] In 1946 the colonial official E. C. Baker, writing in *Mambo Leo* in his capacity as 'Social Welfare Organiser', criticised those who became educated and then forgot their communities. He denied that this was necessary, and argued that in fact *maendeleo* depended not on the rise of individualism but on unity, for 'without unity there will be no true *maendeleo*'.[58] Similar criticisms of educated Africans who embraced individualism and forgot their responsibilities regularly reappeared in the district newspapers of the early 1950s, frequently with the argument that this behaviour was not essential in order to have *maendeleo* and could indeed hold *maendeleo* back. The key to *maendeleo* was not individualism, they argued, but new forms of solidarity, whether through co-operative organisations, political parties, or participation in religious institutions.

So, *maendeleo* was powerful because it was a language which could attract the ear of the colonial state and international institutions, and because it also provided a vocabulary in which to reflect on the ways in which society was changing and the ways in which it ought to change. It was flexible enough to be applied in spiritualor philosophical senses but also in more narrowly defined social and material senses. It could also be exclusionary and served to differentiate between people and between peoples. While the rhetoric of the colonial state and the Trusteeship Council implied a steady trajectory towards increasing progress and development, the letters pages of the Swahili press both demonstrate an anxious spirit of comparison and questioning why some areas were making more and faster progress than others, and a sense that *maendeleo* was fragile and could be reversed.

Comparative thinking took place not just in abstract terms, but often with respect to particular neighbours deemed to have enjoyed more progress. Increasingly, some regions prided themselves on their higher levels of development. Kilimanjaro was a case in point. The Visiting Mission of 1948 was asked by representatives of the Kilimanjaro

Native Co-operative Union what conditions they had found before reaching Kilimanjaro. They gave perhaps the only possible answer to their hosts, which was to say that very few groups had yet reached the level of 'development which you people have here'.[59] Edward Twining, Governor of Tanganyika for the greater part of the 1950s, would praise Kilimanjaro for its level of development on his regular visits to the region. In neighbouring regions, this provoked comparative thinking. The *Kondoa News* frequently contained letters stressing the ways in which Kondoa lagged behind its neighbours. A letter from H. F. Hassan and Shariff Ahmad asked why the people of Kondoa insisted on buying newspapers from outside Kondoa. In contrast, the Chagga newspaper was sufficiently popular to be published twice a month. They asked 'Is this not *maendeleo*? We should try to love our newspaper as others love theirs'.[60] Elsewhere, different neighbours served as models. Thus in 1952 a letter in the Usambara newspaper, *Maendeleo ya Shambalai* called on fellow readers to 'copy others so that we achieve *maendeleo mema*, for the Wapare are now too far in front'.[61]

But there was also a concern that *maendeleo* could go backwards as well as forwards, with jealousy, drunkenness, failure to pay taxes, and corruption all blamed for putting development into reverse. A typical example of this mode of argument can be seen in a letter from a certain Bernard A. M. Daniel, of St Andrew's College in Minaki, to the district newspaper *Habari za Upare* in 1952. He argued that while the Pare had recently made excellent progress in matters of 'farming, business, education and other elements of modern civilization', jealousy, lack of trust, and corruption now endangered this progress. He ended by saying that 'if we do not abandon these bad habits, our *maendeleo* will not come at all quickly'.[62]

In this section we have seen that the power of *maendeleo* lay in its breadth. It could be used to mean the material and cultural attributes of a specific Western definition of progress and modernity, but it could also be used to reflect more broadly on development as human flourishing, as something integral to what it meant to be human. Often employed as a shorthand, it could disguise fundamental disagreements about policy prescriptions. Crucially, as a common language of intellectual life as well as politics, it went beyond merely serving as a tool for the legitimation or acquisition of power by colonial officials or nationalists.

Looking to the future: TANU and maendeleo

Studies of late colonial development discourse have shown that by the late 1950s, any claim to rule by a nationalist party had to encompass a claim to be the best fitted to bring development. The story of how this transition towards development as nation-building best undertaken by independent states came about, is one which cannot be explored here. But what the evidence presented above concerning the concept of *maendeleo* in the Swahili public sphere has shown very clearly is that it was deeply rooted in late colonial intellectual culture in ways that went beyond either the colonial state or the nationalist party. This helps make sense both of the use to which the two terms, *maendeleo* and 'development', were put by the nationalist party, and of the way they outlasted the stigma of association with the authoritarian ends towards which they were increasingly put.

The Tanganyika African National Union (TANU) was founded in 1954, and quickly built up an effective organisational structure on the basis established by the older Tanganyika African Association. In the localities, much of their support was built around their help in opposing new agricultural regulations imposed by the colonial state, while at the centre, they spoke out against the new economic development strategies of the mid-1950s, particularly the argument in favour of privatisation of land put forward by the East Africa Royal Commission. Yet while they opposed colonial development strategies, they were part of a political culture in which they too had to adopt a political language of development.

After 1945 meeting development goals became a standard by which local chiefs and officials were judged. In 1949, a popular movement in Moshi District, the area on the slopes of Mount Kilimanjaro in North-Eastern Tanganyika, led to the election of a Paramount Chief, Thomas Marealle, who pledged his aim as being that of bringing development. When a second popular movement emerged against him in the late 1950s, led by the popular TANU politician Solomon Eliufoo, it too was framed in terms of a charge that Marealle had failed to deliver *maendeleo*. The nationalist newspaper asked, 'Is there *maendeleo* in Kilimanjaro?' A top official working with the Paramount Chief retorted that there was, and listed Marealle's many achievements which had included expanding education and social services and seeking new scholarships and sources of funding from abroad, but Eliufoo won public support for his claim that only TANU could bring true *maendeleo*.[63]

In this sense, the roots of TANU's claims to power on the grounds of its ability to bring *maendeleo* lie in colonial languages of politics. But this local political scuffle is also inseparable from a broader process which was taking place as *maendeleo* was increasingly tied to nation-building. *Maendeleo* had always been part of a network of ideas around progress, self-government, and nation-building, and it was the latter two elements which came to the fore after 1945. India had become independent in 1947, and by the 1950s the Trusteeship Council included a number of new post-colonial states for whom development and nation-building were closely tied together and for whom development provided a mode of conceptualising shared membership of a common project.[64]

As TANU moved increasingly close to national power, particularly after the arrival in the Territory of a new Governor Richard Turnbull in 1958 and its decisive victory in the Legislative Elections of 1958–59, it sought to monopolise *maendeleo* for itself. Nationalist newspapers like *Mwafrika* stressed that only TANU could bring *maendeleo*. In support, they cited Kwame Nkrumah, famous for arguing that the political kingdom must come first and the economic benefits would follow.[65] When in 1960 new political parties emerged calling themselves 'development unions', *Mwafrika*'s response was to defend national unity and TANU. Only TANU could bring development, while the so-called 'development unions' were only interested in the private goods of self-enrichment.[66] There is an important step here, for a few years earlier there was no problem in the idea that *maendeleo* brought self-enrichment or the enrichment of a particular ethnic group. *Maendeleo* had become tied to *national* development.

At the same time, we see TANU making a claim that they were fit to govern, and would deliver the colonial goals of development and order. In this context, the term *maendeleo* served, as James Brennan has argued, to signify their claim to represent order as opposed to disorder, and so the term *maendeleo* signified the opposite of *fujo* or disorder.[67] Taken together with the link between *maendeleo* and nation-building, here are the origins of *maendeleo* being associated with an authoritarian edge.[68] But in a study of the keywords current in Tanzania's public sphere in the 1990s, Denis-Constant Martin found that while many words connected with Tanzania's post-colonial socialist experiment had fallen out of favour, *maendeleo* remained a central keyword in public debate.[69] The roots of this longevity and the ability of the concept to outlive its use by TANU lie in the more expansive intellectual history of the concept examined here.

Conclusion

The chapter has traced the changing scope of the word *maendeleo* as a way of providing a lens on discourses of development within Tanganyika's Swahili public sphere. It has tracked the way in which *maendeleo* underwent an expansion of meaning, from a general sense of progress which could be spiritual or material, to include the more precise meaning of 'development'. As the late colonial discourse of development became increasingly important to both colonial developers and the nationalist party, they operated within a broader discursive context in which the term *maendeleo* was significant.

Yet while this case study tells us something about the intellectual context of politics in late colonial Tanganyika, it also suggests wider lessons, both for the ways in which we might write histories of imperialism and nationalism, and for the way we write the global history of this period. Once the preserve of economic historians or those tracing the roots of contemporary development theory and practice, late colonial concepts of development have now become a central concern of historians of mid-twentieth-century imperialism and nationalism.[70] We now know that in the period after the First World War a language of development became increasingly important, first as a means of legitimising the colonial project, later as a means of critiquing the claims of colonial rulers to rule, and finally as a route to establishing new ties of belonging in the post-colonial state. Studies have shown the political impact of 'developmental' interventions from Kenya to Malaya and uncovered the intellectual processes which led colonial officials to believe schemes devised in Whitehall or Dar es Salaam could remake the economies, political systems, and societies of entire regions.[71]

But the very comprehensiveness of these studies is perhaps leading us towards a sense that a political language of development was omnipresent in the 1940s and 1950s, and that it worked in a similar way in a multitude of different contexts. There is a danger of losing sight of the local contexts in which ideas were debated. New research on the colonial public sphere now makes it possible for us to understand the context in which colonial development discourses operated, and to write an entangled history of a particular context, through tracing the use of one word. We can begin to see the intersections of debate, and the ways in which concepts could shift through those intersections. In this way, this chapter has sought to contribute to the growing body of scholarship which seeks to bring together two historiographical domains, the imperial and the nationalist, once kept firmly apart.

The second broader lesson suggested by this case study concerns the writing of global history. As James Brennan argued in his study of the nationalist party TANU and racial thought in Tanzania, the term *maendeleo* gradually eclipsed the term *ustaarabu* as the 'hub of public discourse' after 1945.[72] In this regard, shifts in the vocabulary found in Tanganyika's public sphere tracked shifts taking place elsewhere. In his study of Nepal's public sphere, Rhoderick Chalmers shows that the word *unnati*, which combined a sense of progress and uplift with a sense of individual progress of character, dominated the public sphere in the interwar period, while the word *bikas* or develop-ment, tied more closely to national or economic development, became ubiquitous later.[73] At an international level, the League of Nations defined its role in terms of the duties owed by a core of countries which had reached requisite standards of civilisation and could govern themselves, towards other countries which were yet to reach that particular construct of what constituted 'civilisation'. In contrast, the United Nations Trusteeship Council saw its task as ensuring that colonial powers contributed towards the economic, political, and social development necessary for self-government and independence.[74]

Viewed in this way, it might seem that we can track a shift from civilisation to development, and that the language of 'development' constituted a new global language of politics. But the fact that very similar languages appear across the world at similar times does not mean that they were used in the same way in all cases. This case study reminds us of the need to be attuned to local contexts and local power relations. Even though, in fact precisely because, they were global concepts, words and concepts had distinctive resonances in local contexts. Thus as we develop our understanding of late colonial discourses of development, we should do so with an eye to languages emerging and shifting above and below, to better contextualise our reading of those late colonial discourses and deepen our understanding of their intellectual context.

Notes

1 Arthur Madan, *Swahili-English Dictionary* (Oxford: Clarendon Press 1903), p. 60. Krapf's 1882 dictionary offers 'progress, advantage' as its translation of *maendeleo*; J. L. Krapf, *A Dictionary of the Suahili Language* (London: Truebner 1892), p. 191.

2 Frederick Johnson, *Standard Swahili-English Dictionary* (London: Oxford University Press 1939), pp. 83–4.

3 Harold A. Goldklang, 'Current Swahili Newspaper Terminology', *Swahili* 37, 2 (1967), pp. 198, 204; C. W. Temu, 'The Development of Political Vocabulary in Swahili', *Swahili* 41, 2 (1971), p. 10.

4 For detailed circulation figures, see Martin Sturmer, *The Media History of Tanzania* (Salzburg: afrika.info 1998). A growing body of scholarship on *Mambo Leo* is begin-ning to emerge, see J. R. Brennan, 'Realizing Civilization through Patrilineal Descent: The Intellectual Making of an African Racial Nationalism in Tanzania, 1920–50', *Social Identities* 12, 4 (2006), pp. 405–23; Katrin Bromber, 'Ustaarabu: A Conceptual Change in Tanganyika Newspaper Discourse in the 1920s', in Roman Loimeier and Rüdiger Seesemann (eds), *The Global Worlds of the Swahili* (Berlin: Lit 2006), pp. 67–81. See also J. F. Scotton, 'Tanganyika's African Press, 1937–1960', *African Studies Review* 21, 1 (1978), pp. 1–18. I explore these themes in more detail in my draft book manuscript, provisionally entitled 'Languages of Freedom: Tanzanian Political Society in an International Age'.

5 The 'letter to the editor' form is attracting increasing attention from historians. See for example Maria Suriano, 'Letters to the Editor and Poems: *Mambo Leo* and

Readers' Debates on *Dansi, Ustaarabu*, Respectability, and Modernity in Tanganyika, 1940s–1950s', *Africa Today* 57, 3 (2011), pp. 39–55.

6 The methodology adopted here combines insights drawn from the study of the history of concepts, from Cambridge School approaches to the history of ideas in context, and from Carol Gluck and Anna Lowenhaupt Tsing's recent edited collection *Words in Motion*, which develops an 'embedded' history of 'words in motion', following their movement across the world, 'changing their impact and meaning as they go'. The empirical basis of the chapter is a close reading of a representative sample of the national and local Swahili press published in Tanzania from 1923 to 1967. This study of *maendeleo* forms part of a wider project which explores debates over the nature of political society in the period of decolonisation. See Carol Gluck and Anna Lowenhaupt Tsing, *Words in Motion: Towards a Global Lexicon* (Durham, NC: Duke University Press 2009), p. 3; Iain Hampsher-Monk, *History of Concepts: Comparative Perspectives* (Amsterdam: Amsterdam University Press 1998); Melvin Richter, *The History of Social and Political Concepts: A Critical Introduction* (Oxford: Oxford University Press 1995); Benjamin Zachariah, *Developing India: An Intellectual and Social History, c. 1930–50* (New Delhi, Oxford: Oxford University Press 2005), pp. 12–14.

7 Tanganyika Territory was renamed Tanzania in 1964 following union with Zanzibar.

8 Michael Ashley Havinden and David Meredith, *Colonialism and Development: Britain and Its Tropical Colonies, 1850–1960* (London, New York: Routledge 1993), p. 281. The scheme had aimed to produce 600,000 tons of groundnuts per year, see Rohland Schuknecht, *British Colonial Development Policy after the Second World War: The Case of Sukumaland, Tanganyika* (Berlin: Lit 2010), p. 206.

9 Schuknecht, *British Colonial Development Policy*, pp. 85–192.

10 Havinden and Meredith, *Colonialism and Development*, p. 276.

11 Peter Pels, 'Creolisation in Secret: The Birth of Nationalism in Late Colonial Uluguru, Tanzania', *Africa* 72, 1 (2002), especially pp. 11–22; Steven Feierman, *Peasant Intellectuals: Anthropology and History in Tanzania* (Madison, WI: University of Wisconsin Press 1990).

12 Feierman, *Peasant Intellectuals*; G. Andrew Maguire, *Toward 'Uhuru' in Tanzania: The Politics of Participation* (London: Cambridge University Press 1969).

13 Joseph Morgan Hodge, *Triumph of the Expert: Agrarian Doctrines of Development and the Legacies of British Colonialism* (Athens, OH: Ohio University Press 2007).

14 Matteo Rizzo, 'What Was Left of the Groundnut Scheme? Development Disaster and Labour Market in Southern Tanganyika, 1946–1952', *Journal of Agrarian Change* 6, 2 (2006), pp. 205–38.

15 Ibid., p. 207.

16 Ibid., p. 212.

17 On the origins of the Sukuma Union see Schuknecht, *British Colonial Development Policy*, pp. 291–3 and Maguire, *Toward 'Uhuru' in Tanzania*, pp. 75–80.

18 Schuknecht, *British Colonial Development Policy*, pp. 291–2.

19 The quote which begins this subsection is taken from a development report for the West Usambara region in 1945: British National Archives, London (hereafter BNA), CO 691/190/6, fo. 7, John Nutman, 'A Development Scheme for West Usambara'. The reference is to Proverbs xxix 18. On development discourse, see recent work by Frederick Cooper including Frederick Cooper, *Decolonization and African Society: The Labor Question in French and British Africa* (Cambridge: Cambridge University Press 1996), and Frederick Cooper and Randall Packard (eds), *International Development and the Social Sciences: Essays on the History and Politics of Knowledge* (Berkeley, Los Angeles, London: University of California Press 1997).

20 Erez Manela, *The Wilsonian Moment: Self-Determination and the International Origins of Anticolonial Nationalism* (Oxford: Oxford University Press 2007).

21 Rajnarayan Chandavarkar, 'Imperialism and the European Empires', in Julian Jackson (ed.), *Europe, 1900–1945* (Oxford: Oxford University Press 2002), pp. 138–72.

22 Nicholas Westcott, 'The Impact of the Second World War in Tanganyika' (PhD dissertation, University of Cambridge, 1982); D. A. Low and John M. Lonsdale,

'Introduction: Towards the New Order, 1945–1963', in D. A. Low and Alison Smith (eds), *History of East Africa*, vol. 3 (Oxford: Clarendon Press 1976), pp. 1–63.

23 Tanganyika Territory, *Development of Tanganyika: Report of the Post-War Planning Advisory Committee* (Dar es Salaam: Government Printer 1944), p. 1. More generally, see BNA CO 691/190, files 1–5.

24 See Tanzania National Archives, Dar es Salaam (hereafter TNA), 5/554, 'Expansion of the Chagga Tribe', and TNA 5/896, 'Chagga Post-War Development'; Emma Hunter, 'Languages of Politics in Twentieth-century Kilimanjaro' (PhD dissertation, University of Cambridge, 2008), pp. 106–7.

25 See T. H. Marshall, *Citizenship and Social Class, and Other Essays* (Cambridge: Cambridge University Press 1950).

26 United Nations Trusteeship Council (hereafter UNTC), First session, 26 March 1947, *Official Records*, p. 5. For the most complete account of Tanganyika's relationship with the Trusteeship Council, see Ulrich Lohrmann, *Voices from Tanganyika: Great Britain, the United Nations and the Decolonization of a Trust Territory, 1946–1961* (Münster: Lit 2006). See also Margaret L. Bates, 'Tanganyika under British Administration, 1920–1955' (PhD dissertation, University of Oxford, 1957); B. T. G. Chidzero, *Tanganyika and International Trusteeship* (London: Oxford University Press 1961).

27 UNTC, First session, 26 March 1947, *Official Records*, p. 5.

28 Bromber, 'Ustaarabu'.

29 'Education Department: Habari za Maendeleo', *Mambo Leo*, December 1929, p. 1194.

30 'Maendeleo Mema', *Mambo Leo*, July 1926, p. 427; Letter from H. Nkonjera, *Mambo Leo*, January 1929, p. 1018.

31 On interwar Tanganyika and indirect rule see John Iliffe, *A Modern History of Tanganyika* (Cambridge: Cambridge University Press 1979).

32 On the ethno-histories see Thomas Geider, 'The Paper Memory of East Africa: Ethnohistories and Biographies Written in Swahili', in Axel Harneit-Sievers (ed.), *A Place in the World: New Local Historiographies in Africa and South Asia* (Leiden: Brill 2002), pp. 255–88.

33 Zachariah, *Developing India*, p. 114.

34 See for example TNA 5/23/25, fo. 7, 'Mkutano no. 13/50 Uliofanyika Hai HQs, 20 October 1950'.

35 Petro Itosi Marealle, *Maisha ya Mchagga Hapa Duniani na Ahera* (Dar es Salaam: Mkuki na Nyota 2002 [ca. 1947]), p. 99. All translations are my own.

36 Ibid., p. 100.

37 Ibid., p. 104.

38 Ibid.

39 J. D. Y. Peel, '*Olaju*: A Yoruba Concept of Development', *Journal of Development Studies* 14, 2 (1978), pp. 139–65.

40 Ibid., pp. 143–4.

41 Zachariah, *Developing India*, p. 13; for parallel examples, in this case 'democracy' and 'civil society', see Michelle L. Browers, *Democracy and Civil Society in Arab Political Thought: Transcultural Possibilities* (Syracuse, NY: Syracuse University Press 2006), p. 5.

42 TNA 215/2818, vol. 1, fo. 53, Letter to Chief Secretary, 25 July 1956.

43 Maswali na Majibu, *Maendeleo ya Shambalai*, October 1952, p. 3. On political conflict in the region, see Feierman, *Peasant Intellectuals*.

44 'Maongezi juu ya Ardhi', *Maendeleo ya Shambalai*, June 1952, pp. 5–6.

45 Editorial, *Maendeleo ya Shambalai*, June 1952, p. 1; Editorial, *Maendeleo ya Shambalai*, September 1952, p. 1.

46 He cites a Saba Saba day speech from 1970 which includes the line: 'Binadamu haridhiki kuishi kama farasi au punda; binadamu ana kitu anakiita maendeleo'; Jan Blommaert, 'Some Problems in the Interpretation of Swahili Political Texts', in Jan Blommaert (ed.), *Swahili Studies: Essays in Honour of Marcel van Spaandonck* (Ghent: Academia Press 1991), p. 120.

47 Editorial, 'Turudi Nyuma?', *Kiongozi*, July 1953.
48 On Mwapachu's career, see references in Iliffe, *Modern History of Tanganyika*, pp. 422, 507.
49 Hamza K. B. Mwapachu, 'Utangulizi', *Ekome wa Bukerebe*, November 1952, p. 1.
50 In a study of a branch of the Anglican Church of the Congo, Emma Wild-Wood offers a fascinating account of the way in which *maendeleo* and *utaratibu* (order) served as two poles of discourse which defined the experience of Church members, one encompassing an idea of spiritual and material change and the other ideas of continuity and stability; Emma Wild-Wood, *Migration and Christian Identity in Congo (DRC)* (Leiden: Brill 2008).
51 Northern Province, 'Welfare ya Moshi', *Mambo Leo*, March 1950, p. 34.
52 'Mikopo ya fedha kwa Waafrika wanaopenda maendeleo', *Kiongozi*, September 1955, p. 3.
53 Letter from Mwl N. Aisario Lemwel and K. Philip Marawiti, 'Impasavyo kila raia kupata riziki', *Komkya*, November 1954, p. 3.
54 Ibid., p. 3.
55 Letter from A. Jidadi, 'Upungufu wa Maendeleo', *Kondoa News*, April/May 1957, p. 4.
56 BNA CO 892/13/1, fo. 273. Though evidence given by Thomas Marealle to the commission and in contemporary newspapers suggests that land was at that time being bought and sold.
57 See for example the missionary Bruno Gutmann's critique in *Africa*: Bruno Gutmann, 'The African Standpoint', *Africa* 8, 1 (1935), pp. 1–19.
58 E. C. Baker, 'Mazungumzo ya Maana', *Mambo Leo*, February 1946, p. 16.
59 TNA 5/237, fo. 91, 'Wageni wa Chama cha Ulinzi Walipozuru K.N.C.U, 10.9.48'.
60 Letter from H. F. Hassan and Shariff Ahmad, 'Gazeti Letu Kwanza', *Kondoa News*, March 1957.
61 TNA 41176, *Maendeleo ya Shambalai*, June 1952, p. 4.
62 TNA 41176, vol. 3, Letter from Bernard A. M. Daniel, 'Maendeleo na ubovu wa Wapare', *Habari za Upare*, November 1952, pp. 8–9.
63 K. R. Baghdelleh, 'Moshi kuna maendeleo?', *Mwafrika*, 7 March 1959; Letter from L. N. Ninatubu, 'Moshi kuna maendeleo?', *Mwafrika*, 28 March 1959, p. 2. For Thomas Marealle's responses to the charge that he had failed to bring development, see United States National Archives II, RG 84, UD 3266, Box 6, File 350, Dar es Salaam to State Department, 'Visit with Chagga Paramount Chief Thomas Marealle', 9 September 1959.
64 On the greater stability of development discourse after 1950, see Zachariah, *Developing India*, pp. 293–8.
65 Mawazo ya Msema Kweli, 'Thamani ya Amani – Uchumi', *Mwafrika*, 1 June 1958, p. 5.
66 For an example see 'Jihadharini na Chama Kipya – TANU', *Mwafrika*, 29 October 1960, p. 8.
67 J. R. Brennan, 'Youth, the TANU Youth League and Managed Vigilantism in Dar es Salaam, Tanzania, 1925–73', *Africa* 76, 2 (2006), pp. 221–46.
68 There are echoes here of the argument made by Cowen and Shenton that development was a way of controlling the disorder caused by 'progress'. Michael Cowen and Robert Shenton, 'The Invention of Development', in Jonathan Crush (ed.), *The Power of Development* (London, New York: Routledge 1995), pp. 27–43.
69 Denis-Constant Martin, *Tanzanie: L'invention d'une culture politique* (Paris: Karthala 1998), p. 65.
70 For the case of Africa, the most important contributions have been those of Frederick Cooper listed above (note 19) and Frederick Cooper, *Africa since 1940: The Past of the Present* (Cambridge: Cambridge University Press 2002).
71 T. N. Harper, *The End of Empire and the Making of Malaya* (Cambridge: Cambridge University Press 2001); Low and Lonsdale, 'Introduction'; Joanna Lewis, *Empire State Building: War and Welfare in Kenya 1925–52* (Oxford: James Currey 2000); Hodge, *Triumph of the Expert*.

72 J. R. Brennan, 'Nation, Race and Urbanization in Dar es Salaam, Tanzania, 1916–1976' (PhD dissertation, Northwestern University, 2002), p. 292.
73 Rhoderick Chalmers, '"We Nepalis": Language, Literature and the Formation of a Nepali Public Sphere in India, 1914–1940' (PhD dissertation, London SOAS, 2003), p. 122. On *bikas* rhetoric, see Mary Des Chene, 'In the Name of Bikas', *Studies in Nepali History and Society* 1, 2 (1996), pp. 1–7.
74 On the discursive transition from 'civilisation' to 'development', see Françoise Dufour, *De l'idéologie coloniale à celle du développement: une analyse du discours France-Afrique* (Paris: L'Harmattan 2010).

PART II

Economic and rural development

CHAPTER FOUR

The 'private' face of African development planning during the Second World War[1]

Billy Frank

In 1942, Barclays Bank (Dominion, Colonial and Overseas) launched an essay competition for its staff on the subject of 'The Bank in relation to post-war colonial development'. In modern business parlance, this 'knowledge management' exercise evinces an interesting insight into capitalist concerns and ideas in relation to colonial economic development and colonial administration in British Africa during the Second World War. In particular, it demonstrates the expatriate business community's disaffection with the British record of economic development and a complete lack of faith in the Colonial Office's ability to forge development policy without the aid of the business community. These essays made numerous proposals: ideas to extend banking facilities for indigenous populations, better support for local business and agriculture, and an increase in the availability of medium and long-term finance for business, the extension of co-operative farming methods, changes to education policy in Britain's African colonies, the creation of a permanent economic staff in colonial governments, and the future federation of certain African colonies. The arguments advanced by the essayists are a significant and underused historical source which this chapter seeks to place in the historical context of the wider efforts by the imperial government to plan for post-war colonial development.

Barclays Bank (Dominion, Colonial and Overseas: DCO)[2] was formed in 1925 as part of the long-term aim of F. C. Goodenough, chairman of Barclays Bank, to move the organisation into the sphere of colonial business.[3] The DCO was formed by the amalgamation of three existing banks gradually brought under Barclays' control. The first of these was the Colonial Bank, whose business was traditionally associated with the West Indies and West Africa. Under its 1916 charter it was empowered to undertake business throughout the empire, an influential factor in F. C. Goodenough's desire to acquire the bank for

Barclays.[4] Negotiation in the early 1920s between the Colonial Bank, now controlled by Barclays, and the National Bank of South Africa and the Anglo-Egyptian Bank, led to a merger in 1925, the organisation being renamed Barclays Bank (Dominion, Colonial and Overseas).[5] The new organisation boasted a branch network that was extensive throughout the British empire, offering local businesses, settlers, and colonial officials a well-known banking brand at the periphery.

During the Second World War, the Colonial Office anticipated a renewed emphasis on colonial development policy after the cessation of hostilities.[6] Various committees, most notably the Colonial Economic Advisory Committee (CEAC), were established within the Colonial Office to discuss possible post-war policy initiatives in the field of colonial development. The CEAC, which was formed in 1943, looked to private business for advice and guidance on colonial economics and invited William Goodenough, son of the Bank's founder and by then its chairman, to join the committee.[7] The Bank's management enjoyed good relations with some of the CO's top officials, most notably Sydney Caine.[8] At its headquarters in Lombard Street in the heart of the City, the DCO's management also enjoyed a close association with London based companies who operated in Africa and elsewhere. This was then mirrored at the periphery where the branch managers worked with local representatives of those London based concerns.

Echoing the post-war colonial development planning within Whitehall, Barclays DCO also looked to the future launching an essay competition in September 1942. The idea came from William Goodenough and Julian Crossley, his brother-in-law and the Bank's General Manager. Any member of the Bank's staff was welcome to participate and cash prizes were promised for the best entries. The Bank was keen to undertake the exercise as a way of pooling ideas from its employees on the periphery, whose local knowledge of economic conditions, development potential, and business opportunities was reliable and up to date. Ten alone were sent from Kenya – the Bank's regional headquarters in East Africa. In addition, a number of essays were submitted from staff at the DCO's headquarters in London, many of whom had recent experience of working for the DCO in Africa and elsewhere.

The range and scope of issues that competition entrants were asked to comment upon is somewhat surprising. For the purpose of the essay, entrants were told to assume that imperial authorities in conjunction with the colonial governments had decided upon a 'long progressive policy' of economic development for the empire aimed at raising the 'material standards of the peoples as well as encouraging the development of the resources of those territories'.[9] Essayists were asked to consider obvious banking issues such as the future employment of funds locally for development purposes, how to extend banking services for Africans, and the extent to which conservative lending policies of the Bank may have previously held back economic progress – especially in the 'more backward territories'. However, those who entered the competition were also asked to comment upon issues such as: the state of agricultural and industrial development and the potentialities for further growth, systems of land tenure and local law with an appeal for suggested 'constructive amendments', the part the Bank might play in helping a colony dependent on export of raw materials to promote local industrial development, and monopolistic crop marketing, and its effects upon conditions in different territories.[10] These were issues that would certainly call for essayists to comment on numerous aspects of colonial administration and policy. In this way, the DCO's managers were gathering intelligence about not only current colonial economic conditions, but the very state of the empire in Africa.

On the periphery the DCO's branch system gave them an impressive geographical network and many essayists believed this could be very attractive to a government whose seeming inability to recruit talented staff in the field hampered their access to reliable and up-to-date information about colonial conditions.[11] Moreover, the Bank's network was seen as more approachable than colonial government. As Dyson (Nairobi) who won first prize, pointed out:

> The State as such has an impersonal flavour, whereas the Bank, with its many branches and the human relationships between the staff and the customer, is in an ideal position to act as a go-between, framing its policy to accord with the State's policy but having the advantage of personal knowledge of its customers when it comes to applying that policy in practice.[12]

The importance of the DCO's branches should not be underplayed; many essayists believed the expansion of its branch network was essential to support a government-sponsored development scheme.[13] Indeed, in the years following the war, the Bank's network in Africa expanded rapidly. In 1946, for example, the Rhodesias and Nyasaland had only 19 DCO branches and 265 members of staff. By 1960 there were 113 branches employing 1,176. During the same period, money deposited in the area rose from £12 million to over £46 million, and the Bank's gross trading profits from these territories rose from £54,000 to £983,000.[14]

The Bank as key development 'partner'

Many of the essays submitted started by acknowledging and accepting the widespread criticism of the British colonial record and suggested ways in which the Bank could support the economic development of the colonies after the war.[15] Most essayists wanted to see this achieved through a strategy of partnership with government, which would provide the leadership in forming development policy. Essay submissions were universally critical of the lack of progress made by pre-war governments in colonial development, and urged the pursuit of a more proactive policy. Many stressed the importance of an effective government-led strategy as a context necessary for the implementation of effective banking policies in Africa. Dyson emphasised:

> It will in fact be essential, if the assistance of the banks is to be obtained and put to good use, for there to be a proper recognition of what a Bank's funds really are, and a proper division as between the Banks and the government of the risks of financing a long-term scheme. This will involve a degree of close cooperation between the Banks and the various governments as well as between their Head Offices and the Colonial Office.[16]

Here Dyson clearly wanted to see the Bank developing a similarly close relationship to the imperial and colonial governments as it enjoyed with big colonial businesses in London and at the periphery.

A recurring theme in the essays was the perceived need for an effective partnership between government and the banks; between public and private finance. The bankers believed that colonial governments should be responsible for welfare projects, soil conservation, educational provisions, communications, and social services. In this way, the British government would set the guidelines for development and then the banks could assist by providing the finance needed for development policy to be implemented. As shall be seen, the notion of centrally driven state-planned development policy was emerging at this time within the Colonial Office.

Various practical ways in which this could be done were put forward, with most staff agreeing that it could be done by the banks subscribing to government loans, indirectly by assisting the private sector, and by providing finance to the government for 'on-lending' to enterprises which were too risky for the banks to undertake on their own. The risk element was particularly high for agricultural loans, and as agricultural development was deemed by many essayists as fundamental to the welfare of the colonial peoples, it was argued that:

> Where credit risks are to be taken in the community's interest, it is the responsibility of the community, not of a particular section, namely

those with credit or banking accounts, to underwrite such risks . . . it is fair that Governments not the Banks should underwrite the credit risks involved if they wish the Banks to assist them in financing the production of any particular commodity as part of a general scheme of development.[17]

Essential large-scale public works in infrastructure, argued Trebble (Jeppestown, Transvaal), would obviously increase the national wealth of the African colonies by opening up access to hitherto inaccessible assets, both agricultural and mineral.[18] Stokes (Nairobi) applauded the advent of the Colonial Development and Welfare Act of 1940 in this respect and correctly predicted its expansion after the war for development of this nature.[19] But it was also stressed that these developments would rely on local business, and here the Bank could play a vital role in support.[20]

Medium- and long-term finance for the private sector

Many writers believed there was a pressing need for more medium and long-term lending in the colonies. This they considered could be met if the colonial governments were prepared to do more in the way of establishing Land Banks, Mortgage Banks, Cooperative Banks or special Corporations. The banks could then find ways of lending to these institutions for the specialist needs of the colonies.[21] In fact the Bank had already undertaken lucrative business of this sort where opportunities had presented themselves, for example in Palestine and Cyprus, and many of the African essayists were keen to see this extended to 'their' colonies.[22]

While the essays display a clear consensus regarding the need for long-term finance to be more readily available, especially for agricultural development, some differences emerge about how this could be best achieved. In Kenya, where a state-funded Land Bank existed, it was argued that the Bank should increase lending on a seasonal basis to farmers as the market for long-term finance was covered,[23] although some essayists suggested that the DCO should enter this long-term business in competition as the anticipated market for long-term finance for mortgages and large loans for investment in buildings and machinery would certainly increase. However, some essayists went further arguing that the Bank itself needed to enter into long-term financing more formally. Evans (Nairobi) and Collins (Swakopmund) amongst others suggested the creation of a new and separate section of the Bank for this purpose, Collins suggesting the establishment of a 'Barclays Bank Colonial Development Corporation' as an empire-wide organisation for making long-term capital available 'in sections of industry selected by the colonial and British governments'.[24] He further suggested that the organisation should adopt a system of inspection to check on the progress of schemes and projects funded by it. Collins envisioned the corporation as being administered at the local level via the Bank's branch network where staff with good local knowledge would be in the best position to adjudge the merits of applications received; this, he argued, would avoid the 'bog of bureaucratic inelasticity' of the state.[25] While many of the essayists put forward the idea that the Bank should move into long-term financing, few fleshed out the idea as practically as Collins. In doing so, Collins pre-empted *modus operandi* of Barclays' own Development Corporation established in 1946 as well as the government's Colonial Development Corporation (CDC) established in 1947.

Some writers correctly predicted that colonial governments would be starved of development capital after the war and believed that 'many tens of millions' would be required from government funds under the auspices of the Colonial Development and Welfare Act in addition to what the banks could contribute.[26] They were not without understanding of the constraints, but one essayist felt that the experiences of the 1920s had driven the colonial banks operating in Africa to adopt an unnecessarily prudent line:

> The banks have had a few sharp lessons of the risks which they run by lending on too generous a scale to [European] farmers who have to face not only the vagaries of weather and climate but also sudden and possibly violent fluctuations in produce prices. These lessons have, it is hoped, been learned thoroughly by lenders and borrowers and past mistakes have been written off to the debit of experience. However, it is suggested that they have had their effect in causing the pendulum to swing rather too far in the direction of restriction of facilities.[27]

As one essayist put it, 'too often the arguments for safety and liquidity are used as a cloak for ultra-caution and timidity'.[28] However, as noted by Mamour (Assiut, Egypt), this conservatism in banking policy in some territories did not detract from the overall fact that the DCO had steadily grown its branch infrastructure and not just in commercial centres but also in the hinterland of certain colonies for the very purpose of extending credit facilities to cultivators.[29]

Another way in which banks could identify more closely with local economic interests and asset development would be to invest locally. In most African colonies there had been few opportunities for this before the war, and essayists suggested that the development of local security markets would be of assistance to colonial governments and profitable for the Bank.[30] Colonial governments would find local borrowing simpler than borrowing in the London market, while the banks would find it 'a welcome outlet for surplus local funds' which had been accumulated.[31] While interest rates were unattractive in London, the banks would find it more profitable to employ the money locally and so avoid the transfer charges of the Currency Boards which were applied in most colonial regions. This type of activity, of course, involved a certain risk, but as the first-prize winner pointed out:

> It is appreciated that if the Bank was to take up local investment of this sort, it would be increasing its stakes in the colony concerned, but it must be borne in mind that this risk would be diminished in proportion as the degree of economic controls and planning in the world is increased. The greater the degree of stability that can be assured both for producer and consumer – and this will be the first object of post-war economic plans – the safer such investments would become.[32]

One of the youngest prize winners went further than most in raising the question of the Bank's own preference for investing in London and South Africa. He did not shy away from deeming this 'exploitation' and suggested a review of the geographical source of all deposits. He felt that banks were very conservative institutions but they might not be able to remain so after the war.[33] These 'hard-nosed business men' were clearly cognisant of the need to see more of the Bank's funds used locally and many made it plain just how much improvement was needed in areas like education and health, even if they did believe the state was responsible for investment in this direction by way of funds under Colonial Development and Welfare.

Dyson (Nairobi) argued that local taxation should be direct rather than indirect, thereby ensuring that companies operating from abroad would contribute directly to local development through taxation.[34] During the war, the DCO and other colonial banks consciously set aside some of their traditional criteria when assessing applications for banking advances. In addition to ascertaining an application's merits from a business perspective, they also adopted a national perspective and looked to encourage investments in agriculture and industrial production that would benefit the colony. This saw the banks favouring such applications rather than those for speculative or 'non-essential' enterprises.[35]

Agricultural development

Many essayists displayed a clear desire to see the territories in which they operated prosper. In asking essayists to consider monopolistic practices, the Bank seemed keen to highlight regions and economic sectors in which this was regarded as problematic and a number of essayists were keen to demonstrate how monopolies impacted locally. Evans (Nairobi) lamented that some large monopolies had moved far beyond the state of solely retailing manufactured goods and large-scale buying of produce, to actually becoming producers themselves. In many instances, local farmers had become tied into contracts to grow certain crops, while the monopoly could switch its focus to another product or region at any time; they were under no public control other than that laid down by Company Laws.[36] Miller (Victoria, Cameroons) highlighted the long-standing grievances of West African cocoa farmers in this respect.[37] For some writers, the real danger in monopolistic practice was in the lack of incentive it gave African farmers to improve production methods and the standard and yield of crops.[38] War-time conditions had brought some stability for growers with a widespread policy of price controls, fixed quotas, and government marketing of African (and European) produce. In Nigeria where pre-war trade in groundnuts and palm oil had been subject to 'violent manipulations', Greenway (Port Harcourt) argued that the continuation of price controls into peacetime would help ensure steady economic growth and would benefit all apart from the monopolistic combines.[39]

Amongst the essayists, the importance of improving agricultural production across the continent was universally regarded as the prime factor in the economic development of the African colonies, however, there were differences expressed about how this should be best achieved. Taking a wider focus, Goss (Kisumu, Kenya) argued that agricultural development should be planned to a greater extent on a regional basis advocating that the Agricultural Departments of the East African colonies should decide upon which areas were best suited to certain crops and the raising of different species of livestock. Goss advocated that the indigenous African people in the identified areas should then be made responsible for production under this system and should be offered a guaranteed price for their surplus production. The storage and marketing of these products could be undertaken by the local government, a practice that was in place for European producers at the time. For Goss, the success of such a scheme would depend heavily on local governments working more effectively with the local African leaders.[40] There were obvious 'snags' with the proposal: the granting of a virtual monopoly to a 'native' marketing board and the possibility that in some years higher prices could be gained outside of the scheme. However, Goss argued that future African development should be judged upon the basis of 'maximum benefit' and believed there would be 'little doubt in which direction that would lie'.[41] Goss and other essayists acknowledged that the colonial prosperity needed would rely on the expansion and improvement of 'native agriculture', but with a strong leadership role required on the part of Europeans for some time to come.

Many essayists from Central and Southern Africa advocated a policy of growth in European immigration into the region for the advancement of agricultural production. Implicit here was the view that 'native farming' was vastly inferior to that of the European. Page (Nairobi) argued that African farmers in Kenya lacked the necessary skill to produce the region's most valuable crops such as tea, sugar, and sisal and advocated an extension of plantation style production under European control.[42] While some regarded immigration as a necessary evil, some advocated it wholeheartedly. Evans (Nairobi) amongst others made the distinction that East Africa needed to attract the 'suitable type' of settler, described by Macdona (Nairobi) as the 'yeoman farmer' who would be prepared to work hard.[43] Page (Nairobi) highlighted the apparent inconsistency between imperial policy which was opposed to further European immigration in Kenya and local policy where white settlers asserted a powerful influence in favour of their own interests.[44]

Industrial and co-operative development

When assessing the possibility of industrial development in Britain's African colonies, most essayists advised caution. In fact, the establishment of secondary industries in the colonies was banned during the 1930s as part of a general policy to protect Britain's economic interests.[45] Several competitors described the impact that the war was having on prospects for local business, the scarcity of essential imports being the main concern.[46] This led to some measure of industrialisation on a relatively small scale in a number of colonies. These secondary industries utilised locally sourced raw materials and crops and produced manufactured items made scarce by the war. However, as Goss (Kenya) argued, while the production of items such as soap, boots, blankets etc. was undoubtedly useful, with the cessation of hostilities and the renewed availability of much cheaper mass-produced goods from Europe, this local production could struggle if not supported by government.[47] Goss questioned whether some vested interests in the colonies would welcome industrial development and whether the imperial government would want to sponsor it as a possible rival to UK manufacture.[48] However, the essays display a consensus that was lukewarm towards the development of any large-scale industry, favouring the advancement of selected secondary industries as long as these were based on local raw materials and fulfilled the consumptive needs of the local population.[49] Most agreed that advances in agriculture offered the most immediate opportunities for widespread economic progress.

Many essayists advocated the development of African co-operative societies as a way of fostering economic development, especially in the agricultural sphere.[50] Some described the advances made by African farming co-operatives before the war. Miller (Victoria, Cameroons) and Peters (Accra, Gold Coast) described the support given by the Bank to African co-operatives in West Africa, in some instances acting as a link between shippers and dealers in the UK.[51] This was in sharp contrast to the southern colonies, where support by the Bank for African co-operatives had been negligible.

Although some essayists like Whitcombe[52] and Evans[53] were alive to the arguments about co-operatives fostering organisation, leadership, shared responsibility, and other characteristics important for the political and social advancement of Africans in the post-war world, the majority saw co-operatives purely as an economic entity that was a safer business prospect to make loans to.[54] This was essentially because of the shared risk inherent in the co-operative model. Whitcombe wanted an extension of the Bank's operations into the marketing of African co-operative societies' produce.[55] He believed that the negotiation of shipping documents, which would be beyond the capabilities of local indigenous producers in East Africa, should be undertaken by the Bank, in effect an extension of the practice occurring in West African colonies described by Miller and, it should be noted, a facility that was already occurring in the region for European co-operatives like the Kenya Farmers Association. He also argued that advances could be made against produce pending favourable opportunities for sale and shipping; this would benefit the colony as it did not leave the producer co-operatives waiting for sale and had the concomitant benefit of allowing more money to circulate freely.[56]

Goss (Kisumu, Kenya) also argued strongly in favour of the development of African co-operatives, however, he also advocated a growth in plantation agriculture under European control. He believed that production of coffee, tea, and sugar should remain in European hands, while African co-operative farmers would be better suited to growing crops such as maize, wheat, vegetables, cotton, barley, sesame, millet, and rice.[57] The essays do demonstrate a clear regional variation in the encouragement of co-operatives. In Britain's few West African territories, Miller (Cameroons) and Peters (Gold Coast) highlighted how co-operatives were actively encouraged by local government, whereas in most of the southern colonies, this had hitherto not been the case, in part due to local settler attitudes and fear of competition.[58]

Africans and Africanisation

The perception of Africans on the part of the bankers was often evidently negative. While some put this down to poor educational policy, some typical settler attitudes to race do emerge and comments such as, 'By nature a lazy and improvident person, the East African Native will live from hand to mouth unless and until he is induced to live otherwise' were not uncommon.[59] It is for this reason that the issue of Africanisation in the banking service itself did not find favour with many essayists. In West Africa the banks had employed Africans in positions of responsibility for some time.[60] The situation was quite different in East and Central Africa where the mores of settler life had prohibited any real advancement in jobs traditionally reserved for whites, so in relation to African bank employees most essayists could not see advancement in this respect for some time. The essay submitted by Major Fanshawe (Northern Rhodesia) does stand out as wholly more positive. The key here is that Fanshawe had been in close contact with local Africans in the armed forces and had seen their potential manifest itself in their army education and training, a point he drove home forcibly in his essay.[61] Few essayists had enjoyed such a close association with Africans, other than in roles of menial subservience.

While critical of the abilities of Africans, essayists did not dispute the need to engage them more readily with banking. Many suggested ways in which the Bank should attempt to increase the account holdings of local people and to seek their business and encourage 'bank mindedness'.[62] Writers showed a practical understanding of the problems involved. Many Africans lacked collateral, what accounts they had were often small, and many were unskilled and illiterate. In the southern colonies fingerprint identification could replace signatures, as was the practice in West Africa.[63] Individual accounts might be small, but they would grow, and in aggregate, savings deposits would be an important source of funds for local lending. The scale of the problem was starkly demonstrated by Rutherford (Northern Rhodesia) who noted that of the 10,000 African wage earners at the Mufilira mines, the DCO had fewer than 100 accounts.[64] Many essayists discussed ways in which Africans could be encouraged to save some of the money they earned rather than spend it on 'shoddy goods'. Soyode, the only African bank employee to enter the essay competition, argued that 'Bestial drunkenness and wasteful luxuries without thought for Savings and hard days are contributing factors for the retrogression of a Colony'.[65] Some essayists suggested the Bank should even play a role in educating Africans in this regard and that employees should endeavour to learn more about local customs, language, and habits.[66]

Money (Nairobi) argued that European bankers coming to the periphery should be properly briefed in this regard and suggested language tuition and libraries be provided at DCO Headquarters in London.[67] However, for Rutherford, the issue of encouraging thrift among Africans was secondary to the much greater problem of overall poverty; he argued 'the Bank cannot encourage thrift in a human being to whom pounds shillings and pence represent the wherewithal to purchase clothing'.[68] Some writers quoted from their personal experience of work with local people. There had been a particularly successful drive by the Bank to encourage saving amongst the relatively prosperous cotton-growing Baganda people in Uganda. The original appeal to the Baganda had been that their money was safe inside the bank, but they quickly showed an appreciation of differentials in interest rates, and the Bank lost business to the Post Office Savings Bank when bank rates on deposits fell.[69] The thrust of the argument was that the Bank must be more imaginative, flexible, and dynamic. After the war, the Bank made strenuous efforts 'to take banking to the people', especially in the African territories.[70]

Colonial administration and development planning

In assessing the potential success of any long-term plan for colonial development, few essayists believed this could be achieved without a huge overhaul of colonial administration. The seemingly poor standard of many colonial officials at the periphery was a common theme. In part, this was a contemporary issue stemming from war-time circumstances as many colonial officials served in the armed forces. However, essayists like Evans (Nairobi) believed there was an innate conservatism about the local colonial administration that stifled any imagination in promoting development at the local level.[71] The poor state of East African agricultural development lay squarely at the feet of the colonial administration according to Goss:

> The point is that the almost criminal apathy which has been exhibited at a time when every acre should have been made to count is characteristic of the pathetic lack of progressive policy, agricultural, industrial, political, social and otherwise which has kept East Africa from attaining anything like her present potentialities.[72]

Money argued that local colonial officials were given very little authority which stymied 'initiative and independent thought', and that promotion in the service was predominantly based upon seniority rather than competency.[73] As Fanshawe (Northern Rhodesia) argued, administrative officers had no training in economic planning, a technical subject that required years of study.[74]

Fanshawe argued that nowhere was this conservatism more visible than in the colonial administration in Northern Rhodesia:

> It was impossible to receive any guarantee, to come to any definite decision, since there was no official willing to accept any responsibility; the smallest and most trivial matters were either shelved or referred back to Whitehall, where apparently they were usually forgotten. In spite of public statements that decisions were usually left to the man on the spot, in view of his greater knowledge or experience, such was not the case in practice.[75]

However, for Fanshawe, the major regional problems – soil erosion, provision of social services, education, infrastructural development, appalling health conditions, widespread poverty, growth of slums near towns, lack of labour protection, and the lack of any adequate political expression – were the result of this malaise in policy at the periphery *and* metropole. The very way in which the Colonial Office gathered its information about local conditions was strongly criticised. Rutherford (Mufilira) argued that the Colonial Office's tendency to utilise visiting Commissions was fatally flawed in that the knowledge they received in the colonies was pre-prepared and they 'only met those people who will say the right thing'.[76] For most essayists, local colonial administrations needed to be far more proactive and take the notion of development planning to heart. What was required was the machinery to put ideals into practice.[77] Roche (DCO Headquarters, London) stressed the urgency of the situation arguing that a 'corps' of experts in surveying, mineralogy, and other areas needed to be established by the imperial government and put to work immediately in order for an empire-wide development scheme to commence after the war.[78] Roche, as was the case with many other essayists, was aware of the need for the detailed assessment of potential locations for development schemes as a precursor to the success of any scheme. What was required was better coordination of efforts. Macdona (Nairobi) and others applauded the recent formation of the East African Industrial Research and Development Board which was jointly funded by the administrations of Uganda, Kenya, and Tanganyika, but reasoned that much more activity like this was required.[79]

Contributors like Stokes saw the scope for change engendered in the Colonial Development and Welfare Act in 1940 as an important step in the right direction towards the conscious planning of development by the imperial government.[80] The Act required local colonial administrations to establish development committees to plan and coordinate development over a ten-year period, many indeed did so, but the onset of war saw little progress. However, such an increase in centralised planning was welcomed, especially as it demonstrated the imperial government's acknowledgement of a lack of state planning before the war. Macdona (Nairobi) cited the well-publicised Development Plan for Tanganyika by a Development Committee that commenced its work before the war, but conceded that similar plans for Kenya had yet to be 'priced'.[81] It is worth noting here that this also displays the sometimes close association between bankers on the periphery and colonial administrators as it is unlikely that this lack of progress in the Kenya Development Plan would have been common knowledge.

At the time the essays were being written, this issue was being examined by the CEAC and there is a clear congruence in the attitudes to state planning demonstrated in Whitehall. One of the fiercest critics of progress made under the Colonial Development and Welfare Act of 1940 was Sir Sydney Caine whose growing influence at the Colonial Office galvanised a new direction in colonial development policy.[82] In an influential memo to his colleague George Gater, Caine set out a number of proposals that he believed were necessary to move colonial development policy forward. He argued that there was a general uneasiness about the slowness of development under the Colonial Development and Welfare Act and pointed out that the excuse of war conditions was 'a little worn with use'.[83] The state had to take a more commanding role. W. Arthur Lewis, a West Indian economist and member of the CEAC, argued that the economic development of the colonies had to be 'carefully planned and as carefully controlled'.[84] Caine also echoed many of Barclays' essayists arguing that there was not enough original and coherent thinking about development possibilities and that 'very little guidance or suggestion of a practical kind has been given to help colonial governments in inventing or working out schemes'. Caine wanted a new proactive state-sponsored development policy characterised by central co-ordination and planning within the Colonial Office. He stated:

> We have to face today a new concept of the place the state must take in planning. There is much nonsense talked which suggests that no development can take place unless it is planned by [colonial] governments. Nothing is more demonstrably untrue for the colonial empire, where tremendous developments have been produced by the planning of private enterprise.[85]

Caine saw private enterprise as an ideal exemplar of good colonial development planning, unsurprising given his position as Head of the

CO's Economic Section. However, despite the praise given to new directions in state planning, essayists like Stokes still maintained that the role of the state should be confined to providing economic assistance for development that would 'no more than touch the fringe of the problem' and the primacy of bank capital would continue.[86] Of course the essayists could not have foreseen the huge rise in state-sponsored colonial development in the shape of the CDC and Overseas Food Corporation created by the British Labour government in 1947.

African advancement

Some essayists believed that too much emphasis in policy statements emanating from London saw post-war reconstruction from an 'ethical and moral view'[87] that suggested a future policy aimed at the advancement of the native as its chief concern and not the development of colonies by European business interests.[88] One policy suggestion in particular from the British Labour Party about the possible extension of the mandate system for territories 'as yet unready for self-government' drew severe criticism from commentators based in East Africa where local knowledge of Tanganyika's slow economic progress was blamed on its mandate status.[89] Inherent in this view was that the mandate system and its openness to 'international supervision' made the 'mandatory power more careful of native interests' in comparison to the more traditional Crown Colony model.[90] For Grylls (Kitale, Kenya) and Evans (Nairobi) the mandate had retarded economic development in neighbouring Tanganyika and thus such pronouncements by the Labour Party were not welcomed.[91]

The 'colour bar', another area of concern expressed 'at home', made little impact in the essays submitted.[92] Indeed, considering the high number of submissions from the settler-dominated southern colonies, few engaged with what was a well-publicised 'evil' of the colonial system in South Africa and the Rhodesias. One exception is the essay by Major Fanshawe who voiced strong criticism of the migrant labour system that had emerged to feed the mines of the Rand.[93] Milward-Oliver (Circus Place, London) who had been based in Nyasaland prior to the war, argued that the well-catalogued problems of labour migration out of Nyasaland to the Rhodesias and the Rand were the result of a level of taxation that was impossible for the local population to muster without resorting to work in southern colonies with well-developed extractive industries.[94] He argued that this could only be addressed if adequate local development and subsequent African employment opportunities were developed in the territory.[95] Fanshawe was generally critical of 'native policy' in the region citing for example the 'particularly disgraceful' land segregation policy which saw increased overcrowding and over-cultivation in the native reserves while large areas of land outside went fallow.[96]

For many essayists, education in the African colonies had hitherto failed to deliver a workforce fit for driving economic development forward. Most commentators argued that not enough educational provision was available, and what there was lacked the necessary emphasis on agriculture and craftsmanship.[97] Most bankers believed education was ancillary to development in agriculture, housing, health, and economic prosperity. Some drew a sharp distinction between West and Southern Africa in the standard of education received by Africans. For Rutherford (Northern Rhodesia) education, which had been left almost entirely to missionary schools, resulted in unequal development and produced what Goss (Kisumu, Kenya) described as 'a half-baked clerk with an unhealthy contempt for any form of manual labour'.[98] Dyson (Nairobi) concluded that British educational policy in the region had to be completely reoriented towards vocational skills.[99] In West Africa, education policy was far more advanced and plentiful. However, even there Greenway (Port Harcourt, Nigeria) argued that huge investment was needed and echoed the call for technical education in areas such as woodworking, masonry, and smith work.[100] Existing higher schools, he argued, had sufficient capacity to produce 'the usual professions sought by Africans – law and medicine'.[101]

Conclusion

The essays submitted by bank staff certainly cover a wide range of topics and are an excellent insight into the colonial mentalities and conditions of the time. As demonstrated, most essayists conceptualised development in somewhat narrow terms, concentrating on local or regional economic activities designed to increase prosperity. This constricted view of 'development' was typical and few writers engaged with wider economic theories. Some did cite the major economists of the time, but did not engage in critical discourse.[102] The majority of essayists saw 'development' in extremely practical banking terms – predominantly in providing short- or medium-term finance for 'sound' commercial ventures that would aid local wealth creation. In this way, the Bank's role would be firmly tied to the commercial sector in the shape of individuals, firms, and companies. Essayists that proposed the Bank enter into longer term finance (in its own right or by the formation of a subsidiary organisation) did envisage a partnership with local government that would see the commercial banks providing finance under government guarantee for road, rail, and other infra-structural improvements, as well as housing, health, and education.[103] Again, this was often with the proviso that the Bank's understanding of local conditions would see it in the best position to direct such investment.

The essays did not always seek to engage with the debates about colonial policy; where they did so the bankers usually exhibited a typically pragmatic attitude. For example, if we consider two of the major strands of the British Labour government's colonial development policy after the war, mass education and the development of co-operatives, the essays strongly evince a pragmatic capitalist attitude: practical vocational education to build a workforce and the improved agricultural organisation and shared responsibility inherent in co-operative farming. Indeed, the essays are certainly 'of their time' – most essayists believed it would be a long time before Africans were in a position to manage their own affairs and that they would be heavily reliant on European leadership and guidance for many years.

Many of the essays display an agreement on numerous issues and this clarity of purpose enabled the bankers in the colonies to exert an important, if indirect, influence over Head Office where the essays were discussed and judged. The close association between the Bank's management and influential officials like Caine seemed to suggest grounds for a continuing dialogue between government and the banks about colonial development. However, on the part of the Bank's foot soldiers at the African periphery, what emerged was a general mistrust of the imperial and colonial governments to put into practice a long-term project of colonial development without better staff and an appreciation of the requirements of the business community with whom lay the long-term economic well-being of the colonies; as Fanshawe acerbically commented, 'the statement that when the war is over, one or two things will disappear, the Empire or the Colonial Office, is too commonly heard'.[104] While many essayists were keen to highlight the Bank's own interwar conservatism, there was a con-sensus about the need for change and perhaps a desire for more appreciation of what the imperial banks could do for Africa – after all, they did facilitate the very cash economy created by colonialism. The vast amount of government finance required for an effective colonial development scheme would need to be channelled into the periphery by agents with a solid understanding of local conditions and potentialities. For the essayists, the Bank was the logical provider of the necessary business acumen. The majority displayed a steadfast belief that the future prosperity of the colonies lay with private enterprise.

Most essayists envisioned a strong partnership at the African periphery between the Bank and colonial governments, the latter providing overall policy direction and the Bank making its local knowledge, expertise, and capital available under government guarantee. Clearly this failed to transpire in any formal manner after the war and the imperial government established its own Colonial Development Corporation (CDC) in 1947, a move strongly opposed by Goodenough when its creation was discussed.[105] However, it should be noted that Barclays did provide the CDC's first chairman.[106] The Barclays Overseas Development Corporation (BODC), established in 1946 before the imperial government's corporation, operated on more modest lines but did make many loans to colonial governments and helped to provide funding for some of the large colonial development schemes.[107] Furthermore, it operated through the Bank's branch system just as Collins had suggested.

Crucially, it was not only the directors of the Bank who took an interest in the results of the essay competition. As we have seen, Goodenough sat on important advisory committees established to examine post-war colonial development. In December 1943 Sydney Caine, the Permanent Secretary of the Colonial Office requested to see some of the essays received by the Bank.[108] Crossley produced an extensive 'digest' of the main points raised in relation to colonial development, and this was given to Caine.[109] The digest was an organised and detailed report of the main arguments put forward by the essayists. The extensive criticism of the colonial and imperial governments would not have made comfortable reading for some members of the Colonial Office, and it is unsurprising that the Bank's management enjoyed a friendly relationship with a strong reformer like Caine who would have found much evidence in the essays to support his desire for a widespread overhaul in colonial economic planning.

Some of the ideas put forward did clearly materialise in post-war policy. The 'corps' of experts called for by Roche did indeed materialise in the late 1940s as famously described by Low and Lonsdale as the 'second colonial occupation'.[110] In 1946, the Colonial Office did create an 'economic section' to examine the needs of colonial business.[111] On some issues the bankers display a consensus with political critics of colonial policy on both sides of the political divide.[112] Both obviously acknowledged the poor place colonial development was in by the start of the war and that the traditional system of financing within the confines of a colony's balance sheet could no longer continue and much more state funding on the lines of the Colonial Development and Welfare Act was required. However, the left's preoccupation with welfare in Africa was not always echoed by the bankers who believed that robust economic growth had to come first. Of course, neither the Bank nor the imperial government could have predicted Britain's post-war economic crisis and the ensuing rise in the importance of colonial development as a means of safeguarding the country's economic interests. During the war, both saw future African development as a necessarily slow process, both economically and politically, but time was running out.

Notes

1 I am indebted to my fellow presenters at the International Workshop 'Developing Africa: Development Discourse(s) in Late Colonialism' at the University of Vienna in January 2011 for their comments and questions that helped me refine this chapter. Thanks also to Maria Sienkiewicz, Nicholas Webb, Kate Raine, and Andrea Waterhouse at Barclays Group Archive, Wythenshawe, Manchester.
2 Henceforth DCO.
3 For an account of the growth of banking practices in East and Central Africa, see Ernst-Josef Pauw, 'Banking in East Africa', in Peter von Marlin (ed.), *Financial Aspects of Development in East Africa* (Munich: Weltforum 1970), pp. 180–225.
4 Julian Crossley and John Blandford, *The DCO Story* (London: Barclays Bank International 1975), p. 2.
5 Ibid., pp. 3–4.
6 Nicholas J. White, *Business, Government, and the End of Empire: Malaya 1942–1957* (Kuala Lumpur, Oxford: Oxford University Press 1996), p. 6. With the loss of the Far Eastern colonies in 1942, the government urged an increase in the development of African resources. See for example British National Archives, London (hereafter BNA), CAB 95/10, A2 (42) 4, 'Policy regarding industrial production in Africa', Colonial Office memo for the War Cabinet, 16 September 1942.
7 Barclays Group Archives, Manchester (hereafter BGA), Barclays Bank (DCO) (hereafter BB/DCO), Julian Crossley, Unpublished diaries, 16 August 1943. Goodenough was already a member of the Colonial Research Council at this time.
8 Caine was put in charge of colonial development planning in April 1943; see Joseph Morgan Hodge, *Triumph of the Expert: Agrarian Doctrines of Development and the Legacies of British Colonialism* (Athens, OH: Ohio University Press 2007), pp. 199–200.
9 BGA BB/DCO, Head Office Circular Letter No. 42/33, 23 September 1942.
10 Ibid.
11 BGA BB/DCO, G. Money (Nairobi), 'The Bank in relation to post-war colonial development', 15 April 1943, p. 17. All essays shared the same title; all are held in the Barclays Group Archives, Manchester (BGA BB/DCO): henceforth only the author and date will be cited.
12 R. G. Dyson (Local Head Office, Nairobi), 12 May 1943, p. 3.
13 P. A. Barnard (Pietersburg, Transvaal), 4 May 1943, p. 2
14 BGA BB/DCO, Leslie Borer, 'History of Barclays Bank DCO 1945–1965' (unpublished manuscript, 1966), pp. 403–4.
15 For example, see essays by G. A. Rutherford (Mufilira, Northern Rhodesia), 26 July 1943, p. 1; B. Macdona (Nairobi, Kenya), April 1943, p. 1; Major G. B. Fanshawe (East Africa Command, Northern Rhodesia), 15 June 1943, p. 4; Barnard (Pietersburg, Transvaal), p. 6; E. V. Whitcombe (Nairobi), 31 May 1943, p. 1.
16 Dyson, pp. 18–19.
17 Ibid. Dyson was making this point because there had been much criticism of banking practice not responding to local conditions, especially related to not supporting agriculturalists through bad harvest years and foreclosing on bank loans.
18 R. Trebble (Jeppestown, Transvaal, South Africa), 7 April 1943, p. 2.

19 D. W. Stokes (Nairobi), 3 April 1943, p. 14.
20 Dyson, p. 7.
21 R. A. Harrison (DCO Gracechurch Street, London), 21 May 1943, p. 6. Like many essayists, Harrison pre-empted the government's post-war commitment to state-sponsored colonial development. He suggested that state-owned colonial industries (such as the coal mines in Nigeria) could assist in stimulating private enterprise in other forms of industry. He suggested that the Bank could offer such industries favourable rates.
22 Barclays supported the establishment of the Cyprus Central Co-operative Bank in 1938 by supplying 45 per cent of the start-up capital, therefore carving a niche in the Cypriot market. Barclays' share of banking business in Cyprus subsequently grew from 4.7 per cent in 1939 to over 13 per cent by 1946; Kate Phylaktis, 'Banking in a British Colony: Cyprus 1878–1959', Business History 30, 4 (1988), pp. 422, 425.
23 Fanshawe, p. 5.
24 J. E. A. Evans (Nairobi), 6 July 1943, p. 10; G. G. Collins (Swakopmund, South West Africa), 8 April 1943, pp. 6–7. Collins's suggested name for such an organisation was included in a digest of the essays given to the Colonial Office in August 1943. This perhaps bore fruit in the creation of the government's Colonial Development Corporation in 1947.
25 Collins, pp. 8–9.
26 C. H. H. Roche (DCO Headquarters, London), 7 July 1943, p. 4; Money, p. 2.
27 Macdona, p. 7.
28 Evans, p. 7.
29 L. H. Mamour (Assiut, Egypt), 17 April 1943, p. 21.
30 BGA BB/DCO, Julian Crossley, 'Banking, Currency and Finance', Part 5 of the Essay Competition Digest for Colonial Office, unnumbered, August 1943.
31 Dyson, p. 7.
32 Ibid.
33 Money, pp. 8–10.
34 Dyson, p. 6.
35 P. G. Grylls (Kitale, Kenya), April 1943, p. 7.
36 Evans, p. 8.
37 P. T. Miller (Victoria, Cameroons), 22 May 1943, p. 5.
38 Rutherford, p. 9.
39 D. R. Greenway (Port Harcourt, Nigeria), 29 May 1943, p. 9.
40 E. V. Goss (Kisumu, Kenya), 1 May 1943, p. 20.
41 Goss, p. 20.
42 J. F. Page (Nairobi), 27 July 1943, p. 11.
43 Evans, p. 3; Macdona, p. 18.
44 Page, p. 9.
45 David Meredith, 'State Controlled Marketing and Economic "Development": The Case of West African Produce after the Second World War', Economic History Review 39, 1 (1986), p. 80.
46 Dyson, p. 3.
47 Goss, p. 11.
48 Ibid., p. 19.
49 See for example Barnard, p. 12.
50 J. Bradbury (Gatooma, Southern Rhodesia), 26 July 1943, p. 1.
51 Miller, pp. 12–13; W. A. Peters (Accra, Gold Coast), 31 May 1943, p. 1.
52 Whitcombe, p. 5.
53 Evans, p. 8.
54 K. M. Wilkinson (Alexandria), 3 April 1943, p. 7.
55 Whitcombe, p. 9. A number of essayists wanted to see the growth of the Bank's marketing operations. This again brought the Bank's network and expertise into play as it was regarded as the best clearing house for intelligence about the supply and demand of commodities. See E. Silverthorne (Windhoek, South West Africa), 9 March 1943, p. 4.

56 Whitcombe, pp. 9–10.
57 Goss, p. 21.
58 It is unfortunate that no essay submission came from Tanganyika, where African coffee growers' co-operatives had emerged during the interwar period.
59 Goss, p. 2.
60 Peters, p. 3.
61 Fanshawe, pp. 11–12.
62 Dyson, p. 6.
63 Dyson and Macdona both make this point in their essays.
64 Rutherford, p. 10.
65 S. O. Soyode (Ibadan, Nigeria), 3 March 1943, p. 2.
66 Peters p. 3; Goss, p. 17.
67 Money, p. 13.
68 Rutherford, p. 10. This essayist noted that Standard Bank, the only other bank in Mufilira, would not open accounts for Africans who could not write their names.
69 Macdona, p. 16.
70 See BGA BB/DCO, Borer, 'History of Barclays Bank DCO', pp. 113–14. In 1947 and 1948 the Bank employed a film maker to produce a 'documentary style' short educational film to encourage African people to open bank accounts; see BGA BB/ DCO, Julian Crossley, Unpublished diaries, 11 May 1948.
71 Evans, p. 5.
72 Goss, p. 9.
73 Money, p. 1.
74 Fanshawe, p. 10. The issue of suitability of colonial staff to undertake economic planning has been taken up by several authors. See for example Barbu Niculescu, *Colonial Planning: A Comparative Study* (London: Allen and Unwin 1958), pp. 37–40.
75 Fanshawe, pp. 2–3.
76 Rutherford, p. 7.
77 Fanshawe, p. 1.
78 Roche, p. 4.
79 See for example Macdona, p. 14, and Evans, p. 5.
80 Stokes, p. 15.
81 Macdona, p. 3.
82 Caine was placed in charge of colonial development policy in April 1943. He headed the 'Economic Section' of the Colonial Office, a position that saw him sometimes come into conflict with the newly created 'Social Services' section. See Martin Petter, 'Sir Sydney Caine and the Colonial Office in the Second World War: A Career in the Making', *Canadian Journal of History* 16, 1 (1981), pp. 73–5.
83 BNA CO 852/588/2, Caine to George Gater, 12 August 1943, p. 166.
84 W. Arthur Lewis, cited in Michael Ashley Havinden and David Meredith, *Colonialism and Development: Britain and Its Tropical Colonies, 1950–1960* (London, New York: Routledge 1993), pp. 216–17. See also BNA T 160/111.
85 Caine to George Gater, 12 August 1943, p. 167.
86 Stokes, p. 9.
87 For example see Silverthorne, p. 1, and Goss, p. 22.
88 Grylls, p. 4.
89 See *A Declaration of Policy by the National Executive of the British Labour Party*, 9 February 1940 (London: Labour Party 1940). This extensive statement of future Labour Party policy was heavily influenced by Fabian thought.
90 See Labour History Archive and Study Centre, Manchester, Labour Party International Sub-Committee, 'Memorandum Formulating Policy for African Colonies and Those in a Similar Stage of Development for the Labour Party After the War', March 1942.
91 Grylls, p. 3.
92 Opposition to 'colour bar' practices in Central and Southern Africa was expressed across the political divide at this time. See for example the House of Commons

Debate 'Northern Rhodesia (African Mineworkers)', 12 March 1941, *Hansard*, vol. 369, cols 1,259–60.

93 Fanshawe, p. 2.
94 The same point was made by the British Labour Party in its declaration of February 1940.
95 C. Milward-Oliver (DCO Circus Place, London), 12 May 1943, p. 30.
96 Fanshawe, p. 1.
97 Goss, p. 15.
98 Rutherford, p. 6; Goss, p. 4.
99 Dyson, p. 7.
100 Greenway, pp. 11–12.
101 Ibid., p. 12.
102 For example, Grylls used a recent statement by Keynes that argued Britain's exports needed to double after the war to question whether HM Government would want to continue its wartime encouragement of secondary industries; Grylls, p. 10.
103 Wilkinson (Alexandria), pp. 2–3.
104 Fanshawe, p. 4.
105 By this time Goodenough sat on the Colonial Economic Advisory Council, the successor to the earlier CEAC. BGA BB/DCO, Julian Crossley, Unpublished diaries, 13 February 1946.
106 BGA BB/DCO, Borer, 'History of Barclays Bank DCO', p. 102.
107 BODC's largest advance was to the Northern Rhodesian Government to help finance the construction of the Kariba Dam.
108 BGA BB/DCO, Julian Crossley, Unpublished diaries, 22 December 1943.
109 BGA BB/DCO, 'Essay Competition Digest – August 1943'. The digest was a very large and detailed document running to over 30,000 words.
110 D. A. Low and John M. Lonsdale, 'Introduction: Towards the New Order 1945–1963', in D. A. Low and Alison Smith (eds), *History of East Africa*, vol. 3 (Oxford: Clarendon Press 1976), p. 12.
111 BGA BB/DCO, Julian Crossley, Unpublished diaries, 12 January 1946.
112 As Lee has demonstrated, this was a period of consensus politics with regard to colonial development; see J. M. Lee, *Colonial Development and Good Government: A Study of the Ideas Expressed by the British Official Classes in Planning Decolonization, 1939–1964* (Oxford: Clarendon Press 1967), p. 15.

CHAPTER FIVE

Ecological concepts of development? The case of colonial Zambia

Sven Speek

The 'greening' of development seems to represent a comparatively recent phase in development thought. Labels like eco-, environmentally sensitive, green, or sustainable development promise an alternative to conventional concepts of development through the integration of ecological principles.[1] A historical analysis of the idea of development, on the other hand, suggests that the contradiction between exploitation and preservation, or, more generally, between progress and order, lies at the core of the modern understanding of development.[2] Environmental historians and historians of science, when tracing the roots of our environmental ideas, have in fact found many continuances between colonial and late-modern concepts of sustainable resource use and several authors have proposed to speak of a 'green' colonialism[3] or have identified an imperial 'legacy of eco-development'.[4] This research adds an important dimension to the already rich literature on the environmental politics of empire.[5] Surprisingly, the science of ecology itself has not been a major focus in these discussions so far, even though recent work suggests that Europe's Ecological Imperialism might well have had a scholarly counterpart in an Imperial Ecology.[6]

Speaking of an 'Imperial Ecology' at all, and on a very basic level, implies that some ecologists were comparatively successful in advertising the use that their science might add to the management of the empire and in attracting colonial funds for ecological research. In other words, they were able to bond with the empire. This was a possibility dependent on existing patronage networks with strong links to the empire, provided, for example, through the Royal Botanic Gardens at Kew, on the establishment of new colonial institutes and advisory boards with an interest in scientific research, and on the integration of scientists as specialist officers into the technical departments of the colonies, who could act as middlemen between science and administration and contributed field data.[7] What I will try to offer here is a single case study of how ecology came to be recognised as a science that could facilitate the development of the empire, how ecological research influenced debates about the meaning of develop-ment, and to what extent colonial research agendas were themselves challenged or transformed by shifts in colonial policy.

The focus of this chapter is plant ecological and agro-ecological research in colonial Zambia (Northern Rhodesia), covering a time span ranging from the Great Depression to the immediate post-war years. Colonial ecological research in Northern Rhodesia contributed to and was structured by a discursive field dominated by the narrative of an impending social and ecological breakdown of 'native subsistence communities' triggered by the impact of colonialism: the unintended consequences of *Pax Britannica*, the introduction of a capitalist eco-nomy, and the creation of reserves. Ecology held the promise not only of helping to come to grips with these complexities, but of serving as a science of planning, opening up the possibility of successfully steering a course between the Scylla of social and ecological breakdown and the Charybdis of stagnation and low productivity.[8] Northern Rhodesia – during the interwar period still a backwater to the empire – consequently became one of the hot spots for the testing out of ecological research methods. Among the ecologically minded scientists visiting the country was Ray Bourne of the Imperial Forestry Institute, Oxford, who conducted a forestry survey in 1927 and tried to assess the usefulness of aerial surveys for ecological mapping.[9] In 1930 and 1931 respectively, Edgar Milne-Redhead, a botanist in the service of the Royal Botanic Gardens, Kew, and Capt. C. R. Robbins, ecological manager of the Aircraft Operating Company Ltd, further elaborated aerial survey methods.[10] A survey party from Oxford University, includ-ing the soil scientists C. G. T. Morison and the botanist A. C. Hoyle, conducted a small ecological survey in 1947 with a view to testing out the extent to which concepts recently developed in soil science were applicable to ecology.[11] Finally, a major ecological and agricultural survey of the whole territory was inaugurated in 1932 by Robert Adamson of Cape Town University and led by Colin Trapnell, formerly of Oxford University, which lasted until 1943.[12]

Plant ecology as a science of empire

Libby Robin has proposed seeing ecology as a science of 'settling' as opposed to sciences of 'exploration' like astronomy or natural history.[13] While ecologists were not primarily concerned with crops of cultiva-tion, ecological research was expected not only to contribute to the management of exploitable 'semi-natural' vegetation like woodlands and pastures, but to provide general insights into the economic potential and the best uses that a given area of land might be put to. This promise carried a strong appeal for a colonial economy that failed to comprehend the dynamics of a foreign environment which defied common expectations of tropical abundance and limitless fertility and showed a marked resistance to Europe's 'Ecological Imperialism'.[14] Seemingly unpredictable weather conditions, soils that were difficult to manage, a high incidence of crop diseases, rapid weed growth on manured fields, tsetse belts acting as barriers to livestock farming, and intricate phenomena like 'veldt poisoning' all provided checks to Europe's exploitation of Africa and spawned concern for a more rational and conservative use of colonial resources. The difficulty of establishing European agriculture was an open invitation to sciences that promised to explain these failures and to help reconcile experience and expectation.

Background: the Agricultural Department in the 1920s, settlers, and Africans

Official interest in ecological research in Northern Rhodesia emerged with the difficulties experienced by the small settler community in establishing agriculture. Local farmers had achieved some success in growing cotton and maize, but yields were far from secure. Following a difficult but promising growing season 1923–24, many farmers had planted large acreages to cotton in the hope of high yields should conditions improve. But both the 1924–25 and the 1925–26 crops turned out to be a failure and many were plunged into financial difficulties. Within the newly established Department of Agriculture serious concern was raised as to the gambling attitude of the European community, and the need to stabilise agriculture and to set it on a scientific basis was emphasised.[15] A first step towards this goal was taken by establishing a combined agricultural and veterinary research station at Mazabuka in 1927 to which Thomas McEwen was appointed Senior Research Officer. In a paper prepared for the first Imperial Agricultural Conference, he outlined Northern Rhodesia's future agricultural research programme. McEwen detailed the many problems that had followed the introduction of exotic cash crops without having reliable scientific data available. Northern Rhodesia presented the bad example of a country where 'occasions have not been lacking when there have been stampedes from one crop to another in periods of depression with disastrous results to the farming community'.[16] McEwen identified the complete lack of knowledge of the country's plant ecology as one of the most pressing problems. He proposed that first of all a botanical survey ought to be undertaken that would map out the territory into natural areas, 'in each of which the relation of vegetation to environment' would be recorded. These detailed insights were to serve as a guide to the country's agricultural potential, making it possible 'to replace by a method of precision the system, if system it can be called, whereby any advisory work undertaken has perforce had to be based on mere impressions of conditions in other places and fancied resemblances'.[17] The research proposal, supplemented by observations of the Secretary of Agriculture, John Smith, on the usefulness of ecological research in livestock management, was submitted to the Empire Marketing Board (EMB) in September 1927.

While Smith wrote up the final memorandum, McEwen toured the country in company with Ray Bourne, an ecologist in the service of the Imperial Forestry Institute. Bourne had been invited to advise the government on its future forest policy, but commented rather broadly on Northern Rhodesia's development strategy. With almost the whole country still 'undeveloped' and covered by forest, one of the main challenges seemed to be to find a scientific strategy for disafforestation. Bourne carefully scrutinised Northern Rhodesia's past development and discussed implications for the future.[18] He criticised the haphazard settlement of inexperienced Europeans on marginal land, warning that 'the extension of white settlement . . . on the existing lines could hardly fail to precipitate a crisis which might set back the country for a generation or more'. To transform a 'gambler's economy' into one dominated by minimised risks, settlement would have to be restricted to select sites based on a careful prior survey of vegetation and soil.[19] While Bourne has been characterised in the literature as an accomplice of colonialism,[20] he actively discouraged extensive European settlement. In fact he saw 'scope for European colonisation as strictly limited' and insisted that 'general development' would have to 'be effected through the native'.[21]

Bourne touched upon politically delicate topics. His emphasis on Africans as agents in the development of the colonial estate to some extent ignored the political situation on the ground and was not immediately followed up by the Agricultural Department. John Smith, Secretary of Agriculture, had depicted African agriculture as a rather neglected affair, the main emphasis being on subsistence production. While he had charged Unwin Moffat, a District Agricultural Research Officer, with the responsibility of studying African agriculture, he was keen to emphasise that there was no intention of increasing competition for European farmers, but rather to teach sound cultivation based on existing subsistence crops.[22] European agriculture was still to be the major focus and the ecological survey was not expected to delve too deeply into African agriculture, but rather to contribute to the solution of practical problems facing the extension of the European agricultural and livestock industry. That Bourne's analysis was nevertheless taken seriously can be gauged from the commitment of the Governor that no settlement schemes for European farmers would be planned until the survey's findings were made available.[23]

While Bourne and McEwen were convinced of the great contribution that an ecological survey could make to Northern Rhodesia's development, metropolitan decision makers were less so. Smith's memorandum had been forwarded by the Governor with a brief remark that the survey had 'the special purpose of assisting in the development of the cattle industry as regards both dairying and beef production'.[24] This left the grant committee of the EMB decidedly unimpressed and the scheme was rejected for having only local significance and not being relevant to export markets. That the scheme was not dropped altogether was probably due to H. C. Sampson, Kew's economic botanist, who was a member of the grant committee. Sampson observed the divergence between McEwen's original research draft and the narrow focus of discussions on livestock farming and it was agreed that the dispatch would be referred to the Royal Botanic Gardens for further observations.[25] At Kew it received immediate support from the Assistant Director, Thomas Ford Chipp, formerly Conservator of Forests, Gold Coast colony. Chipp and the British doyen of ecology, Arthur Tansley, had just edited *Aims and Methods in the Study of Vegetation* (1926): a botanical handbook published by the British Empire Vegetation Committee for use in the colonies, detailing the advantages that ecological work might have in bolstering scientific management of colonial resources.[26] Chipp, who took a strong personal interest in the survey, pointed out that it could serve as an ideal guide 'on which to base all future development of the country'.[27] It was decided that Sampson would redraft the research proposal, fitting it to the EMB's expectations.[28] Sampson detailed the use that an ecological survey might have in studying the prospects of several export crops. Addressing Northern Rhodesia's marginality to the empire, he highlighted that this was probably the first time that a botanical survey had been proposed 'before it was too late to avert the damage which has been caused by both promiscuous and by extensive settlement or by the development of a new phase of native agriculture'.[29] Northern Rhodesia, representing a young colony where comparatively little development had taken place so far, could be seen as an ideal test case for ecological work, with presumably much wider implications for neighbouring territories.[30] The scheme enlisted the support of Frank Stockdale, the Colonial Office's newly appointed Agricultural Adviser, but the finance division of the EMB remained adamantly opposed. It was instead decided that the newly established Colonial Development Fund would take part in financing the survey.

The survey scheme, as worked out by Sampson, had planned for two junior officers, an ecologist and an agronomist, doing most of the field work. A senior officer was to inaugurate the survey and to make sure that it would proceed along the right lines. To find a botanist with tropical experience and a broad ecological outlook willing to take the post of ecologist proved difficult leading to a significant delay. Only in 1931 was the young Colin Trapnell, who had been recommended by Arthur Tansley, appointed leading Ecologist.[31] The post of the agronomist had been reserved for Unwin Moffat, a District Agricultural Officer born in Northern Rhodesia who was already studying African agriculture at Abercorn, but he was not interested. On recommendation of the Governor a graduate of the Imperial College of Tropical Agriculture in Trinidad, J. N. Clothier, was appointed who stayed with the survey for the first half of its work. The survey was inaugurated in 1932 by Professor Robert Scott Adamson of Cape Town University.

The dogma of tropical infertility

The understanding of development displayed by Bourne, Chipp, McEwen, and Sampson was one of constructive development, with the main idea being that of guiding the efficient exploitation of colonial resources. The country, especially the land (e.g. the colonial estate), took the position of the grammatical patient of development. It was in the field of handling the unintended consequences of the capitalist exploitation of Africa that ecology promised to be of the greatest benefit by instilling order and rationality to processes best described as a gamble. Or, as Chipp and Tansley put it when advocating ecology as a 'science of empire':

> The time is now fully ripe for a more consciously directed, systematic, and widespread study of the vegetation as such. Much is already being done, but only a fraction of what urgently requires to be done – urgently, because the natural vegetation of the Empire is being destroyed or radically modified at an increasing pace, and we are not only losing for ever the opportunity of acquiring knowledge, but making mistakes which could be avoided by timely investigation.[32]

The indiscriminate exploitation of vegetation and soils by Europeans and Africans alike was identified by many scientists as an imperial concern of paramount importance. The notion of 'tropical abundance' in particular was made responsible for many mistakes in the colonisation of Africa.[33] The appearance of lush tropical vegetation could be highly misleading, while tropical soils were in fact exhausted quickly and hardly suited for permanent cultivation. Such revelations became commonplace in the literature on tropical ecology and soils. This turn towards a dogma of tropical infertility touched immediately upon the question of the legitimacy of colonial development through settlement. Under the formulation of Indirect Rule and the doctrine of 'native paramountcy', the legitimacy of European colonisation had been based on the assumption that ample land was available and that African farmers – due to a lack of capital, skill, or interest – had simply failed to develop their abundant resources. The failure of European settlers and their dependence on state assistance had to some extent already undermined this ideology. In fact, settlers were often caricatured by government officials as 'shifting cultivators' thus placing them on the same level of supposed skill as African cultivators.[34] Interpreting poor and difficult soils as the reason for the frequent shifting of fields and low population densities put Africans and European settlers in a position where they could be seen as competitors for land. Where land was a scarce resource, settlement implied more trouble than gain. This critical perspective was reiterated by the ecological survey. Judging from the stunted vegetation and the prevalence of 'shifting agriculture', the survey depicted most of the territory as inherently infertile and the proposition of further investigation into the prospects for European settlement was rejected as 'neither practicable nor necessary'. No extended areas of fertile land suitable for European settlement were available.[35] However, with the establishment of economic and agricultural survey commissions in 1931 and 1932 respectively, the Governor, John Maxwell, began to waver on his commitment to base European settlement solely on the findings of the ecological survey. Northern Rhodesia thus still awaited a decision on how to proceed with vast areas of unallocated Crown land.[36] Realising that this was a delicate question, the ecologist Ray Bourne had already advised the government to take care to 'publicly recognise that the area not included in native reserves is not thereby reserved for European settlement'.[37] His main concern had been that the Northern Rhodesian Reserve Commission had been too optimistic in calculating maximum population densities for reserves. Maxwell's successor Hubert Young picked the question up in the mid-1930s and tried to convince the Colonial Office to declare all land which had been identified as unsuited for permanent European settlement as designated native trust land. However, Young also wanted to leave several loop-holes open, so that pockets of land identified by the ecological survey or by a geological survey as suitable for either cash cropping or mineral development, might be reserved for European settlers. Young's interpretation of the doctrine of native paramountcy as being 'the right one . . . in [tracts] in which Europeans will never be able to settle down' did little to impress the Colonial Office, where concern was expressed that a policy of reserving the few pockets of good, fertile land suitable for intensive development for European settlers while leaving the infertile rest for the African was politically untenable.[38] One officer doubted that the interests of settlers and Africans could really be made compatible and questioned whether European settlers were required for the development of the empire.[39] To some extent then, the ecological survey had implicitly undermined its own purpose as serving as a guide for the economic development of Northern Rhodesia.

Settlers and politicians affiliated with settler interests were keenly aware of the grave implications that a paradigm of tropical infertility carried for the position of settlers as legitimate developers of the colonial estate. Speaking in parliament on the Colonial Development and Welfare Bill, Lord Bledisloe, who had just headed a Royal Commission to Northern Rhodesia to advise on the possible amalgamation of Northern Rhodesia with Southern Rhodesia and Nyasaland, felt inclined to explicitly warn the Secretary of State that absolute care should be given, that no money 'is wasted on so-called ecological research'. What had caught his attention was the small sum of £3,070 contemplated for an ecological survey in colonial Basutoland. It was his experience in Northern Rhodesia which had made him a strong critic of ecology: 'We found in Northern Rhodesia that these ecological surveys may result in wholly misleading deductions, tending to inhibit or to restrict development'. Bledisloe accused Trapnell of dogmatism, arguing that a specialised botanist could in no way be expected to give a reliable judgement as to the suitability of the territory for European settlement and should abstain from such speculations.[40] These questions remained a cause for friction. When, after the war, a Land Commission – which was seen by local settlers as strictly biased towards African interests[41] – was set up to decide on the future allocation of Crown land, the ecological survey was again identified as the starting point for the miseries the European settlers found themselves in.[42]

Restoring the balance: ecology and remedial development

The ecological survey itself had turned its interest away from a study of European settlement towards a study of African agriculture. That the investigation of African agriculture would form an important part of the survey was a point on which there had been little disagreement from the start, at least among the outside experts commenting on the scheme. Ray Bourne had already emphasised 'the need for a comprehensive study of native methods of agriculture', from which he hoped that 'not only would much light be thrown on the soil conditions, but a basis would also be established for future technical education'.[43] While the Agricultural Department had so far focused on European farming, 'now the moment appears to have arrived for an investigation of native methods'.[44] Bourne's interest in African agriculture can be explained from different perspectives. Part of it doubtlessly reflects local opinion gathered from officers on the spot.[45] But there were several links through which African agriculture mattered to the study of ecology: first as an impact, second as an indicator. Bourne considered Northern Rhodesia's forests not as pristine, but as shaped by centuries of human intervention. This implied that when studying the correlation between climate, soils, and vegetation biotic factors like cultivation had to be assessed. His second interest stemmed from the observation that African farmers obviously 'took recognition of their environment' and had evolved agricultural practices 'peculiarly suited to local conditions'. From studying these, as Bourne argued, 'it would be surprising, indeed, if the white man learnt nothing'.[46] African farmers thus presented both a problem and a chance. While their cultivation methods tended 'to obscure the issue' by disturbing vegetation and soils and making ecological interpretations more difficult, their 'partiality ... for certain types of soils may even facilitate the identification of others'.[47] A close study of local agriculture was the only possible answer to these problems.

This perspective was shared by other ecologists commenting on the scheme. Kew's economic botanist Sampson observed that the agricultural side of the survey 'would largely consist of enquiry into indigenous agricultural practice such as crops, varieties, soils, seasons and their association one with the other and with the natural vegetation'.[48] Upon inauguration of the survey the South African ecologist Robert Adamson again recommended that 'a detailed study of the native agriculture and its relationship to soil and other factors should prove of considerable interest and importance both in estimating the possibilities of the land and in improvements for the natives'.[49]

The Agricultural Department had started to develop an interest in African agriculture by the mid- to late 1920s. John Smith (Secretary of Agriculture, 1924–32) had outlined the basic policy, arguing that 'it would be unwise to endeavour to change the general principles of native agriculture too suddenly'. While 'many of their methods may be, and are, extremely wasteful . . . some of them are founded upon ideas which are not unsound and all of them are, at present, established as a part of native tradition'. Development on this line came down to an 'investigation of these methods with a view to the gradual elimination of those portions which are inimical to sound agriculture, and the substitution of others which will be of advantage'.[50] The research agenda had the strong support of Smith's successor Claude J. Lewin (Director of Agriculture, 1933–45), formerly Senior Botanist in the non-settler colony of Nigeria. Lewin was probably the key figure in steering the Agricultural Department towards African agriculture. Reflecting on the future of the department shortly after his appointment, he considered that from the standpoint of a European farmer the whole department might be considered an unnecessary luxury. It was African agriculture which was in strongest need of its services:

> At least one-half of the native population is ill-fed and the formation of native reserves has imposed artificial conditions which must eventually lead to radical changes in the traditional agricultural systems, changes which need expert guidance if they are to be accomplished without misery and want.[51]

'Eventually' was the key word. Lewin did not envisage these changes taking place suddenly, but clung to the conservative, research based approach to extension work pioneered by Odin Faulkner and James Mackie in Nigeria:

> No attempt should be made to induce changes in systems of native agriculture until the soundness of the 'improvement' is abundantly proved *under the conditions in which the native farmer himself works*. The present facilities for extension work among natives are very limited and the financial situation is unlikely to permit of any expansion in the immediate future. Progress will therefore be slow until the number of agricultural stations in native areas can be increased, for it is better to attempt nothing than to institute extension work which cannot be supervised and which is based on theory rather than practice.[52]

It was within this framework that the survey's ecologist, Colin Trapnell, developed his idea of applying ecology to the development of African agriculture. The ecological survey was premised on the basic idea that vegetation could be used as an indicator to soil fertility.[53] This promised to be a rapid way to map out the country's productivity by correlating vegetation types with soil types. The link to African agriculture was provided through the reliance that local farmers placed on indicator species in delineating potential sites for gardens. Trapnell attached considerable importance to this observation which seemed to present a shared premise among ecologists and local farmers, making ecology directly applicable to agriculture:

In Northern Rhodesia, if not in other East African territories, the soil is the factor of primary importance in determining vegetation types, these in turn guide the native's land selection and upon his land selection is based the form of his agricultural tradition. For the understanding of that tradition the accomplishment of progress in it or the remedying of departure from it is necessary to look at the soil, and to look at it in the manner of the native, namely through the indications given by the vegetation.[54]

Trapnell and Clothier described the farmer's knowledge as 'intuitive ecology'; an adaptation of agricultural tradition to the surrounding environment. Hierarchies of development were introduced through the social evolutionist notion of 'consciousness' where the 'relative development' of these land-selection systems could vary from instinctive observation to consciously used land selection codes that had become part of a 'tribal tradition'.[55] With agricultural 'tradition reflect[ing] past environment', ecology braced itself as a meta-science without which any attempt to comprehend African production systems was of necessity futile.[56] Where the relationship of man to nature was in equilibrium, ecological research would reveal what was implicit in African land-use practices. But adaptation also implied a close dependence 'on the nature of the country to an extent which it is hard to overestimate', affecting not merely agriculture, but also the 'general development of the tribes': 'poor country and backward people go together'.[57] The idea that African communities developed in accordance with their environment strongly resembled models used in plant ecology. Development's use in ecology was based on the assumption that plant communities behaved similarly to individual organisms and were thus undergoing development in a similar vein, forming more complex, more mature communities until finally reaching a 'fully developed' or 'climax' state. While development described the progressive change of plant communities, the more general term plant succession described both progressive and retrogressive changes. Actual attainment and nature of the climax were determined by the natural environment and by biotic factors like fire or cultivation that could disturb plant succession.[58] The study of ecology then, as defined by Arthur Tansley, aimed 'at the understanding of the conditions which determine the appearance and maintenance of different types of vegetation (plant communities) in different places, and of the laws which govern their development and change under the various influences to which they are exposed'.[59] In the same vein, Trapnell argued, could African agricultural systems be studied, progressive and retro-gressive changes assessed, and remedies be found.

Based on these observations the survey identified three concepts of agricultural development: (1) the introduction of suitable cash crops into existing production systems to provide for an income which was, in part, to serve the stabilisation of village economies which were regarded as suffering from a labour shortage due to the migration of young males to the towns; (2) a local need for remedial measures where African agricultural practices had been adversely affected by contact with Europeans or by concentration of villages in reserves; (3) agricultural development among 'backward tribes', who were – due to 'inferior mentality and lack of initiative, a low standard of living, lack of contact with other tribes, or conservative adherence to an outworn tradition' – not fully adapted to their present environment. Possible improvements were in part to be gauged from a close, eco-logically informed observation of the practices of neighbouring, 'more developed tribes' by which sound improvements could be deduced without having to resort to extensive agricultural experiments. Develop-ment was thus understood to serve the stabilisation of an existing balance of nature while the gradual introduction of ecologically sound improvements and remedies would guide an agricultural evolution 'on native lines'.[60] That the appreciation of African traditional know-ledge could well go hand in hand with strongly paternalistic assump-tions can probably be best gauged from an example drawn from a report on the Gwembe 'famine area' on the Zambezi. As Trapnell and Clothier observed:

> On the Zambezi, adherence to unsuitable land is conditioned by the conservatism of a decrepit headman or the indifference of a slovenly village. The people of the foot-hills, as those of other geographically isolated areas, do not realise the limitations which their country has imposed on them. In either case superstitious grounds of attachment to the site are also to be looked for. A strenuous administration may in course of time remove these obstacles. At the same time a full under-standing of the land question and a study of the gardens will make it possible for the transfer of certain villages to be cautiously encouraged. Reports will be prepared on native land-selection and agricultural prac-tice in Gwembe which will provide a basis for this, and will also indicate agricultural improvements which may have to be considered where, for any reason, transfer cannot be brought about.[61]

A serious threat of degeneration was identified where Africans left their 'natural environment' and migrated to land suitable for Euro-pean farming, thereby entering into competition with the settler community. While in 'his traditional environment he [the African] is infallible in the choice and use of land for his particular purpose', contact with Europeans almost always had 'retrogressive' consequences. People forsake their agricultural traditions and adopted what was at best a 'parody' of European methods.[62] Valuations like these mirror the necessity felt among colonial officers to maintain a divide between Europeans and Africans. This distinction could be expressed through claiming that Africans had a radically different relationship to nature. Europeans progressed through a 'defeat of nature' brought about by the use of fertilisers and mechanisation. African development, by contrast, was characterised by an 'increasingly thorough use of environment'.[63] Similar concerns were raised by ecologists in South Africa, who played an important part in legitimising segregational politics by inscribing Africans into natural habitats quite distinct from those occupied by Europeans, often coupling their arguments with a strong criticism of Western materialism.[64] While ecologists in Northern Rhodesia never dreamt of a comprehensive ecological order of society, these arguments played an important part in the decision to introduce centralised maize marketing which limited the market share of African farmers.[65]

Post-war development and the problem of human ecology

By the late 1930s Northern Rhodesia was seen as moving too slowly in development work and several parliamentary commissions investigating financial and political matters in the colony urged the government to be more ambitious in its efforts. The *Pim Report* in particular emphasised that the reserve policy in Northern Rhodesia had been implemented on the understanding that a comprehensive programme of rural development would follow and that the Northern Rhodesian Agricultural Department had not lived up to the expectations: 'it cannot be said that [the DOA] has made any substantial contribution up to the present to the solution of the problems of native agriculture in the Territory'.[66]

A rough first sketch for a more comprehensive development plan was drawn up in response to the Colonial Development and Welfare Act by the colony's Chief Secretary, Beresford Stooke. Stooke pointed to the problems that the colony would face after the war in absorbing the returning African soldiers, who were used to a much higher standard of living than the villages could offer and made it imperative to bring the 'benefits of civilization' to 'the African'. Stooke defined development broadly as 'all those measures which jointly and severally will have the effect of improving the standards of African life, of improving the conditions under which the African lives, and of enabling him to live a fuller and happier life'.[67] Stooke's definition of development departed in important aspects from the concept of development used in the interwar period. 'The African' now regularly appeared as the grammatical patient of development: 'The standard of life which can be attained by the African depends upon . . . the fullest development of the African himself'; 'It is necessary to teach Africans how to improve their standard of life, how to develop themselves'.[68] While whole 'tribes' had been described by the ecological survey as more or less developed, development here was usually characterised as an evolutionary process: a process which could be guided through the detailed insights offered by ecological analysis. Where development was used as a transitive verb, its patient was almost exclusively the land or a sphere of production like agriculture. This difference is clearly expressed in the ecological report for the year 1934 where 'agricultural development among backward peoples' and 'general progress among backward tribes' is discussed, but never the 'development of backward peoples'.[69] By identifying 'the African' as the patient of development the importance of social and psychological aspects of development was emphasised.

How the ecological approach of the interwar years would fit in with this understanding of development was open to question. In Uganda, the ecologist Edgar B. Worthington aimed at creating 'a new and improved environment' for African farmers through the integrated planning of whole catchment areas.[70] But in Northern Rhodesia detailed ecological investigations of the natural and social environment of African agriculture were still seen as the key to success. Governor John Waddington (1942–47) presented a mash-up of new and old ideas when he argued that the whole problem of development could be framed as one of 'human oecology', of 'the habits and modes of life of individuals in relation to their particular environment'. The main task would be to 'search through simple local investigation for ways and means to raise the mode of life to a level of greater enlightenment and social development'.[71] Balanced progress in all spheres, be it in economy, education, or health, was essential and each unit of population was to be served and studied at the same time by all agencies, otherwise instabilities would be brought about. Ecology – as a kind of meta-approach to development – was thus linked up with a view of how to successfully conduct extension work and with a more general idea about the proper development of societies. The Agricultural Department took this challenge up by forming close bonds with the Rhodes-Livingstone Institute for Social Research, an institution itself firmly committed to the study of change among African societies. In

1945 they conducted a first combined study of the social and natural environment of African agriculture.[72] Colin Trapnell, William Allan and the anthropologist Max Gluckman furthermore proposed to use Colonial Development and Welfare funds to establish a centralised Department of Development Research, which would share facilities with the Rhodes-Livingstone Institute and would focus on socio-ecological surveys and planning. Gluckman even agreed to surrender the Directorship of the Rhodes-Livingstone Institute to the new department.[73]

The Colonial Office, on the other hand, shared Stooke's and Waddington's interest in 'the general uplift of the rural population' and was eager to convince the Northern Rhodesian government to abandon overly conservative strategies of rural development fixated on agriculture and to give more prominence to social welfare and social services. Waddington himself had asked the Colonial Office to supply the territory with an experienced temporary development adviser 'of the Wakefield type',[74] who would help to coordinate development plans across departmental borders. This approach for greater coordination was warmly welcomed in London as marking a step away from Northern Rhodesia's cautious outlook, which had earned them a reputation of being more interested in preserving the privileges of settlers than in developing the reserves.[75] Waddington had planned for a close cooperation between the government ecologist Trapnell and the new development adviser. But his whole idea backfired. At the Colonial Office it was decided that first of all C. J. Lewin, the Director of Agriculture, would have to be dismissed, being emblematic of the conservative approach of the interwar period.[76] In 1945 Geoffrey Clay was appointed Joint-Development Adviser for both Northern Rhodesia and Nyasaland.[77] Clay's appointment signalled a radical break with the Agricultural Department's agenda. In 1932 Lewin had written an editorial for the first studies of African agriculture conducted in Northern Rhodesia, published in the department's *Second Annual Bulletin*. In his editorial he had observed that 'were a history of attempts to improve native agriculture written, it is certain that many passages would substantiate the truth of the proverb concerning the impetuosity of fools and the timidity of angels'.[78] Thirteen years later, Clay took this proverbial wordplay as an invitation to formulate his own vision of development:

> In my view, and I may be accused of subscribing to a policy not favoured by the light-footed and timorous angels, if a healthy rural population is to be developed, fundamental changes in the basic agricultural system will be necessary involving a drastic change from the existing extensive form of agriculture and shifting cultivation, to an intensive form of

agriculture incorporating the wise use of stock and grass leys. In short, I feel that an agricultural revolution is needed, and that the country cannot wait for a gradual process of evolution to effect this change.[79]

Clay envisaged the setting up of several development centres that were to serve as training bases for 1,600 interdisciplinary African rural development teams. This focus on model development zones was intended as an exemplary effort that would show what could be achieved if full use was made of the modern machinery of development. While the Deputy Director of Agriculture, William Allan, admitted that 'more or less radical changes in land usage' were necessary in some restricted problem areas, the department firmly clung to the ideas of the ecological survey. In a territory where the agriculture of neighbouring 'tribes' could differ more widely 'than does the agriculture of Western Europe from that of China', the problem was not one of 'simply teaching the African "good agriculture"'. Allan insisted that 'the problems of African agriculture are indissolubly linked with many others, and they are far too complex to allow of arbitrary answers in simple terms'. Guided evolution, not revolution, was to be aimed at:

> Improvements in traditional usage, based on knowledge of the systems and the adaptations of which they are capable, have been introduced from the beginning. The assumption is that an evolutionary process of agricultural improvement will keep pace with increase of population, and this process must be guided by experiment.[80]

Trapnell and Allan were subsequently transferred to other colonies. With the dismissal of Lewin in 1946 and the retirement of Unwin Moffat in 1951, Northern Rhodesia had lost a complete generation of research officers, each of them with more than fifteen years of service in the department. It was thus in the crucial post-war years, when the course for future development was set, that Northern Rhodesia was almost devoid of a functioning agricultural department. Between 1946 and 1952 the directorship changed almost every year.[81]

Clay's scheme was in many respects typical of the rather short-lived euphoria and patriotism of the immediate post-war years. While some schemes, like the fatal East African Groundnut Scheme, became sinks for millions of pounds, most of them were dissolved in a much less spectacular way. In Northern Rhodesia the settler community, which had gained a stronger hold on territorial politics due to the boom of the Northern Rhodesian copper industry, lobbied successfully against African rural development while the Colonial Office hesitated to commit itself fully to the high expenditures envisaged by Clay. The scheme was curtailed several times and dropped altogether in 1948 when the colony's development aims were redefined as 'more roads, more food, more housing'. A further zoning was introduced, dividing the territory into intensive development areas, development areas, and non-development areas, with a strong bias towards the urban centres of settlement along the railway line, predating Zambia's later policy of 'reinforcement of success'.[82] In the Department of Agriculture itself a technocratic approach based on the separation of laboratory research and field work prevailed.[83]

Conclusion

Ecological development in colonial Zambia was an approach intimately tied to a concern for the preservation and stabilisation of African communities, a concern which became emblematic of the interwar period and the politics of Indirect Rule. While the ecological survey remains exceptional in its breadth and detail, studies into African agriculture proliferated among agronomists and many of them drew on ecological ideas. During the late 1930s, and especially after the Second World War, the political directives changed and concepts of development 'on native lines' lost much of their appeal. This can be attributed to several reasons, not least that development – as Megan Vaughan, Henrietta Moore, and Frederick Cooper, among others, have argued – became a shared (political) discourse between colonisers and certain strata of African societies in which the legitimacy of colonial rule itself was at stake.[84] The colonial governments faced new contradictions as development became an urgent political obligation which could not be left to the goodwill of local administrations. In the interwar years, on the other hand, research had been conducted in a culture of scarcity. Technical departments were poorly staffed, mechanical equipment and artificial fertilisers too expensive, while crop failures alternating with tumbling markets and combined with high transport costs gave little impetus to cash crop production. The popularity of biological concepts like evolution and adaptation in development discourse reflected this constellation: development approaches were expected to stabilise the living conditions of the population, not to disturb them even more. While administrators and scientists alike were aware of radical changes taking place, many of them were doubtful as to where these changes would take them. Sciences like ecology, but also soil science and studies into methods of biological farming, proliferated and challenged the established dogmas of agricultural chemistry. British ecology in particular, with its stronger mechanical orientation and its focus on concepts like the ecosystem, promised a precise managerial approach to these problems. These approaches were not completely lost after the war. Landmark studies like William Allan's *The African Husbandman* (1965) were a direct product of these approaches and agro-ecology was established as an important field of anthropological research. But with the massive inflow of a new generation of young research officers after the war and the parallel setting in of the 'green revolution' these approaches temporarily lost touch with the agricultural establishment until a new emphasis on the 'limits to growth' pushed them back to the centre.

Notes

1 For a discussion of ecological science and its relationship to environmental philosophy see Alan Marshall, *The Unity of Nature: Wholeness and Disintegration in Ecology and Science* (London: Imperial College Press 2002); for standard histories of ecology see Donald Worster, *Nature's Economy: A History of Ecological Ideas* (Cambridge: Cambridge University Press 2007); Jean-Marc Drouin, *L'écologie et son histoire: réinventer la nature* (Paris: Desdée de Brouwer 1991); Pascal Acot, *Histoire de l'écologie* (Paris: Presses universitaires de France, 1988).

2 See Michael Cowen and Robert Shenton, 'The Invention of Development', in Jonathan Crush (ed.), *Power of Development* (London, New York: Routledge 1995), pp. 27–43.

3 Richard H. Grove, *Green Imperialism: Colonial Expansion, Tropical Island Edens and the Origins of Environmentalism, 1600–1860* (Cambridge: Cambridge University Press 1996); Vimbai Kwashirai, *Green Colonialism in Zimbwabe, 1890–1980* (Amherst, NY: Cambria Press 2009).

4 S. Ravi Rajan, *Modernizing Nature: Forestry and Imperial Eco-Development, 1800–1950* (Oxford: Oxford University Press 2006).

5 I will abstain from quoting all of the standard literature on colonialism and environment; for a concise overview see William Beinart and Lotte Hughes, *Environment and Empire* (Oxford: Oxford University Press 2007).

6 Peder Anker, *Imperial Ecology: Environmental Order in the British Empire, 1895–1945* (Cambridge, MA: Harvard University Press 2001); a different perspective, emphasising the liberalising effects of ecology, is offered by Helen Tilley, *Africa as a Living Laboratory: Empire, Development, and the Problem of Scientific Knowledge, 1870–1950* (Chicago: University of Chicago Press 2011), pp. 146–68.

7 This 'Triumph of the Expert' has been traced in detail in Joseph Morgan Hodge, *Triumph of the Expert: Agrarian Doctrines of Development and the Legacies of British Colonialism* (Athens, OH: Ohio University Press 2007). For current debates about the role of science and expertise in colonial Africa see also William Beinart, Karen Brown, and Daniel Gilfoyle, 'Experts and Expertise in Colonial Africa Reconsidered: Science and the Interpenetration of Knowledge', *African Affairs* 108, 432 (2009), pp. 413–33.

8 See William Allan, 'The Resettlement of Native Populations in Northern Rhodesia', in William Allan, *Studies in African Land Usage in Northern Rhodesia* (Cape Town, New York: Oxford University Press 1945), pp. 71–80; for the wider appeal of so-called 'Edenic' narratives see William E. O'Brien, 'The Nature of Shifting Cultivation: Stories of Harmony, Degradation, and Redemption', *Human Ecology* 30, 4 (2002), pp. 483–502; Candace Slater, 'Amazonia as Edenic Narrative', in William Cronon (ed.), *Uncommon Ground: Rethinking the Human Place in Nature* (New York, London: Norton 1996), pp. 114–31.

9 British National Archives, London, Colonial Office Records (hereafter BNA CO), 795/20/9, Ray Bourne, 'The Forests of Northern Rhodesia', 29 November 1927; BNA CO 795/20/10, Ray Bourne, 'Aerial Survey in Relation to the Economic Development of the Empire', 1927, published as Ray Bourne, *Aerial Survey in Relation to the Economic Development of New Countries, with Special Reference to an Investigation*

Carried Out in Northern Rhodesia (Oxford: Clarendon Press 1928). Anker, *Imperial Ecology*, p. 238 has argued that aerial surveys were the most important technology by which ecologists advocated their science. This has been questioned by Chunglin Kwa, 'Painting and Photographing Landscapes: Pictorial Conventions and Gestalts', *Configurations* 16, 1 (2008), p. 64.

10 Royal Botanic Gardens Library, Art and Archives, London (hereafter RBG Kew), 581.501 (10.73), E. Milne-Redhead, 'Report on the Interpretation of Vegetation in Relation to Aerial Survey in Northern Rhodesia', 1931; RBG Kew 2/NR/3/1, 'Captain Robbins' Report', 1933.

11 The history of the survey can be found at BNA CO 927/30/5 and BNA CO 927/130/5.

12 Colin G. Trapnell and J. Neil Clothier, *The Soils, Vegetation, and Agricultural Systems of North-Western Rhodesia: Report of the Ecological Survey* (Lusaka: Government Printer 1937); Colin G. Trapnell, *The Soils, Vegetation, and Agriculture of North-Eastern Rhodesia: Report of the Ecological Survey* (Lusaka: Government Printer 1943); for important discussions of the survey and of agro-ecological research in colonial Zambia in general see Henrietta Moore and Megan Vaughan, *Cutting Down Trees: Gender, Nutrition, and Agricultural Change in the Northern Province of Zambia, 1890–1990* (Portsmouth, NH: Heinemann 1994), pp. 20–45; Tilley, *Africa as a Living Laboratory*, pp. 138–53.

13 Libby Robin, 'Ecology: A Science of Empire?', in Tom Griffiths and Libby Robin (eds), *Ecology and Empire: Environmental History of Settler Societies* (Edinburgh: Keele University Press 1997), pp. 63–4.

14 The term after Alfred W. Crosby, *Ecological Imperialism: The Biological Expansion of Europe, 900–1900* (Cambridge, New York: Cambridge University Press 1986).

15 BNA CO 799/2, Government of Northern Rhodesia, 'Department of Agriculture: Annual Report 1925', 24 August 1926, pp. 4–5.

16 BNA CO 758/53/1, T. McEwen, 'Survey of Agricultural Research Work and Problems of Northern Rhodesia: For the Agricultural Conference', 11 June 1927.

17 Ibid.

18 Bourne, 'The Forests of Northern Rhodesia', p. 31.

19 Ibid.

20 Anker, *Imperial Ecology*, pp. 82–95.

21 Bourne, 'The Forests of Northern Rhodesia', pp. 53–4.

22 Government of Northern Rhodesia, *Department of Agriculture: Annual Report for the Year 1927* (Lusaka: Government Printer 1928), p. 6.

23 BNA CO 795/31/4, J. C. Maxwell to L. S. Amery, 8 April 1929.

24 BNA CO 758/53/1, J. C. Maxwell to L. S. Amery, 12 September 1927.

25 BNA CO 758/53/1, E. M. H. Lloyd to Arthur Hill, 23 December 1927.

26 Anker, *Imperial Ecology*, pp. 35–40.

27 BNA CO 758/53/1, T. F. Chipp to The Secretary, Empire Marketing Board, 3 January 1928; BNA CO 758/53/1, T. F. Chipp (1886–1931) had planned to inaugurate the survey and to supervise the survey party during its first months of work. This was prevented by his death in June 1931.

28 BNA CO 758/53/1, J. C. Maxwell to L. S. Amery, 31 March 1928; BNA CO 758/53/1, A. Hill to S. G. Tallents, 30 June 1928.

29 BNA CO 758/53/1, Vegetation Survey in N. Rhodesia. Memorandum by Mr Sampson, 28 June 1928.

30 BNA CO 758/53/1, E. M. H. Lloyd to J. F. N. Green, 11 January 1928.

31 Trapnell's biography provides an interesting mix: as a co-founder of the Oxford University Exploration Club, having organised its first expedition to Greenland, and with Arthur Tansley as his patron, he exemplified much of what Peder Anker has identified as the North-South axis of early British ecology. But he was actually something of a 'self-made' expert, an amateur naturalist who had read classical greats, not botany. For his biography, see Paul Smith, *Ecological Survey of Zambia: The Traverse Records of C. G. Trapnell, 1932–1943* (Kew: Royal Botanic Gardens 2001).

32 Thomas F. Chipp and Arthur Tansley, *Aims and Methods in the Study of Vegetation* (London: British Empire Vegetation Committee 1926), pp. 2–3.

33 See Helen Tilley, 'African Environments and Environmental Sciences: The African Research Survey, Ecological Paradigms and British Colonial Development, 1920–1940', in William Beinart and JoAnn McGregor (eds), *Social History and African Environments* (Oxford: James Currey 2003), pp. 120–1.

34 See for example Government of Northern Rhodesia, *Department of Agriculture: Annual Report for the Year 1930* (Lusaka: Government Printer 1931), p. 35.

35 Trapnell and Clothier, *The Soils, Vegetation, and Agricultural Systems of North-Western Rhodesia*, p. ix.

36 S. Milligan, *Report on the Present Position of the Agricultural Industry and the Necessity, or Otherwise, of Encouraging Further European Settlement in Agricultural Areas* (Lusaka: Government Printer 1931), pp. 31–2.

37 Bourne, 'The Forests of Northern Rhodesia', p. 55.

38 BNA CO 795/83/6, Hubert Young to John Maffey, 29 April 1936.

39 BNA CO 795/83/6, Note by Trafford Smith, 11 June 1936.

40 House of Lords Debate, 2 July 1940, *Hansard*, vol. 116, cols 743–4.

41 BNA CO 795/130/1, Memorandum for the Farming Development Committee from the Committee of the Midland Farmers' Association: The Land Commission's Report, 2 March 1946; BNA CO 795/130/1, Farming Development Committee to Chief Secretary, 4 March 1946.

42 BNA CO 795/141/5, 'The Grave Limits of Our Settlement', Extract from *Central African Post*, No. 74, 8 September 1949.

43 Bourne, 'The Forests of Northern Rhodesia', p. 55. Bourne even intended to write a separate memorandum on the different agricultural methods followed in Northern Rhodesia, but I am as yet not aware if he ever did so; see BNA CO 795/20/7, R. Bourne to the Undersecretary of State, Colonial Office, 21 December 1927.

44 Bourne, 'The Forests of Northern Rhodesia', p. 39.

45 Ibid., p. 20.

46 Ibid., p. 39. Bourne himself was of the opinion that African cultivators should be employed in forest plantations, where they could combine their 'traditional' methods with modern forest management. This reflects contemporary concern to control 'shifting cultivation' and to capitalise on the labour of African farmers. Among foresters this version of controlled 'shifting cultivation' was known as 'taung-ya' (the Burmese term for 'shifting cultivation'). See ibid., pp. 43–7.

47 Bourne, *Aerial Survey*, p. 24.

48 BNA CO 758/53/1, Vegetation Survey in N. Rhodesia. Memorandum by Mr Sampson, 28 June 1928.

49 RBG Kew PRO 2/NR/4, R. S. Adamson, 'Report on Inauguration of the Ecological Survey', 24 August 1932, p. 21.

50 Government of Northern Rhodesia, *Department of Agriculture: Annual Report for the Year 1928* (Lusaka: Government Printer 1929), p. 5; Northern Rhodesia's Agricultural Department at this point had already inaugurated smaller studies on African agriculture. These were conducted by Unwin Moffat and T. C. Moore. For a discussion see Tilley, *Africa as a Living Laboratory*, pp. 138–44.

51 Government of Northern Rhodesia, *Department of Agriculture: Annual Report for the Year 1932* (Lusaka: Government Printer 1933), p. 3.

52 Ibid., p. 13.

53 Adamson, 'Report on Inauguration of the Ecological Survey', p. 14; for the general background of these ideas see John E. Weaver and Frederic Clements, *Plant Ecology* (New York: McGraw-Hill 1929), pp. 396–420.

54 *Bulletin of Miscellaneous Information (Royal Botanic Gardens, Kew)* 1 (1937); Colin G. Trapnell, 'Ecological Methods in the Study of Native Agriculture in Northern Rhodesia', pp. 9–10; see also RBG Kew PRO 2/N4/4, C. G. Trapnell to A. Hill, 6 November 1932.

55 Government of Northern Rhodesia, *Department of Agriculture: Annual Report for the Year 1932*, p. 23; Trapnell, 'Ecological Methods in the Study of Native Agriculture', p. 6.

56 Ibid., pp. 7, 9–10.

57 Trapnell and Clothier, *The Soils, Vegetation, and Agricultural Systems of North-Western Rhodesia*, p. 24.
58 Arthur Tansley, 'The Classification of Vegetation and the Concept of Development', *Journal of Ecology* 8, 2 (1920), pp. 118–49.
59 Chipp and Tansley, *Aims and Methods*, p. 3.
60 Trapnell, 'Ecological Methods in the Study of Native Agriculture', p. 9; Government of Northern Rhodesia, *Department of Agriculture: Annual Report for the Year 1934* (Lusaka: Government Printer 1935), p. 26.
61 Government of Northern Rhodesia, *Department of Agriculture: Annual Report for the Year 1934*, p. 28.
62 Government of Northern Rhodesia, *Department of Agriculture: Annual Report for the Year 1933* (Lusaka: Government Printer 1934), pp. 23, 26.
63 Trapnell, 'Ecological Methods in the Study of Native Agriculture', p. 8.
64 For the South African 'politics of ecology' see Anker, *Imperial Ecology*, pp. 147–76.
65 Kenneth P. Vickery, 'Saving Settlers: Maize Control in Northern Rhodesia', *Journal of Southern African Studies* 11, 2 (1985), p. 227. Vickery, however, argues that these ecological arguments were merely used to appease the Colonial Office.
66 *Report of the Commission Appointed to Enquire into the Financial and Economic Position of Northern Rhodesia* [the *Pimm Report*] (London: His Majesty's Stationery Office 1938), p. 231.
67 BNA CO 795/125/17, Extract from East Africa and Rhodesia, 9 September 1943: Northern Rhodesia's Plan for Post-War Progress. Text of Memorandum of Instruction by the Chief Secretary, p. 2.
68 Ibid., p. 21.
69 Government of Northern Rhodesia, *Department of Agriculture: Annual Report for the Year 1934*, p. 26.
70 BNA CO 536/218, Extract from Legislative Council Debates, [undated, ca. November 1947]; Edgar B. Worthington, *A Development Plan for Uganda* (Entebbe: Government Printer 1946).
71 BNA CO 795/132/9, J. Waddington to O. Stanley, 18 April 1945.
72 On the RLI see Lyn Schumaker, *Africanizing Anthropology: Fieldwork, Networks, and the Making of Cultural Knowledge in Central Africa* (Durham, NC: Duke University Press 2001). For the cooperation between the DOA and the RLI see the excellent discussion by Andrew Bowman, 'Ecology to Technocracy: Scientists, Survey and Power in the Agricultural Development of Late-Colonial Zambia', *Journal of Southern African Studies* 37, 1 (2011), pp. 135–53.
73 Royal Anthropological Institute, Max Gluckman Papers, Development Plans of Northern Rhodesia. (Gluckman's papers had not been catalogued yet when I last visited the RAI.)
74 BNA CO 795/125/17, Waddington to Stanley, 13 January 1943. Wakefield, a former director of agriculture in Tanganyika, is best known for having devised the notorious East African Groundnut Scheme. See Koponen, this volume, pp. 41–5.
75 BNA CO795/125/17, Minute by Lambert, 1 March 1943.
76 BNA CO 795/123/15, Minute by A. Cohen, Development Machinery in Central Africa, 22 September 1943.
77 Clay, former Director of Agriculture, Uganda, had been occupied with resource planning during the war. After his engagement in Central Africa he became the new Agricultural Adviser to the Secretary of State.
78 Department of Agriculture, *Second Annual Bulletin* (Lusaka: Government Printer 1932), p. 3.
79 Geoffrey F. Clay, *Memorandum on Post-War Planning in Northern Rhodesia* (Lusaka: Government Printer 1945), p. 5.
80 Government of Northern Rhodesia, *Department of Agriculture: Annual Report for the Year 1945* (Lusaka: Government Printer 1946), p. 7.
81 The directors were: C. J. Lewin (1946); W. Allan (1947); E. F. Martin (1948); J. C. Eyre (1949/50); M. Halcrow (1951); C. W. Lynn (1952).

[153]

82 For a discussion of Northern Rhodesia's post-war development strategy see Kusum Datta, 'The Political Economy of Rural Development in Colonial Zambia: The Case of the Ushi-Kabende, 1947–1953', *International Journal of African Historical Studies* 21, 2 (1988), pp. 249–72.
83 See Bowman, *Ecology to Technocracy*, p. 151.
84 Moore and Vaughan, *Cutting Down Trees*, pp. 128–9; Frederick Cooper, *Decolonization and African Society: The Labor Question in French and British Africa* (Cambridge: Cambridge University Press 1996), p. 10.

CHAPTER SIX

Developing rural Africa: rural development discourse in colonial Zimbabwe, 1944–79

E. Kushinga Makombe

In the nine decades of European colonialism in Zimbabwe the theory of rural development passed through many phases – during which different, even opposing points of view assumed orthodoxy. While a simplification, the social psychology of European colonialism was built largely around stereotypes informing perceptions and policies. One such perception was the idea among Europeans that non-European 'native' people or colonial subjects were 'backward', or trapped in tradition. Colonial rule encouraged this idea, as European and non-European cultures were compared within a relationship in which Europe had the powerful military-industrial advantage. This comparison was (mis)interpreted as European cultural superiority or progress. Under these circumstances, the idea of the 'white man's burden' emerged, a concept in which the West viewed itself as a bearer of civilisation to the darker races.[1] This was captured succinctly by an article circulated by the Native Affairs Department (NAD) in 1957 which stated:

> The history of economic development of African agriculture is largely that of Government assistance, organisation and advice to a primitive people whose agriculture was founded on a communal system at a purely subsistence level. The problems of African economic development in the agricultural field are vastly different from those of the European. For the latter with his vastly superior technical skill and experience, the problems are those of adjustment.[2]

The Native Affairs Department and its later mutations following the reorganisation of state departments and ministries in the early 1960s had, over a protracted period of time, made attempts at conceptualising a framework or categorisation that defined their intervention into African rural agrarian practices. By 1979 the 'history of government assistance' had been summarised into the following stages: the Protective Phase 1894–1919, the Technical Development Phase: (a) Progress by Persuasion 1920–42, (b) Progress by Compulsion 1943–62, and the Community Development Phase: (a) Community Extension and Local Government 1963–69, (b) Growth Centres 1969–79. These categorisations however should be viewed more as indicators of differences in stress or purpose rather that as clear cut change from one phase to another.

A whole range of events and processes occurring in and around the Second World War was to force a significant shift in the stress and purpose put around the technical development phase from one of persuasion to compulsion. The immediate post-Second World War era saw the emergence of the modern manufacturing sector. The period also witnessed a boom in the export of primary products on the international market – for example, tobacco, chrome, gold, and asbestos – which earned much needed foreign currency.

Industrial growth greatly increased urban employment opportunities, and cities like Salisbury (now Harare) were expanding rapidly. The number of Africans in wage employment rose from 254,000 in 1936 to 377,000 in 1946 to 600,000 in 1956.[3] Accompanying this was an increase in foreign investment from £13.5 million in 1947 to £50.7 million in 1951.[4] Between 1939 and 1948 factories increased from 294 to 473 with an increase in gross output from £5.4 million to £26.8 million in the same period.[5] Tsuneo Yoshikuni's study of Salisbury reveals that the city experienced a sharp break with its past, at about this time, as it developed socio-economic and cultural links with the broader environs of Mashonaland (Province). After 1945, but more particularly after 1950, large numbers of Shona (indigenous) migrants settled in the town from the nearby reserves such that the city's ecological set-up underwent a profound change. The proportion of Southern Rhodesian Africans rose from 41 per cent in 1951 to 72 per cent in 1962 to 83 per cent in 1969.[6] As Frederick Cooper has put it, 'urbanization, wage labour and commodification had become realities whatever the rhetoric of colonial rule'.[7]

However, conditions in the African demarcated areas were in stark contrast to what was occurring in the urban areas of the country. In the Goromonzi District, for instance, Elizabeth Schmidt illustrates the dramatic decline in peasant production that the passing of the Maize Control Act and the Cattle Levy Act had on the people and the resultant dislocation from the land as Africans sought waged employment in the cities.[8] In response, the colonial government in the 1950s sought to turn other Africans into proletariats so that they could become permanent wage earners. Cabinet ministers supported the move. P. B. Fletcher, then Minister of Native Affairs, remarked that

The Natives must realise that if they want to become great people and to make a contribution to the development of Africa, they must face the fact that as the years go by, a smaller percentage of their people will be . . . in agriculture. Greater and greater numbers must seek a future in industrial development because there is no future for all natives living on the land.[9]

Garfield Todd, the Prime Minister of Southern Rhodesia from 1953 to 1958, echoed this view. He remarked that,

We do not want native peasants. We want the bulk of them working in the mines and farms and the European areas and we could absorb them and their families . . . if 100,000 families moved from the rural area, we can be able to cope with what is left.[10]

Put differently, there was a realisation that the institutional framework of the 1930s had become outmoded as capital penetration undermined the social equilibrium of 'traditional' African society necessitating the control of social and ecological processes in the reserves.

Todd's pronouncement, however, startled other elements within the white community who began to envision being overrun by the growing African settled population. In time, this would develop into a self-fulfilling prophesy as the African urban population more than doubled every decade leading up to the 1970s.[11] Charles Olley, the Mayor of Salisbury from 1943–45 captures such apprehension when he said:

In Salisbury there were about 40,000 natives. If a quarter of them made up their minds that they had wives in the reserves or would buy wives for town life, it was inevitable that eight to ten thousand black piccannins would be born yearly. This would mean that in five years there would be 90,000 natives in Salisbury, of whom 50,000 would be infants [. . .] It will be suicide of the white race in Rhodesia to establish the policy of an employed native having the right to bring his wife into town . . . *It must not be.*[12]

Moreover, the white commercial farmers, to whom the state was beholden because of their economic muscle, were also up in arms as the nascent manufacturing sector was attracting labour away from their employ. However, a more pragmatic and immediate concern had to do with the cost of accommodating such a large number of workers at one time and the attendant cost of administering social services to these people. Hitherto, urban housing policies had favoured the accommodation of single men in hostels or dormitories. Such measures were aimed at turning the urban life of male Africans into a temporary affair and simultaneously reducing the cost of wages by localising social reproduction in the rural areas.[13]

It was therefore as a response to this stark political and planning problematic that Southern Rhodesian 'officials finally began to think in terms of development when considering a remedy for the nexus of poverty and disorder that was striking the parts of the [colony] that were most visibly participating in the imperial economy'.[14] This is precisely what the Chief Native Commissioner in 1946 was alluding to when he remarked, 'To reduce the carrying capacity of many reserves of the present population will make holdings quite uneconomical, so *some solution* will have to be found elsewhere. There is not enough land available for all Natives to be both wage-earners and peasant farmers'.[15]

Towards an alibi for coercive rural development

From a very early stage the settlers had adopted spatial segregation in an attempt to mediate contact between themselves and the indigenous population. This found articulation in the rural-urban divide which had a deep and enduring tension in the imagery of Anglo-Saxon culture. The rural areas were then typecast as the 'proper' and pristine sphere for the non-Europeans and the emergent urban areas were demarcated as European areas and considered the preserve of the white population.

The first reserves for Africans, the arid Gwai and Shangani areas, were designated in 1894. Even the British Deputy Commissioner, Sir Richard Martin, found these reserves to be 'badly watered, sandy and unfit for settlement'.[16] By 1905, the British South Africa Company (BSAC) had created about sixty reserves that occupied only 22 per cent of the new colony; the settler community appropriated the bulk of the rest of the land for themselves. In 1914 a Reserves Commission with the mandate to complete the delimitation of the reserves was established such that by 1922, 64 per cent of all Africans were required to live in the reserves.[17] Initiatives for total spatial segregation were formalised with the appointment in 1924 of the Morris Carter Commission to inquire into views about land segregation.[18] The recommendations of the Commission were incorporated into the Land Apportionment Bill, which became an Act in 1930 and sought to legalise land segregation. Under this Act land was divided into European Areas, Native Areas, Native Purchase Areas, and Forest Areas.

From the first areas demarcated in the last decade of the nineteenth century (see above), the African reserves were the object of diverse and even contradictory depictions. Following the Anglo-Ndebele War of 1893 and the Ndebele-Shona uprisings of 1896–97, fears were expressed that the reserves might allow Africans to re-launch military resistance. Suspicions subsided in the early 1900s, however, as African reserves were increasingly portrayed within white society as mired in rural stasis. They were represented in a monochrome imagery as the traditional, rural end of a rural-urban divide in colonial policy discourse.

When African agricultural production witnessed a pronounced and significant drop in the 1930s, the colonial state blamed poor farming methods on the part of Africans instead of the skewed land distribution pattern and pernicious policies such as the Reserve Pool Act and the Market Stabilisation Act that curtailed African production while simultaneously subsidising European agriculture. Instead of increasing land allocated to the reserves, the colonial state introduced some 'modernisation' initiatives. These included opening two new government schools at Domboshawa in Mashonaland and Tsholotsho in Matabeleland where 'modern' methods of farming were taught. A former American missionary, Emory D. Alvord, became one of the leading agriculturalists responsible for teaching Africans new farming methods, including the use of fertilisers and improved seeds.[19]

This technical development phase through persuasion failed to yield any tangible results, but it wasn't until 1943 that Alvord, the long-serving Agriculturist for the Instruction of Natives,[20] *finally* expressed his disillusion with previous efforts. An exasperated Alvord noted that

> We have wasted our time for 17 years in conducting demonstration work ... average yields on plots have been 10 times the yield on ordinary native lands. The lessons to be learned have been preached for the past 16 years, yet the vast majority ... have made no change ... it is now quite evident that they will never change without compulsion and control ... There are proven methods of cultivation which successfully combat soil erosion, and since natives do not know and cannot be made to realise the danger so as to adopt such methods of their own volition, it is imperative that the Government adopt drastic methods to combat this great evil.[21]

The case for a general change of direction towards a policy of compulsion had just been made. However and perhaps more significantly, this also signalled the adoption of the term 'development' in colonial quotidian nomenclature (rather than retrospectively) and a purposeful partnering with the tools of structural-functionalist analysis.

One of the most influential anthropologists in the 1940s, J. F. Holleman, selected an area in the Buhera District for an anthropological enquiry in 1945, and presented the inhabitants of Buhera as a people 'whose traditional way of life had not yet been profoundly influenced by regular contact with Western society'.[22] He cast a powerful image of 'traditional African society' modelled on his case study and presented rural strategies for making a livelihood in simplistic terms.

The rural community was conceived as a fairly homogeneous and unchanging system. The 'peripheral' economy was said to be based on an undeveloped division of labour, rudimentary technology, partially monetarised markets, and very limited innovativeness. In this depiction the rural people all appeared fairly similar in outlook. They were peasants who toiled the land. They showed parochial values and traits which suppressed any ideas of trying to be different. Teresa Barnes observes that 'spaces in which they (Africans) were allowed some internal mobility were designated as "native kraals", reserves or "locations" and were perceived as primitive, practically foreign territory'.[23]

The anthropologists' representation of African society as traditional and closed was well attuned to the categories of thought of colonial policy discourse in the 1950s. Holleman's book, *Shona Customary Law*, became influential in circles of the Southern Rhodesian Administration.[24] In line with the dominant academic structural-functionalist paradigm of the time, planners in the colonial administration had been armed with the explanation of 'customary laws' and similar background knowledge required for the administration's efforts to 'develop' African society.

The administration found the anthropologists' perspective compelling because it was self-supporting and circular. Development, understood as modernity, was used as a yardstick to measure people. From this perspective Africans seemed to lack everything: tools were poor, harvests unreliable, and the income level low. Indeed seen from the perspective of 'modernisation' the studied areas were truly peripheral and undeveloped. The reserves were thus approached by agricultural economists, anthropologists, and political economists among others with this overriding theme.

The rural reserves were thus no longer singularly portrayed as a mere labour reserve for the settler economy, but were reinvented as 'traditional' rural African society, requiring state intervention in order to develop. In this respect the reinvention of 'tradition' was not only confined to relations of production but also extended to social control of inhabitants in various spaces by buttressing the 'traditional' political authority against challenges presented by missionaries and settler interests.[25] This process also entailed the reformulation of the type of education that Africans could receive in the reserve areas so as to modulate their outlook and expectations; these spaces were not to be contaminated by the educated and semi-educated African 'with a bookish propensity-type of education'.[26] The 1951 Kerr Commission Report on 'native' education even went as far as recommending that

Africans in the country be given the rudiments of education to use only in 'their own villages'.[27]

The rural imagery presented above was aided in no small part by the state's own media such as films produced through the Central African Film Unit and disseminated by a division on Visual Aids in the Native Affairs Department (NAD). The films found a wide audience. In 1958, for example, 746 shows were presented to a total of 281,988 people in both the rural and urban areas averaging 378 persons per show.[28] Chikonzo argues that 'there was a deliberate effort in these films to project the rural area as the legitimate space for the African whilst the city is reserved for whites'.[29] The urban space in colonial films such as *Benzi Comes to Town* and *Mulenga Goes to Town* was reflected as not conducive for Africans because it brings problems. In this regard the rural space was naturalised as the true place of the African.

The comic films gave not only a derogatory identity to the African but also an identity to his physical and social space. Spaces within which the African operates were projected as primitive. Establishing shots of Benzi's and Mulenga's homes as thatched huts in a clustered settlement pattern served to project the backwardness of the 'native' kraals. However, establishing shots of urban areas indicated vibrancy. Scenes of the city were always at the Central Business District where there were tarred roads and high rise buildings that glitter in the sun. This obvious distinction between rural and urban landscapes was meant to show the difference between the people who own those spaces thereby justifying the view of Africans as primitive and whites as civilised.

Coupled with this rural imagery was the 'tribesman' persona. Various reports would define in great detail the psycho-sociological processes that characterise the Africans' day-to-day activities and ultimately conclude that the African is still 'patterned' by factors inherent in 'his' traditional culture and social structure, such as witchcraft, patriarchy, polygamy, the levirate, and so on. Magubane rightly posits: 'If one wanted to improve the efficiency of domination, such information is indispensable'.[30] But I also suggest that such information was intended to assume an instructional/pedagogical authority over the African and in the process purge African knowledge systems from the development circle. The 'tribesman' persona served to exteriorise the African for the purpose of reducing him or imposing upon him what was ultimately meant to be for his benefit. This would then be used to support the notion that Africans had no sense of 'development' unless some exterior force stimulates them and hence justify the prescription of development ideas and ultimately reinforce the supremacy of the moderniser/developer whilst constructing categories of inferiority for the Africans.

Progress by compulsion 1943–62

In the post-Second World War period, government planning, seen as the vehicle of African modernisation, greatly intensified, signalled by the implementation of the Land Apportionment Act (LAA) of 1940 and the Natural Resources Act (NRA) of 1941. The height of 'planned modernisation' in colonial Zimbabwe is generally regarded as occurring in the 1940s and 1950s. As a consequence of the LAA, the reserves in the Shona-speaking areas had to absorb another influx of Africans evicted from alienated lands. At the same time, farming in the reserves became further restricted by the state's conservationist concerns laid down in the NRA.

The Natural Resources Board (NRB) started work in 1942 and at once drew attention to ruination in the reserves commenting that present efforts only touched the fringe of the problem, and that there should be no delay in destocking – a euphemism for culling.[31] The representations by the NRB led to destocking regulations in 1943 and its report on land occupied by Africans induced the Prime Minister to call a conference to discuss the issues with 'stakeholders'. As a result of this the Secretary for Native Affairs was required to put up a plan for 'The *Development* and Regeneration of the Colony's Native Reserves and Areas, and for the Administrative Control and Supervision of the Land Occupied by Natives'.[32] The principal feature of the plan was the building up of a strong professional and technical branch within the NAD, with the addition of an engineering branch and a marketing branch, and the view was accepted that since remedial measures were ascertainable all that was required was finance, staff, equipment, and the co-operation of the African people – but it was also agreed that until this co-operation was forthcoming 'sanctions would have to be imposed from time to time'.[33]

Joseph Hodge observes a similar turn away from the paternalists of the pre-war era towards the more technically oriented officers, in implementing development projects in other parts of Africa, notably in Kenya, during the post-1945 era.[34] There was a renewed onslaught on the rural reserves, this time from officials clutching manuals on soil erosion who believed that they were the bearers of 'development'. Concern over the destruction of natural resources by both African and settler farmers had a long history in Zimbabwe, but by the late 1930s, African cultivators were singled out for special attention.[35] The officials who pursued rural reconstruction at this time brought new certainties.

They were convinced that their policies were scientifically grounded and the only alternative to ecological and economic disaster. However, as Monica van Beusekom and Dorothy Hodgson rightly argue, despite claims to address merely technical problems, the development agenda pursued during the late colonial period was 'deeply intertwined with colonial imperatives to order, control and compel the progress of the most backward subjects'.[36]

While pressure from the NRB was always present, the *Report of the Native Production and Trade Commission* (NPTC) of 1944 can be regarded as the decisive point of departure towards compulsory powers.[37] The NPTC underscored the seriousness of conditions in the reserves and argued that they were at the core of both the problem and the solution to the so-called 'Native question'. The Report stated:

> In our opinion, the maximum benefits, both for the State and for the natives, from Native Agriculture and Animal Husbandry, can only be obtained by compulsory planned production whereby a statutory body should be empowered to direct what crops, acreages and areas should be planted and what livestock should be kept, to enforce good husbandry conditions and to control the distribution and marketing of the consequent products.[38]

S. E. Morris, the Secretary of Native Affairs, in his 1962 report considered this as 'the most authoritative and drastic expression of the proposed policy that had ever been made in this country'.[39] The stated attempt at reorganising African agriculture culminated in the Native Land Husbandry Act (NLHA) of 1951, generally regarded as the 'most ambitious and far-reaching rural intervention programme of the colonial period'.[40]

The NPTC also provided a comprehensive formulation of the nature of the difficulties facing reserve society and a prescription for their solution which, although not accepted in its entirety, was to exercise a powerful influence on the official minds for decades to come. It enlisted the full weight of 'science' to support its conclusions and drew heavily on the testimony of 'expert' witnesses trained in the natural and social sciences. Within this discourse, the 'scientific facts' provided by the literature on soil conservation were given pride of place.

The central premise of the 1944 report was that a primitive subsistence economy co-existed with an advanced money economy in colonial Zimbabwe. While the latter was governed by economic rationality, the former languished in the grip of superstition and an anti-progressive social system. Growing human and stock population in the reserves – the result of benevolent colonial rule in combination

[163]

with the irrational, uneconomic, and unscientific nature of African society and agriculture – had dire consequences for the cultural rather than economic way in which Africans regarded their cattle. In the near future these factors would lead to a near apocalyptic scenario characterised by denudation, siltation, erosion, and other deleterious ramifications. If this impending crisis was not attended to promptly and effectively, the reserves would become wastelands menacing the future of the wider society.

In a fascinating intellectual sleight of hand, the commission laid responsibility for the plight of the reserves squarely on the shoulders of the inhabitants and brushed aside the effects of conquest, land alienation, and segregation. Its solutions displayed equivalent mental dexterity. It rejected arguments that the conditions in the reserves demanded a retreat from segregationist policies and concluded that the solution required effective measures to 'develop' these areas. This prescription involved a comprehensive reorganisation of rural society which would include significant reductions of stock, the fencing of lands, concentrated settlements, improved seed, and an expansion in agricultural education. The commissioners did concede that more land was required in order to relieve congestion in the existing areas and to allow scope for the introduction of better farming methods. But the commissioners also insisted that additional land should not allow the Africans to remain in their backward state and to put back the wheels of progress.

The scenario presented by the NPTC report involved the gradual adaptation of African society together with progress grafted onto the well-rooted stock of African institutions in which chiefs were to play a central role. But this stance did not include any serious consideration of whether African forms of production on the land were effective adaptations to the particular environments and might provide valuable perspectives for both policy makers and practitioners. The recommendations of the NPTC would be the seedbed of the NLHA of 1951 and an investment totalling over £15 million between 1950 and 1958 was directed towards the technical and administrative expense of carrying out this Act.

The result was the era of compulsion; an era in which sociological problems were minimised or rejected and technical planning dominated the whole approach to African life. The prevailing argument at this time was that because African life and economics would be mainly agricultural for a long time to come, the department's efforts had to be concentrated in that direction.[41] While there were some flashes of insight into the importance attached to spreading the risk and a grudging recognition of the 'hardiness of Native cattle', the overwhelming emphasis was on the importance of shouldering aside 'primitive' practices and establishing 'modern' methods. The commission believed that such a shift would enable a large rural African population to support itself on a reasonable basis of agricultural production. The commission failed to give guidance as to how both these objectives could be achieved within the restricted amounts of land available to Africans and it was left to increasingly exasperated NAD officials to attempt to resolve the contradiction.

The African people in virtually every village and household pondered the implications of this new order, which seemed determined to penetrate and dominate every nook and cranny of their world. In the name of 'development' and 'conservation' their cattle were culled, their lands diminished and demarcated. Communities found themselves hemmed in by a host of restrictions, ranging from a ban on cutting trees to prohibitions on keeping donkeys and goats. Households discovered that they had to pay fees for grazing stock and rents for residential sites and new settlements that were laid out in straight lines.

But perhaps most ominous of all were the powers that the NLHA gave to white officials and their agents to interfere in the daily life of communities. Staff serving in the Native Commissioners' (NCs) offices was increased substantially, particularly in the sphere of agricultural and community extension. White Land Development Officers, Forestry Rangers, and Conservation Officers, as well as African Demonstrators were some of the staff appointed to augment the NC. Overall, the appointments considerably enlarged the role of the technical officers within the NAD and enhanced the influence of the Director of Native Agriculture.

Roads were made, villages were laid out in lines, dams were constructed, stockbreeding centres were set up, demonstration centres were established, and irrigation projects were initiated.[42] These policies considered the reserves to be farming areas from which people without farming and grazing rights could, and would, be excluded – to be absorbed in the urban sector of the economy.[43] The colonial reports of the time did not display an understanding of existing land and cattle ownership arrangements or of the relative importance of labour migration, cultivation, and cattle in people's livelihoods. The information gathered served a legal-technical planning exercise that may have had little bearing on actual local situations. Chiefs and headmen who resided on land under control of the NLHA found themselves acting as little more than functionaries in a tightly defined administrative system. These measures were widely detested as intrusive, oppressive, and inimical to the maintenance of even a residual political and economic autonomy.

Community development, 1963–79

The 1960s is often regarded as a period signalling a 'realisation' that 'imposed technical planning has had its day'.[44] The Mangwende Commission report of 1961 for instance stressed that other facets of administration and sociological foundations had been 'overlooked' in the technical development phase and that: 'It is high time that equal weight ... be given to the premises that no sound economy can possibly exist on an unstable social foundation'.[45] The 1960 Select Committee on the Resettlement of Natives also underlined that: 'Emphasis must be laid on the simple fact that people are more important than land'.[46] For the Robinson Commission, technical planning, 'more than anything else, has soured the relations between the Native Commissioner and the rural African'.[47] S. E. Morris was even more forceful by declaring that 'technical desiderata must cease to dominate in administrative planning'.[48]

The Select Committee also reported, rather belatedly, that: 'It does not seem that the implementation of the Land Husbandry Act has yet had the almost revolutionary effect upon agriculture which it was hoped it might have ... productivity of labour has declined'.[49] The Mangwende Commission also concluded that: 'After a quarter of a century of fairly intensive propaganda and concrete demonstration of modern agriculture the measure of appreciation by the mass of the African population has been scant'.[50]

However, given the above, the Select Committee failed to suggest any basic change in approach except for the intensification and transfer of Agricultural Extension out of the hands of administrators into the unrestricted hands of a technical department, with a blue-print on development drawn up by a team of world-recognised agricultural experts. The Committee argued that '[it] could see no reason why, given capital, it should not be possible, by means of an adequate extension service, to bring about the revolution in agriculture originally envisaged in the Native Land Husbandry Act'.[51] A willing financier was found in the World Bank, which gave a loan of £2 million in 1960 to enforce the tenets of the NLHA within a five-year programme costing £11.5 million devised by experts for the development of African agriculture.[52]

In July 1959, the NAD put forward proposals for technical aid in the human sciences to the International Co-operation Administration of the United States, with the result that Dr James Green, a sociologist and an international specialist in Community Development, began working with the department in August, 1960. In July 1961, the government approved the creation of the post of Local Government and Community Development Officer with the appointed officer assigned to understudy and learn the sociological methods and approaches of Dr Green. In 1963, Dr Bonard Wilson, the first of the American Training Advisers sent to Southern Rhodesia under the agreements between the USA and Southern Rhodesia arrived on 6 October and was followed shortly thereafter by Dr Thomas on 20 November to conduct a workshop on community development with Provincial and District Commissioners.[53] Fortified by these visits, the NAD resolved to press ahead in much bolder form and on a much larger scale than before.

However, this 'new' thrust was primarily a restatement of existing policy apart from introducing 'consultation' in pursuing what they termed 'community development', defined in the agreements with the American Agency for International Development (USAID) and the government of Rhodesia as

> The process by which the people of each community are given respons-ibility for their own development, a responsibility which can only be discharged through communal organisation, formally and informally, for democratic planning and action. These bodies of communal self-help make their own plans to meet their needs and solve their own problems, and execute those plans with maximum reliance upon resources found within the community, supplemented when necessary with administra-tive and technical advice and assistance, and financial and material aid from government and other agencies outside the community.[54]

Where the proposals for community development diverged most mark-edly from earlier documents was in the detailed proposal for rural villages to provide suitable houses for the families of Africans regularly employed in industries and other service. It was argued that Africans earning their living in this way could not make efficient use of normal allotments and the establishment of healthy rural villages for their families was the best solution. The colonial state had resigned itself to the fact that there would never be 'enough' land to enable every inhabitant in the reserves to become a full-time peasant farmer.

The NAD had for a long time placed great emphasis on the ideal of long-term racial separation, especially in political and cultural spheres, and a number of axioms had gained influence. Key assump-tions were that cultural differences were divinely ordained and insur-mountable and that chieftainship was the central and authentic institution within African culture, upon which an alternative and distinct domain could be constructed. The 1960s thus witnessed motley attempts at self-government in the African areas through the implementation of the Native Councils Act (NCA) passed in 1957. The state viewed the reorganisation of political relations in the reserves as indispensable to its overarching object of separation and sought to reinforce institutions of patriarchy to regulate the mobility of youth and women into urban/European spaces.[55]

The Mangwende Commission was full of nothing but high praise for the NCA which had ushered in some degree of local government in the reserves describing it as 'A rare and outstanding document'.[56] It didn't take very long however for Native Councils to start languishing and many folded; many more were in a precarious state because of lack of support and because a number were geographically very fragmented. Moreover, while advisory councils were created so that 'trusted' Africans could assist with the practical side of administration, they invariably had little power, even of a patrimonial sort, and were not viable sites for vibrant political activity. Many Africans believed the Native Councils Act had been designed to breach their last lines of defence.

The policy thrust of the 1960s and a desperate effort to curb vivid signs of deterioration in the African reserves necessitated the Land Tenure Act (LTA) of 1969 based on the logic of creating 'African towns in African areas', which would generate African employment and halt the 'influx' to European towns.[57] These towns, termed 'growth points' in the nomenclature of the time, were not real urban centres however – as urban centres existed only in European areas. Colonial administrators were careful not to describe these centres in urban terms because as early as the 1904 European census an urban area had been defined as 'Any centre with a population of more than 25 non-Africans, where individual holdings are less than 15 acres in extent and at least half the adult male inhabitants are employed in industrial sectors other than agriculture'.[58]

The LTA even made it clear that Africans should expect only 'limited civic status' in their urban locations. Officials hoped that these villages, in the context of the large-scale industrial development that had been realised following the federation of Northern and Southern Rhodesia and Nyasaland from 1953 to 1963, would resolve the contradiction between rural restructuring and the continual 'drift to the towns'. Exactly why families denied access to arable land and livestock should wish to remain in these villages was not a question that these rural planners chose to answer.

The Tribal Trust Land Development Corporation (TILCOR) charged with championing the Growth Centre policy identified Sanyati in Mashonaland West (Province) as a prototype, and extensive studies were carried out on the centre and its potential hinterland. The centre was established as the first TILCOR town based largely on an agricultural estate and a cotton growing hinterland. The 1979 Five

Year Public Sector Investment Programme formally adopted the policy of growth points and identified ten centres (Sanyati, Maphisa, Gutu, Mrewa, Nkai, Mtaga, Jerera, Wedza, Chisumbanje, and Mushumbi) for development, with initial investment for each centre tentatively fixed at Z2.8 million spread over five years. This would provide for infrastructure, limited housing, and commercial buildings for letting. The plan formalised what were 'TILCOR growth points' into potential urban areas which would be incorporated into the national urban hierarchy.

The policy of growth points developed through the TILCOR was however closely linked to agricultural development and all the growth points identified were linked to small-scale commercial farming under irrigation. As such the terminology 'growth points', 'growth (urban/service) centres' that developed in the 1970s appears confused because of what Moseley has characterised as the nebulous character of growth centre theory.[59] Colonial planners found the term 'growth' exceedingly seductive, leading even to tiny business centres being termed 'growth centres'. As such most of the rural business centres provided low order retailing services, a phenomenon related to a generally poor rural market. Typical functions included: general dealers, bottle stores, butcheries, supermarkets, grinding mills, and repair services. Because of restrictive business practices, non-agricultural enterprises remained very few. What this reveals, apart from the stubborn insistence on *dualising* space according to race, are the minimalist goals that development had come to assume by the 1970s in stark contrast to the grandiose phrasing and framing of development targets that characterised the NLHA.

While the introduction of growth centres would clearly augment the urban/European/modern versus rural/African/backward cleavage that colonial planners had sought to advance from very early on, the appeal and point of reference for the adoption of such a development path were undoubtedly South African apartheid policies. The idea of applying a growth centre policy was clearly linked to the problems of a polarised economic space. The colonial planners articulated the problems as follows: 'That there was denudation of the natural resources of the tribal areas; there was a massive influx of tribesman into our main towns; and that there was an imbalance between the two sectors of the dual economy – Tribal Trust Lands and European Sector'.[60]

In 1968, R. C. Briggs, the Director of African Administration in the Salisbury Municipality, proposed the setting aside of land for the purposes of accommodating African workers employed in Salisbury in either Domboshawa or Seke (22 and 18 km from Salisbury respectively) and the 'provision of fast rail or mono-rail services to Seke and Domboshawa and the creation in those areas of satellite towns on the lines of Soweto on the Rand'.[61] Briggs, however, felt it was appropriate to dapple his proposal by appealing to the long held conception of the African as a peasant by stating: 'If this was done, it would provide Africans with their own towns in African Tribal areas or African Purchase Areas, and still allow the worker to commute to work in Salisbury and the surrounding Town Management Board areas'. He also pointed out that 'The provision of such towns would be in line with present Government thinking on community development'.[62] This sheds some light on how the state sought to package what was purportedly a different development path to the outside world, while simultaneously pursuing separatist tendencies.

By 1980, the success of the growth points strategy was varied. Sanyati was the most successful both in terms of centre development and the development of the hinterland. Most other centres reflected limited centre development, although agricultural estates run by the state authority thrived. Suffice to say the polarised framework did not encourage flows of investment from the 'core' to the 'periphery'. There were problems of attracting investment because there was no policy on incentives to locate economic activity outside the main urban centres.

In spite of the government policy of continuing to regard the communal areas as a separate and economically insignificant sector, there was a slowly growing awareness in the late 1970s that these areas would have to be brought into the economic mainstream for political as well as economic reasons. This somewhat half-hearted acceptance of change may be deduced from some of the policy measures that were adopted at this time. For instance, in April 1978 the government launched the Small Farm Credit Scheme (SFCS) which was to be administered by the Agricultural Finance Corporation (AFC).[63] The scheme was established to provide credit facilities for the purchase of production inputs by African farmers in the small-scale commercial farming sector (former African Purchase Areas). With the introduction of the scheme, the AFC was, for the first time since its establishment in 1971, authorised to provide agricultural credit to farmers outside the white-owned commercial farming sector. More significant, a section of the legislation barring the AFC from lending to communal area farmers was repealed at the beginning of 1979. The repeal paved the way for the AFC to launch a pilot credit scheme, under the SFCS, in selected communal areas during the 1979–80 season.[64]

Until the establishment of the SFCS, the only sources of agricultural credit available to African farmers had been the Agricultural Loan Fund which was administered by the Ministry of Internal Affairs, or non-governmental organisations such as the African Loan and Development Trust, the African Farming Development Company (which folded in 1969), and the Catholic Association's Silveira House Agricultural Project.[65] The financial resources available for lending by the Loan Fund and by the private organisations were always limited.

In January 1979, the government of Zimbabwe-Rhodesia published its development plan for the country, but it was quickly overtaken by the fast changing political events. It nevertheless remains useful for our purposes by analysing its proposed programmes for agricultural and rural development in the communal areas. The document, titled *Proposals for a Five Year Programme of Development in the Public Sector*, had two annexes, one on the rural sector and the other on the main urban centres.[66] Davies described this plan as 'transitional in conception between traditional "Treasury-type" planning and the ambitious, comprehensive type widely practised in Africa'.[67] However, as far as the ideological framework is concerned, this in no way represented a marked departure from previous policies that had informed the settler colony. The plan proposed to improve agricultural productivity and living standards in the communal areas through the 'trusted' instruments of constructing irrigation schemes and resettlement of underutilised areas. The plan also proposed that the major irrigation schemes 'be developed by private enterprise with Government participation being confined to the provision of storage works and main canals'.[68] The proposal should thus be viewed as the re-articulation of a process (i.e. government disinvestment in the communal/African areas) that had begun in earnest when it adopted the Community Development paradigm in the 1960s.

An anatomy of development in a colonial context

Michael Cowen and Robert Shenton almost resignedly come to the conclusion that 'Development . . . defies definition' precisely because the use of the term depends upon the views and policies on those in positions of authority.[69] As a corollary, Monica van Beusekom and Dorothy Hodgson correctly opine that the very adoption of the term 'development' was a mere lexical turn as 'colonial powers sought to revise their rationales for the legitimacy of the colonial endeavour'.[70] As such, 'longstanding dichotomies such as metropole/colony and civilised/primitive were reworked into the categories of developed/underdeveloped'.[71] Taking my cue from these arguments and following from the discussion in the preceding sections, this section proceeds to highlight some of the key characteristics of the development discourse in colonial Zimbabwe.

What emerges from the notion of development advanced in late colonial Zimbabwe is that 'development' was based on and closely related to the plans and policies which were advocated for the total economic development of the developing countries. The idea was simply that an overall increase in a country's economic development, as measured by Gross National Product (GNP), would of necessity bring about the much needed impetus for rural development. This approach excluded socio-political and socio-cultural changes and considered them closely linked to the index or percentage GNP. Such thinking is captured in the following statement from the NAD:

> In African agriculture the emphasis at this stage is on basic construction so that a system can be developed which will enable the African farmer to make a fuller contribution to the national economy and to shift the emphasis from a subsistence to a market economy which will return to him a large share of the national income to satisfy his rapidly growing needs and desires.[72]

The nonchalance or ambivalence towards the sociological impacts of development efforts among the affected communities was not new. Just as the missionaries had attempted to *preach* 'development', the technical methods following the Second World War informed an

> Approach . . . of goodwill, tolerance and patience, and [that had] to be prepared, as the need arises, to switch our endeavour from an academic approach to the simple and elementary transposing of difficult themes to earthly language . . . with the use of symbols or pictures, on who is entitled to allocations under the Land Husbandry Act; lectures to the more primitive that, in these enlightened days, bodies are not snatched by night for medicinal purposes.[73]

The adjuncts of 'development' in the colonial context of the time necessitated the control and subjection of the very lifestyles of the 'subject' people for the purposes of achieving effective colonisation and this required an objectification where 'target populations' were perceived as all lacking in terms of a key criterion, namely development. This objective in turn propagated a colonialist anthropological discourse and complex that simultaneously condescended to African knowledge systems and championed a Eurocentric model of development.

Even the commitment to 'consultation' (under 'community development') was not based on the premise that rural inhabitants could make a contribution to evolving policy and practice but on the assumption that, given time, they would come to see the wisdom of official designs. This combination of a rhetoric of participation with a reality of imposition set a style which found many imitators in the field of rural development in the decades that followed. The blatant and unashamed paternalism and patronage displayed by colonial officials was evident in the prevalence of terms like 'civilised', 'responsible', and 'advanced' which were found in their correspondences and reports. For instance, S. E. Morris in his 1962 report was bold enough to declare that: 'It is doubtful if any body of men has been more aware of changing African ways and views than the officers of this Department'.[74]

Just as the bold vision advanced by the missionaries bore little relationship to the bleak circumstances of most converts in the 1930s, the brand of 'development' that was rolled out in colonial Zimbabwe was more or less equated to Europeanisation of both space and culture. State development officials would more often than not index development efforts against events in Europe. For instance, the Chief Information Officer in the Native Affairs Department, K. D. Leaver, indicated that one of his division's endeavours had been to 'slowly [bring] home to [the African] that our problems here in Southern Rhodesia are similar to those all over the world – the need for soil conservation is as great in Britain, Fiji and Ghana as it is in Southern Rhodesia'. Leaver went further to state that 'a typical day's work can well be a long discussion on the similarity of the underlying reasons for the Land Husbandry Act with the Industrial Revolution of Britain, coupled with the respective population growths'.[75]

Development was presented as something to aspire to; its exemplars were indexed against the developed nations and modelled against the white-settler paradigm and it displayed a heavy urban bias. As such, the importance of patterns of behaviour generated by the example of white settlers (i.e. high incomes, large homes, many material possessions, the employment of servants and workers, and politico-economic power) in colonial societies should not be underestimated. This made for patterns of development which sought to emulate the West, to appear to be almost natural, and to produce a positive correlation with a European/Western conceptualisation of development. Colonial education was welcomed by some Africans as a vehicle to attain this level of affluence. In fact some believed it was the hallmark of self-advancement. The material accumulation of wealth and the shift towards social arrangements modelled on the West as part of these development schemes such as family planning, monogamy, and nuclear families meant that development became associated with a lifestyle change.

Hence 'development' came to assume a particular meaning – of cumulative change with a specific direction. Development came to be identified with a Western lifestyle appreciated in a Malinowskian perspective by seeing development only in terms of conventional materialist conceptions. Thus, in a very broad sense development came to be appreciated and understood as directional change among certain sections of the African population (who incidentally were to constitute the core of the ruling class in post-independence Zimbabwe).

But perhaps a more profound insight is that the pedagogical authority that the colonial state assumed at the time created in some Africans a permeating guilty conscience that they were somehow responsible for rural poverty and the ecological crisis in the reserves, as the colonialists had deliberately set out to 'blame' the Africans themselves for their current conditions. For instance, Aaron Jacha, the President of the African Farmers Union in the 1950s, remarked in a speech at an African Farmers Union Conference that

> At present we are taken as a section of a people who do not contribute much towards the development of this country . . . because we look like people who do not want to learn . . . we should put our body and soul into hard work so that in the not so far distant future, we can be reckoned together with the important and indispensable European community of farmers who are producing food for the country. We Africans do not as yet understand what agriculture means to mankind. Our ancestors or some of them used to run agriculture as their main pursuit, but it was done in a primitive way. Most of them could hardly produce enough to feed their families. It will not be wrong to say that with the whiteman's knowledge we are now producing more food than we need at home. We must not reject this great knowledge of the whiteman.[76]

The above dictum by the President of the African Farmers Union does indicate that while the colonial agricultural policies projected a derogatory outlook on traditional agricultural technology, there was also a desire among sections of the African community to adopt and concur with those 'progressive' policies. In this regard there was no total polarity of interests between two different cultures or ideologies within any cultural or ideological struggle.

While seemingly extensive in defining the concept of community development, the development of 'growth points' in the 1970s was to take place in such a manner as to consolidate a policy of separate development, and the nationalists were quick to castigate community development for promoting an 'enclave' type development. In theory, the 'growth point policy' was based on identifiable potential and the need to promote industrial development. In reality, the idea of potential was limited in so far as it was only in relationship to already underdeveloped 'tribal' areas. There was also the problem of the racist framework of the policy since it was to be applied to 'African' areas only.

As far as the colonialists were concerned, the development programmes emanating from the First World countries during this time presented them with an opportunity to advance two separate but related agendas: the first was to reassert the niches and binaries along racial and class lines with a view to informing the second goal, which was to maintain and perpetuate the *dualised* structure of the colonial economy. What is discernible nonetheless is that as time went by there was a tacit resignation as to the inability of the 'modern' to imbricate the 'traditional' and such being the case much of the grandiose aims and objectives of earlier development plans of the 1940s and 1950s became minimalist in nature.

Notes

1 See William Easterly, *The White Man's Burden: Why the West's Efforts to Aid the Rest Have Done so Much Ill and so Little Good* (New York: Penguin 2006).

2 Department of Native Affairs/Economic Development, 'African Economic Development in Southern Rhodesia', *Native Affairs Department Annual* (1957), p. 45.

3 Giovanni Arrighi, *The Political Economy of Rhodesia* (The Hague: Mouton 1967), p. 41.

4 Ibid.

5 Ian R. Phimister, *An Economic and Social History of Zimbabwe, 1890–1948: Capital Accumulation and Class Struggle* (New York, London: Longman 1988), p. 253.

6 Tsuneo Yoshikuni, 'Notes on the Influence of Town-Country Relations on African Urban History before 1957: Experiences in Salisbury and Bulawayo', in Brian Raftopoulos and Tsuneo Yoshikuni (eds), *Sites of Struggle: Essays in Zimbabwe's Urban History* (Harare: Weaver Press 1999), p. 120.

7 Frederick Cooper, 'Writing the History of Development', *Journal of Modern European History* 8, 1 (2010), p. 10.

8 Elizabeth Schmidt, *Peasants, Traders and Wives: Shona Women in the History of Zimbabwe, 1870–1939* (Portsmouth, NH: Heinemann; Harare: Baobab; London: James Currey 1992), p. 3.

9 Victor E. M. Machingaidze, 'Agrarian Change From Above: The Southern Rhodesia Native Land Husbandry Act and African Response', *International Journal of African Historical Studies* 24, 3 (1991), p. 565.

10 Arrighi, *Political Economy of Rhodesia*, p. 55.

11 See Diana Patel, 'Some Issues of Urbanisation and Development in Zimbabwe', *Journal of Social Development in Africa* 3, 2 (1988), pp. 17–31, and M. A. H. Smout, 'Urbanization of the Rhodesian Population', *Zambezia* 4, 2 (1975–76), pp. 79–91.

12 Charles Olley quoted in *Rhodesia Herald*, 21 December 1945, my emphasis.

13 The idea was that only able-bodied males would migrate to centres of wage labour during early adulthood. They were expected to return later in life to their home areas. The system was ideologically rationalised as an effort to keep rural societies intact. The objective consequence was a system of super-exploitation. Employers needed to pay only wages sufficient to buy elementary consumer goods and to pay taxes. The rural economy was supposed to care for the workers' families and to provide security in old age and in case of infirmity. In short, to borrow Samir Amin's term, this is the economy of the 'labour reserve'. Samir Amin, 'Underdevelopment and Dependence in Black Africa: Origins and Contemporary Forums', *Journal of Modern African Studies* 10, 4 (1972), pp. 105–20.

14 Cooper, 'Writing the History of Development', p. 10.

15 National Archives of Zimbabwe, Harare (hereafter NAZ), SRG4, Southern Rhodesia, Miscellaneous Reports, 1946–18: CNC's Annual Report 1946, my emphasis.

16 Richard Martin quoted in H. V. Moyana, *The Political Economy of Land in Zimbabwe* (Gweru: Mambo Press 2002), p. 4.

17 Phimister, *Economic and Social History of Zimbabwe*, p. 68.
18 Sabelo J. Ndlovu-Gatsheni, 'Re-thinking the Colonial Encounter in Zimbabwe', *Journal of Southern African Studies* 33, 1 (2007), pp. 188–90.
19 Michael Drinkwater, 'Technical Development and Peasant Impoverishment: Land Use Policy in Zimbabwe's Midlands Province', *Journal of Southern African Studies* 15, 2 (1989), pp. 287–305.
20 Emory Alvord was an American missionary and an agriculturist who had come to the Colony of Southern Rhodesia in about 1909 under the aegis of The American Board Mission in Mount Selinda. His early demonstration fields in Mt Selinda soon caught the attention of the state which appointed him as Agriculturist for the Instruction of Natives in 1919. The colonial state sought to intensify African land use. Alvord promoted intensified agriculture through an agricultural extension programme and land use policies such as 'centralisation' – the reorganisation of land in consolidated grazing and arable blocks, with a line of residential sites in between. The role played by missionaries in development is as significant as their discourse which is very much evident in the quotation cited by using the words 'evil', 'preached', 'Gospel' etc.
21 NAZ SRG/INT4, E. D. Alvord quoted in Southern Rhodesia, Departmental Reports: 'Report of the Secretary for Native Affairs, Chief Native Commissioners and Director of Native Development for the Year 1962', p. 25.
22 J. F. Holleman, *Shona Customary Law: With Reference to Kinship, Marriage, the Family and the Estate* (Manchester: Manchester University Press 1952), pp. 10–11.
23 Teresa A. Barnes, 'The Fight for Control of African Women's Mobility in Colonial Zimbabwe, 1900–1939', *Signs: Journal of Women in Culture and Society* 17, 3 (1992), p. 586.
24 *Shona Customary Law* became part of the inventory of all district stations as well as the curriculum of the training programme for new personnel in the Internal Affairs Department.
25 This period during which Chiefs and Headmen attained some insular authority, through a plethora of pieces of legislation such as the Native Law and Courts Act granting civil jurisdiction to Chiefs, is generally regarded as the 'Rise of the State'.
26 Michael O. West, 'African Middle-Class Formation in Colonial Zimbabwe, 1890–1965' (PhD dissertation, Harvard University, 1990). As early as 1918 the colonialists had appointed a Commission that culminated in the Kegwien Report which urged the introduction of practical subjects in the African's curriculum.
27 Toby Tafirenyika Moyana, *Education, Liberation and the Creative Act* (Harare: Zimbabwe Publishing House 1989), p. 8.
28 NAZ SRG/INT 4, Southern Rhodesia/Native Affairs Department, 'Report of the Chief Information Officer, Division of Native Affairs, Southern Rhodesia for the Year 1958', p. 139.
29 Kelvin Chikonzo, 'The Construction of African Cultural Identities in Zimbabwean Films, from 1948–2000' (MPhil thesis, University of Zimbabwe, 2005), p. 98.
30 Bernard Magubane, 'The "Xhosa" in Town, Revisited. Urban Social Anthropology: A Failure of Method and Theory', *American Anthropologist*, New Series, 75, 5 (1973), p. 1707.
31 In 1939, the Natural Resources Commission had estimated, judging by progress in mechanical conservation so far achieved, that it would take some 250 years to cope with the situation in Native Reserves and hoped that the latest arrangements would speed up matters.
32 Eric K. Makombe, 'A People's Perspective of State Conservation Policies in the Seke Reserve, 1941–1961' (BA Honours dissertation, University of Zimbabwe, 2003), p. 17, my emphasis.
33 Ibid., p. 23.
34 Joseph Morgan Hodge, 'British Colonial Expertise, Post-Colonial Careering and the Early History of International Development', *Journal of Modern European History* 8, 1 (2010), pp. 24–46.

35 This focus remains to be fully explained but appears to have a number of causes. White farmers, alternately insecure in slumps and expansionist booms, railed against the 'destructive' methods of African producers. Droughts, dongas, demographic data, declining yields, 'rivers running brown with mud', and an imperfect understanding of African ecology all helped to fuel official concern. And sensitivity to these issues was considerably enhanced by wider developments. American literature of the 1920s, highlighting the dangers of overtaxing the soil, circulated widely in English-speaking Africa. The warnings offered by these studies proved to be a 'horrific prophecy' as the story of the American 'Dust Bowl' disaster unfolded in the early 1930s.

36 Monica M. van Beusekom and Dorothy L. Hodgson, 'Lessons Learned? Development Experiences in the Late Colonial Period', *Journal of African History* 41, 1 (2000), p. 30.

37 *Report of the Native Production and Trade Commission 1944* (Salisbury: Government Printer 1945).

38 NAZ ZBJ 1/2/1, NPTC Written Memoranda, 1944.

39 Southern Rhodesia, Departmental Reports: 'Report of the Secretary for Native Affairs, Chief Native Commissioners and Director of Native Development for the Year 1962', p. 11.

40 Montague Yudelman, *Africans on the Land: Economic Problems of African Agricultural Development in Southern, Central, and East Africa, with Special Reference to Southern Rhodesia* (Cambridge, MA: Harvard University Press 1964).

41 The growing attention to African farming in colonial policy discourse was equivocal. On the one hand, state intervention attempted to enhance Africans' agricultural practices, but simultaneously sought deliberately to undercut African competitiveness in agricultural produce markets in an attempt to protect the interests of white settler farmers. Two lines of policies can be distinguished in this latter strand. First, the operation of these markets was manipulated. The effect of policies such as the Maize Control Act (1931) and Cattle Levy Act (1934) was that African farmers received lower prices than did their white colleagues. Second, segregationist policies undermined African farmers' ability to produce for markets.

42 For instance, a large irrigation project was set up (at Devuli) in the 1940s, and another, small one, near Murambinda in 1956.

43 Another contradiction on the part of the state becomes apparent in this regard, however, as urban influx regulations (pass laws, registration, and repatriation) appear contradictory to the NLHA. Whereas the pass laws were intended to turn African town life into a temporary affair, the NLHA is generally perceived as an attempt to settle the industrial labour force permanently in towns.

44 Southern Rhodesia, Departmental Reports: 'Report of the Secretary for Native Affairs, Chief Native Commissioners and Director of Native Development for the Year 1962', p. 26.

45 Southern Rhodesia, *Report of the Mangwende Reserve Commission of Inquiry* (Salisbury: Government Printer 1961), p. 1.

46 Southern Rhodesia Legislative Assembly, *Second Report of the Select Committee on the Resettlement of Natives, Presented to the House 18 August 1960* (Salisbury: Government Printer 1961), para. 281.

47 Southern Rhodesia, *Report of the Commission Appointed to Inquire into and Report on Administrative and Judicial Functions in the Native Affairs and District Courts Departments, Presented to the Legislative Assembly 1961* (Salisbury: Government Printer 1961).

48 Southern Rhodesia, Departmental Reports: 'Report of the Secretary for Native Affairs, Chief Native Commissioners and Director of Native Development for the Year 1962', p. 13.

49 Southern Rhodesia Legislative Assembly, *Second Report of the Select Committee on the Resettlement of Natives*, para. 283.

50 Southern Rhodesia, *Report of the Mangwende Reserve Commission*, p. 3.

51 Southern Rhodesia Legislative Assembly, *Second Report of the Select Committee on the Resettlement of Natives*, para. 287.

52 Southern Rhodesia, Departmental Reports: 'Report of the Secretary for Native Affairs, Chief Native Commissioners and Director of Native Development for the Year 1962'.
53 *Community Development and Local Government News Bulletin* 1, 25 November 1963.
54 Ibid., p. 1.
55 E. K. Makombe, 'The Influence of State and Patriarchy on African Migration and Gender: The Case of Zimbabwe (1945–2010)', paper presented to the International Conference on African Migration and Gender in Eastern Africa 'II: Setting the Agenda', organised by IMMIS in partnership with the Mbarara University of Science and Technology (MUST), Uganda, 5–6 July 2010.
56 Southern Rhodesia, *Report of the Mangwende Reserve Commission*.
57 Ministry of Internal Affairs, *Tribal Trust Lands Development Corporation Limited: Urban Development at TILCOR Growth Points* (Salisbury: Government Printer 1976).
58 George L. Kay, *Rhodesia: A Human Geography* (London: University of London Press 1970), p. 15.
59 Malcolm J. Moseley, *Growth Centres in Spatial Planning* (Oxford, New York: Pergamon Press 1974).
60 Ministry of Internal Affairs, *Tribal Trust Lands Development Corporation Limited*, p. 1.
61 NAZ S/SA6175, City of Salisbury, African Administration Report: 'Annual Report of the Director of African Administration for the Year Ending 30th June 1968', p. 57.
62 Ibid., pp. 57–8.
63 Theresa Chimombe, 'The Role of Banks and Financial Institutions in the Accumulation and Reinvestment of Capital in Zimbabwe' (MPhil thesis, University of Zimbabwe, 1983), p. 17.
64 Ibid., p. 19.
65 Ibid., p. 8.
66 Ministry of Finance Zimbabwe-Rhodesia, *Proposals for a Five Year Programme of Development in the Public Sector* (Salisbury: The Ministry 1979).
67 D. Hywel Davies, 'Towards an Urbanisation Strategy for Zimbabwe', *Geojournal*, suppl. 2 (1981), p. 78.
68 Ministry of Finance Zimbabwe-Rhodesia, *Proposals for a Five Year Programme*, p. 51.
69 Michael Cowen and Robert Shenton, 'The Invention of Development', in Jonathan Crush (ed.), *Power of Development* (London, New York: Routledge 1995), p. 28.
70 van Beusekom and Hodgson, 'Lessons Learned?', p. 29.
71 Ibid.
72 Department of Native Affairs/Economic Development, 'African Economic Development', p. 45.
73 NAZ SRG/INT4, Southern Rhodesia/Native Affairs Department, 'Report of the Chief Information Officer, Division of Native Affairs for the Year 1958', p. 139.
74 Southern Rhodesia, 'Report of the Secretary for Native Affairs, Chief Native Commissioners and Director of Native Development for the Year 1962', p. 19.
75 NAZ SRG/INT4, Southern Rhodesia/Native Affairs Department, 'Report of the Chief Information Officer', p. 138.
76 Aaron Jacha quoted in *Bantu Mirror*, 16 September 1950, p. 11.

CHAPTER SEVEN

The tractor as a tool of development? The mythologies and legacies of mechanised tropical agriculture in French Africa, 1944–56

Céline Pessis

(translated by Matthew Vester)

Introduction

During the post-war years, a 'climate of mechanisation'[1] held sway in the new French Union and heavily influenced the formulation of ambitious plans for economic development in the colonies. The machine, a heroic victor in wartime, was destined for a new battleground: Africa. In order to confront the problem of agricultural shortages, planners projected the transformation and mechanised cultivation of hundreds of thousands of hectares of 'new lands'. Vast farms managed by the state were to have formed the redoubts of this mechanised front. Agricultural mechanisation in French overseas territories happened quickly, through new techniques and men, and rendered obsolete the practices and know-how of agricultural services and local farmers. Engineers united around this revolutionary project, which they saw as a good fallback plan, given the conflict in Indochina. Mechanised farming was the flagship instrument of the new interventionism of the colonial state, but its failures also illustrate the limits of post-war planning policies.

The balance sheet of the first Four Year Plan (1948–52) noted that mechanised farms had neither reached their production objectives nor served as the hoped-for catalysts.[2] The following plan (1953–57) reduced funding for mechanisation, whose role shifted from the foreground of the imperial stage to a much more modest part in African rural development. However, during the 1950s the place of tractors in African farming continued to evolve, and during the 1960s and 1970s mechanisation policies were again taken up by new socialist states. How is one to explain this continued push for mechanisation, in light of the monumental failure of the 'mechanising project' of the immediate post-war years?

This chapter intends to show that, surprisingly and paradoxically enough, it was through confrontation with criticisms and obstacles encountered among the wreckage of failed mechanisation efforts that the tractor became a privileged tool of development. The 'mechanising project', as drawn up by metropolitan planning agencies, was subjected to a series of discursive and practical alterations once it was implemented by colonial authorities. This invites consideration of post-war development not as the *sui generis* arrival of a modern rationality, but as the result of challenges, conflicts, and re-appropriations.[3] The history of the mechanisation of tropical agriculture offers a case study that reveals the entire process of decolonisation, from the dream of a modern empire, to its role as a pillar of French reconstruction, to its colonial legacy. It will be examined here as a prism of the interactions between metropole and colonies, taking into careful account the degree to which scientists were invested in this project.

After recounting the genesis of the 'mechanising programme', the chapter will consider the ways in which problems encountered on the ground generated critical and technically oriented feedback. We will then look at how the management of these setbacks created a vast response of adaptation, normalisation, and re-qualification of tractors as instruments of rural development, while obscuring their negative socio-environmental impacts.

The metropolitan mechanisation programme, 1944–48

> It certainly appears that the last and only hope for the modernisation of African agriculture is the machine, which radically expands man's mastery of the land . . . The machine offers, at last, a means of maintaining the organic and mineral fertility of the soil at a satisfactory rate, not subject to the understanding and good will of the farmer, and independently of cultural constraints. (Robert Metge, Director of Agronomic Research at the Office of Niger)[4]

The creation of the Economic and Social Development Investment Fund (*Fonds d'Investissement pour le Développement Économique et Social*, FIDES) in 1946 was a turning point in French colonial policy. For the first time, the metropole began to invest in its colonies on a massive scale. In the agricultural arena, funding sources targeted the development of scientific and technological research and the launching of 'intensive mechanised farming units' that received 8,100 million old francs from the first round of FIDES grants.[5] Together with the development of

transportation and equipment infrastructure, this mechanisation policy oversaw a vigorous development of colonial production resources
aimed primarily at the satisfaction of metropolitan needs. It differed,
though, from a traditional 'value-added' agenda in that it was also
intended to jump-start the development of food processing industries.
This was a matter of solidifying the principle of colonial industrialisation that had been carefully approved at the 1944 Brazzaville conference.[6]

The modernisers wanted to break with the humanist and traditionalist notions that had dominated rural policies before the war.[7] They
criticised the half-measures of the pilot farms that had popularised
(without much success) the use of modest manual and draft-animal
equipment. Their ambition was to move from 'traditional farming to
the latest advances in Technology'.[8] Within this mechanising programme, rural development was addressed only from the perspective
of technological change. How was it that science acquired such a role
in colonial agricultural policies?

The colonial state confronts new production challenges

During the war, as colonial agricultural production declined, the Vichy
government, followed by the administrators of free France, faced serious shortages of raw materials. Both wartime authorities in France,
sensing the crucial importance of the empire and committed to a
planned economy, placed the issue of agricultural mechanisation at
the centre of their policies of imperial reconstruction.[9]

In a context of global shortages, the French colonies were forced to
provide the Germans,[10] then the Allies,[11] and finally France undergoing
reconstruction, with quotas of oilseeds. The provisioning of oilseeds
was a matter of imperial sovereignty and national independence, and
became the main focus of the planned imperial economy established
by Vichy and continuing after the war.[12] This shortage of vegetable
oil drove the most ambitious mechanisation projects: those relating
to groundnut cultivation in Senegal.

Another problem was rice shortages in Africa, which was largely
dependent, according to the system of imperial specialisation, on imports
from Asia, whence supplies were cut off during the war. In January
1940, as part of a last-minute effort to prepare for war, the military
official Annet carried out an initial experimentation with mechanised
rice-farming in Casamance (Senegal).[13] In 1944 the Director of the
Office of Niger, Maurice Rossin, led the first agronomic mission to
the United States, which focused on mechanised rice-farming.[14]

Just after the war, these production priorities were reinforced by
the pressure of the dollar-deficit of French commerce, and also by the

conditions surrounding Marshall Plan aid.[15] Ten per cent of this assistance was designated for the colonies,[16] where it funded the purchase of most of the equipment for agricultural mechanisation.

The demand for increased production in the colonies, a subject of heated debate in post-war conferences, had to confront the chronic problem of labour supply. This obstacle was made worse by the Assembly's abolition of forced labour in 1946, voted in response to heavy pressure from colonial populations and their deputies. The vote delivered on a promise made at the Brazzaville conference in 1944, but generated sharp reactions among industrialists and leading government officials. Mechanisation imposed itself from 1944 on as a way of compensating for the anticipated increase in labour costs.[17]

Some white farm owners sought to bring their plantations, which had been abandoned during the war, back to life through mechanisation. In Madagascar, powerful European planters – who had long refused to resign themselves to the abolition of forced labour – were seized by a veritable frenzy of mechanisation.[18] In 1946 planters in the Ivory Coast created (with the support of the agricultural service of the AOF (*Afrique Occidentale Française*) and financing from the FIDES) the Experimental Committee for Mechanised Farming, in order to offset labour shortages.[19]

But the expensive project of mechanising African agriculture was carried out above all by the state which, in response to the opening of international trade, engaged in a policy of modernising the entire imperial apparatus of production.[20] Propelled by massive public investment through the FIDES, it aimed to leverage these resources and mobilise private capital, embarking on an intensive propaganda campaign among industrialists.[21]

The mechanisation project thus came into being as a result of *metropolitan production demands, the establishment of a free colonial labour force*, and the *opening of international trade*. The tensions generated by these developments seemed like they could be resolved through the power of the machine. At the Institut des Sciences Politiques, the new director of the Office of Overseas Scientific Research (*Office de la Recherche Scientifique Outre-Mer*, ORSOM), Maurice Rossin, taught that this faith in technology was rooted in the practices of warfare and in the 'technological and mechanical victory' of the Allies.[22]

Technicians at the helm in planning agencies

In 1944, equipping farmers and mechanising agriculture thus became consensus priorities in planning meetings where war efforts had propelled industrialists and agricultural experts to the forefront. Along with Rossin, two other agronomists embodied the shift leading to the triumph of the mechanising project as France was liberated. René Dumont had been close to modernising circles in the Vichy regime and repositioned himself among those of free France.[23] André Kopp was the Inspector General of Agriculture in French Equatorial Africa (*Afrique-Équatoriale Française*, AEF) and after the war moved into key positions in the metropole, following his involvement in the French Free Forces (*Forces françaises libres*, FFL).

The mechanisation project marginalised those lands which had been ruined by war and offered few resources. It was developed by the new planning agencies: the Department of Agriculture, Livestock, and Forests and the Department of Plan of the Ministry of French Overseas Territories (created in 1944 and 1945). Also involved were the Plan Commissions[24] and the central committee of the FIDES. All these agencies were closely tied and in all of them expert agronomists played dominant roles.

In anticipation of the early work of the Modernisation Commission, in 1946 the Congress of Agronomic Engineers mobilised elite colleagues to formulate their contributions and research agendas in the context of the Plan which was to 'carry the farmer, in a single step forward, to the forefront of rural technological progress'.[25] From 1946 to 1948 scientific experts at the Modernisation Commission for French Overseas Territories argued for significant state promotion of rural modernisation through capital investment and mechanisation. Proponents of intensive mechanisation of agricultural work (from sowing to harvesting) seemed to have carried the day. These experts were sent to the areas in question to gather information and once there, they were often personally involved in starting up the mechanised farming process. New recruits from the Office of Colonial Scientific Research (*Office de la Recherche Scientifique Coloniale*, ORSC (1943)), which later became ORSOM (1949), and then ORSTOM (1953) also arrived for their 'basic training'.

The mechanisation programme was linked to large-scale accomplishments in transport infrastructure, to great dams, and to smaller water control projects, and thus owed a lot to the engineers of the rural engineering corps. The programme also coincided with the institutionalisation of this agronomic sub-field,[26] which produced the first experts of agricultural machinery, such as Charles Gaury and Robert Dufournet. More broadly, the mechanising project was part of the post-war fascination with technical improvement and motorised engineering. Heavy tractors were then being regularly used in public works and began to appear in the vast silvicultural tracts of the AEF.

The Agriculture Department of the Ministry of French Overseas Territories began pilot projects as a first step in implementing the mechanisation programme. To this end it relied upon the Technical Division of Tropical Agriculture (*Section Technique d'Agriculture Tropicale*, STAT), a subsidiary unit that it planned to transform into the National Institute of Tropical Agronomy.[27] It thus became a competitor of the ORSC in terms of coordinating agronomic research. The STAT, administered by André Kopp, was given the charge of studying agricultural mechanisation in the overseas territories and in the United States.[28]

These initial experiments with agricultural machinery reveal a unitary conception of French empire. In the overseas territories both American machines and French tractor prototypes were tried out.[29] Standard engine types combined with components adapted to specific kinds of tropical or temperate farming conditions were assembled in newly nationalised Renault factories. The decision was made to set up a 'tropicalisation' laboratory in the middle of the greater Paris region in order to test the machinery in artificially created tropical conditions.

Developed according to the measures of rural modernisation in the metropole and the reconstruction of French industry, and piloted by agronomic engineers, mechanisation was promoted as an instrument of the centralisation and technicalisation of colonial agricultural policies.

The environmental justification of the tractor

The immediate post-war years were a key moment of agreement on the importance of environmental issues in the context of inter-colonial and international cooperation (UNESCO, FAO).[30] Numerous experts travelled the globe making inventories and advising on the proper use of resources and land, carrying out technical missions, and participating in international conferences.[31] It was in this climate of awareness and technological optimism that French modernisers offered an environmental justification for the tractor.

French sub-Saharan Africa began to experience an agro-environmental crisis that followed those experienced in North Africa[32] and imperial British Africa.[33] The period of 'reconstruction' favoured a convergence between conservationist and agricultural agendas championed by influential actors such as the forester Aubréville at the Ministry of French Overseas Territories.[34] The proper management of the agricultural environment, whether focusing on the function of regulating water and forests, on soil protection in plantations, or on traditional farming, became a topic of research and of scientific controversy. It also invited administrative directives and various legislative initiatives.

Together with new perspectives on demographic growth, soil erosion became a centre of attention, especially in Madagascar, Senegal, and as Monica von Beusekom has shown, in Sudan.[35] Renewed alarms about desertification prompted a lively debate between agronomists, geographers, and geologists. Enlightened administrators shared the concerns of certain agricultural engineers about damage caused by ploughs. From many quarters, then, came calls to re-examine the practice of farming with draft animals, which had spread during the interwar years.[36] From Brazzaville to the Organisation for European Economic Cooperation (OEEC) and within both the Plan Commissions and the FIDES, planning discourses in the immediate post-war years thus presented the fight against soil exhaustion in the colonies as a key policy for the restoration and development of the empire.[37] A vast investigation carried out in 1945 by the agricultural service of all of the overseas territories revealed significant levels of degradation of colonial soils.[38] The investigation also signalled a growing environmental critique of colonisation. Some began to question the traditional interpretation of erosion: that it was caused by indigenous agrarian practices such as slash-and-burn and nomadic pastoralism. In his response to the investigation, the inspector of the *Eaux et Forêts* (land management bureau) in Senegal, Pierre Bellouard, cited the arguments of Jean-Paul Harroy,[39] who pointed to the structural pressure of export-oriented farming as a cause of soil exhaustion. With the support of the Governor-General, he called for limits to the expansion of groundnut farming (which was being propped up by the administration), and for preference to be given to crops grown under forest cover.[40]

While some agricultural engineers promoted various costly methods for protecting the soil, the modernisers defended mechanisation as an effective way to achieve this goal. At the inter-colonial conference on soil conservation in Goma (1948), the Agricultural Director at the Ministry of French Overseas Territories, Maurice Guillaume, vigorously promoted mechanisation on these grounds.[41] He viewed agricultural mechanisation as a key element in the rational use of arable soils, and delivered the same message to the United Nations Scientific Conference on the Conservation and Utilisation of Resources (UNSCCUR).[42]

Colonial authorities invented a new kind of African rice-growing according to which mechanised farming was practised in irrigated lowlands and was designed to replace peasant rice-growing in mountain regions, which was seen as a cause of environmental disasters. This industrial production of foodstuffs was also intended to free up labour in upland areas for export-oriented tree crops that would not harm the soil. Mechanised irrigated rice-growing also corresponded to the modernisation standard of the FAO at the time.[43] By focusing farming and people on 'centres of mass production' and by privileging the 'improvement' of 'new lands', mechanisation was also meant to have eased demographic pressure in overpopulated areas. It thus promised to re-orient and re-organise the agricultural specialisation of the overseas territories, while adapting farming to the new environmental concerns.

The defenders of the tractor concealed its continuity with draft-animal cultivation, situating it instead within the broader agenda of agro-environmental research: experimental chemical fertilisers and especially green manures. After Harroy, it was indeed no longer possible to plough without replacing organic material. The environmental justification of the tractor was taken up again like a leitmotiv: only the tractor could sow green manure, which was absolutely necessary for intensive, responsible agriculture.[44] For many agronomists, the tractor was the ideal tool for finally breaking with the destructive practices of 'nomadic farming' and for enabling (safely) the agricultural intensification which was out reach for the peasant farmers.[45]

By presenting itself as a solution to soil erosion, the mechanising project also helped to silence the criticisms of colonial farming present in certain environmental warnings. A basic assumption of the mechanisation discourse was that the loss of the environmental equilibrium in rural societies was due not to colonialism but to the inability of peasant societies to adapt to modern realities.[46]

The creed of mechanisation thus set aside the multi-faceted environmental debates of the immediate post-war years and offered instead a monocausal explanation for erosion – archaic peasant practices that harmed the environment – and an unconditional faith in the all-powerful machine.

The tractor as a 'virgin land' assault weapon

Post-war planners thus invented archaic African peasant societies with frozen modes of production and social structures[47] that only the power of the machine would be able to transform. According to the Director of Agriculture, 'one must face the facts: the rural African economy is difficult to improve'.[48] He was resolved to move beyond 'an excessive concern for equity' that 'fragments our efforts, leaving behind disconnected initiatives'.[49] FIDES funding earmarked for general agricultural education was rapidly reallocated for psychotechnical training and for the opening of schools for machine operators and drivers.[50] This focus on machinery demonstrated the limited influence of colonial technicians with rural African populations.[51]

Investments in mechanisation sought to create 'modern zones', while the vast majority of agricultural activity was ignored. Mechanised farms were to be established primarily in 'virgin lands', represented as hitherto under-exploited territories, owing to their roughness and the weak ability of the black man to transform his environment.[52] With colonial engineers, as well as African specialists in heavy machinery as drivers, the tractor relegated the farmers to manual labour and work as assistants of the machine. The tractor embodied a form of development without African farmers, in which French machines and technicians alone confronted the hostile natural conditions of the tropics.

The tractor was seen as offering a radical shift from indigenous to modern agriculture, thereby disrupting the 'poverty equilibrium'. With the help of the lessons of the European agricultural revolution, and through Western capital and know-how, it seemed possible to leap-frog centuries of agricultural evolution by moving directly from manual to mechanical farming. Indeed, the success of these efforts seemed tied to the rapidity and brutality of the changes effected. The decision to launch the first mechanised farms was thus taken in the hallways of the Plan Commissions and the Ministry, even before the Plan of 1948 was unveiled. The agronomist Kopp justified the start-up of industrial farms, without a trial period, in these terms: 'There is no static agronomy. There is no general and definitive agronomic solution. There is a continual evolution; everywhere there is transformation and adaptation. There is thus generalised and continual experimentation'.[53] Salaried labour and wholesale mechanisation were indeed often presented as breakthrough elements facilitating the implantation of mechanisation[54] and leading the way to a less technically advanced 'mechanisation with indigenous characteristics'.

The planners intended for the General Company of Tropical Oilseeds (*Compagnie Générale des Oléagineux Tropicaux*, CGOT) and for the Office of Niger to be two exemplary projects that would drive forward this agricultural revolution. They were, respectively, a semi-public company and one whose capital was 90 per cent state-controlled. These two outfits received about two-thirds of the funds directed towards mechanisation during the first plan to modernise and provide the overseas territories with heavy equipment (1948–52).

The CGOT, created in May 1948, was tasked with piloting five mechanical farming projects in the overseas territories. Its board of directors was a veritable think-tank of mechanisers that gathered together the key personalities of the Plan Commission and by-passed official administrative procedures. Its largest project, inspired by the East Africa Groundnut Scheme,[55] was thus launched against the wishes of the AOF Governor-General.[56] The project's goal was to use intensive mechanisation and a salaried workforce to cultivate 200,000 hectares of grounduts in Senegal. The farm was situated in so-called 'virgin' forested lands in the middle Casamance region, despite the recommendations of Bellouard regarding forest protection. Little attention was given to the reservations of Senegalese elected representatives who stressed the importance of the resources of these lands for peasants migrating south.[57]

The flagship project of the Office of Niger involved cotton and rice farms of 22,000 hectares worked upon by 23,000 peasant farmers and was based on a tight control of farmers. The 1946 decision to mechanise marked a break with the doctrine of the Office of 'Indigenous Colonisation', which was founded to promote farming with draft animals, family structures, and individual land-ownership.[58] On the one hand, it set out to mechanise partially the agricultural work done by African 'colonists'. On the other hand, it envisaged the development of rice paddies of 6,000 hectares, to be farmed on an entirely mechanised basis by salaried workers who were to be managed by a private company. This decision was made by the Office at the time when it was being roiled by technical difficulties and conflicts over lands promised to farmers. The decision was thus met with criticism from office administrators[59] and with discontent from the peasant farmers.[60]

Thus, the mechanisation of tropical agriculture promised a simultaneous resolution of the problems of erosion, raw materials, and labour. Agricultural development assumed the form of a great technological leap forward, from an archaic system to a modern one. This mechanising programme was indeed a key element of development as it was conceived by colonial metropoles anxious to conserve their imperial grandeur in the immediate post-war years. As Frederick Cooper and Joseph M. Hodge have emphasised, development was thus a means of resolving the economic, social, and environmental dimensions of the imperial crisis.[61]

As we have seen, there were multiple ways in which this technicalist faith in the machine demonstrates the state's weakness when confronted with new colonial and international realities. The mechanising programme, which was dependent on American knowledge and goods, and which was debated in international conferences, was itself evidence of how colonial issues were becoming internationalised.

Mechanisation runs out of gas: failures and alternative forms

It took a long time before any fruits of mechanised production were evident. The land-clearing stage took longer than anticipated due to delays in equipment delivery, and was based on desperate technical tinkering that depended on significant input from European technicians, African labour, and outdated locomotives. Thousands of cleared hectares ended up being impossible to farm and were abandoned. Many technical procedures were not adequate for the task at hand and ended up damaging the growing sequence. The mechanical equipment that was delivered was often not the right kind, and soon spare parts were missing. Finally, the clearing of vast surfaces of land, together with deep ploughing, created serious erosion problems in the light soil of the Sahel and made it easier for weeds to grow there.

After a few years, the goals were far from achieved, whether measured in terms of hectares under the plough or agricultural outputs. Thus, in 1952, the CGOT (which had received over two million francs from the FIDES) only had 600 hectares of farmland in operation – land which produced roughly the same amount as the nearby peasant farms.[62] The mechanised rice farms of the Office of Niger operated at serious losses and were afflicted by problems of wild rice and of combines getting stuck in the paddies.

In British East Africa, the huge sums invested in the Groundnut Scheme were all lost, provoking sharp attacks in the press and in the Parliament in 1950, dividing Conservatives and Labour. Such was far from the case in the French Union, where, despite the criticisms of scientists and administrators, agricultural mechanisation in the overseas territories neither captured the attention of the media nor became a political football. A technicalist approach to the difficulties encountered on the ground and the deep technocratisation of colonial affairs helped to mask these failures.

Without questioning the mechanisation model itself, the second plan for development in the overseas territories (1953–57) targeted 'a necessary social and psychological evolution of the peasant masses'[63] and re-oriented FIDES funds towards agricultural training. During the 1950s, when subsidies and responsibilities were being gradually transferred from the metropole to the overseas territories, a new doctrine of mechanisation emerged: the tractor began to be used experimentally in 'rural development'.[64]

'Planned enterprises' and their critics (1948–52)

The planned enterprises that are currently the rage in Africa are state-led ventures that profit large companies, and will soon have completed the task of pumping the tropical lands dry of their abundant natural resources. (Roger Heim, speaking on the radio in 1950)[65]

While more and more problems were being encountered on the ground, critical scientists began to speak out in the metropole. They coalesced around the National Museum of Natural History (*Muséum National d'Histoire Naturelle*, MNHN), directed by Roger Heim, and in the AOF around the research centres of the French Institute for Black Africa (*Institut Français d'Afrique Noire*, IFAN), directed by Théodore Monod. Without really making up a structured network, these voices found a common theme in their criticism of the technological arrogance and the harsh socio-ecological effects of mechanisation. These scientists focused their research on the fragility and complexity of African environments, and on the diversity of agricultural practices there.

At the MNHN, the indefatigable botanist Auguste Chevalier responded to the marginalisation of naturalist knowledge (which resulted from the dominance of agronomic research) by making his *Revue Internationale de Botanique Appliquée et d'Agriculture Tropicale* a site where various kinds of scientists could express their criticism. He himself called the High Commissioner of the AEF to task for failing to insist on more climatological and pedological research, and for promoting mechanisation projects that failed to take into account the needs of peasant farmers.[66] Soil specialists at the MNHN, supported by the dynamic of inter-colonial cooperation following the Goma conference, also willingly sounded the alarm. The geologist Raymond Furon, in addition to engaging in prospecting activities, wrote the internationally acclaimed book *L'érosion*,[67] while the pedologist Jean Guilloteau was named President of the International Soil Conservation Organisation (*Bureau International des Sols*, BIS), created in 1949.

At the IFAN, which did not want to be affiliated with research in the metropole,[68] the naturalists got to know a new generation of geographers and anthropologists. This interaction with the social and human sciences, which took up 'the colonial situation' and 'modernity' as objects of study, thereby inflected the criticisms of mechanisation projects.[69] For example, the young geographer Jacques Richard-Molard, of the IFAN, dedicated himself to describing the dynamics of rural life and the adaptation of peasant societies to their environments. He warned against the opening of a 'third era' in which food crops would be abandoned and food would be supplied by 'entrepreneurs and mechanised workers exploiting the land in an industrialised, scientific manner'.[70] He raised questions about the roles of whites and machines in African development, defending the right of peasants to use their land as they wished, and expressing dismay that they were viewed as obstacles to modernisation. He also pointed to the alternative of intensifying peasant agrarian practices, a solution then being carried out by numerous ethnic groups experiencing demographic pressure.[71]

The naturalists, whose knowledge of tropical flora and fauna was deep and intricate, were sceptical about whether the kind of complete mastery of nature that was presupposed by agro-industrial mechanised farming was possible at all. For instance, the zoologist Pierre-Louis Dekeyser was placed in charge of killing the little birds that flocked on the massive rice paddies. He suggested setting aside mathematical forecasts and trying to understand the natural distortions and dangers created by monocultures. According to him, the sort of chemical eradication that had been proposed would only further destroy the fragile equilibrium of the ecosystems. Dekeyser thought that 'planning in western Africa encountered its first real setbacks' in the form of these little birds.[72]

In 1950 Roland Portères followed Chevalier as the head of Tropical Agronomy at the MNHN. His work in ethno-botany focused on the diffusion of various strains of African rice. Criticising the imposition of an Asian model of rice-farming, he sought to improve traditional rice-growing practices in flooded swales. He proposed a re-orientation of genetic research towards 'artificial, ecologically flexible varieties' that would be able to adapt and survive in different water levels.[73]

But the MNHN, IFAN, and BIS were no match for the iron and concrete that were reshaping Africa. So R. Heim, T. Monod, and R. Furon took their concerns about the negative social and environmental effects of mechanisation to international conferences in 1949, raising the issue in terms of international resource conservation.[74] At the UNSCCUR and in a sub-section of the International Technical Conference on the Protection of Nature (ITPCN) dedicated to the 'repercussion of planned enterprises on natural communities', Théodore Monod called politicians and scientists to account. He argued that, confronted with

the tremendous increase in destructive power represented by the machine in Africa and the obvious perils of certain spectacular clearance operations which posterity may well have cause to regret ... in the face of the ever faster process of evolution that tends to impose on all Africa a civilisation of material progress, the 'benefits' of which are too often doubtful, it is right that human conscience should awaken.[75]

Active members of the new International Union for the Protection of Nature (IUPN), the naturalists of the IFAN went on to make a case for the development of ecological research and became engaged in basic environmental education efforts.[76]

Thus, the critique of planned enterprises was tied to the emergence of a relatively humanist environmentalism and made room for an 'appeal for a new peasantry in Black Africa,'[77] a position that recalled the pre-war ideas of Robert Delavignette and Henri Labouret.[78] The

Senegalese delegate Léopod Sédar Senghor used similar terms when, before the executive committee of the FIDES, he declared his opposition to calls for a new study of mechanised groundnut farming in the AOF. Such a study 'would only interest the big businesses and would ignore the most important issues, which are the problems of soil exhaustion and the work methods of the African peasant farmer'.[79] The elected representatives seated at the Assembly of the French Union, a new organisation whose role was purely consultative, likewise requested (in vain) to review the accounts of the CGOT, calling for its budget to be reduced.[80]

Colonial administrators were not opposed to mechanisation as a matter of principle, but they did not seem to have any sympathy for the state capitalism that appeared to be the order of the day. With respect to the situation in Senegal, the Inspector General of Agriculture of the AOF, Robert Sagot, condemned the fact that 'soil conservation, agricultural mechanisation, and agronomic research, have suddenly become the latest fads and are now the objects of unbridled exaggeration and propaganda'.[81] He opposed the marginalisation of agricultural services and was more inclined to see the tractor as an aid to a popularised kind of agriculture.

The federations of the overseas territories were kept in the dark during metropolitan negotiations, but were eager to tap into Marshall Plan resources, so they took the initiative in creating one motorised farming station in each territory and one division of mechanised agriculture in each federation.[82] At first, the motorised farming stations acted as entrepreneurs, renting their services to the peasants at hourly rates or at a price per hectare. For a time, the low rates of credit they provided to the peasants seemed to guarantee the stations' success. And as we shall see, during the 1950s these structures became new models of mechanisation.

The colonial administrations opposed the project to create a Society for the Development and Equipping of Tropical Agriculture (*Société pour le Développement et l'Equipement de l'Agriculture Tropicale*), which would have had an office and a director in each territory.[83] To counter this kind of metropolitan control, the High Commissioner of the AOF issued a reminder of the importance of being mindful of the diversity of agrarian practices, land tenure, and soil cultivation. The Agricultural Director at the Ministry of the French Overseas Territories then promoted a plan to create Districts of Rural Modernisation, drawing inspiration from the partially state-run farms in North Africa.[84] For two years, conflicts raged over the form that these districts would take. The statute that created the Experimental Districts of Agricultural Modernisation (*Secteurs Expérimentaux de Modernisation Agricole,*

SEMA) on 26 September 1950 enshrined (finally) the principle of working together with the peasants in districts that were limited and experimental.[85] When the heads of the agricultural services were asked whether it would be useful to create SEMAs in their territories, they were generally unenthusiastic, preferring to be prudent and weighing the costs of the project.[86]

Managing difficulties and normalising tractors

The approval of the SEMA plan would have the effect of guaranteeing the survival of numerous mechanisation projects that had burned through their resources without having ever advanced beyond the experimental phase. When it was impossible to find a business interested in managing an area that had been cleared and prepared for agriculture, a SEMA was created instead.[87] The financial autonomy and the experimental nature of these institutions made it possible to overlook their non-viability while continuing to secure investments in them. Administrators were quite dismayed to find that, for the most part, direction of these districts was given to agricultural engineers.[88] This after-the-fact application of a rationalising logic, according to a scientific sensibility, broadly characterised the way in which problems were dealt with and subsequent criticisms were handled.

Neither the experts who were sent into the field to help with mechanised projects nor the technicians on location thought about themselves as facing setbacks, but saw the new problems that they encountered as opportunities to engage in further research with the help of increased funding. This perspective is evident in the three reports that were written by Rossin (director of ORSOM) following his missions to the East Africa Groundnut Scheme and which constitute the bulk of the French records concerning this particular effort. Rather than drawing attention to the paltry production levels achieved and the dead ends faced by the British, he wrote enthusiastically about how rational methods of land-clearing were being perfected.[89]

While the serious lack of necessary preliminary scientific research was widely deplored, it was instead the scientific infrastructure of the mechanised sectors that was reinforced, and research in agricultural machinery took off. In order to render the mechanisation debate morally neutral, Rossin proposed that the tractor be considered a 'tool' that could be used 'for good or for evil'. He popularised the metaphor of 'Aesop's tongue', which stressed using machines in the proper way.[90] Engineers thus calculated the hourly costs and comparative advantages of different machines, defining the conditions in which they should be used and organising the kind of work that they could acomplish.

According to Dumont, this was a matter of researching 'the tractor's best point of impact' while taking the agricultural calendar and the available labour into account.[91] This approach, which sought to target key 'bottle necks' for mechanisation, began gradually to replace the alternative model of wholesale mechanisation, which had become a financial black hole.

At the same time, engineers attempted to adapt and standardise the equipment of mechanised farming. Its resistance to tropical conditions was studied, and filters were developed and installed. French constructors were asked to learn from what the Americans and British had done in terms of integrated growing sequences and field representatives.[92] But here also metropolitan centralisation revealed its limits: locally devised solutions were frequently far more efficient and home-grown inventors were able to offer on-the-spot improvements to 'adapted machinery'.[93]

The environmental problems caused by mechanisation were addressed by a technical and segmented response in which one form of technology tried to outbid another. The attempted solutions for erosion included sub-soiling, ploughing along contour lines, windbreaks, and especially green manures. Although the latter were expensive and their effectiveness was questionable, certain agronomists continued to privilege them. In Senegal, for example, for years they carried out experiments with millet as green manure, despite the lack of interest among the peasants in growing food crops.[94]

Earlier pedological scouting missions had sometimes led to the scaling back of mechanisation projects.[95] But the new experimental orientation of pedological research and its integration into mechanical farming proved more resistant to criticism. When some pedologists, like Roger Fauck at the CGOT, expressed concern about the impact of growing methods on the soil, their expertise carried little weight.[96]

Mechanised areas that experienced difficulties functioned as field laboratories of a sort, where specialists in various agronomic sectors could carry out experiments with chemical fertilisers and insecticides (in Madagascar and Senegal these were applied by airborne methods), or with plant strains that resisted mechanised processes or salinity caused by new hydraulic systems, etc. When the sociologist André Hauser visited the CGOT in 1953, he observed that these experimental stations were the only units that were still expanding, and that they were experiencing housing shortages.[97]

The large-scale agro-industrial farms that never got off the ground were thus re-converted into smaller-scale experimental projects.[98] Wage labour gave way to collaborative efforts with the peasant farmers, following the model initiated by the motorised farming stations managed by local agricultural services, which grew in number and in ambition during the early 1950s.

The tractor in the service of rural development

In 1952 the Marshall Plan came to an end and the International Bank for Reconstruction and Development declined to invest in French tropical mechanisation projects,[99] which thus came to a halt. The executive committee of the FIDES and the Plan Commissions began to scrutinise their disbursements more carefully and scaled back their funding for the mechanisation of tropical agriculture.

There was no getting around the fact that the desired convergence between metropolitan modernisation and overseas development did not occur. In the first place, productivity increases in the metropole made colonial production relatively less important. The development of rapeseed production alleviated the shortages in tropical oilseeds. Second, the French agricultural machinery industry did not experience the kind of rapid, growth-generating expansion that had been expected, and showed no interest in the specific needs of the overseas territories. Finally, state investments overseas did not succeed in priming the pump of private capital.[100]

When the second plan for the development of the overseas territories was put together, the territories were much more involved. A new rural economy commission presented it to the *Commissariat-General of the Plan* (CGP). As far as mechanisation was concerned, rice-growing and local self-sufficiency in food crops were prioritised.[101] The continuation of mechanised groundnut farming in Senegal was negotiated with some difficulty.[102] It only seemed reasonable to continue insofar as it was linked to the manual farming of millet (for which it freed up labour hours) and complemented draft-animal cultivation.[103] Mechanised groundnut farming was saved above all thanks to the intensive efforts of a small team of agronomists who mobilised to have themselves appointed to develop the Plan for the Renovation of the Senegalese Rural Economy.[104]

While the High Commissioner of the AOF and the Governor Roland Pré declared that agricultural policies needed to be re-centred around the African peasantry and its concerns,[105] agricultural technicians continued to defend mechanisation by promoting a new rhetoric that emphasised social and regional development. According to this perspective, bringing modernity into the villages was supposed to have slowed the rates of rural out-migration and stabilised peasants on their lands.

Mechanisation was thus conceptualised in village- and family-friendly terms and presented as a means of renovating and preserving these structures against the forces of social disintegration that threatened the colonial order. As R. Dumont explained, agricultural technicians sought forms of mechanisation that 'would be applied gradually, without creating serious disruptions in the indigenous economy'.[106] In Madagascar, for example, the Modernised Native Rural Collective (*Collectivités Rurales Autochtones Modernisées*, CRAM), created in 1951 to facilitate the rational use of mechanised farming equipment, were based on the traditional peasant structure of the *fokonolona*.[107] Likewise, a key goal was to match mechanisation with family structure according to a logic that was more political than economic. Because it offered flexibility in terms of labour reserves that could be adjusted to the agricultural calendar, 'mechanisation in a family setting' clearly seemed more efficient and less costly than the model of a salaried workforce.

The collective land management and agricultural cooperatives that went along with 'indigenous mechanisation' enabled its advocates to present the idea as the key to professionalising and organising a peasantry that was viewed as weakly structured. Upper Guinea, with its pilot programme for mechanised rice-growing, was thus in 1950 the first Cooperative Section for Land Management and Rural Equipment (*Secteur Coopératif d'Aménagement et d'Equipement Rural*, SCAER).[108] The SCAER provided a structure for the collective use of mechanised equipment, which was placed under the care of a technician. Those in Guinea cleared and prepared vast rice-growing plains, assigned the lands to the peasants, carried out ploughing, and generally organised agricultural work. They were a model for reforming the mutual societies, which had grown very unpopular.[109] The SCAER were a key step in the passage from 'the authoritarian phase of colonisation to its technical phase, from the time of the administrators to that of the agronomists', according to R. Dumont, who (along with other agricultural engineers), defended this transition.[110]

The fabric of colonial agricultural services was strengthened by organisations and concepts such as the SEMA, SCAER, 'modernised hamlets', 'pilot villages', and 'mechanised peasantries'. Agronomic researchers (sometimes assisted by sociologists) committed to popularising their knowledge, envisioned, in terms such as these, an integrated transformation of social structures, agricultural practices, and regional economies.

Although these experiments were carried out on parcels of no more than several hundred hectares in size, they turned village relationships and forms of land tenure upside down. This was also the case when wealthy peasants acquired tractors which they then rented to their neighbours. Tricky questions of landed property and peasant debt seem to have been at the root of numerous conflicts. They also seem to explain a growing reticence of the agricultural service to engage the mechanisation issue.[111]

Conclusion

During the 1950s mechanisation in tropical Africa progressively slowed, while draft-animal cultivation, which was often viewed as an intermediate step in an agricultural evolution leading towards mechanisation, took off. The term 'mechanisation', which in the immediate post-war years signified the use of inanimate motors, was a key element in this teleological perspective and lasted throughout the 1950s, when it came to refer to the use of any agricultural tool, whether manual, harnessed, or motorised. The tractor no longer stood for a necessary rupture, but was rather a developmental goal for agricultural experts, wealthy peasants, and certain governing elites. It was a means of social reproduction or promotion, and even a symbol of national independence, as on a postage stamp issued by the government of Mali in 1961 depicting a combine in action. The various ways by which proto-Socialist African elites in Guinea, Madagascar, Mali, or the Ivory Coast sought to re-appropriate the tractor in the 1960s must be understood as a failure to have learned the lessons of the vast programme of colonial mechanisation and its sorry results.

The beneficiary of huge investments by the metropole in its colonies immediately after the war, agricultural mechanisation conceptualised African agricultural development under the rubric of technological change, and offered itself as a magic pill to cure the social, economic, and environmental ills faced by colonial authorities. An analysis of the emergence of the mechanising project, directed by metropolitan experts in close partnership with the business of imperial planning, demonstrates parallels with what Anglophone historians of the post-war period have referred to as the 'second colonial occupation' or the 'triumph of experts'.[112] Even if this grandiose project of industrialising the African countryside did not succeed, we have seen how the management of its setbacks led to further developments in agronomic research and to the continued control of agricultural technicians over the rural populations of the overseas territories. While the experience of mechanisation gave rise to perceptions in the metropole that the empire was costly, the way in which mechanisation was conceptualised shifted over time (though without much success), from an effort to 'uncover the value' of 'virgin lands' to a goal of developing rural communities.

Even though the tractor's promise was not realised, the voices of criticism did not win the day in the metropolitan political arena, over which the technocratic approach to colonial questions had a strangle-hold. Despite their international activism, the naturalist critics at the IFAN and the MNHN did not succeed in drawing public attention to the problem of the environmental impact of mechanisation, or in launching it as a field of policy research.

On the contrary, the various fields of expertise that were constituted in order to manage the setbacks experienced by the mechanising project imagined the tractor as the end point of agronomic research and as a key feature in the action plans of development projects. The North's construction of an international scientific expertise and the continued post-independence role of agronomists in overseas territories guaranteed the promotion of a development model based on strong technical cooperation between foreign knowledge and foreign capital, driven by state involvement.

Notes

1 In this article, the term 'mechanisation' is used for 'motorisation', according to its meaning in the post-war period. See Archives Nationales d'Outre Mer, Aix en Provence (hereafter ANOM), 58 PA 1, Maurice Rossin, 'La politique des cultures tropicales: sciences politiques, 3 cours', 1951.
2 ANOM 2 FIDES 317, 'Bilan du premier plan de développement économique et social des TOM, présenté par M. Huet à la commission d'étude et de coordination du Plan de Modernisation et d'Equipement des TOM' [ca. 1953], p. 34.
3 Frederick Cooper, 'Modernizing Bureaucrats, Backward Africans, and the Development Concept', in Frederick Cooper and Randall Packard (eds), *International Development and the Social Sciences: Essays on the History and Politics of Knowledge* (Berkeley, Los Angeles, London: University of California Press 1997), pp. 64–92.
4 Robert Metge, 'La mécanisation et le système cultural africain', *L'Agronomie Tropicale* 7, 2 (1952), p. 140.
5 *L'équipement des TOM: Réalisations du FIDES 1947–1950* (Paris: Ministère de la France d'Outre-Mer 1950).
6 *Conférence Africaine Française de Brazzaville, 30 janvier 1944 – 08 février 1944* (Paris: Ministère des colonies 1945).
7 Harry Gamble, 'Peasants of the Empire: Rural Schools and the Colonial Imaginary in 1930s French West Africa', *Cahiers d'Études Africaines* 49, 195 (2009), pp. 775–804.
8 *L'équipement des TOM*, p. 18.
9 ANOM 2 FIDES 317 M22/53, Conférence Africaine Française de Brazzaville, AOF Plan décennal, Section générale, 1944, Comité d'organisation des Productions industrielles coloniales.
10 Chantal Metzger, *L'empire colonial français dans la stratégie du Troisième Reich, 1936–45* (2 vols, Brussels, New York: Peter Lang 2002).
11 John Kent, *The Internationalization of Colonialism: Britain, France and Black Africa, 1939–1956* (Oxford: Clarendon Press 1992).
12 René Dumont, 'Orientation de l'agriculture française et coloniale dans le cadre d'une économie dirigée', *Revue de l'Économie Contemporaine* 17 (September 1943), pp. 19–26.
13 Archives de René Dumont, Musée du vivant et histoire d'AgroParisTech, Paris (hereafter MdV APT), E. Annet, 'Rapport sur l'exécution du programme expérimental de riziculture en Casamance', 26 July 1940.

14 Bibliothèque historique du CIRAD, Nogent (hereafter BH CIRAD), M. Rossin, 'La riziculture aux Etats-Unis', STAT, 1946.
15 European cooperation, which developed along with the Marshall Plan, saw an important role for the overseas territories in helping to balance their budgets, and thus prioritised agricultural projects that were profitable in the short term; see ANOM 2 FIDES 209, 'Le plan quadriennal 1947–1952: Les TOM'.
16 Gérard Bossuat, La France, l'aide américaine et la construction européenne 1944–1954 (Paris: Comité pour l'histoire économique et financière de la France 1997).
17 Frederick Cooper, Décolonisation et travail en Afrique: l'Afrique britannique et française, 1935–1960 (Paris: Karthala 2004).
18 Dominique Desjeux, La question agraire à Madagascar: administration et paysannat de 1895 à nos jours (Paris: L'Harmattan 1979).
19 Archives Nationales du Sénégal, Dakar (hereafter ANS), 1R 161 v158 [ca. 1946].
20 Jacques Marseille, Empire colonial et capitalisme français: histoire d'un divorce (Paris: Albin Michel 1984).
21 This propaganda first appeared in the journals Marchés coloniaux and France Outre Mer, and in 1953 began to be officially disseminated by the Committee of Overseas Rural Machinery (Comité de Machinisme Agricole Outre Mer).
22 Rossin, 'La politique des cultures tropicales'.
23 René Dumont, Plan d'orientation de la production agricole française et coloniale (Paris: Secrétariat Général du Ravitaillement 1944). Created by the Agricultural Ministry and shared with the English, this document also served as a basis of discussion among the Allies.
24 The key Plan Commissions were the sub-commission of agricultural production of the Modernisation Commission for Overseas Territories, and the oil and soap commission, created on 20 February 1947.
25 BH CIRAD, Paul Carton, 'Le plan de modernisation des TOM: le rôle des ingénieurs agronomes dans sa réalisation', Congrès des Ingénieurs agronomes, Paris, 4–6 December 1946 (Paris: Association amicale des anciens élèves de l'Institut national agonomique 1947), p. 37.
26 This took place at the ORSTOM, through the creation of the Rural Economic and Social Development Investment Fund (Fonds d'Équipement Rural et de Développement Economique et Social, FERDES), and by establishing a section of Rural Engineering in the colonial rural services in 1949.
27 ANOM 1 FIDES 70 D747, A. Kopp, 'Note no 68 sur la contribution du FIDES au fonctionnement de la STAT', 5 February 1947.
28 See, for example, BH CIRAD, STAT, Charles Gaury, 'Rapport général de la mission d'information en AOF', 1949; BH CIRAD, STAT, Georges Labrousse, 'Journal de route de la mission T.A. 38/86: machinisme agricole pour les TOM français aux USA du 11/07/1951 au 02/10/1951'.
29 ANOM 1 FIDES 70 D 747, Direction de l'Agriculture, 'Note no 78', 6 January 1947.
30 Björn-Ola Linnér, The Return of Malthus: Environmentalism and Post-War Population-Resource Crises (Isle of Harris: White Horse Press 2003).
31 Colonial engineers gathering information in the United States were very interested in soil conservation techniques, which were a focus of comparative studies and international standardisation. See ANOM FM 2 FIDES 911. See also FAO, Conservation du sol: Etude internationale, Etude agricole de la FAO no 4 (Washington, Rome: FAO 1948).
32 Diana K. Davis, Resurrecting the Granary of Rome: Environmental History and French Colonial Expansion in North Africa (Athens, OH: Ohio University Press 2007).
33 For an overview, see William M. Adams, Green Development: Environment and Sustainability in the Third World (London, New York: Routledge 2001); Joseph Morgan Hodge, Triumph of the Expert: Agrarian Doctrines of Development and the Legacies of British Colonialism (Athens, OH: Ohio University Press 2007); William Beinart and Lotte Hughes, Environment and Empire (Oxford: Oxford University Press 2007).

34 James Fairhead and Melissa Leach, 'Desiccation and Domination: Science and Struggles over Environment and Development in Colonial Guinea', *Journal of African History* 41, 1 (2000), pp. 35–54.

35 Monica M. van Beusekom, 'From Underpopulation to Overpopulation: French Perceptions of Population, Environment, and Agricultural Development in French Soudan (Mali), 1900–1960', *Environmental History* 4, 2 (1999), pp. 198–219.

36 Henri Labouret, *Paysans d'Afrique occidentale* (Paris: Gallimard 1941); Pierre Viguier, 'Les techniques de l'agriculture soudanaise et les feux de brousse', *Revue Internationale de Botanique Appliquée et d'Agriculture Tropicale* 26, 279–80 (1946), pp. 42–51; BH CIRAD, Marchal, 'Les conséquences du labour à la charrue dans les sols légers sahéliens', Conférence africaine des sols, Goma, 8–16 November 1948.

37 *Conférence Africaine Française de Brazzaville: IL'équipement des TOM. Premier rapport de la commission de modernisation des TOM* (Paris: Commissariat Général au Plan 1948); ANOM 2 FIDES 209, 'Le plan quadriennal 1947–1952: Les TOM'.

38 ANS 3R 58 v159. Folder 'Rapports sur la dégradation des sols tropicaux en AOF: enquête de 1945'.

39 Jean-Paul Harroy, *Afrique, terre qui meurt: la dégradation des sols africains sous l'influence de la colonisation* (Bruxelles: Hayez 1944).

40 ANS 3R 58 v159, P. Bellouard, 'La dégradation des sols tropicaux au Sénégal', 1945.

41 BH CIRAD, M. Guillaume, 'La conservation des sols dans les territoires français de l'Afrique noire', Conférence africaine des sols, Goma, 8–16 November 1948.

42 UNSCCUR, 'Soils and forest (discussions)', *Proceedings of the United Nations Scientific Conference on the Conservation and Utilization of Resources (UNSCCUR), 17 August – 6 September 1949, Lake Success*, vol. 1, *Plenary Meetings* (New York: United Nations 1950), p. 90.

43 *Report of the Conference of FAO*. Third Session, Geneva, Switzerland, 25 August – 11 September 1947. Available at: www.fao.org/docrep/x5582E/x5582E00.htm (accessed 25 May 2013); *Report of the Conference of FAO*. Fifth Session, Washington, DC, 21 November – 6 December 1949. Available at: www.fao.org/docrep/x5579E/x5579E00.htm (accessed 25 May 2013).

44 One example is René Dumont, 'Les difficultés de la modernisation de l'agriculture africaine autochtone', *Cahiers des Ingénieurs Agronomes* 6, 2 (1950), pp. 14–20.

45 BH CIRAD, Congrès des ingénieurs coloniaux, Section de l'Agriculture (III), 4 October 1949.

46 On dynamic balance thinking in ecology and its implications for interventionist planning, see Peder Anker, *Imperial Ecology: Environmental Order in the British Empire, 1895–1945* (Cambridge, MA: Harvard University Press 2001).

47 On modernising dualism, see Cooper, 'Modernizing Bureaucrats'.

48 Guillaume, 'La conservation des sols', p. 2243.

49 Ibid., p. 2249.

50 ANOM 2 FIDES 317, 'Bilan du premier plan de développement économique et social des TOM, présenté par M. Huet à la commission d'étude et de coordination du Plan de Modernisation et d'Equipement des TOM'.

51 Metge, 'La mécanisation'.

52 *L'équipement des TOM*, p. 13.

53 André Kopp, 'Réflexions sur la mise en valeur des TOM', *L'Agronomie Tropicale* 2, 9–10 (1947), p. 461.

54 ANOM 2 FIDES 209, 'Procès verbaux des séances du Comité directeur du FIDES, Section TOM', 1947–8.

55 See the essay of Juhani Koponen, 'From dead end to new lease of life: development in South-Eastern Tanganyika' in this volume.

56 Marina Diallo Cô-Trung, *La Compagnie Générale des Oléagineux Tropicaux en Casamance: autopsie d'une opération de mise en valeur colonial, 1948–1962* (Paris: Karthala 1998), p. 30.

57 Ibid.

58 Monica M. van Beusekom, *Negotiating Development: African Farmers and Colonial Experts at the Office du Niger, 1920–1960* (Portsmouth, NH: Heinemann; Oxford: James Currey; Cape Town: D. Philip 2002).
59 BH CIRAD, 'Le riz à l'Office du Niger', 20 April 1950, p. 4.
60 van Beusekom, *Negotiating Development*.
61 Cooper, 'Modernizing Bureaucrats'; Hodge, *Triumph of the Expert*.
62 Diallo Cô-Trung, *La Compagnie Générale des Oléagineux Tropicaux*, p. 216.
63 *Rapport général de la Commission d'étude et de coordination des plans de modernisation et d'équipement des TOM* (Paris: CGP 1954).
64 On the experimental paradigm in the period of development, see Christophe Bonneuil, 'Development as Experiment: Science and State Building in Late Colonial and Postcolonial Africa, 1930–1970', *Osiris*, 2nd series, 15 (2000), pp. 258–81. For a history of medicine perspective, see Guillaume Lachenal, 'Le médecin qui voulut être roi: médecine coloniale et utopie au Cameroun', *Annales: Histoire, Sciences Sociales* 65, 1 (2010), pp. 121–56.
65 Roger Heim, 'Erosion et surpopulation, Protection de la nature no 7', *Culture française*, 8 March 1950. Available at: www.ina.fr/economie-et-societe/environnement-et-urbanisme/audio/PHD86059321/protection-de-la-nature-7–erosion-et-surpopula-tion.fr.html (accessed 24 March 2013).
66 Auguste Chevalier, 'Les essais de cultures nouvelles et de mécanisation de l'agriculture au Moyen Congo Français (Niari et pays Batéké)', *Revue Internationale de Botanique Appliquée et d'Agriculture Tropicale* 31, 347–8 (1951), pp. 506–12.
67 Raymond Furon, *L'érosion du sol* (Paris: Payot 1947).
68 Michel Gleizes, *Un regard sur l'ORSTOM, 1953–1983: témoignage* (Paris: Editions de l'ORSTOM 1985), pp. 34–8.
69 Marie-Albane De Suremain, 'Métamorphoses d'un continent: l'Afrique des Annales de Géographie, de 1919 au début des années 1960', *Cahiers d'Études Africaines* 39, 153 (1999), pp. 145–68.
70 Jacques Richard-Molard, 'Plaidoyer pour une nouvelle paysannerie en Afrique noire', *Présence Africaine* 13 (1952), pp. 170–9.
71 J. Richard-Molard, 'Les terrains tropicaux', *Annales de Géographie* 60, 322 (1951), pp. 349–69.
72 Pierre-Louis Dekeyser, *Quelques aspects du problème des mange-mil* (Dakar: IFAN 1953), p. 8.
73 Roland Portères, 'Le système de riziculture par franges univariétales et l'occupation des fonds par les riz flottants dans l'ouest africain', *Revue Internationale de Botanique Appliquée et d'Agriculture Tropicale* 29, 325–6 (1949), pp. 553–63.
74 Linnér, *The Return of Malthus*.
75 Théodore Monod, 'Education and the Conservation of Natural Resources', in UNSCCUR, *Proceedings of the United Nations Scientific Conference on the Conservation and Utilization of Resources*, vol. 1, pp. 275–8; Théodore Monod, 'Conservation des ressources naturelles en Afrique noire française et éducation', in Secretariat of the International Union for the Protection of Nature (ed.), *International Technical Conference on the Protection of Nature, Lake Success, 22–29 August 1949: Proceedings and Papers* (Paris, Brussels: UNESCO 1950), pp. 242–51. Available at: http://unesdoc.unesco.org/images/0013/001335/133578mo.pdf (accessed 23 March 2013).
76 Institut Français d'Afrique Noire (IFAN), Series 'Protection de la nature: conservation et exploitation rationnelle des ressources naturelles. Education, écologie', 1–22, 1949–59.
77 Richard-Molard, 'Plaidoyer pour une nouvelle paysannerie'.
78 cf. Labouret, *Paysans d'Afrique occidentale*; Robert Delavignette, *Les paysans noirs* (Paris: Stock 1931).
79 ANOM 2 FIDES 183, 'Procès verbaux du Comité directeur du FIDES', 78ème réunion, 10 October 1950.
80 Diallo Cô-Trung, *La Compagnie Générale des Oléagineux Tropicaux*, p. 234.

81 ANS 1R 200 v158, R. Sagot, 'Note au sujet de l'agriculture dans la zone à arachide du Sénégal', September 1951, p. 8.
82 ANS 1R 176 v158, 'Lettre du Haut commissaire aux gouverneurs, Projet de déc. 1947–janv. 1948'.
83 *Premier rapport de la commission de modernisation des TOM.*
84 ANS 1R 176 v158, 'Lettre du Haut Commissaire de l'AOF aux Gouverneurs', 31 August 1948.
85 ANS 1R 176 v158, 'Arrêté ministériel du 26/09/1950, paru au Journal Officiel des 20–21 novembre 1950'. The SEMA model took various forms in different territories; cf. René Tourte, *Histoire de la recherche agricole en Afrique tropicale francophone*, vol. 6, *De l'empire colonial à l'Afrique indépendante, 1945–1960: la recherche prépare le développement* (n.p.: s.n. 2012). Available at: www.fao.org/wairdocs/an500f/an500f00.pdf (accessed 3 April 2013).
86 ANS 1R 176 v158, 'Mémorandum des TOM sur la vulgarisation agricole', 1952.
87 ANS 1R 176 v158, 'Lettre du gouverneur général de l'AOF au Ministère de la France d'Outre-Mer du 22/04/1952'.
88 ANS 1R 176 v158, Folder 'Institution des SEMA dans les TOM'.
89 Maurice Rossin, 'Deuxième compte-rendu sur le développement du plan de culture mécanisée de l'arachide dans l'Est africain anglais: situation en mai 1949', *L'Agronomie Tropicale* 6, 1–3 (1951), pp. 3–28.
90 Paul Coleno and Maurice Rossin, *Le plan de culture mécanisée de l'arachide dans l'Est-africain anglais, situation en mai 1948* (Paris: Ministère de la France d'Outre-Mer 1948).
91 René Dumont, 'La mise en valeur agricole de l'Afrique tropicale', *Economie Contemporaine* (February 1951), pp. 16–28.
92 ANS 1R 161 v158, 'Compte-rendu du voyage d'études accompli par M.P. Lelogeais au Congo belge, en AOF et AEF', Circulaire d'informationdu CEMC, 7 [ca. 1950].
93 Pierre Truteau, *Un paysan français parmi les paysans du Tiers-Monde: vie de Jean Nolle* (Paris: L'Harmattan, 1994); Tourte, *Histoire de la recherche*.
94 ANS 1R 466, 'Conférence franco-britannique Arachide-mil, Contribution du CRA de Bambey', 6–13 September 1954.
95 ANS 1R 318, Georges Aubert, Jacques Dubois, Roger Maignien, 'Les sols à arachides du Sénégal', 1948.
96 BH CIRAD, R. Fauck, 'Erosion et mécanisation agricole', Bureau des sols en AOF, 1956.
97 A. Hauser, *Rapport de mission CGOT* (n.p.: s.n. 1953).
98 For a similar dynamic in the British Empire, see Robert Chambers, *Settlement Schemes in Tropical Africa: A Study of Organizations and Development* (London: Routledge 1969).
99 Bossuat, *La France, l'aide américaine.*
100 Paul Humblot, 'Le plan français de développement économique et social dans les territoires d'Outre-Meret le Plan Marshall', *Economie Contemporaine* (March 1951), pp. 25–32.
101 *Rapport général de la Commission d'étude et de coordination.*
102 See for example, BH CIRAD, 'Procès-verbal de la réunion du 05/06/1953 de la sous-commission d'Economie rurale, CGP'.
103 Mission Roland Portères, *Aménagement de l'économie agricole et rurale au Sénégal* (3 vols, Bambey: Centre de recherches agronomiques 1952).
104 Ibid.
105 *Observations et conclusions personnelles du gouverneur Roland Pré, président de la commission d'Etude et de coordination des plans de modernisation et d'équipement des TOM* (Paris: s.n. 1954); Bernard Cornut-Gentille, 'Allocution prononcée à l'ouverture de la première séance du Grand Conseil de l'AOF', 7 May 1953, quoted in Cooper, *Décolonisation*, p. 407.
106 MdV APT, Archives de René Dumont, 'Notes prises au BEA de Boulel près Kaffrine (Sénégal)', 29 and 30 October 1950, p. 9.

107 MdV APT, 'La Centrale d'Equipement Agricole et de Modernisation du Paysannat: ses attributions, ses moyens, son fonctionnement, ses réalisations' [ca. 1957].
108 ANS 2 G 51 97, 'Rapport annuel du service agricole de Guinée', 1951.
109 *Rapport de la sous-commission Economie rurale, Commission d'étude et de coordination des plans de Modernisation et d'Equipement des TOM* (Paris: CGP 1954).
110 Dumont, 'Les difficultés de la modernisation', p. 19. For a comparable analysis about Madagascar CRAM, see Desjeux, *La question agraire à Madagascar*.
111 Georges Labrousse, 'Tendances de la mécanisation dans nos TOM aujourd'hui', *Bulletin de Liaison du Comité de Machinisme Agricole Outre Mer* 11 (March–April 1958), pp. 1–3; van Beusekom, *Negotiating Development*.
112 See, among others, D. A. Low and John M. Lonsdale, 'Introduction: Towards the New Order, 1945–1963', in D.A. Low and Alison Smith (eds), *History of East Africa*, vol. 3 (Oxford: Clarendon Press, 1976); Hodge, *Triumph of the Expert*.

PART III

Social development and welfare

CHAPTER EIGHT

From precondition to goal of development: health and medicine in the planning and politics of British Tanganyika

Walter Bruchhausen

Whereas health care is an important part of contemporary development co-operation with independent African nations – both in finances and in staff – the same cannot be said of the development discourses in late colonialism. The relationship between health and development was various and changing, thus inviting a closer look. This chapter examines the case of Tanganyika (modern-day Tanzania), and is based on my studies on past and present medical pluralism there.[1] Three concepts of causal relations between health and development can be distinguished in the development strategies since independence. The first is to view health as a precondition for economic development which has been most recently emphasised in reports by the World Bank and WHO on 'investing in health' since the 1990s.[2] The second conceptual approach is to see better health services as a subsequent result of economic development which was assumed in the 'trickle down effect' idea of modernisation theories, especially during the 1960s.[3] Finally, there is health as an explicit goal of development, as in the 'basic needs' strategy of the 1970s when improved health was envisaged even before economic development.[4]

This contribution aims at tracing the earlier beginnings of these different conceptual relationships since the start of policies on colonial economic development in Tanzania under German rule.[5] The first finding is that the word 'development' or its German equivalents entered the discourse on health rather late, only in the 1940s. Thus the third relationship 'health as goal of development' cannot have been conceptualised earlier. The other two usages, however, can be found already in German political and medical discussions on East Africa long before the First World War.

Medical doctors on 'development' in German East Africa

During German colonial rule in East Africa, the word *Entwicklung* (the German equivalent of 'development') was used in the sense of a technical term and nearly exclusively as noun to the adjectives 'economic' or 'colonial' in an affirmative manner. This is the case, for example, with physicians like Otto Peiper who was probably the medical officer most devoted to issues of public health in the whole of German East Africa.[6] Another former medical doctor in German East Africa called the replacing of local healers – with their strong political role in the recent Maji Maji war – with more government doctors a contribution to 'a quiet prosperous development of the colony'.[7] Outside this rather economic use, the word *Entwicklung* had for medical doctors a nearly value-neutral and more descriptive meaning. A major semantic problem is, of course, that *Entwicklung* might translate into English as evolution as well as development, but also as progress, progression, advancement, growth, expansion, or history. The word *Entwicklung* was applied by medical doctors, for example, in order to describe the 'origin and development' ('Ursprung und Entwicklung') of Islam as a religion which is successful in propaganda, but an obstacle towards 'social progress' ('sozialen Fortschritt'), as it means 'stagnation' ('Stagnation') for family life, especially the status of women, and for economics.[8] The main aim was 'culture' ('Kultur') and the way towards it was 'progress' ('Fortschritt'). Thus the metaphors of going, especially departing from some undesired state and reaching new land, were paramount for non-economic issues, not the idea of unfolding some good already there as in 'developing'. The colonial politician Dernburg stated explicitly that 'evolution in the cultural area is very difficult and slow'.[9] Thus the cultural continuation of Darwin's natural evolution tinged the meaning of the German word for development. This evolutionist notion in Germany was taken up by some medical doctors in order to investigate 'primitive' or 'folk' medicine[10] and might have influenced colonial doctors, too, but without obvious traces in the use of the word *Entwicklung*.

Indigenous health as a precondition for development

When the idea of colonial development entered German politics, especially after the major colonial wars in German East and South-West Africa, and the so-called 'Hottentot election' of 1907, preventive medicine or public health was seen as an important tool to further it.[11] The main motivation was the population's importance for economic development, especially considering that many reports described a shrinking and unhealthy population. Several authors offered variations on the idea that the most important asset of the colony was not minerals or natural products but the black inhabitants. This was certainly a major turn as the first European health care personnel in East Africa – that of commercial agencies, Christian missions, and governments – had been intended exclusively for the care of the Europeans and their local employees, mainly servants, clerks, and soldiers.

During the first years of the British mandate in Tanganyika, the argument for the economic importance of health care continued to be heard. Especially in mining, the expectation that better health brought better revenues was investigated and communicated.[12] Yet there was also a change in motives and arguments in favour of health care for the benefit of the local population.

The East Africa Commission of 1925: 'development' and 'improvement'

Unlike the previous German protectorate that had been declared by the German government in order to secure its economic and political interests, and also differing from settler colonies such as Kenya or Southern Rhodesia, Tanganyika Territory was a mandated territory of the League of Nations. Britain, therefore, had 'a special responsibility before the world for insuring its good government and development' as the *Report of the East Africa Commission* stated in 1925.[13] The Commission's statement represents a major argument for social development becoming an end in itself, and not just a contributing factor to an intended economic exploitation. In 1924, the terms of reference for this influential commission had distinguished in their wording, though not in their measures, between 'economic development' on the one side and such changes as 'improvement of health' and 'moral and material improvement' on the other.[14] Both sides were united in the aim of ameliorating 'the social condition of the natives of East Africa'. Accordingly, the chapter on 'Medical Services' does not use the word 'development' other than in the economic sense,[15] although much of its observations and recommendations on medical services were directed towards growth, expansion, improvement, and qualification; that is to concepts that were and became central components of the idea of development. The report observed the tendency to move away from the exclusive responsibility for European health towards allowing for the health problems of the African population – for humanitarian as well as economic reasons.[16] Perceived obstacles included 'venereal disease, malnutrition, ignorance of child welfare, and tribal customs'; that is factors emphasising mainly African behaviour which it felt should be changed.[17] The amount of medical and health work required great numbers of qualified African staff instead of and in addition to the few European health professionals. The number of hospitals for the indigenous population had to be increased enormously. These became in fact the main lines for the health policy of the territory until its end: health education, training of more African staff, and building more health facilities.

This general line was endorsed and modified by a number of factors on the local, territorial, imperial, and international level. There was, for example, a growing demand for medical institutions by the indigenous population and their representatives under Indirect Rule because people could now articulate their wishes for health care services. Such demands were also informed by more African staff working for missions and government health care facilities and by some obvious therapeutic successes such as the mass treatment of yaws, which at the time was an epidemic and crippling bacterial infection. The international wave of 'social medicine' in the 1930s removed health care further from a mere market place commodity and transformed it into a prominent public task and responsibility.

Health care as a case for 'dissociation' instead of 'development'

Yet in this expansion, several points that distinguished the establishment of medical services from political and economic development were made explicit. In 1933, the Director of Medical Services, John Shircore, observed: 'Native Administrations are attempting to develop themselves from existing native laws and customs, whereas the native medical service, at present at least, dissociates itself completely from native medicine'.[18] In a similar way five years later William Macmillan's influential report on Africa counted health as one of the areas where the idea of starting development from native practices – as is fundamental to the concept of Indirect Rule – was not applicable: 'The new system [of Indirect Rule], therefore, does not necessarily help and may even impair the energy applied to the work of reconstruction – the promotion of health, education, and scientific agriculture. In this sphere, moreover, there is little that is African to build on, and a good deal of deeply rooted custom standing in the way of essential changes'.[19] Thus Macmillan titled the chapter on health services, education, and agriculture, 'The Attack on Backwardness', and not 'development' as in the chapters on mining (IX) and on colonial economy (XII).

This idea that development means improvement or modernisation of pre-existing local institutions whereas medicine demands a complete break away from and replacement of previous indigenous practices made health policy, perhaps together with education, a special case. In the British colonies of Asia where written medical traditions and indigenous medicine was practised as a scholarly pursuit and intense exchange with European physicians dated back to the eighteenth century, the case was somewhat different although not completely. In colonial India, European anatomy and medicine had already been integrated into studies of Ayurveda and Yunani medicine at the beginning of the nineteenth century. Whereas the colonial administration attempted to stop this syncretism, the movement for independence was connected to a combination of Ayurvedic and Western medicine whose relationship was academically and politically discussed in the years before independence including by Western scholars.[20] After independence, in Sri Lanka and India a heated debate arose as to whether Ayurveda should be kept 'pure' or, as already had been the case in practice and even in colleges for indigenous medicine, combined with such facilities as the x-ray and laboratory.[21] The question discussed by nationalist politicians and physicians was whether 'progress' – the word 'development' does not seem to have been prominent in these debates – meant the integration or the separation of Western and traditional Indian types of medicine. As in Communist China the actual national policy in India became a separate professional and academic institutionalisation of 'traditional' medicine.[22]

Given such syncreticisation in Asia, one may wonder what the reasons were for the allegedly necessary, complete rupture from indigenous knowledge and practices in health and medicine in colonial Africa. Why could administrative functions relate to traditional institutions but health care could not? One issue was the recruitment of personnel. Wherever traditional authorities still existed there was an attempt to involve them in the territorial administration. In health care, the predominating idea was quite the opposite. Traditional experts where usually regarded as completely useless, if not a hindrance. This became quite clear in the question of who should be trained as midwives. The Protestant missionary Mrs Maynard had been quite outspoken about this in 1927 when she voted for training 'girls who are not yet deeply contaminated by native customs, as are all the mature women . . . There is too much to train out of older women'.[23] This view that training in midwifery had to be based on school education and not on traditional experience was also the common view in the Pan-African conference that the League of Nations' Health Organisation held in Cape Town in 1932.[24] Health care was not regarded as an improved continuation of African practices but as a completely new start from scratch.

Medical theories on development in East Africa

This sceptical view of African achievements corresponded to another debate of the time that related medical science to development. Especially in Kenya where scientific racism was flourishing at this time medical doctors posed the question of whether and to what degree the native Africans were suited for progress. In his address to the East African branches of the British Medical Association in 1936, the psychiatrist H. L. Gordon stated: 'The present state of the East African . . . is a non-progressive state showing deficiencies of physical, mental, moral, and social development according to the standards of a progressive people. To this state, commonly called backwardness, I give the more scientific name *bradyphysis*'. For Gordon, the enquiry 'into the nature and the causes' of this so called 'bradyphysis', which literally meant the 'slow natural constitution', involved four approaches: the social, the environmental, the psychological, and the physical.[25] His medical colleague Vint, a pathologist, concentrated on the latter two and explained the alleged mental difference to Europeans as being the result of a different morphological structure of the brain. Gordon's and Vint's approaches were soon opposed by new trends in anthropology, but they expressed wide-spread attitudes and views in the medical profession and white society of East Africa at the time.

Some of the perceived obstacles to the desired progress, however, could be tackled by the means of medicine and science of the human body. A considerable part of alleged physical and intellectual deficiencies of Africans was explained by preventable or curable infectious diseases and by nutritional deficiencies. Thus such research resulted in demands for more funds for medicine and emphasised the importance of promoting agriculture. By these arguments, representatives of medical science claimed at the same time to explain development problems of East Africa and to offer solutions to them.

Health services as depending on colonial economy

That health services were dependent on the economic situation of a colony was already clear from the British idea of financial 'self-sufficiency'.[26] As the social scientist Walter Morris-Hale described it: 'The guiding principle of the British Government had always been that "A colony should have only those services which it can afford to maintain out of its own resources"'.[27] Accordingly, the Colonial Development Act and Fund of 1929 was an idea of the Conservatives taken up by the Labour Party in order to fight unemployment in Britain,[28] and can hardly be seen as oriented towards African interests. Yet ten years later, in 1938, less from such British interests than out of responsibility for sub-Saharan Africa, the two major reports, Lord Hailey's *African Survey* and William Macmillan's *Africa Emergent*, demanded a 'constructive' function of colonial administration instead of the previous rather 'protective' role. It would require promoting better living conditions instead of merely keeping up law and order.[29] Hailey's biographer John Cell[30] characterised Hailey's position on Africa as emphasising the colonial task of 'material betterment', thus making a distinction between the political and welfare: 'Promising eventual self-government was all very well but Africa's first priority should be decent health, nutritional, and living standards, for which massive aid would be required'.[31] This idea was not complete selflessness, but had then already acquired a short history in British justifications for keeping its colonial territories. In 1935, for example, the British Prime Minister Ramsay MacDonald 'had concluded that a much more aggressive welfare-development approach was needed if Britain were to justify its refusal to transfer the three High Commission territories to South Africa'.[32]

The terms 'development' and 'welfare' in relation to health

One result of this turn towards social policy was the addition of the term 'welfare' in the Colonial Development and Welfare Act of 1940, which included among other things funding for education and health services.[33] According to this terminology, health was regarded as part of welfare, not development. In East Africa in the same year, however, a new Central Development Committee for Tanganyika devoted nearly a hundred paragraphs of its report to health care.[34] The Director of Medical Services, Ralph Roylance Scott, noted these paragraphs 'cover a wide range of matters directly and indirectly affecting the health of the people and were made in the light of the Committee's wide interpretation of the word "development" and of their objectives, which included "a healthy population, an increased non-native and native population and a greatly improved standard of living"'.[35] For a physician at the time, health being an objective of development obviously sounded somehow unusual. Nevertheless, 1940 seems to have been the turning point in using the concept (or at least the word) 'development' to encompass health care too. Before, reports and memoranda had used the term 'extension of medical [especially health] services'.[36] In 1942, the same director of medical services titled his memorandum 'on the Future Development of the Medical Services'.[37]

This growing reception of the word 'development' in medical circles does not necessarily mean an integration of health care into the overall idea of development. In Tanganyika in the 1940s and even the 1950s, the word development continued to refer rather to material extension, not to anything like 'community development'. It signified the physical infrastructure including numbers of staff – for example, when a proposal for the 'Development of Native Administration Dispensaries' from 1946 spoke of the 'centrifugal development' of dispensaries,[38] or when the responsibility for hospital building in the 1950s was assigned to the government's 'Member for Communications, Works and Development Planning'.

At the metropolitan level of the British empire, the distinction between 'development' and 'welfare' implied in the Colonial Development and Welfare Act of 1940 influenced or reflected the terms in official and semi-official reports. Lucy P. Mair's study of *Welfare in the British Colonies*, written for the Royal Institute of International Affairs in 1944, largely avoids the word 'development' and uses it mainly just in the plural, that is in a non-technical meaning. Health, as one of the four areas studied (the others being education, labour, and social welfare), is rather referred to by terms such as 'improvement' or 'expansion of services'. To a great extent, it is discussed as a question of international co-operation, organisation of health services, and control of diseases. 'Progress' in 'the promotion of good health', as the aim is titled, varies greatly, and depends 'upon local conditions, in particular the finances available, the standard of education of the community and the stage of development reached'.[39] Thus good health is rather seen as a possible result of development, not so much as part and condition of development. Even as late as in 1953, the *Review of the Development Plans* in the Southern Province of Tanganyika did not include health services, and only mentioned health at all briefly in the remarks on 'industrial health'.[40] And in 1956, the only chapters in the second edition of Lord Hailey's *An African Survey* (as in the first of 1938), which had 'development' in the title were the two on 'Economic Development' (chapters XVIII and XIX, 1956 (XIX and XX, 1938)). Only within the chapter on health (XVII, 1938 or XVI, 1956) was the section originally titled 'The Beginnings of Medical Work in Africa' renamed as 'The Development of Medical Activities' in the second edition. Notwithstanding the change of name, the section was still exclusively devoted to the history from early missionary work to the first decades of the twentieth century.[41] Thus even in 1956, the word 'development' referred to past extension rather than ongoing trends or plans in the health services.

Post-war debates: development of health care in quantity or quality?

Apart from the perhaps formal question of whether the word 'development' was used or not within documents on health care, it has to be asked whether the content of the concept, that is the idea of what later or in other contexts has been named development, was not already planned and pursued in health care as well. It might be argued that certain policies could be called development issues 'avant la lettre' as they did not only try to preserve the status quo, in the sense of reacting to urgent needs by repairing damage to health, but aimed through more sophisticated planning at social services closer to those of industrialised nations – repeating the way Europe had taken in health care not that much earlier in time. There was quite an elaborate debate on the future directions for the health services, with intense conflict over the decision whether to favour quantity or quality in the promotion of rural health services. The protagonists of this heated debate, which started around the end of the Second World War, were the so-called Native Authorities and the political administration on the one side, with the government's medical department on the other.

The new appointment of Paul Arthur Theodore Sneath as Director of Medical Services in 1945 marked the beginning of the debate. Sneath, who had already served as Acting Director since 1944, was a Canadian-born physician with a postgraduate qualification in Public Health from Johns Hopkins University, a leading centre in that field, and several years of experience in the public health service of other British territories, namely the Gold Coast and British New Guinea. Sneath argued that the work of African staff, the 'tribal dressers' and other medical aids, should be confined to those dispensaries that could be supervised by a European medical doctor.[42] Underpinning his justification was a notion of development that compared the African present to the Western past:

> The principle at dispute here, in my opinion, is one of intellectual honesty vs. charlatanism . . . Our own history of development is marked by the herbalist, the itinerant vendor of snake-bite or some other kind of cure, the patent medicine racket, and the shilling doctor . . . I question whether such a medical service, on which we are placing a cloak of respectability by calling them dispensaries of one kind or another, is in fact one with better than the native medical practices that we are attempting to displace.[43]

Here scientific evidence makes the decisive difference for development proper. The improvement of health indicators, by disease control, hygiene, and health education, thus demanded certain alterations in life. This for Sneath was the true meaning of progress and development, not the numbers of staff and institutions.

For the Native Administration and their white counterparts in the political administration, however, 'development' meant precisely the increase in health care facilities and personnel, whatever their quality was.[44] The demand of the population for such services, fuelled by the obvious success of injections in treating widespread infectious diseases, counteracted the restrictions desired by the Medical Department. Thus, competing views dominated the debate: the individual perspective of accessible curative services versus the epidemiological perspective of decreasing morbidity and mortality; the expectation of some further benefits from the administration versus the appeal to change one's behaviour. In the end, both sides got at least partly what they wanted. The drugs and other therapeutic procedures allowed for the use of local staff were restricted, but no dispensaries were closed.

Although Sneath was opposed as being a backward spokesman for the professional dominance of physicians instead of accepting political interests, his proclaimed aim sounds quite progressive, even prophetic.[45] It was 'creating an African community conscience directed towards reducing the burden of recognisable, controllable illness falling within the scope of the community's own efforts and fostering the positive objective of the attainment and maintenance of health and community responsibility for their fulfilment'.[46] With words that might have been taken out of a WHO document in the 1970s, Sneath was probably too far ahead of East African realities during his time and, therefore, he was forced to retire in early 1950, after having applied without success for a job with the WHO and a professorship in Manitoba.[47]

Preventing future instead of treating actual disease: health centres vs. hospitals

Yet despite Sneath's personal defeat, his view of strengthening preventive in relation to curative medicine became part of the official colonial policy at that time. It can only be speculated whether the main motivation was more the humanitarian one to avoid unnecessary suffering or the economic intelligence that prevention is less costly than the cure. Economic considerations that health care would pay off in economic growth or should be sacrificed to it were certainly less present than in earlier documents, if not altogether absent.

The turn towards a more preventive approach was supported by hints from the Colonial Office in London, albeit a bit less radical than what Sneath had intended. In 1949 the Chief Medical Officer for the colonies, Eric Pridie, wrote a report after a journey to East Africa. This report was accepted by the Legislative Council of Tanganyika and thereby replaced the recommendations of the Committee on Rural Medical Services of 1948.[48] The report remained official policy for the development of health services in Tanganyika until independence. Yet the actual planning often did not follow the intended balance between curative and preventive services. For despite the official emphasis on rural health centres, the bulk of investment continued to be in the area of curative services. The *Revised Development and Welfare Plan* for Tanganyika for 1950–56, for example, distributed two-thirds of the funds for construction to the two largest hospitals, whereas the construction of health centres together with that of smaller hospitals received less than 20 per cent of the whole budget.[49] Most of the dispensaries were left to the responsibility of the Native Administration or local governments.

Only in the next and last *Draft Plan for the Development of Medical Services in Tanganyika with Special Reference for the Period 1956–1961*, did the health centres receive more attention, five pages in comparison to two on hospitals.[50] The building and maintenance of the centres together with equipment and provision as well as the employment of subordinate staff were the responsibility of the Local Government (the new name for Native Authorities/Administration), while the training, supervision, and employment of qualified staff was the task of the central government's Medical Department.[51]

Conclusion: development and health care

For the sake of drawing some crude lines into this complex history it could be said that in the earlier years of colonial rule in German East Africa/Tanganyika, the main emphasis was on health services in relation to ('economic' or 'colonial') development. The causal relationship moved in both directions; it was assumed that economic improvement with its effects on nutrition, water supply, sanitation, and housing would eventually lead to improved health, but it was also argued that better health as a result of improved public health measures was important for the colonial economy. For this approach the native staff had to be trained in European science in order to replace European experts as well as African traditional medicine and to extend the services.

Only with the later intrusion of the new ideas on welfare and social medicine did health become an indicator for development and increasingly a goal in itself. It was no longer mainly a precondition or result of development but part of it. Health care was seen as a responsibility of the local community, not just of the individual, health professionals, and the government. There are two possible interpretations for this shift, both of which are valid to a certain degree in the always mixed motivations for health care stemming from altruism, sympathy, and social justice, as well as enlightened egotism und utility.

First, the role of health in the development discourses on East Africa, and probably also more generally, could serve as an example of the increasingly broader notion of development that emerged in the mid-twentieth century, and especially for the qualitative shift towards 'human development'. Yet this conceptual integration of health care into development was obviously not unanimous and rather delayed. In the papers from an Oxford conference on 'Alternatives in Development' which took place in 1973, for example, the author of the first contribution on health began by justifying health care in the context of development. According to the author, areas such as health were generally postponed until sufficient economic development had been achieved.[52] Only in the 1970s, with Robert McNamara's Nairobi Speech on 24 September 1973 or the Declaration of Cocoyoc from 23 October 1974 and their basic needs approach,[53] did health care become fully part of 'development aid'. It is thus not until the 1970s that we find such demands as 'the integration of health services into development services as a whole'.[54]

Nevertheless, a second, perhaps quite the opposite interpretation of taking up health as a development issue is possible as well. Transferring the responsibility for better health from the public services to the local communities relieves the government to a certain degree of substantial obligations in both finances and staff. If communities are able to avoid the effects of widespread ill-health through preventive practices, then future development replaces the need for immediate social services. Seen in this light, the controversy between the US-trained public health expert Sneath and the British colonial administrators was a clash not only between modern science-based disease prevention and old-fashioned curative care, but also between American liberalism with its principle of individual responsibility and the emerging British welfare state.

In either case – development as embracing or as replacing welfare activities – the role of health in colonial development remained ambiguous. It continued to oscillate between the aspects of promoting, indicating, and presupposing economic development. Therefore the study of late colonial policies on health does not give any definitive answer to the question what were the driving motives informing development discourses. But at the same time, as the study of health and medicine in colonial Tanganyika illustrates, it warns against a one-dimensional view of colonial interests.

Notes

1 Walter Bruchhausen, *Medizin zwischen den Welten: Vergangenheit und Gegenwart des medizinischen Pluralismus im südöstlichen Tansania* (Göttingen: v&r University Press, Bonn University Press 2006).

2 World Bank, *World Development Report 1993: Investing in Health* (Washington, DC: World Bank 1993); World Health Organization, Commission on Macroeconomics and Health, *Macroeconomics and Health: Investing in Health for Economic Development* (Geneva: WHO 2001).

3 Walt W. Rostow, *The Stages of Economic Growth: A Non-Communist Manifesto* (Cambridge: Cambridge University Press 1960).

4 International Labour Organization, *The Basic Needs Approach to Development: Some Issues Regarding Concepts and Methodology* (Geneva: International Labour Office 1980); World Bank, *First Things First: Meeting Basic Human Needs in the Developing Countries* (New York: Oxford University Press 1981).

5 Juhani Koponen, *Development for Exploitation: German Colonial Policies in Mainland Tanzania, 1884–1914* (Helsinki, Hamburg: Lit 1994).

6 Otto Peiper, 'Der Bevölkerungsrückgang in den tropischen Kolonien Afrikas und der Südsee, seine Ursachen und seine Bekämpfung', *Veröffentlichungen aus dem Gebiete der Medizinalverwaltung* 11, 7 (Berlin: Schoetz 1920), p. 440.

7 'eine ruhige gedeihliche Entwicklung der Kolonie': Hans Krauss, 'Der Suaheli-Arzt', *Münchener Medizinische Wochenschrift* 55 (1908), p. 519.

8 Peiper, 'Der Bevölkerungsrückgang in den tropischen Kolonien', pp. 25–6 and 437–8.

9 Bernhard Dernburg, 'Rede in der Sitzung der Budgetkommission des Reichstags vom 18. Februar 1908 besonders über Fragen der Eingeborenenpolitik', *Deutsches Kolonialblatt* 19 (1908), p. 221.

10 Reinhard Hofschlaeger, 'Die Entstehung der primitiven Heilmethoden und ihre systematische Weiterentwicklung', *Archiv für Geschichte der Medizin* 3 (1910), pp. 81–103; Hugo Magnus, *Die Volksmedizin, ihre geschichtliche Entwicklung und ihre Beziehung zur Kultur* (Breslau: Kern 1905).

11 Walter Bruchhausen, '"Practising Hygiene and Fighting the Natives' Diseases": Public and Child Health in German East Africa and Tanganyika Territory, 1900–1960', *Dynamis* 23 (2003), pp. 85–114.

12 Tanzania National Archives, Dar es Salaam (hereafter TNA), 11568, Investigations and treatment of worm infections (ankylostomiasis), 1927–38, nos. 1–3, Letter Shircore to Chief Secretary, 13 December 1927, refers to studies by Dr Giglioli, Demera Bauxite Company in 1924: 60 per cent of labourers infected with hookworm, mass treatment of ca. 800 in September 1923, six months later only 12 per cent infected; increase in tons per man per ten-hour day to 5.1 in November and in February to 6.76, equalling an increase of $1^3/_4$ tons five months after mass treatment.

13 *Report of the East Africa Commission* (London: HMSO 1925), p. 113.

14 Ibid., p. 3.

15 Ibid., p. 53.

16 Ibid., pp. 53–61.

17 Ibid., p. 54.

18 TNA 13571, vol. 1, Native Administration: Tribal Dressers, 1928–34, nos. 157–71, Memorandum by the Director of Medical Services on 'Tribal dressers', 16 May 1933, p. 165.

19 William MacMillan, *Africa Emergent: A Survey of Social, Political, and Economic Trends in British Africa* (London: Faber and Faber 1938), p. 317.

20 Henry E. Sigerist, 'The Need for an Institute of the History of Medicine in India', in *India: Report of the Health Survey and Development Committee*, vol. 3, *Appendices* (Delhi: Manager of Publications 1946), pp. 204–13.

21 Charles Leslie, 'Interpretations of Illness: Syncretism in Modern Āyurveda', in Charles Leslie and Allan Young (eds), *Paths to Asian Medical Knowledge* (Berkeley: University of California Press 1992), pp. 178–85.

22 Carl E. Taylor, 'The Place of Indigenous Medical Practitioners in the Modernization of Health Services', in Charles Leslie (ed.), *Asian Medical Systems: A Comparative Study* (Berkeley: University of California Press 1976), p. 290.

23 TNA 10409, vol. 1, Training of Native: Of Midwives, Village and Welfare Workers, 1927, no. 11, N. H. Maynard to District Officer McMahon, 27 June 1927.

24 Cape Town Conference, 'Report of the International Conference of Representatives of the Health Services of Certain African Territories and British India, held at Cape Town, November 15th to 25th, 1932', *Quarterly Bulletin of the Health Organisation of the League of Nations* 2 (1933), p. 106.

25 H. L. Gordon, 'A Rumination of Research and Eye-wash', *East African Medical Journal* 13, 4 (1936–37), p. 114.

26 Rudolf von Albertini, *Dekolonisation: die Diskussion über die Verwaltung und Zukunft der Kolonien, 1918–1960* (Köln: Westdeutscher Verlag 1966), p. 123.

27 Walter Morris-Hale, 'British Administration in Tanganyika from 1920 to 1945' (PhD dissertation, University of Geneva, 1969), p. 235.

28 Albertini, *Dekolonisation*, pp. 127–9; Morris-Hale, *British Administration in Tanganyika*, p. 235.

29 Stephen Constantine, *The Making of British Colonial Development Policy, 1914–1940* (London: Frank Cass 1984), p. 232.

30 John W. Cell, *Hailey: A Study in British Imperialism, 1872–1969* (Cambridge: Cambridge University Press 1992).

31 John W. Cell, 'Lord Hailey and the Making of the African Survey', *African Affairs* 88, 353 (1989), p. 505 with reference to [Lord] William Malcolm Hailey, 'Some Problems Dealt with in the African Survey', *International Affairs* 18, 2 (1939), pp. 194–210.

32 Cell, 'Lord Hailey and the Making of the African Survey', p. 505, referring to a Letter of MacDonald, cited in David John Morgan, *The Official History of Colonial Development*, vol. 1, *The Origins of British Aid Policy, 1924–1945* (London: Macmillan 1980), pp. xiv–xv.

33 Albertini, *Dekolonisation*, p. 137.

34 Tanganyika Territory, *Report of the Central Development Committee* (Dar es Salaam: Government Printer 1940), pp. 419–517.

35 Tanganyika Territory, *Memorandum on the Future Development of the Medical Services of Tanganyika Territory by the Director of Medical Services, 1942* (Dar es Salaam: Government Printer 1944), pp. 3–4.

36 TNA 25473, vol. 1, Medical Auxiliaries, 1937, no. 4, Notes on the Extension of Health Services in Rural Areas, p. 1; and Tanganyika Territory, *Memorandum on Medical Policy* (Dar es Salaam: Government Printer 1938), p. 3.

37 Tanganyika Territory, *Memorandum on the Future Development of the Medical Services*.

38 TNA 12602, vol. 2, Rural Medical Services: Village Dispensaries Maintained by Native Treasuries, 1946–47, no. 4a, R. de Z. Hall, Provincial Commissioner for the Central Province/Dodoma, proposal for the Provincial Commissioners' conference, 'Development of Native Administration Dispensaries', May 1946.

39 Lucy P. Mair, *Welfare in the British Colonies* (London: Royal Institute of International Affairs 1944), p. 90.

40 Tanganyika Territory, *A Review of the Development Plans in the Southern Province* (Dar es Salaam: Government Printer 1953), p. 36.

41 [Lord] William Malcolm Hailey, *An African Survey: A Study of Problems Arising in Africa South of the Sahara*, rev. edn (Oxford: Oxford University Press 1957 [1938]), pp. 1064–9.

42 Tanganyika Territory, *A Ten-Year Development and Welfare Plan for Tanganyika Territory: Report by the Development Commission* (Dar es Salaam: Government Printer 1946), p. 48.

43 TNA 12602, vol. 2, Rural Medical Services: Village Dispensaries Maintained by Native Treasuries, 1946–47, no. 7, Sneath, Address to Provincial Commissioners, 6 June 1946.

44 See, for example, TNA 12602, vol. 2, Rural Medical Services: Village Dispensaries Maintained by Native Treasuries, no. 10, Extract from proceedings of the Provisional Commissioners' Conference 'Development of Native Administration Dispensaries', 3 June 1946.

45 John Iliffe, *East African Doctors* (Cambridge: Cambridge University Press 1998), p. 45.

46 TNA 12602, vol. 3, Rural Medical Services: Village Dispensaries Maintained by Native Treasuries, 1948–49, no. 189, Sneath, 'Rural Medical Services: Group A Dispensaries', 6 January 1949, p. 3.

47 Rhodes House Library, Oxford, MSS Brit. Emp.s. Sneath, Paul A., Tanganyika Correspondence and Medical Papers 1950, Confidential letter Chief Secretary to Sneath, 6 March 1950, p. 56.

48 Legislative Council of Tanganyika Territory, *A Review of the Medical Policy of Tanganyika*, Sessional Paper 2 (Dar es Salaam: Government Printer 1949).

49 Tanganyika Territory, *Revised Development and Welfare Plan for Tanganyika, 1950–1956* (Dar es Salaam: Government Printer 1951), p. 35.

50 Tanganyika Territory, Medical Department, *A Draft Plan for the Development of Medical Services in Tanganyika with Special Reference for the Period 1956–1961* (Dar es Salaam: Government Printer 1956), pp. 2–7.

51 Ibid., p. 4.

52 Ole David Koht Norbye, 'Adequate Health Services for Poor Countries: How Can the Rich Countries Contribute to Reaching such a Goal?', *World Development* 2, 2 (1974), pp. 13–18.

53 'The Declaration of Cocoyoc', *World Development* 3, 2–3 (1975), pp. 141–8.

54 Dag Hammarskjöld Foundation, *What Now? Another Development* (Uppsala: Dag Hammarskjöld Foundation 1975), p. 32.

CHAPTER NINE

'Keystone of progress' and *mise en valeur d'ensemble*: British and French colonial discourses on education for development in the interwar period

Walter Schicho

The 1920s marked a turning point in colonial policy, which evolved from predatory colonialism to planned exploitation during the decade after the First World War. France and Great Britain, as well as Portugal somewhat belatedly, began to conceive new strategies for the handling of their colonised African territories. The new colonial policies were an answer both to the economic and political losses caused by the First World War[1] and to pressures from private metropolitan capital for the government to take over full responsibility for the improvement of infrastructure and the allocation of disciplined manpower. In Portugal, the change in colonial policies came with the rise of the fascist state (Estado Novo) under Salazar, while colonial capital in French and British occupied Africa succeeded in obtaining exclusive rights over lucrative economic domains (or else built oligopolies) after squeezing out or buying up smaller Western and African companies. Colonial government was then the ideal partner for big enterprises, taking over the costly side of doing business in Africa.

The primary target of colonial development planning was to achieve economic benefits for the metropole, along with safeguarding imperial power and gaining international recognition. To secure the sustainable growth of an export-oriented production of raw materials and to assure political and economic control in the occupied territories, colonial governments and private enterprises needed the training of agricultural producers, craftspeople, clerks, and wage earners in mining and transport as well as the formation of a local elite willing to collaborate with colonial power and capital. Therefore, colonial powers invested not only in infrastructure, but also in social development, especially in health and education.

While fascist Portugal up to the late 1950s drew its local adminis-trative and entrepreneurial petty bourgeoisie mainly from the planned migration of poor, unemployed Portuguese (or migrants from Cape Verde) to its African colonies, French and British authorities saw the key to development in the education and Westernisation of a certain number of Africans.[2] There was an undeniable discrepancy between colonial, especially metropolitan, authorities, and settlers concerning the structure and aims of 'native education', but in the end both sides agreed on the principles of an education based on selection and colonial role-attribution: 'la politique d'association'[3] or 'la politique indigène' in French colonial discourse and 'adapted education' in the British.

According to Veronique Dimier, French colonial discourse in the 1890s and in the first decade of the twentieth century was marked by 'the progressive replacement of the concept *"assimilation"* by *"association"* or *"politique indigène"* . . . a political concept directed towards the well-being of the colonised'.[4] That is too optimistic of a position; the aim of the colonial powers in the years between the two World Wars, the period Franz Ansprenger called the 'high noon of the colonial Empires',[5] was to modernise colonialism or, with allusion to the implementation of Structural Adjustment during the last two decades of the twentieth century, to make it 'colonialism with a human face' without en-dangering colonial dominance. During the early phases of colonial rule, education was on the one hand a domain assigned to religious actors (especially Christian missions, but also Islamic movements), and on the other an instrument used by the colonial government to influ-ence and control local elites.[6] After the end of the First World War education became one of the most important instruments of colonial control, replacing brute force as a prevalent means of domination.

The following analysis of texts delves into a specific discourse strand[7] centred on 'colonial education'. It covers a wide range of sub-topics: 'adapted education', 'character training', 'education of women', 'institu-tions and structures', 'language and acquisition of knowledge', and 'higher education'. The texts show entanglement with other discourse strands, especially discourses on economic and social development, progress, and colonial responsibility for metropolitan interests. Also addressed are aspects of inter-textual relationship, validity claims of rightness, and finally nomination and predication strategies concern-ing the construction of difference between coloniser and colonised.

Owners of discourse

Colonial history reveals a wide range of actors who assumed more or less power over the discourse on 'native education': missionaries, administrators, metropolitan politicians, business representatives, African traditional authorities, Westernised African elites, civil society activists, and last but not least, scholars of different scientific disciplines. It was politicians and administrators whose concepts and practices shaped the landscape of late colonialism most profoundly, but they were strongly influenced by ideological, scientific, and economic arguments.

The overseas 'education for development' policies of the French and British were closely linked to the names of two prominent colonial planners of the interwar period, whose publications and public interventions constitute the main focus of this contribution: the French Minister of Colonies, Albert Sarraut, and Sir Frederick Gordon Guggisberg, the British Governor of the Gold Coast.[8] To Guggisberg education was the 'keystone of progress' and 'what is uppermost in the thoughts of all Africans'.[9] His planning efforts concerned first and foremost the Gold Coast. Albert Sarraut composed his plan, which encompassed a complex set of values, for the development of the colonial empire as a whole. Economic progress had to be supported by education, welfare, and health to further the development of what he called 'la civilisation coloniale'. Both authors conceived education not only as a means of knowledge transfer and professional instruction, but also as 'training of the character', which made Africans 'valuable' subjects of the colonial project. Both were committed to key metropolitan values and to colonial models of education, but Guggisberg went further, maintaining that education was what the local elite desired to obtain, and that it had to be provided in an African context.

In 1921 Albert Sarraut and his collaborators[10] submitted a substantial proposal to the National Assembly, providing economic data and development plans for each territory of the colonial empire. The Members of Parliament considered the project to be too expensive and chose to pass the proposal on to local assemblies. The high costs, for Sarraut 'a delicate question, but not at all unsolvable',[11] should have been covered by German war reparations. As Germany did not pay, financing had to be obtained by other means: loans taken out by the colonies, the sale of concessions to private enterprises, and government grants. Sarraut's compilation of policies and data which formed the background for his proposal was published in 1923 as a book, which became a foundational text of reference for local colonial authorities claiming support for infrastructural development.[12] The idea to combine economic growth with social development, as Albert Sarraut proposed in his publications and in various manuscripts, seldom reappeared in their projects.[13]

Gordon Guggisberg's text, written 'at sea' in spring 1924, is a much smaller booklet written in reference to 'the Gold Coast and nowhere else'[14] and intended as an exercise in public awareness and information about ongoing projects in education in the Gold Coast Colony. He repeated and expanded his arguments at different opportunities, for instance, during the the Governor's annual addresses to the Legislative Council.

The difference in style of these two colonial actors and also in the publics they addressed is worth noting: on the one hand a French statesman, devoted to the glory and honour of his country, believing in the 'benevolent spirit' ('le génie bienfaisant') of 'his race',[15] and addressing the metropolitan elite; on the other an upright administrator, imbued by the conviction of British superiority and racialised world views, but also convinced of the fact, that 'if Government's plans for education were better known, there would be better cooperation with the people'.[16]

The discourse on education

Basically both Albert Sarraut's and Governor Guggisberg's concepts of education correspond to what Patti McGill Peterson described as 'educational colonialism': 'The British colonial idea of careful, limited access to higher education for the African or the French colonial idea of *instruire la masse et dégager l'élite'*.[17] Governor Guggisberg referred to the writings of Thomas Jesse Jones and James Aggrey, both close to the American Phelps-Stokes Fund, and their concept of 'educational adaptation' of African Americans, who were supposed to accept their status of submission to white supremacy and prove themselves 'worthy of attaining higher goals'.[18] The Fund's African Education Commission strongly influenced the Colonial Office's education policy for Africa in the early 1920s.[19] The British White Paper *Education Policy in British Tropical Africa*, published in the same year as Guggisberg's *Keystone*, reproduced what had been already fiercely rejected by critics in the United States, namely that 'education should be adapted to the mentality, aptitudes, occupations and traditions of the various peoples'.[20]

In a similar way, Albert Sarraut's concepts of education can be traced back to the writings and proposals of George Hardy, mastermind behind colonial education in French West Africa from 1912 to 1920 and later Director of the École coloniale in Paris. Although Hardy dismissed Gobineau's extreme racist arguments, he believed in the existence of a fundamental difference between the French and the colonised, who were 'able to learn, but unable to understand and to appropriate the [French] culture which was essentially different from their way of thinking'. Hardy therefore proposed segregated systems of education for French and Africans, the latter with a strong orientation towards professional formation and practical skills and 'adapted to the intellectual capacities of the children and the cultural development of their country'.[21]

To Minister Sarraut, who dealt with the vast field of development or 'enhancement of the colonies' (*la mise en valeur*), education was part of France's 'mission humaine'[22] and an essential component of its 'politique indigène'.[23] In his text he used a number of terms such as 'enseignement', 'éducation', or 'instruction (publique)' without defining appropriate meanings for these terms or instruments for their implementation. Education and knowledge transfer were subordinate elements in a complex enterprise aiming at economic progress, stability and security of the empire, marked by 'human justice' and the 'civilising mission', and contributing 'also' to the progress and advantages of the colonies.[24] The British-American colonial 'education for the heart and hand' (as Booker T. Washington had called it[25]), was amended by the French policy of 'heart and reason, duty and interests' ('le cœur et la raison, le devoir et l'intérêt').[26]

Guggisberg's and Sarraut's discourses on education are marked by two topics: 'adapted education' and 'character building'. While Guggisberg discusses both topics as central elements of his plan for education in the Gold Coast, they figure only as sub-topics to 'progress' and 'politique indigène' in Sarraut's texts.

Adapted education

Guggisberg had to defend his model of education against a rival system implemented by Christian missions in secondary schools such as Mfantsipim School and Adisadel College but also on the primary level, where the missionaries considered widespread literacy among the African population to be just as important as the training of practical skills for economic gains.[27] While the Governor's approach at the primary level and in terms of vocational education was heavily influenced by the American model of 'adapted education', the programme for the Prince of Wales School at Achimota had to combine both approaches – the locally modified 'adapted education' in conjunction with the grammar school approach of British origin. While the former 'promoted the Africanisation of the curriculum and adaptation to the rural environment, emphasising manual labor and agriculture', the latter 'provided an elitist, academic "grammar" education for the training of the "gentleman" scholar and politician of England'.[28]

French administrators in the occupied territories of West Africa considered mission schools not so much as rivals, than as an additional resource, especially when government schools were overflowing with pupils. The AOF was even disposed to support them financially.[29] Guggisberg was less satisfied with the products of mission schools but he was equally convinced that higher education by itself would not be sufficient to develop the country. Higher education, he felt, 'must be accompanied by a better system of training in handicrafts, agriculture, and all those trades that go to provide for the necessities of a community; for although higher education may be the brain of a country, its productive capacity is its heart'.[30]

Nevertheless, Guggisberg and Sarraut shared the belief that education had to be selective and adapted to relevant social dimensions of the colonised world; it was the coloniser's duty to define and to curtail content and frames of education for the colonised. In Albert Sarraut's wording it was 'le bon sens' which had to guide the specification and 'wise delimitation' of education attributed to a given territory.[31] His mighty position as a minister allowed the French politician to argue with reference to common sense, while Guggisberg had to refer to conservative educational authorities, accepted by powerful actors of British colonial policy, but already heavily criticised back in their American social and professional environment.[32]

Sarraut and Guggisberg were both more or less enlightened evolutionists believing in the backwardness of their colonised subjects, and the obligation (but also the right) of the coloniser to define 'tradition' as the starting point for their social and economic development.[33] Colonial education had to guide the people under colonial 'wardship' in their evolution without imposing Western democratic patterns, which – as Albert Sarraut wrote in *La mise en valeur* – would result in turning the colonised into caricatures rather than producing true and successful models of the coloniser.[34]

The use of 'traditional' elements, the mix of Western knowledge and African ritual, of drumming, dancing, and parading 'took the form chiefly of buffoonery in one or other of the local languages' as Francis Agbodeka wrote concerning Achimota College,[35] but it efficiently divided education in the colonial world between education for citizens with full rights (*citoyens de plein droit*) and that for colonial subjects (*sujets coloniaux*).

Colonial government, elites, and missionaries did not share the same objectives in education, but Guggisberg could rely on the support of the traditional elite, the chiefs and their councillors. It was in point of fact the 'Paramount Chiefs and the people of the Gold Coast and Asante', as the Ghanaian historian Adu Boahen wrote,[36] who paid for Guggisberg's gravestone when the Governor prematurely died in 1930.

When Guggisberg claimed 'a better education for Africans than our present schools are capable of providing',[37] he was arguing not only for an 'enlightened educational colonialism',[38] but also defending his concept of 'adapted education' against the more academically oriented mission schools. The educated African elite also did not agree with his emphasis on 'character building' and 'practical skills', showing strong preference instead for an academic education modelled after the British public school. But from a colonial state's perspective, 'adapted education' not only served to appease the local patriarchal authorities, but also created a divide between the emerging elite and the masses, between urban and rural societies, and between the 'modern' and the 'backward' section of the populace.

Character training and leadership

'Brain – to a leader – is of no use, is a positive danger, unless backed by force of character. Britain herself, mother of the greatest Empire the world has ever seen, owes her position far more to the force of character of her sons than to their brain'.[39] This statement seems to be typical for the British colonial regime, which prized physical fitness and straight, hardworking officers.[40] To Guggisberg it was obvious that character training needed to be given a prominent place in the educational curriculum. He quoted Thomas Jesse Jones approvingly in describing the virtues which made up his 'force of character': 'perseverance, thoroughness, order, cleanliness, punctuality, thrift, temperance, self-control, obedience, reliability, honesty, and respect for parents', and to these he added'a correct appreciation of responsibility'.[41]

Guggisberg called character training an 'important factor in the happiness and success of the artisan's life as [it is] in that of the highly educated barrister',[42] and although he claimed a place for character training in every type of education, he considered it to be especially 'the all-essential factor in higher education'[43] because in his words, 'the greater the learning the greater the opportunity and the capacity for doing harm unless knowledge is backed up by character'.[44]

What the Governor considered important concerning labour and character training he listed in the chapter on technical training: the pupils had to work in the garden to produce their own food; they were to be organised in the tradition and following the rules of boy scouts; parading, discipline, working for money, punctuality, and physical strength were considered preconditions for developing leadership and a sense of responsibility. 'The object of these schools is to turn out a good, if not a highly skilled, craftsman who will be able to earn a living in the country, and who will take away with him ideas of sanitation – an important subject in the curriculum – and the general conduct of life that will in due course spread among the people around him'.[45] The theme of 'cleanliness' is also documented in French colonial discourse. In 1952, for instance, the district commissioner (*Commandant du cercle*) Gienger argued in his annual report in favour of a better education for the spouses of African civil servants, because only education could guarantee the cleanliness of the homes, and in consequence the right 'character' of their husbands.[46]

Guggisberg, when discussing character training became exclusively Western-oriented, as if character was something completely foreign to African society, imported by the coloniser and obtainable only through instruction by the colonial administrator and his staff. Neither the traditional authorities, nor the Christian missionaries, were granted the capacity to train leaders.

Albert Sarraut was far less elaborate in his argument on character training, but he too assigned the power to train leaders to French educators, who alone were able to convey to their 'protégés' the sense of collaboration, in order to share responsibility and benefits with their colonisers.[47] Education was to better their consciousness until they became aware of their obligations towards the French and the necessity to defend the 'common heritage'.[48] If the education project failed, and the character training for leadership had ended in producing 'ignorant, stupid and inexperienced' elites it would have meant the 'end of civilisation' and the 'return to the old servitude'.[49]

Education of women

While Guggisberg devoted a chapter of his book to the 'education of women' as a priority of his policy, the French authors[50] of *La mise en valeur* in the early 1920s were less disposed to consider women as subjects of the colonial project. Guggisberg's position was straightforward: 'there can be no real civilisation if the women of the race are left uneducated'.[51] He considered resistance to education for women as a sign of cultural backwardness.[52] In his undated manuscript 'Programme coloniale', Albert Sarraut finally argued in the same manner: 'Without extending instruction and education to the female gender we may never be able to attain our targets ... To reduce opposition and to overcome the inconsistencies linked to our activities, to build up without destroying too much, to modernise without demoralising people, we must gain the support of the women and we have to convince them without scaring them'.[53] But while Guggisberg discussed education for women as a sub-topic of 'social evolution/progress', Sarraut considered it to be an essential element of 'colonial interests and control'. The above quoted example on 'cleanliness' is a good example of this discursive strand.

Social evolution is closely bound to Western education – there is no alternative to it from the colonial point of view, but in promoting female education Guggisberg ignored that gender-based discrimination still existed in metropolitan education. As his project for Achimota provided the necessary infrastructure for female students,[54] it was, at least in theory, more egalitarian and progressive than the mission school system which was marked by separateness.

Co-education, Guggisberg was convinced, had to start in primary school, not later, and as far as public opinion was concerned, he believed that it would become 'more enlightened in the course of the next few years'. In discussing the subject he referred to Lord Cromer, General Consul in Egypt, who wrote that the younger generation of men in Egypt at the beginning of the twentieth century asked for a better education for their spouses. 'This is a remark which applies with great force to the Gold Coast, for nothing more detrimental to the progress of this race can be imagined than the present system of educated husbands and illiterate wives'.[55] Unfortunately the Governor did not explain how or why the difference in education was 'detrimental to the progress of this race' (and also why this should apply to 'this race', but not to the Britons). The merging of the Victorian social model and the African patriarchal system finally led to an enforcement of the existing inequality instead of making gender relations more equal.

Institutions and structures

The mid-1920s were for Guggisberg 'a critical point in the Gold Coast's history'. His answer to the aspirations and claims of the West African national elite was an initiative for a new and holistic system of education, which had to provide institutions from the primary to the university level, but also 'ample training facilities for all the trades and professions ... but first of all for the good citizen'.[56] The list of professions and experts ranged from brick-makers to engineers, barristers, and doctors. To avoid alienation and anti-colonial indoctrination of the elite and population he recommended institutions, qualified staff and instruments for colonial education in the Gold Coast in order to prevent the local elite from sending their sons to Europe. Even if the Gold Coast Colony in the 1920s could not provide studies necessary to produce experts of every profession needed, he was convinced that 'gradually we should arrive at the moment when everything that is taught at an English college can be adopted at Achimota'.[57]

The French system was based on a strict duality – 'adapted education for the masses' and 'carefully chosen individuals for higher education'. Higher education for the latter was provided in a few centres, most notably the 'schools for the sons of chiefs and the translators', the most famous of which was the École William Ponty, founded in 1903 in St Louis, Senegal, and attended by personalities such as Félix Houphouet-Boigny and Modibo Keita, the 'fathers of independence' of Côte-d'Ivoire and Mali. Those who received their secondary education and academic formation in France, usually supported by grants from the French government, had an even better chance of climbing up to the top of the professional and social ladder. The model for such a career was certainly Léopold S. Senghor, the poet and President of Senegal, and member of the Académie Française.

Following Guggisberg's concept, education was to be predominantly located in boarding schools where character training was uppermost in the curriculum. To guarantee that character training took place, the schools had to follow 'Scout and Guide lines, which contain a practical application of the principles of Christianity and citizenship that is invaluable'.[58] The main characteristics of the system were 'orderliness, punctuality and a sense of subordination to one's seniors' and 'the sense of initiative and leadership' was closely linked to these qualities.[59] Guggisberg saw the 'slow but inevitable' progress from 'primitive to modern civilisation' as the joint work of 'devoted' colonial agents and 'honest' African subjects. It was the government's responsibility to provide education and character training. The African's share, marked by 'hard and steady work', was the application of the colonial plans, the acceptance of being educated, submission and 'an honest determination to prove himself worthy'.[60]

Guggisberg appointed education committees or supported the creation of metropolitan committees to evaluate the educational institutions and to serve as advisers. Among the members of the Colonial Office's Advisory Committee on Native Education in Tropical Africa, which was formed in 1924, were such famous personalities as Sir Frederick Lugard and William Ormsby-Gore, later Parliamentary Under-Secretary for the Colonies. In the French system control and programming was by far more centralised. The local administration had to follow instructions of the colonial ministry, and was supervised by officers affiliated with the ministry in Paris.[61] High ranking officers appointed by the colonial minister, such as George Hardy, *inspecteur de l'enseignement* in French West Africa, produced the blue-prints for education in the colonies.[62]

Sarraut and Guggisberg shared the same opinion as far as the development process was concerned: to both, the colonised societies were not advancing fast enough. But while the British governor argued for more power to be given to local institutions and more African initiative to speed up development,[63] Sarraut considered local initiatives and individual designs to be responsible for the retarding of development.[64]

In the end, the outcome of both educational systems showed similar shortcomings: urban regions were privileged compared to rural areas, central or coastal regions of the colonial territories privileged compared to the rest, and female students more disadvantaged compared with male students.[65] Professional education and the predominance of human sciences resulted in a lack of university-trained experts in economics and natural sciences. By the time Ghana gained independence in 1957, the country was somewhat better off educationally than the former French colonies, which was due in part to Governor Guggisberg and his belief in education as a keystone, but also to the long tradition of education linked to the early activities of Christian missions in the region.

Language and acquisition of knowledge

Guggisberg's plan provided for the use of African languages in primary schooling. It was the Phelps-Stokes Commission which had recommended the use of 'tribal languages' in lower elementary classes and of a lingua franca of African origin later on. Only upper standards should be taught in English or other European languages.[66] To provide a solid foundation for his educational model Guggisberg drafted sixteen principles, one of which states: 'Whilst an English Education Must be Given It Must be Based Solidly on the Vernacular'. He also proposed that European teachers should learn a local language, to 'get an insight into the minds of the teachers and their pupils'.[67]

But Guggisberg also argued that the use of English in the Gold Coast educational system was indispensible, because of the lack of a local (written) literature and the linguistic diversity of the country. For this reason, he argued, 'the language must obviously be English . . . And as knowledge of the language gradually increases *until the African can think in English*, so can the highest form of education be given to him'.[68] Although Guggisberg was one of the most progressive colonial officers of his time, he firmly believed in two principles: the acquisition of knowledge was not possible without a good command of the colonial language and knowledge as such could not be other than Western.

For the French authorities it was clear that French was the exclusive medium of education, and as the state controlled most of the colonial schools, there was also considerably less competition from the mission school system which usually gave preference to local languages in primary education because this facilitated proselytisation.[69] Evidently, colonial minister Sarraut considered the use of French as the common base and the fundamental principle of the colonial school system.[70] Guy Camille in his review of Sarraut's *La mise en valeur* expounded the position of a colonial scientist in a rather matter-of-fact way: 'Our indigenous overall have to speak French . . . without necessarily cramming their brain with theoretical or confusing knowledge which they will never need'.[71]

Higher education

Guggisberg in presenting his plans for educational reform announced also the foundation of a university in the Gold Coast, but declared, at the same time, that it was necessary to lay first the foundation in the form of an efficient primary school education to produce 'suitably educated scholars'. Secondary schools and the university would come 'in due course', but in his opinion the time was not yet ripe for a university. What he foresaw was a common institution for all British West African territories in order to find enough sufficiently educated students to fill this university.[72] This was, naturally, his answer to the demands of the West African nationalists for higher education, but at the same time a tool to protect British colonial interests against the development of anti-colonial currents supported by members of the elite who had not been subject to British 'character training'.

As the Gold Coast government had only limited funds it had to give preference to secondary education and to the training of teachers. Guggisberg focused on teacher training, because the shortage of qualified teaching staff had 'compelled [him] to go slow in building primary schools'.[73] His policy ran contrary to the intentions and strategies of the Christian missions, who as he put it opened 'bush schools' and employed poorly trained teachers, because they considered literacy for all a precondition for their task of spreading Christianity among the colonised population.

Guggisberg argued in two ways against 'literary education', which he considered to be in danger of inflation, 'turning out annually some 4,000 to 5,000 boys who are only fitted to be clerks, and, what is worse, the majority of whom could not, from their education, be anything but inferior clerks'.[74] One reason for the alleged inefficiency of the mission school system was the low quality of teachers and teaching; the other, as he put it, was the lack of 'character-training'. 'We are flooding the market with semi-educated youths for whom, owing to their disdain of manual labour, there is annually less employment. The very fact that they are educated tends to separate them in thought

and sympathy from their less advanced relations ... Failing employment in an office, and strongly imbued with an unhealthy dislike
to manual labour, they fall a natural victim to discontent and consequently to unhappiness'.[75]

Sarraut did not discuss higher education in *La mise en valeur*. It
was Jules Carde, Governor General of French West Africa from 1923
to 1930, who composed the famous phrase: 'Instruct the masses and
capture the elite *(Instruire la masse et dégager l'élite)*'.[76] Higher education in the French colonised territories was at the beginning earmarked
for the offspring of the traditional elite; but later on colonial officials
and people with influence in the colony extended selection to those
they felt were 'marked with the noble seal reserved for the elite',[77] a
quality similar in outcome to what Guggisberg meant by 'character'.

Albert Sarraut in 'Programme coloniale' argued that higher education had to be provided with wise clear-sightedness, and – although
the 'indigenous' elites were not be excluded from attaining higher
education – it had to be dealt with prudentially and without hastiness.
He concluded his argument with a metaphorical warning comparing
knowlege (which he depicts as 'scientific speculations') to strong wine
'which easily turns the head'.[78]

Formation of an African elite

The formation of an African elite through colonial education was
linked to 'character training' or 'proof of [the African's] competence
(preuve de ses capacités)' as Sarraut called it. The existence of an elite,
as Sarraut argued, 'was absolutely necessary for the public life of any
country. It guaranteed progress in an orderly and disciplined way'.[79]

Both Sarraut and Guggisberg emphasised the importance of education to breed a Westernised elite, but they had different views on how,
when, and where this should take place. Guggisberg considered local
education, accessible to many, as the right solution in contrast to
'education in Europe of a few [Africans], an education that invariably
lacks character training and that more often than not results in bad
European habits replacing good African characteristics'.[80] In that he
differed from the French model, which was in favour of a separate
education for the African masses (following the principle of 'association') but considered assimilation appropriate for the elite.[81] Sarraut
in his plan, according to what had been designed by George Hardy,[82]
saw above all the need for 'general education of a practical and realist
type',[83] followed by technical and professional formation. Of highest
importance was the economic usefulness of mass instruction ('l'utilité
économique de l'instruction de la masse').[84] The formation of an
African elite was a carefully planned process of selection and Sarraut's

discourse underscores that the indigenous elite should be chosen on proof of their capacities: 'If there came up from the masses and different populations under the protection of our flag some individuals whom natural predestination or proven ability in intellectual hard work had marked with the noble seal reserved for the elite, then it is our duty as a ward to help them to arrive at the position they merit to achieve'.[85]

According to Sarraut, the 'generous and clear-sighted' policy of association ('la généreuse et clairvoyante application d'une politique d'association') would allow colonised people access to political institutions of the colonial system, while the formation of character and capacities would lay the foundation for a useful and reasonable collaboration between the rising elite and the colonial rulers.[86] Sarraut's discourse corresponds to the mainstream sentiments of his epoch, while Guggisberg's plan to create leaders 'to cope with the changing conditions that are daily being wrought by the advance of European civilization'[87] was well in advance, although he did not betray the 'principles of colonial rule'. He designed Achimota College to be 'an institution at which the African youth will receive, first and foremost, character-training of such a nature as will fit him to be a good citizen; and secondly, the higher education necessary to enable him to become a leader in thought, in the professions, or in industry among his fellow-countrymen'.[88]

The discourse on progress and development

In the texts under review, both Guggisberg and Sarraut use the terms 'progress' and 'development' in a similar manner with overlapping realms of meaning. Progress and development are therefore considered as realisations of the same concept, although diachronically they are quite different in meaning and use.[89] Both can designate either a state or a process and can be used in transitive and intransitive modes. Arguments which justify colonial rule as furthering development refer on the one hand to 'moral obligation' ('la mission civilisatrice'), and on the other, to economic and political necessity.[90] In the following section, three sub-topics are treated: education as a precondition for development, economic development, and progress of people or social development.

Education as the keystone of progress

In Guggisberg's presentation education and progress or development are related twofold. On the one hand it is a precondition for the access to (higher) education to have attained a certain stage on 'the road of progress'.[91] On the other, it is education which leads to progress: 'Once, however, that a nation has emerged from the primitive phases of its existence, education and all that it comprises becomes not only the first but the only step towards progress'.[92]

Albert Sarraut on the other hand did not assume a direct relation between education and development. In his description better conditions for health came before instruction and education: 'Après l'hygiène, l'instruction'. Education was an instrument to contribute to the success of the colonial project, and the colonial project in consequence guaranteed progress of both coloniser and colonised.[93] Instruction and education had to increase colonial production, and economic growth meant development. Economic growth was the main objective of the colonial project which had to guarantee the 'joint profit of the warden and the ward (*le profit commun du protecteur et du protégé*)'[94] but still, 'joint profit' did not mean that individual and social well-being of the colonised were equivalent to the well-being of the coloniser.

Following Guggisberg, it was argued that government's duty lay in creating the foundations of development by, among others, organising 'a system of schools where Africans can obtain better and higher education'.[95] Sarraut was convinced that education was something the West provided with good grace to 'those [for whom] we have assumed custodianship'.[96] Guggisberg also acknowledged that there was a demand for better education by the colonised, which he saw as closely linked to the amelioration of living conditions.[97] For him education (including the transfer of knowledge) and the demand for social (individual) development were two sides of the same coin. He stated that the demand of the educated African 'for an education and training that will fit him to take a greater share in the development of his own land'[98] was not only genuine, but right – and in the interest of the coloniser, because denying education would alienate the local elite and create problems for the empire. As Western socialisation and education had started quite early in the Gold Coast and the colonial economy flourished (gold, rubber, cocoa), Guggisberg – referring to the economic progress of its coastal regions since the mid-nineteenth century[99] – considered the colony to be a special case compared to other British colonies, especially those in Central and East Africa.

Economic versus social development

While Guggisberg addressed various purposes and priorities concerning development, economic progress was not in the fore of his arguments – at least not in *The Keystone*. Already in 1919, at the beginning of his governorship, he had presented a ten-year development programme to the Legislative Council. The plan mainly focused on the improvement of infrastructure, but besides investing in roads and the building of a seaport at Takoradi, he also emphasised the need for social infrastructure including water supply, schools, and hospitals.[100]

Minister Sarraut, in contrast, argued predominantly in favour of the 'benefit' or the 'economic benefit for the Empire'; in his world view the benefit of empire included the benefit of the colonised – if and when they decided to collaborate and to join the coloniser 'in solidarity'.[101] 'Progress of people' and 'metropolitan gains', in Sarraut's words, were one and the same. It was the coloniser ('la France') who made sure that there was economic growth, the 'development of the riches of the colonies', which was closely linked to France's 'civilising mission'. From this social development ('le développement humain') would automatically follow.[102] For Sarraut, development needed especially investment to improve the economy; 'soft investments' such as education and social assistance ranged far behind.[103]

Governor Guggisberg referred to the 'pressure brought to bear on the Arch of Progress by the hurricane of material development', which could only be endured through carefully planned education.[104] Sarraut on the other hand, in his bid for the enhancement of the colonies, repeatedly opposed the devastating exploitation linked to the 'Pacte Colonial'[105] and claimed to be opening the way for the more efficient use of the colonies' natural resources and for allowing them the right to trade with neighbouring countries.[106] The difference between the two approaches is clearly visible: while the economy dominates social development from the French perspective, Guggisberg believes in interdependency if not in the precedence of social development.

Progress of people

At least twice in his short text Guggisberg alluded to the 'well-being and development of peoples not yet able to stand by themselves' as being the colonial government's main policy. The main instrument to implement this policy was education – not simply 'education' but rather 'education and all that it comprises'.[107] What he meant by 'all that it comprises' is open to a contextual interpretation.

Comparing the social and political advancement of the Gold Coast with that in other British occupied territories, one can say that Guggisberg promoted progressive colonial policies far ahead of what his fellow administrators were prepared to do elsewhere. He addressed them by asking: 'Do the critics honestly believe that we have the right to deny the African the chance of proving that his race is capable of doing what other races have done in the past?' In his answer to this question, Guggisberg was careful not to challenge the colonial world view of difference and evolutionary hierarchy, but instead appealed to the self-perception of the British: 'If so, they have forgotten that

Britain stands where she does to-day by giving her peoples and her opponents alike a "sporting chance"'.[108]

Minister Sarraut also dealt with critics of his approach to colonial policy, but he pretended that French colonial policy for a long time had overcome 'the brutal conception of the old colonial pact based on the never-ending inequality of races and the law of the strongest'.[109] For Sarraut, 'progress of people' was equivalent to some kind of development which French colonial civilisation ('civilisation coloniale') owed to the dignity of humankind ('la dignité même de l'espèce humaine').[110]

'Development' in Guggisberg's discourse means a state or a step in the evolution of humankind, as when he underscores that 'a human being can rise from a lower to a higher plane of development',[111] but can also refer to a transitive action, having the coloniser as actor and the colonised as object. In this sense he refers to 'Britain's recently self-imposed task of tutelage and development'.[112] In Albert Sarraut's text 'development' is used in general as a transitive action, closely linked to economic changes, but he also points to the 'different levels of intellectual and political development of diverse parts of our colonial domain'.[113] 'Progress' on the other hand is an intransitive process, concerning both 'the people', the 'local' or 'native races', and the colonial authority.[114] Sarraut links 'progress' especially to education, instruction, morality, and science. In this, his use of 'progress' is different from his use of 'development', with the latter term being directed mainly towards economic enhancement.

Education to serve colonial interests

The discourse on colonial interests and support for the colonial government of both planners is linked to four sub-topics: workforce, power and security of the metropolis, the prevention of anti-colonial activities, and elite formation, a topic already discussed above.

Workforce

The main argument concerning the workforce was the high cost – at least in the eyes of the colonial administration and metropolitan members of parliament – of employing Europeans in administration and private enterprises: 'the development of the country necessitates an annual increase in staff. No Government in the world could afford proportionately, the immense financial burden of European salaries, passages and long furloughs that would fall on the Gold Coast if this increase was to consist of Europeans only'.[115] Both authors proposed to replace expensive European staff by cheaper African manpower, because 'practically every one of our Departments has vacancies which an African suitably qualified in education and character could fill with advantage to the service'.[116] In a similar way Albert Sarraut asked for the well-directed formation of local employees to relieve the fast increasing colonial budgets.[117] However, while Guggisberg already in the 1920s proposed the employment of Africans in senior positions in administration and Albert Sarraut wrote that locals should get advancement in the colonial hierarchy,[118] the British did not put it into practice until after the Second World War and the French placed metropolitan staff in key positions of administration up to the end of the colonial regime and even after independence.

Another argument was that there was a need for qualified workers and for African employees in administration and business management. Both colonial administration and the colonial economy developed rapidly in the 1920s creating demand for the recruitment of local staff in order to make the colonial project profitable. Colonial minister Sarraut argued that the 'improvement of intelligence' and the development of competencies of local African workers was a precondition for substantially augmenting the value of colonial production.[119] And while Guggisberg conceived of a qualified African workforce as supplementing a European workforce, Guggisberg intended to substitute Europeans with Africans.

Power and security

The question of power and security of the imperial state preoccupied especially Albert Sarraut, while Guggisberg steadfastly believed in 'Britain . . . mother of the greatest Empire the world has ever seen'.[120] The French colonial minister repeatedly referred to the German occupation during the First World War and the military support of the colonies in France's struggle against the Central Powers. His concept of a 'Greater France' was based on the assumed solidarity of 60 million colonised people with 40 million inhabitants of the home country and on military forces recruited in the colonies.[121] He therefore argued for the formation of indigenous non-commissioned officers who should acquire 'a clear notion of the beneficence of our civilisation, and the deep-rooted conviction that they had to be at France's service and ready for her defence'.[122] While Guggisberg saw no reason to discuss power and security of the metropolis, he joined Sarraut in the discourse on power over colonised peoples, which also centred on the sub-topic of prevention of anti-colonial activities.

Prevention of anti-colonial activities

Education and elite formation held an ambiguous position with colonial discourse: on the one hand they were considered to be *the* means to secure colonial control and to support colonial government, but on the other they were suspected of instigating anti-colonial activities and resistance. As Guggisberg argued: '[Some] critics have it that, in advocating the provision of a higher education locally for Africans, we are deliberately inviting political troubles in the Gold Coast. Surely the absolute contrary is the case. If politics are to come – and come they must if history is of any value as a guide – surely the safeguard *against* trouble is the local education of the many, accompanied by character-training, rather than the education in Europe of a few'.[123]

Guggisberg saw a steadily growing gap between more and less educated people in the colonies; between those who were rich enough to obtain higher education in England or somewhere else in Europe or the United States and those who could not and remained at home. He feared that the African educated overseas (and therefore lacking the 'necessary character-training') would undo what Guggisberg called 'the legitimate aspirations of the African for advancement and for a greater share in the government of his country'. He therefore saw the necessity 'to protect the masses from the hasty and ill-conceived schemes of possible local demagogues'.[124] Lord Cromer had discussed this question already with relevance to India and warned that the common people would be left intellectually defenceless 'in the presence of the hair-brained and empirical projects which the political charlatan, himself but half-educated, will not fail to pour into their credulous ears'.[125] To protect those whom Lord Cromer considered 'the natural prey' of these 'political charlatans' education was needed – and Guggisberg fully agreed with him.

Guggisberg's ideas influenced politics in the Gold Coast even after he left as governor. In 1936 Arku Korsah, member of the Legislative Council, pleaded for more widespread education claiming that 'a little learning is a dangerous thing'. Only an educated person could not be impressed by 'an evil disposed person'.[126]

To both the Governor and the French colonial minister the danger of foreign influence, 'modernist ideas', and ideologies directed against colonial rule seemed to be quite imminent. Lord Cromer, Guggisberg, and Arku Korsah spoke of 'half-educated charlatans', 'evil disposed persons', and 'imposters' influenced and guided by ideas brought back from overseas study visits. Sarraut especially warned of foreign educated members of the elite,[127] yet he saw those who received higher education in France as the ideal, assimilated partners of the colonial regime. Unlike the British, who called them 'charlatans' and 'evil disposed persons', French authorities (and in particular Minister Sarraut) saw them as corrupted by 'communist agitation'.[128] Sarraut warned the colonial governments against immigrants from Anglophone neighbouring countries, who brought with them anti-colonial, 'communist' ideas, Anglo-American Pan-Africanism, and African nationalism.[129] His 'natural' partners against foreign evil and influence were members of the 'traditional' elite ('les chefs indigènes'), who were trained to serve as intermediaries between the colonised and the coloniser.[130]

With lofty words Sarraut warned against 'an enormous flood of non-western peoples (*races de couleur*) due to the awakening of new aspirations which would inevitably endanger European civilisation (*la civilisation européenne*)'.[131] Guggisberg was more optimistic believing education would steer the awakening of the 'local races: in no other way shall we fit them to absorb European civilisation unhurt – and it is my belief that in no other way shall we keep them permanently the loyal and worthy members of our Empire that they now are'.[132]

'We' and 'they': coloniser vs. colonised

While on the one hand education was the means of modernising African societies and economies and furthering colonial exploitation, on the other, it was also a space in which to differentiate between actors and subjects, between 'us' and 'them'. The actor's position and the differentiation between Self and Other are clearly visible in the two analysed texts. Guggisberg, for example, contrasted 'a Government composed of men of European civilisation' to 'primitive people of tropical Africa'.[133] Sarraut attributed to the French coloniser ('la France') the role of a creator and a custodian, endowed with 'le génie civilisateur',[134] and saw the colonised as the recipient, the ward and the protected. In both tracts, Europeans are portrayed as uniform in character and culture, while the colonised peoples are depicted as heterogeneous and particular social entities are assigned different positions in the European-defined hierarchy of evolution.

Guggisberg's description of the laying of the foundation stone of Achimota College on 24 March 1924 offers an insight into how the Governor perceived Gold Coast society at the time. The Europeans at the top were 'those who had inherited for many generations the qualities conferred on them by the education of their forbears', which limited the capacity of others to inherit the cultural and social knowledge of the British. African knowledge, customs, and traditions were vaguely referenced when discussing 'adapted education', and disappear altogether when Guggisberg drew the frontiers between coloniser and colonised.[135]

Next to the Europeans on the right side of the Governor stood the 'European-clad' African 'barristers, doctors, teachers and traders', with 'their faces ample proof of their satisfaction that, at long last, the dream they had dreamed was approaching realisation';[136] the Chiefs and their councillors had their place on the left side. While the Westernised 'pioneers of the progress of their race' were depicted as oriented towards future development and prepared to take over roles in a colonial-designed society and economy, the 'Chiefs in their robes and insignia of State' were part of the past, although they had to appreciate 'what was coming'. Boy scouts and the Gold Coast Regiment – 'hardy fighting men from the far North whose breasts carried evidence of their readiness to defend their country against aggression' – enclosed the participants of the ceremony and represented the basement of the colonial project. Absent were the masses, the people of rural origin, and the picture we get from our sources is that he deliberately ignored those who – according to his argument – had 'by no means reached the point on the Road of Progress at which a higher education is either within their intellectual grasp or would be good for their future'.[137]

Albert Sarraut used almost the same argument to exclude the marginalised majority of the Africans from colonial development: 'Sometimes immense distances separate the evolutionary states of the different indigenous races' and some pages later he contrasts the 'three-quarter savages' of the equatorial forests to the intellectual 'évolué' from Senegal.[138] Writing about the capacity to access higher education – 'nos hautes études littéraires et scientifiques', he qualified students from Algeria, Tunisia, Vietnam, and Madagascar as 'brilliant', but did not mention others.[139]

Guggisberg was concerned about the education of skilled craftsmen, clerks, and teachers, and he supported the work of African physicians, surgeons, officers of health, nurses, and midwives. He also developed plans for the professional formation of 'carpenters, metal workers, concrete workers, bridge and culvert builders, and roadmakers'[140] – but he never mentioned peasants or farmers, the majority of the African population. In a similar way Sarraut discussed the evolution of a 'valuable workforce' and members of the local elite, but farmers and pastoralists were only of limited importance, although he wrote: 'For the moment being it might be more profitable to train good agriculturalists then lawyers'.[141]

Guggisberg and Sarraut thus saw themselves as 'enlightened colonialists'.[142] Arguing about the French right to colonise, Sarraut declared that France had 'since long dismissed the brutal idea of the old colonial contract concerning the never-ending inequality of the races and the law of the strongest'.[143] And Guggisberg accused his critics of believing they had 'the right to deny the African the chance of proving that his race is capable of doing what other races have done in the past'.[144]

But both were colonialists and would have never done away with the distinction between themselves, who had the right to conquer, to plan, to decide, and to educate, and the Other, whose role it was to receive, to obey, and to accept the need for character training. Sarraut questioned the capacity of Africans to understand the core values – social and intellectual – of European civilisation and argued with subtle opaqueness regarding the granting of French citizenship to Africans: 'Under the condition which is based on common sense that the indigenous are people as we are, we have to treat them as people like we are'.[145]

Colonial education and development: concluding remarks

To summarise the outcome of this analysis of colonial documents, we could briefly say that Sarraut and Guggisberg drafted two different strategies for education, which had the same targets: making the colonised ideal subjects of the colonial government and defining development both as a process and an objective dominated by Western interests.

The findings can be categorised in three groups according to their implication for colonial and post-colonial practices. To group one belong means, strategies, and practices relevant only for the colonial regime, to group two are those which deeply influenced and changed African societies and prepared the way for social and economic development after independence, and to group three belongs what can be considered as the inherent property of asymmetric relations; in today's wording the characteristics of 'North-South relations'.

Of actual relevance for the colonial regime was the transformation of colonialism into 'colonialism with a human face', which was not only economically sound but also essential to counter the emerging international discourse of self-determination[146] and the claims of African nationalists. There was also the role of education as a means of control, leading to co-operation with and acceptance of the colonial government, and the formation of a disciplined workforce through professional training and instruction in practical skills. Education was furthermore, at least for the British, a space to challenge and to reduce the influence of the Christian missions, who had many more years of colonising experience than administrators and politicians.

The efforts to include women in the education project did not change African societies, but rather strengthened patriarchal power and male dominance. Social and economic changes introduced by colonial rule created tensions and fractures within African society, leading especially to the formation of African elites, which – despite the emphasis on character building – turned into a predatory class after independence.

'Adapted education' from the colonial perspective not only served to appease the local patriarchal authorities, but also created a divide between the emerging elite and the masses, between urban and rural societies, and between the 'modern' and the 'backward' segments of the populace. In this, the colonial model of education prepared the ground for the implementation of the concept of the 'dual economy'[147] which dominated development discourse and practice after the Second World War for at least two decades.

Education and elite formation, but also the introduction of colonial languages as the dominant means of communication, paved the way for neo-colonial domination after independence. Albert Sarraut forecasted the creation of a shared patrimony ('patrimoine solidaire'),[148] in which 'The colonies . . . have the right to their own life, their own interests and to the interest of their people. What ties them to the metropolis is less servitude than solidarity, it is family bonds'.[149] And in a strange way, at least from the French perspective, his prediction has subsequently become reality.

Some implications of British and French colonial education discourse are directly related to global inequality and the North-South divide: Sarraut defined education of the colonised ('les indigènes') as a moral obligation of the coloniser, but this obligation was also 'in accordance with [France's] self-evident interests in economy, administration, defence, and politics'.[150] Anyone who is familiar with today's aid business recognises that the core message is not all that different from contemporary development discourse with its focus on 'partnership', 'ownership', a 'common global system', and the moral obligation for the donors.

Guggisberg was even closer to today's discourse when he claimed it was the colonised people themselves who demanded what he felt was the appropriate way to develop the colonised target group. There was no question of rights in colonial times, not even of 'giving a sporting chance'. 'Progress of the people' was what colonialism had brought for and to the colonised – but if we compare the wording to the discourse of today we have to admit that the former was by far more sincere than the latter. Actors and experts in development make a fuss about 'rights based development', but those concerned don't know they have rights, and if they don't know how can they claim their rights?

Notes

1 To damages and debts caused by a costly war, which German reparations could never cover, but still more to losses closely linked to the rise of the United States of America as a creditor and the new hegemonic power in global politics and economy.

2 Belgium, by the way, did both; therefore, after the Second World War, the Congo not only had to house an important number of settlers, industrial and administrative staff, and especially missionaries from Europe, but also had one of the highest rates in primary school enrolment in Africa south of the Sahara. The latter was the outcome of intense (especially Catholic) mission activities supported by the government.

3 Jules Harmand, claiming for the French the 'right to rule based on moral superiority' defined his 'policy of association' as a strategy which should assign specific roles and duties to the different social groups of the colonial project: 'Elle n'entend pas du tout préparer et réaliser une égalité à jamais impossible, mais établir une certaine équivalence ou compensation de services réciproques'. See Jules Harmand, *Domination et colonisation* (Paris: Flammarion 1910), pp. 156, 160.

4 Veronique Dimier, 'Politiques indigènes en France et en Grande-Bretagne dans les années 1930: aux origines coloniales des politiques de développement', *Politique et Sociétés* 24, 1 (2005), pp. 80, 74. This and the following translations from French are mine.

5 Franz Ansprenger, *Politische Geschichte Afrikas im 20. Jahrhundert* (Munich: Beck 1999), p. 38.

6 Accordingly, Governor Faidherbe called the institution he founded in Senegal in 1855 École des otages (the hostages' school); it was then re-named École des fils de chefs et des interprètes (School for the sons of chiefs and for translators).

7 My analysis is based on methodological approaches of Critical Discourse Analysis. The emphasis is on a content-orientated structural analysis. For a general overview, see Siegfried Jäger and Florentine Maier, 'Theoretical and Methodological Aspects of Foucauldian Critical Discourse Analysis and Dispositive Analysis', and Martin Reisigl and Ruth Wodak, 'The Discourse-Historical Approach (DHA)', in Ruth Wodak and Michael Meyer (eds), *Methods of Critical Discourse Analysis* (London: Sage 2009), pp. 34–61, pp. 87–121.

8 See Albert Sarraut, *La mise en valeur des colonies françaises* (Paris: Payot 1923); [Sir] Frederick Gordon Guggisberg, *The Keystone* (London: Simpkin, Marshall, Hamilton, Kent and Co. 1924).

9 Guggisberg, 'Address to the Legislative Assembly 1924', quoted in T. David Williams, 'Sir Gordon Guggisberg and Educational Reform in the Gold Coast, 1919–1927', *Comparative Education Review* 8, 3 (1964), p. 290.

10 The colonial minister in particular expressed his gratitude to Governor André Touzet.

11 Sarraut, *La mise en valeur*, p. 20.

12 While there are references to the concept *mise en valeur* in the reports of the colonial government of French West Africa during the 1920s, the reports of the 1930s are dominated by measures against the impact of the Great Depression. See Archives Nationales d'Outremer, Aix en Provence (hereafter ANOM), 1affpol 536 to 538, Rapports d'Ensemble du Gouvernement Générale de l'Afrique Occidentale Française; Archives Départementales de l'Aude, Carcassonne (hereafter ADA), Albert Sarraut Papers, 12J163, 'Programme de la mise en valeur et d'intensification de la production coloniale', November 1926.

13 Sarraut, *La mise en valeur*; and Albert Sarraut, *Grandeurs et servitudes coloniales* (Paris: Sagittaire 1931). The 'Fonds Albert Sarraut', ADA, provides also a number of manuscripts and drafts of speeches, dealing with the necessity to amend or change colonial policies.

14 Guggisberg, *The Keystone*, p. 2.

15 'La France doit envisager ses devoirs non seulement vis-à-vis d'elle-même, mais vis-à-vis de l'Europe et de l'univers; et je crois ardemment que son génie bienfaisant peut exercer sur la paix du monde et le progrès humain une influence décisive, par l'effet des hautes et généreuses disciplines morales qui composent sa tradition d'altruisme'. Sarraut, *La mise en valeur*, p. 19.
16 Guggisberg, *The Keystone*, p. 1.
17 Patti McGill Peterson, 'Colonialism and Education: The Case of the Afro-American', *Comparative Education Review* 15, 2 (1971), pp. 147–8.
18 Ibid., p. 150.
19 Edward H. Berman, 'American Influence on African Education: The Role of the Phelps-Stokes Fund's Education Commissions', *Comparative Education Review* 15, 2 (1971), p. 132.
20 *Education Policy in British Tropical Africa* (1924), quoted in Gita Steiner-Khamsi and Hubert O. Quist, 'The Politics of Educational Borrowing: Reopening the Case of Achimota in British Ghana', *Comparative Education Review* 44, 3 (2000), pp. 273–4.
21 Carole Reynaud Paligot, 'Les *Annales* de Lucien Febvre à Fernand Braudel: entre épopée coloniale et opposition Orient/Occident', *French Historical Studies* 32, 1 (2009), p. 128.
22 'La France . . . ne peut pas abdiquer l'essence même de son génie, de sa mission humaine, qui est d'agir dans le droit et pour le droit, de civiliser au sens plein du mot'. Sarraut, *La mise en valeur*, p. 84.
23 'L'enseignement, l'instruction publique, est un autre article essentiel du programme de politique indigène'. Ibid., p. 95.
24 Ibid., p. 87.
25 Peterson, 'Colonialism and Education', p. 150.
26 Sarraut, *La mise en valeur*, p. 87.
27 For these differences between the Governor and the mission see the handwritten remarks a reader of *The Keystone* left in a copy of the book belonging to the library of the Basle Mission. The reader underlines phrases dealing with 'desire for better conditions of living', questions the remark that 'character training . . . has hitherto been omitted from the African's curriculum' and comments as 'not true' Guggisberg's statement that the government could provide more trained teachers than the Mission.
28 Steiner-Khamsi and Quist, 'The Politics of Educational Borrowing', p. 279.
29 ANOM, 1affpol 539, Rapport Politique et Administratif d'Ensemble du Gouvernement AOF, 1933.
30 Guggisberg, *TheKeystone*, pp. 7–8.
31 Sarraut, *La mise en valeur*, pp. 96–7.
32 Peterson, 'Colonialism and Education', p. 154.
33 Dimier, 'Politiques indigènes en France et en Grande-Bretagne', p. 76.
34 Sarraut, *La mise en valeur*, p. 104.
35 Francis Agbodeka, *Achimota in the National Setting* (Accra: Afram 1977), quoted in Steiner-Khamsi and Quist, 'The Politics of Educational Borrowing', p. 291.
36 Adu Boahen, *Ghana: Evolution and Change in the Nineteenth and Twentieth Centuries* (London: Longman 1975), p. 118.
37 Guggisberg, *The Keystone*, p. 5.
38 This is what Gita Steiner-Khamsi and Hubert Quist call 'old wine repackaged in new bottles'. See Steiner-Khamsi and Quist, 'The Politics of Educational Borrowing', p. 289.
39 Guggisberg, *The Keystone*, p. 14.
40 Peter Holt and M. Daly described in their *History of the Sudan* the colonial government as 'composed, in the words of a British newspaper, of "athletic public school boys accustomed to hard work rather than to hard thinking"'. Peter M. Holt and M. W. Daly, *A History of the Sudan from the Coming of Islam to the Present Day* (London: Longman 1988), p. 123.
41 Guggisberg, *The Keystone*, pp. 16–17.

42 Ibid., p. 42.
43 Ibid., p. 8.
44 Ibid., p. 42.
45 Ibid., p. 45.
46 ANOM, 14MI2738, 2G/214, Territoire du Sénégal, Cercle Linguere, Rapport Politique du Commandant du Cercle Gienger, 1952.
47 'l'instruction doit développer parmi eux leurs facultés et les capacités d'une utile et raisonnable collaboration avec nous'. ADA, Albert Sarraut Papers, 12J162, 'Programme coloniale', [n.d.], pp. 32–3.
48 Sarraut, *La mise en valeur*, p. 89.
49 'Abdiquer cette force entre des mains ignorantes, débiles ou inexpérimentées, ce serait décréter l'arrêt de la civilisation, la fin des bienfaits qu'elle garantit, l'anarchie et le retour des masses en tutelle vers les servitudes anciennes'. Ibid., p. 103.
50 Although Albert Sarraut apparently did most of the conceptual work for this book he had to rely on collaborators who did the economic and demographic sections concerning single territories and the empire as a whole.
51 Guggisberg, *The Keystone*, p. 41.
52 Ibid., p. 38.
53 ADA, Albert Sarraut Papers, 12J162, 'Programme coloniale', pp. 38–9.
54 Guggisberg, *The Keystone*, p. 39.
55 Ibid., p. 40.
56 Ibid., p. 36.
57 Ibid., p. 20.
58 Ibid., pp. 26, 18.
59 Steiner-Khamsi and Quist, 'The Politics of Educational Borrowing', p. 283.
60 Guggisberg, *The Keystone*, p. 11.
61 Sarraut, *La mise en valeur*, p. 97.
62 Georges Hardy, *Une conquête morale: l'enseignement en A.O.F.* (Paris: Armand Colin 1917).
63 'As for going slow, we are going too slow. Although it is perfectly true that the races of the Gold Coast are now in a phase through which every other race has had to pass since time immemorial, yet every century sees a quicker rate of advance made by the primitive peoples of the world. Therefore, although we may draw lessons from the past experience of other nations, it is essential that we should move faster, quicker even than the educational authorities did in the days of our youth'. Guggisberg, *The Keystone*, p. 11.
64 Sarraut, *La mise en valeur*, p. 25.
65 Remi P. Clignet and Philip J. Foster, 'French and British Colonial Education in Africa', *Comparative Education Review* 8, 2 (1964), pp. 191–8.
66 Hans-Georg Wolf, 'British and French Language and Educational Policies in the Mandate and Trusteeship Territories', *Language Sciences* 30, 5 (2008), p. 559.
67 Williams, 'Sir Gordon Guggisberg and Educational Reform in the Gold Coast', p. 293.
68 Guggisberg, *The Keystone*, p. 48, emphasis in the original.
69 Bob W. White, 'Talk about School: Education and the Colonial Project in French and British Africa, 1860–1960', *Comparative Education* 32, 1 (1996), pp. 11–12.
70 Sarraut, *La mise en valeur*, p. 97.
71 Guy Camille, 'La mise en valeur des colonies françaises', *Annales de Géographie* 32, 177 (1923), p. 267.
72 Guggisberg, *The Keystone*, p. 27.
73 Ibid., p. 22.
74 Ibid., pp. 24–5.
75 Ibid., p. 25.
76 Peterson, 'Colonialism and Education', pp. 147–8.
77 Sarraut, *La mise en valeur*, p. 98.
78 'Les hautes spéculations scientifiques sont un vin capiteux qui tourne facilement les têtes'. ADA, Albert Sarraut Papers, 12J162, 'Programme coloniale', p. 35.

79 Sarraut, *La mise en valeur*, p. 101.
80 Guggisberg, *The Keystone*, p. 10.
81 'notre rôle est de créer, dans une élite que les progrès de l'éducation feront sans cesse plus nombreuse, cette conscience civique, formée de devoirs et de droits, qui permettra aux meilleurs d'entre nos protégés de partager avec nous les responsabilités de l'action et de l'administration de leur pays'. Sarraut, *La mise en valeur*, p. 101.
82 Hardy, *Une conquête morale*.
83 ADA, Albert Sarraut Papers, 12J162, 'Programme coloniale', p. 33.
84 Sarraut, *La mise en valeur*, pp. 97–8.
85 Ibid., p. 98.
86 Ibid., p. 96.
87 Guggisberg, *The Keystone*, p. 14.
88 Ibid., p. 30.
89 'The races of Africa are in such varying *stages of development* that some of them have by no means reached the point on the *Road of Progress* at which a higher education is either within their intellectual grasp or would be good for their future'. See Guggisberg, *The Keystone*, p. 2, my emphasis.
90 'Instruire les indigènes est assurément notre devoir: c'est une obligation morale impérieuse que nous créent les responsabilités de la souveraineté vis-à-vis des populations indigènes dont nous avons assumé la tutelle. Mais ce devoir fondamental s'accorde par surcroît avec nos intérêts économiques, administratifs, militaires et politiques les plus évidents'. Sarraut, *La mise en valeur*, p. 95.
91 Ibid.
92 Guggisberg, *The Keystone*, p. 19.
93 'il faut que l'indigène soit instruit, et éduqué. Instruit, afin de pouvoir donner à l'œuvre commune toutes les ressources de son esprit. Eduqué, afin que, éveillé par nous, le sentiment de sa Dignité personnelle dirige son instruction'. ADA, Albert Sarraut Papers, 12J162, 'Programme coloniale', p. 30.
94 Sarraut, *La mise en valeur*, p. 89.
95 Guggisberg, *The Keystone*, p. 7.
96 Sarraut, *La mise en valeur*, p. 95.
97 Guggisberg, *The Keystone*, p. 6.
98 Ibid., pp. 5–6.
99 Ibid., p. 6.
100 F. M. Bourret, *Ghana: The Road to Independence, 1919–1957* (Oxford: Oxford University Press 1960), pp. 26–35.
101 '[l]'instruction, qui en éclairant leurs cerveaux, les fait plus conscients de la gratitude qu'ils nous doivent et mieux capables de collaborer avec nous pour la bonne exploitation du patrimoine commun'. Sarraut, *Grandeurs et servitudes coloniales*, p. 170.
102 Sarraut, *La mise en valeur*, pp. 19–23.
103 'Les œuvres d'enseignement, d'éducation, d'hygiène et d'assistance indigènes qui, en aménageant les fortes bases de l'avenir de progrès que la civilisation coloniale doit à la dignité même de l'espèce humaine, affirment et consacrent les obligations supérieures de la politique d'expansion lointaine'. Ibid., p. 83.
104 Guggisberg, *The Keystone*, p. 19.
105 '[a] policy known initially as the Colonial Pact, and later as the *économie du traite*. Under either name, it required the French colonies to export the raw materials to France and to import French merchandise in a close economic circuit designed to exclude foreign traders and shipping'. Virginia Thompson and Richard Adloff, 'French Economic Policy in Tropical Africa', in Peter Duignan and L. H. Gann (eds), *Colonialism in Africa, 1870–1960*, vol. 4, *The Economics of Colonialism* (Cambridge: Cambridge University Press 1975), p. 128.
106 Sarraut, *La mise en valeur*, p. 85.
107 Guggisberg, *The Keystone*, pp. 19, 24.
108 Ibid., p. 9.

109 Sarraut, *La mise en valeur*, p. 19.
110 Ibid., p. 83.
111 Guggisberg, *The Keystone*, p. 8.
112 Ibid., p. 14.
113 Sarraut, *La mise en valeur*, p. 117. The former Governor General of French Indochina especially refers to the difference between Asians and Africans.
114 'To comply with all these demands, to cope with rapidly changing conditions, Government acting by itself will make insufficient progress; its efforts must be supplemented by African enterprise'. Guggisberg, *The Keystone*, p. 6.
115 Ibid., p. 10.
116 Ibid., p. 28.
117 Sarraut, *La mise en valeur*, p. 96.
118 ADA, Albert Sarraut Papers, 12J162, 'Programme coloniale', p. 30.
119 Sarraut, *La mise en valeur*, p. 95.
120 Guggisberg, *The Keystone*, p. 14.
121 'Hier, la France a eu besoin, pour le combat, des contingents coloniaux. Elle en aura besoin demain pour reforger son instrument militaire. Sa sécurité est désormais tributaire de ses colonies. La Chambre des Députés n'a pu voter la réduction du service à dix-huit mois qu'en escomptant les contributions d'un recrutement indigène progressivement accru'. Sarraut, *La mise en valeur*, p. 17.
122 Ibid., p. 96.
123 Guggisberg, *The Keystone*, p. 10, emphasis in the original.
124 Ibid., p. 30.
125 Lord Cromer, quoted ibid., pp. 29–30.
126 Arku Korsah, quoted in Williams, 'Sir Gordon Guggisberg and Educational Reform in the Gold Coast', p. 298.
127 Sarraut, *La mise en valeur*, p. 99.
128 See ANOM, 1affpol 536 to 538, Rapports d'Ensemble du Gouvernement Générale de l'Afrique Occidentale Française, during the 1920s and 1930s.
129 French colonial officers and politicians did not differentiate between 'communists' and Anglophone Pan-Africanists, while Guggisberg responded positively to the latter's requests. In 1920 Casely-Hayford and others had founded the National Congress of British West Africa, which among other things called for the creation of an African university – a claim answered by Guggisberg through the foundation of the Prince of Wales College in Achimota.
130 Sarraut, *La mise en valeur*, p. 96.
131 '[l]'immense flot des races de couleur, marquent le réveil nouveau d'aspirations qui ne seraient point sans danger pour la civilisation européenne, le jour où elles coaliseraient encore les vieux fanatismes, les nationalismes ou les mysticismes contre les lumières venues de l'Occident'. Ibid., p. 18.
132 Guggisberg, *The Keystone*, p. 12.
133 Ibid., p. 19.
134 Sarraut, *La mise en valeur*, pp. 15, 89.
135 Guggisberg, *The Keystone*, pp. 2–4.
136 The foundation of a university, or at least a college which might become a university in the future. Ibid., p. 3.
137 Guggisberg, *The Keystone*, p. 2.
138 Sarraut, *La mise en valeur*, pp. 96, 118.
139 ADA, Albert Sarraut Papers, 12J162, 'Programme coloniale', p. 35.
140 Guggisberg, *The Keystone*, p. 44.
141 ADA, Albert Sarraut Papers, 12J162, 'Programme coloniale', pp. 37–8.
142 Dimier, 'Politiques indigènes en France et en Grande-Bretagne', pp. 83–4.
143 Sarraut, *La mise en valeur*, p. 19.
144 Guggisberg, *The Keystone*, p. 9.
145 'Sous cette réserve, qui est le simple bon sens, les indigènes étant des hommes comme nous, il faut les traiter en hommes comme nous'. ADA, Albert Sarraut Papers, 12J162, 'Programme coloniale', pp. 45–6.

146 As background we have to consider the efforts of the American President Woodrow Wilson to find a new, more peaceful basis for international relations and the discussions of the League of Nations.

147 'The economic system may be divided into two sectors – the advanced or modern sector, which we will call, somewhat inaccurately, the manufacturing sector, and the backward or traditional sector, which may be suggestively denoted agriculture'. Dale W. Jorgenson, 'The Development of a Dual Economy', *Economic Journal* 71, 282 (1961), p. 311.

148 Sarraut, *La mise en valeur*, p. 89.

149 Ibid., p. 113.

150 Ibid., p. 95.

CHAPTER TEN

Development and education in British colonial Nigeria, 1940–55

Uyilawa Usuanlele

Education, by which I mean the imparting of knowledge and new skills to people for the efficient utilisation of resources, as well as for sustaining and enhancing society, was an issue of significant concern to European colonialists and their African subjects. The need for education was widely shared, but disagreements arose between colonisers and colonised over the ends to be served by Western education as well as the quality and quantity of instruction to be provided. Although the question of African capabilities and ability had been resolved by some Christian missionaries who converted and educated Africans, many colonial officials who held essentialist views of Africans insisted on a different type of education. Education of Africans came to be tied to the indirect system of rule and development 'along native lines' policy that was adopted by various colonial administrations.[1]

The introduction of colonial development policies from the late 1920s, particularly the Colonial Development and Welfare Act (CDWA) of 1940 which had a welfare component, is said to have had a beneficial impact on education in Africa. But did the adoption of a more development-oriented approach really change the policy measures and practices established for education of Africans, or was it a medium employed to further enhance the exploitation of Africans? This chapter examines the officially assigned role of education in development and vice versa in colonial Nigeria, and discusses the politics of implementation and its impact. It argues that although education was viewed by local colonial officials as a medium for improving welfare, the overriding view of education as a means of training skilled personnel needed for increasing productivity prevailed despite shifts in Colonial Office rhetoric. The characteristic neglect of primary and secondary education continued, even after the Second World War, with consequences for the development of Nigeria. The chapter is divided into three sections with the first part focusing on the policy and state of education before the introduction of the colonial development policies of the 1930s and 1940s. The second part looks at the views of the various actors, particularly the Colonial Office and local officials, on the role and place of education within the development project and the politics of its implementation. Finally, section three discusses what were termed as adult and mass education schemes as a component of colonial development and its objectives.

Early colonial education in Nigeria: towards development 'along native lines'

In the nineteenth century, European Christian missionaries and freed African slaves heralded Western education in the territory that became known as Nigeria. When the colonisation of Nigeria commenced in 1861, there existed a small educated African population in Lagos who were interested in the further expansion and development of Western education. In 1863, shortly after the colonisation of Lagos, the newspaper, *Anglo-African*, voiced the opinion of a section of the educated African inhabitants by stating: 'In order to elevate a people of whom the chief part is sunk into a state of mental darkness and moral depredation, there seems but a single course to be pursued, namely, to provide for proper direction and development of the minds of their youth . . . as a rule education must be begun in youth in order to have its due effect on our habits and life'.[2] But British colonial administration in Lagos did not share even this paternalistic view of the education of the inhabitants of its West African colonies, preferring instead to not educate them at all. It was not until the 1880s that Inspectors of Schools were appointed. Lagos Colony was placed under an Inspector in faraway Gold Coast colony and his visits were few and far between.[3] With only a perfunctory interest in education, the administration voted a mere pittance of £700 for education out of a total budget of £45,000, whereas a robust £16,000 was allocated for prisons in 1880. Such a paltry sum so alarmed *The Times* newspaper that it queried: 'Is crime considered a more respectable thing than education?' The paper went on to demand 'the establishment or support of good elementary schools by the Government with an efficient inspector at their head . . . because no people, as a people, are more anxious for the advantages of liberal education than the people of Lagos. From time to time, we see the strenuous efforts put forth, and the enormous sacrifice made by parents to secure the great boon for their children'.[4]

This media outcry was also prompted by the low quality of education provided by missionaries, which was so poor that Lagos Colony had sufficiently qualified pupils neither to fill a proposed high school nor to be employed as confidential clerks to the Governor.[5] Though an Education Code was passed in 1882 partly to improve the quality of its products for colonial administrative work and trade needs, the missions were opposed to government inspection, which they viewed as an attempt to change the religious orientation of their schools.

Beyond the Indian Mutiny of the 1850s which initiated a change in British attitudes towards the education of colonial subjects,[6] the late nineteenth century was also a period of critical change in British–African relations. It was one of high imperialism and racial hardening which impacted European attitudes towards educated Africans, who were increasingly viewed as distinct and inferior and expected to chart a different course of development 'along their own lines'. Educated Africans reacted to the shifting European attitudes with virulent criticisms (and cultural nationalism), which further reinforced European stereotypes and negative views of them.

In spite of the development and adoption of what was referred to as Indirect Rule, colonial administration still required a small number of literate personnel with skills and rates of efficiency necessary for the functioning of the government and trading.[7] This left the colonial administration with not much choice other than to recruit some of its personnel from this educated African population and provide small financial grants to missions to supply education services. In the evolving colonial economic system, the need for Western education was supported by Ralph Moor, Consul General of the Niger Coast Protectorate as a means to 'improve the lot' of the uncivilised people.[8] To this end, Moor and Governor William McGregor of Lagos Colony invited Frederick Lugard, the High Commissioner of the Protectorate of Northern Nigeria, to jointly establish a Normal and High School for the three administrations. In the event, Lugard declined the offer as he was against literary education for Africans.[9] And in the Protectorate of Southern Nigeria, where missionaries preceded colonialism with some welfare work, complete government control proved impossible despite the various attempts that characterised the pre-development era.

In addition, various attempts were made at designing a different type of education that would maintain Africans in their assumed life's station. Contrary to Clive Whitehead's claim,[10] British colonial officials were already urging the adaptation of 'native education' to the local environment and culture well before the arrival of British anthropologists in the 1920s and 1930s. The stated aim of education in the revised rules of the Education Code formulated by Governor McGregor of Lagos was 'not to divert the education of the boys into unnatural and unserviceable channels but rather to keep in touch with the development actually going on in the Colony and the requirements of ordinary life'.[11] McGregor's 'unnatural and unserviceable channels' as well as 'ordinary life' in the Colony were euphemisms for his perception of African 'primitive life'. His introduction of vernacular education in the code was a pointer to the native lines philosophy. Moor, though a most zealous advocate of government funding and the establishment of secular educational institutions, shared the prevailing views of most administrators of using education to conserve African societies. He argued that 'The aping of the European destroys the independence of character and the initiative of the native of these territories and certainly during the period of their education, I consider it infinitely preferable to keep them clothed in some suitable native garb with a view of maintaining their distinct native character'.[12]

He therefore opposed the establishment of a full-fledged secondary school because 'the education necessary to enable the Natives ... to take their place as useful members of their community need not necessarily include the entire secondary course'.[13] Moor's successor, Egerton, who had a seemingly more liberal attitude, introduced the defining issue in so-called 'Native education' which was compulsory manual and agricultural training to re-orientate African youths into taking to agricultural production rather than seeking clerical employment. Lugard's successors in the Protectorate of Northern Nigeria went further and designed a unique educational system that excluded missionaries and gave the government monopoly control over the content, quality, and quantity of recipients of Western education and thereby minimised, if only temporarily, the envisaged problems of political agitation and unemployment of educated subjects.[14]

Education thus remained a medium for the production of clerks, artisans, and low level staff for the various departments of government and for meeting the needs of commercial and trading firms. Even when secondary schools were established later on, such as King's College in 1906 and the Government Colleges in 1927, they served the same ends with added emphasis on producing teachers for government elementary schools. In the Protectorate of Northern Nigeria, the government's tight control over administration led to a system that was unable to produce enough personnel to meet its needs,[15] while in the Southern Provinces, the mushrooming of Christian mission schools created an over-production of school leavers who were insubordinate to the administration and customary authority. As a result educational development remained poor in quality, while increases in quantity were experienced in the Southern Provinces.

Education policy received a jolt from the Colonial Office in the early 1920s. Some scholars have pointed out that the demand of the League of Nations' Permanent Mandate Commission that colonial powers should treat their subjects humanely had some influence on the Colonial Office after the First World War.[16] The extent of this influence is not known, but the criticisms of education in British colonies by the Phelps-Stokes Commission Report of 1922 surely had a great influence. As a result of this development as well as the promptings of Christian missionaries who wanted primacy of place in African education, the Colonial Office's Advisory Committee on Native Education in Tropical Africa (ACNETA) was established in 1924. The Advisory Committee came largely under the influence of Christian missionaries and some of the early colonial officials such as Lugard and Hanns Vischer[17] who designed education policies to keep Africans in their assigned inferior 'life stations' as agricultural producers. Their influence can be seen in the first memorandum of the Advisory Committee, the 1925 White Paper, *Education Policy in British Tropical Africa*, and the subsequent 1935 *Memorandum on the Education of African Communities*, whose primary objective was to adapt Western education to the life of agricultural and handicraft occupations in African communities and to instil moral and character training in the youths through the medium of local vernacular languages. The *Memorandum* only reinforced what early colonial officials had for long been advancing, but failed to achieve in Nigeria.

Rather than turn education mainly into an instrument of religious conversion by leaving it entirely in the hands of Christian missions as recommended by Governor Hugh Clifford (1919–25),[18] the Advisory Committee demanded

> that education should be adapted to the mentality, occupations and traditions of the people, conserving as far as possible all sound and healthy elements in the existing fabric of their social life. Its aim should be to render the individual more efficient and to promote the advancement of the community as a whole through the improvement of agriculture, the development of native industries, the improvement of health, the training of the people in the management of their domestic affairs; and it must include the raising of capable, trustworthy, public spirited leaders of the people belonging to their own race. Every department of government concerned with the welfare of the natives or vocational training, including especially the Health and Agricultural Departments should co-operate closely in the educational policy.[19]

The Committee recognised 'that the rapid development of the African Dependencies on the material and economic side both demands and warrants a corresponding advance in the expenditure on education'.[20] But apart from establishing Katsina College in 1922 and two teacher training colleges to train teachers for the few government elementary schools in 1927, and expanding the European inspectorate staff in

Southern Nigeria, investment in the education of Nigerians remained low and poor at a time of rapid increases in the demand for education. As a result, Africans resorted to self-help in education provisioning which aroused the Committee's fear of losing control to African initiative, with the accompanying political consequences that this entailed.[21] Despite such fears, funding for education in Nigeria remained low with only £231,983 or 3.5 per cent of total expenditure devoted to it in 1937.[22] In spite of a slight improvement in funding in 1938, the Secretary of State for Colonies was exasperated enough to complain in 1941 that 'expenditure on Education for 1938/39 represents only 4.3 per cent of the Government's total recurrent expenditure and the approximate number of Government and assisted schools per thousand of the population is lower than in any other British territory but one in East or West Africa'.[23] In 1939 there were only two government secondary schools and three teacher training colleges for a population of over 20 million and only 350,000 (about 10 per cent) out of three million school age children were reported to be enrolled in school.[24]

Development and education

Political agitations and crises throughout the empire in the late 1930s forced Britain to pass the Colonial Development and Welfare Act (CDWA) in 1940. Despite the novelty of the 1940 Act, it is still plausible to assert that Britain was not really committed to addressing the welfare problems of its colonies. Some British officials were candid enough to admit that there might not be money to implement the new development mission.[25] For the first time British colonial development policy alluded to providing assistance for the improvement of education. The CDWA Memo stated that 'assistance will be available both for schemes involving capital expenditure necessary for Colonial development in the widest sense and to assist in meeting recurrent expenditure in the colonies in certain specific services such as agriculture, *education*, health and housing'.[26] Education, particularly the school based type, though highlighted was still not viewed as critical to the kind of development envisaged and was thus put on the recurrent list. This was because the main goal of 'colonial development [was to be] the promotion of productivity in the colonies, which will enable them to increase their local supplies of food and to support to the maximum extent possible out of their own resources those governmental and other services which are required to give their people a good life'.[27]

But the underlying objective of increased productivity was advocated not so much for the 'good life' of colonial people, as for the benefit and profit needs of the metropole, which needed to be sustained particularly during and after the war. The logic of increased productivity as the basis of African welfare was not entirely accepted by all in the colonies including some colonial officers. It was faulted, for example, by the Resident of Bornu who argued that the Secretary of State's Memo on the CDWA 'proposed to start at the wrong end' because 'at the same time it may well be argued that a general advance in education is a necessary preliminary to the promotion of productivity'.[28] The Chief Commissioner of Northern Nigeria concurred that if 'the chief aim of the scheme is to promote productivity and so gradually increase wealth and provide greater revenue for social needs', it would not be successful because 'in Nigeria the increase in taxable capacity would be so slow that our social expenditure would remain stagnant for a great number of years'. Instead, he argued that 'we must therefore include medical and health work, and increased expenditure on education – both of which tend to raise the wealth of the community'.[29]

Apart from some officials faulting the logic of the Colonial Office and the CDWA, the new Act was received with enthusiasm by many local officials who rightly hinged its success on education. Governor Bernard Bourdillon (1935–44) enthusiastically instructed the Director of Education to make proposals on developing the education sector. In Mr Morris, the Director of Education's opinion,

> educational services in Nigeria have been starved, and that [the Nigerian] Government has not fulfilled its obligations. The expenditure during the last decade in Nigeria compared most unfavourably with that of other British colonial territories in Africa. In consequence there is much leeway to make up, and this task must have the first call on any funds available. The money required represents a debt of honour, which government has contracted at the expense of the Missionaries and the teachers, it should be discharged before any applications from other Departments of Government are given consideration.[30]

A proposal based on the overarching role of education in development was sent by the Governor to the Colonial Office requesting £102,050 for grants-in-aid for 1940–41 and an additional £32,000 to pay European teachers. It also requested that an annual increment of teachers' salaries should be paid from Colonial Development and Welfare funds to solve the lingering teacher's salary problem, particularly in the mission schools. The Nigerian government made a commitment to contribute an annual £100,000 for grants-in-aid. The requested funds, according to the Director of Education, in a view echoed by the Governor, were to be used 'for repairing defects in the machinery which maintained existing services' instead of an 'extension of social and developmental services'.[31]

The Secretary of State for Colonies viewed matters differently. He attributed the poor funding of education, manifested in the government's inability to meet the increasing cost of grants-in-aid, to the failure of the Nigerian colonial government to exercise control over the expansion of mission schools. He opined that 'the relative poverty of Nigeria will necessitate substantial assistance from United Kingdom funds to enable any improvement to take place', but warned the Nigerian government not to be too optimistic as he did not know how much would be available and that any funding provided would be for the 'necessary minimum personnel'.[32]

The Colonial Office did not share the local officials' critical view of education in relation to development. In 1944, Oliver Stanley, the Secretary of State for Colonies, made this clear by unbundling the relationship between development and education. As far as the CDWA was concerned, Stanley clarified that

> without belittling the need for welfare expenditure, the basic objective of sound development in any dependency must be the improvement of productive and earning power (in which health and *education* services *may* well play an important part) not simply additions to income at the UK taxpayers' expense, the ultimate objective being to place the dependency in a position to support itself without external assistance.[33]

Given the above directive from the CO, the Nigerian government had little choice but to toe the official line. In its development policy and planning objectives, the government agreed 'to ignore for the present all subjects that were already well in hand under a Department of Government, e.g. *Education*, Medical and Health, Labour; and to concentrate on those subjects upon which little or no progress had been made during the past years because there was no adequate Government organization set up to deal with them'.[34] Not all local officials were willing to relegate education to the backburner, especially given its obvious critical role in colonial development. The introduction of planning provided these local Nigerian colonial officials with another opportunity to press home their viewpoint. This was forcefully made by Mr Davidson, the new Director of Education, in drawing up the ten-year development plan of his department, which stressed that education affected development in all its ramifications. Firstly, he pointed out that 'Indeed, a spread of rudimentary education, even if this extends only to modest literacy in the vernacular, is necessary to ensure a receptive public for development'.[35] He went further to buttress this linkage asserting:

> Educational and general development are closely interlocked and bear directly on one another at all points. Moreover, it appears that *all* the

Departments will have two urgent needs in common, first, many more Africans with post-secondary education and, second, a very considerable increase in European staff to give the necessary technical training to these Africans. Until these needs are met, no large development in any sphere will be possible.[36]

The use of the above and other arguments that emphasised the gross neglect of education and poverty were employed by Governor Arthur Richards[37] to persuade the CO to prioritise education as critical to development. Such arguments, however, met with little success in Whitehall.

Though officials in Nigeria showed some enthusiasm, given the limitations of their powers, their implementation of the CDWA in the field of education was restricted to attempts at 'repairing defects in the machinery which maintained existing services'. To this end, their aim was to raise government expenditure on education from a miserly 4.3 per cent to 11–12 per cent of total expenditure in order to increase the percentage of school-age children enrolled in school from 11 per cent to 17 per cent.[38] The other aims were to increase the efficiency of schools in the Southern Provinces and increase the training of teachers to facilitate the expansion of education in the Northern Provinces. The proposed plan concentrated on enhancing secondary school education with courses that would be more practical and 'suited to rural environment' in the absence of large-scale employment prospects for secondary school leavers, improving the working conditions of teachers, and improving the quality of education through the building of new schools by the government and funding the expansion of mission schools. The total cost of the revised plan was £3,572,075. Nigeria was expected to contribute £164,000 in the first year and increase this annually up to £300,000 in the tenth year, while the Colonial Development and Welfare funds' contribution was to increase from £147,000 in year one to £500,000 in the tenth year.[39]

This proposed education plan was based on discussions between the Director of Education and the Boards of Education which were dominated by European missionaries and colonial officials, which probably accounts for the plan being skewed largely towards satisfying the missions. The unofficial African members of the Legislative Council criticised the proposed plan because they viewed the expenditure on education as being too small and demanded that a greater portion of Colonial Development and Welfare funds be expended for the purpose. They called for the introduction of compulsory education, no restrictions on the number of schools to be built, equal treatment of the different categories of teachers (Europeans, Africans, and the 'uncertificated'), employment of more African education officers, increased

African representation on the Board of Education, and the use of the Public Works Department's apprenticeship training programme for technical education.[40]

The Advisory Committee and the Colonial Office viewed the African members' demands as unrealistic because of the scale of 'poverty' in Nigeria. As the British government was unwilling to fully fund the improvement and expansion of education in Nigeria, they requested a more detailed education plan that could be sustained after the expiration of Colonial Development and Welfare funds and the Ten Year Development Plan in 1954. The subsequently revised plan advised caution, noting that

> it involves a temporary neglect of primary education which, in itself, requires a massive development ... When we speak of neglecting primary education we mean the neglect of regularly constituted schools with properly trained staff. These must await the teachers which it is the business of the secondary schools and the Training Centres to produce. Their turn will come a little later.[41]

Even the revised plan went through more protracted processes of revision entailing major cost cutting and reductions in the duration of British financial contributions (from ten to six years) that were expended on British personnel. The bulk of the funding was transferred to the Nigerian taxpayer through the use of pre-existing Nigerian funds as well as loans and new taxes. These measures further watered down the plan and restricted access to education for the vast majority of Nigerian children, thus retarding their social development. The neglect of primary education under the plan no doubt affected the quality of education provided in these schools during this period. More importantly, the policy kept many school aged children out of school because of inadequate facilities. At the end of the period in 1954, there were 1,216,421 pupils in primary school. Over the next two years, with the introduction of universal, free primary education by nationalist politicians, enrolments doubled to 2,528,801 pupils.[42] The neglect of the most basic stage of education contradicted the objectives of development planning in Nigeria which were '(a) to develop the resources of Nigeria or (b) to promote the wellbeing of the people'.[43]

Mass education and depoliticisation of development

Apart from the huge financial cost,[44] the Colonial Office disfavoured school-based education because of its destabilising effect on the existing social order by producing unemployed and embittered school leavers. Other forms of education that promoted production-oriented development while preserving the existing social order were preferred. The Colonial Advisory Committee on Native Education in Tropical Africa had since the 1930s tried to develop a non-school based education policy that would conserve communal social obligation while also promoting increased productivity. This was partly a response to the African independent school initiatives that were producing new political leadership among Africans[45] at the expense of traditional leaders and thereby weakening the pillars of Indirect Rule. In addition school-based education was viewed as promoting migrancy and 'detribalisation', which were seen as hindering increased agricultural productivity as well as communal obligations and loyalty. African communities were claimed to be undergoing disintegration and polarisation caused by economic change and Western education. According to Sivonen, Arthur Creech Jones, the Labour Party member of ACNETA, feared that 'rapid changes produced by economic and social force within the Empire created restless activity and legitimate political ambition . . . The problem of direction must be admitted if repeated obstructions and disorder were to be avoided in certain colonies'.[46] It was argued that these changes had produced a dangerous state of 'partial development'. The solution was to help people adjust and thus to restore social cohesion in the community.[47]

Creech Jones, who subsequently became Secretary of State for Colonies, initiated the re-direction of the Advisory Committee away from school-based education towards adult and later mass education. He borrowed some of his ideas from the experience of workers' education in Britain and the mass literacy successes of the Soviet Union. Adult, mass education was thought to be the means of increasing productivity while simultaneously improving African communities and weaning them from disloyal leadership. This resulted in a 1935 report of the Committee on Adult Education which advocated the use of adult literacy to promote the 'betterment' of Africans. Betterment was to be achieved through the combined work of the education, health, and agriculture departments and the use of their expert knowledge to promote the better use and protection of land for increased agricultural productivity. The memo was yet to be implemented in Nigeria when the Second World War broke out.

However, the Memorandum on Adult Education was criticised by Creech Jones for not going far enough and another memorandum was drafted by the Adult and Mass Education Sub-Committee in 1944, entitled 'Mass Education in African Society'.[48] This 1944 report was aimed at instilling a sense of belonging and social obligation of Africans to their 'community'. These goals were to be achieved through the promotion of literacy and the participation of Africans in activities

which the colonial administration deemed necessary for the improvement of African community life. This new scheme, which focused on
literacy education, was to be co-ordinated with the activities of other
social service agencies including agriculture and health.

Apart from the objective of increasing agricultural productivity, the
scheme and report had other underlying political objectives. The underlying political aim of the report was to steer African communities
towards pursuits that were

> worth sustained effort . . . secured through the leadership from among
> the people themselves, but it must not be forgotten that wise leadership
> is not likely to emerge and take effect in a community that has not
> learned to discriminate between the true leader and the plausible *self-
> seeking misleader*. Instances are not unknown of the *astute adventurer*
> exploiting for his own ends people lacking experience whom he professes
> to lead. The surest form of protection for a people in such circumstances
> consists in the development of their own power of criticism and dis-
> crimination. If that development is to be effective there must be provi-
> sion in mass education to secure freedom of discussion and criticism,
> and there must be opportunity for extending the range of knowledge
> relevant to the changing conditions. Free discussion in itself is valuable
> but it is not a substitute for being well informed.[49]

The 'self-seeking misleader' and 'astute adventurer' were euphemisms
for emergent Western educated nationalists of various shades. The
fear of the emergence of African anti-colonial agitators had long
influenced British colonial policies. The dissemination of leftist and
anti-colonial ideas before and during the war further heightened this
fear.[50] It was also feared that the war itself would throw up more
'misleaders' or 'adventurers' from among the demobilised soldiers who
might not easily fit back into their communities after exposure to
new ideas abroad. Adult or mass education was thus to provide a level
playing field that would mitigate against the advantage of the Western
educated over the illiterate peasant population. This would be achieved
through providing the illiterate peasant with some level of literacy
and opportunities for participation that would enable them to remain
influential in their communities. In addition, the 'community development' aspect (which was added to the scheme in 1948) was also seen
as a means of mobilising unpaid labour for projects that facilitated
increased agricultural production.

The Colonial Office directive on mass education was distributed
in Nigeria along with a memorandum titled 'Reflections' written by
Mr Davidson, Director of Education in Nigeria.[51] He recommended that
the 'the approach from above would be more effective and . . . assistance
from below would follow'.[52] Both the directive and memorandum were

received by local officials with mixed feelings. Many of the District Officers and Residents drew attention to the likely difficulties of dependence on unpaid volunteers, the hostile attitude of peasants to education, the lack of operational materials and funds, and dearth of population literate in the roman script in Northern Nigeria. Both the Chief Commissioners of the Northern and Western Provinces, in spite of their misgivings, recommended its implementation. They viewed the scheme as an aspect of rural development that should begin in areas that had the material preconditions for potential success.[53] Like previous schemes and directives received during this period, implementation was to wait until after the war.

The mass education scheme received little funding after its introduction and the Education Department showed little commitment to its implementation. Since the mass education scheme was not funded by the central administration and the CDWA, the Nigerian provinces approached its implementation in divergent ways, depending on the disposition and revenue of the provincial administration. The implementation in the Eastern Provinces entailed both social and literacy education, the Northern Provinces placed emphasis on village reorganisation/reconstruction or rural development based on the Anchau Scheme Model,[54] while the Western Provinces attempted adult education in conjunction with other schemes decided on at the district level.[55]

Shortly after the war, the Director of Education drafted a ten-year development plan for adult literacy. His stated that the reason for doing so was the need to have such a proposal to present to the Colonial Office or Parliament 'when the inevitable request for information appears on the scene'.[56] The scheme was to cost £14,000 in the first year with additional support from the Native Authorities and fees in the Southern Provinces to pay honoraria to volunteer teachers.[57] However, only £10,000 was approved for inclusion in the 1948 estimates for the scheme's implementation in areas which showed enthusiasm and initiative in response to the propaganda of the Education Department.[58]

According to the assessment of A. B. Cohen of the Colonial Office, the implementation of the mass education scheme was poor.[59] As a result, Creech Jones, by now the Secretary of State for Colonies, directed that there should be no large financial provisions for adult literacy as an adjunct of education.[60] The Governor concurred, but disagreed with the report of poor implementation in Nigeria, claiming that adult literacy work 'has so far outstripped public relations and welfare departments which are both in the early stages of development'.[61]

Following the regionalisation of administration in 1948, adult education came under the jurisdiction of the central government and was co-ordinated through the Department of Education. Because of differing approaches adopted by the regional administrations to the scheme, it was consequently resolved that each government should assist only so far as funds and personnel allowed, and that the scheme should use the spoken language of the people, assist with the distribution of literature, and employ mature and experienced people as adult education officers.[62] Though Creech Jones blamed the failure of mass education on misunderstanding and criticism by Africans and the inadequacies of the local administrative machinery,[63] in truth the scheme foundered because the people were mainly interested in the provision of regular schools for their children that would lead to their employment and were not inclined towards unpaid voluntary labour. Its death knell was sounded by the introduction of community development under Creech Jones's auspices in 1948.

Community development was the engagement of people in projects and programmes that were capable of simultaneously increasing their productive capacity and preserving the social fabric of the community against forces of disintegration. As conceived by Creech Jones, the projects were supposed to develop from the peoples' initiative and involve their participation. But in its implementation in Nigeria, the peoples' initiative was constrained by the Chief Secretary, who listed the village improvements that did not qualify for funding as 'post offices, schools, maternity homes and leper villages, or the building of palm presses and similar commercial activities' as 'none of these subjects can be considered as true village reconstruction and in some instances are the normal responsibilities either of government or Native Administration', while those that qualified were 'some form of amenity such as market place, playing field, village hall and other suitable facility or improvement'.[64] Funding of the projects was partial and limited to a refund of 10 per cent of the cost by government while the balance was funded through free labour. Apart from absorbing the former Urban and Town Planning and Village Reconstruction Schemes of the CDWA, community development also incorporated the adult literacy schemes, which as noted above were restricted to communities that showed enthusiasm. It was against this background of the Colonial Office's refusal to give education its primacy of place in development, that nationalist politicians like Obafemi Awolowo and Nnamdi Azikiwe proclaimed free, universal primary education as the cornerstone of their social programme immediately after power started to be devolved to them in 1955 and 1957 respectively.

Conclusion

This chapter has examined the role assigned to education in the colonial enterprise before and after the proclamation of a development policy in colonial Nigeria. It has shown that the colonial view towards education was deeply ambivalent, perceiving it both as a civilising agent and as a destabilising institution that needed to be closely controlled and managed. Though education remained largely ancillary to the colonial development project, various measures were taken to control the quality and quantity of recipients as well as to re-orient its products towards agriculture and a subordinate station in life. This chapter has argued that the proclamation of the CDWA in 1940 did not bring about a radical departure in approach to education because of the Colonial Office's overriding interest in using its development policy to increase productivity, which they saw as the basis of welfare. As a result, education remained ancillary and funds continued to be provided partially by the Nigerian taxpayers. Only certain aspects were 'repaired', such as the training of a few technical personnel for departments involved with development projects. At the same time, a cheap non-school based mass education scheme geared towards the depoliticisation of the populace and exploiting their free labour in the name of development was promoted by the Colonial Office. It was only after the nationalist politicians introduced free universal primary education in 1955 that education was brought to the centre of the development debate.

Notes

1 The idea of promoting a different line of development in Africa was in the late nineteenth century canvassed by some Europeans who came to be known as the 'Third Party' in opposition to Crown Colony administration in West Africa. A leading member and publicist Edmund Morel admonished the British to 'develop the native people along lines of their own civilisation'. See E. D. Morel, *Affairs of West Africa* (London: Frank Cass 1968 [1902]), p. 15.
2 Michael J. C. Echeruo, *Victorian Lagos: Aspects of Nineteenth Century Lagos Life* (London: Macmillan 1977), p. 50.
3 Ibid., p. 53.
4 *The Times*, as quoted in Echeruo, *Victorian Lagos*, p. 55.
5 Echeruo, *Victorian Lagos*, p. 53.
6 Mahmood Mamdani, *Citizen and Subject: Contemporary Africa and the Legacy of Late Colonialism* (Kampala: Fountain Publishers 2002), pp. 49–50.
7 Indirect Rule was a form of political authority and power that relied largely on indigenous African rulers and agents to mediate between the vast majority of Africans, most of who had been transformed into primary commodity producers and labourers, and the European colonisers.
8 National Archives of Nigeria, Ibadan (hereafter NAI), CSO 1/13 vol. 7, Despatch 159 Niger Coast Protectorate, Annual Report for the Year 1896–97, Moor to Foreign Office, 10 December 1897, p. 384; NAI CSO 1/13 vol. 14, Despatch 29 Moor to Secretary of State, Colonial Office, 6 February 1901, pp. 68–9.

9 NAI CSO 520, Moor to Secretary of State for Colonies, 28 February 1900; Sonia F. Graham, *Government and Mission Education in Northern Nigeria, 1900–1919* (Ibadan: Ibadan University Press 1966), p. 8; Adewunmi Fajana, *Education in Nigeria, 1842–1939: An Historical Analysis* (Ikeja: Longman 1978), p. 71.

10 Clive Whitehead, 'The Historiography of British Imperial Education Policy, Part II: Africa and the Rest of the Colonial Empire', *History of Education* 34, 4 (2005), p. 445.

11 Quoted in Fajana, *Education in Nigeria*, p. 65.

12 NAI CSO 1/13 vol. 15, Despatch 160 Moor to Rev. J. Buchanan, 15 June 1901, pp. 480–1.

13 Ibid., p. 482.

14 Charles Temple was the ideologue of the post-Lugard administration and had a great influence on Governor Girouard. Temple argued that the Muslims were too intelligent to be exposed to literary education in both English and Arabic which would bring them in touch with subversive political ideas, while the pagans were too attached to 'tribe' and 'customs' to be easily influenced by Christian missionary evangelisation. Temple and his boss further believed that Western education would 'denationalise' the natives and create problems for the administration as it was incompatible with Indirect Rule particularly in the Muslim emirates. Also, he opined that evangelisation activities required Christian missionaries to interactwith 'natives' that would harm their religious and cultural sensibilities and lead to conflict and disintegration or loss of 'Native character' which would undermine the authority of the native rulers. This situation could only be pre-empted by segregation of the races and tribes. See Charles P. Temple, *Native Races and their Rulers: Sketches and Studies of Official Life and Administrative Problems in Nigeria* (London: Frank Cass 1968 [1918]), pp. 183–90 and pp. 213–17.

15 By 1914 the system had only been able to establish eight elementary schools for Muslims in the protectorate, while one school for non-Muslims had just begun. It was also yet to produce a single clerk, and over 90 per cent of the clerks in the administration were foreigners. As late as 1943, the system was still so inefficient that only two Middle IV graduates were produced by all the Northern Provinces in 1943. See National Archives of Nigeria, Kaduna (hereafter NAK), SNP 17 File 36861 E. W. Thompstone, Resident, Borno Province to The Secretary, Northern Provinces, 11 October 1944, p. 60.

16 Ann Beck, 'Colonial Policy and Education in British East Africa, 1900–1950', *Journal of British Studies* 5, 2 (1966), p. 122; Whitehead, 'The Historiography of British Imperial Education Policy', p. 441.

17 Joseph Morgan Hodge, 'Development and Science: British Colonialism and the Rise of the "Expert", 1895–1945' (PhD dissertation, Queen's University Kingston [Canada], 1999), p. 399. Sir Hanns Vischer, 1876–1945, was born in Basel, Switzerland of Evangelical Christian parentage and studied languages in higher institutions in England. He joined the Anglican Church Missionary Society group and came to Nigeria in 1900 as a lay missionary. He left the Mission in 1902 and joined the British colonial administration in the Protectorate of Northern Nigeria under Governor Frederick Lugard in 1903. He served as Resident of Bornu Province, and in 1908, he was sent to study the educational systems of some colonies to design an educational system for the Protectorate. He later became the Director of Department of Education of the Northern Provinces until the outbreak of the First World War when he went for military service. After the war, he stayed in England and was in 1923 appointed as Secretary of the Colonial Office Advisory Committee on Education in Tropical Africa. Stephan Winkler, 'Vischer, Sir Hanns (1876–1945), educationist', *Oxford Biographical Dictionary*, Oxford University Press, 2004–13, www.oxforddnb.com/view/printable/40720.

18 British National Archives, London (hereafter BNA), CO 879/121/4 ACNETA Minutes of meetings, memoranda and reports, and correspondence: Memorandum for Despatch to Nigeria, Meeting held on 16 and 28 January 1925, fo. 58/310.

19 Ibid., fo. 58/310.

20 Ibid., fo. 59/311.
21 Seppo Sivonen, *White-Collar or Hoe Handle? African Education under British Colonial Policy, 1920-1945* (Helsinki: Suomen Historiallinen Seura 1995), pp. 207-16.
22 James S. Coleman, *Nigeria: Background to Nationalism* (Berkeley: University of California Press 1965), pp. 126, 134.
23 NAI CSO 26/2 File 36644/S.14, Secretary of State for Colonies to Officer Administering the Government of Nigeria, 5 June 1941, p. 66.
24 Coleman, *Nigeria: Background to Nationalism*, p. 126.
25 Cited in Toyin Falola, *Development Planning and Decolonization in Nigeria* (Gainesville, FL: University Press of Florida 1996), p. 37.
26 NAI CSO 26/2 File 36644/S14 vol. 1 Colonial Development Fund: Education Department – Inclosure: 'Statement of Policy on Economic Development and Welfare in the Colonial Empire', Actingg Chief Secetary to the Government, Memo to Secretaries, Commissioners and Directors, 23 March 1940, fo. 3/5, my emphasis.
27 Ibid., fo. 3/7.
28 NAK SNP 17 File 36644/S.12 Colonial Development Fund: Proposals by Residents – Acting Resident, Bornu Province to Secretary, Northern Provinces, 1 May 1940, p. 4.
29 NAI CSO 26/2 File 36644/S.21 Colonial Development Fund: Chief Commissioner, Northern Nigeria – Memorandum by T. S. Adams, Chief Commissioner, Northern Provinces, 1 June 1940, p. 2.
30 NAI CSO 26/2 File 36644/S.14 vol. 1 Colonial Development Fund: Education Department – Director of Education to The Chief Secretary, 30 May 1940, p. 13.
31 NAI CSO 26/2 File 36644/S.14 vol. 1 Colonial Development Fund: Education Department – B. H. Bourdillon, Governor, to Secretary of State for Colonies, 18 October 1940, p. 61.
32 NAI CSO 26/2 File 36644/S.14 vol. 1 Colonial Development Fund: Education Department – Secretary of State for Colonies to Officer Administering the Government of Nigeria, 5 June 1941, p. 66.
33 NAI CSO 26/2 File 41557 Planning and Development, General – Oliver Stanley to Sir Richards, 28 April 1944, p. 52, my emphasis.
34 NAI CSO 26/2 File 41557 Planning and Development, General – 'Particular Objectives of Development Policy in Nigeria', [1944], p. 45, my emphasis.
35 NAI CSO 41426/S.15 Government Post-War Reconstruction Programme 1943: Education – Sketch of a ten-year plan of educational development by Director of Education, in Development Secretary to Governor, 22 September 1944, p. 17.
36 Ibid. Emphasis in original.
37 This plan emphasised that 'Nigeria is considerably backward in the provision of educational services'. See BNA CO 583/272/4 Planning and Reorganisation: Education – Nigeria: Development of Educational Services; Application for a free grant of £913,600 C.D.W.A. Scheme No. D, October 1945, p. 25.
38 David B. Abernethy, *The Political Dilemma of Popular Education: An African Case* (Stanford, CA: Stanford University Press 1969), p. 95.
39 NAI CSO 26/2 File 36644/S.14, Notes by D. E. Morris, Ten-Year Development Plan, n.d. [1942], pp. 99-102.
40 NAI CSO 26/2 File 36644/S.14, A. C. Burns to Chief Secretary of Government, 25 March 1942, p. 97.
41 NAI CSO 26/2 File 36644/S.14, p. 4 (59).
42 Colonial Office, *Nigeria: Report for the Year 1954* (London: HMSO, 1958), p. 105; Coleman, *Nigeria: Background to Nationalism*, p. 134.
43 NAI CSO 26/2 File 41557 Planning and Development, General – 'Particular Objectives of Development Policy in Nigeria', p. 46.
44 The findings of a Colonial Office study group indicated that, excluding the cost of grants-in-aid and other tiers of education in 1950-51, £3 per child or one-third of Nigeria's annual revenue would be required to put all primary school age pupils, who constituted a quarter of the population, into primary schools. See Saheed Adejumobi, '"Life more Abundant": Colonial Transition, the Yoruba Intelligentsia

and the Politics of Education and Social Welfare Reform in Nigeria, 1940–1970'
(PhDdissertation, University of Texas/Austin, 2001), p. 306.
45 Seppo Sivonen, *White-Collar or Hoe Handle?*, p. 208.
46 Ibid., p. 217.
47 Advisory Committee on Education in the Colonies, *Report of Adult and Mass
Education Sub-Committee: Mass Education in African Society* (London: HMSO
1943), p. 5.
48 NAK SNP 17 File 36861, Secretary, Northern Provinces to Residents, 24 July 1944,
p. 22.
49 Advisory Committee on Education in the Colonies, *Report of Adult and Mass
Education Sub-Committee*, p. 9, my emphasis.
50 Coleman, *Nigeria: Background to Nationalism*, pp. 248–50; Hakeem Ibikunle Tijanni,
'Britain, Leftist Nationalists and the Transfer of Power in Nigeria, 1945–1965' (PhD
dissertation, University of South Africa/Pretoria, 2005), pp. 56–92.
51 Davidson's memorandum argued that the implementation of mass education
could only be done from above because of the inadequacies of existing educational
facilities. He opined that this would entail the employment of many Europeans;
a measure that he feared would be unpopular with educated Africans who sought to
be the only decisive voice of Africans in the colonies. He recommended propaganda,
a survey of the existing personnel, structures and materials, training of personnel,
production of necessary and relevant literature in the dominant vernacular, acquisition of broadcasting and film materials, and the use of Provisional Education Boards,
Provincial Economic and Welfare Boards, the Nigerian Union of Teachers and tribal
associations for implementation. Davidson advised against the participation of trade
unions because, given the history of their development in Nigeria, they were 'unlikely
to play a prominent part'. See NAK SNP 17 File 36861, Adult and Mass Education
– 'Some Reflections on Colonial 186', 1944, pp. 18–26.
52 NAK SNP 17 File 36861, Adult and Mass Education – 'Some Reflections on Colonial
186', 1944, p. 20.
53 NAK SNP 17 File 36861, Secretary, Northern Provinces to The Chief Secretary to
the Government, 7 December 1944, p. 71a; NAK SNP 17 File 36861, Acting Secretary,
Western Provinces to The Chief Secretary to the Government, 10 February 1945,
p. 97.
54 Anchau Scheme was a localised development scheme used to eradicate sleeping
sickness in the Anchau village area of Zaria Province in the 1930s. It involved the
clearing of the river banks and resettlement of the village inhabitants in planned
new sites and their education in sanitation and agriculture.
55 NAK SNP 17 File 36861, Secretary, Western Provinces to The Chief Secretary to
the Government, 18 July 1947, pp. 130–1; NAK SNP 17 File 36861, Secretary,
Northern Provinces to The Chief Secretary to the Government, 28 July 1947,
pp. 133–5.
56 NAK SNP 17 File 36861, Director of Education to The Chief Secretary, 9 September
1946, p. 92.
57 Under the plan, 6,000 classes were proposed to be established in 2,000 centres and
supported with grants for 4–5 years before becoming self-supporting. Only those
schemes that emphasised agricultural training would receive further assistance from
CDWA funds. The draft plan was not approved.
58 NAK SNP 17 File 36861, Chief Secretary to the Government to Director of Education,
4 March 1947, p. 111.
59 For instance, the adult literacy scheme in Ijebu Province was reported to have
dwindled with the loss of enthusiasm of the students and it was only in Ilaro and
Ado Ekiti in the whole of the Western Provinces that schemes similar to mass
education were reported to be functioning. NAK SNP 17 File 36861, Secretary,
Western Provinces to The Chief Secretary to the Government, January 1947,
pp. 105–6.
60 NAK SNP 17 File 36861, Arthur Creech Jones, Secretary of State for Colonies, to
Sir Arthur Richards, Governor of Nigeria, 25 July 1947, p. 114.

61 NAK SNP 17 File 36861, Arthur Richards, Governor, to Secretary of State for Colonies, 20 August 1947, pp. 136–40.
62 NAK SNP 17 File 36861, Minutes of First Meeting of the Central Board of Education, Lagos, 22–5 February 1949, pp. 236–8.
63 NAK SNP 17 File 36861, Arthur Creech Jones, Secretary of State for Colonies to Sir John Macpherson, Governor of Nigeria, 10 November 1948, p. 147; Sivonen, *White-Collar or Hoe Handle?*, p. 221.
64 NAI BP 2305B Community Development: General – Circular on Village Reconstruction and Grants under Colonial Development and Welfare Scheme D.547 by Chief Secretary to the Government, 15 January 1946, pp. 45–7.

CHAPTER ELEVEN

Motherhood, morality, and social order: gender and development discourse and practice in late colonial Africa

Barbara Bush

Since the 1990s there has been a marked growth of interest in the colonial origins of development discourse and practice. Insufficient attention, however, has been given to the importance of gender, particularly the complex and often contradictory ways in which African women have been represented in such discourse. This has resulted in an assumption that concepts relating to women and development only date from the era of decolonisation and after.[1] This chapter builds a gender dimension into pioneering studies of colonial development discourse that have demonstrated how such discourse was intimately linked to practice and contributed to the failure of development in pre- and post-colonial Africa.[2] First, I examine representations of African women and how these influenced conceptions of tradition versus modernity in development discourse. Second, I demonstrate how representations of African gender identities and relations, domesticity, morality, and sexuality permeated colonial discourse and influenced practice. Finally I provide a critique of gendered colonial development discourse and its implications for post-colonial African development. Fundamental to my analysis is the link between this gendered discourse and strategies to control and discipline African men and women as economic and social change accelerated and the legitimacy of colonial rule was challenged.

Development is a much contested concept but in colonial development discourse orthodox modernisation theory dominated, that is economic development and related social and political changes followed a development trajectory modelled on Western Europe and the United States as the norm. In this discourse, women were excluded as active agents of development in favour of the male African worker who produced agricultural and mineral export commodities. Colonial officers only dealt with male authority as family heads and had few dealings with African women unless they became a threat to the authorities. Most domestic servants employed by Europeans were men and it was mission educated African men who were appointed to lower positions within the colonial administration or joined the privileged professional elite. It was colonised men who learnt the language of the colonial powers which also gave them an advantage over women.

As development discourse and practice was generated and implemented primarily by European men for the benefit of Europeans and collaborative male African elites, I adopt a dual focus: the representation of African women in colonial and post-colonial development discourse and the contribution European women made to the evolution of such discourse and practice. I draw mainly on British colonial discourse and practice which was arguably highly influential in post-colonial development.[3] Given, however, that the major colonial powers differed little in their perceptions of African and European gender roles and relations, the themes I develop have broader relevance.

'Tradition', modernity, and the conceptualisation of African gender roles in colonial development discourse

European representations of African women are fundamental to understanding the evolution of gendered development discourse and practice and the problems inherent in a simplistic binary of tradition, associated with a 'primitive' and 'backward' Africa, versus modernity. Representations of African women as the embodiment of the primitive can be traced back to the earliest contact between Africans and Europeans, and permeated the colonial development discourse of all the major colonial powers. The main threads of this discourse were African women's oppression in polygamous marriages, their association with 'pagan' religion and associated beliefs and practices, and their uncontrolled sexuality. Women epitomised the simultaneous repulsion and fascination whites felt for 'mysterious', 'timeless' Africa. In colonial narratives African women are silent, nameless ciphers most commonly represented as labouring 'beasts of burden'.[4] Their oppression under African male patriarchy was contrasted with the strength and freedom of emancipated European women who saw them as 'their own jailers in the subjection in which they were held'.[5] Within this racial discourse, however, the oppressed victim was also the promiscuous, sexualised woman, the temptation of lonely colonial officers.[6] Thus it was African women who came to epitomise the 'dark' continent and 'sensuality' of the African bush.

Embedded within colonial discourse, then, were both paternalistic concern for the welfare of African women and fears of powerful female agency that had to be firmly controlled. Women's uncontrolled sexuality threatened racial orders and, argues Megan Vaughan, older women's association with 'all that was dark and evil in African culture' posed a danger to colonial stability.[7] This discourse evoked a feminised, primitive Africa in need of a white male vitalising force that would introduce 'modernity' in the form of the masculine virtues of order, enterprise, and patriarchal 'management' of women.[8] Progress was contingent on the eradication of 'barbaric' cultural practices such as female circumcision, polygamy, and forced marriage. But, equally, African male agency was to be harnessed to control women and minimise any threats they posed to colonial order and development.

After the First World War, the colonies were increasingly conceptualised as 'laboratories of modernity'.[9] Numerous official publications elaborated on development but few addressed women directly. In the new coupling of development with welfare after 1940, African men were the agents of economic development, while women were the passive recipients of welfare. Women were thus conceptualised as only marginal to economic development as wives, mothers, and pivots of family life, and remained associated with the 'traditions' of undeveloped Africa. It is from this time that we can chart the evolution of a modern development discourse; the prior emphasis on 'civilising' and converting the 'heathen' was supplanted by concepts of tradition versus modernity and, by the Second World War, by development and underdevelopment.[10]

Gendered development discourse, however, constituted an uneasy mingling of a conservative, paternalistic commitment to protecting traditional cultures from the pollution of modernity, and the ambitions of liberal modernisers who wished to transform these 'backward' cultures. This is evident in debates over forced marriage and the status of women which were framed in conceptions of superior European values and practices and which reinforced the discourse of African culture as primitive and backward. For modernisers, the spread of Christian marriage and modern gender roles were regarded as crucial to successful development. Traditional patriarchal pressures to force girls into marriage were at odds with modern European conceptions of individual freedom and the rights of women.

In May of 1936 a young woman in Tanganyika was sentenced to fifteen months hard labour for stabbing a man she was betrothed to against her will. This led to criticisms of the colonial government and the Labour MP, Eleanor Rathbone, called for action to prevent forced marriage. Subsequently the Secretary of State for Colonies, William Ormsby-Gore, elicited informed opinion and wrote to colonial governors requesting information regarding the extent of coercion into marriage. Responses imply a lack of interest in women's problems and irritation with liberal 'do-gooders' who raised the issue. The official line was that since slavery was abolished 'the old idea of coercion is completely eradicated'.[11] Governors claimed that girls could report coercion or maltreatment to the colonial and other authorities, a right that was 'freely exercised'.[12]

The debate over forced marriage reflects the wider discourse of female welfare but also the masculine bias of male administrators. The colonial authorities in Northern Rhodesia wished to protect girls but did not want to 'over-interfere' with the business of (male) native authorities who were anxious that girls were becoming 'too independent' and 'tending to flout the influence which parents might rightly exercise over them'. The Acting Governor of Kenya Colony warned against interference with 'deep rooted tribal customs... however deplorable' as 'any sudden removal of parental control [of girls] would have disastrous results'. He added that the whole question of the status of native women should be approached 'with the greatest caution and sympathy'.[13] The Governor of Gambia reported that 'older members of native society' were already alarmed by 'the liberties being demanded and taken by their women' and also warned against any interruption of 'the gradual process of [women's] emancipation by means of intangible forces of civilisation already at work'.[14] The only respondent to diverge from this tacit support for male control of women was Mrs (Isabel) McGregor Ross, an influential liberal critic of settler colonialism with East African experience, who advocated that girls should be given 'the best education' as 'only by education could they deal with the problem of African women in marriage'.[15]

This relegation to the private sphere restricted women's opportunities for education, further confirming their association with the traditional, pre-literate past. Colonial authorities, African parents, and the Christian mission schools prioritised boys' education. Even white women sympathetic to improving the status of women through education, such as the Canadian anthropologist Margaret Wrong, who was the Secretary of the International Committee on Christian Literature for Africa (ICCLA), continued to link literacy education with training for modern domesticity.[16] The monumental, *An African Survey* (1938), commissioned by the British government and collated by Malcolm Hailey, reported that there were no facilities for secondary education of girls in Kenya, Tanganyika, Zanzibar, Nyasaland, Northern Rhodesia, and Uganda, and a similar pattern existed in the French colonies. By this time there was a growing demand for girls' education but Hailey revealed his own masculine bias by attributing this to the fact that 'educated men needed wives who can help with their leading positions in native society'.[17] Women, it seems, had no independent desires for education.

After the Second World War, international humanitarian groups as well as the new United Nations organisation emphasised equality of access to education as fundamental to raising women's status and developing their potential as citizens rather than subjects under the control of fathers and husbands. In response, British colonial development discourse began to stress the need to 'swell the band of trained and educated women on whom the development of a balanced society depends'. Nevertheless emphasis remained on 'modernising [women's] outlook on home-making' and literacy education to help them support educated men who would become future leaders.[18] In colonial development discourse and practice women thus remained excluded from the public sphere. After 1918, however, limited entrée of women into Western modernity became central to colonial stability and re-establishing a moral framework undermined by economic development and urbanisation.

Gender and the discourse of colonial morality

Migration and urbanisation evoked the spectre of unregulated male sexuality and an increase in prostitution and venereal diseases, regarded as 'among the most difficult of medical problems' which would only be resolved when 'moral and educational standards' were raised.[19] A new strand to gendered colonial discourse now emerged: single female migrants in urban areas as polluting, destabilising influences, superfluous to the urban male workforce and outside traditional gender discipline.[20] Such women were often only seeking work but, as Margaret Wrong observed of Kenya, Africans, missionaries, and officials were all concerned about the dangers of girls 'flocking into towns'. In mining areas such as Northern Rhodesia it was alleged that the absence of men from home created prostitution in mining districts and women got free passages on lorries of 'boys' recruited for the mines by 'passing as wives'.[21] In colonial discourse, the single African girl/woman and the prostitute thus became increasingly conflated. The Governor of Uganda argued that it was not coercion of oppressed women that was the problem in modern Africa but 'the breakdown of moral restraints and the spread of prostitution'; the most serious danger for African women was not 'excessive restraint' but 'excessive licence' exhibited by young women.[22]

Sexual and physical pollution thus became associated particularly with African women affected by, or moving into, the realm of the modern. In colonial discourse, such uncontrollable women had no place in ordered urban development that segregated European from African. Loss of control over women's sexuality also increased the potential for inter-racial sexual relations and dangerous breaches in race boundaries that threatened white prestige. As Governor of Nigeria, Frederick Lugard was particularly concerned to clean up and regulate urban 'native' markets that were dominated by women, in order to exclude 'objectionable persons . . . thieves and prostitutes' who frequently adopted the role of 'itinerant hawker' and were 'dirty and unsanitary'.[23] In Belgian Africa, unmarried urban women were taxed and in South Africa, where racial segregation was most rigidly policed, the authorities, concerned about the 'alarming influx of native females into towns', subjected African women entering urban areas to 'degrading and humiliating' medical examinations in addition to making them carry passes.[24] For differing reasons, it was in the interests of both European and African authorities to collude in preventing women from leaving rural areas and keeping them in their place as the bearers of 'tradition'.[25]

This discourse of moral chaos and physical dangers, closely linked to the eugenicist discourse of sexual hygiene and the health of societies, informed a two pronged strategy: first, the strengthening of indigenous patriarchy to control female migration and/or sexual autonomy; second, the promotion of Christian marriage, and 'home life' education emphasising health, cleanliness, and hygiene. Modernisers believed that if the colonised shared 'modern', Western notions of domesticity, colonial societies would be stabilised and greater consent secured for the imperial 'civilising' mission. Colonisation, argue Comaroff and Comaroff, entailed the 'reconstruction of the ordinary' and this emphasis on reshaping the contours of everyday life was reflected in both discourse and practice.[26]

Gendered colonial development discourse was thus premised on the reconstruction of a moral order disrupted by colonialism, through a process of 'education and enlightenment'.[27] This assumed the stabilising influence of superior Western concepts of 'correct' gender roles. Christian organisations and the Girl Guides and Boy Scouts movements were dedicated to socialising the young colonised to Western values including gender roles and moral codes. In South Africa, where economic development was most advanced, 'remaking' the 'primitive' African man centred on 'moralising' migrant workers through philanthropic initiatives such as the Bantu Men's Social Clubs which emphasised superior white masculine values.[28] In attempts to stabilise labour, the Union Minière de Haut Katanga assisted workers to provide a dowry for their marriage and provided maternity and child welfare services.[29]

It was colonised women, however, who were targeted as the key to taming potentially rebellious men and ensuring the modernisation of colonial society through Western domesticity. As stressed above, in official discourse training for domesticity (homecraft and mothercraft skills) and the education of girls was indivisible. Hailey's report notes that by the late 1930s mission stations provided some 'valuable, if limited, training in domestic sciences, the care of children, nursing and midwifery and as teachers'; in Northern Rhodesia, the Jeanes School for Girls, subsidised by the Carnegie Corporation and the government, provided an education that prepared girls for marriage and motherhood.[30]

With rapid post-war economic development and urbanisation, interventions in colonial gender orders to diffuse discontent through the spread of domesticity were intensified as, in the words of the colonial expert, Margery Perham, 'raw tribesmen turned proletariat' and 'runaway tribal girls' became prostitutes.[31] Education of women was placed higher on the development agenda; homecraft and mothercraft training now incorporated literacy but the emphasis on domestic science training to bring health and stability to the African home persisted. Homecraft clubs for women flourished throughout colonial Africa, now increasingly directed to incorporation of the wives of male African elites into a gender ideology of the white elite class.[32] In this discourse women were the key to 'taming' men as mass nationalism gained pace. In Kenya, for example, a Provincial Homecrafts Officer was appointed by the colonial authorities and the East African Woman's League established an African Welfare Section which initiated uplift schemes for African women, including homecrafts courses, summer schools, and 'Better Homes' competitions.[33]

In addition to marriage training for women, the discourse of modern domesticity included dissemination of Western conceptions of morality and sexual hygiene. The British Social Hygiene Council, which received a grant from the Colonial Development Fund, assisted in the campaign against venereal diseases with educational films and handbooks on 'biological teachings'.[34] Sexual 'discipline' for men was advocated, reinforcing ideas of a superior white masculinity in control of base urges, a control inferior African men lacked and must develop in order to progress. With the spread of literacy, certain books that instilled appropriate moral values were regarded as suitable reading for African men and women such as Dr Janet Welch, *Health and the Home*, the Library of the African Home produced by the Society for the Promotion of Christian Knowledge (SPCK) which included a pamphlet on 'Women's work in the home', and H. C Trowell's 1940 book *The Passing of Polygamy: A Discussion of Marriage and of Sex for African Christians*.[35]

The Passing of Polygamy was an attempt to discuss 'the position of marriage and morality' in the 'tribes of Africa who have been exposed to the disruptive forces of culture contact with Europe'. Trowell, a lecturer in medicine at the Ugandan Medical School, promoted the 'discipline of sex' and advocated that a Christian African man must control his desire for women and the 'promiscuous intercourse' common in African communities. He advocated better sex education and envisaged that with development men would have a better standard of living to support women in the home, cleaning, making clothes, and cooking. Such marriages were based on an 'equality of labour' and sharing of money and property, supposedly absent in polygamous marriages.[36]

This vision of perfect middle class English domesticity and marriage and the need to modernise African gender roles along the same lines was also shared by metropolitan anti-imperialists. When Fenner Brockway was invited to Kenya by nationalist leaders he uncritically accepted representations of Kikuyu women as 'beasts of burden', failed to acknowledge their active role in anti-colonial protest, and advised Jomo Kenyatta, who defended traditional gender orders, that Kikuyu men should adopt a 'new attitude' to women and embrace Western concepts of 'equal marriage'.[37] Initiatives to 'domesticate' African men and women thus constituted a discourse of lack, in that the moral values of a superior European culture were lacking, but also a discourse of difference, in that superior European gender roles and behaviour were contrasted with inferior African cultural practices. This discourse of lack also informed initiatives directed to 'remaking' African mothers.

African motherhood and the 'biomedical discourse' of progressive imperialism

Biomedical discourse and associated public health initiatives were closely linked to the 'health' of the imperial mission and progress towards civilised modernity. By the 1930s Hailey recorded a 'very substantial' expansion of state health services, throughout colonial Africa, including more training for African nurses, popular education in hygiene, and an increase in research into African health questions.[38] Development discourse now employed the language of modern science and medicine in conceptualising an Africa cleansed of harmful customs, traditions, and practices. The disciplining of African sexuality, prevention of venereal diseases, promotion of public health, and improvements in maternal and infant health were key elements of this new biomedical discourse of progressive imperialism.[39]

African women as mothers and pivots of family life were targeted as central to public health projects, in particular tackling high infant and maternal mortality which modernisers such as the Governor of the Gold Coast, Sir Frederick Gordon Guggisberg, regarded as a major impediment to development.[40] As Nancy Rose Hunt has pointed out in relation to her study of interventions into women's lives in the Belgian Congo, colonialism entered 'some of the most intimate aspects' of colonised women's lives' including the birth process, breast feeding, weaning, dietary choices, and sexual activity. This arguably led to an obsession in colonial development discourse with the control of African women's bodies.[41]

'Making mothers', observed Jean Allman, was women's work.[42] White women were thus instrumental in the development of colonial discourse and practice centred on the health and welfare of African women and children. Before the First World War colonial discourse emphasised military pacification, and a 'muscular' Christianity defined the civilising mission; only white missionary women had any concern for the 'uplift' of African women. After the war, the greater emancipation of women, most notably in Britain and its white settler colonies, enabled them to take a more active role in the imperial mission.[43] More white women went to the colonies as wives of officials and as settlers and missionaries or were recruited to the colonial service as nurses, doctors, welfare workers, and teachers. 'Welfare' and social policy were associated with feminine qualities of 'empathy' and were thus regarded by the Colonial Office as a useful way in which educated white women could participate in colonial development.

Colonial governments appointed women medical officers to promote maternal and infant health in clinics but, with the exception of the Gold Coast, there was little interest in welfare issues and funding was inadequate. Embedded within this discourse of welfare is also an emerging construct of the 'uncooperative' African. An example here is the mining areas of Northern Rhodesia where the government was concerned about problems created by migration and the need for welfare centres. During her field work among the Bemba of Northern Rhodesia, the anthropologist, Audrey Richards, met a government-appointed female health worker who was 'worn out by the struggle to get a welfare scheme going due to constant delay over funding and lack of interest in natives in medical welfare'. She wanted to start a welfare centre 'with lessons on mosquitoes and tidy houses' but complained about the 'boredom of women'.[44]

Given the lukewarm commitment of the colonial authorities, infant and maternal welfare and health education was largely the province of female missionaries who were engaged in Christian conversion of

African women. African women also became the object of elite white women's philanthropic initiatives. Lady Joan Grigg, wife of the Kenyan Governor, Sir Edward Grigg, was an 'enthusiastic fund raiser' for her 'African welfare work' and in 1926 founded a Native Maternity Home.[45] Princess Christian, a member of the British royal family, founded the Princess Christian Cottage Hospital in Freetown, Sierra Leone, the first to employ white nurses, provide maternity services for African women, and run weekly child welfare clinics. The matron was Mary Alexandria Ward, a nurse in West Africa from 1894–1930 who was closely involved in the training of African nurses and midwives. Princess Christian's daughter, Princess Marie Louise, continued her mother's charitable work as patron of the West African Nursing Service and in 1926 officially opened the Princess Marie Louise Hospital for Mothers and Infants in Accra, the first of its kind in the Gold Coast.[46] Such women were also sponsors of another cultural import, the baby show, where prizes were given for 'bonny' babies. These women, though well intentioned, assumed a maternalist superiority and duty to ensure the 'uplift' of inferior, downtrodden women and had negligible practical involvement in the schemes they sponsored.

More influential were the women with medical expertise who were at the forefront of educating African women in modern Western practices in maternity and infant care, and challenging the knowledge and practices of traditional midwives or 'nanas' or 'mammies'. From 1919, the Overseas Nursing Association played an active role in developing health services for African women and children in the British colonies, and nurses who were recruited were expected to have training and experience in midwifery.[47] By the 1930s more European women were involved in training African women as nurses and midwives primarily in missionary institutions.[48] However, provision varied from colony to colony. In her tour of Africa, Margaret Wrong observed that the government-run hospital in the Gold Coast was 'unique in West Africa in size and equipment' and had a 'well patronised' maternity hospital with a hostel for training midwives who were taking over from the 'mammies'. In Omdurman in Northern Sudan training was more basic. The Misses Wolfe, known as 'the Wolves', founded a government centre for training midwives; 'illiterate women' came from villages all over the Sudan for a six month course but, observed Wrong, teaching was by 'demonstration' and they were not taught to read.[49]

White women's practical interventions and health related publications entrenched differences between 'superior', civilised Europeans, and 'inferior' African women. In 1936, for instance, Dr Mary Blacklock of the Liverpool School of Tropical Medicine, a pioneer of public health education in Africa and a member of the Colonial Advisory Medical

Committee, published an influential article which reiterated the need to challenge and change traditional cultural practices around childbirth and child rearing and made a strong case for more extensive modern maternity services and better education for girls.[50] Biomedical discourse also targeted African women's child rearing practices as a major factor in the poor nutrition that undermined children's health. In her study of the Bemba, Audrey Richards observed crucial differences between European and African practices in the use of supplementary cereal practically from birth and lengthy breast feeding. But, she added, Bemba women were resistant to change and critical of European mothers who breast-fed for six months without additional food.[51] Breast feeding practices starkly illuminated the contrast between 'primitive' and civilised that threaded through development discourse and the deep gulf between European and African women. 'Women suckle openly', wrote Audrey Richards, 'but have a general belief that the mission mamas don't like their nakedness' and this 'deterred them from going to the infant clinics'.[52]

When African women persisted in their 'inferior practices', European women revealed irritation and also their own arrogance as 'superior' European women. In *Health and the Home*, based on talks given to mothers at welfare clinics and student midwives on health subjects, Dr Janet Welch, an expert in public health, offered ideas that 'may be of use to teachers of mothercraft classes'. She complained, however, of the difficulties of getting medical teaching accepted by village women because of 'the fundamental difference between Western and African ideas of health, disease and the art of healing'. Welch gave African women no option; the only way forward was in accordance with current Anglo-American trends in mothercraft. 'It is a mother's duty', she wrote, 'to attend the Infant Welfare Clinic or Mothercraft Class if there is one in her district'.[53] Women may also have been coerced into attending clinics. In Tanganyika numbers at one maternity clinic had jumped from 120 to 1,200 but allegedly this was due to the imposition of a 5 shillings tax for failing to bring the child in to be born. In the same clinic women were berated by the matron for not adopting European, as opposed to African, practices regarding care of new-born infants.[54]

This discourse of women's resistance to intrusions into their intimate lives is also evident in Audrey Richards' field diaries relating to a fertility study of the Buganda funded by UNESCO in the early 1950s. At the time Richards was Director of the influential, government-funded East African Institute of Social Research based at Makerere College, Uganda. She was reluctant to take on the research as she regarded it as a 'bore' but in a letter to a colleague claimed that 'the medicos here are rather keen and want to prod vaginas'.[55] The study thus involved personal questions about cultural practices and medical histories. Richards visited baby clinics, interviewed women about, for instance, the age of menarche, and researched girls' initiations. Despite help from local research assistants and interpreters, she had problems interviewing women and was deeply frustrated by the responses: elderly women refused to speak and some women were 'angry and hostile' when approached.[56] In a letter to a close colleague she conceded that the fertility survey was the 'first piece of fieldwork I have found difficult'; the women were insolent and laughed at her questions and she referred to the 'futility [of] having a heart to heart with successful prostitutes [to] learn what are mysteriously called their "values"'.[57] These encounters with female intransigence raise the wider issue of the contribution female academics such as Richards made to a gendered development discourse.

Gender and the emergence of an academic development discourse

With the emancipation of women in the USA, and Britain and its white dominions, more women received a higher education and thus, in addition to participating in practical schemes to improve the welfare of women, women academics in the metropolitan centre began to make their mark on colonial research and related African studies. Notable here are the pro-imperialist Margery Perham, the anthropologists Lucy Mair, Audrey Richards, Phyllis Kaberry, and Margaret Wrong, the educationalist, Margaret Read, and Sally Chilver, a historian of Cameroonian society. The Fabian socialist, Rita Hinden, a critic of pre-1939 colonial development practice, contributed to the new discourse of colonial reform, welfare, and development in Africa which became orthodoxy after 1945.

From the 1930s women were engaged in anthropological research in Africa, reflecting the need for colonial governments to gain more knowledge of African cultures to aid governance.[58] Two of the earliest studies of African women, by Sylvia Leith-Ross, the wife of a colonial officer, who subsequently worked in the Nigerian colonial service, and the anthropologist Margaret Green, were funded as an adjunct to colonial policy making after the 1929 'Women's War' in Southern Nigeria and retained a conceptual framework based on a crude dichotomy between 'primitive' and 'sophisticated' women.[59] Audrey Richards carried out research among the Bemba in the 1930s and subsequently became Secretary to the Colonial Social Welfare Committee which dealt with questions of training of medical aides and African nurses, and maternal and infant welfare. She was sent to East Africa by the Colonial Office to examine the possibilities of setting up social welfare schemes although she later confessed she 'knew little about the subject'.[60]

Developments during the war opened up more opportunities for women researchers. Both the British and French governments allocated more funding to colonial research in response to the evolving discourse of development and the new social welfare agenda and in 1944 the British Colonial Office set up the Colonial Social Science Research Council (CSSRC).[61] Audrey Richards, now seconded to the Colonial Office, contributed to the planning stages, Sally Chilver was Secretary from the late 1940s, and from the Council's inception women academics were involved in decision making. Female post-graduates and research fellows also received funding for a range of projects. One of the most important of these projects in understanding the evolution of gendered development discourse is Phyllis Kaberry's *Women of the Grassfields* (1952). This study reflected the new humanitarian development discourse influencing the agenda of the United Nations, which emphasised improving social and economic conditions in the colonies, including the status of women, and obliged colonial governments to provide information on development indicators.

The idea for the grasslands study is attributed to the educationalist, Dr Margaret Read, who drew attention to the need for research into the low status of women in Bamenda society after a visit to West Africa. She consulted Daryll Forde, Director of the International African Institute, about organising a field study which was supported by the Cameroons Development Corporation. The Governor of Nigeria, who was responsible for British Cameroon, the part of the former German colony placed under a British mandate, sent a despatch to the Colonial Office which drew attention to the problem of under-population among the Bamenda peoples. He argued this was an obstacle to economic development of 'considerable natural resources' and attributable partly to 'a very high infant mortality and low status of women'. More women educationalists were needed 'in order to assist the adaptation of a backward society to changing conditions' but, he added, these would need advice from a social anthropologist familiar with the culture. Thus the immediate need was for a study of general social and economic conditions funded through the Colonial Research Fund.[62]

Kaberry had carried out research on aboriginal women in her native Australia. She came to London in 1936 and subsequently became Audrey Richards' research assistant at the London School of Economics. As a lecturer in Social Anthropology at University College London from 1949 until her death in the 1970s she continued her research among the Bamenda, collaborating at times with Sally Chilver, and was given the honorary title of Queen Mother. Kaberry was appointed to the Grassfields Project in 1945, which was supervised by the CSSRC and completed in 1951. Her research was confined mainly to the economic position of women as that was emphasised in the terms of reference provided but her findings contested representations of women in ortho-dox colonial development discourse. Kaberry's research emphasised female agency rather than passivity; in orthodox discourse men, as heads of household, held the land, whereas, in effect, their wives retained customary rights and control over land and the crops they grew. Women and girls, she added, produced most of the food and enjoyed considerable economic independence and in this sphere of their lives there had been less change than in others as a result of interventions by missionaries and colonial officials. Any changes in the use and allocation of land or in farming techniques, she concluded, should take this into account.[63]

Given her brief from the CSSRC, which was based on Margaret Read's perceptions of the low status of women, and the limitations placed on her research, Kaberry was unsure of the value of her research in addressing the problems identified by Read. She found it difficult to disassociate women's economic role from social factors and cultural changes that had resulted from colonial rule. She queried the mono-lithic and paternalistic discourse of female welfare and regarded pres-sure from the UN Trusteeship Council (via regular questionnaires) to make generalisations as to whether the status of women was high or low, good or bad, as 'profitless' – a point she made with 'monotonous regularity' in her reports to the CSSRC. She also felt that she was being pushed into 'applied' anthropology, which was not as prestigious as the anthropological research carried out by the male anthropologists who dominated the CSSRC.[64]

Anthropology was a masculine province and a key discipline in the evolution of development discourse in the interests of colonial powers: most anthropological studies remained gender blind or androcentric. Audrey Richards claimed in retrospect that women often did better than men in relations with Africans; as all colonial administrators were men, the women anthropologists 'could appear free of the dread-ful colonial taint'.[65] Yet 'Africans' implied men rather than women; the writings of women academics mostly ignore women or confirm the cultural gulf between European and African women. As a young anthropologist Audrey Richards' first encounter with Bemba women proved less 'reverent' than she had anticipated, as they frequently teased her and laughed. In a small 'unappetising' village, however, she was faced with the 'abysmal stupidity' of the chief's wives. With a degree of relief, perhaps, she recorded that these were the first women she encountered who justified the warnings of district officers and male anthropologists that 'you will never get anything out of the women. They will sit and giggle'.[66]

Richards' inability to communicate with African women was compounded by language problems and her struggles to understand cultural meanings. Moreover, she had little interest in women's issues and her published research *Land, Labour and Diet in Northern Rhodesia: An Economic Study* (1939) focuses mainly on male migration and the impact this had on food production. Her later field diaries from the 1950s confirm that she remained ill at ease with African women, even the trained African nurses she met. She recorded that she had difficulty 'rounding up' women to interview which made her feel 'slightly embarrassed and reluctant'.[67] In her letters and field diaries she uses unflattering terms to describe African women such as 'stupid' and 'unattractive' and frequently refers to 'prostitutes' and 'illegitimate children'.

Whether women 'feminised' academic development discourse is thus debatable. Although women were represented on the CSSRC, for instance, the Council was dominated by powerful male academics and the research agenda prioritised masculine agents of development. Most social and anthropological studies reflected government prioritisation of research into migration, urbanisation, ethnicity, and conflict to manage rapid social and political change. Margery Perham's copious writings on colonial administration and the growth of nationalism also say little about women, and the Africans she had personal contact with were mainly from the Western-educated male elites. Similarly, in her *Plan for Africa* (1941), Hinden advocated support for small-scale farmers and development of cooperatives but assumes the small cocoa farmers on the Gold Coast were men helped by the 'family'. She omits to mention female cocoa growers and traders and uses the genderless term 'African' throughout when, in effect, she means men. Gender is only relevant where she discusses women's welfare and in her continued feminisation of Africa as a recipient of European tutelage; for Hinden the colonies were like 'growing daughters [who] must be provided with dowries . . . to help them find their feet in the adult world'.[68]

Women academics were, of course, in the minority in a male dominated world and their careers depended on 'fitting in'; the evolving discourse of welfare and development was thus determined primarily by male 'experts'. Foremost among these was Sir (later Lord) William Malcolm Hailey, who became the official guru of colonial policy during the Second World War when more money was made available for social welfare. His mammoth *African Survey*, which covered the whole of sub-Saharan Africa, articulated a discourse of accelerated modernisation and partnership through gradual incorporation of the colonial intelligentsia into governance, expansion of welfare programmes, education for boys and girls, and the promotion of cooperative production. Audrey Richards contributed as a researcher but there were no women on the survey's general committee. Despite the twinning of welfare and development, the overwhelming emphasis is on the masculine agents of economic, agricultural, and political development. Thus, as independence approached, African women remained firmly located in colonial development discourse as passive objects of health and welfare initiatives. Even in the 1950s, as colonies were given more self-government, women were still regarded simply as adjuncts of African men. An example here, cited by Richards, is the first Buganda elections in 1953 in which 'a number of women [illegally] voted' although the colonial government had not provided for this in the belief that Bugandan men 'wouldn't hear of such a thing'.[69]

Rhetoric and reality: a critique of gendered development discourse and practice

Gendered development discourse was based on assumptions about African gender roles and relations that did not match with reality and contained inherent weaknesses. First, there were no typical women that fitted the homogenised 'African woman' that permeated development discourse: women's status and gender roles were mediated by education, religion, class position, and levels of Westernisation. In colonies where there was a large Moslem population, different perceptions of gender roles existed to those in non-Moslem populations; women were more tightly controlled and there was greater resistance from men to, for instance, women's education.[70]

Second, gendered discourse originated in Eurocentric readings of African cultures that, in practice, involved the dissemination of superior European cultural values. Domestic and marriage training and infant welfare clinics assumed inferior African practices, were poorly attended by women, and thus had only a marginal impact. Projects to spread European concepts of domesticity and morality failed to stabilise a colonial society in flux. As Luise White points out, in Kenya during the Mau Mau uprising, Kikuyu wives not only failed to 'tranquilise' their men folk and quell political discontent but also became Mau Mau fighters.[71] Kikuyu women also actively opposed missionary campaigns against circumcision, which endowed them with certain traditional rights but which missionaries and liberal colonial reformers regarded as a barbaric practice and evidence of women's oppression. Kikuyu opposition and reluctance of the government to intervene in traditional practices, resulted in a compromise whereby African women were employed to perform safe, hygienic operations.[72]

Third, the rhetoric of raising women's status through development was not reflected in reality and, arguably, women's welfare and education remained neglected in favour of men, whose political activism was seen as a greater threat to colonial stability.[73] Projects to 'remake' African womanhood were patchy and limited in scope and largely dependent on missionaries and philanthropic initiatives. Rita Hinden claimed that 'practically no maternity or child welfare work was done', social services and public health services were inadequate, and poor nutrition persisted. Northern Rhodesia had a particularly bad record but even in the progressive Gold Coast, provision was still inadequate.[74] Additionally, deep contradictions existed between a gendered discourse centred on 'welfare' and domestic stability and the colonial labour policies that took men away from their villages to work in the modern sector of mining and large-scale agricultural production for export. Male migration undermined domestic life and created what Audrey Richards described as 'hungry manless areas'.[75] Yet there were no practical initiatives to support women's agriculture even though women remained responsible for subsistence production through most of sub-Saharan Africa.[76]

Fourth, women's economic autonomy and the decline of traditional moral constraints were targeted as prime causes of the moral crisis resulting from colonial development. The solution was the strengthening of allegedly traditional African patriarchal controls. Colonial administration was through male authority, hereditary or created, and, as Terence Ranger argued, rural chiefs and the urban intelligentsia colluded in the colonial 'invention' of African 'traditions' in order to keep women in their place. However, an essentialist notion of 'tradition' as the polarised opposite to 'modernity' is much contested, as it implies an unchanging past. As Thomas Spear has argued, 'tradition' was a complex discourse in which the past was continually re-interpreted in the context of the present; tradition was not invented but 'reformed and reconstructed by subjects and rulers alike'.[77] Additionally, the colonial authorities subscribed to the essentialist notion of 'tradition' when it worked in their interests but, as van Beusekom and Hodgson point out, they also blamed setbacks in development on the failure to transform practices and beliefs regarded as hindering progress.[78]

Seminal studies have demonstrated how relegation of African women to the realm of unchanging 'tradition' failed to acknowledge the continuous dynamic of cultural change that adversely impacted on women's autonomy in African gender relations; women, they conclude, lost more under colonial rule than men.[79] Gendered development discourse in practice undermined women's role as guardians of the land and led to the commoditisation of land and loss of their customary land rights. It failed to acknowledge the importance of women as the main producers of subsistence food supplies and, in the West African colonies, as powerful market women and traders in export commodities such as palm oil and cocoa.[80] As Kathleen Staudt has stressed, the colonial state structured gender relations to facilitate the development of the colonial economy in gender specific ways.[81] African men were co-opted by the colonial administration to police women and exploit women's labour to produce export crops. Support for African patriarchy, concludes April Gordon, was not so much an effort to preserve 'backward customs' but a creative response to preserve male privilege in a new, underdeveloped capitalist system.[82]

Assumptions of patriarchal control and resultant deterioration in women's economic and political status could evoke strong resistance. Yet colonial officials were often unable to understand, or indeed control the resistant behaviour of women. Women's resistance to both elite African men and colonial authorities when their rights and economic autonomy were threatened, as during the serious disturbances in Southern Nigeria in 1925 and 1929, only confirmed elements of gendered discourse that focused on the primitive, uncontrollable nature of African women. When so challenged European men had no hesitation in abandoning paternalist concern for women's welfare for force and violence.[83]

Finally, the gendered development discourse that informed colonial practice was re-articulated in the context of a masculine African nationalist discourse and thus perpetuated the inherent contradictions and weaknesses into the post-colonial era. As anti-colonialism intensified, new conflicts erupted between male nationalists and Europeans over differing conceptions of gender orders and control of the development agenda. Throughout colonial Africa restoration of positive masculine identities and control over the domestic sphere became central to nationalist ideology and the re-validation of African culture. Women's bodies now became a site of conflict between colonial rulers and male nationalists who reclaimed greater control over 'their women' and pre-empted the colonial government's role as protector of women's welfare. Women remained excluded from economic planning. This gendering of nationalist discourse by colonised men, the colonial authorities, and the new academic 'development' experts, male and female, obscured the significant contribution women made to nationalist struggles and post-colonial development. Thus the development agenda, integral to the transformation of colonies into new, modern

African states was appropriated by male African nationalist elites in conjunction with powerful male dominated international aid agencies.

Conclusion

In gendered colonial development discourse men were targeted as the prime agents of economic and political development; women were represented as passive victims in need of help and protection from European men and women, ignorant mothers who were to be taught superior modern health practices, or sexually abandoned girls and women in need of re-moralisation through the strengthening of traditional African patriarchy or Christian marriage. Such deep interventions in the domestic lives of women were based on misrepresentations of African gender roles and failed to pay due regard to the cultural context and spiritual world view of women. In consequence, practical initiatives premised on this discourse undermined rather than promoted sustainable development. Gender, as it related to the respective contributions of white men and women, is also important to understanding the evolution and practical implementation of gendered colonial development discourse. However, whether implementing welfare programmes, contributing to academic development discourse, or campaigning in the metropolitan centre to raise the status of African women, white women generally concurred with the discourse of female passivity and oppression that threaded through official literature relating to colonial development.

With decolonisation and independence, an influential academic clique in the US re-defined the conceptual framework of a post-colonial 'development studies' discourse. Western governments and new international agencies provided more money for development but macroeconomic strategies continued to prioritise men and marginalise women. As in the colonial era, women remained relegated to the more marginal 'welfare' sector and gender inequalities persisted.[84] International development discourse was thus directly influenced by the gendered 'development discourse' that informed British, French, and Belgian colonial policies. From the late colonial era onward, failure to recognise women's economic contribution, particularly to subsistence farming and domestic markets, resulted in greater reliance on food imports, environmental degradation, wasted aid money, and failed schemes.[85] It was only in the 1990s, after a decade of worsening poverty, that the World Bank and other powerful development agencies integrated a gender approach into strategic policies. As the failures of the colonial era indicate, sustainable development and poverty reduction in Africa can only be achieved when women are able to fully participate in political and economic development.

Notes

1 See, Margaret C. Snyder and Mary Tadesse, *African Women and Development: A History* (London: Zed 1995), p. 8.

2 For instance Monica M. van Beusekom and Dorothy L. Hodgson, 'Lessons Learned? Development Experiences in the Late Colonial Period', *Journal of African History* 41, 1 (2000), pp. 29–30; Frederick Cooper, 'Writing the History of Development', *Journal of Modern European History* 8, 1 (2010), pp. 5–23.

3 See, for instance, Joseph Morgan Hodge, 'British Colonial Expertise, Post-Colonial Careering and the Early History of International Development', *Journal of Modern European History* 8, 1 (2010), pp. 24–44.

4 For example the historian William Macmillan's comments on Kikuyu women in Colonial Office, *Correspondence Relating to the Welfare of Women in Tropical Africa* (London: HMSO 1938), p. 5.

5 Elspeth Huxley, *The Mottled Lizard* (London: Chatto and Windus 1962), pp. 123–4. Women's travelogues are good sources of such contemporary representations of African women, see, for instance, [Lady] D. R. M. Mills, *The Golden Land: A Record of Travel in West Africa* (London: Duckworth 1929) and *Episodes from the Road to Timbuktu: The Record of a Woman's Adventurous Journey* (London: Duckworth 1927).

6 As represented, for instance, in E. F. G. Haig, *Nigerian Sketches* (London: Allen and Unwin 1931), pp. 231–3; Richard Oakley, *Treks and Palavers* (London: Seeley Service 1938), pp. 43, 95–6.

7 Megan Vaughan, *Curing their Ills: Colonial Power and African Illness* (Cambridge: Polity Press 1991), pp. 22–3, 69–70.

8 Implicit, for instance, in Frederick D. Lugard's influential guidelines for colonial administration *Political Memoranda: Revision of Instructions to Political Officers on Subjects Chiefly Political and Administrative, 1913–1918*, edited and with an introduction by A. H. M. Kirk Greene (London: Frank Cass 1970). *Political Memoranda* was revised and reprinted in 1919 and was passed to successive governors as model practice.

9 Ann Laura Stoler and Frederick Cooper, 'Between Metropole and Colony: Rethinking a Research Agenda', in Ann Laura Stoler and Frederick Cooper (eds), *Tensions of Empire: Colonial Cultures in a Bourgeois World* (Berkeley, Los Angeles, London: University of California Press 1997), pp. 5, 16.

10 Michael Cowen and Robert Shenton, *Doctrines of Development* (London, New York: Routledge 1996), pp. 2–9, 27.

11 William Ormsby-Gore in Colonial Office, *Correspondence Relating to the Welfare of Women*, p. 9.

12 Charles Dundas, Deputy to the Governor, Northern Rhodesia, and Harold MacMichael, Governor of Tanganyika, ibid., pp. 11, 27–8.

13 A. de V. Wade, Acting Governor of Kenya Colony, Dundas and B. H. Bourdillon, Governor of Nigeria, ibid., pp. 11, 24–6, 35.

14 W. T. Southorn, ibid., p. 13.

15 Mrs McGregor Ross, ibid., p. 4.

16 Margaret Wrong, *Across Africa* (London: International Committee on Christian Literature for Africa 1940), pp. 8, 15–16, 58.

17 [Lord] William Malcolm Hailey, *An African Survey: A Study of Problems Arising in Africa South of the Sahara*, rev. edn (Oxford: Oxford University Press 1957 [1938]), p. 1125 and also pp. 1242–3, 1255–6, 1287.

18 Colonial Office, *The Colonial Territories, 1948–1949* (London: HMSO 1949), pp. 82–3.

19 Hailey, *An African Survey*, pp. 1129–30.

20 For instance Elizabeth Schmidt, *Peasants, Traders and Wives: Shona Women in the History of Zimbabwe, 1870–1939* (Portsmouth, NH: Heinemann; Harare: Baobab; London: James Currey 1992), pp. 98–106; Jean Allman, '"Rounding up Spinsters": Gender Chaos and Unmarried Women in Colonial Asante', *Journal of African History* 37, 2 (1996), pp. 195–214.

21 Archives of the London School of Economics and Political Science, London (hereafter LSE), Richards Papers, 3/1, Audrey Richards, Bemba Diaries, 14 April 1930; Wrong, *Across Africa*, p. 8.
22 P. E. Mitchell in Colonial Office, *Correspondence Relating to the Welfare of Women*, p. 16.
23 Lugard, *Political Memoranda*, pp. 33, 419.
24 University of South Africa Archives, Pretoria, RSA (hereafter UNISA), Box 4, 9.2.2, Champion Papers, Annual Report: Women's Section of the National Congress, Natal province, 1948; see also Nancy Rose Hunt, 'Noise over Camouflaged Polygamy: Colonial Morality, Taxation and a Woman-Naming Crisis in Belgian Africa', *Journal of African History* 32, 3 (1991), pp. 47–94.
25 As demonstrated in Samwel Ong'wen Okuro, 'Our Women Must Return Home: Institutionalized Patriarchy in Colonial Central Nyanza District, 1945–1963', *Journal of Asian and African Studies* 45, 5 (2010), pp. 522–33.
26 Jean Comaroff and John Comaroff, 'Home-made Hegemony: Modernity, Domesticity and Colonialism in South Africa', in Karen Transberg Hansen (ed.), *African Encounters with Domesticity* (New Brunswick, NJ: Rutgers University Press 1992), p. 67.
27 Ormsby-Gore in Colonial Office, *Correspondence Relating to the Welfare of Women*, p. 35.
28 UNISA, Box 1, 4.2, Champion Papers, Bantu Men's Social Centre Information Leaflet.
29 Hailey, *An African Survey*, p. 681.
30 Ibid., pp. 1255–6.
31 Margery Perham, 'The Colonial Dilemma', *The Listener*, 15 July 1949, reproduced in Perham, *Colonial Sequence, 1930–1949: A Chronological Commentary upon British Colonial Policy, especially in Africa* (London: Methuen 1967), p. 335.
32 Sita Ranchod Nillson, 'Educating Eve: The Woman's Club Movement and Political Consciousness among Rural African Women in Southern Rhodesia, 1950–1980', in Tranberg Hansen (ed.), *African Encounters with Domesticity*, p. 195.
33 Rhodes House Library, Oxford (hereafter RHO), Huxley Papers, 3/6, Nellie Grant to Elspeth Huxley, 13 September 1945; 6 January 1953; 7 June, 24 August, 1953.
34 Hailey, *An African Survey*, p. 1199.
35 Wrong, *Across Africa*, p. 87.
36 H. C. Trowell, *The Passing of Polygamy: A Discussion of Marriage and of Sex for African Christians* (Oxford: Oxford University Press 1940), pp. 46–9, 67–75.
37 Fenner Brockway, *African Journeys* (London: Gollancz 1955), pp. 93–7, 114, 195–6.
38 Hailey, *An African Survey*, p. 1121.
39 Vaughan, *Curing their Ills*, p. 16 and chapter 6, 'Syphilis and Sexuality: The Limits of Colonial Medical Power', pp. 129–54.
40 Princess Marie Louise, *Letters from the Gold Coast* (London: Methuen 1926), p. 225.
41 Vaughan, *Curing their Ills*, p. 16; Nancy Rose Hunt, '"Le bébé en brousse": European Women, African Birth Spacing, and Colonial Intervention in Breast Feeding in the Belgian Congo', in Stoler and Cooper (eds), *Tensions of Empire*, pp. 307–8.
42 Jean Allman, 'Making Mothers: Missionaries, Medical Officers and Women's Work in Colonial Asante, 1924–1945', *History Workshop Journal* 38, 1 (1994), pp. 23–47.
43 See Barbara Bush, 'Gender and Empire: The Twentieth Century', in Philippa Levine (ed.), *Gender and Empire* (Oxford: Oxford University Press 2004), pp. 77–111.
44 LSE, Richards Papers, 3/1, Audrey Richards, Bemba Diaries, 14 April; 10 August, 1930.
45 Letters to Ingeborg Dinesen, 1 August 1926; 24 August 1928, in Isak Dinesen, *Letters from Africa, 1914–1931*, ed. Frans Lasson (London: Weidenfeld and Nicolson 1981), pp. 268, 369.
46 Princess Marie Louise, *Letters from the Gold Coast*, pp. 5–6, 225–6. See also Mary Alexandra Ward Collection. Royal Commonwealth Society Archives, Cambridge University Library, Cambridge, RCMS 134/Y, Biographical Material.
47 Mary G. Blacklock, 'Cooperation in Health Education', *Africa* 4, 2 (1931), pp. 202–8.

48 Jane Turrittin, 'Colonial Midwives and Modernising Childbirth in West Africa', in Susan Geiger, Jean Marie Allman, and Nakanyike Musisi (eds), *Women in African Colonial Histories* (Bloomington, IN: Indiana University Press 2002), pp. 71–93.
49 Wrong, *Across Africa*, pp. 26, 59–60.
50 Mary G. Blacklock, 'Certain Aspects of the Welfare of Women and Children in the Colonies', *Annals of Tropical Medicine and Parasitology* 30, 2 (1936), pp. 221–64.
51 Audrey Richards, *Land, Labour and Diet in Northern Rhodesia: An Economic Study of the Bemba Tribe* (Oxford: Oxford University Press 1939), pp. 67–71.
52 LSE, Richards Papers, 3/1, Bemba Diaries, 19 July 1930.
53 Janet Welch, *Health and the Home* (London: Sheldon Press 1940), pp. viii, x, 7, 14.
54 LSE, Richards Papers, 3/3, Audrey Richards, Bemba Diaries, 1 August 1931.
55 LSE, Richards Papers, 16/7, Audrey Richards to Sally Chilver (Secretary of the CSSRC), n.d. [ca. 1952].
56 LSE, Richards Papers, 8/1, Buganda 1, Audrey Richards, Buganda Diaries, 1950–51, 13 February; 8 June 1951.
57 LSE, Richards Papers, 16/7, Richards to Chilver, 14 August 1952.
58 For the importance of anthropological research to colonial policy, see Hailey, *An African Survey*, pp. 40–59, and for a critique of the contribution of such research to development, see James Ferguson, 'Anthropology and Its Evil Twin: "Development" in the Constitution of a Discipline', in Frederick Cooper and Randall Packard (eds), *International Development and the Social Sciences: Essays on the History and Politics of Knowledge* (Berkeley: University of California Press 1997), pp. 150–76.
59 M. M. Green, *Igbo Village Affairs* (London: Frank Cass 1947); Sylvia Leith-Ross, *African Women: A Study of the Ibo of Nigeria* (London: Faber and Faber 1939).
60 LSE, Richards Papers, 16/26, Audrey Richards to Richard Brown, 27 February 1978.
61 C. Y. Carstairs, 'Colonial Research', *African Affairs* 44, 174 (1945), pp. 19–26. For similar developments in France, see Frederick Cooper and Randall Packard, 'Introduction', in Cooper and Packard (eds), *International Development and the Social Sciences*, pp. 7–8.
62 Phyllis M. Kaberry, *Women of the Grassfields: A Study of the Economic Position of Women in Bamenda, British Cameroons*, preface by Daryll Forde (London: HMSO 1952).
63 Ibid., p. vii.
64 LSE 8 /1/108, Firth Papers, File 1 of 2, Audrey Richards to Raymond Firth, 20 February 1978; Kaberry, *Women of the Grassfields*, p. vi.
65 LSE, Richards Papers, 8/1, Richards to Chilver, 22 November 1983.
66 LSE, Richards Papers, 3/1, Audrey Richards, Bemba Diaries, 17 September 1930.
67 LSE, Richards Papers, 8/1, Buganda 1, Audrey Richards, Buganda Diaries, 1950–51, 13 February 1951.
68 Rita Hinden, *Plan for Africa: A Report Prepared for the Colonial Bureau of the Fabian Society*, with a foreword by Arthur Creech Jones (London: Allen and Unwin 1941), pp. 117, 194, 214–17.
69 LSE, Richards Papers, 16/7, Richards to Chilver, 21 November 1953.
70 See for instance the Tanzanian example provided by Denise Roth Allen, *Managing Motherhood, Managing Risk: Fertility and Danger in West Central Africa* (Ann Arbor, MI: University of Michigan Press 2002), pp. 88–90.
71 Luise White, 'Separating the Men from the Boys: Colonial Constructions of Gender, Sexuality and Terrorism in Central Kenya, 1930–1959', *International Journal of African Historical Studies* 23, 1 (1990), p. 19.
72 RHO, Huxley Papers, 2/7, Nellie Grant to Elspeth Huxley, 23 July 1945. For opposition to circumcision see Bruce Berman and John Lonsdale, *Unhappy Valley: Conflict in Kenya and Africa*, Book Two, *Violence and Ethnicity* (London: James Currey; Nairobi: Heinemann Kenya; Athens: University of Ohio Press 1992), pp. 237, 385–6.
73 A point made in Joanna Lewis, 'Tropical East Ends and the Second World War: Some Contradictions in Colonial Office Welfare Initiatives', *Journal of Imperial and Commonwealth History* 28, 2 (2000), p. 47.
74 Hinden, *Plan for Africa*, pp. 171, 106–7, 294–5.

75 LSE, Richards Papers, 3/3, Audrey Richards, Bemba Diaries, 13 May 1931.
76 Ester Boserup, *Women's Role in Economic Development*, with a new introduction by Nazneen Kanji, Su Fei Tan, and Camilla Toulmin (London: Earthscan 2007 [1970]), pp. 3–5.
77 Thomas Spear, 'Neo-Traditionalism and the Limits of Invention in British Colonial Africa', *Journal of African History* 44, 1 (2003), pp. 4–5; Terence Ranger, 'The Invention of Tradition in Africa', in Eric Hobsbawm and Terence Ranger (eds), *The Invention of Tradition* (Cambridge: Cambridge University Press 1983), pp. 258–9.
78 van Beusekom and Hodgson, 'Lessons Learned?', p. 31.
79 Catherine Coquery-Vidrovitch, *African Women: A Modern History* (Boulder, CO: Westview Press 1997), p. 59. Other studies recovering women's lives from the objectification in colonial discourse include Geiger, Allman, and Musisi (eds), *Women in African Colonial Histories*; and Andrea Cornwall (ed.), *Readings in Gender in Africa* (Oxford: James Currey 2005).
80 For women's economic power in West Africa see Nwando Achebe, *Farmers, Traders, Warriors, and Kings: Female Power and Authority in Northern Igboland, 1900–1960* (Portsmouth, NH: Heinemann 2005). Land rights are discussed in Ingrid Yngstrom, 'Women, Wives and Land Rights in Africa: Situating Gender beyond the Household in the Debate over Land Policy and Changing Tenure Systems', *Oxford Development Studies* 30, 1 (2002), pp. 21–40.
81 Kathleen Staudt, 'The State and Gender in Colonial Africa', in Sue Ellen Charlton, Jana Everett, and Kathleen Staudt (eds), *Women, the State and Development* (Albany, NY: State University of New York Press 1989), p. 68.
82 April A. Gordon, *Transforming Capitalism and Patriarchy: Gender and Development in Africa* (London: Lynne Rienner 1996), p. 31.
83 For women's challenges to colonial authority, see Marc Matera, Misty L. Bastian, and Susan Kingsley Kent, *The Women's War of 1929: Gender and Violence in Colonial Nigeria* (Basingstoke: Palgrave Macmillan 2011). In crushing the disturbances colonial officers shot at women, who were armed only with sticks, resulting in an official casualty list of 48, including 18 deaths. In parallel riots in Opobo, over 30 women were shot dead. See *Report of a Commission of Enquiry into the Disturbances at Aba and other Places in South Eastern Nigeria in November and December 1929* (London: HMSO 1930), pp. 4–5.
84 Naila Kabeer, *Reversed Realities: Gender Hierarchies in Development Thought* (London: Verso 1994), p. 5; Snyder and Tadesse, *African Women*, pp. 9–10.
85 For a detailed analysis of consequences of leaving women out of the development agenda, see Michael Kevane, *Women and Development in Africa: How Gender Works* (London: Lynne Rienner 2004).

PART IV

Discourse-analytical and literary perspectives on colonial development

CHAPTER TWELVE

The world the Portuguese developed:[1] racial politics, luso-tropicalism and development discourse in late Portuguese colonialism

Caio Simões de Araújo and Iolanda Vasile

'This is Portugal!' With this cheerful title, the Portuguese newspaper, *Diário Popular*,[2] described the visit of the Brazilian anthropologist Gilberto Freyre throughout the colonial territories in 1951, which he had previously described as 'the world the Portuguese created'.[3] The article narrates how Freyre had accurately noticed that the 'unique capacity' of the Portuguese, and their fundamental contribution to the world, was a 'Franciscan love for all the peoples, for men of all colours'. In the late phase of Portuguese colonialism, however, it was clear that it was not enough to give birth to a new type of 'pluri-racial civilisation'. On the contrary, in a post-war period of global change and rapid reconstruction, economic growth and improvement of social conditions – 'development', in a general sense – was also required as living proof of the benefits of colonial intervention. How would the Portuguese negotiate its colonial project, premised on a discourse of 'humanity' and 'cosmopolitan love', with the material demands of the world economy? What kinds of mediation would be required? And more to the point, which narratives would be employed in order to sustain and accommodate clearly different, and sometimes conflicting, political, cultural, and economic interests? This chapter addresses the tortuous paths of late Portuguese colonialism in negotiating and putting forward a development project that would be presented as the *raison d'etre* of the Portuguese presence in Africa. More precisely, we will interrogate how the notion of 'development' was articulated to, and in the process re-framed by, a broader political and anthropological discourse constituting the very fabric of Portuguese rule and racial politics: luso-tropicalism.

Our analysis is influenced by a number of studies that have recently analysed development from a critical or discursive perspective. In particular we highlight the theoretical contributions of Arturo Escobar, who has drawn a 'genealogy of development' as a discursive practice, relating the concept to a broader set of historical processes such as colonialism and the uneven distribution of global power and wealth. Assuming an anthropological criticism of 'development', Escobar demonstrates how the concept, and the practices underlying it, were invented by discursive strategies that legitimised economic and political intervention over zones defined as 'underdeveloped'.[4] Drawing on these insights, we assume that a critical discursive analysis of 'development', grounded on anthropological criticism, may help us to unveil and address the hidden signifying strategies embedded in the political and epistemic languages of world power and processes of capitalist production associated with it.

In our narrative, we follow Escobar methodologically, resorting not only to his 'anthropology of development' as a discursive regime, but also to the 'historical ethnographies' proposed by Comaroff and Comaroff.[5] As our analysis makes clear, it is precisely in the interstices of history and other narratives of temporal power that the ethnographical gaze can generate its very counter-image of modernity in its route towards development. However, if Escobar has focused on the development regime as a new economic paradigm and discourse of power emerging mostly after 1945, we are inclined to point out that the concept is better understood if related to earlier modes of thinking and historical processes, particularly the rise of European evolutionary thought and the colonial encounter, in relation to which it was generated. For example, Cowen and Shenton locate the genesis of the concept in some of the canonical figures of Western thought, such as Comte, Spencer, Durkheim, and Weber, all of who contributed to the rise of 'development' as a scientific notion capable of establishing order in a continuously changing and increasingly hierarchical world. Moreover, development issues entered the realm of world politics long before 1945, during the late nineteenth and early twentieth centuries, when colonial powers took labour and industry as critical elements to improve their colonial empires.[6]

Furthermore, in his well-known study of the narrative and material production of the 'Other' through temporalisation, Fabian analyses how the 'periodisation of modernity' in a temporal sequence was only possible through the 'naturalisation' of linear time operated by European evolutionary thought after the Industrial Revolution. The firm belief in natural, evolutionary, time 'promoted a scheme in terms of which not only past cultures, but all living societies were irrevocably placed on a temporal slope'.[7] The notion of 'development' was a direct product of such temporal arrangement. Similarly, in a fascinating reading of the articulations between the temporal rationality of development and the politics of identity of the modern subject, Ferguson demonstrates that modernity is a *telos* that settles the path, and therefore the stage of each actor towards an ideal end defined in Western terms. He goes further to insist that, as a narrative, the 'developmental time' of world history 'transforms a spatialized global hierarchy into a temporalized (putative) historical sequence'.[8] When we focus on the colonial encounter, Meneses demonstrates how, once naturalised, 'time' was appropriated by the colonial project, creating the categories of the archaic, the barbarian, and the savage, which were used to justify 'progress' and legitimise the civilising mission on the route to the supreme stage of development – European modernity.[9] In this process, as 'the temporal axis [of evolution] was projected over the spatial axis [of the empire], history was made global'.[10] It is at this point that Africa could be invented, narrated, and administered as a 'place of backwardness'.

The critical assessment of these entanglements between histories and stories of colonialism and development must, however, avoid generalisation and simplification. As Nederveen Pieterse points out, critical development studies and particularly development discourse analysis often tend to 'homogenise developmental thinking', failing to draw a more sophisticated analysis of development discourse in the West as it was, frequently, 'replete with moments of improvisation, dissonance, discontinuity'.[11] This observation could not be more fitting to the Portuguese case. Throughout the history of the empire, development was a contested terrain upon which highly heterogeneous actors – from Portugal, the colonies or even global locations – negotiated their interests, confronted competing projects, and settled their power disparities. Therefore, the meanings of development were largely flexible and ready to be appropriated, re-articulated, and changed in a number of complex ways. Nonetheless, we are mostly interested in describing how, in the post-1945 global arena, Portugal was compelled to ascribe a hegemonic meaning to the 'development' of its territories in Africa, mostly as a discursive and political strategy to secure the viability of its political project on the continent.

In this context, 'development discourse' emerges as a legitimising imagery fully integrated into processes of colonialism and subalternisation. However, if we intend to challenge totalising notions of history and avoid over-simplifications of the meanings of 'development', then we are forced to recognise that 'colonialism' and 'empire' are also problematic notions that only make sense according to a politics of location. Therefore, the way different European empires mediated their experience of modernity and coloniality with specific uses of time and discourses of development can only be specific to each context. In this perspective, the Portuguese empire went through a particular trajectory in the context of European imperial order and deployed specific discursive strategies associated with the notions of modernity, colonialism, and development.

Portugal's *sui generis* position in international politics, world history, and global economy has been largely explained through the country's semi-peripheral position in the world system.[12] Taken from Immanuel Wallerstein's influential work, the category of 'semi-periphery' describes the condition of those countries of 'intermediate' development that mediate the economic (and often political) relations between the 'centre' and the 'periphery' of the world system.[13] This 'semi-peripheral condition' is said to have underlined the whole history of Portuguese colonialism until its late end in 1975.[14] Furthermore, it can also explain why, from the late seventeenth century onwards, the Portuguese empire was no longer able to follow the rhythm of global political and economic forces on an equal footing, since the mercantile capitalism on which it was based began to decline under the tension of a world-economy increasingly centred on industrial activities.[15] In 1986, some years after the Portuguese accession to the European Union, Santos invoked the semi-peripheral condition of the country in order to explain how the image of 'Europe' provided the marginal state the discursive conditions it needed to imagine itself as a 'centre'.[16] Ribeiro takes this point further to clarify the relations between, on the one hand, a 'semi-peripheral' reality, and, on the other, an 'imagination of the centre' in the context of European colonial modernity. The author goes on to argue that the symbolic constitution of Portugal as a 'centre' is only fully accomplished through the country's imagining of itself as an 'imperial nation', and cognisant of its imperial history. In this perspective, while masking the experienced reality associated with its 'semi-peripheral' condition, Portugal, as a precarious centre of an empire or as an imperial periphery in Europe, 'imagines the "centre", by symbolically participating of it'.[17]

As is well known, post-colonial studies have extensively documented the ambivalent and arbitrary nature of colonial discourse.[18] However, such ambivalence is particularly deep and sharp in the case of Portugal as an imperial nation and as a source of colonial discourse, since it was produced not only by the ambiguity of colonial authority *tout court*, but also by the problematic, precarious, and unstable position of the country itself as a 'legitimate' empire. Portugal lacked the material (by which we mean primarily the historical, economic, and geo-political conditions) to impose itself as a colonial power in its own right among the European imperial order,[19] and its colonial discourse was embedded in a complex and contradictory tapestry of images and signs meant to mediate narratives of powerlessness and poverty with histories and stories of glory, civilisation, and progress. The critical issue is to understand how all these signifying processes were negotiated and worked out.

As both the practices and the discourses of European colonialism, particularly the British and the French, became the norm, Portuguese colonialism was always trapped in a dialectic between a discursive excess and a material lack of colonialism.[20] The Portuguese empire had to develop a set of specific practices and discourses in order to cope with its position as a marginal colonial power. In fact, since the late nineteenth century, but especially from the first quarter of the twentieth century onwards, the colonial project assumed a central place in the Portuguese economy, which was then just about to undergo the concomitant processes of industrialisation and agrarian modern-isation.[21] Obviously, this particular economic condition and global political status would lead the country to attribute very specific meanings to what development is or should be. It goes without saying that Portuguese marginality did not prevent it from reproducing and confronting general colonial tendencies of the time. On the contrary, our analysis here will draw mostly and more precisely on these tensions and mediations between specificity and sameness, localised and global narratives, pride and modesty, and the way these notions are conveyed with meaning and put into circulation in the semantic networks of the empire.

Despite the broad scope of our analysis, we concur with Neto that Portuguese colonialism is an expression devoid of meaning unless localised in time and space.[22] In this sense, although we probe the wider angle of the empire, we will be particularly focused on Angola, the African colony considered throughout most of the twentieth century to be the 'jewel' of the empire. Precisely because of its natural resources and territorial extension, in Angola the tensions and nego-tiations around questions of development were particularly intense. By the same token, 'colonial discourse' is a highly ideal notion that means little unless we can 'grasp' it in some material form. In this perspective, our gaze centres on two specific sets of sources. Firstly, we analyse the issues of the Overseas General Bulletin (*Boletim Geral do Ultramar*) published from 1945 to 1970, when it was shut down. Established in 1924 as a sub-agency of the General Overseas Agency (*Agência Geral do Ultramar*),[23] the *Boletim* was a central vehicle of colonial propaganda meant to 'exalt' and 'defend' the empire and 'demonstrate the colonising abilities and capacity of the Portuguese'.[24] Secondly, we look at publications of the Institute for Overseas Research (*Junta de Investigações do Ultramar*), created in 1936 to produce 'useful knowledge' about the overseas provinces, from natural to social sciences.[25] If the *Boletim* published a highly heterogeneous set of texts, from official speeches, newspaper articles, and reports, to interviews and articles by prominent figures of the empire, the publications of the *Junta* were mostly, but not absolutely, policy-oriented, designed to provide scientific and technical information related to issues of political, economic or social relevance to the Portuguese administration.[26] As we will see in what follows, both sets of publications can be understood as privileged symbolic spaces in which development discourse is materialised and put into action.

Luso-tropicalism as development discourse in late Portuguese colonialism

After 1945, with the rise of the US and the USSR as the world's foremost super powers and the explosive spread of anti-colonialism in Africa and Asia, the Portuguese empire was faced with a radically new international arena, particularly in regard to its political economy and the legitimacy of its colonial possessions. The newly created United Nations (UN) and the emerging post-colonial states, backed by the USSR, increasingly managed to push a radical anti-colonial agenda in world politics and obliged the Portuguese empire to re-adapt its doctrine in order to achieve at least some international recognition. Moreover, after the hangover of the war, the international economy was about to go through a period of state-induced intense growth – what the French demographer Jean Fourastié would later call 'Les Trente Glorieuses'.[27] Although this interplay of increasing public investment, economic growth, and state intervention expressed a new moment in global political economy, marked by a geo-economic struggle between American and Soviet interests for 'spheres of influence', it also reflected the rising of what Escobar terms the post-war 'development industry', both in the West and in the 'Third World'.[28] In this rapidly shifting geo-political context, in which development – and, of course, under-development – was emerging as an important *topos* upon which power politics and economic competition would be expressed, the future of Portuguese presence in Africa depended not only on a meaningful increase in development policies and investments,[29] but also on a shift within the regime's discourse.

Under the influence of both the Marshall Plan in Europe and the emerging field of development economics, a public debate emerged in

Portugal over the insufficiencies of the regime's budgetary austerity, which highlighted the need for a new economic agenda, based on massive and planned public investment.[30] It was under these circumstances that the government approved a plan of economic stimulation – the *Plano de Fomento* – to be implemented in Portugal and its overseas territories from 1953 to 1958. Focused mostly on agricultural development, production and distribution of electrical power, basic industries, transport and communications, and technical education, the first *Plano de Fomento* was programmatic and had full employment as an underlying goal. Even if criticised for the restrictive overall budget,[31] this first initiative opened the way for economic planning to be accepted as the basic principle of the regime's economic policy until its end.[32] For instance, the second *Plano de Fomento*, executed from 1959 to 1964, was already conceived, according to Marcello Caetano, by then Head of the University of Lisbon, 'not as a simple administrative government programme, but as the defining instrument of an economic policy'.[33]

It hardly needs saying that this major shift in the economic organisation of the empire was closely related to broader and analogous changes within the political and legal structure of Portuguese colonialism. In fact, a new legal framework was adopted in 1951, with the total abolition of the Colonial Act of 1930, whose dispositions were directly integrated into the new Constitution. This legal change produced a radical re-structuring of Portuguese colonial discourse, since the very notion of the Portuguese Colonial Empire (*Império Colonial Português*) was simply abolished and replaced by the Portuguese Overseas (*Ultramar*),[34] in an attempt to invent the political and symbolic unity of the Portuguese nation: what Alexandre has called the 'nationalisation of the Empire'.[35] By the same token, the Portuguese territories in Africa and Asia became 'overseas provinces', instead of 'colonies', in a more cosmetic than substantive change meant to symbolically erase any vestige of colonial relations from the Portuguese space.[36] In this particular context, development discourse was heavily employed to explain the different levels of 'regional development' of the Portuguese multi-continental nation, providing the regime with the economic rationale with which to justify its political and economic intervention in Africa. In this regard, economist Vasco Fortuna pointed out the articulations between Portuguese sovereignty and public finances, when affirming that 'the financial unity of the Portuguese world, performed by the *Planos de Fomento* in terms of public investment in Portugal and the overseas provinces, will be an affirmation of sovereignty equivalent to running up the flag. It will be the consecration of our efforts of centuries of civilising mission on the Portuguese overseas'.[37]

Nevertheless, the emergence of modalities of economic and social intervention – Escobar's development industry – that promised to fight poverty in underdeveloped zones with no resort to direct colonial relations meant that fulfilling an 'obligation to develop' would hardly be enough to legitimise Portuguese presence in Africa. In fact, it became clear that the re-structuring of the political economy of the empire needed to be articulated to a whole reformulation of the symbolic economy of late Portuguese colonialism. In the context of African anti-colonialism and its underlying criticism of the generalised racism of European empires, it became necessary to purge Portuguese discourse of its racial bias, especially as it was, so far, based on generally outdated and increasingly discredited theories of anthropometric or eugenic inclination. The answer to this deep symbolic dilemma was provided by the Brazilian anthropologist, Gilberto Freyre. Having received his training at Columbia University in the American School of Cultural Anthropology, Freyre had developed, since the mid-1930s, a whole theory – which he named 'luso-tropicalism' – about what, he believed, was a specific Portuguese way of engaging with cultures and peoples of tropical zones.

Briefly put, 'luso-tropicalism' was based on the premise that, largely because of its racially mixed origin, the Portuguese people in general – and the Portuguese coloniser in particular – was not only naturally devoid of racism, but also respectful of the cultural differences of other peoples. According to Freyre, throughout history the Portuguese love for other races was expressed by the high levels of miscegenation and cultural syncretism easily noticeable in all the parts of what he later called the 'world the Portuguese created'. Moreover, Freyre looked at the encounter of the *Luso* and the *Tropics* and saw strong bonds of solidarity and multi-cultural co-existence, which led him to conclude that Portuguese colonisation in America, Africa, and Asia fostered the development of racially and culturally integrated societies, parts of a broader 'luso-tropical complex of civilisation'.[38] As Cláudia Castelo reveals in her path-breaking study, although Freyre's theory had been seen with caution and clear discomfort by Salazar's Estado Novo during the 1930s and early 1940s, in the post-1945 context luso-tropicalism was fully embraced and incorporated into the official discourse of the regime.[39] In fact, in 1951, Sarmento Rodrigues, by then Minister of Overseas Provinces, invited Freyre to travel throughout the Portuguese 'pluri-racial and multi-continental nation'. Freyre's official visit to the Portuguese territories signified his conscious positioning as an 'organic intellectual' of the empire,[40] and also marked the foundational moment of the political appropriation of the luso-tropical discourse by the Salazarist regime.[41]

In the turbulent period of decolonisation and international pressure, the *luso-tropical* ideology served the Portuguese designs in three main respects. Firstly, it gave full support to the ideas of internal diversity and discontinuous unity of the nation, so central to the Portuguese discourse. In this perspective, Angola and Mozambique, for example, were not colonies, but the material expression of an esoteric 'Portugality' in the tropics, being harmoniously integrated into the unitary space of the 'luso-tropical civilisation', reaching from 'Minho to Timor'. Secondly, in a context when Portugal was openly accused of resisting the 'winds of change' expressed by decolonisation, luso-tropicalism allowed the regime to claim a double-sided historical legitimacy. On the one hand, decolonisation struggles were seen with scepticism, as African peoples were accused of leaving behind one form of colonialism, imposed by Europe, only to find another one, led by the US and the Soviet Union. In this view, a true model of decolonisation meant 'integration' and full 'emancipation' of the peoples involved, both of which, according to the regime, had been Portuguese practices for centuries. Therefore, in the words of Cunha, Under-Secretary of Overseas Administration, Portugal had already promoted 'decolonization through History'.[42] On the other hand, in a context in which Africa was raging with anti-racism and Europe was only beginning to face its own multi-culturalism, Portugal considered itself to be the pioneer of harmonious inter-racial relations. According to Salazar, in an interview given to the American journal, *Foreign Affairs*, 'Multi-racialism, that today is beginning to be admitted by those who practically never accepted it, can be said to be a Portuguese creation . . . Thus, we do not have to change our path; the others, in their own interest, should follow us'.[43] Thirdly, the figure of Gilberto Freyre himself was instrumental in assuring the validity of the luso-tropical doctrine. As a prominent cultural anthropologist, whose scientific competence had already been recognised in different instances, Freyre was an authorised voice on the study of cultural dynamics. Thus, his scientific legitimacy meant, in the regime's strategy, that his findings and assumptions about the 'Portuguese world' were accurate, impartial, and reliable. Moreover, Freyre was Brazilian. As a post-colonial subject and citizen of a country that had already been 'peacefully' and 'successfully' colonised by the Portuguese, Freyre's rhetoric of solidarity, cultural bonds, and brotherhood not only gave some picturesque authenticity to the luso-tropical discourse, but also allowed Portugal to use the image of the 'South-American brother' in order to nourish projects of building other 'Brazils' in Africa, especially in the case of Angola.[44]

Regarding the Portuguese 'developmental' project of the post-1945 period, it is important to notice the complex ways in which the luso-tropical doctrine interacted with, fertilised, and meaningfully colonised other political, economic, and racial discourses and ideologies. One of the important outcomes of these rhetorical and symbolic contact zones is that it was mostly through luso-tropicalism, or at least with a luso-tropical bias, that the 'human' factor was incorporated into Portuguese development policies. This is not to say that 'human resources' were not taken into account in previous periods. On the contrary, issues of indigenous labour and white settlement had for a long time been fundamental to the political economy of colonial development, surely at least since the late nineteenth century onwards. However, and perhaps precisely because in the 1950s and 1960s these same problems re-emerged under a particularly critical light, luso-tropicalism was the privileged way through which the Estado Novo could manage, in a 'coherent' manner, the role of the 'human factor' in colonial development discourse. As we will explore in the next section, it was precisely around issues of culture, labour, Christian morals, education, race, and body politics, that luso-tropicalism was called into action and provided important signifying elements to the regime's narrative of progress and redemption.

Luso-tropical humanism and the symbolic economy of colonial development

By the late 1940s Portugal lacked the technical and financial means to put forward the ambitious development programme it needed. At the same time, it was rather reticent about opening the economy to foreign investments, which were then seen as external interference on domestic affairs.[45] The success of Portuguese developmental policies, thus, was highly dependent on the capacity to efficiently activate ready-available resources, with labour, indigenous and white, being the most obvious one. On the other hand, if the discourse of the 'unity of the nation' was to work, it was necessary to improve labour conditions and indigenous welfare and, at the same time, increase the waves of white settlement, which was, in the early 1950s, below the desired level, especially in the vast territories of Angola and Mozambique. Moreover, although the emigration of white settlers to the overseas provinces was also meant to alleviate white poverty in the metropolis,[46] it had the fundamental political function of consolidating the Portuguese political presence in the African territories,[47] thus offering a new argument against international demands for decolonisation. In this complex conjuncture, luso-tropicalism was a powerful discursive strategy through which the ongoing tensions between the regime's precarious resources and its trans-continental ambitions were mediated.

On the one hand, in the official discourse of the regime, economic and social development in Africa could only be achieved with massive white settlement. While this idea was dependent on the implicit – and sometimes explicit – assumption about indigenous backwardness, commonly framed in a rhetoric of lack of 'preparation', 'instruction' or 'education', it was also associated with images of the 'whites' as the only group with full capacity, and even with the 'noble' responsibility of promoting development in the continent. Since white settlers had to 'justify their presence' in Africa, as the former Minister of Colonies Marcello Caetano himself recognised, they would have to work on both the 'improvement of the land' and 'indigenous education', thus encouraging 'culture and civilization'.[48] Luso-tropicalism provided yet another sort of justification for white European settlement: as the luso-tropical narrative was centred on the figure of an individualised *Luso* and a generalised *Tropic*, it basically meant that whatever the territory in which it flourished and developed, the 'luso-tropical complex of civilisation' could not exist without the input of the European element. Thus in official discourse, the political and economic requirements behind the increase of white emigration to the overseas provinces were disguised precisely under the need to foster inter-racial contact. For instance, Adriano Moreira, Minister of Overseas Provinces, declared that white settlement was the necessary condition for 'the formation of multiracial integrated communities, without which in Africa there will be neither progress nor order, civilisation or human rights'.[49] What is more important, Freyre's theory provided the regime with the rhetorical tools it needed to justify white settlement on mainly humanitarian grounds, thus hiding or at least strategically displacing the centrality of the racial line – and the 'white body' – in assuring the economic and political project of late colonialism. The 'humanist' justifications behind development efforts were meaningfully expressed in an official report on the second *Plano de Fomento*, in which the engineer, Trigo de Morais, who was a representative of the Corporative Chamber (*Câmara Corporativa*),[50] affirmed:

> We wish that the greatest number possible of white families of the metropolis [will] constitute vigorous *foci* of colonisation in the overseas territories ... exercising there their traditional virtues of Portuguese settlers, [maintaining] well alive the sense of fraternal collaboration with the indigenous Portuguese of the overseas provinces, loving them and respecting them ... with the fecund aspiration of assimilation by example and by heart, under the illumination of the doctrine of Christ.[51]

On the other hand, another central element of *luso-tropicalism* was the way it constructed a linear trajectory of indigenous development. According to this narrative, the races and cultures in contact would be necessarily incorporated into 'the world the Portuguese created' through racial miscegenation and/or cultural syncretism of Portuguese dominance. This linear transformation allowed the regime to think of its so-called 'policies of integration' of the indigenous population in terms of 'cultural development'. In fact, in 1954, the Executive Order no. 39.666 of 20 May, introduced the Statute of the Portuguese Indigenous of the Provinces of Guinea, Angola and Mozambique (*Estatuto dos Indígenas Portugueses das Províncias da Guiné, Angola e Moçambique*), which divided the Portuguese population into three groups: white citizens with rights and duties as established by modern law, indigenous populations subjected to customary authorities, and those Africans who had been fully incorporated into the Portuguese culture and, thus, could also be granted citizenship rights: the assimilated or *assimilados*. The *assimilado* had to be: (a) civilised, in terms of language and culture (education and religion); (b) integrated into capitalist economy through wage labour; and (c) free of 'anti-social' tribal customs. The *estatuto* was not only based on the presumed public responsibility to 'protect' and 'defend the rights' of those generally found in a 'state of natural incapacity', to use the terms employed by the General-Secretary of the Ministry of Overseas Provinces, José Bossa,[52] but heavily dependent on the idea that acknowledging the different kinds of people was precisely meant to sustain 'diversity in unity', assuring the respect for 'each of the groups that united themselves to form the Portuguese people'.[53] Thomaz accurately noticed that luso-tropicalism, when working together with this legal framework and its underlying notion of 'stages of cultural development', 'legally establishes the structural inequalities of the Empire while attributing to the State the role of controlling and administering the progressive assimilation of the native population to the *political* and *spiritual* body of the nation'.[54] Therefore, it is worth noting that while the *assimilados* were taken as those individuals who had already gone through the developmental and civilising activities of the state, the indigenous were the ones who were still in this evolutionary process, to be completed through Christian education and, above all, labour. In this regard, Salazar himself declared that there was no 'other escape from the underdevelopment cycle than through the path of labour'.[55] Moreover, the trajectory of indigenous cultural development should be complemented by the improvement of living conditions, which was a moral as much as a material issue. In this perspective, journalist Forjaz Trigueiros observed, in an essay published by the *Boletim Geral do Ultramar*, that

> Among the most important principles defined by the Statute of the Portuguese Indigenous] are those establishing the right of citizenship, and the promotion, through all means, of the material and moral improvement of indigenous life, the development of its natural capabilities and

faculties, and the access to education as the superior form of moving towards civilisation.[56]

Of course, the over-representation of the 'humanistic' or 'humanitarian' side of colonial development cannot be completely attributed to luso-tropicalism, but is also connected to the Catholic missionary ethos that dominated Portuguese social service and the generalised presence of Christian values in the regime's discourse at large. Nevertheless, the particular Luso-tropical modality of development discourse had a specificity related to the very nature of Freyre's cultural anthropology. During his training in the US, Freyre had had Franz Boas as his superviser, thus incorporating in his work a Boasian approach, and thus more sensitive to 'definite cultural phenomena' such as cooking, folk tales, clothing, sensorial notions, and subjective perceptions, than orthodox streams of anthropology. Freyre's focus on aspects of culture – taken as disconnected from or independent of social realities – meant that his luso-tropical approach could basically document the presence of 'cultural harmony' and 'spiritual and sentimental unity' even when the existence of discriminatory or anti-democratic social, cultural, and political structures would show otherwise. As Thomaz has already highlighted, this was quite handy to the Estado Novo's dictatorial political project, since it allowed the regime to claim a democracy based on 'cultural integration' rather than on political or social rights.[57] Taking this argument further, we can say that the luso-tropical discourse had a similar effect on the symbolic economy of development, since it added a thick layer of 'humanism' to what had been so far largely regarded as an eminently economic process. That is not to say that the purely economic or material side of development was dismissed. It was not. What we want to point out is that the luso-tropical text co-existed with and, to some extent, colonised already existing discourses of materiality and civilisation, such as the multiple redemptive images of progress involving railways, hygiene, rural mechanisation, hospitals, schools, and industries.[58]

The anti-economistic ethos in Portuguese colonial discourse was, furthermore, also meant to address some of the accusations circulating in the international sphere. Because 'colonialism' was increasingly criticised in the post-1945 era, Portugal had to make an effort to attest her specificity as a non-imperial nation. If luso-tropicalism had already evidenced the qualities of Portuguese racial politics of miscegenation, its encounter with development economics would produce, paradoxically, the vivid proof that Portuguese intervention in Africa was more 'humanistic' than economic. In fact, Gilberto Freyre himself pointed out that if Portugal had failed in keeping up with the rhythm of capitalism – as opposed to the leading European states – it was nonetheless much more advanced in humanistic fields such as arts and culture generally speaking.[59] Similarly, the Minister of Finance, Águedo de Oliveira, in his speech at the first Conference of Portuguese Economists (*Congresso de Economistas Portugueses*), held in Luanda in 1955, argued that other European powers would be 'surprised' to notice that, contrary to their own practices, the Portuguese administration was based on policies made 'from man to man', thus constituting a mission of 'civilisation and settlement' rather than 'a great technological and capitalist endeavour', one in which the natives were seen in their 'human and spiritual' aspects rather than in their implicit economic value.[60] By the same token, some years later, the Under-Secretary of State for Overseas Development, Mário de Oliveira, fully demonstrated the extent to which Portuguese development discourse was deeply embedded in an anti-economicist ethos. According to Oliveira:

> In the Portuguese case, above all, we have to focus on the human factors that actively participate in the multiple manifestations of our national life, which is constituted by multiple ethnic groups, bonded together by the Portuguese feeling that is the common denominator of this singular nation that is Portugal . . . It is thus important to highlight . . . how necessary it is to look at the lives of the populations of the overseas provinces, understanding their movements in the flows of their anxieties, hopes, aspirations or inquietudes. Only after that we will be able to give a pragmatic expression to a policy of economic development.[61]

Furthermore, as a general theory of inter-racial sociality, luso-tropicalism had the potential to explain and justify a fundamental contradiction of Portuguese political economy: the problem of how to articulate the racial discrimination produced by the *estatuto* with the goal of encouraging full economic integration. Especially because colonial development was focused on the problem of the so-called 'African Duality', that is the co-existence of two independent and non-communicative economic systems, the 'indigenous' and the 'modern', luso-tropicalism constituted a valuable theory of how to manage the harmonious integration of 'traditional' systems of production into a 'modern' capitalist economy. Because the trajectory of cultural development and legal entitlement envisaged by the *estatuto* involved, necessarily, indigenous labour, the system of racial regimentation served economic purposes as long as it assured a cheap and accessible workforce, therefore pushing African populations towards the national economy by means of voluntary – and sometimes mandatory – labour. With its a discursive stance, on the other hand, the encounter of 'traditional' and 'modern' economies was framed as a sectoral expression of the broader luso-tropical politics of integration. A meaningful example of these entanglements was given in the opening session of the Colloquium on the Second *Plano de Fomento* (*Colóquio sobre o II Plano de Fomento*), in which the Under-Secretary of State for Overseas Development, Carlos Abecasis, argued that the 'preferable' means of promoting the integration of the indigenous economies was to induce their 'disarticulation' by 'transferring' the workforce to the '"islands" of monetary economy'. Abecasis goes further to point out that such 'economic evolution [would have to] be systematically juxtaposed with the integration of the indigenous masses in the spiritual community of the Nation'.[62] In this context, the economic appropriation of indigenous labour or colonisation of the traditional farm was an element of the broader process of the harmonious integration of the indigenous peoples into the 'pluri-racial integrated society'. What is most interesting in this perspective is how development is implicitly understood as the successful articulation of these contradictory economic and political projects of discrimination and integration. As we will see below, the rise of anti-colonial violence in the overseas territories would introduce profound challenges to late Portuguese rule and require further accommodation of development discourse to new domestic and international pressures.

Decolonisation, colonial war, and the securitisation of development

By February of 1961, a violent uprising in Luanda's prison as well as organised subversion against colonial authorities in the north-west region marked the outburst of colonial war in Angola. Soon enough, the military conflict reached Mozambique and Portuguese Guinea. Only a few months later, by mid-December, the enclaves of Goa, Daman, and Diu were occupied by Indian troops and incorporated into the post-colonial Republic of India. The violent attacks against Portuguese rule in Africa and the sudden expulsion from the Indian subcontinent took the Portuguese by surprise and forced the regime to face the contentious nature of its political sovereignty in the overseas territories. To the problem of the profound, and obvious, contradiction between a discourse of harmonic integration and a context of military confrontation, Portugal reacted with more luso-tropicalism. As international pressure rose and condemnations of the regime's policy in Africa gained terrain in the UN, the *Estatuto dos Indígenas* was abolished and efforts were made towards commercial and monetary integration through the suppression of trade tariffs and the creation of an Escudo Zone (Zona Escudo) between Portugal and the overseas provinces.[63] Needless to say, both measures had the clear objective of deepening the unity of the 'Portuguese World' on legal-political and economic grounds, respectively. In the official discourse, the war was narrated as a conflict insidiously inflicted from the outside, associated with foreign ambitions and with no connection with the empire's internal tensions whatsoever. In fact, liberation movements were never recognised as such, but were commonly described as 'terrorist' or 'subversive' groups that were advancing, in Portuguese soil, the political interest of foreign agents.[64] In this context, the Soviet Union was often accused of aiming to expand its imperial project over the Portuguese provinces, while the neighbouring independent African states were seen as propagating racist sentiments and ideologies throughout the continent.

For that matter, anti-colonialism in general was understood as an insidious form of 'black racism' whose main goal was to expel from Africa the white groups that, nonetheless, should have their 'rights of settlement' recognised. Previously existing associations between white intervention and development were, in this moment, re-framed as an argument against decolonisation. For instance, Salazar himself affirmed that 'black racism' would forsake the benefits the 'progressive white [settler] 'could bring to the black populations in terms of 'capital, labour and culture'. He went further concluding that 'economic, social and political progress' in Africa would be possible only as far as 'racial exclusivism' was replaced by collaboration 'on a multicultural basis'.[65] The idea that without the white element no development was possible also reveals an underlying scepticism, in Portuguese discourse, about the very political or economic viability of post-colonial states. In this regard, in an article published in the journal *Ultramar*, Afonso Mendes argued that anti-colonialism was connected to the insecurity felt by newly formed African states and their fear that 'the administration and economic development of colonial territories show progress that may discredit the governmental capacity of their own countries'.[66]

Needless to say, after 1961, the symbolic and material efforts put forward by the Portuguese evidenced the centrality of development in the politics of late colonialism. Especially in its *luso-tropical* modality, development discourse provided the answer to Portuguese challenges in Africa. As the result of the centuries-old encounter between the *Luso* and the *Tropic*, development was presented as a peaceful process of gradual economic change and cultural elevation, therefore regarded as a much better alternative for Africa than the radical – and violent – change promoted by anti-colonial revolutions. The luso-tropical doctrine was extended to unprecedented degrees, particularly in a period in which the developmental efforts in the overseas provinces were being constantly undermined by the costs and the destruction imposed by the war. More precisely, luso-tropicalism played a major role in symbolically structuring the nexus between development and security in late colonialism. In fact, it clearly demonstrated the corelation between pursuing developmental goals, on the one hand, and protecting the pluri-racial national community from the dangers of anti-colonial terrorism, on the other. In this highly militarised context, the luso-tropical politics of integration as an ideological weapon was easily appropriated as an important modality of 'preventive action'. The securitisation of colonial development was fully expressed by A. Correia de Araújo in his *Aspects of Economic and Social Development of Angola*. According to Araújo:

> The economic development that we have been defending for our national community will only be possible and efficient as long as it encompasses, indistinctly, the harmonious and collective promotion of all ethnic groups, in the economic and social fields. Of course, this premise that does not constitute any novelty in our already centuries-old activities in the overseas provinces. Given, however, that our overseas territories have become a field of ideological battle, in a struggle for life or death upon which our future depends, everything suggests that we, now more than ever, pay special attention to the economic and social development of the ethnic groups that for so long we have been integrating and assimilating. We cannot in any way overlook this enormous and noble national task, or we will fail.[67]

From 1961, this triangulation between luso-tropicalism, national security, and development was materialised in two particular policies: rural resettlement (*re-ordenamento rural*) and community development (*desenvolvimento comunitário*).[68] The policy of *re-ordenamento rural* was reactive to the common Portuguese anxiety about what was perceived as insufficient control over vast areas of the territory, particularly in Angola and Mozambique. In this perspective, it was urgent to increase the Portuguese presence in certain zones, and particularly focus on the national integration of remote rural communities that otherwise were seen as susceptible to the ideological threat of terrorism. *Re-ordenamento rural*, briefly put, meant the dislocation and concentration of these rural populations to designated areas, in which technical assistance would be provided in order to improve living conditions and direct their agricultural production so as to fit into the broader framework of the 'Portuguese Economic Space'. It hardly needs saying, *re-ordenamento rural* expresses the securitisation of development as it posed the double-sided goal of integrating 'isolated' indigenous populations into the 'spiritual community' of the nation – therefore keeping them safe from 'terrorists' – and of integrating their traditional economies into the Portuguese economy at large. In addition, the idea of *desenvolvimento comunitário* proposed that development projects should be conceived so as to respect grassroots realities instead of disrupting them, therefore assuring the reduction of the political costs of social and economic change. Moreover, in this framework development plans should be consistently based on the participation and active consent from the communities involved. This point is made clear by a policy-oriented report prepared by the Mozambique Working Group on Social Promotion (*Grupo de Trabalho de Promoção Social de Moçambique*): 'In order to succeed in leading native rural communities out of the backward stage in which they have vegetated for thousands of years, it has been recognised that it is indispensable first to attain their good will and active collaboration. We have to admit the failure and even the counter-productive results of methods of coercion'.[69]

As conjoint policies, *re-ordenamento rural* and *desenvolvimento comunitário* showed how the *luso-tropical* notions of harmonious integration, inter-racial respect, and national unity were articulated with the securitisation of development in the context of war and African decolonisation. As such, they came in quite handy to the regime's politics in three ways. Firstly, these were relatively inexpensive policies, in the sense that the responsibility of development was partly transferred from the state alone to the communities to which public investment was directed. Secondly, after all the criticism directed to the *Estatuto dos Indígenas* regarding its policies of unilateral integration, *desenvolvimento comunitário* was based on a 'democratic' and humanist rhetoric that seemed to be much more adequate to cope with international pressures. As a matter of fact, it enabled Portuguese colonial doctrine to accommodate emerging notions such as the human element of economic change or 'community participation', both of which were in this period receiving the increasing attention of the international community and UN-related institutions. As Adriano Moreira, in a speech presented at the Oporto Trade Association (*Associação Comercial do Porto*) pointed out, 'those who have recently acknowledged the importance of *desenvolvimento comunitário* [in international organs], will be able to understand, perhaps with some discontent, that once again they have met Portuguese solutions'.[70] Thirdly, as policies of *desenvolvimento comunitário* were mostly focused on inter-subjective processes, their outcomes could hardly be measured or proven in any statistical sense. In this context, the luso-tropical argument about the Portuguese natural respect for indigenous peoples worked as 'evidence' that attested to the largely presumed efficacy of such methods. For example, in an article written in 1963 originally for the newspaper *Diário de Notícias*, Alfredo de Sousa declared that even if the results of *desenvolvimento comunitário* were 'difficult to evaluate, as the major achievements are not expressed in numbers . . . it is easy to deduce that the mental and social evolution of the populations represent a great move towards development'.[71]

Furthermore, the securitisation of development in late Portuguese colonialism was also related, in the regime's discourse, to broader efforts and responsibilities to be carried out in a context of the spread of communism. In this regard, the Portuguese efficiently made use of the international political context of the Cold War in order to obtain some international support from the 'Free World', particularly from the US, but also from the two major anchors on the opposite sides of a Southern Atlantic security system: Brazil and South Africa. Luso-tropicalism, in this context, gained a clear geo-political function, expressed in the idea of the Portuguese nation – overseas territories included – as a Euro-Africa, constituted as a 'protective belt' against communist expansion in the southern portion of the continent. As development needs were often subsumed to or jeopardised by security or military needs, the war efforts in the overseas territories were considered not only, or even primarily, as a struggle to preserve Portuguese sovereignty in the provinces, but as a moral commitment to the defence of Western values and civilisation, of which the very notion of development was associated and derived. In this perspective, several times the regime described the pair 'communism' and 'anti-colonialism' not as a threat to its own interests, but as an outrage to Europe, the West, and the whole 'Free World'. For example, in a report on the efforts of development in times of military conflict, the National Service of Information (*Serviço Nacional de Informação*) recognised that, even if it was a heavy burden on the economy, the war was necessary as a 'responsibility derived from [our] participation in the security system of the free world'.[72] To the political and spiritual threat posed by communism and the 'black racism' of decolonisation, thus, luso-tropicalism and its implied inter-racial cooperation for development was the obvious answer. Portugal would be, once again, the country to lead the West towards the future, as it had already done five centuries before, during the Great Navigations. However, in the years to come the regime's dream of geo-political glory, trans-continental salvation, and humanitarian development would perish under the carnage and destruction of the war, and the Portuguese developmental ambitions would be nothing more than a mirage in the mist.

Conclusion

If luso-tropicalism emerged as a discourse of strong anthropological impetus, limited, thus, to the workings of culture as the privileged object of the anthropological gaze, the appropriation of its narrative by the Estado Novo would turn it into a 'total theory' of nearly cosmological ambitions. As a matter of fact, the new rhetoric of the regime would take the luso-tropical sign to its exhaustion by applying it, whenever needed, to all possible fields of colonial intervention, from indigenous policies and local administration to international politics. Even with the outbreak of anti-colonial struggles in 1961, the Portuguese myth of colonial harmony would have to wait many years to fall apart. According to Fernando Rosas, the symbolic moment of the luso-tropical debacle can be identified in a speech delivered in September of 1970 by Marcello Caetano, who took over the direction of the empire after Salazar's removal from office in 1968. As Rosas indicates, on that occasion Caetano explicitly abandoned the ideological, spiritual, and ontological integrity of the *Ultramar*, by recognising, rather pragmatically, that the interests and lives of the Portuguese white settlers in the overseas provinces were the only reasons for proceeding with the war efforts. Even if we are not sure if it is possible to so clearly demarcate the demise of the luso-tropical myth, we nonetheless agree that, as Rosas highlighted, once colonial 'transcendence' was denied, the war and decolonisation could be looked upon as the political – and not moral or spiritual – issues that they were.[73] A similar argument could be raised regarding the symbolic economy of development, as the material traumas of the war tended to displace the centrality of luso-tropical humanism, which gradually faded from Portuguese discourse. Devoid of meaning, *luso*-tropicalism was no longer an option for the Estado Novo, which, with no ideological or material support, could not avoid political subversion at home and succumbed to the Carnations Revolution in 1974. In 1975, the newly elected democratic government would return sovereignty to the overseas territories, bringing the final end to the Portuguese colonial adventure and its ambivalent trajectory of development.

As our narrative has shown, 'the world the Portuguese created' was deeply embedded in complex networks of global power and local sacrifice, negotiating sharp tensions between meta-narratives of inter-racial conviviality and the violence of administrative abstraction. In this context, development – the idea and the ideal – was one of the central means through which late Portuguese colonialism tried to put a happy ending to its long history of adventure and redemption. For in the Portuguese case, what is now a fully operating structure of development co-existed with the symbolic economy of the empire. The critical analysis of this historical conjuncture, we contend, may shed some light on current debates on the coloniality of world politics, and particularly on the insidious fixation of images of backwardness on the black body. More precisely, late Portuguese colonialism managed to sustain a highly racialised development project with no reference to race as such, focusing rather on 'culture' as the critical element of its evolutionary ethos. It hardly needs saying that connections and continuities with our contemporary times are, to our deep discomfort, abundant. During the 1990s, some scholarly works addressed the cultural politics of development, arguing that the roots of under-development may be found in the 'inadequate' culture of impoverished countries and populations.[74] David Landes in particular affirmed that Portuguese colonisation was an underdeveloping factor, mostly due to the conservative morals and rudimentary economy it introduced in the colonies.[75] In 2010, Portuguese diplomat José Fernandes Fafe, published a response, noting that if Brazil is now in full development, being the emerging economy that it is, it means that Portuguese colonialism was not so bad after all – quite on the contrary.[76] Obviously, these are all contemporary expressions of deep historical entangle-ments, through which colonial discourses on development, fetishising fixations of culture, and globalised political hierarchies are deeply intertwined. These texts can only indicate how a mirage of the empire still haunts our modern imagination. They show, finally, that the disclosure of these hidden ties – how development came into being in history – is critical for the understanding of our contemporary predicament.

Notes

1 We want to express our special thanks to Maria Paula Meneses and Margarida Calafate Ribeiro for constantly encouraging the study of Portuguese post-colonial studies. We are also grateful to Andreas Dafinger and Cláudia Castelo, who were kind enough to comment on earlier versions of this chapter. We also want to acknowledge the work of Debjyoti Ghosh and Eszter Timar in the editing of this text.

2 The article was written by the poet and literary critic José Osório de Oliveira and published in *Diário Popular* in 1951. See José Osório de Oliveira, 'Portugal é Isto!', *Boletim Geral do Ultramar* 27, 317 (1951), pp. 118–19. All translations from Portuguese by Araújo and Vasile.

3 See Gilberto Freyre, *O mundo que o português criou: aspectos das relações sociaes e de cultura do Brasil com Portugal e as colónias portuguesas* (Rio de Janeiro: Livraria Jose Olympio 1940).

4 Arturo Escobar, *Encountering Development: The Making and Unmaking of the Third World* (Princeton, NJ: Princeton University Press 1995).

5 John Comaroff and Jean Comaroff, *Ethnography and the Historical Imagination* (Oxford, Boulder, CO: Westview Press 1992).

6 Michael Cowen and Robert Shenton, *Doctrines of Development* (London, New York: Routledge 1996).

7 Johannes Fabian, *Time and the Other: How Anthropology Makes Its Others* (New York: Columbia University Press 1983), p. 17.

8 James Ferguson, 'Decomposing Modernity: History and Hierarchy after Development', in Ania Loomba et al. (eds), *Postcolonial Studies and Beyond* (Durham, NC: Duke University Press 2005), p. 167.

9 Maria Paula Meneses, 'O "indígena" africano e o "colono" europeu: a construção da diferença por processos legais', *E-cadernos CES* 7 (2010), pp. 68–93. Available at: www.ces.uc.pt/e-cadernos/media/ecadernos7/04%20-%20Paula%20Meneses%2023_06.pdf (accessed 17 March 2013).

10 'O eixo temporal [da evolução] foi projectado sobre o eixo do espaço [do Império] e a história tornou-se global'. Ibid., p. 72.

11 Jan Nederveen Pieterse, 'The Development of Development Theory: Towards Critical Globalisation', *Review of International Political Economy* 3, 4 (1996), pp. 543, 546.

12 The notion of semi-periphery was introduced in Portuguese sociology to some extent by influence of an article published by Boaventura de Sousa Santos in 1985. See Boaventura de Sousa Santos, 'Estado e sociedade na periferia do sistema mundial: o caso português', *Análise Social* 21, 87–9 (1985), pp. 869–901.

13 Carlos Fortuna, *O fio da meada: o algodão de Moçambique, Portugal e a economia-mundo, 1860–1960* (Porto: Afrontamento 1993); Immanuel Wallerstein, *The Modern World System* (New York: Academic Press 1974); Immanuel Wallerstein, *The Capitalist World Economy* (Cambridge: Cambridge University Press 1979).

14 Boaventura de Sousa Santos, 'Between Prospero and Caliban: Colonialism, Post-colonialism, and Inter-identity', *Luso-Brazilian Review* 39, 1 (2002), pp. 9–43.

15 Maria Helena da Cunha Rato, 'O colonialismo português, factor de subdesenvolvimento nacional', *Análise Social* 19, 3–5 (1983), pp. 1121–9.

16 Boaventura de Sousa Santos, 'O Estado, as relações salariais e o bem-estar social na semiperiferia: o caso português', in Boaventura de Sousa Santos (ed.), *Portugal: um retrato singular* (Porto: Afrontamento 1993), pp. 17–58.

17 '"imagina o centro", participando simbolicamente dele'. Margarida Calafate Ribeiro, 'Uma história de regressos: império, guerra colonial e pós-colonialismo', *Oficina do CES* 188 (2003), p. 2. Available at: www.ces.uc.pt/publicacoes/oficina/ficheiros/188.pdf (accessed 25 May 2013).

18 See, for example, Edward Said, *Culture and Imperialism* (New York: Vintage 1994) and Homi K. Bhabha, *The Location of Culture* (London: Routledge 1994).

19 See Santos, 'Between Prospero and Caliban'.

20 Ibid., p. 11.

21 Fernando Rosas, 'Estado Novo, império e ideologia imperial', *Revista de História das Ideias* 17 (1995), pp. 19–32.

22 Maria da Conceição Neto, 'Ideologias, contradições e mistificações da colonização de Angola no século XX', *Lusotopie* (1997), pp. 327–59.

23 Changes to the administrative structure of the empire throughout the twentieth century affected both institutions. In 1924, the Bulletin was named *Boletim da Agência Geral das Colónias* (Bulletin of the General Agency of the Colonies). In 1935, it was renamed *Boletim Geral das Colónias* (General Bulletin of the Colonies), in an attempt to attest its autonomy from the Agency, thereby supposedly offering a general and 'impartial' view on the colonial world. In 1951, following a constitutional change on the organisation of the empire, the Bulletin was again re-named to *Boletim Geral do Ultramar* (Overseas General Bulletin). The *Agência Geral das Colónias* (General Agency of the Colonies), created in 1924 to centralise power and authority on colonial issues, was also renamed in 1951, becoming the *Agência Geral do Ultramar* (General Overseas Agency).

24 'fazer propaganda do nosso património colonial, contribuindo por todos os meios para o seu engrandecimento, defesa, estudo das suas riquezas e demonstração das aptidões e capacidade colonizadora dos portugueses'. *Boletim da Agência Geral das Colónias* 1, 2 (1925), p. 231.

25 The *Junta de Investigações do Ultramar* was a development of the *Comissão de Cartographia* (Commission of Cartography), created in 1883 with the goal of assuring the 'scientific occupation' of the colonies. In 1936, the *Comissão de Cartographia* was enlarged and replaced by the *Junta das Missões Geográficas e de Investigação Coloniais* (Colonial Committee of Geographic and Research Missions), in 1951 being renamed *Junta das Missões Geográficas e de Investigação do Ultramar* (Overseas Committee of Geographic and Research Missions), abbreviated to *Junta de Investigações do Ultramar*. For a full account of the history of scientific institutions in the Portuguese empire, see Ana Cristina Martins and Teresa Albina (eds), *Viagens e missões científicas nos trópicos, 1883–2010* (Lisbon: Instituto de Investigação Científica Tropical 2010).

26 It is worth noting the close association between the production of scientific knowledge, particularly in terms of applied science, and the developmental goals of the Portuguese administration. The *Junta de Investigações do Ultramar*, thus, is explicitly understood as enabling and serving the 'improvement of the quality of life of populations and the more efficient use of the resources available on the overseas provinces' / 'a melhoria do nível de vida das populações e para um melhor aproveitamento dos recursos ultramarinos'. *Boletim Geral do Ultramar* 35, 407–8 (1959), p. 181.

27 Jean Fourastié, *Les Trente Glorieuses, ou la révolution invisible de 1946 à 1975* (Paris: Fayard 1979).

28 See Escobar, *Encountering Development*.

29 Yves Léonard,'O Ultramar Português', in Francisco Bethencourt and Kirti Chaudhuri (eds), *História da expansão portuguesa*, vol. 5, *Último império e recentramento, 1930–1998* (Lisbon: Círculo de Leitores 1999), pp. 31–50.

30 This idea is well expressed in the words of the Portuguese economist Vasco Fortuna, to whom it was fundamental to create 'favourable conditions to economic development: power production, lines of communication, technical assistance, cheap habitation, commercial, industrial and banking organisation, public services, access to culture, scientific research, etc. In a word: investment! The economic progress of underdeveloped regions, as with some of our overseas provinces, requires a massive investment policy capable of furnishing the lack of fixed capital, and a re-investment policy capable of retaining the primary benefits of investments' / 'condições favoráveis ao desenvolvimento económico: produção de energia, vias de comunicação, assistência técnica, habitações baratas, organização comercial, industrial e bancárias, serviços públicos, acesso à cultura, investigação científica, etc. Numa palavra: investimentos! O progresso económico das regiões subdesenvolvidas, como o são algumas das nossas províncias ultramarinas, requer uma política de investimentos maciços capaz de suprir a falta de capital fixo, e uma política de reinvestimentos capaz de reter os benefícios primários dos investimentos'. Vasco Nunes Pereira Fortuna, 'As finanças públicas do mundo português', *Boletim Geral do Ultramar* 27, 317 (1951), pp. 41–2.

31 Salazar himself acknowledged that, even if justified in terms of the possibilities at hand, the budget of 13.5 million *contos* was 'insufficient for our necessities, and certainly timid for our ambitions' / 'insuficientes para nossas necessidades, e certamente acanhada para nossas ambições'. António de Oliveira Salazar, 'Plano de Fomento Nacional', *Boletim Geral do Ultramar* 29, 336–7 (1953), p. 31.

32 The regime executed three plans of planned economic stimulation: *I Plano de Fomento* (1953–58), *II Plano de Fomento* (1959–64), and *III Plano de Fomento* (1968–73). An intercalary plan was also executed from 1965 to 1967, the *Plano Intercalar de Fomento*.

33 'não já como um simples programa administrativo do Estado, mas como o instrumento de definição de uma política económica'. Marcelo Caetano, 'O planeamento económico em Portugal', in Marcelo Caetano and Carlos Krus Abecasis (eds), *Colóquio sobre o II Plano de Fomento: Ultramar* (Lisbon: Junta de Investigações do Ultramar – Centro de Estudos Políticos e Sociais 1959), p. 10.

34 In academic literature or in the documentation published in English by the Estado Novo, we could find no consensus regarding this nomenclature. Although, in

Portuguese, the term *Ultramar* (Overseas), stands as a noun to refer to the totality of the Portuguese territories in Africa and Asia, in English 'overseas' is generally, but not always, used as an adjective, thus associated with other terms, such as 'provinces', 'territories', 'administration', or 'development'. Although we have found publications in which the word 'Overseas' is used as a literal translation of *Ultramar*, in this paper we have chosen to employ the term as an adjective. In this regard, we have largely followed the terminology used in the English Section of the *Boletim Geral do Ultramar*. We must highlight, however, that the word *Ultramar* expresses better the Portuguese designs than the translation 'overseas provinces'. As a singular noun, *Ultramar* is the linguistic expression of the transcendental unity of the Nation, which is not so well captured by the term 'overseas provinces' or 'overseas territories'.

35 Valentim Alexandre, 'Ideologia, economia e política: a questão colonial na implantação do Estado Novo', *Análise Social* 28, 123–4 (1993), pp. 1117–36.

36 Heriberto Cairo, '"Portugal is not a small country": Maps and Propaganda in the Salazar Regime', *Geopolitics* 11, 3 (2006), pp. 367–95; see also Léonard, 'O Ultramar Português'.

37 'A unidade financeira do Mundo Português será uma afirmação de soberania equivalente a um bastear de bandeira. Será a consagração dos esforços de muitos séculos de acção civilizadora no Ultramar. Facilitará a circulação interna das pessoas, dos capitais e das mercadorias'. Fortuna, 'As finanças públicas do mundo português', p. 47.

38 Freyre, *O mundo que o português criou*; Gilberto Freyre, *O Luso e o Trópico: sugestões em torno dos métodos portugueses de integração de povos autóctones e de culturas diferentes da europeia num complexo de civilização: o luso-tropical* (Lisbon: Comissão Executiva das Comemorações do Infante D. Henrique 1961).

39 Cláudia Castelo, '*O modo português de estar no mundo': o luso-tropicalismo e a ideologia colonial portuguesa, 1933–1961* (Porto: Afrontamento 1998).

40 João Alberto da Costa Pinto, 'Gilberto Freyre e a intelligentsia salazarista em defesa do Império Colonial Português, 1951–1974', *História* 28, 1 (2009), pp. 445–82.

41 Castelo, '*O modo português de estar no mundo'*.

42 'Portugal [realizou] a descolonização através da História'. Joaquim Moreira da Silva Cunha, 'Portugal e o fenómeno da descolonização', *Boletim da Agência Geral do Ultramar* 39, 454–5 (1963), p. 47.

43 'O multi-racialismo, que hoje começa a ser citado e admitido pelos que praticamente o não aceitaram nunca, pode dizer-se uma criação portuguesa [...] Desse modo, não somos nós que temos de desviar-nos do caminho; são os outros que, em seu próprio interesse, deverão toma-lo'. António de Oliveira Salazar, 'Realidades da política portuguesa', *Boletim Geral do Ultramar* 39, 454–5 (1963), p. 16.

44 In fact, the Newspaper *O Século* describes the first official travel of the Minister of Finance, Águedo de Oliveira, to Angola, in which he defined the province as 'a new Brazil, that will remain forever Portuguese' / 'um novo Brasil, que ficará sempre português'. See 'Angola, um novo Brasil', *Boletim Geral do Ultramar* 27, 317 (1951), pp. 115–18.

45 For instance, Rosas and Brito describe how Portugal at first refused to adopt the Marshall Plan. The country would apply for US funding under the Plan only by the early 1950s, when it realised that it needed the funds for its development plans. Although Portugal did not receive the full value of what it had applied for, the capital was crucial in allowing the *Planos de Fomento* to proceed. See Fernando Rosas and José Maria Brandão de Brito, *Dicionário de História do Estado Novo* (Lisbon: Círculo de Leitores 2006).

46 Cláudia Castelo, *Passagens para África: o povoamento de Angola e Moçambique com naturais da metrópole, 1920–1974* (Porto: Afrontamento 2007).

47 In this sense, it was instrumental to early post-war discourse to compare Portuguese provinces with Rhodesia and South Africa, in order to make a point that in all these territories there was a population of 'white Africans' who should have their 'rights to Africa' recognised. However, with the increasing international criticism

of apartheid and other policies of racial discrimination, Portuguese discourse tended to highlight its provinces' difference from South Africa precisely through luso-tropicalism, while advancing the ambiguous argument that Portuguese settlers in the provinces should be taken as both 'Europeans' and 'white Africans'. In this regard, it is worth noting that luso-tropicalism also allowed Portugal to narrate itself as a Euro-African nation.

48 Marcello Caetano, 'Angola e Moçambique', *Boletim Geral do Ultramar* 30, 348–9 (1954), p. 95.

49 'a formação de comunidades multirraciais integradas, sem as quais não haverá em África nem progresso, nem ordem, nem civilização, nem direitos do homem'. Adriano Moreira, 'Política de integração', *Boletim Geral do Ultramar* 37, 434–5 (1961), p. 28.

50 The Corporative Chamber was an advisory body that represented the interests of cultural, economic, and social corporations in legislative matters, mainly by publishing reports and issuing statements on legislative matters. For an in-depth analysis of the role of the Corporative Chamber, see Nuno Miranda, 'A Câmara Corporativa no Estado Novo: composição, funcionamento e influência' (PhD dissertation, University of Lisbon, 2009). Available at: www.estig.ipbeja.pt/~ac_direito/MirandaF.pdf (accessed 14 March 2013).

51 'Deseja-se ainda que o maior número de famílias brancas das províncias da metropole constitua nas províncias ultramarinas núcleos vigorosos de colonização, . . . exercendo ali as suas tradicionais virtudes de colono português, [mantendo] bem vivos os sentimentos de colaboração fraternal com os outros portugueses indígenas do ultramar, amando-os e respeitando-os . . . sob o anseio fecundo da assimilação pelo exemplo e pelo coração, sob a iluminação da doutrina de Cristo'. Trigo de Morais 1953, quoted in José Fernando Nunes Barata, *Para uma política de população* (Lisbon: Junta de Investigação do Ultramar – Centro de Estudos Político-Sociais 1963), p. 144.

52 See José Bossa, 'Resumo dos princípios constitucionais por que se rege o território ultramarino de Portugal', *Boletim Geral do Ultramar* 28, 329 (1951), pp. 17–26.

53 'cada um dos grupos que se uniram para formar o povo português', Adriano Moreira, 'A unidade política e o estatuto das populações', *Boletim Geral do Ultramar* 36, 417 (1960), p. 120.

54 'consagrava legalmente a desigualdade estrutural no império e atribuía ao Estado o papel tutelar e de administração da progressiva assimilação da população nativa ao corpo político e espiritual da nação'. Omar Ribeiro Thomaz, '"O bom povo português": usos e costumes d'aquém e d'alem-mar', *Mana* 7, 1 (2001), p. 63, emphasis in the original.

55 'não haverá outra saída do ciclo de subdesenvolvimento que não seja pela via do trabalho'. Salazar, 'Realidades da política portuguesa', p. 20.

56 'Entre os princípios mais importantes que o Estatuto define estão aqueles em que estabelece o direito á cidadania, e promoção, por todos os meios, da melhoria das condições materiais e morais da vida dos indígenas, o desenvolvimento das suas aptidões e faculdades naturais, e o acesso ao ensino como forma superior de encaminhamento para a civilização'. Luís Forjaz Trigueiros, 'O estatuto dos indígenas e os valores morais', *Boletim Geral do Ultramar* 29, 347 (1954), p. 24.

57 Omar Ribeiro Thomaz, 'Tigres de Papel: Gilberto Freyre, Portugal e os países africanos de língua oficial portuguesa', in Cristina Bastos, Miguel Vale de Almeida, and Bela Feldman-Bianco (eds), *Trânsitos coloniais: diálogos críticos Luso-Brasileiros* (Lisbon: Imprensa de Ciências Sociais 2002), pp. 39–63.

58 For instance, during its existence the *Boletim Geral do Ultramar* published a very heterogeneous group of texts with the objective of documenting the material progress of the provinces. In this regard, there are numerous newspaper articles and reports on urbanisation, industries, railways, living conditions, medicine, and so on.

59 Freyre, *O Luso e o Trópico*.

60 'Assim que admira [a outras potências Europeias] que fizéssemos obra de homem para homem, mais do que construção onde avultasse o dinheiro e que levássemos

os nativos mais no humano e no espiritual que no económico; obra civilizadora e povoadora em vez de grande empreendimento tecnológico capitalista?!' Águedo de Oliveira, 'Velhas e novas ideias económicas: ao encontro da dualidade africana e das pressões internacionais', *Boletim Geral do Ultramar* 31, 363 (1955), p. 42.

61 'No caso Português, sobretudo, há que ter bem presentes of factores humanos que participam activamente nas múltiplas manifestações da vida activa nacional, na plena consciência de que nesta avultam etnias várias, ligadas entre si pelo sentimento lusíada, que é denominador comum desta singular nação que é Portugal . . . Importa por isso sublinhar . . . quão necessário é debruçarmo-nos sobre a vida das populações ultramarinas, pescrutar-lhes os movimentos no fluir das suas ansiedades, esperanças, aspirações ou inquietações. Só depois disso poderá dar-se expressão pragmática a uma política de desenvolvimento económico'. Águedo de Oliveira, 'Para uma política de desenvolvimento económico no ultramar português', *Boletim Geral do Ultramar* 39, 458–60 (1963), p. 74.

62 'O esforço nacional terá de visar à integração global da economia agrícola indígena, de preferência à sua desarticulação pela transferência de mão-de-obra para as "ilho-tas" da economia monetária, como haverá de procurar que à evolução económica se justaponha sistematicamente a integração das massas indígenas na comunidade espiritual da Nação'. Carlos Krus Abecasis, 'Prefácio', in Caetano and Abecasis (eds), *Colóquio sobre o II Plano de Fomento*, p. xii.

63 A full assessment of monetary and trade policies after 1961 is beyond the scope of this chapter. For a detailed description of these measures, see Adelino Torres, 'Mécanismes de la Zone Escudo, années 60–70', in Comité pour l'histoire économique et financière de la France (ed.), *La France et l'Outre-Mer: un siècle de relations monétaires et financières* (Paris: Ministère de l'économie, des finances et de l'industrie 1998), pp. 615–43.

64 For instance, in 1967, thus in the middle of the colonial war, Américo Tomás, Head of the State, read the following message to the Portuguese people: 'Our policy in Africa, product of some centuries of experience and wise conviviality, did not show to be wrong so far, as opposed to the ones adopted by other nations, less sensitive to the environment. And if we ignore the infiltrations from other nations that do not know the rules of good conviviality . . . we can affirm that in our territories in Africa there are peace, order and progress'/'A nossa política em África, fruto de alguns séculos de experiência e de sábio convívio, não se mostrou até agora errada, ao invés das adoptadas por outras nações, menos conhecedoras do meio. E se abstrairmos as infiltrações provenientes de países que não conhecem as regras de boa convivência . . . podemos afirmas que nos nossos territórios de África há paz, há ordem e há progresso'. Américo Tomás, 'Mensagem do Chefe de Estado', *Boletim Geral do* Ultramar 43, 499–500 (1967), p. 7.

65 'O racismo negro tenderá a prescindir de tudo quanto o branco mais progressivo pode levar [ao negro] em capital, trabalho, cultura. Seria mais assisado substituir o exclusivismo rácico pela colaboração que vimos ser imprescindível. É por isso que nós entendemos que o progresso económico, social e político daqueles territórios só será possível numa base multiracial'. Salazar, 'Realidades da política portuguesa', p. 23.

66 'A administração e o desenvolvimento económico dos territórios coloniais demon-strem progressos que desacreditem a capacidade governativa dos seus próprios países'. Afonso Mendes, 'Portugal em face do anticolonialismo: estudos e ensaios', *Ultramar* 6 (October–December 1961), p. 29.

67 'O desenvolvimento económico que temos vindo a pugnar para a nossa Comunidade Nacional só sera possível e eficiente desde que englobe, indistintamente, a promoção harmonica e conjunta de todas as etnias, nos campos económico e social, linha de rumo esta que não constitui qualquer novidade na nossa já tão longa acção ultramarina. Dado porém, que o nosso Ultramar se tornou num campo de bata de ideologias opostas, numa luta de vida ou de morte, da qual dependerá o nosso futuro, tudo nos aconselha a que, agora mais do que nunca, dediquemos uma atenção muito especial ao desenvolvimento económico e social das etnias que desde velha data

temos vindo a integrar e a assimilar. Não podemos de forma alguma descurar esta ingente e magna tarefa nacional, sob pena de retumbante fracasso'. A. Correia de Araújo, *Aspectos do desenvolvimento económico e social de Angola* (Lisbon: Junta de Investigações do Ultramar 1964), pp. 137–8.

68 A full assessment of these policies both in terms of their conceptualisation and implementation goes beyond the scope of our study. Here we are mostly interested in highlighting the ways in which they express the nexus between development and security, i.e. the securitisation of colonial development, during late Portuguese rule. For a detailed and extremely interesting study of both policies, see Gerald J. Bender, *Angola under the Portuguese: The Myth and the Reality* (Berkeley, Los Angeles: University of California Press 1978). Particularly in chapter 6, the author explores both military and developmental projects of *re-ordenamento rural*, while also discussing the paradigm of *desenvolvimento comunitário*.

69 'Para se conseguir arrancar as comunidades rurais nativas do nível atrasado em que por milénios têm vegetado, reconhece-se ser indispensável conquistar a boa vontade e activa colaboração. Há que admitir o fracasso ou mesmo os resultados contraproducentes dos métodos de coerção'. Grupo de Trabalho de Promoção Social de Moçambique, *Promoção Social em Moçambique* (Lisbon: Junta de Investigação do Ultramar 1964), p. 27.

70 'aqueles que recentemente descobriram a importância do desenvolvimento comunitário [em fóruns internacionais] estarão habilitados a entender, porventura com algum desgosto, que mais uma vez se encontram com soluções portuguesas'. Moreira, 'Política de integração', p. 14.

71 'são difíceis de avaliar, sobretudo porque os principais sucessos não são traduzíveis em números . . . é fácil deduzir que a evolução mental e social da população representa um grande passo no sentido do desenvolvimento'. Alfredo de Sousa, 'Desenvolvimento Comunitário', *Boletim Geral do Ultramar* 39, 454–5 (1963), p. 242.

72 'responsabilidade resultante da . . . participação no sistema defensivo do mundo livre'. Serviço Nacional de Informação, *O esforço do desenvolvimento económico português: o II Plano de Fomento* (Lisbon: Serviço Nacional de Informação 1959), p. 4.

73 Rosas, 'Estado Novo, império e ideologia imperial'.

74 Lawrence E. Harrison, *Who Prospers? How Cultural Values Shape Economic and Political Success* (New York: Basic Books 1992); David S. Landes, *The Wealth and Poverty of Nations: Why Some Are so Rich and Some so Poor* (New York: W.W. Norton 1998).

75 Landes, *The Wealth and Poverty of Nations*.

76 José Fernandes Fafe, *A colonização portuguesa e a emergência do Brasil* (Lisbon: Temas e Debates 2010).

CHAPTER THIRTEEN

The notion of 'développement' in French colonial discourses: changes in discursive practices and their social implications[1]

Françoise Dufour

The period between the end of the First World War and the independence of African nations around 1960 was marked by the passage from a colonial Discourse[2] based on 'progress of civilisation' ('progrès de la civilisation') to a post-colonial Discourse based on 'development', in which the development of Africa ('développement de l'Afrique')[3] refers to the process undertaken by former African colonies to achieve a certain level of economic development and well-being. The term *développement* had already been in use in colonial discourses, as part of the more general notion of 'civilisation' ('civilisation'). It definitively entered mainstream dialogue from the moment of independence onwards, but the term was not new. Already, at the beginning of the 1930s, it came to designate a shared, ideological notion.

This shift in the notions attached to the discursive use of *développement* could be considered the keystone of the French 'post-colonial order of discourse'. 'Post-colonial' in this context does not refer to a historical period, but to a Discourse which gradually emerged after the First World War and materialised with the rise of the Non-Aligned Movement following the Bandung Conference of 1955 and with the independence of most former colonies in the 1950s and 1960s.

In this chapter, I analyse the emergence of *développement* as an ideological notion on the basis of a corpus of French discourses on colonial and post-colonial Africa. The period that extends from the end of the First World War to the realisation of independent states, that is to say from the 1920s to the 1960s, saw changes in discursive practices, with the formation of development Discourse as a dominant ideological Discourse. What I propose here is to analyse the reformulation of the 'colonial Discourse' becoming a 'development Discourse', focusing specifically on the discursive shifts in the *linguistic* representations of African nations and peoples as 'engines of social change'.[4]

The discourse analysis methodology

Researchers dealing with issues of development, colonialism or post-colonialism encounter a broad variety of texts: political speeches, legal documents (decrees and laws), reports, projects and programmes, letters, diaries, texts from newspapers and other media. Research in history or political science relies mainly on the content of these documents. The content analysis is based on the transparency of discourse, whereas discourse I would maintain is opaque: there is an 'illusion that the map corresponds to the territory'.[5] Historical events pertain to the past and researchers have no direct access to them. As Paul Veyne sets out: 'History is a narrative of events . . . in no case is what historians call an event captured directly and fully: it is always captured incompletely and sideways through documents or testimony, that is to say through *tekmeria*, traces'.[6]

Events and acts related to the construction of French dominance over Africa are only attainable by means of discourses which capture and objectify them. The scholarly works of historians and anthropologists, but also literary work and popular reports have contributed to the production of knowledge concerning the relations between France and Africa. What can be accessed are not these relations in their essence, but the discourses on them, and accordingly I agree with Pierre Achard: 'Discourse on history makes part of history'.[7]

Discourse Analysis offers a different approach to the analysis of corpora. It is interested not only in what the writers tell us about the events but first and foremost in analysing the ways in which they express their narrative, i.e. the very forms of the linguistic elements[8] they use – reformulations, various modalities, the way the discourse is organised and structured, the agency of representations, echoes of voices, and so on – which constitute the 'materiality' of discourse.

Analysing the linguistic materiality in a variety of discourses that address the same object during the same period in similar contexts makes it possible to identify recurring discursive practices. Discourses, with reference to Michel Foucault, are not simply treated as sets of signs which denote objects 'but as practices that systematically form the objects of which they speak'. Foucault expanded his argument as follows: 'Of course, discourses are composed of signs; but what they do is more than use these signs to designate things. It is this *more* that renders them irreducible to the language (*la langue*) and to speech. It is this "more" that we must reveal and describe'.[9]

Discursive practices are made up through the use of cognitive[10] representations or 'notions', which Antoine Culioli describes as 'complex bundle[s] of structured physico-cultural properties'.[11] Notions are 'constructions of organized representations', linked to states of knowledge and to the activity of elaboration of experiences that 'allow intersubjective adjustment'.[12] They 'are apprehended and established through occurrences', but 'should not be equated with lexical labels or actual items'.[13] The occurrences are terms with a high degree of generality which best embody the notions and constitute notional domains. The recurrent use of *développement* representing the corresponding notion of development constitutes discursive practices shared by a community.

Discursive practices are one form of social practices which interact with and act on the production of other social practices. The methodological apparatus in discourse analysis enables the researcher 'to look at language in society in ways that allow [her or him] simultaneously to focus on linguistic form and on social environment and to avoid a discontinuity between various levels of explanation'.[14] The way linguistic forms constructing utterances are organised (or 'enunciative agency') lays out ways of acting, that is to say it maps out the actor's respective experiences. The particular discursive representations of experience and degree of responsibility in the act determine the status of social actors. The placing of linguistic forms therefore may have socio-political implications and play a role in the configuration of the socio-political arena.

By using recurring discursive practices shared by her or his community the speaker (or writer) identifies her/himself – wittingly or unwittingly – with the dominant ideology. The term 'ideology', as defined by Louis Althusser,[15] means an imaginary representation of the reality that is shared and taken for granted by a socio-discursive community. It exists through acts inserted into practices regulated by social rituals: a phrase, a prayer, a look, a handshake, a verbal discourse, external or internal conscience. For his part, Foucault decided to coin the concept of 'discursive formation', 'thus avoiding words that are already over laden with conditions and consequences, and in any case inadequate to the task of designating such a dispersion, such as "science", "ideology", "theory", or "domain of objectivity"'.[16]

The plurality of discourses on development constitutes the discursive formation of development, or development ideology (what we commonly express through 'development Discourse'), even if such discourses are antagonistic. Indeed, any notion – such as development – is constructed with and from antagonistic points of view: pros and cons. To Foucault, 'a discursive formation is not, therefore, an ideal, continuous, smooth text that runs beneath the multiplicity of contradictions . . . It is rather a space of multiple dissensions, a set of different oppositions whose levels and roles must be described'.[17]

Any notional domain pertaining to a given discursive formation is composed of two facets: the interior or positive facet and the exterior or negative facet, which is the complement of the positive one. In *La force du préjugé: essai sur le racisme et ses doubles* (1988), Pierre-André Taguieff for instance defends the idea that anti-racism is the negative double of racism.[18] Anti-racism Discourse, when opposing racism with the use of the term, activates the interior of the notional domain of racism (which is 'primitive' in the construction of the domain) and contributes to its existence. Concerning development, although the universality of the notion is controversial, it connotes, to many, a positive representation difficult to oppose.

A discursive formation can be characterised as a set of discursive practices that pervade time, space, and events. It is inside a discursive formation, as Michel Pêcheux suggested, that meaning is constituted: 'A word, a phrase, or a proposition do not have a meaning fixed to their literal form, but their sense originates in each discursive formation in relation to other words, phrases or propositions of the same formation'.[19] A change in meaning depends on the (ideological) position of the speaker or writer, but may also be induced by a transfer of elements from one discursive formation to another. In a preceding argument Pêcheux also argued: 'If one acknowledges that words, phrases or propositions change their sense passing from one discursive formation to another, one has also to concede that *literally different*[20] words, phrases and propositions may, within a given discursive formation, have the same meaning'.[21]

It is therefore interesting to reason whether the post-colonial term *développement* produces the same meaning as the prevailing colonial notion of '(progrès de la) civilisation'. The discursive shift from 'civilisation' to 'développement' could be interpreted as indicative of a recomposed discursive formation and consequently have impacts in social terms. A discursive analysis of linguistic markers on a long-term basis may provide an answer to this question.

The different discursive uses of 'development'

It has been said that the term 'development' was popularised as an international catchword by the Inaugural Address of US President Harry Truman on 20 January 1949 when he spoke of 'a bold new program for making the benefits of our scientific advances and industrial progress available for the improvement and growth of *underdeveloped areas*' and announced that the United States ('we') would 'foster capital investment in *areas needing development*'.[22]

[325]

This announcement is commonly perceived as the starting point for the global business of development aid and development planning. In many scientific and public discourses Truman's speech is treated as 'the invention of development'. Nevertheless, the word 'development' was not unknown in the discursive formation up to then and already had a long history.[23] Layers of meaning had accumulated in its extensive journey through previous discourses.

In my research I explore the uses of the term *développement* over a period of more than two hundred years in different sources. The corpus consists of roughly 150 texts representing multiple genres such as scientific treatises, accounts of projects of colonisation, travel reports, development programmes, political speeches, and essays. These documents highlight three different periods: the early phase of the construction of a colonial matrix, the colonial epoch, and the era of development aid.

The exploration of the corpora with the textometry software Hyperbase[24] helps to identify various uses of the word *développement* in different sources and by various speakers and writers: philosophers, anthropologists, ministers, army colonels, colonial governors, and so on. The following list gives a rough overview of the outcome: (a) 'the development of our abilities' ('le développement de nos facultés'),[25] 'the intellectual and moral development of these primitive peoples' ('le développement moral et intellectuel de ces populations primitives');[26] (b) 'the development of the social and intellectual state; the development of the external and general circumstances and of the internal and personal human nature, in a word, the development of society and humanity' ('le développement de l'état social, et celui de l'état intellectuel; le développement de la condition extérieure et générale, et celui de la nature intérieure et personnelle de l'homme; en un mot, le perfectionnement de la société et de l'humanité'),[27] 'the development of societies' ('le développement des sociétés'),[28] 'the development of the human race' ('le développement de l'humanité');[29] (c) 'the development of civilization' ('le développement de la civilisation');[30] (d) 'the development of agriculture or trade' ('le développement agricole ou commercial'),[31] 'the development of trade in this region' ('le développement du commerce dans cette région'),[32] 'economic development' ('le développement économique'),[33] 'the economic development of underdeveloped countries' ('le développement économique des pays sous-développés');[34] (e)'the development of our French Sudan' ('le développement de notre Soudan français'),[35] 'the development of our African Empire' ('le développement de notre empire africain'),[36] 'the development of West and East Africa' ('le développement de l'Afrique occidentale et orientale'),[37] 'You will explore ... which conditions ... may seem possible to you to apply gradually in each of our territories, so that, by their very development and the progress of their people, they may integrate into the French community' ('Vous étudierez ... quelles conditions ... vous paraissent pouvoir être progressivement appliquées dans chacun de nos territoires, afin que, par leur développement même et le progrès de leur population, ils s'intègrent dans la communauté française'),[38] 'the development of our Overseas Territories' ('le développement de nos Territoires d'Outre-Mer'),[39] 'the whole of our views and approaches which guide [the French Sudan's] development' ('l'unité de vues et de doctrines qui préside à son [le Soudan] développement'),[40] 'the development of Black Africa' ('le développement de l'Afrique noire').[41]

The listing above highlights what is extensively documented in my dissertation: a gradual decrease of discursive uses (a), (b), and (c), which first appeared in the Enlightenment discourse.[42] They were later re-activated in the colonial context, having their emphasis on the development of civilisation, humanity and society. Uses of (d) and (e) are characteristic for the later period of colonialism, particularly after the First World War, and have a focus on the economic component: 'economic development' and 'development' of a given country or region.

'Développement' as a property of the 'progrès de la civilisation' in the Enlightenment

The examples presented above under (a), (b), and (c) show how early French colonial Discourse was inspired by the Discourse of the Enlightenment. We know from their life stories that certain colonial politicians were influenced by this ideology.[43] Jules Ferry (1832–93), who several times served as the Minister of Public Instruction and is considered one of the chief architects of French colonisation, had read the works of Condorcet, the famous Enlightenment philosopher and mathematician, especially his *The Nature and Purpose of Public Instruction* (1791–92).[44]

One of the declared goals of French colonisation was the 'progress of civilisation' ('progrès de la civilisation') everywhere in the world and especially in territories whose inhabitants were considered to be 'savages' ('sauvages') or 'primitives' ('primitifs'). 'Progrès de la civilisation' referred to the 'humanitarian' motive for colonisation which was invoked to justify the safeguarding of French economic and political interests.[45] In the Enlightenment Discourse, 'développement' was one of the characteristic properties of 'progrès de la civilisation'. 'Civilisation', both as a state and a process, was shaped by the idea of 'infinite advancement', the limits of which were constantly being pushed forward. Condorcet (and others) considered the French and the Anglo-Americans to represent the most advanced state of civilisation. He doubted if those defined as 'Others' and characterised by 'bondage', 'ignorance', and 'savagery', could ever transcend the 'immense distance' separating them from 'civilisation'.[46]

The notion of civilisation has often been defined in conjunction with progress and development, both of which served as reformulations for civilisation, as in the following description by François Guizot, a French historian and Minister of Public Instruction (1832–34): 'It seems to me that the first idea comprised in the word civilisation ... is the notion of progress, of development'.[47] In Guizot's discourse, civilisation consists in the development of the intellectual and of the social spheres: 'the development of society and humanity' as quoted above.[48]

In Condorcet's discourse, civilisation is a process to develop human perfectibility in a universalist vision of 'Humanity', that is nonetheless evolutionist and ethnocentric. In the Discourse of the Enlightenment, all humanity moves towards civilisation, often designated as 'la Civilisation' in French discourses, with an uppercase character C and the definite article *la*, which implies a unique civilisation for the whole world. Consequently, the 'most civilised' peoples identified as 'the French and the Anglo-Americans' are located at the top of the ladder leading up to progress and conversely the 'savages' identified as the 'African tribes' are on the lowest rung, at the 'first [lowest] position of civilisation'.[49] In this typology, development of human perfectibility was part of a quest for civilisation.

The emergence of the ideology of development as a shared notion

Recent critical approaches to development have identified President Truman's 1949 inaugural speech as the place where the term 'development' was introduced first without any nominal expansion.[50] This signifies a process towards the essentialisation of the notion and the forming of a shared ideology. Following the discursive strands of 'civilisation' and 'development' we can observe that they are both nouns derived from verbal roots and experienced the same discursive evolution. The following examples may illustrate the argument. First, extended by a nominal expansion (adjective or noun) *développement* and *civilisation* were used, on the one hand, to denote the process (of developing or civilising), and on the other, for the result that follows the process, the state of being civilised or developed. For example, 'civilisation of primitive peoples' can express both the action

[328]

of civilising peoples and the state of civilisation reached by primitive peoples. Laurent-Basile Hautefeuille, a lawyer at the royal court presented in 1830 his 'Project to colonise the French possessions in West Africa by means of the civilisation of the indigenous negroes' (*Plan de colonisation des possessions françaises dans l'Afrique occidentale au moyen de la civilisation des nègres indigènes*). Here, the word *civilisation* refers to a process of 'civilising' the indigenous, but in the same text, Hautefeuille also uses *civilisation* to denote a state of being: 'We have to analyse carefully what is the state of the negroes' civilisation'.[51] In the same way, when in 1960 de Gaulle calls for the 'development of our territories of Africa' he means both the process of development (the action of developing territories) and its result (the state of development reached by the said territories): 'Within the *Communauté*, Mali and the French Republic ... will cooperate with all their zeal to further their own development and that of all people'.[52] Or, as Moreau phrases it: 'Black Africa ... must be supported by the Metropolis to reach its complete development'.[53]

Secondly, *développement* and *civilisation* without nominal expansion express the notions of 'civilisation' or 'development' in general: they are self-sufficient. This use bestows a kind of legitimacy and high value to the act and the result, as in: 'These tribes have never understood the benefits of civilization';[54] or: 'Our commitment towards West Africa, towards Equatorial Africa, is to ensure that they attain the [degree of] development that we have been able to give to North Africa'.[55]

While the early phase of French colonialism was justified by referring to the 'mission to civilise', a new argument came to the fore at the end of the First World War: 'The enhancement of the French colonies' ('La mise en valeur des colonies françaises'). The proliferation of the phrase can be linked to a draft law put before the French Parliament in 1921 by Albert Sarraut, the Minister of Colonies (1920–24 and 1932–33). Although Sarraut saw his initiative blocked for financial reasons, his programme which was published as a book in 1923 influenced colonial policies in several territories.[56] The project focused on the improvement of colonial infrastructure and on productive investment, but also included aspects of social development: its holistic approach addressed 'amendments of a moral, intellectual, political and social kind, closely linked to concrete, material implementations'.[57]

The formula 'mise en valeur' was not completely new in the colonial discursive formation. Other occurrences are to be found earlier in the corpus of texts, as for instance in Etienne Richet's *Le problème colonial*, published 1919, or George Hardy's 1921 dissertation, *La mise en valeur du Sénégal de 1817 à 1854*. Although not fully implemented, Sarraut's programme signified the transition from the colonial pact of dependence (which obliged the colonies to produce raw materials for the profit of the metropole) to a development based on the French model of 'association', which assigned each participant his specific role in a modernised colonial system of exploitation. Sarraut's description of 'association' attempts to paper over the exploitative aspects of modernisation by projecting a more idealistic and collaborative relationship: 'The operation is no longer unilateral: it is conceived for the advantage and the good of both parties; there is no more spoliation of one race by another but *association*, according to the successful formula that has become the motto of our colonial policy'.[58]

The colonial infrastructure programme included railway projects in Africa, among which the Trans-Saharan was meant to answer the twofold goal of transporting raw material to the metropolis and bringing 'social progress' to the local population. As the Comité du Transsaharien which was founded in 1927 optimistically forecasted: '[The Trans-Saharan railway] will allow the *mise en valeur* of our Black Africa. It will promote the development of raw materials that we need for our industries and drain them to the metropolitan area. The Trans-Saharan railway will be an instrument of social progress in French Africa and an element of national safeguard for France itself'.[59]

The formula 'mise en valeur des colonies' in Sarraut's discourse thus has a value of what Quentin Skinner called 'linguistic action', in which the claimant uses the 'inherited normative vocabularies [in] ways in which we are capable of reappraising and changing our world by changing the ways in which these vocabularies are applied'.[60] The conceptual change then is used as a political instrument. As Kari Palonen notes: 'For Skinner, concepts are not stable entities, they can be changed at any moment, and they exist only "in movement", that is, when they are used as moves, as political instruments of action'.[61]

From Sarraut's perspective, the colonial 'territories' are viewed as enterprises or ventures and the local populations as a workforce that needs to be educated to produce and to consume in accordance with the logic of the market economy. This way of associating the social progress of the populations in the overseas territories with their direct inclusion both as a workforce and as a future consumer market occurs repeatedly in colonial documents and speeches of French politicians.

With the use of 'development' as a term focusing on economic aspects, a new discursive practice emerged in the 1920s and 1930s in conjunction with 'civilisation', which was still in circulation. There is a system of co-occurrence of both terms in the same discursive formation during this period. Both terms may even appear together within a single discourse, such as 'civilising' and 'development' in the discourse of a Malian radio officer in 1951: 'Settlers, traders, colonial officers brought the civilising mandate . . . The successful evolution of our old Sudan lies in the unity of views and doctrines that govern its development'.[62] Although both terms are used in this discourse fragment, we can nevertheless observe that 'civilising' is linked to past events ('settlers *brought*') whereas 'development' is associated with the present.

This emerging practice of a development Discourse can be explained by the impact of various circumstances, including, for example, the rising demand for emancipation in the colonies, the weakening of France in the two world wars, a growing number of French educated African intellectuals critical of colonial rule, and the foundation of the United Nations organisation. In this emerging new political context the paradigm of 'civilisation' was increasingly perceived as Eurocentric while the prevalence of 'development' as a shared notion led to the emergence of a new paradigm: 'underdeveloped' vs. 'developed' countries, which increasingly served as a substitute, and eventually replacement, for the henceforth politically incorrect 'savage' vs. 'civilised'. Consequently, 'development' was no longer conceived as a property of the more general notion of 'progress of civilisation' ('progrès de la civilisation'), but gained the full status of a notion *per se*. The notion or term 'development' began to be operator in the redistribution of roles in the enunciative agency as well as in the social order.

'Development': an integrative process

The very forms of the new paradigm derived from the term 'development' indicate a new 'order of discourse' in the Foucauldian sense that is characterised by a continuous process of integration of the 'Other', recognised as a potential, future 'Same'.[63] The main change lies in the names given to groups of countries according to their level of development: 'developed' vs. 'underdeveloped'. Both adjectival past participles share the same verbal root 'develop', whereas previously in the colonial ideology of civilisation only one part of the world was considered as 'civilised', so that consequently there was no term derived from the root 'civilise' that might have been attributed to the less civilised or under-civilised. People regarded as 'not civilised' were called 'primitives', 'savages', 'barbarians', or 'backward people', as shown in the following quotation: 'The territory of the black barbarians will certainly open to European civilisation and the immense backward family is ready to answer ourcall'.[64]

In the colonial Discourse, the names given to different groups of people constitute two distinct categories separated by a 'boundary'.[65] The constitutive properties of one group are not to be found in the other. While in civilisation's discourses, some peoples in Africa are said to be 'oppressed', civilised nations are known to be 'free': freedom is one of the properties of civilisation identified in Condorcet's *Esquisse* (1794). African people were said to be 'retarded' or 'backward' while France, as a 'civilised' nation, was an 'advanced' nation ('pays avancé'). 'Progress' is also a property of civilisation. In the colonial Discourse, which was inspired by Enlightenment values that were manipulated to benefit colonial policies, the category of the 'Same', called the 'civilised', is organised through a 'predicative relation'[66] that could be expressed as follows: 'to be civilised' or 'to have the properties of civilised nations'. It could also be realised through the word that has the highest capacity of generalisation, what Pierre Achard called an 'operator'; that is 'civilization'.[67]

The linguistic units identified as possessing the necessary and sufficient properties of 'civilisation' constitute the category of the 'Same': progress, freedom, family, political institutions, laws, government, property, sciences, industry, education, written language. The linguistic units inverting those properties form a 'complement' by way of 'differentiation': backwardness, ignorance, tribes, orality.[68] The 'Same' and its complement constitute a class of occurrences associated with a 'notional domain' in which the 'Same' is the Interior (I) and the complement is the Exterior (E): the complement is constitutively defined by not possessing the properties of the 'Same'. E is constructed from I by differentiation (E = non I). Consequently, the message contained in I is dominant and because of this dominance, the predicative relation acts like an injunction: 'Be civilised!' which means: 'Be free, advanced, rich, industrialised!' The role of an operator (as in this case 'civilisation') is to generate a family of 'derived forms (from which it will be possible to construct a paraphrastic family of *énoncés*)'[69] and to organise all the occurrences which lie in its enunciative scope.

The emergence of the new paradigm of development integrating all humanity into one is then a 'linguistic action' which has the dimension of a social and political act. The very forms of designations such as 'pays *en développement*', or 'pays *en voie de développement*'[70] enjoin the so-called countries to advance gradually towards the same state of progress (the Western dominant one). The linguistic evidence of this integrative process is the sharing of the same verbal root (develop-) forming the linguistic names of the different elements constituting the notional domain: *dévelop*pé, sous-*dévelop*pé, en *dévelop*pement. The operator *développement* organises a domain, where the 'Others' are in the process of entering the Interior to become more or less adapted to the 'Same'.

The following examples highlight how these new ways of naming indicate a willingness of integration into the Interior of the notional domain. The UN General Assembly called its Resolution 198 (III) (4 December 1948) 'Economic Development of *underdeveloped* countries'. The title was translated into French as '*Développement économique des pays* insuffisamment développés', which, translated back into English, literally gives: 'Economic development of *insufficiently developed* countries'. In a similar way, the French Ministry for the Colonies (1894–1945) became the Ministry for Overseas France (1946–58).

Integration, but into the margins of the category

The phrase 'insufficiently developed countries' indicates a lack of development. Nevertheless the countries are not considered 'undeveloped'. The adverb 'insufficiently' imparts that there is deficiency, but not that there is no development at all. In other words, entities described as 'underdeveloped' are located in the margins of the category of developed countries. As such, they are encouraged to strive for a standard of living and to act politically and economically in ways that are considered acceptable, based on (mainly economic) criteria established by international political and scientific actors.

The French epithet *sous-développés* troubled French speakers and they tried to replace it, as illustrated by the following discourse fragment: 'Countries we call "underdeveloped" but which we could also call countries "with retarded economic development" . . . Which countries are they? . . . let us simply say that they are countries or regions which have not yet fully exploited their natural resources and where, for various reasons, the standard of living is very low'.[71]

Another strategy to distance oneself from a name is also encountered in regard to the use of the nominal locution 'least developed countries' ('pays les moins avancés'), which is very often used in French texts with quotes and the expression 'so-called', as in the so-called 'less advanced' countries.[72] Western politicians and journalists feel uncomfortable when those epithets are directed at their African counterparts because they perceive that the representation of African peoples as inferiors might cause them 'to lose face'. Reformulations such as 'pays en développement' or 'pays en voie de développement' were coined as a consequence to pay tribute to the request for 'political correctness', which characterises the discourses of the global aid community since the late 1980s.

But in 1956 'insufficiently developed' was still being used and discussed. Luc Fauvel back then published an article with the title 'L'O.N.U. et les pays insuffisamment développés'. In the article, he admonished the United Nations for being responsible for a misleading discussion on the subject: 'What does one mean by underdeveloped countries? It is difficult to give a scientific definition and it is indeed a fine subject of discussion for experts, because the concept has swiftly met with passionate responses. The vocabulary has evolved. At first we talked of *economically backward* countries. But the word "backward" carries pejorative connotations for many people. So we came to "underdeveloped". This epithet has in turn been worn out. "Under" may offend the hyper-sensitive. So we prefer to use the adverb "insufficiently" that, for the time being seems more diplomatic'.[73]

One way of making sensitive attributes such as 'backward' acceptable has been to restrict the 'backwardness' to economics alone. GDP (Gross Domestic Product) has thus been instituted as the major evaluator of the level of development in a country, in economic terms, as declared in UN Resolutions 198 (III) (4 December 1948) – 'Economic Development of underdeveloped countries' – and in 142 (VII) (11 August 1948) – 'Development of the under-industrialised countries'.

Preservation of the order of dominance

In the dialectic paradigm 'developed vs. underdeveloped' or 'insufficiently developed', the 'developed' countries that best represent the notion of development are recognised as poles of reference or 'types'.[74] In previous discursive formations based on 'civilisation', occidental nations appear as the actors 'on top of the ladder' (as documented above through reference to Condorcet). In a similar way, France and its allies (mainly Great Britain and the United States) were designated types for 'developed' nations or the best representatives of development in the development Discourse. That Great Britain, and later the United States, were France's main competitors in the colonial conquest and later in the contest for economic and political control over Africa, did not matter in this context.

France offered itself as a leader and role-model for other countries: a 'type' in discursive terms. When in the mid-1940s Charles de Gaulle opened the Brazzaville Conference (which he himself called an 'African conference', even though the attendees were all French colonial officers and Western journalists), he called France 'the nation whose immortal genius is designated for initiatives which, by degrees, raise men to the heights of dignity and fraternity where, someday, all may unite' and therefore he saw no other nation more suited to lead the sixty million colonised subjects into new, modern times than France.[75] More than sixty years later another French President, Nicolas Sarkozy, made a similar declaration, but worded in a quite different way. In a speech at the University of Dakar he presented a long list of duties to young

Africans and defined France as the actor who was ready to join them in their efforts, if, and only if, they accepted the French to-do list – 'if you choose democracy, liberty, justice and the law', thus defining the necessary and sufficient features to engage in 'codéveloppement', one of the recently introduced reformulations of the notion of development: 'What France wants to do with Africa is co-development, that is to say shared development'.[76] The order of dominance is clearly visible: in the enunciative agency, the 'developed countries' are positioned as agents of processes, as the responsible actors, while 'under-developed countries' are 'experiencing actants', partakers who are the location of ascriptions.[77]

In the dominant discourses, under-developed countries are not represented as agents of the processes whereby they might transform their conditions on their own. What they do at most is to express a 'need', a 'want' or an 'intention': 'Ten million Algerians need to solve the problem of food and underemployment, millions of blacks want access to a modern economy. They all intend to produce for a better living'.[78]

While 'development' is conceived as an integrative notion, the distribution of roles in the enunciative agency helps to produce and maintain dominance. The representation of 'Others' as non-agents is a means of confining them to a certain type of social role. The inequality represented in the enunciative agency carries the implicit value of an injunction: it designates a dominated social place while there is an injunction to reach the heart of the category of 'Others' by raising standards of living.

Conclusion

Development as Discourse constitutes the materiality of an integrative ideology compared to the colonial Discourse which places a 'frontier' between the 'Same' and the 'Others'. Within the period 1920–60 when post-colonial Discourse came to the fore, particular attention was paid to the well-being of the colonised for both humanist and economic reasons. All discursive actants – and the social actors they represent – became included within the unique category of development. The former colonies, renamed as the Territories of Overseas France after the Second World War, entered the 'development family' and as such they were (and still are) subjected to the ideology of economic growth.

Although the post-colonial Discourse places the colonised within the notional domain of 'development', they are represented as situated in and belonging to the margins of the category. Marginal elements, formerly the 'Third World' and today the global 'South', are represented as not controlling their destiny, traced by the dominant values of the 'North'.[79] To gain independence could have been considered a threshold of entry into a new discursive formation, the era of development. But for African societies this was not the moment when a paradigmatic shift occurred; the same agency which perpetuates the prevailing order of dominance was and is maintained.

The co-occurrence of an injunction for integration and the unequal status that appears in the enunciative agency has the character of a contradiction. This apparent contradiction is constitutive of the discursive formation of development. At the one hand, we have the search for integration and the broad constitution of the 'Same' (recently realised by overwhelming discourses on partnership and participation), and on the other, the globalised context of the market economy, subject to the political and economic constraints of marking differences. While the colonial ideology of civilisation was imposed by force against the will of the colonised peoples, development is a shared ideology which it seems difficult to oppose. There are nevertheless activists (belonging to civil society or the academic community) who became aware of the new type of dominance encapsulated in 'development'. Former Malian Minister of Culture, Aminata Traoré, commented on the linguistic aspect of dominance as follows: 'How then should we name the legitimate hope of recovering our economic, political, social and cultural rights, when words, not only ring false, but add to human misery. Why couldn't we be creative and draw on the rich linguistic heritage of the continent for the concepts that speak of humanity and its environment, and that make sense for the peoples ... It is up to the actors and organizations of African societies to make this creative effort'.[80]

Aminata Traoré had clearly perceived that appropriating dominant words and expressions that circulate the related ideology helps to perpetuate a certain state of power. It is indeed a characteristic of ideology that using one element of the paradigm – even in an opposing sense – activates the ideology, helps its circulation, and contributes to the preservation of dominance. It is, therefore, indeed difficult to escape! The re-organisation of the enunciative agency in the development Discourse, visible for instance in the use of euphemisms like 'the South' for naming the poorest countries of the planet is a 'politically correct' way to maintain a certain distribution of roles and places in the social sphere.[81] As for *civilisation* in the colonial Discourse, the post-colonial use of *développement* produces effects of consensus, and the term can be seen as a watchword for countries evaluated by the international community as 'insufficiently' developed. It is not only the strength of the semantic content of the word itself that has social implications, but the reproduction of the same agency of representations that reproduces a form of dominant model taken for granted all over the world. To refer again to Michel Pêcheux on the change (respective retention) of meaning, 'one has also to concede that literally different words, phrases and propositions may, within a given discursive formation, have the same meaning'.[82]

Notes

1 I should like to thank Janice Valls-Russell for reading this essay and her suggestions and Walter Schicho for editing the first version of my essay.

2 I use 'Discourse' with a capital D in reference to the discursive materiality of the ideology circulating through a 'discursive formation' and 'discourse' with a small 'd' when I refer to the discursive activity of a specific speaker or writer.

3 The meaning of key terms discussed here – such as *développement* – in the context of French colonial and post-colonial Discourse might not match the meaning that their translation into English could produce. That is why I propose a translation of these terms in brackets when they first occur in the text, but stick to the use of the French form in the following occurrences.

4 Quentin Skinner, *Visions of Politics*, vol. 1, *Regarding Methods* (Cambridge: Cambridge University Press 2002), p. 178.

5 Pierre Achard, 'La passion du développement: une analyse de l'économie politique' (Thèse de lettres, Université Paris 7, 1989), p. 12. This and the following quotations from French sources are my translations.

6 Paul Veyne, *Comment on écrit l'histoire: essai d'épistémologie* (Paris: Éditions du Seuil 1971), pp. 14–15.

7 Achard, 'La passion du développement', p. 834.

8 What, in linguistics, we call 'linguistic markers'.

9 Michel Foucault, *The Archeology of Knowledge and the Discourse on Language* (New York: Vintage Books 2010), p. 49, emphasis in the original.

10 'Cognitive' is used in an extensive way – not only restricted to mental cognition but also including social cognition.

11 Antoine Culioli, *Pour une linguistique de l'énonciation*, vol. 1, *Opérations et représentations* (Paris: Ophrys 1990), p. 69.

12 Antoine Culioli, *Pour une linguistique de l'énonciation*, vol. 2, *Domaine notionnel* (Paris: Ophrys 1999), p. 12.

13 Culioli, *Pour une linguistique de l'énonciation*, vol. 1, p. 69.

14 Jan Blommaert, *Discourse* (Cambridge: Cambridge University Press 2005), p. 16.

15 Louis Althusser, 'Idéologie et appareils idéologiques d'état (Notes pour une recherche)', in Louis Althusser, *Positions, 1964–1975* (Paris: Les Éditions sociales 1976), pp. 106–8.

16 Foucault, *The Archeology of Knowledge*, p. 38.

17 Ibid., p. 155.

18 André Taguieff, *La force du préjugé: essai dur le racisme et ses doubles* (Paris: Gallimard 1988).

19 Michel Pêcheux, *Les vérités de La Palice: linguistique, sémantique, philosophie* (Paris: Maspéro 1975), p. 145.

20 Here and elsewhere in the text, the emphasis is mine, unless otherwise stated.

21 Pêcheux, *Les vérités de La Palice*, p. 144.

22 Harry S. Truman, 'Inaugural Address', 20 January 1949. Available at: www. trumanlibrary.org/calendar/viewpapers.php?pid=1030 (accessed 25 March 2013).

23 For the history of the notion/term *développement*/'development' see Françoise Dufour, 'Des rhétoriques coloniales à celles du développement: archéologie discursive d'une dominance' (Thèse de doctorat, Université de Montpellier, 2007), pp. 143–71.

Available at: http://tel.archives-ouvertes.fr/docs/00/20/26/72/PDF/TheseFDufour.pdf (accessed 8 May 2013).

24 Hyperbase is a documentary and statistical software for textual data analysis (textual statistics) developed by Etienne Brunet in Nice (BCL laboratory).

25 Marquis de Condorcet, Jean-Antoine-Nicolas de Caritat, *Esquisse d'un tableau historique des progrès de l'esprit humain* (Paris: Flammarion 1998 [1794]), p. 87.

26 Archives Nationales d'Outremer, Aix en Provence (hereafter ANOM), Alg/gga/24H/73, manuscript of Antoine Marie Paul Godefroy, *Transsahariens et transafricains* (Paris: Laroze 1919), no pagination.

27 François Pierre Guillaume Guizot, *Cours d'histoire moderne: histoire de la civilisation en France depuis la chute de l'Empire romain jusqu'en 1789*, vol. 1 (Paris: Pichon et Didier 1829), p. 8.

28 Paul Leroy-Beaulieu, *De la colonisation chez les peuples modernes* (Paris: Guillaumin 1870), p. xv.

29 Olivier de Sanderval, *Kahel: carnet de voyages* (Paris: Félix Alcan 1893), p. 28.

30 Laurent-Basile Hautefeuille, *Plan de colonisation des possessions françaises dans l'Afrique occidentale au moyen de la civilisation des nègres indigènes* (Paris: Librairie de Levasseur 1830), p. 15.

31 ANOM, FM SG SEN/IV/46, Prosper de Chasseloup-Laubat, 'Rapport à l'Empereur', June 1860.

32 Louis Léon César Faidherbe, *Le Soudan français: chemin de fer de Médine au Niger* (Lille: Danel 1881), p. 505.

33 Archives Nationales du Mali, Notes and documents, R. R. 'Le rapport de l'organisme d'études', 1928.

34 UN General Assembly, December 1948; quoted after Gilbert Rist, *Le développement: histoire d'une croyance occidentale* (Paris: Presses de Sciences Po 1996), p. 121.

35 ANOM, BIB AOM B/7070, Gustave Humbert, 'La France au Soudan'. Paper presented at the Congrès annuel de la Société d'Économie Sociale, Paris, 26 May 1891, p. 23.

36 B. Vivier de Streel, *Le transsaharien, instrument indispensable de la défense et de l'expansion nationale* (Angoulême: Coquemard 1922), not paginated.

37 Eugène Gross, *Faut-il faire le Transsaharien?* (Oran: Éditions Heinz 1927), p. 23.

38 Charles de Gaulle, 'Discours de Brazzaville, 30 Janvier 1944'. Available at: www.charles-de-gaulle.org/pages/l-homme/accueil/discours/pendant-la-guerre-1940–1946/discours-de-brazzaville-30–janvier-1944.php (accessed 14 May 2013).

39 Edmond Giscard d'Estaing, 'Marchés tropicaux il y a dix ans', *Marchés tropicaux* 744 (1950), p. 447.

40 Macalou Fily, 'Le Soudan et l'expansion française', *Le Soudan français* 27 (1951), p. 4.

41 Jean-Paul Moreau, Yves Pasquier and Marianne Ozouf, *Nouveau cours de géographie pour l'enseignement du second degré* (Paris: Nathan 1956), p. 450.

42 Dufour, 'Des rhétoriques coloniales à celles du développement', pp. 381–590.

43 *Ideology* is still used here in the Althusserian sense (see note 15 above).

44 Jean-Michel Gaillard, *Jules Ferry* (Paris: Fayard 1989), pp. 129–33.

45 See Jules Ferry, 'Discours du 28 juillet 1885', in Paul Robiquet (ed.), *Discours et opinions de Jules Ferry*, vol. 5 (Paris: Armand Colin 1893), pp. 172–220.

46 Condorcet, *Esquisse*, p. 194.

47 François Pierre Guillaume Guizot, *General History of Civilization in Europe*, ed. George Wells Knight (New York: Appleton 1896), p. 11.

48 Guizot, *Cours d'histoire moderne*, p. 8.

49 Condorcet, *Esquisse*, p. 81.

50 Nominal expansions such as 'développement *économique et social*' or 'développement *de l'Afrique*'.

51 'Il faut chercher avec soin quel est l'état de civilisation des nègres'. See Hautefeuille, *Plan de colonisation*, p. 119.

52 'Au sein de la Communauté, le Mali et la République française . . . coopéreront de toute leur ardeur à leur propre développement et à celui de tous les homes'. ANOM, SOM P1119, Charles de Gaulle, 'Message du Président de Gaulle à l'occasion de la déclaration de l'indépendance de la Fédération du Mali', 20 June 1960.

53 'L'Afrique noire . . . doit être aidée par la Métropole à atteindre son plein développement'. Moreau, *Nouveau cours de géographie*, p. 450.
54 'Ces peuplades n'ont jamais compris les bienfaits de la civilisation'. See Gilbert Jaime, *De Koulikoro à Tombouctou à bord du Mage* (Paris: É. Dentu 1890), pp. 344–8.
55 'Notre devoir envers l'Afrique occidentale, envers l'Afrique équatoriale est donc de leur assurer le développement que nous avons su donner à l'Afrique du Nord'. Gross, *Faut-il faire le Transsaharien?*, p. 23.
56 Albert Sarraut, *La mise en valeur des colonies françaises* (Paris: Payot 1923).
57 'Il s'ensuit que ce n'est pas uniquement un programme "d'outillage économique" qui a été dressé: c'est le plan d'une "mise en valeur d'ensemble" dans laquelle les améliorations d'ordre moral, intellectuel, politique et social sont étroitement liées aux réalisations d'ordre matériel'. Ibid., p. 83.
58 'L'opération n'est plus unilatérale: elle est conçue pour l'avantage et le bien des deux parties; il n'y a plus spoliation d'une race par l'autre mais association, suivant la formule heureuse qui est devenue la devise de notre politique coloniale'. Ibid., p. 88, emphasis in the original.
59 'Il permettra la mise en valeur de notre Afrique noire. Il favorisera le développement des matières premières nécessaires à notre industrie et les draînera vers la métropole. Le transsaharien sera un instrument de progrès social dans l'Afrique française et un élément de sauvegarde nationale pour la France elle-même'. Personal Archive of Paul Pandolfi, Montpellier, Comité du Transsaharien, 'Il faut faire le Transsaharien', leaflet, 1930.
60 Skinner, *Visions of Politics*, vol. 1, p. 178.
61 Kari Palonen, 'Rhetorical and Temporal Perspectives on Conceptual Change: Theses on Quentin Skinner and Reinhard Kosseleck', in Kari Palonen (ed.), *Finnish Yearbook of Political Thought* 3 (1999), p. 46.
62 'Les colons, commerçants, fonctionnaires ont apporté l'œuvre civilisatrice . . . L'heureuse évolution de notre vieux Soudan réside dans l'unité de vues et de doctrines qui président à son développement'. Fily, 'Le Soudan et l'expansion française', pp. 1–2.
63 Michel Foucault, *L'ordre du discours: leçon inaugurale au Collège de France prononcée le 2 Décembre 1970* (Paris: Gallimard 1971).
64 'La barbarie noire s'ouvrira certes à la civilisation européenne et l'immense famille attardée est prête à accourir à notre appel'. Lucien Hubert, 'Conférence sur l'Afrique Occidentale Française', *Le Mois Colonial et Maritime* 4 (April 1907).
65 Culioli, *Pour une linguistique de l'énonciation*, vol. 1, pp. 83–90.
66 Ibid., p. 205.
67 Achard, 'La passion du développement', p. 821.
68 Culioli, *Pour une linguistique de l'énonciation*, vol. 1, p. 194.
69 Ibid., p. 79. In French in Culioli's quotation (utterances).
70 Both translations of the Anglo-American 'developing', used in the United Nations' resolutions.
71 'Des pays qu'on appelle "sous-développés" mais qu'on pourrait appeler "pays à évolution économique attardée" . . . De quels pays s'agit-il? . . . disons seulement que ce sont des pays ou des régions qui n'ont pas encore exploité à plein leurs ressources naturelles et où, pour des raisons multiples, le niveau de vie est très bas'. ANOM, Cbr6418, 'La coopération dans les pays à évolution économique attardée', 1953.
72 Françoise Dufour, 'De l'effet de l'interdiscours colonial dans la production du sens de la nomination "pays dits *les moins avancés*"', in Virginie Doubli *et al.* (eds), *Le sens c'est de la dynamique: la construction du sens en sciences du langage et en psychologie* (Montpellier: Presses Universitaires de la Méditerranée 2009), pp. 61–73.
73 Luc Fauvel, 'L'O.N.U. et les pays insuffisamment développés', *Annales Africaines* 2 (1956), p. 179.
74 '"Types" are, in enunciative terms, the equivalent of the prototypes in the cognitive approach'. Culioli, *Pour une linguistique de l'énonciation*, vol. 2, p. 12.
75 'parce que cette guerre a pour enjeu ni plus ni moins que la condition de l'homme et que, sous l'action des forces psychiques qu'elle a partout déclenchées, chaque

individu lève la tête, regarde au-delà du jour et s'interroge sur son destin. S'il est une puissance impériale que les événements conduisent à s'inspirer de leurs leçons et à choisir noblement, libéralement, la route des temps nouveaux, où elle entend diriger les soixante millions d'hommes qui se trouvent associés au sort des quarante-deux millions d'enfants, cette puissance c'est la France. En premier lieu parce qu'elle est la France, c'est-à-dire la nation dont l'immortel génie est désigné pour les initiatives qui, par degrés, élèvent les hommes vers les sommets de dignité et de fraternité où, quelque jour, tous pourront s'unir'. Charles de Gaulle, 'Discours de Brazzaville, 30 Janvier 1944'.

76 'Ce que veut l'Afrique est ce que veut la France, c'est la coopération, c'est l'association, c'est le partenariat entre des Nations égales en droits et en devoirs. Jeunesse africaine, vous voulez la démocratie, vous voulez la liberté, vous voulez la justice, vous voulez le droit? C'est à vous d'en décider. La France ne décidera pas à votre place. Mais si vous choisissez la démocratie, la liberté, la justice et le droit, alors la France s'associera à vous pour les construire . . . Ce que veut faire la France avec l'Afrique, c'est regarder en face les réalités. C'est faire la politique des réalités et non plus la politique des mythes. Ce que la France veut faire avec l'Afrique, c'est le codével-oppement, c'est-à-dire le développement partagé'. Nicolas Sarkozy, 'Discours à l'Université de Dakar', 26 July 2007. Available at: www.afrokanlife.com/politique/think-tank/discours_sarkozy_universite_de_dakar_26_juillet_07 (accessed 20 March 2013).

77 Gilbert Lazard, *L'actance* (Paris: Presses Universitaires de France 1994), p. 64.

78 'Dix millions d'Algériens ont besoin de résoudre le problème de l'alimentation et du sous-emploi, des millions de noirs veulent accéder à l'économie moderne. Tous entendent produire pour mieux vivre'. See Jean Depret, 'Trait d'union entre deux mondes: le "Méditerranée-Niger" ', *Sahara de Demain* (October 1958), p. 31.

79 Françoise Dufour, 'Dire le "Sud"': quand nommer l'autre catégorise le monde', *Autrepart: Revue des Sciences Sociales du Sud*, 41 (2007), pp. 27–39.

80 Aminata D. Traoré, 'L'oppression du développement', *Manière de Voir* 79 (2005), pp. 50–2.

81 However, countries such as Australia or New Zealand, also located on the southern half of the planet, are not part of the 'South' as defined by the UNDP.

82 Pêcheux, *Les vérités de La Palice*, p. 144.

CHAPTER FOURTEEN

Developing Africa in the colonial imagination: European and African narrative writing of the interwar period[1]

Martina Kopf

Development under colonial rule, as it emerged from the 1920s onwards, was first and foremost a political concept and an ideology of the metropolis, the colonial state, and the League of Nations' mandate system.[2] It was understood primarily in economic and, to a lesser degree, social terms. Novels, and fictional and semi-fictional narratives of the period on and from Africa are not the first place, then, where one would start researching the history of development. Suppose that we put on a particular set of glasses and look at colonial fiction with a conceptual history of development in mind. What would we see? Can we read its traces in and through the imagination and narratives that both shaped and reflected the colonial encounter of Africans and Europeans in the first half of the twentieth century?

This chapter takes its point of departure from the intersection of colonial discourses of development and narrative writing on Africa in France and Great Britain during the interwar period. After theoretical and methodological reflections on the contribution of literature studies to the history of development it will proceed to analyse five texts published between 1931 and 1943.[3] The texts have in common that their authors – a French and an English colonial official, an English missionary educationist, a Ugandan intellectual and anthropologist, and a Canadian literacy advocate – were agents in state-governed economic development, education, health care, and higher education. It is this mutual relationship of social practice, (imaginative) representation, and communication with a wider public that guided the selection of the texts. The analysis focuses on three issues that were of importance in colonial development policies and at the same time turned up as subjects and motives of colonial narratives: 'making the colony productive', 'developing the human being', and 'negotiating knowledge'. The selected texts are part of a larger corpus mainly based on the novels promoted by the French Colonial Writers' Society on the one hand, and on the book reviews of the journal *East Africa* on the other.

Colonial literature and development discourse

In 1921 the French colonial minister Albert Sarraut, author of the famous doctrine on the *mise en valeur* of the French colonies,[4] initiated a prize for colonial literature, an annual award that should support writing on and from the colonies and make it more popular in the metropolis. The Colonial Writers' Society took up Sarraut's doctrine – which set out principles for the economic and social development of the colonies and shaped the French colonial discourse of the inter-war period – in its founding statement.[5] Throughout the 1920s and 1930s its members did not tire in promoting colonial literature and propagating its important role in the colonial project. In 1932 and 1935 the Society awarded two novels which both told stories of French technological and administrative intervention in West African agricultural production. The first one was *Black Peasants* (1931) by Robert Delavignette, the second *Black Soil* (1935) by Oswald Durand.[6] Delavignette wrote his novel about an industrial oil press – referred to as 'the Machine' – and how its installation transforms the agricultural practices and the social structure of a peasant community in colonial Burkina Faso. In Durand's *Black Soil* it is the introduction of ploughs in a Guinean rural community, told in terms of a techno-logical and social revolution, that leads to economic growth and frees the peasants from the yoke of their feudal masters.[7] Both authors had started their careers as civil servants of the French colonial administration in the respective regions where they set the plot of their novels.

At about the same time, in 1933, Ferdinand Stephen Joelson, founder and chief editor of the London-based magazine *East Africa*, initiated a debate on the importance of 'good fiction' on and from colonial East Africa. It was taken up and pursued in letters to the editor and book reviews over the following years.[8] Some years before he had already launched a challenge to writers in a book review:

> East Africa has repeatedly said that it is awaiting with eager anticipation the publication of an East African novel which it can recommend to all and sundry as a happy, healthy, and true portrayal of life in the Dependencies. The novelist has great scope for the propagation of accurate information and for the creation of the right atmosphere, for tens of thousands of people who will read an East African novel through to the end will resolutely refuse to do more than glance at a more serious work.[9]

Looking at the book reviews and literary criticism that appeared in the magazine in the 1930s gives an impression of how writing and the functions of writing changed simultaneously with an increasing interest in the economic development of East Africa. The first productions had a predominantly technical character focused on trade and agriculture; the books reviewed and advertised were above all manuals on farming, hunting, and the like. In the years to follow the magazine opened its scope to other facets and subjects of colonial life and discourse, reporting on the activities of the International Institute of African Languages and Cultures, and on issues of colonial administration such as 'native education', or printing lectures of anthropologists and historians on East and Central Africa. Its book pages that observed and covered Anglophone book publications on and from East, Central, and Southern Africa became more varied with reviews more informative and controversial. They discussed a growing proportion of narrative literature that reflected and dealt with the colonial situation in a more realistic way than did adventure and safari stories and settler romances that formed the bulk of popular English literature on East Africa. There was a period of about ten years when the magazine took a keen interest in realist fiction and non-fiction during which its book pages mirrored a varied and multi-faceted writing culture, reaching from Elspeth Huxley's early novels; *East Africa*'s own edited series of country reports; stories and accounts of colonial servants such as Kenneth Bradley in Zambia, missionary teachers such as Cicely Hooper in Kenya or Mabel Shaw in Zambia, or medical doctors; to publications by African authors such as Parmenas Githendu Mockerie's account *An African Speaks For His People* (1934) or Akiki Nyabongo's novel *The Story of an African Chief* (1935), which will be discussed below. At the same time there was a visible and significant rise of the terms 'development' and 'develop' in the magazine's reporting. There were periodic columns entitled 'Developing Nyasaland' or 'Developing Tanganyika', and in the second half of the 1930s there was not a single issue that did not use either of the terms in at least one of its headlines.

In what follows, I interpret these two cases – the activities of the Colonial Writers' Society in France and the debate on 'good' novels in the British magazine *East Africa* – as expressions of an intersection that is characteristic of European colonialism in Africa during the interwar period, despite the formative differences of their respective national and colonial contexts. First, the economic and – to a lesser degree – social development of the colonies emerged as a powerful concept and ideology of European colonial politics and rhetoric after the First World War.[10] The terms 'development' and 'develop' joined the semantic field that characterises the colonial discourse on Europe's presence in Africa. The concept gained strength in the face of related notions like 'civilisation' or 'progress', and would in time lead to the displacement of the previous colonial opposition of 'civilised' v. 'savage' by 'developed' and 'under-developed'.[11] Second, the colonial appropriation of Africa inspired, nourished, and occupied European imagination. The territorial occupation was accompanied by cognitive, narrative, visual, and scientific appropriations that resulted in an enormous production of texts and knowledge. Colonial servants, missionaries, teachers, travellers, entrepreneurs, settlers, anthropologists – men and women of a variety of professions turned to writing, obviously convinced that their presence and experience in Africa endowed them with something meaningful to share with a wider public. The role of art and literature and more generally of language, discourse, and rhetoric in European imperialism must not be underestimated. Imperialism produced, was shaped by, and depended on discursive strategies of colonisation.[12]

Finally, there was a shift in Europe's narrative culture on Africa as well as in contemporary discourses on colonial literature. Romantic and exotic representations of the continent, which were common in adventure stories and romances, found an articulate opposition in critical debates which demanded realistic, informed, and demystifying portrayals of Africa. This kind of meta-discourse was most explicit in France, where writers, academics, and colonial activists led a vivid debate on colonial literature that resulted in a number of book publications and articles in print media.[13] As Bernard Mouralis put it, 'colonial literature' as a concept both emerged from and produced a specific intersection of 'l'écriture, le réel et l'action',[14] which I would circumscribe as an intersection of discursive and social practices and the experience of the real. The shift from the exotic to the (imagined) realistic was not only a literary phenomenon, but can be observed in other European 'imaginings' of Africans as well, as Jeater has shown in her article on changing representations of Africans in the records of the colonial government of Zimbabwe.[15]

Reading fiction as a source of knowledge

Approaching the history of development through fictional and semi-fictional narratives necessarily entails the question, what kind of knowledge can be gained from them? There are a growing number of interesting studies from social, historical, and even political science backgrounds that deal with fiction as a source of knowledge in the context of African history, imperial studies, and development studies.[16]

Obviously, academic research on colonial writing has been continually crossing the bridge between fiction and history for decades, with post-colonial theory and the establishment of post-colonial studies acting as important catalysts. But until recently it seemed to be a one way road from literature and language studies to historical, anthropological, and social themes and subjects while the social and historical disciplines have remained reluctant to venture into using fiction as a source of knowledge.[17] Historians, sociologists, or anthropologists have occasionally referred to novels and works of imagination, but rarely have they developed methodological approaches that go beyond looking at fiction as a mere illustration, a parabolic insertion to make one's point or a subordinate addition to the archive.[18]

Looking for theoretical and methodological approaches to colonial narratives with the intention of shedding more light on the conceptual history of development, I encountered several problems. There exists a considerable body of post-colonial literature studies and analyses of colonial discourse. While these are helpful in seizing and analysing the 'colonial' in narratives of colonial development, they have not shown much interest in 'development' as a concept. The second question is what *are* 'narratives of colonial development'? How do I define them? The question is easier to answer when dealing with texts that explicitly deal with 'development' – such as the development plans of the respective colonial governments that proliferated especially after the Second World War, or journalistic writing that took up the concept and used the term. Colonial fiction, however, did not participate that obviously in the discourse of development. Few are the cases like Delavignette's novel *Black Peasants*, which can be read as a fictionalised *mise en scène* of contemporary development policies. And even this tale does not use the terms 'development' or 'develop' but requires an informed reader who is already familiar with thinking of the narrated processes in terms of 'development'.

In their inspiring article, 'The Fiction of Development', Lewis, Rodgers, and Woolcock diagnose a crisis of representation in development studies. They suggest including literary fiction as a potential source of knowledge in development studies to 'widen the scope of the development knowledge base conventionally considered to be "valid"'.[19] With the socio-economist Thea Hilhorst, for instance, they juxtapose Helen Fielding's novel *Cause Celeb* with mainstream academic writing on non-governmental organisations. While the latter remains bound up with formal organisational structures, the novel achieves more depth and complexity by portraying the interplay of different actors in the field of international development work.[20] Lewis, Rodgers, and Woolcock's diagnosis echoes – without explicitly referring to it – Spivak's impulse to rethink the problem of representation in subaltern studies,[21] with the difference being the authors are much more optimistic that there is something like an authentic representation of experience in and through acts of storytelling and narration. Basing their approach upon post-colonial, literary, and sociological theories of narrative, they see storytelling in fiction and non-fiction as a fundamental tool to transmit experience and to transform experience into knowledge. Accordingly, they argue for a complementary use of empirical research and portrayals of development-related themes and subjects in popular fiction.

In this chapter, I adopt Lewis, Rodgers, and Woolcock's argument on literature as a site of knowledge production in development studies that should be approached in a complementary, non-hierarchical way. However, I want to refine it in two critical aspects. First, it is important to define the criteria of selection. It is problematical how the above authors construct categories such as 'fiction of development' or 'development writing' without explaining what 'development' means and contains. Of course we can think of certain types of texts in these terms. But is writing a story that deals with poverty, migration, gender relations, economic exploitation – or other subjects that have been claimed as 'development issues' at a given period and in a given social, economic, and political context – 'development writing'? Or, regarding development under colonial rule, is any colonial narrative of the twentieth century also a narrative on 'colonial development'? In this chapter 'development' is understood as an intentional practice defined as an improvement of economic and social practices and processes. The terms, objects, and aims of improvement are not stable but have been part of power struggles of various agents with conflicting interests.

The second concern refers to the methodological approach. From a literature studies point of view Lewis, Rodgers, and Woolcock perform and present basically positivist, content-based readings of fictional literature. Literature or more specifically narrative literature, however, constitutes a particular kind of discursive practice. It distinguishes itself by the deliberate use of imagination, by its dialogic or rather polylogic structure, and by the polyvalence of meaning. Narrative literature has different layers of meaning that are to be found in the narrative techniques, the language employed, the narrative composition as much as in the content of the story. The Russian literary theorist Mikhail Bakhtin coined the term 'heteroglossia', meaning the co-existence of and conflict between different types of speech in the text.[22] Rather than expressing only the views and perspectives of an individual author any literary narrative represents a performative and mimetical act, which opens up the text for different readings and interpretations.

Based on this understanding of development and of narrative literature I approach the selected texts and explore if and how they represent what Lewis, Rodgers, and Woolcock would call 'development knowledge'. The criteria of selection are – to describe them in empirical terms – less quantitative than qualitative, meaning that I chose individual texts that I found particularly interesting and at the same time representative of three kinds of agency: the colonial administrator's intervention, the white missionary's intervention, and the African intellectual's intervention. Although the analysis does not explicitly make use of the category 'gender', it was implicitly present in my intention to assemble a diversity of voices. Similarly, I did not systematically theorise on differences between African and European perspectives, but ensured that they were both represented. This should make the reader aware that writing the history of colonial development must involve the perspectives, authorship and agency of women, men, colonised, and colonisers alike.

Making the colony productive

The transition from colonial conquest to securing the European occupation through administrative structures did not only determine European colonial politics in Africa in the early twentieth century, but also had effects on the European narrative culture on Africa. Colonial fiction of the period is characterised by the advent of the colonial official, as author, as narrative perspective, as character, and as subject of narration.[23] The *administrateur* becomes a central character of the French colonial novel after 1918, as Steins observes in his comprehensive study on French colonial literature, a hero who has to confront enormous challenges.[24] The colonial novel, as Kirk-Greene has declared, can also be used as an important source to study colonial service in the field.[25] Colonial servants, at the same time, were central in executing and shaping colonial policies that increasingly presented themselves as development policies. Their fictional, semi-fictional, and autobiographical narratives, diaries, and popular accounts allow for insights into the imagination that governed these policies, their ideological framing, and the discursive strategies in communicating colonial practices of development to the metropolitan public. This section takes a closer look at Robert Delavignette's novel *Black Peasants* and Kenneth Bradley's *Diary of a District Officer*. I read them as texts that document the discursive inventiveness in putting the contradictions and double binds of development under colonial rule into coherent, meaningful narratives, and the manifold doubts, tensions, and insecurities that accompanied the enterprise.

Black Peasants is a most fascinating text that manages to put the French doctrine of agricultural development in French West Africa of the period successfully into the form of a novel and, what is perhaps more astounding, one which still convinces as a novel. Its author, Robert Delavignette, was an active and multi-faceted protagonist, thinker, and writer of French colonialism in West Africa from the 1930s until after independence. His publications include books and articles on colonial issues as well as four novels.[26] He held several positions in French West Africa and in France, and was a district officer in Niger and Burkina Faso, head of the Ecole Coloniale, the French training institution for colonial officials (renamed Ecole Nationale de la France d'Outre-mer after the Second World War), and for a brief period High Commissioner in the Cameroons.

Black Peasants is part of a larger discourse that discovered and invented the West African peasants as subjects and agents of the economic development of French West Africa.[27] Its historical context is the efforts of the colonial governments in French West Africa of the interwar period to push export production for the metropolitan market by encouraging and at times forcing African farming communities grow cash crops. The dependence on coercive labour was one of the central problems and contradictions that threatened the success of the *mise en valeur* of French West Africa in the interwar period.[28] In *Black Peasants*, Delavignette sketches a vision of how to integrate the peasants' interests and needs and thus to negotiate the imminent coercion and pressure of the economic process. The title is programmatic, and misleading as well. The novel represents peasants as subjects and gives them a voice, but the central character and agent of the narrated process is not a peasant, but a colonial servant. The district officer in *Black Peasants* is an embodiment of the Saint-Simonian doctrine of development analysed by Cowen and Shenton.[29] His intervention negotiates the destructive effects of uncontrolled industrial progress and moderates the potential exploitation of labour through private capital, represented by the company that runs the oil mill. He understands and exerts his position as one of trusteeship over the African peasants. The novel starts with a seemingly desperate deadlock. The Compagnie Française de la Côte d'Ivoire (CFCI) has installed a peanut oil press in Nérigaba – referred to as 'the Machine' – and the colonial administration agrees to provide 6,000 tons of groundnuts in the first years. It obliges the feudal elite of the Dioula to supply the amount, considered 'too much' by the subordinate peasants. The district officer as a result becomes the victim to a plot. Into this tense and entrenched situation comes a new district officer who mobilises all he can to resolve the seemingly desperate situation.[30] In a metaphorical sense, his arrival represents the replacement of the 'old' order of exploitation by a 'new' order of development. The new *commandant* does not reduce the promised amount, but starts intervening into and transforming the modes of production and social structures in order to raise productivity. He counts upon the *soukala* – the compound – as social nucleus and central unit of production. To achieve the required surplus he intends to work with, not against, the *soukalas*.[31]

It is interesting how Delavignette narratively performs this story. The realist style converges with the features of a parable where elements involved have a highly symbolic and exemplary character – expressed, for instance, in the capital letters of 'Machine' and 'Pays'. The initial struggle between the district officer and the village authorities is verbalised as a struggle over 'l'arachide-trop',[32] literally 'the too-much-groundnut', and over the possible meaning and effects of this *trop*. Indeed, the whole narrative seems to spring from the word *trop* – a signifier of incommensurability, 'too much' – as if the story was meant to undermine its potential immobilising effect and to transform it into an impulse.

The novel represents the paradoxical effort to reconcile capitalist growth and surplus production with peasant culture, the factual coercion exerted by the colonial government with its self-representation of liberating French West Africa from slavery and feudalism. The author tells a story that not only reconciles irreconcilable differences and conflicts but also performs this reconciliation on the narrative level. He embeds his success story of progress and capitalist growth into a cyclical temporal structure. The subtitle of the novel is *Récit soudanais en douze mois* (Sudanese tale in twelve months). The titles of the twelve chapters – 'The Sowing Month', 'The Month of the Decisive Rain', 'The Month of Marriages' – reflect cycles of rural production and culture. By inventing 'new' seasons – such as 'The Month of the Railway', 'The Month of the Machine and the Corncob' – the author integrates the signs of the new mode of production, making them part of the agricultural cycle, while at the same time transcending it. But even if the novel creates this vision of an enduring reconciliation between colonised peasant culture and the interests of metropolitan capital, the railways and factories did not follow rural cycles of production. Ironically, Delavignette's fiction would prove more enduring than the factual background; the oil mill whose installation he administrated not as a writer, but as the district officer of Banfora, was closed after some years.[33]

A much more pessimistic impression is given in Kenneth Bradley's *Diary of a District Officer* (1943), where the impermanence of European initiated and administered measures of development is a strong element.[34] Bradley started his career as a district officer in colonial Zambia. In the 1930s and 1940s he held appointments in the Colonial Service in Zambia, Ghana, and the Falkland Islands. After his return to England in 1949 he became editor of *Corona*, the Colonial Office's newly founded monthly publication, then Director of the Imperial Institute (later Commonwealth Institute) from 1955 to 1969, and finally, Vice-President of the Council of the Royal African Society from 1969 to 1976. During his assignment in Zambia Bradley published several books and articles. His first major publication was *Africa Notwithstanding* (1932), a collection of stories, followed by the novel *Hawks Alighting* (1933). Soon after his return to England the Colonial Office published his work *The Colonial Service as a Career* (1950), re-edited five years later under the title *A Career in the Oversea Civil Service*.

Diary of a District Officer (1943) was introduced by Lord Malcolm Hailey, director of *An African Survey* (1938), one of the most influential colonial publications on Africa. In the foreword, Hailey wrote:

> In many of the Dependencies there is a great mass of primitive people who are still far off the stage in their development when politics can have any meaning for them. For them 'the Government' is a remote and shadowy abstraction. They see it only through its visible embodiment, the administrative officer. It is he who wields its powers; and for them it is he who is the dispenser of its benefits.[35]

This foreword, together with the fact that Bradley later wrote an introduction to the colonial service for the Colonial Office and became – as editor of *Corona* – an important figure in the Office's public relations, allows for reading his writings as insights into the imagination and ideological framing that governed British colonial development policies at the time.

Diary of a District Officer relates six inspection tours in the Fort Jameson District in Zambia, which Bradley undertook from May to December 1938. Each tour forms one chapter in the book, and it concludes with one final chapter 'Preparing to Leave'. In his daily notices from the tours Bradley tells about his inspection of villages, meetings with the native authorities and so on. The immediate account of events is accompanied by a meta-narration, where the narrator reflects and comments upon colonial administration, Indirect Rule, and the 'natives' as well as his role and function as a district officer. The author conceptualises British interventions in terms of 'civilisation' and 'civilise' rather than in terms of 'development'. This means that 'develop' or 'development' does not play a significant role in the wording of the text. The one moment where the term 'development' features prominently in the book is the above quoted foreword by Lord Hailey.

[350]

So the DO's narrative is framed by development discourse, although the narrative itself on the level of wording remains tangential to it. Or, from an alternative perspective, it gets appropriated by the development discourse. On the level of themes and contents, however, the narrative overlaps with and takes part in the conceptualisation of 'developmentalist colonialism'.

The narrator conceives of the British administration and his function as district officer above all in terms of 'improving' African society, life, and productivity in the reservations. The sectors he designates for improvement are mainly infrastructure, agricultural methods, hygiene, education, and 'native' administration. European intervention materialises in the realisation of 'buildings': there is a strong emphasis throughout the narration on the building of schools, courthouses, latrines, streets, dams, and wells. In *Diary* as well as in the introduction to his earlier collection of stories *Africa Notwithstanding* (1932) Bradley constructs 'Africa' as the counterpart to innovation, change, permanence, and civilisation. Every effort to build up something or to change a pattern is threatened by destructive forces – be they those of nature like white ants, baboons, elephants, and the fast growing vegetation or those of human society like fatalistic mentality, laziness, or despotism. It is a recurrent rhetorical device of the narrative that those phenomena which are identified as hindrances to development are subsumed under the term 'Africa'. So, each individual hindrance always forms part of the larger concept 'Africa':

> There is no middle-age in Africa, no modest antiquity of man's handiwork – only the ancient earth, and on it huts and fields which have been made this year – or last – and which in a year or two will have vanished as though they had never been. Even in the towns and settlements there is the same contrast, *as if Africa intends to offer the same resistance to any permanent mark upon her*, even our European, civilisation.[36]

Throughout the narration the administrator and the order he represents are constructed as the realisation of permanence. But in the last chapter 'Preparing to leave' this construction for a moment disintegrates when the narrator receives a letter confirming his leave: 'Already I feel curiously detached from it all. What does it all amount to? Perhaps it is like the roads, this season's camber is next year's ditch. This year's forest is next year's fire. This year's planting is next year's bread – or famine'.[37]

In this scene the motive of impermanence, which was an attribute of the other, 'Africa' side of the binary discursive order, suddenly appears on the 'wrong' side. This comes as a surprise within the narrative order. Suddenly the central opposition shifts and the structure, which

[351]

was an integral and defining part of the construction of Africa, appears within the construction of administration and all it represents. This unexpected rupture works like a question mark to the binary construction and opens another layer of meaning. Is it 'Africa's' opposition against permanence which intrudes on the identity of the colonial official? Or is it the impermanence that defines his own work and that he has projected all along on the side of the other?

Developing the human being

In 1935 Mabel Shaw, head of a girls' boarding school in colonial Zambia, wrote a letter to the director of native education of the colonial government, noting that 'a feature of our School is the long period of training our children have – the whole girlhood is spent in school with a consequent maximum of influence and Christian development'.[38] 'Development' here is to be understood as a pedagogical concept, as a development of the character in accordance with Christian values and principles. At the same time, we can assume that the term has a strategic function in this communication between a missionary educationalist and the representative of the colonial government's education policy.

Mabel Shaw was a member of the London Missionary Society, a renowned educationalist and book author. At the beginning of the twentieth century she came to the mission station of Mbereshi, Zambia, and some years later initiated the Mbereshi Girls' Boarding School, which was to become the station's most prestigious institution. Shaw was its Principal from 1915 until 1940. During her time as principal she published four books reflecting the missionary project and experience in Mbereshi, the lives and training of Bemba girls and women, gender relations in Bemba society, and the changes this society underwent at the time.[39] In the 1930s the school came increasingly under pressure. Its pedagogical concept came to be seen as too individualistic, expensive, and exclusive by a colonial government that started to define education as a sector of development and became more interested in cheaper and less exclusive models of 'mass education'.[40] Designating the school's impact as 'Christian development' thus expresses both a reference to the development discourse and an alternative vision. The following analysis explores how this concept of 'Christian development' comes across in Shaw's narratives.

In *A Treasure of Darkness* (1936) Shaw narrates the story of a girl, a half-orphan who was brought to the mission as an almost starved newborn. The missionaries named her Mary Livingstone and raised her as an adopted child. The 'realness' of the account is additionally highlighted through a foreword that informs the readers that all characters in the story actually exist[41] and through inserted photographs that show and document the 'real' Mary to the readers of the book. The text thus creates a strong impression of authenticity and non-fiction.

At the same time this portrayal of a happy, beloved, and rich childhood conveys a story of successful interventions into and transformations of modes of child care, communal behaviour, education, and learning. The child's salvation is narrated as the result of one of the first experiments with industrial child nutrition in the region. In one scene the African school girls question the child care methods of the missionary hospital's white doctor, who leaves the baby most of the time by itself sleeping in a cradle. The girls want to tie the baby to their backs as their mothers do and confront the doctor with the following dialogue:

> 'She is living like a white baby'.
> 'Yes, but she is growing into a lovely, happy, healthy, black baby, isn't she?'
> 'Yes, she's the best black baby we have ever seen'.[42]

As is typical for European discourses on Africa at the time, Shaw's narratives are structured by binary oppositions, the most salient being 'light' v. 'dark'; 'educated' v. 'savage'; 'new' v. 'old', 'clean' v. 'dirty', 'white' v. 'black', 'knowing' v. 'ignorant', '(reformed) village life' v. 'urban life', 'Christian belief' v. 'native custom', and 'child' v. 'adult'.[43] Yet the oppositions are not static, but operate in a dynamic, fluid way. Time and again, the hierarchy between the two is subverted – which happens often unexpectedly and surprisingly. There is an interesting dialogue in *A Treasure of Darkness*, when Mary's father hands over the infant to the missionaries for them to take care of her:

> 'Just look at the towel,' said Mama Sabin, 'it will take days to get her clean, the dirt is caked on; and look at her little head, it is plastered with mud'.
> 'The father put mud there to protect that little thin part where the pulse throbs,' said tall Chungu, the cook, who had come from the kitchen to help.[44]

In the discursive context the first sentence evokes the image of 'savage/dirtiness' versus 'educated/clean'. 'Dirtiness' is a signifier which Europeans of the time frequently used when describing African culture and surroundings. 'Cleanliness' in the same discursive order thus becomes a marker for Western education, civilisation, knowledge, and change.

The interesting thing in the above passage is that the utterance is not left without comment. The narrator introduces a second view and a second voice, which is that of a Bemba woman and former pupil of the school. Through Chungu's comment and the information she gives, the discursive order is shifted. The infant's 'dirtiness' is no longer a sign of ignorance and backwardness – as it was when read by European readers with no understanding of local African practices. On the contrary it is revealed as a cultural technique used in child care. The dialogue, which started out as a hierarchy of knowledge-versus-ignorance, turns – through Chungu's intervention – into a negotiation of knowledge and techniques. This is such an unusual moment in colonial narratives that I was literally stunned when I came across it. This moment of surprise also made me aware of how strongly the ideological frame of colonial narratives works: how it creates and fulfils expectations within a closely knit pattern.

In Shaw's *A Treasure of Darkness* as well as in her earlier texts there are quite a number of similar moments where expectations are subverted by unanticipated turns or interventions. This results in a certain negotiability and flexibility of opposites and their ascribed values. Rather than constructing 'Africa' and 'Christian development' as antagonistic – as we find in Bradley's depiction – Shaw's writing heads for a synthesis. The implicit goal of her vision of Christian development is the African subject who incorporates the 'good' elements of both sides. This 'best black baby ever seen' will ideally grow into an adult with 'the knowledge of two languages, her own Chibemba and English' and 'learning the courteous and gracious ways of Africa and England'.[45] Projected onto society, the 'Christian development' of the individual results in a reformed, Christianised African village life.

Through these moments of subverting and shifting dichotomies Shaw's writing anticipates narrative strategies that have been assigned to post-colonial writing. If we understand the 'post' in 'post-colonial' not so much as a temporal marker, but in the sense of moving or thinking 'beyond' colonial structures, then Shaw's text also proves that Europeans in colonial Africa had the potential and the possibility to transcend the rules of the colonial discourse they created. Or, to put it differently, they were not only subjects, but also agents of colonial discourse. This quality becomes even more visible when we read the text against the background of subject-constructions of Western-educated Africans in colonial fiction of the time. Colonial fiction on Africa of the period as a rule displayed a strong bias against the 'Westernised' African or against 'half-castes' of mixed belonging.[46] Characters such as the Oxford-trained Nigerian aristocrat Aladai in Joyce Cary's *The African Witch*[47] are invariably doomed to fail. These literary constructions formed a counter-current to the discourse on colonial development by ridiculing and belittling its prospective outcome. Shaw's construction of the developing subject and future agent of Christian development on the continent shows confidence in the potential of a synthesis of European and African knowledge, values, and techniques.[48]

However, this subject-construction bears another problem. Mary Livingstone, the bilingual eight-year-old girl that surpasses her age mates in reading skills, wit, and social behaviour, epitomises this ideal as a half-orphan, raised on mission grounds, outside the reach of her African family and the social control of the village. Mary's mother died at childbirth exhausted of the travel back from town, where her husband worked, to her home village. Her early death evokes the strains of labour migration in colonial Zambia.[49] Thus Shaw's metaphor and prospective agent of successful Christian development in Africa implies a radical rupture with the social surroundings. Mary's inexhaustible happiness in the narrative covers the violence and loss inherent in this rupture. Her happiness is a signifier used in a way to let the reader feel at ease with this subject-construction and to cut short any doubts and questions that might arise from it, just as it erases the doubts of the schoolgirls when they question the 'Mama Doctor's' methods in bringing up the baby. The Doctor asks the schoolgirls:

> 'Does Mary cry when she is all alone?'
> 'No, she smiles and smiles'.
> 'Then it must be good for her'.[50]

Reading Shaw's fictionalised accounts of the missionary educational endeavour is an ambiguous experience. On the one hand, Shaw's writing displays a post-colonial openness to subject-positions and voices of the colonised. This holds true also for Shaw's portrayal of the Bemba girls attending the mission school in her earlier book *Dawn in Africa* (1927). The girls and young women in *Dawn in Africa* like Mary in *A Treasure of Darkness* are not mere objects of narration or passive embodiments of Shaw's development vision. They act through dialogues and the author creates a textual space where their voices, emotions, minds, resistance as well as their creativity are represented. There are situations and dialogues that effectively portray the girls as agents. The narrative does not construct them as passive and voiceless recipients of education, but as agents who interpret, apply, and adapt what they learn in sometimes surprising and unexpected ways. If read with awareness, Shaw's narratives transmit – maybe unwillingly – a dense description of the ambiguities and double binds that rule the students' journey between the opposing demands of their communities, the missionaries, and their own desires. This represents a difference from contemporary programmatic writing on female education in Africa.

But, on the other hand, Shaw is not an uninvolved storyteller but an engaged – and as such interested – protagonist in the processes she portrays in her accounts. The girl protagonists are all portrayals of factual students of the Mbereshi school. While the narration gives an idea of their factual agency, interests, and desires, they also act on behalf of, or rather *perform* the author's vision of Christian development. The students' agency is authored and staged through an omniscient narrator who, in the last chapter, reveals herself as the autobiographical 'I' of the author.[51] Shaw's skill as a storyteller makes it difficult to discern where the act of representation merges into an act of replacement – or, to put it differently, to discern how far the girl protagonists are representations in the storyteller's tale and how far they are metaphors in the author's tale of 'Christian development'.

Negotiating knowledge

Development is intrinsically linked with the production and transfer of knowledge. Knowledge and knowledge production under colonial rule, on the other hand, have been fundamentally related to power, to the suppression and exclusion of African systems of knowledge. Táíwò, for instance, argues that in the case of Nigeria, colonialism did not transform pre-colonial modes of knowledge production or replace them by new ones, but was essentially characterised by exclusions that eventually pre-empted the creation of new modes of knowledge production.[52] The question of whether knowledge and knowledge systems of the colonised were merely excluded or appropriated or if they even contributed actively in the production of knowledge under colonial rule, is a subject of debate. Wagoner identifies two positions in this debate. The first, which he refers to as 'post-colonialist', holds that knowledge was as much a part of colonial conquest and power as were military, economic, and political power and that the colonised were merely assigned to deliver 'raw material' for the production of colonial knowledge. The second position, while agreeing with the first assumption, sees colonised subjects not only as passive 'patients' in the processes of knowledge production, but attributes more importance to their contributions and agency in these processes.[53] This agency is at the heart of the following reading of *The Story of an African Chief*, written by Akiki Nyabongo, a Ugandan academic intellectual in 1935.[54] My focus is on how the text represents knowledge production and the transfer of knowledge in the context of development.

Nyabongo's novel *The Story of an African Chief* (1935) first appeared in New York and was re-edited in 1936 in Great Britain under the title *An African Answers Back*. The text combines collective biography, autobiography, and fiction. The author, member of the Buganda aristocracy, was a trained anthropologist with a Master's degree from Harvard University in the United States and a PhD in anthropology from Oxford. After his studies at Oxford, Nyabongo returned to the USA, where he was a professor at the University of Alabama and later North Carolina.[55] The novel, dedicated to the author's mother, is set in Uganda and covers the period from the reign of Mwanga II and the wars that accompanied his early reign, through to the early British protectorate until about the first decade of the twentieth century. It tells the story of the boy Abala Stanley Mujungu, son of a Buganda chief, born about fifteen years after Henry Morton Stanley met Mutesa, King of Buganda in 1875, as a narrative of the conflictual encounter between a Buganda elite who actively sought to profit from European knowledge, and the English missionaries who used their influence on the students to intervene into the Buganda social structures. It is a witty, subversive text written by a member of a self-confident elite who meets the new European players, moves between and compares different systems of knowledge, and offers ways of adapting and reforming African communities. What is particularly interesting are the many dialogues in which the chief, the chief's wives, the reverend and head of the mission school, Mujungu and other boys of his age, the clan elders, and European medical doctors negotiate their knowledge, their interests, their influence, and their perspectives.

The book was not received well by the colonial press. The *East Africa* review pages, for example, commented on the second edition critically, noting: 'The author is in a position to render a service of great value to his people, and to assist those – missionaries, officials and others – who are endeavouring to raise their moral, intellectual and economic standards, and it may be hoped that he will be encouraged to turn his attention to problems of African culture and development more worthy of his gifts and education'.[56] The tone of the review reproduces the colonialist bias against Western-educated Africans, assuming on the one hand that Western education endows the colonised with the necessary tools to contribute to 'African development' and diagnosing on the other hand a failure of the other to use the tools accordingly. An earlier review of the first edition dismissed the book as an unreliable source of knowledge on African life.[57] The struggle over the production of knowledge and over the right way to use that knowledge to achieve development frames the contemporary reception of the book from the outset, as much as Nyabongo makes it part of the narration.

Similar to Shaw, Nyabongo's writing exposes the notion of a productive synthesis of European and African knowledge, values, and techniques. It is an interesting parallel that the protagonist carries the name of a European explorer. The name is of highly symbolic value and the act of naming is made part of the narration. The symbolism of the name, however, already shows that Africans have a say in the rules and conditions that govern this synthesis. It is Stanley's father who decides to give his son two new names, going against the clan's tradition: 'Stanley' in reference to Henry Morton Stanley and 'Mujungu', the Swahili word for the white 'roamers', from and about whom the boy shall later learn.[58] The text hitherto refers to him as 'Mujungu', which also has an ironic aspect. Significantly, the initiative to open autochthonous systems of knowledge and beliefs to the impact of European migrants comes from an African chief and representative of the pre-colonial social elite. And, significantly again, while he succeeds in convincing the clan to accept this new procedure of naming, he fails in convincing the white Reverend. The Reverend's refusal to baptise the child as long as the father practises polygamy reveals that the initiated process of change is from the beginning marked by struggles over its control.

Abala Stanley Mujungu is constructed as a developing subject,[59] who turns into a potential agent of development. The text comments on the moment when its protagonist, Mujungu, succeeds his father to a position of effective power: 'He felt proud and confident and knew that he would develop the possibilities in his people and country'.[60] Being the son and successor of a chief, attending a mission school and, after being expelled, graduating from a private school, he has – just like the protagonist in Cheikh Hamidou Kane's famous novel *Ambiguous Adventure* (1961) – a privileged access to two systems of knowledge. Unlike the orphaned Mary in Shaw's narrative he enters the school not as a blank slate. His social status and background endow him with the necessary prestige, self-confidence, and symbolic capital to confront the new system of knowledge and beliefs as an already informed subject and an equal. This is highlighted in the continued struggles and conflicts with the Reverend that will eventually lead to his expulsion from the school.

And yet, the novel does not offer a counter-narrative to European discourses on colonial development. Instead, the protagonist's vision of 'develop[ing] the possibilities in his people and country' replicates colonial concepts regarding the means, sectors, and aims of intervention. For example, when Mujungu reaches a position of authority he dissolves the polygamous household of his deceased father and decides to lead a monogamous life. Dressed in European clothes he goes on an inspection tour of the villages under his authority and makes plans for the beginning of a school system.[61] The image is one of mimicry of the European district officer. Before that he had actively sought the help of European doctors to fight a smallpox epidemic. His focus on education, gender relations, and health is in line with key sectors of intervention in colonial development policies and discourse.

In contrast to Shaw, Nyabongo shifts the productive synthesis between African and European knowledge and cultural practices from the religious to the secular, from religion to science. Missionary practices relying on religious belief are not constructed as a driving force, but as a hindrance to a development based on synthesis. The 'best practice' in improving the living standards of the population is the successful interaction of European and African knowledge and techniques in medicine and communications that brings the smallpox epidemic to an end.[62]

While the novel does not significantly differ from European versions of development under colonial rule in terms of the underlying concept of development, it makes a difference in highlighting the role of African knowledge in processes of development. Moreover, it brings knowledge, as a highly contested and competitive terrain, to the forefront of the narration. The transfer of knowledge in European narratives is predominantly represented as a one-way process of superior European practices and techniques being introduced to African societies. The knowledge of Africans is either not represented at all, or it is represented as knowledge without effects or as something other than knowledge. Read between the lines, however, European narratives do show an awareness that knowledge existed on the side of the colonised and that the transfer of knowledge moved in both directions.

A good example can be found in the work of Margaret Wrong. Wrong was the Head of the International Committee on Christian Literature for Africa, as well as being a book author and an important agent in the field of literacy development. In her book, *Land and Life of Africa*, Wrong depicts a dialogue between a European doctor and her clients – all elderly African women – in a government hospital in Accra:

> 'It is true that many babies die,' said one old woman, 'and it is true that cleanliness is good and may save some lives, but there are causes of death, such as the curse of an enemy, which clean hands will not touch. But in our talks with you we have learned many things.'
>
> 'I, too, have learned from you,' replied the doctor.[63]

The passage indicates there is a process of learning taking place on both sides, but while it makes clear that the African women received European knowledge on hygiene it does not indicate the kind of knowledge that passed from the African women to the European doctor. Her statement remains rhetorical in a way that may be read as politeness, and the text leaves the knowledge it alludes to without content and meaning.

Another example is the passage in *A Treasure of Darkness* quoted in the previous section. It goes a step further in its representation of the technique – covering the infant with mud in order to protect her from the sun – which Europeans would not have recognised as such without the interference of an African interpreter of this knowledge. But even though Shaw represents it as knowledge, it remains without meaning and without effects on the progress of the story. It is, in effect, washed away like the mud from the baby's head. European narratives developed quite a number of strategies to include the – obviously undeniable – presence of African knowledge, skills, and techniques and simultaneously exclude it from the narrated development processes. What is interesting is not so much *what* they tell about African knowledge, but the narrative strategies they apply to conceal its presence.

In Nyabongo's narrative knowledge is not a neutral condition of development, but a site of continuous negotiation of power, of the terms and conditions of its control, as we will see in the following two text passages. In one passage, Stanley's mothers and his father ask him to show them his newly acquired reading skills and he reads to them from the 'Book of Solomon'. His father is stupefied when he hears his son reciting from the Bible that the King had a large number of wives and lovers. When accompanying his son back to the mission school he confronts the Reverend, who refused to baptise Stanley as long as the chief lives in polygamy. Consequently the Reverend forbids all pupils from reading to their relatives at home, declaring that: 'From now on and forever, I want students to stop this reading of magazines, newspapers, and books to their parents during vacations. You must talk only in ordinary conversation with your people. Don't try to explain the things which you learn here. Your people can't understand you properly, as you can when I teach you'.[64]

In another text passage the grown-up Stanley prevents the white medical doctors from treating the broken arm of one of his people. While he fully promotes their vaccination programme he does not approve of their methods in treating bone fractures but explains to them that the local methods are more efficient. When the whites show interest Stanley orders one of the village's doctors[65] to demonstrate his skill. Reluctantly the latter shows the whites, whom he perceives as rivals, how he locates the exact spot of the fracture and treats it successfully with a combination of manual therapy and an embrocation of butter and herbal medicine. Answering their questions he explains to them how often the treatment has to be repeated, but he does not share his full knowledge with them.

Both sequences are narrative moments unheard of in European narratives and versions of development processes I have read. I do not read them in a positivist way as authentic reports of incidents that happened exactly this way. Rather, I read them as discursive events that interpret and give meaning to the role played by the transfer of knowledge in the context of colonial development. These two sequences are subversive in the sense that they subvert the narrative patterns through which the transfer of knowledge is constructed in European narrative representations of development processes. Their meaning within colonial development discourse resides in the way they reveal what European narratives omit and conceal.

As for the first sequence, I have not found a single instance in European narratives showing European agents of development processes who explicitly hold back, refuse or deny Africans (the application of) knowledge – as does the Reverend who forbids the students to read to their relatives at home – and thus exert authoritative control on the transfer of knowledge. Europeans tend to represent themselves as giving and bringing knowledge and techniques, not restricting them or holding them back. It is through the narratives of Africans that these blind spots in European self-representations are illuminated. Nyabongo's Reverend is but one facet of asserting a monopolist position in transfers of knowledge. The Kenyan intellectual Parmenas Githendu Mockerie, for instance, relates other versions of the same motive. In *An African Speaks for His People* (1934) he gives voice to African teachers in Kenya, who were not allowed to teach the English language without the supervision of a European teacher, as well as workers on European plantations, who were forbidden to apply their experience and knowledge in coffee growing for their own profit and start their own plantations.[66]

The second text passage on competing treatments of bone fractures is a rare incidence of a narrative representation of effective African medical knowledge. What is equally interesting is the way it is made part of a whole communication process. The plot is simple and could be quickly told, but in the novel its narration covers several pages. Mujungu first just tells the white doctors that his people know more effective ways of treating broken bones. It is only after one of the whites explicitly asks to learn this method that the knowledge is put in practice and demonstrated. Through his narrative representation Nyabongo highlights the significance of communication and dialogue in transfers of knowledge and how much they determine whether the exchange succeeds and produces effects, or fails. By representing the thoughts and feelings of the Buganda doctor, his fears that 'giving' his knowledge to the whites might result in 'giving it away', the narrative also creates awareness of the competitive nature of the situation.

Through the narrative representation of knowledge and control in processes of development Nyabongo's writing differs significantly from contemporary European colonial writing. Neither Nyabongo nor Mockerie – as two cases of African intellectuals writing during the colonial period – construct European culture as a superior entity. Rather, they portray Europeans in control of useful and powerful knowledge, skills, and technologies that are objects of desire and can be learned, but not in possession of a superior culture as a whole.

Conclusion

In this chapter I have featured some of the diversity of voices, stories, experiences, positions, visions, and interests that make up the some- what colourless term 'colonial fiction'. The particular intersection of professional practice – be it in the sectors of governing and adminis- tration, education, or academic careers – with acts of storytelling and fictional writing produced a body of narrative literature that constitutes a valuable source for research on the colonial history of development in Africa.

On the epistemological level, the terms 'development' or 'develop' seldom appear in narrative literature on Africa of the interwar period – much in contrast to the contemporary French and English colonial press where the term was rapidly gaining importance. This holds not only true for the texts discussed in this chapter, but also for the larger corpus of fictional and semi-fictional texts awarded by the French Colonial Writers' society and reviewed in the British journal *East Africa* which formed the basis of this research. 'Developing Africa' did not – and in fact has not until today – become an integral part of the language and terminology of popular literature on Africa. I inter- pret this as a sign that the discourse of development was – and maybe still is – a discourse of 'experts', assigned to other social spheres than those of narrative literature. Nevertheless narrative writing by colonial servants, missionaries or African intellectuals of the colonial period reflected the intentional practices and interventions designed for and defined as improvement that made up the discourse of colonial devel- opment. Not only did their narratives take part in the discursive formation of development, but they also worked as translation and intermediary between the experts' discourse on the one hand and the reading public on the other. Furthermore, they served to mediate experience, visions, and critique – as is particularly the case with the writing of African authors – among the social and professional groups who took an interest into the transformation of African social, political, and economic structures under colonial rule.

Reading fiction as a source of knowledge implies an awareness of how narrative literature works, of the different layers of meaning it opens. My question is not so much, what do the texts tell us, but rather, how do they work as narratives? Concerning the history of development, colonial fiction does not tell us anything factually new that cannot be, or has not already been, discovered through empirical historical research and studying colonial archives. The concepts of development that speak through the writings of district officers such as Robert Delavignette or Kenneth Bradley, for instance, were part of colonial policies which we can access through colonial records as well. Shifting the focus from *what* the stories tell to *how* they work as narratives, however, I have tried to show how a close reading of narrative representations and imaginations of processes of development gives insights into the communicative patterns, subject constructions, the conflicts, contradictions, and mental structures decisive for how these processes were put into practice. The narratives of the colonised, in particular, are sources of knowledge on more than one level. They document and reflect how knowledge was produced, excluded, (de)valued, and refused within colonial conceptualisations of development. 'Colonial', here, is to be understood as a structural and not so much as a temporal category, meaning that colonial conceptualisations of development are as much part of the present as they are of the past.

In 'The Fiction of Development' Lewis, Rodgers, and Woolcock provide a useful appendix with a selection of novels suggested as sources of knowledge for academics and practitioners of development.[67] The decades of colonial development in Africa, however, are left completely blank. The list includes Joseph Conrad's novels, some novels from the late 1950s, and some post-colonial fiction that deals with colonial history – such as Chinua Achebe's *Things Fall Apart*. But it remains silent on the writings of colonial servants, missionaries, teachers, anthropologists – African and European, women and men – who nourished the imagination of European as well as African readers mainly of the colonial educational institutions with stories of a continent 'in development'. This chapter, it is hoped, may serve as a contribution to complement Lewis, Rodgers and Woolcock's list of recommended reading for contemporary thinkers and practitioners of development.

Notes

1 This chapter resulted from an interdisciplinary research project funded by the Austrian Science Fund at the University of Vienna/Department of African Studies. The author would like to thank her project partner Gerald Hödl for all his discussions, suggestions, and advice that went into this text. She is also grateful to her colleague Inge Grau who read and commented on an earlier version of this article.

2 Antony Anghie, 'The Evolution of International Law: Colonial and Postcolonial Realities', *Third World Quarterly* 27, 5 (2006), pp. 739–53; Monica M. van Beusekom and Dorothy L. Hodgson, 'Lessons Learned? Development Experiences in the Late Colonial Period', *Journal of African History* 41, 1 (2000), pp. 29–33; Frederick Cooper, 'Writing the History of Development', *Journal of Modern European History* 8, 1 (2010), pp. 5–23.

3 Although it was published in 1943, I included Kenneth Bradley, *Diary of a District Officer*, in the selection since it dates back to the notes Bradley took on an inspection tour in 1938.

4 Albert Sarraut, *La mise en valeur des colonies françaises* (Paris: Payot 1923).

5 Marius-Ary Leblond, 'A quoi doit servir la littérature coloniale: La Société des Écrivains Coloniaux', *Monde Colonial Illustré* (April 1926), p. 95.

6 Robert Delavignette, *Les paysans noirs* (Paris: Stock 1931) and Oswald Durand, *Terre noire* (Paris: Fournier 1935).

7 Martina Kopf, 'A Peasant, a Governor and a Plough: Development Discourse and the French Colonial Novel in the 1930s', *Stichproben-Vienna Journal of African Studies* 26 (2014).

8 The weekly appeared from 1924 until 1966, changed its title to *East Africa and Rhodesia* in 1936, and reflected above all perspectives and interests of settlers and European private capital in East Africa, its chief editor being, by his own words, a former 'planter' in Tanganyika.

9 Ferdinand Stephen Joelson, 'A First Novel of East Africa: German Designs in Tanganyika Territory, *East Africa* (29 August 1929), p. 1687.

10 van Beusekom and Hodgson, 'Lessons Learned?', p. 33.

11 See Françoise Dufour's chapter in this volume.

12 For a critical investigation of this relationship see for example Christa Knellwolf King and Margarete Rubik (eds), *Stories of Empire: Narrative Strategies for the Legitimation of an Imperial World Order* (Trier: wvt 2009); Valentin Y. Mudimbe, *The Invention of Africa: Gnosis, Philosophy, and the Order of Knowledge* (Bloomington, IN: Indiana University Press 1988); Edward Said, *Culture and Imperialism* (New York: Vintage 1994); David Spurr, *The Rhetoric of Empire: Colonial Discourse in Journalism, Travel Writing, and Imperial Administration* (Durham, NC: Duke University Press 1993].

13 Jean-Marc Moura, 'Littérature coloniale et exotisme: examen d'une opposition de la théorie littéraire coloniale', in Jean-François Durand (ed.), *Regards sur les littératures coloniales: Afrique francophone. Découvertes*, vol. 1 (Paris, Montreal: L'Harmattan 1999), pp. 21–39.

14 Bernard Mouralis, 'L'écriture, le réel et l'action: le cas de Georges Hardy dans *Ergaste ou la vocation colonial'*, in Durand (ed.), *Regards sur les littératures coloniales*, vol. 1, pp. 63–84.

15 Diana Jeater, 'Imagining Africans: Scholarship, Fantasy, and Science in Colonial Administration, 1920s Southern Rhodesia', *International Journal of African Historical Studies* 38, 1 (1999), pp. 1–26.

16 Philip Darby, *The Fiction of Imperialism: Reading Between International Relations and Postcolonialism* (London, Washington, DC: Cassell 1998); David Lewis, Dennis Rodgers, and Michael Woolcock, 'The Fiction of Development: Literary Representation as a Source of Authoritative Knowledge', *Journal of Development Studies* 44, 2 (2008), pp. 198–216; Nancy Rose Hunt, 'Between Fiction and History: Modes of Writing Abortion in Africa', *Cahiers d'Études Africaines* 47, 186 (2007), pp. 277–312.

17 See for instance Abdul JanMohamed, *Manichean Aesthetics: The Politics of Literature in Colonial Africa* (Amherst, MA: University of Massachusetts Press 1983); Anne McClintock, *Imperial Leather: Race, Gender and Sexuality in the Colonial Contest* (London, New York: Routledge 1995); Bernard Mouralis, *Littérature et développement: essai sur le statut, la fonction et la représentation de la littérature négro-africaine d'expression française* (Paris: Silex 1984); Hans-Jürgen Lüsebrink, *La conquête de l'espace public colonial: prises de parole et formes de participation d'écrivains et d'intellectuels africains dans la presse à l'époque coloniale, 1900–1960* (Frankfurt-on-Main; London: IKO 2003); Spurr, *The Rhetoric of Empire*.

18 A rare exception is Nancy Rose Hunt, 'Between Fiction and History'. The article treats novels as sources *and* artefacts, which speak not only through their content, but also through the way the story is organised, structured, and shaped.

19 Lewis, Rodgers, and Woolcock, 'The Fiction of Development', p. 199.

20 Ibid., pp. 204–5.

21 Gayatri Chakravorty Spivak, 'Can the Subaltern Speak?', in Laura Chrisman and Patrick Williams (eds), *Colonial Discourse and Postcolonial Theory: A Reader* (New York: Columbia University Press 1994 [1988]), pp. 66–111.

22 Mikhail M. Bakhtin, 'Discourse in the Novel', in Michael Holquist (ed.), *The Dialogic Imagination: Four Essays by M. M. Bakhtin* (Austin: University of Texas Press 2008), pp. 301–31.

23 Léon Fanoudh-Siefer, *Le mythe du nègre et de l'Afrique noire dans la littérature française, de 1800 à la Deuxième Guerre Mondiale* (Paris: Klincksieck 1968), p. 113.

24 Martin Steins, *Das Bild des Schwarzen in der europäischen Kolonialliteratur, 1870–1918: ein Beitrag zur literarischen Imagologie* (Frankfurt-on-Main: Thesen Verlag 1972), p. 57.

25 Anthony Kirk-Greene, *On Crown Service: A History of HM Colonial and Overseas Civil Services, 1837–1997* (London, New York: I. B. Tauris 1999), p. 150.

26 See the bibliography in Bernard Mouralis and Anne Piriou (eds), *Robert Delavignette: savant et politique, 1897–1976* (Paris: Karthala 2003), pp. 333–5.

27 Robert Delavignette, 'Le Paysannat', in Robert Delavignette, *Service coloniale* (Paris: Gallimard 1946), pp. 172–221.

28 Alice L. Conklin, *A Mission to Civilize: The Republican Idea of Empire in France and West Africa, 1895–1930* (Stanford, CA: Stanford University Press 1997), pp. 212–325; Catherine Coquery-Vidrovitch, 'La politique économique colonial', in Catherine Coquery-Vidrovitch and Odile Goerg (eds), *L'Afrique occidentale au temps des français: colonisateurs et colonisés, c. 1860–1960* (Paris: La Découverte 1992), pp. 105–40.

29 Michael Cowen and Robert Shenton, *Doctrines of Development* (London, New York: Routledge 1996), pp. 32–5.

30 Delavignette, *Les paysans noirs*, pp. 9–26.

31 Ibid., p. 27.

32 Ibid., pp. 22–3.

33 For a detailed account of the historical and autobiographical background, see Michèle Dacher, 'Une épopée gouin: *Les paysans noirs* à Banfora aujourd'hui', in Mouralis and Piriou (eds), *Robert Delavignette*, pp. 29–60.

34 Kenneth Bradley, *The Diary of a District Officer* (London: Harrap 1943).

35 William Malcolm Hailey, 'Foreword', in Bradley, *Diary*, p. 5.

36 Bradley, *Diary*, pp. 68–9, my emphasis.

37 Ibid., p. 177.

38 Quoted in Sean Morrow, '"No Girl Leaves the School Unmarried": Mabel Shaw and the Education of Girls at Mbereshi, Northern Rhodesia, 1915–1940', *International Journal of African Historical Studies* 19, 4 (1986), p. 615.

39 Mabel Shaw, *Children of the Chief* (London: London Missionary Society 1921); *Dawn in Africa: Stories of Girl Life* (London: Edinburgh House Press 1927); *God's Candlelights: An Educational Venture in Northern Rhodesia* (London: Edinburgh House Press 1932); *A Treasure of Darkness: An Idyll of African Child Life* (London, New York, Toronto: Longmans, Green and Co. 1936).

40 Morrow, '"No Girl Leaves the School Unmarried"', p. 633.
41 E. R. Micklem, 'Foreword', in Shaw, *Treasure of Darkness*, p. viii.
42 Shaw, *Treasure of Darkness*, pp. 53–4.
43 In Shaw's writing the child tends to symbolise the pure and the presence of God.
44 Shaw, *Treasure of Darkness*, p. 34.
45 Ibid., p. 74.
46 André Viola, 'L'angoisse devant l'autre et le même: le demi-sauvage (civilisé, métis) dans le roman populaire anglais du vingtième siècle', in Jean-François Durand and Jean Sévry (eds), *Regards sur les littératures coloniales: Afrique anglophone et lusophone*, vol. 3 (Paris: L'Harmattan 1999), pp. 109–27.
47 Joyce Cary, *The African Witch* (London: House of Stratus 2000 [1936]).
48 The last chapter ends with a vision of the author-narrator showing the adult Mary as future head of a flourishing mission; Shaw, *Treasure of Darkness*, p. 158.
49 Shaw gives this realist account a metaphorical dimension by paralleling the journey of the young African couple with the evangelical journey of Mary and Joseph to Bethlehem. The biblical story works as a frame that makes of the infant's salvation through the missionaries a re-enactment of Mary's salvation in the Gospel. The author thus (ab)uses the factual death of a Bemba woman to turn it into a message of religious supremacy: the ancestral gods that her husband evokes to save her do not have the power of the Christian god who saved Mary in the Gospel.
50 Shaw, *Treasure of Darkness*, p. 53.
51 Shaw, *Dawn in Africa*, pp. 60–2.
52 Olúfémi Táíwò, 'Colonialism and Its Aftermath: The Crisis of Knowledge Production', *Callaloo* 16, 4 (1993), pp. 895–8.
53 Phillip B. Wagoner, 'Precolonial Intellectuals and the Production of Colonial Knowledge', *Comparative Studies in Society and History* 45, 4 (2003), pp. 783–5.
54 Akiki K. Nyabongo, *The Story of an African Chief* (New York: Charles Scribner's Sons 1935).
55 Marc Matera, 'Colonial Subjects: Black Intellectuals and the Development of Colonial Studies in Britain', *Journal of British Studies* 49, 2 (2010), p. 395.
56 '"A Uganda Native's Book": Review of *An African Answers Back*, by Akiki K. Nyabongo', *East Africa* (8 August 1936), p. 1034.
57 '"Mis-remembering Africa: An African's Literary Effort": Review of "The Story of an African Chief"', by Akiki K. Nyabongo', *East Africa* (16 January 1936), p. 407.
58 Nyabongo, *African Chief*, pp. 62–3.
59 The text comments on Mujungu's first holidays at home: 'Many people from the uncle's village came to see him. They had a great feast that evening. And all the people went back talking of how fine Mujungu was and how well he had developed as a man'. Ibid., p. 210.
60 Ibid., p. 307.
61 Ibid., p. 308.
62 Ibid., pp. 273–89.
63 Margaret Wrong, *The Land and Life of Africa* (London: Cargate Press 1935), p. 39. The book is a semi-documentary collection of impressions of one of the author's numerous professional travels to East, Central and West Africa.
64 Nyabongo, *African Chief*, p. 244.
65 The text uses the term 'doctor' for Africans as well as for Europeans. The terminology differs from European texts that tend to call Africans skilled in treating illness and injuries anything from 'healer', 'native doctor' to 'charlatan'.
66 Parmenas Githendu Mockerie, *An African Speaks for His People* (London: Hogarth Press 1934), pp. 58–9; 71.
67 Lewis, Rodgers, and Woolcock, 'The Fiction of Development', pp. 214–16.

Epilogue: taking stock, looking ahead[1]

Joseph M. Hodge

Writing a truly comprehensive history of colonial development in Africa may be too tall an order for any book, regardless of its size or the skill of its authors, to ever claim. It is hoped, however, that the work presented here has made a modest contribution towards such a lofty goal. In this concluding epilogue, I would like to take stock of what I see as the common patterns and distinctive features that the fourteen case studies compiled for this volume reveal about development in colonial Africa. Much more, of course, could and should be done. I end, therefore, by looking ahead with some ideas and suggestions for further study.

Perhaps the most significant observation – one which all fourteen contributors have emphasised to varying degrees – is that the concept and practice of 'development' in colonial Africa was never static or monolithic in contruction or implementation. Instead, it evolved and shifted, taking on multiple meanings and forms in different contexts over the course of the century. Claudia Castelo's chapter documents the evolving nature of Portuguese colonial development doctrine under the Estado Novo, from Salazar's emphasis on the private sector as the engine of progress in the 1930s, through to the series of *Planos de Fomento* of the 1950s, with their emphasis on communications, transport, and white settlement, to the onset of the colonial wars in the 1960s in which the 'human factor', social investment, and regional integration feature more prominently. Similarly, Françoise Dufour's analysis of recurring discursive practices in French writing reveals a broad landscape of successive phases of development discourse stretching back two hundred years. Dufour identifies five main usages of the term *développement*, starting with the Enlightenment and early French colonial discourse, which stressed the goal of 'progress of civilisation' in which development refers to moral and intellectual development or the development of society or of the human race, or of civilisation more generally. It is not until the period from 1920 to 1960 that notions of economic development or the development of a specific country or region are introduced and become more commonly used.

On a more localised level, Eric Makombe explains how the theory of rural development in colonial Zimbabwe also passed through many phases, from the protective phase (1894–1919), to the technical development phase (1920–62), to the community development phase (1963–79), while Emma Hunter stresses that the Swahili word *maendeleo* shifted in meaning from simply referring to 'progress towards civilisation', with clear Christian undertones before the Second World War, to being associated more with new forms of social services, especially housing and education, and even with new political arrangements like local democratic government after 1945. Several contributors, including Castelo, Frank, Speek, Makombe, Pessis, Bruchhausen, Aráujo and Vasile, see the Second World War or the decade of the 1940s more generally, as a decisive turning point or sharp break either in the conceptual and policy framework for colonial development or in its actual practices or in both.

It might be more helpful, as Emma Hunter suggests, to think of these alterations and deflections as an expansion of the term creating a web of meanings and associations. Dufour implies something similar when she notes that development is a discourse with layers of accumulated meaning. Or, to paraphrase Juhani Koponen, development had many uses and meant different things, depending on who was using it to what end. Development provided a common language, broad enough to allow it to be used by a range of actors and for a variety of purposes. It is this amorphous and flexible nature, as Hunter argues, that is key to understanding its enduring power. It is a global concept with distinctive local resonances, and it is these specific instances and usages that need to be examined, not in isolation, but in conjunction and juxtaposition with one another.

The most obvious agents, as several chapters document (Koponen, Castelo, Makombe, Pessis, Aráujo and Vasile), were colonial state administrators and planners who utilised 'development' to legitimate and extend state intervention and control over African societies and communities. But as Hunter, and to a lesser extent Uyilawa Usuanlele and Martina Kopf, stress, African political leaders and nationalist parties also shared the goal of development and used it to critique government policies and practices as well as to support their own programmes of nation-building. The business community, as Billy Frank's piece on Barclays Bank reminds us, was also critical of large-scale state sponsored schemes, and offered a distinctive model of public-private financial partnership, lobbying the Colonial Office to ensure policies favourable to private enterprise. And in colonies dominated by white settlers, as Makombe shows, the language of development could be employed to perpetuate the segregation (separate development) and the unequal treatment of Africans by containing them in distinct, spatial 'niches'. Even missionaries, as Kopf's essay suggests, articulated their version of 'Christian development' that was projected as an alternative to the government's 'mass education' policies, through mission boarding schools. Perhaps the most paradoxical set of actors, as several chapters touch on (Castelo, Speek, Pessis, Bush), were scientists and various types of experts – agronomists, engineers, ecologists, public health experts, etc. – who both reinforced dominant development paradigms and were instrumental in planning and advising for many of the large-scale schemes and projects, but also played leading roles in re-shaping and reforming colonial policies towards a more 'humanist' and 'welfarist' emphasis.

The flexibility and amorphous nature of 'development' contributed to another prominent feature stressed by many of the contributors to the collection: colonial development was a deeply ambiguous and contradictory enterprise. Both Walter Schicho and Usuanlele, for example, note that education held a deeply ambiguous position in British and French colonial discourses. On the one hand, it was seen as an instrument of control, helping to shape African minds through 'character training' and 'adapting' them to a life of manual and agricultural labour. But on the other hand, colonial officials were reluctant to provide adequate educational services to Africans, especially literary education, for fear of 'flooding the market' with unemployed school leavers who were ripe for anti-colonial agitation. Similarly, Makombe notes that rural development strategies in colonial Zimbabwe were riddled with contradictions encouraging Africans to become wage earners living permanently with their families in towns in order to absorb 'surplus labour' from the reserves, while at the same time, working with African political authorities to 're-invent' rural African society in order to preserve the reserves.

Perhaps the most contradictory regime of all, however, was Portugal's Estado Novo which, as Aráujo and Vasile argue, developed a deeply ambiguous set of practices and discourses to cope with its relative powerlessness and inability to impose its imperial will. To legitimate its continuing presence in Africa, the regime adopted the concept of lusotropicalism, as well as the 'softer' rhetoric of a more 'humanist' colonial development doctrine, as discursive strategies to mediate the tensions of continuing economic exploitation and emigration of white settlers. Portugal and its colonies were projected as a multi-racial, multi-continental 'nation', in which white settlers in Angola and Mozambique were justified as the key agents fostering cultural harmony and promoting greater economic integration, despite the existence of discriminatory legal and political structures and glaring disparities in rural and regional living standards.

[369]

Colonial development was not only plagued by tensions and contradictions, it was also controversial, debated and frequently contested.
Indeed, ambiguity fostered doubt and dissent. Castelo, Pessis, Speek,
and Bush all emphasise the complex role of experts who lent legitimacy to colonial state power but also challenged and questioned
orthodox thinking on colonial development policy. At times, as both
Castelo and Pessis observe, they became highly vocal critics of the
post-war technocratic approach, uncovering abuses, calling into question political motives, and offering 'alternative visions' of development.
Makombe notes how the settler community in colonial Zimbabwe
was divided over the state's policy to encourage African labour stabilisation in urban areas, with some whites fearful of being 'swamped' by
Africans. White commercial farmers and estate owners also opposed
the policy, fearful that it would lead to greater competition for African
labour. Both Speek and Pessis emphasise that the post-war push
for mechanisation and technocratically driven development was
often opposed by local colonial administrators, especially agricultural
officers, who saw their power and authority being by-passed by new
state agencies and procedures. Speek notes how the leading officials in
the Northern Rhodesian Department of Agriculture, who advocated a
more ecologically informed and guided approach to developing African
agriculture, were either transferred or pushed into retirement after
the war, thus leaving the department devoid of leadership at the very
moment the new technocratic model was introduced. Frank in his
survey of the views of Barclays Bank field staff notes that there was
considerable debate within the Bank on what was necessary for
development in Africa to happen. Finally, Bruchhausen, Schicho and
Usuanlele all make mention of debates between those who advocated
quantity and those in favour of quality of colonial health and educational services. After the passing of the CDWA, for example, some
officials in Nigeria argued that education should be the first priority
in terms of investment and requested substantial sums under the new
Act for teacher salaries and for hiring more teachers, only to be blocked
by the CO which insisted that the dependencies had to be made productive first. Some local officials, however, continued to push back
insisting that development required substantial increases in Africans
with post-secondary education and technical training.

The fourteen case studies brought together for this compilation also
reveal some distinctive patterns and marked contrasts between sectors
as well as between different empires and regions. The chapters on economic and rural development show that ideologically the emphasis
on increasing the production and productivity of economic resources
was consistently advocated as part of colonial development. As Koponen

argues, 'development' has been part of colonialism from the outset, and should be regarded as the condition that made colonial exploitation possible. This imperative was expressed and dominant throughout, although there is a shift in the 1930s and 1940s to emphasising development as mutually beneficial with African populations gaining from raising colonial standards of living. Thus in terms of economic development, the Second World War was a turning point not so much at the policy or conceptual level as it was at the level of state practice, which – as Speek, Makombe, and Pessis all agree – saw a sharp and dramatic break in terms of urgency, compulsion, and the use of intrusive new methods such as mechanisation.

In contrast, the chapters on social development and welfare reveal a significant shift in the discourse towards a greater emphasis on the 'human' side of development, which in the case of Britain and France occurs in the 1930s and 1940s and for Portugal somewhat later in the 1950s and 1960s. But what is striking is the degree of continuity at the level of actual practice in the areas of health, education, and the representation and role of African women within colonial development. There is a strong continuity of pre-war patterns. As Bruchhausen and Usuanlele demonstrate for British colonial Africa, with the emphasis on the 'welfare' of African communities in the late 1930s and 1940s, there was a shift from seeing health and education as preconditions for development (Guggisberg's 'keystone of progress'), to viewing them more as the results of development, to be paid for by revenues generated from increased colonial production. But throughout the colonial period such 'recurrent expenditures' were never treated by colonial regimes as explicit goals of development and were never given priority in practice in terms of government investment. Barbara Bush comes to a similar conclusion when she notes that despite the new emphasis on a social welfare agenda, which opened up new opportunities for female medical experts, educationalists, anthropologists, and other researchers, it cannot really be claimed that academic development discourse was 'feminised'; just as before the Second World War, in the 1940s and 1950s male agents still dominated research, it was still assumed that peasant farmers were men, and African women remained passive objects of health and other welfare initiatives.

Another distinction that stands out from the essays has to do with the diversity of colonial rule in Africa rather than sectoral divergences. There was, as this volume has shown, considerable overlap in development trends across all the major colonial powers in Africa in the twentieth century. At the same time, both Portuguese colonialism and settler colonialism in southern Africa followed trajectories that were in many ways atypical and exhibited unique patterns not seen elsewhere. As noted in the introduction to this volume, scholars such as Penvenne have stressed the distinctiveness of late Portuguese colonialism, noting that 'Portugal settled [Angola and Mozambique] against the tide, promoting substantial state-sponsored projects at the very moment that other colonial powers began to reconsider their colonial empires'.[2] From a southern African perspective, however, as Makombe's chapter reminds us, Portugal's bolstering of settler colonialism doesn't seem so out of step, nor does its emphasis on large-scale settlement schemes which other late colonial and early post-colonial states also sponsored across sub-Saharan Africa at the time.

Nonetheless, one has to admit that the Portuguese experience deviated in significant ways, and that the enigmatic nature of Portuguese colonialism was, as Araújo and Vasile suggest, rooted in the country's precarious position within the international political and economic system. Portugal's 'semi-peripheral condition' within Europe made it an uncertain and contested centre of empire, forcing it to mediate 'narratives of powerlessness and poverty' with 'histories . . . of glory, civilisation and progress'. It lacked the material capacity to implement a large-scale development project in Africa and therefore had to mobilise the existing resources of indigenous labour and the inflow of white settlers. Its perceived need to maintain the 'mirage' of being an imperial nation may have also contributed to its persistence in fighting protracted colonial wars long after the imperial endgame had been decided in the rest of sub-Saharan Africa.

Nor was Portugal the only hold out, as the case of colonial Zimbabwe (and indeed South Africa under apartheid) reminds us. Significantly, Zimbabwe's development path has also been viewed by scholars as unique, designed 'to meet a set of rather specific requirements' that gave rise to a variety of 'idiosyncratic practices'.[3] As Makombe's study indicates, Southern Rhodesia was one of the only areas outside South Africa to witness the emergence of a manufacturing sector and industrial growth leading to significant rural migration to urban areas and the formation of a sizeable class of African wage earners. Simultaneously, skewed land distribution patterns favouring white farmers along with growing population pressures among Africans accelerated the deterioration of the reserves. These conditions reflected the size and dominance of the white settler community and their influence on local politics which to a large degree explains the particular response of the colonial state. It was only after the Second World War, Makombe notes, that policies similar to Indirect Rule appear as part of a strategy to re-invent and stabilise the reserves, and it was only in the 1960s with the promotion of 'community development', that the regime finally began to put more emphasis on people and social issues rather than land management.

The case studies presented here, as evidenced by the synopsis above, have given us much to think about. Needless to say, there is still much that needs to be done before a complete history of colonial development in Africa can be written. Such a history will have to explore the multiple links between various colonial state formations and their respective approaches to development. It will have to delineate the numerous flows and transfers of ideas, practices, and norms not only between supra-national bodies and imperial states, but also within imperial states themselves (between, for example, the metropolitan state and colonial governments, or among various branches of colonial administration). It will have to take account of cultural representations of development discourse in literature, film, visual media, and popular culture, which as Kopf and Makombe have shown with regard to colonial narratives and films, played a significant role in communicating concepts and practices of development to a wider public. Finally, it will have to include perspectives on development from colonised peoples as well as development concepts and practices derived from non-Europhone sources. In short, such a history will have to assemble a complex cartography of interconnections, intersections and influences.

By way of conclusion, I would like to lay out some possible directions for future research that have been suggested by the work of the scholars in this book. First and foremost, it is clear that more research needs to be done on African perspectives and the role of Africans, from various social backgrounds, as actors and agents of development. Up until now, most scholars have treated 'development' as a Western or Eurocentric concept in origin that was imposed on Africa from outside, and which was met by indifference and outright hostility among Africans. But scholars are now beginning to think of development and modernisation as a global project with a common history.[4] Emma Hunter's study, for example, shows how the concept was taken up in the Swahili language and public sphere in Tanzania. The example of Tanzanians taking diverse, and even conflicting, interest in *maendeleo* is instructive. It makes plain that colonial restrictions and exclusions of the colonised did not prevent Africans altogether from dealing with development, adopting, confronting or challenging it and evolving concepts and practices in the name of development and its respective translations. As Fred Cooper observes: 'The turning of the French and British towards a development-minded colonialism – the desire to expand empire resources while legitimizing colonial rule – became the basis for a profound engagement of African and European actors, which in turn changed the meanings of "development", of "citizenship", and of "self-government"'.[5]

Recent studies have begun to probe the perspective not just of nationalist leaders and political parties, who saw development as a way of building constituencies, but of everyday African workers and farmers. Sometimes even development projects typically judged as failures, such as the East Africa Groundnut Scheme, might be interpreted as beneficial from the perception of the African workers involved.[6] The influx of monetary income, as noted in Chapter 1 by Koponen, may have stimulated the local economy allowing some to accumulate enough savings to invest in trade, transport, or farming activities. In other cases, Africans transformed the technologies of colonial development, such as automobiles and roads, into – as Joshua Grace remarks – tools that 'could be used to undercut the logic of imperial rule'. Grace's research demonstrates that although 'roads and motor vehicles were supposed to transform African economies and societies by carrying the civilizing mission throughout . . . their introduction also offered African colonial employees . . . opportunities for social mobility as well as the skills and tools to contest racial hierarchies of technology and movement'.[7]

A second, related field of enquiry that requires further study is the role of African women in colonial development. Although Barbara Bush's chapter provides an excellent overview, both of representations of African women in colonial development discourses, and of the contributions of European women experts and academics to the formation of colonial policies and practices, we need much more research on specific cases of African women as actors and agents of development. Here too, recent work promises to fill the gap. Laura Ann Twagira's examination of the Office du Niger scheme, for example, shows how despite efforts to recruit whole families, the scheme suffered from a chronic absence of women, especially young unmarried women and wives, which doomed the Office's settlements to severe food shortages, population losses, and ultimately to failure. As Twagira writes:

> The problem was not just the lack of food stores, it was the lack of women to prepare even the small amount food available. The whole event centered on women. They were the ones who sold small bits of cotton in the market for sauce ingredients. They pounded millet for the main dish *toh* and carried the meal to the fields. Women assured daily survival; young men also needed wives to establish themselves . . . without women there was nothing to eat and little for young men to demonstrate any wealth or material standing.[8]

Other research avenues worth pursuing include more studies that are truly inter disciplinary in nature and scope. By bringing together scholars from Africa, Europe, and North America, *Developing Africa* has sought to foster a uniquely international dialogue on the history of colonial development. We regard the authors' diverse origins, both in terms of geography and disciplinary background, to be a valuable and noteworthy attribute of the book. But scholars should be encouraged to do more, by which I mean not simply the fostering of further dialogue between scholars from different disciplinary backgrounds, but the producing of studies, written by scholars or groups of scholars, that fuse together different methodological approaches into an integrated framework of analysis. Such studies are rare, and difficult to produce, but may ultimately be necessary for comprehending such an all-encompassing phenomenon as the history of development in Africa. There also needs to be more comparative work done on the diversity of different colonial experiences. Particularly valuable would be case studies that situate the Belgian Congo, or South Africa under the apartheid regime, within the continent-wide development trends and patterns identified and examined in this edited collection.

Finally, there needs to be more research on the interconnections among colonial empires in terms of horizontal flows and networks of personnel, ideas, debates, practices, and techniques. Christophe Bonneuil's examination of the pre-packaged settlement schemes implemented by colonial governments and post-independence regimes alike across tropical Africa is a good example of the kind of research I have in mind.[9] There are also clear parallels between the Portuguese colonies of Angola and Mozambique and colonial Zimbabwe which deserve further attention. In both cases, for example, we see a belated shift towards the 'human factor' and an emphasis on 'community development' and the idea of 'growth poles' in the 1960s.[10] We need to better understand, as David Simon suggests, how different former colonial territories were in touch with each other and how different indigenous communities were in touch with each other within and often across these colonial territories.[11]

Such interconnections must also be viewed through a more global or international lens, bringing in institutions such as the World Bank and the United Nations specialised agencies and programmes, as well as the strategic imperatives and dynamics of Cold War geo-politics. Continuing with the comparison of colonial Zimbabwe and Portuguese Africa, for example, it is significant that both regimes were able to prolong their grasp on power through indirect support from Washington, pitching their development efforts ideologically as part of the global Cold War.[12] The Rhodesians and the Portuguese, along with South Africa, attempted to justify their suppression of anti-colonial guerrilla wars by casting themselves as a 'protective belt' in the fight against communism in southern Africa. Much can be gained, I believe, from understanding how the global forces of the Cold War and the imperatives of the developmentalist state were intertwined and resonated across the continent and across the rupture of decolonisation. We need to know more – and hopefully future studies will help to clarify – how these forces and imperatives played themselves out in specific contexts and settings, and what the consequences and legacies have been for the countries and people affected.

Notes

1 I would like to thank my co-editors, Gerald Hödl and Martina Kopf, for their helpful comments and suggestions in writing the epilogue.
2 Jeanne Marie Penvenne, 'Settling Against the Tide: The Layered Contradictions of Twentieth-Century Portuguese Settlement in Mozambique', in Caroline Elkins and Susan Pedersen (eds), *Settler Colonialism in the Twentieth Century: Projects, Practices, Legacies* (New York, London: Routledge 2005), p. 80.
3 Eric Worby, '"Discipline without Oppression": Sequence, Timing and Marginality in Southern Rhodesia's Post-War Development Regime', *Journal of African History* 41, 1 (2000), p. 102. Other scholars have tended to view the Southern Rhodesian government's conservation and rural development polices as part of a wider, distinctive southern African experience; see Leonard Leslie Bessant, 'Coercive Development: Land Shortage, Forced Labor, and Colonial Development in the Chiweshe Reserve, Colonial Zimbabwe, 1938–1946', *International Journal of African Historical Studies* 25, 1 (1992), pp. 39–65; Michael Drinkwater, 'Technical Development and Peasant Impoverishment: Land Use Policy in Zimbabwe's Midlands Province', *Journal of Southern African Studies* 15, 2 (1989), pp. 287–305.
4 David C. Engerman and Corinna R. Unger, 'Introduction: Towards a Global History of Modernization', *Diplomatic History* 33, 3 (2009), pp. 375–85.
5 Frederick Cooper, *Africa since 1940: The Past of the Present* (Cambridge: Cambridge University Press 2002), p. 39.
6 Matteo Rizzo, 'What Was Left of the Groundnut Scheme? Development Disaster and Labour Market in Southern Tanganyika, 1946–1952', *Journal of Agrarian Change* 6, 2 (2006), pp. 205–38.
7 Joshua Grace, 'Heroes of the Road: Race, Gender, and the Politics of Mobility in Twentieth-Century Tanzania', *Africa: Journal of the International African Institute* 83, 3 (August 2013). Also see his dissertation 'Modernization *Bubu*: Cars, Roads, and the Politics of Development in Tanzania, 1870s to 1980s' (PhD dissertation, Michigan State University, 2013).
8 Laura Ann Twagira, 'Peopling the Landscape: Colonial Irrigation, Technology, and Demographic Crisis in the French Soudan, ca. 1926–1944', *PSAE Research Series* 10 (2012), pp. 26–7.
9 Christophe Bonneuil, 'Development as Experiment: Science and State Building in Late Colonial and Postcolonial Africa, 1930–1970', *Osiris*, 2nd series, 15 (2000), pp. 258–81.
10 See the chapters by Castelo, Makombe, and Aráujo and Vasile in this volume. Also see Jocelyn Alexander, 'Technical Development and the Human Factor: Sciences of Development in Rhodesia's Native Affairs Department', in Saul Dubow (ed.), *Science and Society in Southern Africa* (Manchester: Manchester University Press 2000), pp. 212–37.
11 Comments made by David Simon during the concluding roundtable session at the 'Developing Africa' International Workshop, University of Vienna, January 2011.
12 Odd Arne Westad, *The Global Cold War: Third World Interventions and the Making of Our Times* (Cambridge: Cambridge University Press 2005), pp. 207–49.

BIBLIOGRAPHY

Archives

Archives Départementales de l'Aude, Carcassonne
Archives of the London School of Economics and Political Science (LSE), London
Archives Nationales du Mali
Archives Nationales d'Outremer (ANOM), Aix en Provence
Archives Nationales du Sénégal (ANS), Dakar
Arquivo Histórico Ultramarino (AHU), Lisbon
Barclays Group Archives (BGA), Manchester
Bibliothèque Historique du CIRAD (BH CIRAD), Nogent
British National Archives (BNA), London
Centre de Recherche et de Documentation du Sénégal (CRDS), Saint-Louis
Ghana National Archives, Accra
Labour History Archive and Study Centre, Manchester
Musée du vivant et histoire d'AgroParisTech (MdV APT), Paris
National Archives of Nigeria (NAI), Ibadan
National Archives of Nigeria (NAK), Kaduna
National Archives of Zimbabwe (NAZ), Harare
Rhodes House Library (RHO), Oxford
Royal Anthropological Institute (RAI), London
Royal Botanic Gardens, Library, Art, and Archives (RBG Kew), London
Royal Commonwealth Society Archives, Cambridge University Library, Cambridge
Tanzania National Archives (TNA), Dar es Salaam
United States National Archives II, College Park, Maryland
University of South Africa Archives (UNISA), Pretoria, RSA

Printed sources

Abbott, George C., 'Re-examination of the 1929 Colonial Development Act', *Economic History Review*, New Series, 24, 1 (1971): 68–81.
Abecasis, Carlos Krus, 'Prefácio', in Marcello Caetano and Carlos Krus Abecasis (eds), *Colóquio sobre o II Plano de Fomento: Ultramar* (Lisbon: Junta de Investigações do Ultramar – Centro de Estudos Políticos e Sociais 1959): ix–xii.
Abernethy, David B., *The Political Dilemma of Popular Education: An African Case* (Stanford, CA: Stanford University Press 1969).
Achard, Pierre, 'La passion du développement: une analyse de l'économie politique' (Thèse de lettres, Université Paris 7, 1989).
Achebe, Nwando, *Farmers, Traders, Warriors and Kings: Female Power and Authority in Northern Igboland, 1900–1960* (Portsmouth, NH: Heinemann 2005).

BIBLIOGRAPHY

Acot, Pascal, *Histoire de l'écologie* (Paris: Presses universitaires de France 1988).

Adams, William M., *Green Development: Environment and Sustainability in the Third World* (London, New York: Routledge 2001).

Adamu, E. S. S., 'Small-holder Cashew Farmers in Mtwara Region: A Case Study', *Journal of the Geographical Association of Tanzania*, 5 (1969): 71–93.

Adas, Michael, *Dominance by Design: Technological Imperatives and America's Civilizing Mission* (London, Cambridge, MA: Belknap 2006).

Adejumobi, Saheed, '"Life more Abundant": Colonial Transition, the Yoruba Intelligentsia and the Politics of Education and Social Welfare Reform in Nigeria, 1940–1970' (PhD dissertation, University of Texas/Austin, 2001).

Advisory Committee on Education in the Colonies, *Report of Adult and Mass Education Sub-Committee: Mass Education in African Society* (London: HMSO 1943).

Advisory Committee on Native Education in Tropical Africa, *Education Policy in British Tropical Africa* (London: HMSO 1925).

Agência Geral do Ultramar, 'Junta de Investigações do Ultramar', *Boletim da Agência Geral do Ultramar* 35, 407–8 (1959): 181–2.

Albertini, Rudolf von, *Dekolonisation: Die Diskussion über die Verwaltung und Zukunft der Kolonien, 1918–1960* (Köln: Westdeutscher Verlag 1966).

Alcalde, Javier Gonzalo, *The Idea of Third World Development: Emerging Perspectives in the United States and Britain, 1900–1950* (Lanham, NY, London: University Press of America 1987).

Alexander, Jocelyn, 'Technical Development and the Human Factor: Sciences of Development in Rhodesia's Native Affairs Department', in Saul Dubow (ed.), *Science and Society in Southern Africa* (Manchester: Manchester University Press 2000): 212–37.

Alexandre, Valentim, *A questão Colonial no Parlamento, 1821–1910* (Lisbon: Publicações Dom Quixote 2008).

——, 'Ideologia, economia e política: a questão colonial na implantação do Estado Novo', *Análise Social* 28, 123–4 (1993): 1117–36.

——, *Velho Brasil, novas Áfricas: Portugal e o Império, 1808–1975* (Porto: Afrontamento 2000).

Allan, William, 'The Resettlement of Native Populations in Northern Rhodesia', in William Allan, *Studies in African Land Usage in Northern Rhodesia* (Cape Town, New York: Oxford University Press 1949): 71–80.

Allman, Jean, 'Making Mothers: Missionaries, Medical Officers and Women's Work in Colonial Asante, 1924–1945', *History Workshop Journal* 38, 1 (1994): 23–47.

——, '"Rounding up Spinsters": Gender Chaos and Unmarried Women in Colonial Asante', *Journal of African History* 37, 2 (1996): 195–214.

Althusser, Louis, 'Idéologie et appareils idéologiques d'état (Notes pour une recherche)', in Louis Althusser, *Positions, 1964–1975* (Paris: Les Éditions sociales 1976): 67–125.

Anderson, David, *Eroding the Commons: The Politics of Ecology in Baringo, Kenya, 1890s–1963* (Athens, OH: Ohio University Press 2003).

Anghie, Antony, 'The Evolution of International Law: Colonial and Postcolonial Realities', *Third World Quarterly* 27, 5 (2006): 739–53.

Anker, Peder, *Imperial Ecology: Environmental Order in the British Empire, 1895–1945* (Cambridge, MA: Harvard University Press 2001).

Ansprenger, Franz, *Politische Geschichte Afrikas im 20. Jahrhundert* (Munich: Beck 1999).

Araújo, A. Correia de, *Aspectos do desenvolvimento económico e social de Angola* (Lisbon: Junta de Investigações do Ultramar 1964).

Arce, Alberto and Norman Long, *Anthropology, Development, and Modernities: Exploring Discourses, Counter-Tendencies, and Violence* (London, New York: Routledge 1999).

Arrighi, Giovanni, *The Political Economy of Rhodesia* (The Hague: Mouton 1967).

Ashton, S. R. and S. E. Stockwell (eds), *Imperial Policy and Colonial Practice 1925–1945: British Documents on the End of Empire*, vol. 1/A (London: HMSO 1996).

——, 'Introduction', in S. R. Ashton and S. E. Stockwell (eds), *Imperial Policy and Colonial Practice 1925–1945: British Documents on the End of Empire*, vol. 1/A (London: HMSO 1996).

Bakhtin, Mikhail M., 'Discourse in the Novel', in Michael Holquist (ed.), *The Dialogic Imagination: Four Essays by M. M. Bakhtin* (Austin: University of Texas Press 2008): 259–422.

Barata, José Fernando Nunes, *Para uma política de população* (Lisbon: Junta de Investigação do Ultramar – Centro de Estudos Político-Sociais 1963).

Barnes, Teresa A., 'The Fight for Control of African Women's Mobility in Colonial Zimbabwe, 1900–1939', *Signs: Journal of Women in Culture and Society* 17, 3 (1992): 586–608.

Barnett, Tony, *The Gezira Scheme: An Illusion of Development* (London: Frank Cass 1977).

Bates, Margaret L., 'Tanganyika under British Administration, 1920–1955' (PhD dissertation, University of Oxford, 1957).

Beck, Ann, 'Colonial Policy and Education in British East Africa, 1900–1950', *Journal of British Studies* 5, 2 (1966): 115–38.

Beinart, William, 'Soil Erosion, Conservationism and Ideas about Development: A Southern African Exploration, 1900–1960', *Journal of Southern African Studies* 11, 1 (1984): 52–83.

Beinart, William and Lotte Hughes, *Environment and Empire* (Oxford: Oxford University Press 2007).

Beinart, William, Karen Brown, and Daniel Gilfoyle, 'Experts and Expertise in Colonial Africa Reconsidered: Science and the Interpenetration of Knowledge', *African Affairs* 108, 432 (2009): 413–33.

Bender, Gerald J., *Angola under the Portuguese: The Myth and the Reality* (Berkeley, Los Angeles: University of California Press 1978).

Berman, Bruce and John Lonsdale, *Unhappy Valley: Conflict in Kenya and Africa*, Book Two, *Violence and Ethnicity* (London: James Currey; Nairobi: Heinemann Kenya; Athens, OH: University of Ohio Press 1992).

Berman, Edward H., 'American Influence on African Education: The Role of the Phelps-Stokes Fund's Education Commissions', *Comparative Education Review* 15, 2 (1971): 132–45.

Berman, Marshall, *All that is Solid Melts into Air: The Experience of Modernity* (Harmondsworth: Penguin 1988).

Bessant, Leonard Leslie, 'Coercive Development: Land Shortage, Forced Labor, and Colonial Development in the Chiweshe Reserve, Colonial Zimbabwe, 1938–1946', *International Journal of African Historical Studies* 25, 1 (1992): 39–65.

Bhabha, Homi K., *The Location of Culture* (London: Routledge 1994).

Blacklock, Mary G., 'Certain Aspects of the Welfare of Women and Children in the Colonies', *Annals of Tropical Medicine and Parasitology* 30, 2 (1936): 221–64.

——, 'Cooperation in Health Education', *Africa* 4, 2 (1931): 202–8.

Blommaert, Jan, *Discourse* (Cambridge: Cambridge University Press 2005).

——, 'Some Problems in the Interpretation of Swahili Political Texts', in Jan Blommaert (ed.), *Swahili Studies: Essays in Honour of Marcel van Spaandonck* (Ghent: Academia Press 1991): 109–35.

Boahen, Adu, *Ghana: Evolution and Change in the Nineteenth and Twentieth Centuries* (London: Longman 1975).

Bonneuil, Christophe, *Des savants pour l'empire: la structuration des recherches scientifiques colonials au temps de 'La mise en valeur des colonies françaises', 1917–1945* (Paris: L'ORSTOM 1991).

——, 'Development as Experiment: Science and State Building in Late Colonial and Postcolonial Africa, 1930–1970', *Osiris*, 2nd series, 15 (2000): 258–81.

Boserup, Ester, *Women's Role in Economic Development*, with a new introduction by Nazneen Kanji, Su Fei Tan, and Camilla Toulmin (London: Earthscan 2007 [1970]).

Bossa, José, 'Resumo dos princípios constitucionais por que se rege o território ultramarino de Portugal', *Boletim Geral do Ultramar* 28, 329 (1952): 17–26.

Bossuat, Gérard, *La France, l'aide américaine et la construction européenne, 1944–1954* (Paris: Comité pour l'histoire économique et financière de la France 1997).

Bourne, Ray, *Aerial Survey in Relation to the Economic Development of New Countries, with Special Reference to an Investigation Carried Out in Northern Rhodesia* (Oxford: Clarendon Press 1928).

Bourret, F. M., *Ghana: The Road to Independence, 1919–1957* (Oxford: Oxford University Press 1960).

Bowman, Andrew, 'Ecology to Technocracy: Scientists, Survey and Power in the Agricultural Development of Late-Colonial Zambia', *Journal of Southern African Studies* 37, 1 (2011): 135–53.

Bradley, Kenneth, *Africa Notwithstanding* (London: Lovat Dickson 1932).

——, *The Colonial Service as a Career* (London: Colonial Office 1950).

——, *The Diary of a District Officer* (London: Harrap 1943).

——, *Hawks Alighting* (London: Lovat Dickson 1933).

Brantlinger, Patrick, *Rule of Darkness: British Literature and Imperialism, 1830–1914* (Ithaca, NY, London: Cornell University Press 1988).

Brennan, J. R., 'Nation, Race and Urbanization in Dar es Salaam, Tanzania, 1916–1976' (PhD dissertation, Northwestern University, 2002).

——, 'Realizing Civilization through Patrilineal Descent: The Intellectual Making of an African Racial Nationalism in Tanzania, 1920–50', *Social Identities* 12, 4 (2006): 405–23.

——, 'Youth, the TANU Youth League and Managed Vigilantism in Dar es Salaam, Tanzania, 1925–73', *Africa* 76, 2 (2006): 221–46.

Brockway, Fenner, *African Journeys* (London: Gollancz 1955).

Bromber, Katrin, 'Ustaarabu: A Conceptual Change in Tanganyika Newspaper Discourse in the 1920s', in Roman Loimeier and Rüdiger Seesemann (eds), *The Global Worlds of the Swahili* (Berlin: Lit 2006): 67–81.

Browers, Michelle L., *Democracy and Civil Society in Arab Political Thought: Transcultural Possibilities* (Syracuse, NY: Syracuse University Press 2006).

Bruchhausen, Walter, *Medizin zwischen den Welten: Vergangenheit und Gegenwart des medizinischen Pluralismus im südöstlichen Tansania* (Göttingen: v&r University Press, Bonn University Press 2006).

——, '"Practising Hygiene and Fighting the Natives' Diseases": Public and Child Health in German East Africa and Tanganyika Territory, 1900–1960', *Dynamis* 23 (2003): 85–114.

Bush, Barbara,'Gender and Empire: The Twentieth Century', in Philippa Levine (ed.), *Gender and Empire* (Oxford: Oxford University Press 2004): 77–111.

Butler, L. J., 'British Decolonization, Insurgency and Strategic Reverse: The Middle East, Africa and Malaya, 1951–1957', in Martin Thomas, Bob Moore, and L. J. Butler (eds), *Crises of Empire: Decolonization and Europe's Imperial States, 1918–1975* (London: Hodder Education 2008): 73–96.

Caetano, Marcello, 'Angola e Moçambique', *Boletim Geral do Ultramar* 30, 348–9 (1954): 95–8.

——, 'Discurso de S. Ex.ª o Ministro das Colónias no acto de posse do Director Geral, Interino, de Fomento Colonial e do Inspector Superior de Fomento Colonial', *Boletim Geral das Colónias* 21, 236 (1945): 3–15.

——, 'O planeamento económico em Portugal', in Marcello Caetano and Carlos Krus Abecasis (eds), *Colóquio sobre o II Plano de Fomento: Ultramar* (Lisbon: Junta de Investigações do Ultramar – Centro de Estudos Políticos e Sociais 1959): 1–16.

——, *Os nativos na economia africana* (Coimbra: Coimbra Editora 1954).

——, 'Plano de fomento para 1959–64: exposição do sr. prof. dr. Marcello Caetano ao Conselho Económico', *Boletim Geral do Ultramar* 33, 379 (1957): 9–46.

Cairns, Alan C., *Prelude to Imperialism: British Reactions to Central African Society, 1840–1890* (London: Routledge and Kegan Paul 1965).

Cairo, Heriberto, '"Portugal is not a small country": Maps and Propaganda in the Salazar Regime', *Geopolitics* 11, 3 (2006): 367–95.

Camille, Guy, 'La mise en valeur des colonies françaises', *Annales de Géographie* 32, 177 (1923): 265–71.

Cape Town Conference, 'Report of the International Conference of Representatives of the Health Services of Certain African Territories and British India, held at Cape Town, November 15th to 25th, 1932', *Quarterly Bulletin of the Health Organisation of the League of Nations* 2 (1933): 3–115.

BIBLIOGRAPHY

Carneiro, Rui de Sá, 'Fomento colonial', *Boletim Geral das Colónias* 18, 204 (1942): 37–63.

Carstairs, C. Y., 'Colonial Research', *African Affairs* 44, 174 (1945): 19–26.

Cary, Joyce, *The African Witch* (London: House of Stratus 2000 [1936]).

Castelo, Cláudia, *'O modo português de estar no mundo':o luso-tropicalismo e a ideologia colonial portuguesa, 1933–1961* (Porto: Afrontamento 1998).

——, *Passagens para África: o povoamento de Angola e Moçambique com naturais da metrópole, 1920–1974* (Porto: Afrontamento 2007).

Cell, John W., *Hailey: A Study in British Imperialism, 1872–1969* (Cambridge: Cambridge University Press 1992).

——, 'Lord Hailey and the the Making of the African Survey', *African Affairs* 88, 353 (1989): 481–505.

Chafer, Tony, 'Friend or Foe? Competing Visions of Empire in French West Africa in the Run-up to Independence', in Martin Thomas (ed.), *French Colonial Mind*, vol. 1, *Mental Maps of Empire and Colonial Encounters* (Lincoln, NE, London: University of Nebraska Press 2012): 275–97.

Chalmers, Rhoderick, '"We Nepalis": Language, Literature and the Formation of a Nepali Public Sphere in India, 1914–1940' (PhD dissertation, London SOAS, 2003).

Chamberlain, Joseph, 'British Trade and the Expansion of Empire: Speech given before the Birmingham Chamber of Commerce, 13 November 1896', in Joseph Chamberlain, *Foreign and Colonial Speeches* (London: Routledge 1897): 140–58.

——, 'Speech at Walsall, 15 July 1895', in George Bennett (ed.), *The Concept of Empire: Burke to Attlee, 1774–1947* (London: Adam & Charles Black 1953): 313–14.

Chambers, Robert, *Settlement Schemes in Tropical Africa: A Study of Organizations and Development* (London: Routledge 1969).

Chandavarkar, Rajnarayan, 'Imperialism and the European Empires', in Julian Jackson (ed.), *Europe, 1900–1945* (Oxford: Oxford University Press 2002): 138–72.

Charlton, Sue Ellen M., Jana Everett, and Kathleen Staudt (eds), *Women, the State and Development* (Albany, NY: State University of New York Press 1989).

Chevalier, Auguste, 'Les essais de cultures nouvelles et de mécanisation de l'agriculture au Moyen Congo Français (Niari et pays Batéké)', *Revue Internationale de Botanique Appliquée et d'Agriculture Tropicale* 31, 347–8 (1951): 506–12.

Chidzero, B. T. G., *Tanganyika and International Trusteeship* (London: Oxford University Press 1961).

Chikonzo, Kelvin, 'The Construction of African Cultural Identities in Zimbabwean Films, from 1948–2000' (MPhil thesis, University of Zimbabwe, 2005).

Chimombe, Theresa, 'The Role of Banks and Financial Institutions in the Accumulation and Reinvestment of Capital in Zimbabwe' (MPhil thesis, University of Zimbabwe, 1983).

Chipp, Thomas F. and Arthur Tansley, *Aims and Methods in the Study of Vegetation* (London: British Empire Vegetation Committee 1926).

Clarke, Sabine, 'A Technocratic Imperial State? The Colonial Office and Scientific Research, 1940–1960', *Twentieth Century British History* 18, 4 (2007): 453–80.

Clay, Geoffrey F., *Memorandum on Post-War Planning in Northern Rhodesia* (Lusaka: Government Printer 1945).

Clignet, Remi P. and Philip J. Foster, 'French and British Colonial Education in Africa', *Comparative Education Review* 8, 2 (1964): 191–8.

Cohen, Andrew, *British Policy in Changing Africa* (London: Routledge and Kegan Paul 1959).

Cohn, Bernard S., *Colonialism and Its Forms of Knowledge: The British in India* (Princeton, NJ, Chichester: Princeton University Press 1996).

Coleman, James S., *Nigeria: Background to Nationalism* (Berkeley: University of California Press 1965).

Coleno, Paul and Maurice Rossin, *Le plan de culture mécanisée de l'arachide dans l'Est-africain anglais, situation en mai 1948* (Paris: Ministère de la France d'Outre-Mer 1948).

Colonial Office, *Correspondence Relating to the Welfare of Women in Tropical Africa* (London: HMSO 1938).

Comaroff, John and Jean Comaroff, *Ethnography and the Historical Imagination* (Oxford, Boulder, CO: Westview Press 1992).

——, 'Home-made Hegemony: Modernity, Domesticity and Colonialism in South Africa', in Karen Tranberg Hansen (ed.), *African Encounters with Domesticity* (New Brunswick, NJ: Rutgers University Press 1992): 37–74.

Condorcet, Jean-Antoine-Nicolas deCaritat, Marquis de, *Esquisse d'un tableau historique des progrès de l'esprit humain* (Paris: Flammarion 1998 [1794]).

Congresso de Povoamento e Promoção Social, Luanda, 4 a 9 de Outubro de 1970 (Luanda: Asociações Econòmicas de Anglola 1970).

Conklin, Alice L., *A Mission to Civilize: The Republican Idea of Empire in France and West Africa, 1895–1930* (Stanford, CA: Stanford University Press 1997).

Constantine, Stephen, *The Making of British Colonial Development Policy, 1914–1940* (London: Frank Cass 1984).

Cooper, Frederick, *Africa since 1940: The Past of the Present* (Cambridge: Cambridge University Press 2002).

——, *Colonialism in Question: Theory, Knowledge, History* (Berkeley, London: University of California Press 2005).

——, *Decolonization and African Society: The Labor Question in French and British Africa* (Cambridge: Cambridge University Press 1996). French edition: *Décolonisation et travail en Afrique: l'Afrique britannique et française, 1935–1960* (Paris: Karthala 2004).

——, 'Development, Modernization and the Social Sciences in the Era of Decolonization: The Examples of British and French Africa', *Revue d'Histoire des Sciences Humaines* 10 (2004): 9–38.

——, 'Modernizing Bureaucrats, Backward Africans, and the Development Concept', in Frederick Cooper and Randall Packard (eds), *International Development and the Social Sciences: Essays on the History and Politics of Knowledge* (Berkeley, Los Angeles, London: University of California Press 1997): 64–92.

——, 'Reconstructing Empire in British and French Africa', *Past and Present* 210, suppl. 6 (2011): 196–210.

——, 'Writing the History of Development', *Journal of Modern European History* 8, 1 (2010): 5–23.

Cooper, Frederick and Randall Packard (eds), *International Development and the Social Sciences: Essays on the History and Politics of Knowledge* (Berkeley, Los Angeles, London: University of California Press 1997).

——, 'Introduction', in Frederick Cooper and Randall Packard (eds), *International Development and the Social Sciences: Essays on the History and Politics of Knowledge* (Berkeley, Los Angeles, London: University of California Press 1997): 1–41.

Coquery-Vidrovitch, Catherine, *African Women: A Modern History* (Boulder, CO: Westview Press 1997).

——, 'La mise en dépendance de l'Afrique noire: essai de périodisation, 1800–1970', *Cahiers d'Études Africaines* 16, 61 (1976): 7–58.

——, 'La politique économique colonial', in Catherine Coquery-Vidrovitch and Odile Goerg (eds), *L'Afrique occidentale au temps des français: colonisateurs et colonisés, c. 1860–1960* (Paris: La Découverte 1992): 105–40.

Cornwall, Andrea (ed.), *Readings in Gender in Africa* (Oxford: James Currey 2005).

Costa, Manuel Rafael Amaro da, *Humanismo económico no Ultramar: conferência proferida pelo Subsecretário de Estado do Fomento Ultramarino, Eng.º Manuel Rafael Amaro da Costa, em 5 de Junho de 1962, no anfiteatro do Instituto de Medicina Tropical* (Lisbon: Agência Geral do Ultramar 1962).

Cowen, Michael and Robert Shenton, *Doctrines of Development* (London, New York: Routledge 1996).

——, 'The Invention of Development', in Jonathan Crush (ed.), *Power of Development* (London, New York: Routledge 1995): 27–43.

Crosby, Alfred W., *Ecological Imperialism: The Biological Expansion of Europe, 900–1900* (Cambridge, New York: Cambridge University Press 1986).

Crossley, Julian and John Blandford, *The DCO Story* (London: Barclays Bank International 1975).

Crush, Jonathan (ed.), *Power of Development* (London, New York: Routledge 1995).

Culioli, Antoine, *Pour une linguistique de l'énonciation*, vol. 1, *Opérations et représentations* (Paris: Ophrys 1990).

——, *Pour une linguistique de l'énonciation*, vol. 2, *Domaine notionnel* (Paris: Ophrys 1999).

Cullather, Nick, 'Development? It's History', *Diplomatic History* 24, 4 (2000): 641–53.

Cunha, Joaquim Moreira da Silva, *Cabora-Bassa: The Signing of the Cabora Bassa Agreement on the 19th September 1969* (Lisbon: Agência Geral do Ultramar 1970).

——, 'Portugal e o fenómeno da descolonização', *Boletim da Agência Geral do Ultramar* 39, 454–5 (1963): 43–50.

Dacher, Michèle, 'Une épopée gouin: *Les paysans noirs* à Banfora aujourd'hui', in Bernard Mouralis and Anne Piriou (eds), *Robert Delavignette: savant et politique, 1897–1976* (Paris: Karthala 2003): 29–60.

Dag Hammarskjöld Foundation, *What Now? Another Development* (Uppsala: Dag Hammarskjöld Foundation 1975).

Danquah, Francis K., 'Rural Discontent and Decolonization in Ghana, 1945–51', *Agricultural History* 68, 1 (1994): 1–19.

Darby, Philip, *The Fiction of Imperialism: Reading between International Relations and Postcolonialism* (London, Washington, DC: Cassell 1998).

Darwin, John, 'What was the Late Colonial State?', *Itinerario* 23, 3–4 (1999): 73–82.

Datta, Kusum, 'The Political Economy of Rural Development in Colonial Zambia: The Case of the Ushi-Kabende, 1947–1953', *International Journal of African Historical Studies* 21, 2 (1988): 249–72.

Davies, D. Hywel, 'Towards an Urbanisation Strategy for Zimbabwe', *Geojournal*, suppl. 2 (1981): 73–84.

Davis, Diana K., *Resurrecting the Granary of Rome: Environmental History and French Colonial Expansion in North Africa* (Athens, OH: Ohio University Press 2007).

'The Declaration of Cocoyoc', *World Development* 3, 2–3 (1975): 141–8.

de Gaulle, Charles, 'Discours de Brazzaville, 30 Janvier 1944'. Available at: www.charles-de-gaulle.org/pages/l-homme/accueil/discours/pendant-la-guerre-1940–1946/discours-de-brazzaville-30–janvier-1944.php (accessed 14 March 2013).

Dekeyser, Pierre-Louis, *Quelques aspects du problème des mange-mil* (Dakar: IFAN 1953).

Delavignette, Robert, *Les paysans noirs* (Paris: Stock 1931).

——, *Service coloniale* (Paris: Gallimard 1946).

Department of Agriculture, *Second Annual Bulletin* (Lusaka: Government Printer 1932).

Department of Native Affairs/Economic Development, 'African Economic Development in Southern Rhodesia', *Native Affairs Department Annual* (1957): 45–56.

Dernburg, Bernhard, 'Rede in der Sitzung der Budgetkommission des Reichstags vom 18. Februar 1908 besonders über Fragen der Eingeborenenpolitik', *Deutsches Kolonialblatt* 19 (1908): 216–31.

Des Chene, Mary, 'In the Name of Bikas', *Studies in Nepali History and Society* 1, 2 (1996): 1–7.

Desjeux, Dominique, *La question agraire à Madagascar: administration et paysannat de 1895 à nos jours* (Paris: L'Harmattan 1979).

De Suremain, Marie-Albane, 'Métamorphoses d'un continent: l'Afrique des Annales de Géographie, de 1919 au début des années 1960', *Cahiers d'Études Africaines* 39, 153 (1999): 145–68.

de Wilde, John Charles, assisted by Peter F. M. McLoughlin et al., *Experiences with Agricultural Development in Tropical Africa*, vol. 2, *The Case Studies* (Baltimore: Johns Hopkins Press 1967).

Diallo Cô-Trung, Marina, *La Compagnie Générale des Oléagineux Tropicaux en Casamance: autopsie d'une opération de mise en valeur colonial, 1948–1962* (Paris: Karthala 1998).

Dimier, Véronique, 'Politiques indigènes en France et en Grande-Bretagne dans les années 1930: aux origines coloniales des politiques de développement', *Politique et Sociétés* 24, 1 (2005): 73–99.

Dinesen, Isak, *Letters from Africa, 1914–1931*, ed. Frans Lasson (London: Weidenfeld and Nicolson 1981).

Drinkwater, Michael, 'Technical Development and Peasant Impoverishment: Land Use Policy in Zimbabwe's Midlands Province', *Journal of Southern African Studies* 15, 2 (1989): 287–305.

Drouin, Jean-Marc, *L'écologie et son histoire: reinventer la nature* (Paris: Desdée de Brouwer 1991).

Dufour, Françoise, 'De l'effet de l'interdiscours colonial dans la production du sens de la nomination "pays dits *les moins avancés*"', in Virginie Doubli, Laurent Bénédicte, Lecler Aude et al. (eds), *Le sens c'est de la dynamique: la construction du sens en sciences du langage et en psychologie* (Montpellier: Presses Universitaires de la Méditerranée 2009): 61–73.

——, *De l'idéologie coloniale à celle du développement: une analyse du discours France-Afrique* (Paris: L'Harmattan 2010).

——, 'Des rhétoriques coloniales à celles du développement: archeologie discursive d'une dominance' (Thèse de doctorat, Université de Montpellier, 2007). Available at: http://tel.archives-ouvertes.fr/docs/00/20/26/72/PDF/TheseFDufour.pdf (accessed 8 May 2013).

——, 'Développement durable, humain: la cohérence discursive des contradictions', *Mots: Les Langages du Politique*, 96 (2011): 81–96.

——, 'Dire le "Sud": quand nommer l'autre catégorise le monde', *Autrepart: Revue des Sciences Sociales du Sud* 41 (2007): 27–39.

Dumont, René, 'Les difficultés de la modernisation de l'agriculture africaine autochtone', *Cahiers des Ingénieurs Agronomes* 6, 2 (1950): 14–20.

——, 'La mise en valeur agricole de l'Afrique tropicale', *Economie Contemporaine* (January 1951): 24–34; (February 1951): 16–28.

——, 'Orientation de l'agriculture française et coloniale dans le cadre d'une économie dirigée', *Revue de l'Économie Contemporaine*, 17 (September 1943): 19–26.

——, *Plan d'orientation de la production agricole française et coloniale* (Paris: Secrétariat Général du Ravitaillement 1944).

Durand, Oswald, *Terre noire* (Paris: Fournier 1935).

Easterly, William, *The White Man's Burden: Why the West's Efforts to Aid the Rest Have Done so Much Ill and so Little Good* (New York: Penguin 2006).

Echeruo, Michael J. C., *Victorian Lagos: Aspects of Nineteenth Century Lagos Life* (London: Macmillan 1977).

Ehrlich, Cyril, 'The Poor Country: The Tanganyika Economy from 1945 to Independence', in D. A. Low and Alison Smith (eds), *History of East Africa*, vol. 3 (Oxford: Clarendon Press 1976): 290–330.

Engerman, David C., Nils Gilman, Mark H. Haefele, and Michael E. Latham (eds), *Staging Growth: Modernization, Development, and the Global Cold*

War (Amherst, MA: University of Massachusetts Press; London: Eurospan 2003).

Engerman, David C. and Corinna R. Unger, 'Introduction: Towards a Global History of Modernization', *Diplomatic History* 33, 3 (2009): 375–85.

Escobar, Arturo, *Encountering Development: The Making and Unmaking of the Third World* (Princeton, NJ: Princeton University Press 1995).

Fabian, Johannes, *Time and the Other: How Anthropology Makes Its Others* (New York: Columbia University Press 1983).

Fafe, José Fernandes, *A colonização portuguesa e a emergência do Brasil* (Lisbon: Temas e Debates 2010).

Faidherbe, Louis Léon César, *Le Soudan français: chemin de fer de Médine au Niger* (Lille: Danel 1881).

Fairhead, James and Melissa Leach, 'Desiccation and Domination: Science and Struggles over Environment and Development in Colonial Guinea', *Journal of African History* 41, 1 (2000): 35–54.

Fajana, Adewunmi, *Education in Nigeria, 1842–1939: An Historical Analysis* (Ikeja: Longman 1978).

Falola, Toyin, *Development Planning and Decolonization in Nigeria* (Gainesville, FL: University Press of Florida 1996).

Fanoudh-Siefer, Léon, *Le mythe du nègre et de l'Afrique noire dans la littérature française, de 1800 à la Deuxième Guerre Mondiale* (Paris: Klincksieck 1968).

Fauvel, Luc, 'L'O.N.U. et les pays insuffisamment développés', *Annales Africaines* 2 (1956): 179–211.

Feierman, Steven, *Peasant Intellectuals: Anthropology and History in Tanzania* (Madison, WI: University of Wisconsin Press 1990).

Ferguson, James, 'Anthropology and Its Evil Twin: "Development" in the Constitution of a Discipline', in Frederick Cooper and Randall Packard (eds), *International Development and the Social Sciences: Essays on the History and Politics of Knowledge* (Berkeley, Los Angeles, London: University of California Press 1997): 150–76.

——, *The Anti-Politics Machine: 'Development', Depoliticization, and Bureaucratic Power in Lesotho* (Cambridge: Cambridge University Press 1990).

——, 'Decomposing Modernity: History and Hierarchy after Development', in Ania Loomba, Suvir Kaul, Matti Bunzl et al. (eds), *Postcolonial Studies and Beyond* (Durham, NC: Duke University Press 2005): 166–81.

Ferreira, Eduardo de Sousa, 'A lógica da consolidação da economia de mercado em Angola, 1930–74', *Análise Social* 21, 1 (1985): 83–110.

Ferry, Jules, 'Discours du 28 juillet 1885', in Paul Robiquet (ed.), *Discours et opinions de Jules Ferry*, vol. 5 (Paris: Armand Colin 1893), pp. 172–220.

Fieldhouse, D. K.,'Decolonization, Development, and Dependence: A Survey of Changing Attitudes', in Prosser Gifford and William Roger Louis (eds), *The Transfer of Power in Africa: Decolonization 1940–1960* (New Haven, CT: Yale University Press 1982): 483–515.

——, *The West and the Third World: Trade, Colonialism, Dependence, and Development* (Oxford, Malden, MA: Blackwell 1999).

Fortuna, Carlos, *O fio da meada: o algodão de Moçambique, Portugal e a economia-mundo, 1860–1960* (Porto: Afrontamento 1993).

Fortuna, Vasco Nunes Pereira, 'As finanças públicas do mundo português', *Boletim Geral do Ultramar* 27, 317 (1951): 27–47.

Foucault, Michel, *L'archéologie du savoir* (Paris: Gallimard 1969). English translation quoted: *The Archeology of Knowledge and the Discourse on Language* (New York: Vintage Books 2010).

——, *L'ordre du discours: leçon inaugurale au Collège de France prononcée le 2 Décembre 1970* (Paris: Gallimard 1971).

Fourastié, Jean, *Les Trente Glorieuses, ou la révolution invisible de 1946 à 1975* (Paris: Fayard 1979).

Frankel, Herbert S. 'The Kongwa Experiment: Lessons of the East African Groundnut Scheme', in Herbert S. Frankel (ed.), *The Economic Impact on Underdeveloped Societies: Essays on International Investment and Social Change* (Cambridge, MA: Harvard University Press 1953): 141–53.

Freund, Bill, *The Making of Contemporary Africa: The Development of African Society since 1800* (Boulder, CO: Lynne Rienner 1998).

Freyre, Gilberto, *Casa-grande e senzala: formação da família Brasileira sob o regime de economia patriarcal* (Lisbon: Livros do Brasil 1933). English edition: *The Masters and the Slaves: A Study in the Development of Brazilian Civilization*, translated from the Portuguese by Samuel Putnam (New York: Knopf 1946).

——, *O Luso e o Trópico: sugestões em torno dos métodos portugueses de integração de povos autóctones e de culturas diferentes da europeia num complexo de civilização: o luso-tropical* (Lisbon: Comissão Executiva das Comemorações do Infante D. Henrique 1961).

——, *O mundo que o português criou: aspectos das relações sociaes e de cultura do Brasil com Portugal e as colônias portuguesas* (Rio de Janeiro: Livraria Jose Olympio 1940).

——, *Um brasileiro em terras portuguesas* (Rio de Janeiro: José Olympio 1953).

Fuggles-Couchman, N. R., *Agricultural Change in Tanganyika, 1945–1960* (Stanford, CA: Stanford University, Food Research Institute 1964).

Furon, Raymond, *L'érosion du sol* (Paris: Payot 1947).

Gaillard, Jean-Michel, *Jules Ferry* (Paris: Fayard 1989).

Gaitskill, Arthur, *Gezira: A Story of Development in the Sudan* (London: Faber and Faber 1959).

Gamble, Harry, 'Peasants of the Empire: Rural Schools and the Colonial Imaginary in 1930s French West Africa', *Cahiers d'Études Africaines* 49, 195 (2009): 775–804.

Geider, Thomas, 'The Paper Memory of East Africa: Ethnohistories and Biographies Written in Swahili', in Axel Harneit-Sievers (ed.), *A Place in the World: New Local Historiographies in Africa and South Asia* (Leiden: Brill 2002): 255–88.

Geiger, Susan, Jean Marie Allman, and Nakanyike Musisi (eds), *Women in African Colonial Histories* (Bloomington, IN: Indiana University Press 2002).

Gilman, Nils, *Mandarins of the Future: Modernization Theory in Cold War America* (Baltimore, London: Johns Hopkins University Press 2003).

Gleizes, Michel, *Un regard sur l'ORSTOM, 1953–1983: témoignage* (Paris: Editions de l'ORSTOM 1985).

Gluck, Carol and Anna Lowenhaupt Tsing, *Words in Motion: Towards a Global Lexicon* (Durham, NC: Duke University Press 2009).

Goldklang, Harold A., 'Current Swahili Newspaper Terminology', *Swahili* 37, 2 (1967): 194–208.

Gordon, April A., *Transforming Capitalism and Patriarchy: Gender and Development in Africa* (London: Lynne Rienner 1996).

Gordon, H. L., 'A Rumination of Research and Eye-wash', *East African Medical Journal* 13, 4 (1936–37): 110–19.

Grace, Joshua, 'Heroes of the Road: Race, Gender, and the Politics of Mobility in Twentieth-Century Tanzania', *Africa: Journal of the International African Institute* 83, 3 (August 2013): 403–25.

Graham, Sonia F., *Government and Mission Education in Northern Nigeria, 1900–1919* (Ibadan: Ibadan University Press 1966).

Green, M. M., *Igbo Village Affairs* (London: Frank Cass 1947).

Grove, Richard H., *Green Imperialism: Colonial Expansion, Tropical Island Edens and the Origins of Environmentalism, 1600–1860* (Cambridge: Cambridge University Press 1996).

Gruhn, Isebill V., 'The Commission for Technical Co-operation in Africa, 1950–65', *Journal of Modern African Studies* 9, 3 (1971): 459–69.

Guggisberg, [Sir] Frederick Gordon, *The Keystone* (London: Simpkin, Marshall, Hamilton, Kent & Co. 1924).

Guizot, François Pierre Guillaume, *Cours d'histoire moderne: histoire de la civilisation en France depuis la chute de l'Empire romain jusqu'en 1789*, vol. 1 (Paris: Pichon et Didier 1829).

——, *General History of Civilization in Europe*, ed. George Wells Knight (New York: Appleton 1896).

Gutmann, Bruno, 'The African Standpoint', *Africa* 8, 1 (1935): 1–19.

Haig, E. F. G., *Nigerian Sketches* (London: Allen and Unwin 1931).

Hailey, [Lord] William Malcolm, *An African Survey: A Study of Problems Arising in Africa South of the Sahara*, rev. edn (Oxford: Oxford University Press 1957 [1938]).

——, 'Foreword to *The Diary of a District Officer*, by Kenneth Bradley' (London: Harrap 1943): 5.

——, 'Some Problems Dealt with in the African Survey', *International Affairs* 18, 2 (1939): 194–210.

Hampsher-Monk, Iain, *History of Concepts: Comparative Perspectives* (Amsterdam: Amsterdam University Press 1998).

Haqqi, Anwarul Haque, *The Colonial Policy of the Labour Government, 1945–51* (Aligarh: Muslim University 1960).

Hardy, Georges, *Une conquête morale: l'enseignement en A.O.F.* (Paris: Armand Colin 1917).

Harmand, Jules, *Domination et Colonisation* (Paris: Flammarion 1910).

[389]

Harper, T. N., *The End of Empire and the Making of Malaya* (Cambridge: Cambridge University Press 2001).

Harrison, Lawrence E., *Who Prospers? How Cultural Values Shape Economic and Political Success* (New York: Basic Books 1992).

Harroy, Jean-Paul, *Afrique, terre qui meurt: la dégradation des sols africains sous l'influence de la colonisation* (Bruxelles: Hayez 1944).

Hautefeuille, Laurent-Basile, *Plan de colonisation des possessions françaises dans l'Afrique occidentale au moyen de la civilisation des nègres indigènes* (Paris: Librairie de Levasseur 1830).

Havinden, Michael Ashley and David Meredith, *Colonialism and Development: Britain and Its Tropical Colonies, 1850–1960* (London, New York: Routledge 1993).

Hetherington, Penelope, *British Paternalism and Africa, 1920–1940* (London: Frank Cass 1978).

Hill, J. F. R. and J. P. Moffett (eds), *Tanganyika: A Review of its Resources and their Development* (Dar es Salaam: Government of Tanganyika 1955).

Hinden, Rita, *Plan for Africa: A Report Prepared for the Colonial Bureau of the Fabian Society*, with a foreword by Arthur Creech Jones (London: Allen and Unwin 1941).

Hobsbawm, Eric and Terence Ranger (eds), *The Invention of Tradition* (Cambridge: Cambridge University Press 1983).

Hodge, Joseph Morgan, 'British Colonial Expertise, Post-Colonial Careering and the Early History of International Development', *Journal of Modern European History* 8, 1 (2010): 24–46.

——, 'Development and Science: British Colonialism and the Rise of the "Expert", 1895–1945' (PhD dissertation, Queen's University Kingston [Canada], 1999).

——, *Triumph of the Expert: Agrarian Doctrines of Development and the Legacies of British Colonialism* (Athens, OH: Ohio University Press 2007).

Hofschlaeger, Reinhard, 'Die Entstehung der primitiven Heilmethoden und ihre systematische Weiterentwicklung', *Archiv für Geschichte der Medizin* 3 (1910): 81–103.

Hogendorn, Jan S. and K. M. Scott, 'Very Large-Scale Agricultural Projects: The Lessons of the East African Groundnut Scheme', in Robert I. Rotberg (ed.), *Imperialism, Colonialism and Hunger: East and Central Africa* (Lexington, MA: Lexington Books 1983): 167–98.

Holleman, J. F., *Shona Customary Law: With Reference to Kinship, Marriage, the Family and the Estate* (Manchester: Manchester University Press 1952).

Holt, Peter M. and M. W. Daly, *A History of the Sudan from the Coming of Islam to the Present Day* (London: Longman 1988).

Hubert, Lucien, 'Conférence sur l'Afrique Occidentale Française', *Le Mois Colonial et Maritime* 4 (April 1907): 1–32.

Humblot, Paul, 'Le plan français de développement économique et social dans les territoires d'Outre-Mer et le Plan Marshall', *Economie Contemporaine* (March 1951): 25–32.

Hunt, Nancy Rose, '"Le bébé en brousse": European Women, African Birth Spacing, and Colonial Intervention in Breast Feeding in the Belgian Congo', in Ann Laura Stoler and Frederick Cooper (eds), *Tensions of Empire: Colonial Cultures in a Bourgeois World* (Berkeley, Los Angeles, London: University of California Press 1997): 287–321.

——, 'Between Fiction and History: Modes of Writing Abortion in Africa', *Cahiers d'Études Africaines* 47, 186 (2007): 277–312.

——, 'Noise over Camouflaged Polygamy: Colonial Morality, Taxation and a Woman-Naming Crisis in Belgian Africa', *Journal of African History* 32, 3 (1991): 47–94.

Hunter, Emma, 'Languages of Politics in Twentieth-century Kilimanjaro' (PhD dissertation, University of Cambridge, 2008).

Huxley, Elspeth, *The Mottled Lizard* (London: Chatto and Windus 1962).

Iliffe, John, *A Modern History of Tanganyika* (Cambrige: Cambridge University Press 1979).

——, *East African Doctors* (Cambridge: Cambridge University Press 1998).

Internation Labour Organization, *The Basic Needs Approach to Development: Some Issues Regarding Concepts and Methodology* (Geneva: International Labour Office 1980).

Jäger, Siegfried and Florentine Maier, 'Theoretical and Methodological Aspects of Foucauldian Critical Discourse Analysis and Dispositive Analysis', in Ruth Wodak and Michael Meyer (eds), *Methods of Critical Discourse Analysis* (London: Sage 2009): 34–61.

JanMohamed, Abdul, *Manichean Aesthetics: The Politics of Literature in Colonial Africa* (Amherst, MA: University of Massachusetts Press 1983).

Jätzold, Ralph, 'Die Nachwirkungen des fehlgeschlagenen Erdnuss-Projekts in Ostafrika', *Erdkunde* 19, 3 (1965): 210–32.

Jeater, Diana, 'Imagining Africans: Scholarship, Fantasy, and Science in Colonial Administration, 1920s Southern Rhodesia', *International Journal of African Historical Studies* 38, 1 (2005): 1–26.

Jennings, Christian, 'Unexploited Assets: Imperial Imagination, Practical Limitations, and Marine Fisheries Research in East Africa, 1917–53', in Brett Bennett and Joseph Hodge (eds), *Science and Empire: Knowledge and Networks of Science across the British Empire, 1800–1979* (Basingstoke: Palgrave Macmillan 2011): 253–74.

Jerónimo, Miguel Bandeira, *Livros brancos, almas negras: a 'missão civilizadora' do colonialismo português, c. 1870–1930* (Lisbon: Imprensa de Ciências Sociais 2010).

Joelson, Ferdinand Stephen, 'A first Novel of East Africa: German Designs on Tanganyika Territory', *East Africa* (29 August 1929): 1687.

Johnson, Frederick, *Standard Swahili-English Dictionary* (London: Oxford University Press 1939).

Jorgenson, Dale W., 'The Development of a Dual Economy', *Economic Journal* 71, 282 (1961): 309–34.

Kabeer, Naila, *Reversed Realities: Gender Hierarchies in Development Thought* (London: Verso 1994).

Kaberry, Phyllis M., *Women of the Grassfields: A Study of the Economic Position of Women in Bamenda, British Cameroons*, preface by Daryll Forde (London: HMSO 1952).

Kane, Cheikh Hamidou, *Ambiguous Adventure* (London: Heinemann 1972 [1961]).

Kay, George L., *Rhodesia: A Human Geography* (London: University of London Press 1970).

Kent, John, *The Internationalization of Colonialism: Britain, France and Black Africa, 1939–1956* (Oxford: Clarendon Press 1992).

Kevane, Michael, *Women and Development in Africa: How Gender Works* (London: Lynne Rienner 2004).

Kirk-Greene, Anthony, *On Crown Service: A History of HM Colonial and Overseas Civil Services, 1837–1997* (London, New York: I. B. Tauris 1999).

Knellwolf King, Christa and Margarete Rubik (eds), *Stories of Empire: Narrative Strategies for the Legitimation of an Imperial World Order* (Trier: wvt 2009).

Kopf, Martina, 'A Peasant, a Governor and a Plough: Development Discourse and the French Colonial Novel in the 1930s', *Stichproben-Vienna Journal of African Studies* 26 (2014).

Koponen, Juhani, *Development for Exploitation: German Colonial Policies in Mainland Tanzania, 1884–1914* (Helsinki, Hamburg: Lit 1994).

Koponen, Juhani, 'Maji Maji and the Making of the South', *Tanzania Zamani* 7, 1 (2010): 1–58.

Kopp, André, 'Réflexions sur la mise en valeur des TOM', *L'Agronomie Tropicale* 2, 9–10 (1947): 454–61.

Krapf, J. L., *A Dictionary of the Suahili Language* (London: Truebner 1892).

Krauss, Hans, 'Der Suaheli-Arzt', *Münchener Medizinische Wochenschrift* 55 (1908): 517–19.

Kriesel, Herbert C., Charles K. Laurent, Carl Halpern, and Henry E. Larzelere, *Agricultural Marketing in Tanzania: Background Research and Policy Proposals* (East Lansing, MI: Michigan State University 1970).

Kubicek, Robert V., *The Administration of Imperialism: Joseph Chamberlain at the Colonial Office* (Durham, NC: Duke University Press 1969).

Kwa, Chunglin, 'Painting and Photographing Landscapes: Pictorial Conventions and Gestalts', *Configurations* 16, 1 (2008): 57–75.

Kwashirai, Vimbai, *Green Colonialism in Zimbabwe, 1890–1980* (Amherst, NY: Cambria Press 2009).

Labouret, Henri, *Paysans d'Afrique occidentale* (Paris: Gallimard 1941).

Labrousse, Georges, 'Tendances de la mécanisation dans nos TOM aujourd'hui', *Bulletin de Liaison du Comité de Machinisme Agricole Outre Mer* 11 (March–April 1958): 1–3.

Lachenal, Guillaume, 'Le médecin qui voulut être roi: médecine coloniale et utopie au Cameroun', *Annales: Histoire, Sciences Sociales* 65, 1 (2010): 121–56.

Landes, David S., *The Wealth and Poverty of Nations: Why Some Are so Rich and Some so Poor* (New York: Norton 1998).

Lazard, Gilbert, *L'actance* (Paris: Presses Universitaires de France 1994).

League of Nations, 'The Covenant of the League of Nations', 28 April 1919. Available at: http://avalon.law.yale.edu/20th_century/leagcov.asp (accessed 14 April 2013).

Leblond, Marius-Ary, 'A quoi doit servir la littérature coloniale: La Société des Écrivains Coloniaux', *Monde Colonial Illustré* (April 1926): 95.

Lee, J. M., *Colonial Development and Good Government: A Study of the Ideas Expressed by the British Official Classes in Planning Decolonization, 1939–1964* (Oxford: Clarendon Press 1967).

Leith-Ross, Sylvia, *African Women: A Study of the Ibo of Nigeria* (London: Faber and Faber 1939).

Léonard, Yves, 'O Ultramar Português', in Francisco Bethencourt and Kirti Chaudhuri (eds), *História da expansão portuguesa*, vol. 5, *Último império e recentramento, 1930–1998* (Lisbon: Círculo de Leitores 1999): 31–50.

——, 'Salazarisme et lusotropicalisme: histoire d'une appropriation', *Lusotopie* (1997): 211–26. Available at: www.lusotopie.sciencespobordeaux. fr/l%C3%A9onard97.pdf (accessed 20 May 2013).

Leslie, Charles, 'Interpretations of Illness: Syncretism in Modern Āyurveda', in Charles Leslie and Allan Young (eds), *Paths to Asian Medical Knowledge* (Berkeley: University of California Press 1992): 177–208.

Lewis, David, Dennis Rodgers, and Michael Woolcock, 'The Fiction of Development: Literary Representation as a Source of Authoritative Knowledge', *Journal of Development Studies* 44, 2 (2008): 198–216.

Lewis, Joanna, *Empire State Building: War and Welfare in Kenya, 1925–52* (Oxford: James Currey 2000).

——, 'Tropical East Ends and the Second World War: Some Contradictions in Colonial Office Welfare Initiatives', *Journal of Imperial and Commonwealth History* 28, 2 (2000): 42–66.

Leys, Colin, *The Rise and Fall of Development Theory* (Nairobi: EAEP; Bloomington and Indianapolis: Indiana University Press; London: James Currey 1996).

Liebenow, J. Gus, *Colonial Rule and Political Development in Tanzania: The Case of the Makonde* (Nairobi: East African Publishing House 1971).

Linnér, Björn-Ola, *The Return of Malthus: Environmentalism and Post-War Population-Resource Crises* (Isle of Harris: White Horse Press 2003).

Lohrmann, Ulrich, *Voices from Tanganyika: Great Britain, the United Nations and the Decolonization of a Trust Territory, 1946–1961* (Münster: Lit 2006).

Low, D. A. and John M. Lonsdale, 'Introduction: Towards the New Order, 1945–1963', in D. A. Low and Alison Smith (eds), *History of East Africa*, vol. 3 (Oxford: Clarendon Press 1976): 1–63.

Ludden, David, 'India's Development Regime', in Nicholas B. Dirks (ed.), *Colonialism and Culture* (Ann Arbor, MI: University of Michigan Press 1992): 247–87.

Lugard, Frederick D., *The Dual Mandate in British Tropical Africa* (Edinburgh, London: Blackwood 1922).

——, 'Education in Tropical Africa', *Edinburgh Review* 242, 493 (1925): 1–19.

——, *Political Memoranda: Revision of Instructions to Political Officers on Subjects Chiefly Political and Administrative, 1913–1918*, edited and with an introduction by A. H. M. Kirk Greene (London: Frank Cass 1970 [1919]).

Lunstrum, Elizabeth, 'State Rationality, Development, and the Making of State Territory: From Colonial Extraction to Postcolonial Conservation in Southern Mozambique', in Christina Folke Ax, Niels Brimnes, Niklas Thode Jensen, and Karen Oslund (eds), *Cultivating the Colonies: Colonial States and their Environmental Legacies* (Athens, OH: Ohio University Press 2011), pp. 209–74.

Lüsebrink, Hans-Jürgen, *La conquête de l'espace public colonial: prises de parole et formes de participation d'écrivains et d'intellectuels africains dans la presse à l'époque coloniale, 1900–1960* (Frankfurt-on-Main, London: IKO 2003).

Machingaidze, Victor E. M., 'Agrarian Change From Above: The Southern Rhodesia Native Land Husbandry Act and African Response', *International Journal of African Historical Studies* 24, 3 (1991): 557–88.

Macmillan, William, *Africa Emergent: A Survey of Social, Political, and Economic Trends in British Africa* (London: Faber and Faber 1938).

Madan, A., *Swahili-English Dictionary* (Oxford: Clarendon Press 1903).

Magnus, Hugo, *Die Volksmedizin, ihre geschichtliche Entwicklung und ihre Beziehung zur Kultur* (Breslau: Kern 1905).

Magubane, Bernard, 'The "Xhosa" in Town, Revisited. Urban Social Anthropology: A Failure of Method and Theory', *American Anthropologist*, New Series 75, 5 (1973): 1701–15.

Maguire, G. Andrew, *Toward 'Uhuru' in Tanzania: The Politics of Participation* (London: Cambridge University Press 1969).

Mahoney, Michael, 'Estado Novo, Homem Novo (New State, New Man): Colonial and Anti-colonial Development Ideologies in Mozambique, 1930–1977', in David C. Engerman, Nils Gilman, Mark H. Haefele, and Michael E. Latham (eds), *Staging Growth: Modernization, Development, and the Global Cold War* (Amherst, MA: University of Massachusetts Press; London: Eurospan 2003): 165–98.

Mair, Lucy P., *Welfare in the British Colonies* (London: Royal Institute of International Affairs 1944).

Makombe, Eric K., 'A People's Perspective of State Conservation Policies in the Seke Reserve, 1941–1961' (BA: Honours dissertation, University of Zimbabwe, 2003).

Malcom, D. W., *Sukumaland: An African People and Their Country. A Study of Land Use in Tanganyika* (London: Oxford University Press 1953).

Mamdani, Mahmood, *Citizen and Subject: Contemporary Africa and the Legacy of Late Colonialism* (Kampala: Fountain Publishers 2002).

Mandal, R. C., *Cashew: Production and Processing Technology* (Jodhpur: Agrobios 2007).

Manela, Erez, *The Wilsonian Moment: Self-Determination and the International Origins of Anticolonial Nationalism* (Oxford: Oxford University Press 2007).

Marealle, Petro Itosi, *Maisha ya Mchagga Hapa Duniani na Ahera* (Dar es Salaam: Mkuki na Nyota 2002 [1947]).

Marie Louise, Princess, *Letters from the Gold Coast* (London: Methuen 1926).

Marseille, Jacques, *Empire colonial et capitalisme français: histoire d'un divorce* (Paris: Albin Michel 1984).

——, 'The Phases of French Colonial Imperialism: Towards a New Periodization', *Journal of Imperial and Commonwealth History* 13, 3 (1985): 127–41.

Marshall, Alan, *The Unity of Nature: Wholeness and Disintegration in Ecology and Science* (London: Imperial College Press 2002).

Marshall, T. H., *Citizenship and Social Class, and Other Essays* (Cambridge: Cambridge University Press 1950).

Martin, Denis-Constant, *Tanzanie: l'invention d'une culture politique* (Paris: Karthala 1998).

Martins, Ana Cristina and Teresa Albina (eds), *Viagens e missões científicas nos trópicos, 1883–2010* (Lisbon: Instituto de Investigação Científica Tropical 2010).

Matera, Marc, 'Colonial Subjects: Black Intellectuals and the Development of Colonial Studies in Britain', *Journal of British Studies* 49, 2 (2010): 388–418.

Matera, Marc, Misty L. Bastian, and Susan Kingsley Kent, *The Women's War of 1929: Gender and Violence in Colonial Nigeria* (Basingstoke: Palgrave Macmillan 2011).

Matos, Norton de, *A nação una: organização política e administrativa dos territórios do ultramar português* (Lisbon: Paulino Ferreira Filhos 1953).

Maxwell, Kenneth, 'Portugal and Africa: The Last Empire', in Prosser Gifford and William Roger Louis (eds), *The Transfer of Power in Africa: Decolonization 1940–1960* (New Haven, CT: Yale University Press 1982): 337–86.

McClintock, Anne, *Imperial Leather: Race, Gender and Sexuality in the Colonial Contest* (London, New York: Routledge 1995).

McMichael, Philip, *Development and Social Change: A Global Perspective*, 2nd edn (London, Thousand Oaks, CA: Pine Forge 2000).

Mendes, Afonso, 'Portugal em face do anticolonialismo: estudos e ensaios', *Ultramar* 6 (October–December 1961): 25–38.

Meneses, Maria Paula, 'O "indígena" africano e o colono "europeu": a construção da diferença por processos legais', *E-cadernos CES* 7 (2010): 68–93. Available at: www.ces.uc.pt/e-cadernos/media/ecadernos7/04%20–%20 Paula%20Meneses%2023_06.pdf (accessed 17 March 2013).

Meredith, David, 'State Controlled Marketing and Economic "Development": The Case of West African Produce after the Second World War', *Economic History Review* 39, 1 (1986): 77–91.

Metge, Robert, 'La mécanisation et le système cultural africain', *L'Agronomie Tropicale* 7, 2 (1952): 136–49.

Metzger, Chantal, *L'empire colonial français dans la stratégie du Troisième Reich, 1936–1945* (2 vols, Brussells, New York: Peter Lang 2002).

Milligan, S., *Report on the Present Position of the Agricultural Industry and the Necessity, or Otherwise, of Encouraging Further European Settlement in Agricultural Areas* (Lusaka: Government Printer 1931).

Mills, [Lady] D. R. M., *Episodes from the Road to Timbuktu: The Record of a Woman's Adventurous Journey* (London: Duckworth 1927).

——, *The Golden Land: A Record of Travel in West Africa* (London: Duckworth 1929).

Ministry of Finance Zimbabwe-Rhodesia, *Proposals for a Five Year Programme of Development in the Public Sector* (Salisbury: The Ministry 1979).

Miranda, Nuno, 'A Câmara Corporativa no Estado Novo: composição, funcionamento e influência' (PhD dissertation, University of Lisbon, 2009). Available at: www.estig.ipbeja.pt/~ac_direito/MirandaF.pdf (accessed 14 March 2013).

Mission Roland Portères, *Aménagement de l'économie agricole et rurale au Sénégal* (3 vols, Bambey: Centre de recherches agronomiques 1952).

Mockerie, Parmenas Githendu, *An African Speaks for His People* (London: Hogarth Press 1934).

Monod, Théodore, 'Conservation des ressources naturelles en Afrique noire française et éducation', in Secretariat of the International Union for the Protection of Nature (ed.), *International Technical Conference on the Protection of Nature, Lake Success, 22–29 August 1949: Proceedings and Papers* (Paris, Bruxelles: UNESCO 1950): 242–51. Available at: http://unesdoc. unesco.org/images/0013/001335/133578mo.pdf (accessed 23 March 2013).

——, 'Education and the Conservation of Natural Resources', in UNSCCUR, *Proceedings of the United Nations Scientific Conference on the Conservation and Utilization of Resources (UNSCCUR), 17 August – 6 September 1949, Lake Success*, vol. 1, *Plenary Meetings* (New York: United Nations 1950): 275–8.

Monteiro, Armindo, *Da Governação de Angola* (Lisbon: Agência Geral das Colónias 1935).

——, 'Directrizes duma política ultramarina', *Boletim Geral das Colónias* 9, 97 (1933): 11–33.

——, *Para uma política imperial: alguns discursos do Ministro das Colónias Doutor Armindo Monteiro* (Lisbon: Agência Geral das Colónias 1933).

Moore, David B., 'Development Discourse as Hegemony: Towards an Ideological History, 1945–1995', in David B. Moore and Gerald J. Schmitz (eds), *Debating Development Discourse: Institutional and Popular Perspectives* (Basingstoke, London: Macmillan Press; New York: St. Martin's Press 1995): 1–53.

Moore, Henrietta and Megan Vaughan, *Cutting Down Trees: Gender, Nutrition, and Agricultural Change in the Northern Province of Zambia, 1890–1990* (Portsmouth, NH: Heinemann 1994).

Moreira, Adriano, 'A unidade política e o estatuto das populações', *Boletim Geral do Ultramar* 36, 417 (1960): 101–20.

——, 'Política de integração', *Boletim Geral do Ultramar* 37, 434–5 (1961): 3–28.

Morel, E. D., *Affairs of West Africa* (London: Frank Cass 1968 [1902]).

Morgan, David John, *The Offical History of Colonial Development* (5 vols, London: Macmillan 1980).

Morris-Hale, Walter, 'British Administration in Tanganyika from 1920 to 1945' (PhD dissertation, University of Geneva, 1969).

Morrow, Sean, '"No Girl Leaves the School Unmarried": Mabel Shaw and the Education of Girls at Mbereshi, Northern Rhodesia, 1915–1940', *International Journal of African Historical Studies* 19, 4 (1986): 601–35.

Moseley, Malcolm J., *Growth Centres in Spatial Planning* (Oxford, New York: Pergamon Press 1974).

Moura, Jean-Marc, 'Littérature coloniale et exotisme: examen d'une opposition de la théorie littéraire coloniale', in Jean-François Durand (ed.), *Regards sur les littératures coloniales: Afrique francophone. Découvertes*, vol. 1 (Paris, Montreal: L'Harmattan 1999): 21–39.

BIBLIOGRAPHY

Mouralis, Bernard, 'L'écriture, le réel et l'action: le cas de Georges Hardy dans *Ergaste ou la vocation colonial*', in Jean-François Durand (ed.), *Regards sur les littératures coloniales: Afrique francophone. Découvertes*, vol. 1 (Paris, Montreal: L'Harmattan 1999): 63–84.

——, *Littérature et développement: essai sur le statut, la fonction et la représentation de la littérature négro-africaine d'expression française* (Paris: Silex 1984).

Mouralis, Bernard and Anne Piriou (eds), *Robert Delavignette: savant et politique, 1897–1976* (Paris: Karthala 2003).

Moyana, H. V., *The Political Economy of Land in Zimbabwe* (Gweru: Mambo Press 2002).

Moyana, Toby Tafirenyika, *Education, Liberation and the Creative Act* (Harare: Zimbabwe Publishing House 1989).

Mudimbe, Valentin Y., *The Invention of Africa: Gnosis, Philosophy, and the Order of Knowledge* (Bloomington, IN: Indiana University Press 1988).

Murteira, Mário, 'Formação e colapso de uma economia nacional', in Francisco Bethencourt and Kirti Chaudhuri (eds), *História da expansão portuguesa*, vol. 5, *Último império e recentramento, 1930–1998* (Lisbon: Círculo de Leitores 1999): 108–30.

——, 'Planos de Fomento', in A. Barreto and M. F. Mónica (eds), *Dicionário de história de Portugal*, vol. 9, *Suplemento* (Porto: Figueirinhas 1999): 99–102.

Ndlovu-Gatsheni, Sabelo J., 'Re-thinking the Colonial Encounter in Zimbabwe', *Journal of Southern African Studies* 33, 1 (2007): 173–91.

Nederveen Pieterse, Jan, 'The Development of Development Theory: Towards Critical Globalisation', *Review of International Political Economy* 3, 4 (1996): 541–64.

——, *Development Theory: Deconstructions/Reconstructions* (New Delhi: Vistaar 2001).

Neto, Maria da Conceição, 'Ideologias, contradições e mistificações da colonização de Angola no século XX', *Lusotopie* (1997): 327–59.

Niculescu, Barbu, *Colonial Planning: A Comparative Study* (London: Allen and Unwin 1958).

Nillson, Sita Ranchod, 'Educating Eve: The Woman's Club Movement and Political Consciousness among Rural African Women in Southern Rhodesia, 1950–1980', in Karen Tranberg Hansen (ed.), *African Encounters with Domesticity* (New Brunswick, NJ: Rutgers University Press 1992): 195–221.

Nisbet, Robert A., *Social Change and History: Aspects of the Western Theory of Development* (New York, London: Oxford University Press 1969).

Norbye, Ole David Koht, 'Adequate Health Services for Poor Countries: How Can the Rich Countries Contribute to Reaching such a Goal?', *World Development* 2, 2 (1974): 13–18.

Nwauwa, Apollos O., 'University Education for Africans, 1900–1935: An "Anathema" to British Colonial Administrative Policy', *Asian and African Studies* 27, 3 (1993): 263–92.

Nyabongo, Akiki K., *The Story of an African Chief* (New York: Charles Scribner's Sons 1935).

Nyerere, Julius, *Freedom and Unity – Uhuru na umoja: A Selection from Writings and Speeches, 1952–65* (London: Oxford University Press 1967).

Oakley, Richard, *Treks and Palavers* (London: Seeley Service 1938).

O'Brien, William E., 'The Nature of Shifting Cultivation: Stories of Harmony, Degradation, and Redemption', *Human Ecology* 30, 4 (2002): 483–502.

Oliveira, Águedo de, 'Para uma política de desenvolvimento económico no ultramar português', *Boletim Geral do Ultramar* 39, 458–60 (1963): 72–90.

——, 'Velhas e novas ideias económicas: ao encontro da dualidade africana e das pressões internacionais', *Boletim Geral do Ultramar* 31, 363 (1955): 21–63.

Oliveira, José Osório de, 'Portugal é Isto!' *Boletim Geral do Ultramar* 27, 317 (1951): 118–19.

Oliveira, Mário de, *Problemas do ultramar no Plano Intercalar de Fomento: comunicação feita por Sua Excelência o Subsecretário de Estado do Fomento Ultramarino na sessão plena do Conselho Ultramarino do dia 5 de Novembro de 1964, seguida do colóquio que teve lugar no final da mesma* (Lisbon: Agência Geral do Ultramar 1964).

Ong'Wen Okuro, Samwel, 'Our Women Must Return Home: Institutionalized Patriarchy in Colonial Central Nyanza District, 1945–1963', *Journal of Asian and African Studies* 45, 5 (2010): 522–33.

Palonen, Kari, 'Rhetorical and Temporal Perspectives on Conceptual Change: Theses on Quentin Skinner and Reinhart Koselleck', in Kari Palonen (ed.), *Finnish Yearbook of Political Thought* 3 (1999): 41–59.

Patel, Diana, 'Some Issues of Urbanisation and Development in Zimbabwe', *Journal of Social Development in Africa* 3, 2 (1988): 17–31.

Paulo, João Carlos, 'Vantagens da instrução e do trabalho: "Escola de massas" e imagens de uma educação "colonial portuguesa"', *Educação, Sociedade e Culturas* 5 (1996): 99–128.

Pauw, Ernst-Josef, 'Banking in East Africa', in Peter von Marlin (ed.), *Financial Aspects of Development in East Africa* (Munich: Weltforum 1970): 180–225.

Pêcheux, Michel, *Les vérités de La Palice: linguistique, sémantique, philosophie* (Paris: Maspéro 1975).

Pedersen, Susan, 'Settler Colonialism at the Bar of the League of Nations', in Caroline Elkins and Susan Pedersen (eds), *Settler Colonialism in the Twentieth Century: Projects, Practices, Legacies* (New York, London: Routledge 2005): 113–34.

Peel, J. D. Y., 'Olaju: A Yoruba Concept of Development', *Journal of Development Studies* 14, 2 (1978): 139–65.

Peiper, Otto. 'Der Bevölkerungsrückgang in den tropischen Kolonien Afrikas und der Südsee, seine Ursachen und seine Bekämpfung', *Veröffentlichungen aus dem Gebiete der Medizinalverwaltung* 11, 7 (Berlin: Schoetz 1920).

Pels, Peter, 'Creolisation in Secret: The Birth of Nationalism in Late Colonial Uluguru, Tanzania', *Africa* 72, 1 (2002): 1–28.

Penvenne, Jeanne Marie, 'Settling Against the Tide: The Layered Contradictions of Twentieth-Century Portuguese Settlement in Mozambique', in Caroline Elkins and Susan Pedersen (eds), *Settler Colonialism in the Twentieth Century: Projects, Practices, Legacies* (New York, London: Routledge 2005): 79–94.

Pereira, Victor, 'A economia do Império e os Planos de Fomento', in Miguel Bandeira Jerónimo (ed.), *O Império Colonial em questão, sécs. XIX–XX* (Lisbon: Edições 70 2012): 251–86.

Perham, Margery, *Colonial Sequence, 1930–1949: A Chronological Commentary upon British Colonial Policy, especially in Africa* (London: Methuen 1967).

Peterson, Patti McGill, 'Colonialism and Education: The Case of the Afro-American', *Comparative Education Review* 15, 2 (1971): 146–57.

Petter, Martin, 'Sir Sydney Caine and the Colonial Office in the Second World War: A Career in the Making', *Canadian Journal of History* 16, 1 (1981): 67–85.

Phimister, Ian R., *An Economic and Social History of Zimbabwe, 1890–1948: Capital Accumulation and Class Struggle* (New York, London: Longman 1988).

Phylaktis, Kate, 'Banking in a British Colony: Cyprus 1878–1959', *Business History* 30, 4 (1988): 416–31.

Pinto, João Alberto da Costa, 'Gilberto Freyre e a intelligentsia salazarista em defesa do Império Colonial Português, 1951–1974', *História* 28, 1 (2009): 445–82.

Porter, Bernard, *Critics of Empire: British Radical Attitudes to Colonialism in Africa, 1895–1914* (London: Macmillan; New York: St. Martin's Press 1968).

Portères, Roland, 'Le système de riziculture par franges univariétales et l'occupation des fonds par les riz flottants dans l'ouest africain', *Revue Internationale de Botanique Appliquée et d'Agriculture Tropicale* 29, 325–326 (1949): 553–63.

Portugal, Presidência do Conselho, *III Plano de Fomento para 1968–1973*, vol. 1 (Lisbon: Presidência do Conselho 1968).

Proença, M. Cândida, 'A questão colonial', in Fernando Rosas and Maria Fernanda Rollo (eds), *História da Primeira República Portuguesa* (Lisbon: Tinta da China 2009): 503–21.

Rajan, S. Ravi, *Modernizing Nature: Forestry and Imperial Eco-Development, 1800–1950* (Oxford: Oxford University Press 2006).

Ranger, Terence, 'The Invention of Tradition in Colonial Africa', in Eric Hobsbawm and Terence Ranger (eds), *The Invention of Tradition* (Cambridge: Cambridge University Press 1983): 211–62.

Rato, Maria Helena da Cunha, 'O colonialismo português, factor de sub-desenvolvimento nacional', *Análise Social* 19, 3–5 (1983): 1121–9.

Reisigl, Martin and Ruth Wodak, 'The Discourse-Historical Approach (DHA)', in Ruth Wodak and Michael Meyer (eds), *Methods of Critical Discourse Analysis* (London: Sage 2009): 87–121.

Report of the Commission Appointed to Enquire into the Financial and Economic Position of Northern Rhodesia (London: HMSO 1938).

Report of the Commission Appointed to Inquire and Report on Administrative and Judicial Functions in the Native Affairs and District Courts Departments (Salisbury: Government Printer 1961).

Report of a Commission of Enquiry into the Disturbances at Aba and other Places in South Eastern Nigeria in November and December 1929 (London: HMSO 1930).

BIBLIOGRAPHY

Report of the East Africa Commission (London: HMSO 1925).

Report of the East Africa Royal Commission 1953–1955 (London: HMSO 1955).

Report of the Native Production and Trade Commission 1944 (Salisbury: Government Printer 1945).

Reynaud Paligot, Carole, 'Les *Annales* de Lucien Febvre à Fernand Braudel: entre épopée coloniale et opposition Orient/Occident', *French Historical Studies* 32, 1 (2009): 121–44.

Ribeiro, Margarida Calafate, 'Uma história de regressos: império, guerra colonial e pós-colonialismo', *Oficina do CES* 188 (2003). Available at: www.ces.uc.pt/publicacoes/oficina/ficheiros/188.pdf (accessed 25 May 2013).

Ribeiro, Orlando, 'Problemas humanos de África', in Junta de Investigações do Ultramar (ed.), *Colóquios sobre problemas humanos nas regiões tropicais* (Lisbon: Junta de Investigações do Ultramar – Centro de Estudos Políticos e Sociais 1961): 1–22.

Richard-Molard, Jacques, 'Plaidoyer pour une nouvelle paysannerie en Afrique noire', *Présence Africaine*, 13 (1952): 170–9.

——, 'Les terrains tropicaux d'Afrique', *Annales de Géographie* 60, 322 (1951): 349–69.

Richards, Audrey, *Land, Labour and Diet in Northern Rhodesia: An Economic Study of the Bemba Tribe* (Oxford: Oxford University Press 1939).

Richter, Melvin, *The History of Social and Political Concepts: A Critical Introduction* (Oxford: Oxford University Press 1995).

Rist, Gilbert, *Le développement: histoire d'une croyance occidentale* (Paris: Presses de Sciences Po 1996). English edition: Rist, Gilbert, *The History of Development: From Western Origins to Global Faith* (London: Zed Books; New York: St. Martin's Press 1997).

Rizzo, Matteo, 'What Was Left of the Groundnut Scheme? Development Disaster and Labour Market in Southern Tanganyika, 1946–1952', *Journal of Agrarian Change* 6, 2 (2006): 205–38.

Robin, Libby, 'Ecology: A Science of Empire?', in Tom Griffiths and Libby Robin (eds), *Ecology and Empire: Environmental History of Settler Societies* (Edinburgh: Keele University Press 1997): 63–75.

Rocha, Edgar, 'Portugal, anos 60: crescimento económico acelerado e papel das relações com as colónias', *Análise Social* 13, 51 (1977): 593–617.

Rolo, José Manuel, 'Entrevista a Mário Murteira', *Análise Social* 46, 200 (2011): 564–73.

Rosas, Fernando, 'Estado Novo, império e ideologia imperial', *Revista de História das Ideias* 17 (1995): 19–32.

——, *Portugal entre a paz e a guerra, 1939–1945* (Lisbon: Estampa 1990).

Rosas, Fernando and José Maria Brandão de Brito, *Dicionário de História do Estado Novo* (Lisbon: Círculo de Leitores 2006).

Rossin, Maurice, 'Deuxième compte-rendu sur le développement du plan de culture mécanisée de l'arachide dans l'Est africain anglais: situation en mai 1949', *L'Agronomie Tropicale* 6, 1–3 (1951): 3–28.

Rostow, Walt W., *The Stages of Economic Growth: A Non-Communist Manifesto* (Cambridge: Cambridge University Press 1960).

Roth Allen, Denise, *Managing Motherhood, Managing Risk: Fertility and Danger in West Central Africa* (Ann Arbor, MI: University of Michigan Press 2002).

Said, Edward, *Culture and Imperialism* (New York: Vintage 1994).

——, *Orientalism* (New York: Pantheon Books 1978).

Salazar, António de Oliveira, 'Declaração sobre política ultramarina', *Boletim Geral do Ultramar* 39, 458–60 (1963): 5–50.

——, 'O império colonial na economia da Nação', in António de Oliveira Salazar, *Discursos e notas políticas*, vol. 2 (Coimbra: Coimbra Editora 1937): 153–71.

——, 'Plano de Fomento Nacional', *Boletim Geral do Ultramar* 29, 336–7 (1953): 27–54.

——, 'Realidades da política portuguesa', *Boletim Geral do Ultramar* 39, 454–5 (1963): 3–24.

Salazar, António de Oliveira and Armindo Monteiro, *Conferência do Império Colonial: discursos pelos srs. Presidente do Conselho e Ministro das Colónias* (Lisbon: Agência Geral das Colónias 1933).

Salgueiro, João, 'Política de investimentos nos territórios do Ultramar', in Junta de Investigações do Ultramar (ed.), *Colóquios sobre o II Plano de Fomento: Ultramar* (Lisbon: Junta de Investigações do Ultramar – Centro de Estudos Políticos e Sociais 1959): 35–56.

Samuel, Frank,'Economic Potential of Colonial Africa', *Tropical Agriculture* 28, 7–12 (1951): 138–50.

Santos, Boaventura de Sousa, 'Between Prospero and Caliban: Colonialism, Postcolonialism, and Inter-identity', *Luso-Brazilian Review* 39, 1 (2002): 9–43.

——, 'Estado e sociedade na periferia do sistema mundial: o caso português', *Análise Social* 21, 87–9 (1985): 869–901.

——, 'O Estado, as relações salariais e o bem-estar social na semiperiferia: o caso português', in Boaventura de Sousa Santos (ed.), *Portugal: um retrato singular* (Porto: Afrontamento 1993): 17–58.

Sarkozy, Nicolas, 'Discours à l'Université de Dakar', 26 July 2007. Available at: www.afrokanlife.com/politique/think-tank/discours_sarkozy_universite_de_dakar_26_juillet_07 (accessed 20 March 2013).

Sarmento Rodrigues, Manuel Maria, 'O plano de fomento no ultramar: aproveitamento de recursos e povoamento', in Secretariado Nacional da Informação (ed.), *O plano de fomento: conferências ministeriais inauguradas pelo Presidente do Conselho em 28 de Maio* (Lisbon: SNI 1953): 81–106.

——, 'Plano de fomento do ultramar', *Boletim Geral do Ultramar* 29, 336–7 (1953): 55–81.

——, *Unidade da nação portuguesa* (2 vols, Lisbon: Agência Geral do Ultramar 1956).

Sarraut, Albert, *Grandeurs et servitudes coloniales* (Paris: Sagittaire 1931).

——, *La mise en valeur des colonies françaises* (Paris: Payot 1923).

Schmidt, Elizabeth, *Peasants, Traders and Wives: Shona Women in the History of Zimbabwe, 1870–1939* (Portsmouth, NH: Heinemann; Harare: Baobab; London: James Currey 1992).

Schuknecht, Rohland, *British Colonial Development Policy after the Second World War: The Case of Sukumaland, Tanganyika* (Berlin: Lit 2011).

Schumaker, Lyn, *Africanizing Anthropology: Fieldwork, Networks, and the Making of Cultural Knowledge in Central Africa* (Durham, NC: Duke University Press 2001).

Scott, James C., *Seeing Like a State: How Certain Schemes to Improve the Human Condition Have Failed* (New Haven, CT, London: Yale University Press 1998).

Scotton, J. F., 'Tanganyika's African Press, 1937–1960', *African Studies Review* 21, 1 (1978): 1–18.

Serviço Nacional de Informação, *O esforço do desenvolvimento económico português: o II Plano de Fomento* (Lisbon: Serviço Nacional de Informação 1959).

Shaw, Mabel, *Children of the Chief* (London: London Missionary Society 1921).

——, *Dawn in Africa: Stories of Girl Life* (London: Edinburgh House Press 1927).

——, *God's Candlelights: An Educational Venture in Northern Rhodesia* (London: Edinburgh House Press 1932).

——, *A Treasure of Darkness: An Idyll of African Child Life* (London, New York, Toronto: Longmans, Green and Co. 1936).

Shipway, Martin, *Decolonization and Its Impact: A Comparative Approach to the End of the Colonial Empires* (Malden, MA: Blackwell 2008).

Sieberg, Herward, *Colonial Development: Die Grundlegung moderner Entwicklungspolitik durch Großbritannien, 1919–1949* (Stuttgart: Steiner 1985).

Sigerist, Henry E., 'The Need for an Institute of the History of Medicine in India', in *India: Report of the Health Survey and Development Committee*, vol. 3, *Appendices* (Delhi: Manager of Publications 1946): 204–13.

Silva, Antonio Burity da, 'Os princípios português da integração racial', *Boletim Geral do Ultramar* 43, 499–500 (1967): 75–89.

Simon, David, 'Development Reconsidered: New Directions in Development Thinking', *Geografiska Annaler. Series B, Human Geography* 79, 4 (1997): 183–201.

Sivonen, Seppo, *White-Collar or Hoe Handle? African Education under British Colonial Policy, 1920–1945* (Helsinki: Suomen Historiallinen Seura 1995).

Skinner, Quentin, *Visions of Politics*, vol. 1, *Regarding Methods* (Cambridge: Cambridge University Press 2002).

Slater, Candace, 'Amazonia as Edenic Narrative', in William Cronon (ed.), *Uncommon Ground: Rethinking the Human Place in Nature* (New York, London: Norton 1996): 114–31.

Smith, Adam, *An Inquiry into the Nature and Causes of the Wealth of Nations* (2 vols, London: W. Strahan and T. Cadell 1776).

Smith, Paul, *Ecological Survey of Zambia: The Traverse Records of C. G. Trapnell, 1932–1943* (Kew: Royal Botanic Gardens 2001).

Smout, M. A. H., 'Urbanization of the Rhodesian Population', *Zambezia* 4, 2 (1975–76): 79–91.

Smouts, Marie-Claude (ed.), *La situation postcoloniale: les postcolonial studies dans le débat français* (Paris: Presses de Sciences Po 2007).

Snyder, Margaret C. and Mary Tadesse, *African Women and Development: A History* (London: Zed 1995).

Sousa, Alfredo de, 'Desenvolvimento Comunitário', *Boletim Geral do Ultramar* 39, 454–5 (1963): 237–43.

——, 'Desenvolvimento comunitário em Angola', in Instituto Superior de Ciências Sociais e Politica Ultramarina (ed.), *Angola: curso de extensão universitária ano lectivo de 1963–1964* (Lisbon: Junta de Investigações do Ultramar 1964): 5–22.

Spear, Thomas, 'Neo-Traditionalism and the Limits of Invention in British Colonial Africa', *Journal of African History* 44, 1 (2003): 3–27.

Spivak, Gayatri Chakravorty, 'Can the Subaltern Speak?', in Laura Chrisman and Patrick Williams (eds), *Colonial Discourse and Postcolonial Theory: A Reader* (New York: Columbia University Press 1994 [1988]): 66–111.

Spurr, David, *The Rhetoric of Empire: Colonial Discourse in Journalism, Travel Writing, and Imperial Administration* (Durham, NC: Duke University Press 1993).

Staples, Amy L. S., *The Birth of Development: How the World Bank, Food and Agriculture Organization, and World Health Organization Have Changed the World, 1945–1965* (Kent, OH: Kent State University Press 2006).

Staudt, Kathleen, 'The State and Gender in Colonial Africa', in Sue Ellen Charlton, Jana Everett, and Kathleen Staudt (eds), *Women, the State and Development* (Albany, NY: State University of New York Press 1989): 66–85.

Steiner-Khamsi, Gita and Hubert O. Quist, 'The Politics of Educational Borrowing: Reopening the Case of Achimota in British Ghana', *Comparative Education Review* 44, 3 (2000): 272–99.

Steins, Martin, *Das Bild des Schwarzen in der europäischen Kolonialliteratur, 1870–1918: ein Beitrag zur literarischen Imagologie* (Frankfurt-on-Main: Thesen Verlag 1972).

Stoler, Ann Laura and Frederick Cooper, 'Between Metropole and Colony: Rethinking a Research Agenda', in Ann Laura Stoler and Frederick Cooper (eds), *Tensions of Empire: Colonial Cultures in a Bourgeois World* (Berkeley, Los Angeles, London: University of California Press 1997): 1–56.

—— (eds), *Tensions of Empire: Colonial Cultures in a Bourgeois World* (Berkeley, Los Angeles, London: University of California Press 1997).

Sturmer, Martin, *The Media History of Tanzania* (Salzburg: afrika.info 1998).

Suret-Canale, Jean, 'From Colonization to Independence in French Tropical Africa: The Economic Background', in Prosser Gifford and William Roger Louis (eds), *The Transfer of Power in Africa: Decolonization 1940–1960* (New Haven, CT: Yale University Press 1982): 445–81.

Suriano, Maria, 'Letters to the Editor and Poems: *Mambo Leo* and Readers' Debates on *Dansi, Ustaarabu*, Respectability, and Modernity in Tanganyika, 1940s–1950s', *Africa Today* 57, 3 (2011): 39–55.

Taguieff, Pierre-André, *La force du préjugé: essai sur le racisme et ses doubles* (Paris: Gallimard 1988).

Táíwò, Olúfémi, 'Colonialism and Its Aftermath: The Crisis of Knowledge Production', *Callaloo* 16, 4 (1993): 891–908.

[403]

——, *How Colonialism Preempted Modernity in Africa* (Bloomington, IN: Indiana University Press 2010).

Tanganyika Territory, *Development of Tanganyika: Report of the Post-War Planning Advisory Committee* (Dar es Salaam: Government Printer 1944).

——, *Memorandum on the Future Development of the Medical Services of Tanganyika Territory by the Director of Medical Services, 1942* (Dar es Salaam: Government Printer 1944).

——, *Memorandum on Medical Policy* (Dar es Salaam: Government Printer 1938).

——, *Report of the Central Development Committee* (Dar es Salaam: Government Printer 1940).

——, *A Review of the Development Plans in the Southern Province* (Dar es Salaam: Government Printer 1953).

——, *Revised Development and Welfare Plan for Tanganyika, 1950–1956* (Dar es Salaam: Government Printer 1951).

——, *A Ten-Year Development and Welfare Plan for Tanganyika Territory: Report by the Development Commission* (Dar es Salaam: Government Printer 1946).

——, Medical Department, *A Draft Plan for the Development of Medical Services in Tanganyika with Special Reference for the Period 1956–1961* (Dar es Salaam: Government Printer 1956).

Tansley, Arthur, 'The Classification of Vegetation and the Concept of Development', *Journal of Ecology* 8, 2 (1920): 118–49.

Taylor, Carl E., 'The Place of Indigenous Medical Practitioners in the Modernization of Health Services', in Charles Leslie (ed.), *Asian Medical Systems: A Comparative Study* (Berkeley: University of California Press 1976): 285–99.

Temple, Charles P., *Native Races and their Rulers: Sketches and Studies of Official Life and Administrative Problems in Nigeria* (London: Frank Cass 1968 [1918]).

Temu, C. W., 'The Development of Political Vocabulary in Swahili', *Swahili* 41, 2 (1971): 3–17.

Thomas, Martin, 'Albert Sarraut, French Colonial Development, and the Communist Threat, 1919–1930', *Journal of Modern History* 77, 4 (2005): 917–55.

——, 'Contrasting Patterns of Decolonization: Belgian and Portuguese Africa', in Martin Thomas, Bob Moore, and L. J. Butler (eds), *Crises of Empire: Decolonization and Europe's Imperial States, 1918–1975* (London: Hodder Education 2008): 385–410.

——, 'Decolonizing the French African Federations after 1945', in Martin Thomas, Bob Moore, and L. J. Butler (eds), *Crises of Empire: Decolonization and Europe's Imperial States, 1918–1975* (London: Hodder Education 2008): 152–81.

——, 'The Roots of French Decolonization: Ideas, Economics, and Reform, 1900–1946', in Martin Thomas, Bob Moore, and L. J. Butler (eds), *Crises of Empire: Decolonization and Europe's Imperial States, 1918–1975* (London: Hodder Education 2008): 127–51.

Thomaz, Omar Ribeiro, ' "O bom povo português": usos e costumes d'aquém e d'alem-mar', *Mana* 7, 1 (2001): 55–87.

——, 'Tigres de Papel: Gilberto Freyre, Portugal e os países africanos de língua oficial portuguesa', in Cristina Bastos, Miguel Vale de Almeida, and Bela Feldman-Bianco (eds), *Trânsitos coloniais: diálogos críticos Luso-Brasileiros* (Lisbon: Imprensa de Ciências Sociais 2002): 39–63.

Thompson, Virginia and Richard Adloff, 'French Economic Policy in Tropical Africa', in Peter Duignan and L. H. Gann (eds), *Colonialism in Africa, 1870–1960*, vol. 4, *The Economics of Colonialism* (Cambridge: Cambridge University Press 1975): 127–64.

Throup, David, *Economic and Social Origins of Mau Mau, 1945–53* (London: James Currey 1987).

Tijanni, Hakeem Ibikunle, 'Britain, Leftist Nationalists and the Transfer of Power in Nigeria, 1945–1965' (PhD dissertation, University of South Africa/Pretoria, 2005).

Tilley, Helen, *Africa as a Living Laboratory: Empire, Development, and the Problem of Scientific Knowledge, 1870–1950* (Chicago: University of Chicago Press 2011).

——, 'African Environments and Environmental Sciences: The African Research Survey, Ecological Paradigms and British Colonial Development, 1920–1940', in William Beinart and JoAnn McGregor (eds), *Social History and African Environments* (Oxford: James Currey 2003): 109–30.

Tomás, Américo, 'Mensagem do Chefe de Estado', *Boletim Geral do Ultramar* 43, 499–500 (1967): 3–11.

Topper, Clive P., 'The Historical and Institutional Background of the Tanzanian Cashew Industry', in Clive P. Topper, P. D. S. Caligari, A. K. Kullaya et al. (eds), *Proceedings of the International Cashew and Coconut Conference: Trees for Life – the Key to Development, Held at Kilimanjaro Hotel, Dar es Salaam, 17–21 February 1997* (Reading: BioHybrids International 1998): 76–83.

Torres, Adelino, 'Mécanismes de la Zone Escudo, années 60–70', in Comité pour l'histoire économique et financière de la France (ed.), *La France et l'Outre-Mer: un siècle de relations monétaires et financières* (Paris: Ministère de l'économie, des finances et de l'industrie 1998): 615–43.

Tourte, René, *Histoire de la recherche agricole en Afrique tropicale francophone*, vol. 6, *De l'empire colonial à l'Afrique indépendante, 1945–1960: la recherche prépare le développement* (n.p.: s.n. 2012). Available at: www.fao.org/wairdocs/an500f/an500f00.pdf (accessed 3 April 2013).

Tranberg Hansen, Karen (ed.), *African Encounters with Domesticity* (New Brunswick, NJ: Rutgers University Press 1992).

Traoré, Aminata D., 'L'oppression du développement', *Manière de Voir* 79 (2005): 50–2.

Trapnell, Colin G., 'Ecological Methods in the Study of the Native Agriculture in Northern Rhodesia', *Bulletin of Miscellaneous Information (Royal Botanic Gardens, Kew)* 1 (1937): 1–10.

——, *The Soils, Vegetation, and Agriculture of North-Eastern Rhodesia: Report of the Ecological Survey* (Lusaka: Government Printer 1943).

Trapnell, Colin G. and J. Neil Clothier, *The Soils, Vegetation, and Agricultural Systems of North-Western Rhodesia: Report of the Ecological Survey* (Lusaka: Government Printer 1937).

Trigueiros, Luís Forjaz, 'O estatuto dos indígenas e os valores morais', *Boletim Geral do Ultramar* 29, 347 (1954): 21–43.

Trowell, H. C., *The Passing of Polygamy: A Discussion of Marriage and of Sex for African Christians* (Oxford: Oxford University Press 1940).

Truman, Harry S., 'Inaugural Address', 20 January 1949. Available at: www.trumanlibrary.org/calendar/viewpapers.php?pid=1030 (accessed 25 March 2013).

Truteau, Pierre, *Un paysan français parmi les paysans du Tiers-Monde: vie de Jean Nolle* (Paris: L'Harmattan 1994).

Turrittin, Jane, 'Colonial Midwives and Modernising Childbirth in West Africa', in Susan Geiger, Jean Marie Allman, and Nakanyike Musisi (eds), *Women in African Colonial Histories* (Bloomington, IN: Indiana University Press 2002): 71–93.

Twagira, Laura Ann, 'Peopling the Landscape: Colonial Irrigation, Technology, and Demographic Crisis in the French Soudan, ca. 1926–1944', *PSAE Research Series* 10 (2012): 1–29.

Twining, Sir Edward, 'The Situation in Tanganyika', *African Affairs* 50, 201 (1951): 297–310.

United Nations Development Programme, *Africa Human Development Report 2012: Towards a Food Secure Future* (New York: United Nations 2012).

Unschuld, Paul U., *Medicine in China: A History of Ideas* (Berkeley: University of California Press 1985).

van Beusekom, Monica M., 'Colonisation *Indigène*: French Rural Development Ideology at the Office du Niger, 1920–1940', *International Journal of African Historical Studies* 30, 2 (1997): 299–323.

——, 'Disjunctures in Theory and Practice: Making Sense of Change in Agricultural Development at the Office du Niger, 1920–1960', *Journal of African History* 41, 1 (2000): 79–99.

——, 'From Underpopulation to Overpopulation: French Perceptions of Population, Environment, and Agricultural Development in French Soudan (Mali), 1900–1960', *Environmental History* 4, 2 (1999): 198–219.

——, *Negotiating Development: African Farmers and Colonial Experts at the Office du Niger, 1920–1960* (Portsmouth, NH: Heinemann; Oxford: James Currey; Cape Town: D. Philip 2002).

van Beusekom, Monica M. and Dorothy L. Hodgson, 'Lessons Learned? Development Experiences in the Late Colonial Period', *Journal of African History* 41, 1 (2000): 29–33.

Vaughan, Megan, *Curing their Ills: Colonial Power and African Illness* (Cambridge: Polity Press 1991).

Veyne, Paul, *Comment on écrit l'histoire: essai d'épistémologie* (Paris: Éditions du Seuil 1971).

Vickery, Kenneth P., 'Saving Settlers: Maize Control in Northern Rhodesia', *Journal of Southern African Studies* 11, 2 (1985): 212–34.

Viguier, Pierre, 'Les techniques de l'agriculture soudanaise et les feux de brousse', *Revue Internationale de Botanique Appliquée et d'Agriculture Tropicale* 26 (1946): 42–51.

Viola, André, 'L'angoisse devant l'autre et le même: le demi-sauvage (civilisé, métis) dans le roman populaire anglais du vingtième siècle', in Jean-François Durand and Jean Sévry (eds), *Regards sur les littératures coloniales: Afrique anglophone et lusophone*, vol. 3 (Paris: L'Harmattan 1999): 109–27.

Wagoner, Phillip B., 'Precolonial Intellectuals and the Production of Colonial Knowledge', *Comparative Studies in Society and History* 45, 4 (2003): 783–814.

Wallerstein, Immanuel, *The Capitalist World Economy* (Cambridge: Cambridge University Press, 1979).

——, *The Modern World System* (New York: Academic Press 1974).

Watts, Michael, '"A New Deal in Emotions": Theory and Practice and the Crisis of Development', in Jonathan Crush (ed.), *Power of Development* (London, New York: Routledge 1995): 44–62.

Weaver, John E. and Frederic Clements, *Plant Ecology* (New York: McGraw-Hill 1929).

Welch, Janet, *Health and the Home* (London: Sheldon Press 1940).

West, Michael O., 'African Middle-Class Formation in Colonial Zimbabwe, 1890–1965' (PhD dissertation, Harvard University, 1990).

Westad, Odd Arne, *The Global Cold War: Third World Interventions and the Making of Our Times* (Cambridge: Cambridge University Press 2005).

Westcott, Nicholas, 'The Impact of the Second World War in Tanganyika' (PhD dissertation, University of Cambridge, 1982).

Wheeler, Douglas L. and René Pélissier, *Angola* (London: Pall Mall Press 1971).

White, Bob W., 'Talk about School: Education and the Colonial Project in French and British Africa, 1860–1960', *Comparative Education* 32, 1 (1996): 9–25.

White, Luise, 'Separating the Men from the Boys: Colonial Constructions of Gender, Sexuality and Terrorism in Central Kenya, 1930–1959', *International Journal of African Historical Studies* 23, 1 (1990): 1–25.

White, Nicholas J., *Business, Government, and the End of Empire: Malaya 1942–1957* (Kuala Lumpur, Oxford: Oxford University Press 1996).

——, 'Reconstructing Europe through Rejuvenating Empire: The British, French, and Dutch Experiences Compared', *Past and Present* 210, suppl. 6 (2011): 211–36.

Whitehead, Clive. 'The Historiography of British Imperial Education Policy, Part II: Africa and the Rest of the Colonial Empire', *History of Education* 34, 4 (2005): 441–54.

Wild-Wood, Emma, *Migration and Christian Identity in Congo (DRC)* (Leiden: Brill 2008).

Williams, T. David, 'Sir Gordon Guggisberg and Educational Reform in the Gold Coast, 1919–1927', *Comparative Education Review* 8, 3 (1964): 290–306.

Wittgenstein, Ludwig, *Philosophical Investigations* (Oxford: Blackwell 1995 [1953]).

Wolf, Hans-Georg, 'British and French Language and Educational Policies in the Mandate and Trusteeship Territories', *Language Sciences* 30, 5 (2008): 553–74.

Wood, Alan, *The Groundnut Affair* (London: The Bodley Head 1950).

Worboys, Michael, 'The Emergence of Tropical Medicine: A Study in the Establishment of a Scientific Specialty', in Gerard Lemaine, Roy MacLeod, Michael Mulkay, and Peter Weingart (eds), *Perspectives on the Emergence of Scientific Disciplines* (The Hague: Mouton; Paris: Maison des Sciences de l'Homme 1976): 75–98.

——, 'Manson, Ross and Colonial Medical Policy: Tropical Medicine in London and Liverpool, 1899–1914', in Roy MacLeod and Milton Lewis (eds), *Disease, Medicine and Empire: Perspectives on Western Medicine and the Experience of European Expansion* (London, New York: Routledge 1988): 21–37.

——, 'Science and British Colonial Imperialism' (PhD dissertation, University of Sussex, 1979).

Worby, Eric, '"Discipline without Oppression": Sequence, Timing and Marginality in Southern Rhodesia's Post-War Development Regime', *Journal of African History* 41, 1 (2000): 101–25.

World Bank, *Africa's Future and the World Bank's Support to It* (n.p.: s.n. 2011).

——, *First Things First: Meeting Basic Human Needs in the Developing Countries* (New York: Oxford University Press 1981).

——, *World Development Report 1993: Investing in Health* (Washington, DC: World Bank 1993).

World Health Organization, Commission on Macroeconomics and Health, *Macroeconomics and Health: Investing in Health for Economic Development* (Geneva: WHO 2001).

Worster, Donald, *Nature's Economy: A History of Ecological Ideas* (Cambridge: Cambridge University Press 2007).

Worthington, Edgar B., *A Development Plan for Uganda* (Entebbe: Government Printer 1946).

Wrong, Margaret, *Across Africa* (London: International Committee on Christian Literature for Africa 1940).

——, *The Land and Life of Africa* (London: Cargate Press 1935).

Yngstrom, Ingrid, 'Women, Wives and Land Rights in Africa: Situating Gender beyond the Household in the Debate over Land Policy and Changing Tenure Systems', *Oxford Development Studies* 30, 1 (2002): 21–40.

Yoshikuni, Tsuneo, 'Notes on the Influence of Town-Country Relations on African Urban History before 1957: Experiences in Salisbury and Bulawayo', in Brian Raftopoulos and Tsuneo Yoshikuni (eds), *Sites of Struggle: Essays in Zimbabwe's Urban History* (Harare: Weaver Press 1999): 113–28.

Young, Crawford, *The African Colonial State in Comparative Perspective* (New Haven, CT, London: Yale University Press 1994).

Young, Roland and Henry Fosbrooke, *Land and Politics among the Luguru of Tanganyika* (London: Routledge and Kegan Paul 1960).

Yudelman, Montague, *Africans on the Land: Economic Problems of African Agricultural Development in Southern, Central, and East Africa, with Special Reference to Southern Rhodesia* (Cambridge, MA: Harvard University Press 1964).

Zachariah, Benjamin, *Developing India: An Intellectual and Social History, c. 1930–50* (New Delhi, Oxford: Oxford University Press 2005).

INDEX

Notes: literary works can be found under authors' names; 'n.' after a page reference indicates the number of a note on that page.

EU authorised representative for GPSR:
Easy Access System Europe, Mustamäe tee 50,
10621 Tallinn, Estonia
gpsr.requests@easproject.com